BOLLINGEN SERIES LXXVI

MIRCEA ELIADE

SHAMANISM

Archaic Techniques
of Ecstasy

Translated from the French by
WILLARD R. TRASK

BOLLINGEN SERIES LXXVI

PRINCETON UNIVERSITY PRESS

THIS IS THE SEVENTY-SIXTH IN A SERIES OF WORKS
SPONSORED BY
BOLLINGEN FOUNDATION

Originally published in French as
Le Chamanisme et les techniques archaïques de l'extase
by Librairie Payot, Paris, 1951
Revised and enlarged for the present edition

Princeton University Press books are printed on acid-free
paper, and meet the guidelines for permanence and
durability of the Committee on Production Guidelines for
Book Longevity of the Council on Library Resources

First Princeton/Bollingen Paperback Printing, 1972
Second Printing, 1974

19   18   17   16   15   14   13   12

Library of Congress Catalogue Card No. 63–10339
ISBN 0–691–01779–4 (paperback edn.)
ISBN 0–691–09827–1 (hardcover edn.)
Manufactured in the United States of America
Text designed by Andor Braun

*Cover: An Eskimo ceremonial mask, courtesy of Staatliche
Museen Preussischer Kulturbesitz, Museum für Völkerkunde,
Berlin (West). Cover design: Frank Mahood. Cover
photograph: Waldtraut Schneider-Schütz*

To my French masters and colleagues

CONTENTS

Foreword   xi

Note on Orthography   xxiii

I. General Considerations. Recruiting Methods. Shamanism and Mystical Vocation   3

Approaches, 3 — The Bestowal of Shamanic Powers, 13 — Recruiting of Shamans in Western and Central Siberia, 15 — Recruiting among the Tungus, 17 — Recruiting among the Buryat and the Altaians, 18 — Hereditary Transmission and Quest in Obtaining Shamanic Powers, 20 — Shamanism and Psychopathology, 23

II. Initiatory Sicknesses and Dreams   33

Sickness-Initiation, 33 — Initiatory Ecstasies and Visions of the Yakut Shamans, 35 — Initiatory Dreams of the Samoyed Shamans, 38 — Initiation among the Tungus, the Buryat, and Others, 43 — Initiation of Australian Magicians, 45 — Australian — Siberian — South American and Other Parallels, 50 — Initiatory Dismemberment in North and South America, Africa, and Indonesia, 53 — Initiation of Eskimo Shamans, 58 — Contemplating One's Own Skeleton, 62 — Tribal Initiations and Secret Societies, 64

III. Obtaining Shamanic Powers   67

Siberian Myths concerning the Origin of Shamans, 68 — Shamanic Election among the Goldi and the Yakut, 71 —

vii

*Election among the Buryat and the Teleut, 75 — The Shaman
Female Tutelary Spirits, 79 — Role of the Souls of the Dea
81 — "Seeing the Spirits," 85 — The Helping Spirits, 88 -
"Secret Language" — "Animal Language," 96 — The Que
for Shamanic Powers in North America, 99*

IV. Shamanic Initiation   110

*Initiation among the Tungus and the Manchu, 110 — Yaku
Samoyed, and Ostyak Initiations, 113 — Buryat Initiatio
115 — Initiation of the Araucanian Shamaness, 122 — Ritu
Tree Climbing, 125 — Celestial Journey of the Carib Shama
127 — Ascent by the Rainbow, 131 — Australian Initiation
135 — Other Forms of the Rite of Ascent, 139*

V. Symbolism of the Shaman's Costume and Drun
                                                        1

*Preliminary Remarks, 145 — The Siberian Costume, 148
The Buryat Costume, 149 — The Altaic Costume, 152 — T
Shaman's Mirrors and Caps, 153 — Ornithological Symbolis
156 — Symbolism of the Skeleton, 158 — Rebirth from t
Bones, 160 — Shamanic Masks, 165 — The Shamanic Dru
168 — Ritual Costumes and Magical Drums throughout t
World, 176*

VI. Shamanism in Central and North Asia: 1
     I. Celestial Ascents. Descents to the Underwor

*The Shaman's Functions, 181 — "Black" and "Whit
Shamans. "Dualistic" Mythologies, 184 — Horse Sacrifice a
the Shaman's Ascent to the Sky (Altaic), 190 — Bai Ülg
and the Altaic Shaman, 198 — Descent to the Underwor
(Altaic), 200 — The Shaman as Psychopomp (Altaia
Goldi, Yurak), 205*

II. Shamanism in Central and North Asia: 215
II. Magical Cures. The Shaman as Psychopomp

Summoning and Searching for the Soul: Tatars, Buryat, Kazak-Kirgiz, 217 — The Shamanic Séance among the Ugrians and Lapps, 220 — Séances among the Ostyak, the Yurak, and the Samoyed, 225 — Shamanism among the Yakut and the Dolgan, 228 — Shamanic Séances among the Tungus and the Orochi, 236 — Yukagir Shamanism, 245 — Religion and Shamanism among the Koryak, 249 — Shamanism among the Chukchee, 252

I. Shamanism and Cosmology 259

The Three Cosmic Zones and the World Pillar, 259 — The Cosmic Mountain, 266 — The World Tree, 269 — The Mystical Numbers 7 and 9, 274 — Shamanism and Cosmology in the Oceanian Region, 279

Shamanism in North and South America 288

Shamanism among the Eskimo, 288 — North American Shamanism, 297 — The Shamanic Séance in North America, 300 — Shamanic Healing among the Paviotso, 302 — The Shamanic Séance among the Achomawi, 305 — Descent to the Underworld, 308 — Secret Brotherhoods and Shamanism, 313 — South American Shamanism: Various Rituals, 323 — Shamanic Healing, 326 — Antiquity of Shamanism in the Two Americas, 333

Southeast Asian and Oceanian Shamanism 337

Shamanic Beliefs and Techniques among the Semang, Sakai, and the Jakun, 337 — Shamanism in the Andaman Islands and Nicobar, 342 — Malayan Shamanism, 344 — Shamans and Priests in Sumatra, 346 — Shamanism in Borneo and Celebes, 349 — The "Boat of the Dead" and the Shamanic Boat,

355 — *Otherworld Journeys among the Dyak*, 359
Melanesian Shamanism, 361 — *Polynesian Shamanism*, 3

XI. Shamanic Ideologies and Techniques among th
Indo-Europeans 375

Preliminary Remarks, 375 — *Techniques of Ecstasy among t*
Ancient Germans, 379 — *Ancient Greece*, 387 — *Scythia*
Caucasians, Iranians, 394 — *Ancient India: Ascensional Rit*
403 — *Ancient India: Magical Flight*, 407 — *Tapas* and *Dīks*
412 — "*Shamanic*" *Symbolisms and Techniques in Ind*
414 — *Shamanism among the Aboriginal Tribes of India*, 4

XII. Shamanic Symbolisms and Techniques in Tib
China, and the Far East 428

Buddhism, Tantrism, Lamaism, 428 — *Shamanic Practi*
among the Lolo, 441 — *Shamanism among the Moso*, 444
Shamanic Symbolisms and Techniques in China, 447
Mongolia, Korea, Japan, 461

XIII. Parallel Myths, Symbols, and Rites 466

Dog and Horse, 466 — *Shamans and Smiths*, 470 — "*Mag*
Heat," 474 — "*Magical Flight*," 477 — *The Bridge and*
"*Difficult Passage*," 482 — *The Ladder* — *The Road of*
Dead — *Ascension*, 487

XIV. Conclusions 495

The Formation of North Asian Shamanism, 495

Epilogue 508

List of Works Cited 513

Index 571

FOREWORD

> the best of our knowledge the present book is the first to cover
> entire phenomenon of shamanism and at the same time to
uate it in the general history of religions. To say this is to imply
 liability to imperfection and approximation and the risks that
takes. Today the student has at his disposition a considerable
antity of documents for the various shamanisms—Siberian,
rth American, South American, Indonesian, Oceanian, and so
 Then too, a number of works, important in their several ways,
ve broken ground for the ethnological, sociological, and
chological study of shamanism (or rather, of a particular type
shamanism). But with a few notable exceptions—we refer
ecially to the studies of Altaic shamanism by Holmberg
arva)—the immense shamanic bibliography has neglected to
erpret this extremely complex phenomenon in the framework
he history of religions. It is as a historian of religions that we,
ur turn, have attempted to approach, understand, and present
manism. Far be it from us to think of belittling the admirable
dies undertaken from the viewpoints of psychology, sociology,
ethnology; we consider them indispensable to understanding the
ious aspects of shamanism. But we believe that there is room
another approach—that which we have sought to implement in
 following pages.

he writer who approaches shamanism as a psychologist will be
 to regard it as primarily the manifestation of a psyche in crisis
even in retrogression; he will not fail to compare it with
ain aberrant psychic behavior patterns or to class it among
ital diseases of the hysteroid or epileptoid type.

We shall explain why we consider it inacceptable to assimilate

xi

shamanism to any kind of mental disease.[1] But one point remain (and it is an important one), to which the psychologist will alway be justified in drawing attention: like any other religious vocatio the shamanic vocation is manifested by a crisis, a temporar derangement of the future shaman's spiritual equilibrium. All th observations and analyses that have been made on this point a particularly valuable. They show us, in actual process as it wer the repercussions, within the psyche, of what we have called th "dialectic of hierophanies"—the radical separation betwee profane and sacred and the resultant splitting of the world. To sa this is to indicate all the importance that we attribute to su studies in religious psychology.

The sociologist, for his part, is concerned with the soci function of the shaman, the priest, the magician. He will stud prestige originating from magical powers, its role in the structu of society, the relations between religious and political leade and so on. A sociological analysis of the myths of the First Sham will elicit revealing indications concerning the exceptional positi of the earliest shamans in certain archaic societies. The sociolo of shamanism remains to be written, and it will be among the mo important chapters in a general sociology of religion. T historian of religions must take all these studies and their co clusions into account. Added to the psychological conditic brought out by the psychologist, the social conditions, in t broadest sense of the term, reinforce the element of human a historical concreteness in the documents that he is called upon handle.

This concreteness will be accentuated by the studies of t ethnologist. It will be the task of ethnological monographs situate the shaman in his cultural milieu. There is danger of m understanding the true personality of a Chukchee shaman, example, if one reads of his exploits without knowing anythi about the life and traditions of the Chukchee. Again, it will be the ethnologist to make exhaustive studies of the shama

[1] See below, pp. 23 ff.

ostume and drum, to describe the séances, to record texts and
melodies, and so on. By undertaking to establish the "history" of
one or another constituent element of shamanism (the drum, for
example, or the use of narcotics during séances), the ethnologist—
joined when circumstances demand it, by a comparatist and a historian—will succeed in showing the circulation of the particular
motif in time and space; so far as possible, he will define its center
of expansion and the stages and the chronology of its dissemination.
In short, the ethnologist will also become a "historian," whether or
not he adopts the Graebner-Schmidt-Koppers method of cultural
cycles. In any case, in addition to an admirable purely descriptive
ethnographical literature, there are now available numerous works
of historical ethnology: in the overwhelming "gray mass" of cultural data stemming from the so-called "ahistorical" peoples, we
now begin to see certain lines of force appearing; we begin to distinguish "history" where we were in the habit of finding only
"Naturvölker," "primitives," or "savages."

It is unnecessary to dwell here on the great services that
historical ethnology has already rendered to the history of
religions. But we do not believe that it can take the place of the
history of religions. The latter's mission is to integrate the results
of ethnology, psychology, and sociology. Yet in doing so, it will
not renounce its own method of investigation or the viewpoint
that specifically defines it. Cultural ethnology may have demonstrated the relation of shamanism to certain cultural cycles, for
example, or the dissemination of one or another shamanic complex; yet its object is not to reveal the deeper meaning of all these
religious phenomena, to illuminate their symbolism, and to place
them in the general history of religions. In the last analysis, it is
for the historian of religions to synthesize all the studies of
particular aspects of shamanism and to present a comprehensive
view which shall be at once a morphology and a history of this
complex religious phenomenon.

But an understanding must be reached concerning the importance to be accorded to "history" in this type of investigation. As

we have said more than once elsewhere, and as we shall hav
occasion to show more fully in the complementary volume (i
preparation) to *Patterns in Comparative Religion*, although the hi
torical conditions are extremely important in a religious phenome
non (for every human datum is in the last analysis a historic
datum), they do not wholly exhaust it. We will cite only o
example here. The Altaic shaman ritually climbs a birch tree
which a certain number of steps have been cut; the birch syn
bolizes the World Tree, the steps representing the various heave
through which the shaman must pass on his ecstatic journey to t
highest heaven; and it is extremely probable that the cosmologic
schema implied in this ritual is of Oriental origin. Religio
ideas of the ancient Near East penetrated far into Central a
North Asia and contributed considerably to giving Central Asi
and Siberian shamanism their present features. This is a go
example of what "history" can teach us concerning the di
semination of religious ideologies and techniques. But, as
said above, the *history* of a religious phenomenon cannot reveal
that this phenomenon, by the mere fact of its manifestation, seeks
show us. Nothing warrants the supposition that influences fr
Oriental cosmology and religion *created* the ideology and ritual
the ascent to the sky among the Altaians; similar ideologies a
rituals appear all over the world and in regions where anci
Oriental influences are excluded a priori. More probably, the O
ental ideas merely *modified* the ritual formula and cosmologi
implications of the celestial ascent; the latter appears to be a p
mordial phenomenon, that is, it belongs to man as such, not to m
as a historical being; witness the dreams, hallucinations, and ima
of ascent found everywhere in the world, apart from any histori
or other "conditions." All these dreams, myths, and nostalgias w
a central theme of ascent or flight cannot be exhausted by a psyc
logical explanation; there is always a kernel that remains refract
to explanation, and this indefinable, irreducible element perha
reveals the real situation of man in the cosmos, a situation that,
shall never tire of repeating, is not solely "historical."

Thus the historian of religions, while taking historico-religious
cts into account, does his utmost to organize his documents in the
storical perspective—the only perspective that ensures their
ncreteness. But he must not forget that, when all is said and done,
e phenomena with which he is concerned reveal boundary-line
uations of mankind, and that these situations demand to be
derstood and made understandable. This work of deciphering
e deep meaning of religious phenomena rightfully falls to the
storian of religions. Certainly, the psychologist, the sociologist,
e ethnologist, and even the philosopher or the theologian will
ve their comment to make, each from the viewpoint and in the
rspective that are properly his. But it is the historian of religions
o will make the greatest number of valid statements on a
igious phenomenon *as a religious phenomenon*—and not as a
ychological, social, ethnic, philosophical, or even theological
enomenon. On this particular point the historian of religions
o differs from the phenomenologist. For the latter, in principle,
ects any work of comparison; confronted with one religious
enomenon or another, he confines himself to "approaching"
nd divining its meaning. Whereas the historian of religions does
t reach a comprehension of a phenomenon until after he has
npared it with thousands of similar or dissimilar phenomena,
til he has situated it among them; and these thousands of
enomena are separated not only in time but also in space. For a
e reason, the historian of religions will not confine himself
rely to a typology or morphology of religious data; he knows
t "history" does not exhaust the content of a religious phe-
nenon, but neither does he forget that it is always in History—
the broadest sense of the term—that a religious datum develops
its aspects and reveals all its meanings. In other words, the
torian of religions makes use of all the *historical* manifestations
a religious phenomenon in order to discover what such a phe-
nenon "has to say"; on the one hand, he holds to the historically
crete, but on the other, he attempts to decipher whatever
nshistorical content a religious datum reveals through history.

We need not dwell here on these few methodological considera tions; to set them forth adequately would require far more space than a foreword affords. Let us say, however, that the word "his tory" sometimes leads to confusion, for it can equally well mean historiography (the act of *writing* the history of something) and simply "what has happened" in the world. This second meaning of the word itself comprises several special meanings: history in the sense of what happened within certain spatial or temporal bounda ries (history of a particular people, of a particular period), that is the history of a continuity or of a structure; but then again, history in the general sense, as in the expressions "the historical existence of man," "historical situation," "historical moment," or even in the existentialist use of the term: man is "in situation," that is, in history.

The *history* of religions is not always necessarily the *histor ography* of religions. For in writing the history of one or another religion or of a given religious phenomenon (sacrifice among the Semites, the myth of Herakles, and so on), we are not always able to show everything "that happened" in a chronological perspec tive; we can do so, of course, if the documents permit, but we are not obliged to practice *historiography* in order to claim that we are writing the history of religions. The polyvalence of the term "history" has made it easy for scholars to misunderstand one another here; actually, it is the philosophical and general meaning of "history" that best suits our particular discipline. To practice that discipline is to study religious facts as such, that is, on the specific plane of manifestation. This specific plane of manifestation is always *historical*, concrete, existential, even if the religious facts manifested are not always wholly reducible to history. From the most elementary hierophanies—the manifestation of the sacred in some stone or tree, for example—to the most complex (the "vi sion" of a new "divine form" by a prophet or the founder of a re ligion), everything is manifested in the historically concrete and everything is in some sort conditioned by history. Yet in the hum blest hierophany there is an "eternal new beginning," an etern eturn to an atemporal moment, a desire to abolish history, to blot ut the past, to recreate the world. All this is "shown" in religious cts; it is not an invention of the historian of religions. Obviously, historian bent on being only a historian has the right to ignore he specific and transhistorical meanings of a religious fact; an hnologist, a sociologist, a psychologist may do likewise. A historian of religions cannot ignore them. Familiar with a considerable umber of hierophanies, his eye will have learned to decipher the operly religious meaning of one or another fact. And to return to he very point from which we set out, this book strictly deserves to e called a study in the history of religions even if it does not follow he chronological course of historiography.

Then too, this chronological perspective, however interesting certain historians, is far from having the importance commonly tributed to it. For, as we have attempted to show in *Patterns in omparative Religion*, the very dialectic of the sacred tends definitely to repeat a series of archetypes, so that a hierophany ealized at a certain "historical moment" is structurally equivalent a hierophany a thousand years earlier or later. This tendency on he part of the hierophanic process to repeat the same paradoxical cralization of reality ad infinitum is what, after all, enables us to nderstand something of a religious phenomenon and to write its history." In other words, it is precisely because hierophanies peat themselves that we can distinguish religious facts and ccceed in understanding them. But hierophanies have the peculiarity of seeking to reveal the sacred in its totality, even if the uman beings in whose consciousness the sacred "shows itself" sten upon only one aspect or one small part of it. In the most ementary hierophany *everything is declared*. The manifestation of he sacred in a stone or a tree is neither less mysterious nor less oble than its manifestation in a "god." The process of sacralizing eality is the same; the *forms* taken by the process in man's eligious consciousness differ.

This is not without its bearing on the conception of a chronological perspective of religion. Though a *history* of religion exists, it is

xvii

not, like all other kinds of history, irreversible. A monotheis
religious consciousness is not necessarily monotheistic through
its span of existence for the reason that it forms part of a mor
theistic "history," and that, as we know, within that history c
cannot revert to polytheism or paganism after having known a
practiced monotheism. On the contrary, one can perfectly well b
polytheist or indulge in the religious practices of a totemist wh
thinking and maintaining that one is a monotheist. The dialectic
the sacred permits all reversibilities; no "form" is exempt fr
degradation and decomposition, no "history" is final. Not o
can a community—consciously or unconsciously—practice ma
religions, but the same individual can have an infinite variety
religious experiences, from the "highest" to the most undevelop
and aberrant. This is equally true from the opposite point of vie
any cultural moment whatever can provide the fullest revelation
the sacred to which the human condition is capable of accedi
Despite the immense historical differences involved, the expe
ences of the monotheistic prophets can be repeated in the m
"backward" of primitive tribes; the only requirement is "re
zation" of the hierophany of a celestial god, a god attested nea
everywhere in the world even though he may be absent from
current practice of religion. No religious form, however vitiat
is incapable of producing a perfectly pure and coherent mysticis
If exceptions of this kind are not numerous enough to impr
observers, this is due not to the dialectic of the sacred but to hum
behavior in respect to that dialectic. And the study of hum
behavior lies beyond the field of the historian of religions; it is
concern of the sociologist, the psychologist, the moralist,
philosopher. In our role of historian of religions, it suffices us
observe that the dialectic of the sacred makes possible the spon
neous reversal of any religious position. The very fact of t
reversibility is important, for it is not to be found elsewhere. T
is why we tend to remain uninfluenced by certain results attai
by historico-cultural ethnology. The various types of civilizat
are, of course, organically connected with certain religious for

ut this in no sense excludes the spontaneity and, in the last analysis, the ahistoricity of religious life. For all history is in some measure a fall of the sacred, a limitation and diminution. But the sacred does not cease to manifest itself, and with each new manifestation it resumes its original tendency to reveal itself wholly. is true, of course, that the countless new manifestations of the sacred in the religious consciousness of one or another society repeat the countless manifestations of the sacred that those societies knew in the course of their past, of their "history." But it is equally true that this history does not paralyze the spontaneity of hierophanies; at every moment a fuller revelation of the sacred remains possible.

It happens—and this brings us back to our discussion of chronology in the history of religions—that the reversibility of religious positions is even more striking in the case of the mystical experiences of archaic societies. As we shall frequently show, particularly coherent mystical experiences are possible at any and every degree of civilization and of religious situation. This is as much as to say that, for certain religious consciousnesses in crisis, there is always the possibility of a historical leap that enables them to attain otherwise inaccessible spiritual positions. Certainly, "history"—the religious tradition of the tribe in question—really intervenes to subject the ecstatic experiences of certain privileged persons to its own canons. But it is no less true that these experiences often have the same precision and nobility as the experiences of the great mystics of East and West.

Now, shamanism is precisely one of the archaic techniques of ecstasy—at once mysticism, magic, and "religion" in the broadest sense of the term. We have sought to present it in its various historical and cultural aspects, and we have even tried to outline a brief history of the development of shamanism in Central and North Asia. But what we consider of greater importance is presenting the shamanic phenomenon itself, analyzing its ideology, discussing its techniques, its symbolism, its mythologies. We believe that such a study can be of interest not only to the specialist but also to the cultivated man, and it is to the latter that this boo[k] is primarily addressed. For example, facts that we could hav[e] adduced concerning the dissemination of the Central Asian dru[m] in the Arctic regions, while of intense interest to a small group [of] specialists, would probably leave the majority of readers cold. B[ut] things change—or, at least, so we hope—when it becomes a matt[er] of entering so vast and varied a mental universe as that of shama[n]ism in general and the techniques of ecstasy that it implies. In th[is] case we are dealing with a whole spiritual world, which, thoug[h] differing from our own, is neither less consistent nor less interes[t]ing. We make bold to believe that a knowledge of it is a necessi[ty] for every true humanist; for it has been some time since humanis[m] has ceased to be identified with the spiritual tradition of the We[st,] great and fertile though that is.

Conceived in this spirit, this work cannot possibly exhaust any [of] the aspects that it approaches in its several chapters. We have n[ot] undertaken a complete study of shamanism; we lack both the [?] sources and the will for such a task. It is always as a comparat[ist] and a historian of religions that we have treated our subje[ct;] admitting which, we plead guilty in advance to the inevitable ga[ps] and imperfections in a work that, in the last analysis, represe[nts] an effort toward a synthesis. We are neither an Altaicist nor [an] Americanist nor an Oceanicist, and it is probable that a cert[ain] number of specialized studies have escaped our notice.

Even so, we do not believe that the over-all picture drawn he[re] would have been modified in its general outlines: many stud[ies] merely repeat, with slight variants, the accounts of the earli[er] observers. Popov's bibliography, published in 1923 and confi[ned] exclusively to Siberian shamanism, lists 650 works by Russ[ian] ethnologists. The bibliographies of North American shamani[sm] and Indonesian shamanism are similarly extensive. One cann[ot] read everything. And we repeat: we have no thought of tak[ing] the place of the ethnologist, the Altaicist, or the American[ist.] However, we have supplied footnotes throughout, indicating

incipal works to which the reader may turn for supplementary
formation. Naturally, we could have greatly increased the
ocumentation, but that would have meant a work in several
olumes. We did not see the value of such an undertaking;
ur aim is not a series of monographs on the various shamanisms,
ut a general study addressed to nonspecialist readers. Then too,
number of subjects to which we have merely referred will be
udied in greater detail in other works (*Death and Initiation,
ythologies of Death*, etc.).

We could not have completed this book without the help and
ncouragement we received, during these five years of work,
om General N. Radesco, former Prime Minister of Romania;
om the Centre National de la Recherche Scientifique (Paris);
om the Viking Fund (New York); and from Bollingen Founda-
on (New York). To them all, we offer our most sincere thanks
re. We have taken the liberty of dedicating this book to our
ench masters and colleagues, as a modest testimony of gratitude
· the encouragement that they have never ceased to lavish on us
nce our arrival in France.

We have already partially set forth the results of our researches
certain articles—"Le Problème du chamanisme," *Revue de l'his-
re des religions*, CXXXI (1946), 5–52; "Shamanism," in *For-
tten Religions*, edited by Vergilius Ferm (New York, 1949), pp.
9–308; and "Einführende Betrachtungen über den Schamanis-
is," *Paideuma*, V (1951), 88–97—and in lectures that we had
e honor to deliver, in March, 1950, at the University of Rome
d the Istituto Italiano per il Medio ed Estremo Oriente, at the
·itation of Professors R. Pettazzoni and G. Tucci.

MIRCEA ELIADE

ris, March, 1946–March, 1951

FOREWORD

POSTSCRIPT (1962)

Translations of this work into Italian, German, and Spanish were pu[b]lished in 1953, 1957, and 1960, and each time we took the opportunity [to] make corrections and improvements in a book that, for all its sho[rt]comings, was the first to treat shamanism as a whole. But it has been [in] preparing the text for the present edition in English that we have th[or]oughly corrected and considerably added to the original work. Numero[us] studies of the various shamanisms have been published during the pa[st] ten years. We have attempted to make use of these in our text, or at le[ast] to mention them in the notes. Though we have recorded nearly two hu[n]dred new publications (that is, which have appeared since 1948), we l[ay] no claim to have exhausted the recent bibliography of shamanism. But, [as] we said before, this book is the work of a historian of religions, who a[p]proaches the subject as a comparatist; it cannot take the place of sp[e]cialists' monographs devoted to various individual aspects of shamanis[m]. The present English translation may be considered the second editi[on,] corrected and enlarged, of the volume published in 1951 under the ti[tle] *Le Chamanisme et les techniques archaïques de l'extase.* Cf. also our arti[cle] "Recent Works on Shamanism: a Review Article," *History of Religio[ns,]* I (summer, 1961), 152–86.

Once more we wish to express our gratitude to Bollingen Foundati[on:] the grant that it accorded us has enabled us to continue our study [of] shamanism long after the publication of the French edition.

By relieving us from teaching during the third trimester in 1958 a[nd] 1959, Dean Jerald Brauer, of the Federated Theological Faculty of [the] University of Chicago, made it possible for us to devote ourselves to p[re]paring the present edition. We tender him sincere thanks.

Finally, we are glad to have this opportunity to express all our gra[ti]tude to our loyal translator and friend, Willard R. Trask, who, on[ce] again, has devoted his best skill to producing an adequate rendering [of] our book. Also, special thanks are due to Miss Sonia Volochova a[nd] William McGuire for their assistance in editing the manuscript and [to] A. S. B. Glover for preparing the index.

MIRCEA ELIAD[E]

University of Chicago
June, 1962

NOTE ON ORTHOGRAPHY

ranscriptions of Russian names and terms and of names and
rms derived, through Russian transliterations, from the lan-
ages of the various Siberian tribes follow in general the trans-
eration system adopted by the Joint Committee on Slavic Studies,
pointed by the American Council of Learned Societies and the
cial Science Research Council. The system is not applied to the
tual names of the Siberian tribes or to personal names that have
tablished spellings: e.g., Sandschejew, Shirokogoroff.

The spelling of names of tribes, including names of Siberian
bes, follows that established in George Peter Murdock, *Outline
World Cultures* (Human Relations Area Files Press, New Haven,
58).

For names and terms transliterated from Oriental and other non-
ropean languages, the usages of current English and American
holarship are followed in so far as possible, except in quotations.

Where necessary, variant spellings of forms of authors' names
d variant transliterations of foreign words are given in paren-
ses: e.g., Waldemar G. Bogoras (V. G. Bogoras); *tabjan
ibyan*).

ll references for works cited in the footnotes are given in the
st of Works Cited.

SHAMANISM

Archaic Techniques

of Ecstasy

CHAPTER ONE

General Considerations.
Recruiting Methods. Shamanism
and Mystical Vocation

Approaches

SINCE the beginning of the century, ethnologists have fallen into the habit of using the terms "shaman," "medicine man," "sorcerer," and "magician" interchangeably to designate certain individuals possessing magico-religious powers and found in all "primitive" societies. By extension, the same terminology has been applied in studying the religious history of "civilized" peoples, and there have been discussions, for example, of an Indian, an Iranian, a Germanic, a Chinese, and even a Babylonian "shamanism" with reference to the "primitive" elements attested in the corresponding religions. For many reasons this confusion can only militate against any understanding of the shamanic phenomenon. If the word "shaman" is taken to mean any magician, sorcerer, medicine man, or ecstatic found throughout the history of religions and religious ethnology, we arrive at a notion at once extremely complex and extremely vague; it seems, furthermore, to serve no purpose, for we already have the terms "magician" or "sorcerer" to express notions as unlike and as ill-defined as "primitive magic" or "primitive mysticism."

We consider it advantageous to restrict the use of the words "shaman" and "shamanism," precisely to avoid misunderstandings and to cast a clearer light on the history of "magic" and "sorcery." For, of course, the shaman is also a magician a medicine man; he is believed to cure, like all doctors, and perform miracles of the fakir type, like all magicians, wheth primitive or modern. But beyond this, he is a psychopomp, and may also be priest, mystic, and poet. In the dim, "confusionisti mass of the religious life of archaic societies considered as a who shamanism—taken in its strict and exact sense—already sho a structure of its own and implies a "history" that there is eve reason to clarify.

Shamanism in the strict sense is pre-eminently a religio phenomenon of Siberia and Central Asia. The word comes to through the Russian, from the Tungusic *šaman*. In the oth languages of Central and North Asia the corresponding terms a Yakut *ojuna* (*oyuna*), Mongolian *bügä*, *bögä* (*buge*, *bü*), and *udag* (cf. also Buryat *udayan*, Yakut *udoyan*: "shamaness"), Turk Tatar *kam* (Altaic *kam*, *gam*, Mongolian *kami*, etc.). It has be sought to explain the Tungusic term by the Pali *samaṇa*, and shall return to this possible etymology (which is part of the gr problem of Indian influences on Siberian religions) in the l chapter of this book.[1] Throughout the immense area compris Central and North Asia, the magico-religious life of soci centers on the shaman. This, of course, does not mean that h the one and only manipulator of the sacred, nor that religi activity is completely usurped by him. In many tribes the sa ficing priest coexists with the shaman, not to mention the fact t every head of a family is also the head of the domestic c Nevertheless, the shaman remains the dominating figure; through this whole region in which the ecstatic experience is c sidered the religious experience par excellence, the shaman, he alone, is the great master of ecstasy. A first definition of complex phenomenon, and perhaps the least hazardous, will shamanism = *technique of ecstasy*.

As such, it was documented and described by the earl travelers in the various countries of Central and North A

1 Pp. 495 ff.

ter, similar magico-religious phenomena were observed in
orth America, Indonesia, Oceania, and elsewhere. And, as we
all soon see, these latter phenomena are thoroughly shamanic,
d there is every reason to study them together with Siberian
shamanism. Yet one observation must be made at the outset: the
esence of a shamanic complex in one region or another does not
cessarily mean that the magico-religious life of the corre-
onding people is crystallized around shamanism. This can occur
s, for example, in certain parts of Indonesia), but it is not the
ost usual state of affairs. Generally shamanism coexists with
her forms of magic and religion.

It is here that we see all the advantage of employing the term
shamanism" in its strict and proper sense. For, if we take the
ouble to differentiate the shaman from other magicians and
edicine men of primitive societies, the identification of shamanic
mplexes in one or another region immediately acquires definite
nificance. Magic and magicians are to be found more or less
 over the world, whereas shamanism exhibits a particular
gical specialty, on which we shall later dwell at length: "mas-
y over fire," "magical flight," and so on. By virtue of this fact,
ough the shaman is, among other things, a magician, not every
gician can properly be termed a shaman. The same distinction
st be applied in regard to shamanic healing; every medicine
n is a healer, but the shaman employs a method that is his and
 alone. As for the shamanic techniques of ecstasy, they do not
aust all the varieties of ecstatic experience documented in the
ory of religions and religious ethnology. Hence any ecstatic
not be considered a shaman; the shaman specializes in a trance
ing which his soul is believed to leave his body and ascend to
 sky or descend to the underworld.

A similar distinction is also necessary to define the shaman's
tion to "spirits." All through the primitive and modern worlds
 find individuals who profess to maintain relations with
irits," whether they are "possessed" by them or control them.
eral volumes would be needed for an adequate study of all the

problems that arise in connection with the mere idea of "spiri
and of their possible relations with human beings; for a "spir
can equally well be the soul of a dead person, a "nature spirit,
mythical animal, and so on. But the study of shamanism does
require going into all this; we need only define the shama
relation to his helping spirits. It will easily be seen wherei
shaman differs from a "possessed" person, for example;
shaman controls his "spirits," in the sense that he, a human bei
is able to communicate with the dead, "demons," and "nat
spirits," without thereby becoming their instrument. To be su
shamans are sometimes found to be "possessed," but these
exceptional cases for which there is a particular explanati

These few preliminary observations already indicate the cou
that we propose to follow in order to reach an adequate und
standing of shamanism. In view of the fact that this magico-r
gious phenomenon has had its most complete manifestation
North and Central Asia, we shall take the shaman of these regi
as our typical example. We are not unaware, and we shall endea
to show, that Central and North Asian shamanism, at least in
present form, is not a primordial phenomenon free from
external influence; on the contrary, it is a phenomenon that h
long "history." But this Central Asian and Siberian shaman
has the advantage of presenting a structure in which elements
exist independently elsewhere in the world—i.e., special relati
with "spirits," ecstatic capacities permitting of magical fli
ascents to the sky, descents to the underworld, mastery over
etc.—are here already found integrated with a particular ideo
and validating specific techniques.

Shamanism in this strict sense is not confined to Central
North Asia, and we shall endeavor later to point out the grea
possible number of parallels. On the other hand, certain sham
elements are found in isolation in various forms of archaic m
and religion. And they are of considerable interest, for they s
to what extent shamanism proper preserves a substratum
"primitive" beliefs and techniques and to what extent it has

vated. Always endeavoring to define the place of shamanism
thin primitive religions (with all that these imply: magic,
lief in Supreme Beings and spirits, mythological concepts,
:hniques of ecstasy, and so on), we shall constantly be obliged to
fer to more or less similar phenomena, without implying
it they are shamanic. But it is always profitable to compare and
point out what a magico-religious element similar to a certain
amanic element has produced elsewhere in a different cultural
semble and with a different spiritual orientation.[2]

For all that shamanism dominates the religious life of Central
l North Asia, it is nevertheless not *the* religion of that vast
;ion. Only convenience or confusion has made it possible for
ne investigators to consider the religion of the Arctic or Turko-
tar peoples to be shamanism. The religions of Central and
rth Asia extend beyond shamanism in every direction, just as
/ religion extends beyond the mystical experience of its
vileged adherents. Shamans are of the "elect," and as such they
'e access to a region of the sacred inaccessible to other members
the community. Their ecstatic experiences have exercised, and
l exercise, a powerful influence on the stratification of religious
ology, on mythology, on ritualism. But neither the ideology nor
mythology and rites of the Arctic, Siberian, and Asian peoples
the creation of their shamans. All these elements are earlier
n shamanism, or at least are parallel to it, in the sense that they
the product of the *general* religious experience and not of a
ticular class of privileged beings, the ecstatics. On the contrary,

2 In this sense, and only in this sense, do we regard identifying "sha-
ic" elements in a highly developed religion or mysticism as valuable.
:overing a shamanic symbol or rite in ancient India or Iran begins to
: meaning only in the degree to which one is led to see shamanism as a
rly defined religious phenomenon; otherwise, one can go on forever talk-
of "primitive elements," which can be found in any religion, no matter
"developed." For the religions of India and Iran, like all the other re-
•ns of the modern or ancient East, display a number of "primitive ele-
ts" that are not necessarily shamanic. We cannot even consider every
nique of ecstasy found in the East "shamanic," however "primitive"
ay be.

7

as we shall see, we frequently find the shamanic (that is, ecstati
experience attempting to express itself through an ideology that
not always favorable to it.

In order not to encroach on the subject matter of the followi
chapters, we will here say only that shamans are persons who sta
out in their respective societies by virtue of characterist
that, in the societies of modern Europe, represent the signs o
vocation or at least of a religious crisis. They are separated fr
the rest of the community by the intensity of their own religi
experience. In other words, it would be more correct to cl
shamanism among the mysticisms than with what is commo
called a religion. We shall find shamanism within a considera
number of religions, for shamanism always remains an ecsta
technique at the disposal of a particular elite and represents, a
were, the mysticism of the particular religion. A comparison
once comes to mind—that of monks, mystics, and saints wit
Christian churches. But the comparison must not be pushed too
In contrast to the state of affairs in Christianity (at least during
recent history), peoples who profess to be shamanists accord c
siderable importance to the ecstatic experiences of their shama
these experiences concern them personally and immediately; fc
is the shamans who, by their trances, cure them, accompany tl
dead to the "Realm of Shades," and serve as mediators betw
them and their gods, celestial or infernal, greater or lesser. 7
small mystical elite not only directs the community's religious
but, as it were, guards its "soul." The shaman is the great spec
ist in the human soul; he alone "sees" it, for he knows its "fo
and its destiny.

And wherever the immediate fate of the soul is not at is
wherever there is no question of sickness (= loss of the soul
death, or of misfortune, or of a great sacrificial rite involving s
ecstatic experience (mystical journey to the sky or the un
world), the shaman is not indispensable. A large part of relig
life takes place without him.

The Arctic, Siberian, and Central Asian peoples are mad

iefly of hunters-fishers or herdsmen-breeders. A degree of no-
adism is typical of them all. And despite their ethnic and linguis-
: differences, in general their religions coincide. Chukchee,
ungus, Samoyed, or Turko-Tatars, to mention only some of the
ost important groups, know and revere a celestial Great God, an
-powerful Creator but on the way to becoming a *deus otiosus*.[3]
metimes the Great God's name even means "Sky" or "Heaven";
ch, for example, is the Num of the Samoyed, the Buga of the
ungus, or the Tengri of the Mongols (cf. also Tengeri of the
ryat, Tängere of the Volga Tatars, Tingir of the Beltir, Tangara
the Yakut, etc.). Even when the concrete name of the "sky"
lacking, we find some one of its most characteristic attributes—
igh," "lofty," "luminous," and so on. Thus, among the Ostyak
the Irtysh the name of the celestial god is derived from *sänke*, the
imitive meaning of which is "luminous, shining, light." The
kut call him "Lord Father Chief of the World," the Tatars of
 Altai "White Light" (Ak Ayas), the Koryak "The One on
gh," "The Master of the High," and so on. The Turko-Tatars,
ong whom the celestial Great God preserves his religious cur-
cy more than among their neighbors to the north and northeast,
 call him "Chief," "Master," "Lord," and often "Father." [4]
This celestial god, who dwells in the highest sky, has several
ns" or "messengers" who are subordinate to him and who oc-
y lower heavens. Their names and number vary from tribe to
e; seven or nine "sons" or "daughters" are commonly men-
ied, and the shaman maintains special relations with some of
n. These sons, messengers, or servants of the celestial god are
rged with watching over and helping human beings. The
theon is sometimes far more numerous, as, for example, among

3 This phenomenon, which is especially important for the history of
ions, is by no means confined to Central and North Asia. It is found
ughout the world and has not yet been entirely explained; cf. Eliade,
erns in Comparative Religion, pp. 46 ff. If only indirectly, it is hoped
the present work will throw some light on this problem.
4 See Eliade, *Patterns*, pp. 60 ff.; J.-P. Roux, "Tängri. Essai sur le ciel
des peuples altaïques."

the Buryat, the Yakut, and the Mongols. The Buryat mentic
fifty-five "good" and forty-four "evil" gods, who have been fo
ever opposed in unending strife. But, as we shall show later,[5] the
is reason to believe that both this multiplication of gods and the
mutual hostility may be comparatively recent innovations.

Among the Turko-Tatars goddesses play a rather minor rol
The earth divinity is not at all prominent. The Yakut, for exampl
have no figurines of the earth goddess and offer no sacrifices
her.[7] The Turko-Tatar and Siberian peoples know several femini
divinities, but they are reserved for women, their spheres bei
childbirth and children's diseases.[8] The mythological role of wom
is also markedly small, although traces of it remain in some sh
manic traditions. The only great god after the God of the Sky
the Atmosphere [9] is, among the Altaians, the Lord of the Und
world, Erlik (= Ärlik) Khan, who is also well known to the sh
man. The very important fire cult, hunting rites, the conception
death—to which we shall return more than once—complete this br
outline of Central and North Asian religious life. Morphologica
this religion is, in general, close to that of the Indo-Europeans:
both there is the same importance of the great God of the Sky or
the Atmosphere, the same absence of goddesses (so characteris
of the Indo-Mediterranean area), the same function attributed
the "sons" or "messengers" (Aśvins, Dioscuri, etc.), the sa
exaltation of fire. On the sociological and economic planes the si
larities between the protohistorical Indo-Europeans and the a
cient Turko-Tatars are even more strikingly clear: both societ
were patriarchal in structure, with the head of the family enjoy

5 Below, pp. 184 ff.

6 Cf. Eveline Lot-Falck, "À propos d'Ätügän."

7 Uno Harva (formerly Holmberg), *Die religiösen Vorstellungen
altaischen Völker*, p. 247.

8 Cf. Gustav Ränk, "Lapp Female Deities of the Madder-Akka Grou
especially pp. 48 ff.

9 For in Central Asia, too, we find the well-known transition
celestial god to a god of the atmosphere or of storm; cf. Eliade, *Patte
pp. 91 ff.

reat prestige, and on the whole their economy was that of the
unters and herdsmen-breeders. The religious importance of the
orse among the Turko-Tatars and the Indo-Europeans has long
een noted. And the most ancient of Greek sacrifices, the Olympian,
as been shown to possess characteristics of the sacrifice practiced
y the Turko-Tatars, the Ugrians, and the Arctic peoples—pre-
sely the typical sacrifice of the primitive hunters and herdsmen-
eeders. These facts have their bearing on the problem with which
e are concerned. Given the economic, social, and religious paral-
ls between the ancient Indo-Europeans and the ancient Turko-
atars (or, better, Proto-Turks),[10] we must determine to what
tent the various historical Indo-European peoples still preserve
amanic survivals comparable to Turko-Tatar shamanism.

But, as can never be sufficiently emphasized, nowhere in the
orld or in history will a perfectly "pure" and "primordial" re-
ious phenomenon be found. The paleoethnological and pre-
storic documents at our disposition go back no further than the
leolithic; and nothing justifies the supposition that, during the
undreds of thousands of years that preceded the earliest Stone
ge, humanity did not have a religious life as intense and as various
in the succeeding periods. It is almost certain that at least a part
prelithic humanity's magico-religious beliefs were preserved in
er religious conceptions and mythologies. But it is also highly
obable that this spiritual heritage from the prelithic period un-
rwent continual changes as a result of the numerous cultural
ntacts among pre- and protohistorical peoples. Thus, nowhere in
 history of religions do we encounter "primordial" phenomena;
 history has been everywhere, changing, recasting, enriching, or
poverishing religious concepts, mythological creations, rites,
hniques of ecstasy. Obviously, every religion that, after long

0 On the prehistory and earliest history of the Turks, see René Grousset's
 mirable synthesis, *L'Empire des steppes.* Cf. also W. Koppers, "Urtürken-
 m und Urindogermanentum im Lichte der völkerkundlichen Universal-
 chichte"; W. Barthold, *Histoire des Turcs d'Asie Centrale;* Karl Jettmar:
 ur Herkunft der türkischen Völkerschaften"; "The Altai before the
 ks"; "Urgeschichte Innerasiens," pp. 153 ff.

processes of inner transformation, finally develops into an autono
mous structure presents a "form" that is its own and that is accepte
as such in the later history of humanity. But no religion is com
pletely "new," no religious message completely abolishes the pas
Rather, there is a recasting, a renewal, a revalorization, an inte
gration of the elements—the most essential elements!—of an imme
morial religious tradition.

These few remarks will serve for the present to delimit the his
torical horizon of shamanism. Some of its elements, which we sha
indicate later, are clearly archaic, but that does not mean that the
are "pure" and "primordial." In the form in which we find i
Turko-Mongol shamanism is even decidedly marked by Orient
influences; and though there are other shamanisms without suc
definite and recent influences, they too are not "primordial."

As for the Arctic, Siberian, and Central Asian religions, in whi
shamanism has reached its most advanced degree of integratio
we may say that they are characterized on the one hand by t
scarcely felt presence of a celestial Great God, and on the other
hunting rites and an ancestor cult that imply a wholly differe
religious orientation. As will be shown later, the shaman is more
less directly involved in each of these religious areas. But one h
the impression that he is more at home in one area than in anothe
Constituted by the ecstatic experience and by magic, shamanis
adapts itself more or less successfully to the various religious stru
tures that preceded or are cotemporal with it. Replacing t
description of some shamanic performance in the frame of the ge
eral religious life of the people concerned (we are thinking,
example, of the celestial Great God and the myths about him),
sometimes find ourselves amazed; we have the impression of t
wholly different religious universes. But the impression is false;
difference lies not in the structure of the religious universes but
the intensity of the religious experience induced by the shama
performance. The shaman's séance almost always has recourse
ecstasy; and the history of religions is there to show us that no ot
religious experience is more subject to distortion and aberrati

To close these few preliminary observations here: In studying hamanism we must always remember that it values a certain number of special and even "private" religious elements and that, at the same time, it is far from exhausting the religious life of the rest of the community. The shaman begins his new, his true life by a "separation"—that is, as we shall presently see, by a spiritual crisis that is not lacking in tragic greatness and in beauty.

The Bestowal of Shamanic Powers

In Central and Northeast Asia the chief methods of recruiting shamans are: (1) hereditary transmission of the shamanic profession and (2) spontaneous vocation ("call" or "election"). There are also cases of individuals who become shamans of their own free will (as, for example, among the Altaians) or by the will of the clan (Tungus, etc.). But these "self-made" shamans are considered less powerful than those who inherited the profession or who obeyed the "call" of the gods and spirits.[11] As for choice by the clan, it is dependent upon the candidate's ecstatic experience; if that does not follow, the youth appointed to take the place of the dead shaman is ruled out.[12]

However selected, a shaman is not recognized as such until after he has received two kinds of teaching: (1) ecstatic (dreams, trances, etc.) and (2) traditional (shamanic techniques, names and functions of the spirits, mythology and genealogy of the clan, secret language, etc.). This twofold course of instruction, given by the spirits and the old master shamans, is equivalent to an initiation. Sometimes initiation is public and constitutes an autonomous ritual in itself. But absence of this kind of ritual in no sense implies absence of an initiation; the latter can perfectly well occur in dream or in the neophyte's ecstatic experience. The available documents on shamanic dreams clearly show that they involve an initiation

11 For the Altaians, see G. N. Potanin, *Ocherki severo-zapadnoi Mongolii*, , 57; V. M. Mikhailowski, "Shamanism in Siberia and European Russia," 90.   12 See below, p. 17.

whose structure is well known to the history of religions. In an
case, there is no question of anarchical hallucinations and of a pure
ly individual plot and dramatis personae; the hallucinations and th
mise en scène follow traditional models that are perfectly consister
and possess an amazingly rich theoretical content.

This fact, we believe, provides a sounder basis for the proble
of the psychopathy of shamans, to which we shall soon returr
Psychopaths or not, the future shamans are expected to pas
through certain initiatory ordeals and to receive an education tha
is sometimes highly complex. It is only this twofold initiation–
ecstatic and didactic—that transforms the candidate from a possib
neurotic into a shaman recognized by his particular society. Th
same observation applies to the origin of shamanic powers: it
not the point of departure for obtaining these powers (heredit
bestowal by the spirits, voluntary quest) that is important, but th
technique and its underlying theory, transmitted through initia
tion.

This observation seems important, for more than one schol
has sought to draw major conclusions concerning the structure ar
even the history of this religious phenomenon from the fact that
certain shamanism is hereditary or spontaneous, or that the "cal
that determines a shaman's career appears to be conditioned (
not) by his psychopathic constitution. We shall return to the
methodological problems later. For the moment we will confi
ourselves to reviewing some Siberian and North Asian documen
on the "election" of shamans, without attempting to arrange the
under headings (hereditary transmission, call, appointment by t
clan, personal decision), for, as we shall presently see, the m
jority of the peoples with whom we are concerned have more th
one method of recruiting their shamans.[13]

13 On the grant of shamanic powers, see Georg Nioradze, *Der Schaman
mus bei den sibirischen Völkern*, pp. 54–58; Leo Sternberg, "Divine Elect
in Primitive Religion," passim; id., "Die Auserwählung im sibirisc
Schamanismus," passim; Harva, *Die religiösen Vorstellungen*, pp. 452
Åke Ohlmarks, *Studien zum Problem des Schamanismus*, pp. 25 ff.; Urs
Knoll-Greiling, "Berufung und Berufungserlebnis bei den Schamanen."

Recruiting of Shamans in Western and Central Siberia

Among the Vogul, N. L. Gondatti reports, shamanism is hereditary and is also transmitted in the female line. But the future shaman exhibits exceptional traits from adolescence; he very early becomes nervous and is sometimes even subject to epileptic seizures, which are interpreted as meetings with the gods.[14] Among the eastern Ostyak the situation appears to be different; according to S. A. Dunin-Gorkavich, shamanism is not learned there, it is a gift from heaven, received at birth. In the Irtysh region it is a gift from Sänke (the Sky God) and is manifest from earliest years. The Vasyugan also hold that one is born a shaman.[15] But, as Karjalainen remarks,[16] hereditary or spontaneous, shamanism is always a gift from the gods or spirits; viewed from a certain angle, it is hereditary only in appearance.

Generally the two forms of obtaining shamanic powers coexist. Among the Votyak, for example, shamanism is hereditary, but it is also granted directly by the Supreme God, who himself instructs the future shaman through dreams and visions.[17] Exactly the same is true among the Lapps, where the gift is transmitted in a family but the spirits also grant it to those on whom they wish to bestow it.[18]

Among the Siberian Samoyed and the Ostyak shamanism is hereditary. On the shaman's death, his son fashions a wooden image of his father's hand and through this symbol inherits his powers.[19] But being the son of a shaman is not enough; the neophyte must also be accepted and approved by the spirits.[20] Among

14 K. F. Karjalainen, *Die Religion der Jugra-Völker*, III, 248.
15 Ibid., pp. 248–49.   16 Ibid., pp. 250 f.
17 Mikhailowski, p. 153.
18 Ibid., pp. 147–48; T. I. Itkonen, *Heidnische Religion und späterer Aberglaube bei den finnischen Lappen*, pp. 116, 117, n. 1.
19 P. I. Tretyakov, *Turukhansky krai, evo priroda i zhiteli*, p. 211; Mikhailowski, p. 86.
20 A. M. Castrén, *Nordische Reisen und Forschungen*, IV, 191; Mikhailowski, p. 142.

the Yurak-Samoyed the future shaman is marked from birth
infants born with their "shirt" (i.e., caul) are destined to become
shamans (those born with the "shirt" covering only the head will
be lesser shamans). Toward the approach of maturity the candidate
begins to have visions, sings in his sleep, likes to wander in soli
tude, and so on; after this incubation period he attaches himself to
an old shaman to be taught.[21] Among the Ostyak it is sometime
the father himself who chooses his successor among his sons; in
doing so, he does not consider primogeniture but the candidate'
capacities. He then transmits the traditional secret knowledge to
him. A shaman without children transmits it to a friend or disciple
But in any case those destined to become shamans spend their
youth mastering the doctrines and techniques of the profession.[22]

Among the Yakut, W. Sieroszewski writes,[23] the gift of sha
manism is not hereditary. However, the *ämägät* (sign, tutelar
spirit) does not vanish after the shaman's death and hence tends to
incarnate itself in a member of the same family. N. V. Pripuzov
supplies the following details: One destined to shamanship begin
by becoming frenzied, then suddenly loses consciousness, with
draws to the forests, feeds on tree bark, flings himself into water
and fire, wounds himself with knives. The family then appeals to a
old shaman, who undertakes to teach the distraught young man the
various kinds of spirits and how to summon and control them. Thi
is only the beginning of the initiation proper, which later includes
series of ceremonies to which we shall return.[25]

Among the Tungus of the Transbaikal region he who wishes to
become a shaman announces that the spirit of a dead shaman has
appeared to him in dream and ordered him to succeed him. For
this declaration to be regarded as plausible, it must usually be ac
companied by a considerable degree of mental derangement.[26] Ac
cording to the beliefs of the Turukhansk Tungus, one destined

21 T. Lehtisalo, *Entwurf einer Mythologie der Jurak-Samojeden*, p. 14
22 Belyavsky, cited by Mikhailowski, p. 86.
23 "Du chamanisme d'après les croyances des Yakoutes," p. 312.
24 Cited by Mikhailowski, pp. 85 f.
25 Cf. below, pp. 113 f.   26 Mikhailowski, p. 85.

become a shaman has dreams in which he sees the devil called Khargi perform shamanic rites. In this way he learns the secrets of the profession.[27] We shall return to these "secrets," for they constitute the essence of the shamanic initiation that sometimes takes place in seemingly morbid dreams and trances.

Recruiting among the Tungus

Among the Manchu and the Tungus of Manchuria there are two classes of "great" shamans—those of the clan and those independent from the clan.[28] In the former case the transmission of shamanic gifts usually takes place from grandfather to grandson, for, engaged in supplying his father's needs, the son cannot become a shaman. Among the Manchu the son can succeed; but if there is no son the grandson inherits the gift, that is, the "spirits" left available after the shaman's death. A problem arises when there is no one in the shaman's family to take possession of these spirits; in such a case a stranger is called in. As for the independent shaman, he has no rules to obey.[29] We take this to mean that he follows his own vocation.

Shirokogoroff describes several cases of shamanic vocation. It seems that there is always a hysterical or hysteroid crisis, followed by a period of instruction during which the postulant is initiated by an accredited shaman.[30] In the majority of these cases the crisis occurs at maturity. But one cannot become a shaman until several years after the first experience.[31] And recognition as a shaman is bestowed only by the whole community and only after the aspirant has undergone the initiatory ordeal.[32] In default of this, no shaman can exercise his function. Many renounce the profession if the clan does not recognize them as worthy to be shamans.[33]

Instruction plays an important role, but it does not begin until

27 Tretyakov, p. 211; Mikhailowski, p. 85.
28 S. M. Shirokogoroff, *Psychomental Complex of the Tungus*, p. 344.
29 Ibid., p. 346.   30 Ibid., pp. 346 ff.   31 Ibid., p. 349.
32 Ibid., pp. 350–51. On this initiation, see below, pp. 111 ff.
33 Ibid., p. 350.

after the first ecstatic experience. Among the Tungus of Man
churia, for example, the child is chosen and brought up with a view
to becoming a shaman; but the first ecstasy is decisive: if no ex
perience supervenes, the clan renounces its candidate.[34] Sometime
the young candidate's behavior determines and hastens his con
secration. Thus it may happen that candidates run away to th
mountains and remain there seven days or longer, feeding o
animals "caught . . . directly with their teeth," [35] and returnin
to the village dirty, bleeding, with torn clothes and hair disheveled
"like wild people." [36] It is only some ten days later that the can
didate begins babbling incoherent words.[37] Then an old shama
cautiously asks him questions; the candidate (more precisely, th
"spirit" possessing him) becomes angry, and finally designate
the shaman who is to offer the sacrifices to the gods and prepar
the ceremony of initiation and consecration.[38]

Recruiting among the Buryat and the Altaians

Among the Alarsk Buryat studied by Sandschejew shamanism i
transmitted in the paternal or maternal line. But it is also spor
taneous. In either case vocation is manifested by dreams and con
vulsions, both provoked by ancestral spirits (*utcha*). A shaman
vocation is obligatory; one cannot refuse it. If there are no suitabl
candidates, the ancestral spirits torture children, who cry in the
sleep, become nervous and dreamy, and at thirteen are designate
for the profession. The preparatory period involves a long series
ecstatic experiences, which are at the same time initiatory; t

34 Shirokogoroff, *Psychomental Complex*, p. 350.

35 Which indicates transformation into a wild beast, that is, a sort
reintegration into the ancestor.

36 All these details have an initiatory bearing, which will be explain
later.

37 It is during this period of silence that the initiation by the spirits
completed, concerning which Tungus and Buryat shamans supply mo
valuable details; see below, pp. 75 ff.

38 Shirokogoroff, p. 351. On the continuation of the ceremony prop
see below, pp. 111 ff.

ancestral spirits appear in dreams and sometimes carry the candidate down to the underworld. Meanwhile the youth continues to study under the shamans and elders; he learns the clan genealogy and traditions, the shamanic mythology and vocabulary. The teacher is called the Father Shaman. During his ecstasy the candidate sings shamanic hymns.[39] This is the sign that contact with the beyond has finally been established.

Among the Buryat of Southern Siberia shamanism is usually hereditary, but sometimes one becomes a shaman after a divine election or an accident; for example, the gods choose the future shaman by striking him with lightning or showing him their will through stones fallen from the sky; [40] one who had chanced to drink *tarasun* in which there was such a stone was transformed into a shaman. But these shamans chosen by the gods must also be guided and taught by the old shamans.[41] The role of lightning in designating the shaman is important; it shows the celestial origin of shamanic powers. The case is not unique; among the Soyot, too, one who is touched by lightning becomes a shaman,[42] and lightning is sometimes portrayed on the shaman's costume.

In the case of hereditary shamanism, the souls of the ancestral shamans choose a young man in the family; he becomes absent-minded and dreamy, loves solitude, and has prophetic visions and sometimes seizures that make him unconscious. During this period, the Buryat believe, the soul is carried off by the spirits—eastward if the youth is destined to become a "white" shaman, westward if a "black." [43] Received in the palace of the gods, the neophyte's soul is instructed by the ancestral shamans in the secrets of the profession, the gods' forms and names, the cult and names of the spirits, and so on. It is only after this first initiation that the soul

---

39 Garma Sandschejew, "Weltanschauung und Schamanismus der Alaren-urjaten," pp. 977–78.

40 On "thunder-stones" fallen from the sky, see Eliade, *Patterns*, pp. 9 ff.

41 Mikhailowski, p. 86.   42 Potanin, IV, 289.

43 For the distinction between these two types of shaman, see below, p. 184 ff.

returns to the body.[44] We shall see that the initiatory process continues long after this.

For the Altaians the shamanic gift is generally hereditary. While still a child, the future shaman, or *kam*, proves to be sickly, withdrawn, contemplative. But his father gives him a lengthy preparation, teaching him the tribe's songs and traditions. When a young man in a family is subject to epileptic attacks, the Altaians are convinced that one of his ancestors was a shaman. But it is also possible to become a *kam* of one's own volition, though this kind of shaman is considered inferior to the others.[45]

Among the Kazak Kirgiz (Kirgiz-Kaisak) the profession of *baqça* (shaman) is usually transmitted from father to son; exceptionally, the father transmits it to two of his sons. But there is a memory of an ancient time when the neophyte was chosen directly by the old shamans. "In former days the *baqças* sometimes enlisted very young Kazak Kirgiz, usually orphans, in order to initiate them into the profession of *baqça*; however, to succeed in the profession a predisposition to nervous disorders was essential. The subjects intending to enter the *baqçylyk* were characterized by sudden changes in state, by rapid transitions from irritability to normality, from melancholia to agitation."[46]

Hereditary Transmission and Quest in Obtaining Shamanic Powers

Two conclusions already appear from this rapid examination of Siberian and Central Asian data: (1) that a hereditary shamanism

---

44 Mikhailowski, p. 87; W. Schmidt, *Der Ursprung der Gottesidee*, X, 395 ff.

45 Potanin, IV, 56–57; Mikhailowski, p. 90; W. Radlov, *Aus Sibirien*, II, 16; A. V. Anokhin, *Materialy po shamanstvu u altaitsev*, pp. 29 ff.; H. von Lankenau, "Die Schamanen und das Schamanenwesen," pp. 278 ff.; W. Schmidt, *Der Ursprung*, IX, 245–48 (Altaic Tatars), 687–88 (Abakan Tatars).

46 J. Castagné, "Magie et exorcisme chez les Kazak-Kirghizes et autres peuples turcs orientaux," p. 60.

exists side by side with a shamanism bestowed directly by the gods and spirits; (2) that morbid phenomena frequently accompany both spontaneous manifestation and hereditary transmission of the shamanic vocation. Let us now see what the situation is in regions other than Siberia, Central Asia, and the Arctic.

It is unnecessary to dwell at length on the question of hereditary transmission or spontaneous vocation in the case of the magician or medicine man. In general, the situation is the same everywhere: the two ways of access to magico-religious powers coexist. A few examples will suffice.

The profession of medicine man is hereditary among the Zulu and the Bechuana of South Africa,[47] the Nyima of the southern Sudan,[48] the Negritos and the Jakun of the Malay Peninsula,[49] the Batak and other peoples of Sumatra,[50] the Dyak,[51] the sorcerers of the New Hebrides,[52] and in several Guianan and Amazonian tribes (Shipibo, Cobeno, Macusi, etc.).[53] "In the eyes of the Cobeno, any shaman by right of succession is gifted with a higher power than one whose title is due only to his own seeking."[54] Among the Rocky Mountain tribes of North America shamanic power can also be inherited, but the transmission always takes place through an ecstatic experience (dream).[55] As Willard Z. Park observes,[56] inheritance seems rather to be a tendency in a child or other relative to acquire the power by drawing from the same source as the sha-

47 Max Bartels, *Die Medizin der Naturvölker*, p. 25.

48 S. F. Nadel, "A Study of Shamanism in the Nuba Mountains," p. 27.

49 Ivor H. N. Evans, *Studies in Religion, Folk-lore, & Custom in British North Borneo and the Malay Peninsula*, pp. 159, 264.

50 E. M. Loeb, *Sumatra*, pp. 81 (the northern Batak), 125 (Menang-kabau), 155 (Nias).

51 H. Ling Roth, *The Natives of Sarawak and British North Borneo*, I, 260; also among the Ngadju Dyak, cf. H. Schärer, *Die Gottesidee der Ngadju Dajak in Süd-Borneo*, p. 58.

52 J. L. Maddox, *The Medicine Man: a Sociological Study of the Character and Evolution of Shamanism*, p. 26.

53 Alfred Métraux, "Le Shamanisme chez les Indiens de l'Amérique du Sud tropicale," pp. 200 f.

54 Ibid., p. 201.   55 *Shamanism in Western North America*, p. 22.

56 Ibid.; p. 29.

man. Among the Puyallup, Marian Smith remarks, the power tends to remain in the family.[57] Cases have also been known in which the shaman transmits the power to his child during his own lifetime.[58] Inheritance of shamanic power appears to be the rule among the Plateau tribes (Thompson, Shuswap, southern Okanagon, Klallam, Nez Perce, Klamath, Tenino) and those of northern California (Shasta, etc.), and it is also found among the Hupa, Chimariko, Wintu, and western Mono.[59] Transmission of the "spirits" always remains the basis of this shamanic inheritance, in distinction from the more usual method among most North American tribes—acquiring "spirits" by a spontaneous experience (dream, etc.) or by a deliberate quest. Among the Eskimo shamanism is occasionally hereditary. An Iglulik became a shaman after being wounded by a walrus, but in a sense he inherited his mother's qualification, she having become a shamaness as the result of a fireball entering her body.[60]

The office of medicine man is not hereditary among a considerable number of primitive peoples, whom it is unnecessary to cite here.[61] This means that all over the world magico-religious powers are held to be obtainable either spontaneously (sickness, dream, chance encounter with a source of "power," etc.) or deliberately (quest). It should be noted that nonhereditary acquisition of magico-religious powers presents an almost infinite number of forms and variants, which are of concern rather to the general history of religions than to a systematic study of shamanism; for this type of acquisition includes not only the possibility of obtaining

57 Cited by Marcelle Bouteiller, "Du 'chaman' au 'panseur de secret,'" p. 243. "A girl known to us acquired the gift of curing burns from an old woman neighbor, now dead, who taught her the secret because she had no family but had been initiated herself by an older relative."

58 Park, p. 30.

59 Ibid., p. 121. Cf. also Bouteiller, "Don chamanistique et adaptation à la vie chez les Indiens de l'Amérique du Nord."

60 Knud Rasmussen, *Intellectual Culture of the Iglulik Eskimos*, pp. 120 ff. Among the Diomede Islands Eskimo the shaman sometimes transmits his powers directly to one of his sons; see E. M. Weyer, Jr., *The Eskimos*, p. 429.

61 Cf. Hutton Webster, *Magic*, pp. 185 ff.

magico-religious powers spontaneously or deliberately and thus becoming a shaman, medicine man, or sorcerer, but also the possibility of obtaining such powers for one's own safety or personal advantage, as is the case almost everywhere in the archaic world. The latter method of acquiring magico-religious powers implies no distinction in religious or social practice from the rest of the community. The man who, by using certain rudimentary but traditional techniques, increases his magico-religious potential—to ensure the abundance of his crop, to defend himself against the evil eye, and so on—does not intend to change his socio-religious status and become a medicine man by this act of reinforcing his potential for the sacred. He simply wishes to increase his vital and religious capacities. Hence his moderate and limited quest for magico-religious powers falls in the most typical and rudimentary category of human behavior in the presence of the sacred. For, as we have shown in *Patterns in Comparative Religion*, in primitive man as in all human beings the desire to enter into contact with the sacred is counteracted by the fear of being obliged to renounce the simple human condition and become a more or less pliant instrument for some manifestation of the sacred (gods, spirits, ancestors, etc.).[62]

In the following pages the deliberate quest for magico-religious powers or the grant of such powers by gods and spirits will concern us only in so far as it entails a massive acquisition of the sacred destined to make a radical change in the socio-religious practice of the subject, who finds himself transformed into a specialized technician. Even in cases of this kind we should discover a certain resistance to "divine election."

Shamanism and Psychopathology

Let us now examine the relations allegedly discovered between Arctic and Siberian shamanism and nervous disorders, especially

---

62 On the meaning of this ambivalent attitude to the sacred, see Eliade, *Patterns*, pp. 459 ff.

the various forms of arctic hysteria. From the time of Krivoshapkin (1861, 1865), V. G. Bogoraz (1910), N. Y. Vitashevsky (1911), and M. A. Czaplicka (1914), the psychopathological phenomenology of Siberian shamanism has constantly been emphasized.[63] The last investigator to favor explaining shamanism by arctic hysteria, Å. Ohlmarks, is even led to distinguish between an Arctic and a sub-Arctic shamanism, according to the degree of neuropathy exhibited by their representatives. In his view shamanism was originally an exclusively Arctic phenomenon, due in the first place to the influence of the cosmic milieu on the nervous instability of the inhabitants of the polar regions. The extreme cold, the long nights, the desert solitude, the lack of vitamins, etc., influenced the nervous constitution of the Arctic peoples, giving rise either to mental illnesses (arctic hysteria, *meryak*, *menerik*, etc.) or to the shamanic trance. The only difference between a shaman and an epileptic is that the latter cannot deliberately enter into trance.[64] In the Arctic the shamanic ecstasy is a spontaneous and organic phenomenon; and it is only in this zone that one can properly speak of a "great shamanizing," that is, of the ceremony that ends with a real cataleptic trance, during which the soul is supposed to have left the body and to be journeying in the sky or the underworld.[65] But in the sub-Arctic the shaman, no longer the victim of cosmic oppression, does not spontaneously obtain a real trance and is obliged to induce a semitrance with the help of narcotics or to mime the journey of the soul in dramatic form.[66]

63 Ohlmarks, *Studien zum Problem des Schamanismus*, pp. 20 ff.; Nioradze, *Der Schamanismus*, pp. 50 ff.; M. A. Czaplicka, *Aboriginal Siberia*, pp. 179 ff. (Chukchee); V. G. Bogoraz (Waldemar G. Bogoras), "K psikhologi shamanstva u narodov severo-vostochnoi Azii," pp. 5 ff. Cf. also W. I. Jochelson: *The Koryak*, pp. 416–17; *The Yukaghir and the Yukaghirized Tungus*, pp. 30–38.

64 *Studien*, p. 11. See Eliade, "Le Problème du chamanisme," pp. 9 f. Cf. Harva, *Die religiösen Vorstellungen*, pp. 452 ff. See also D. F. Aberle " 'Arctic Hysteria' and Latah in Mongolia." On ecstasy as a specific characteristic of Arctic religion, cf. R. T. Christiansen, "Ecstasy and Arctic Religion."

65 Concerning these journeys, see the following chapters.

66 Ohlmarks, pp. 100 ff., 122 ff., etc.

I. General. Recruiting Methods. Mystical Vocation

The thesis equating shamanism with mental disorder has also been maintained in respect to other forms of shamanism than the Arctic. As long as seventy-odd years ago, G. A. Wilken asserted that Indonesian shamanism had originally been a real sickness, and it was only later that the genuine trance had begun to be imitated dramatically.[67] And investigators have not failed to note the striking relations that appear to exist between mental unbalance and the different forms of South Asian and Oceanian shamanism. According to Loeb, the Niue shaman is epileptic or extremely nervous and comes from particular families in which nervous instability is hereditary.[68] On the basis of Czaplicka's descriptions, J. W. Layard believed that there was a close resemblance between the Siberian shaman and the *bwili* of Malekula.[69] The *sikerei* of Mentawei [70] and the *bomor* of Kelantan [71] are also neuropaths. In Samoa epileptics become diviners. The Batak of Sumatra and other Indonesian peoples prefer to choose sickly or weak subjects for the office of magician. Among the Subanun of Mindanao the perfect magician is usually neurasthenic or at least eccentric. The same thing is found elsewhere: in the Andaman Islands epileptics are considered great magicians; among the Lotuko of Uganda the infirm and neuropathic are commonly candidates for magic (but must, however, undergo a long initiation before being qualified for their profession).[72]

According to Father Housse, candidates for shamanship among the Araucanians of Chile "are always sickly or morbidly sensitive, with weak hearts, disordered digestions, and subject to vertigo. They claim that the divinity's summons to them is irresistible and that a premature death would inevitably punish their resistance

67 *Het Shamanisme bij de Volken van den Indischen Archipel*, passim.

68 "The Shaman of Niue," p. 395.

69 "Shamanism: an Analysis Based on Comparison with the Flying Tricksters of Malekula," p. 544. The same observation is made in Loeb, "Shaman and Seer," p. 61.

70 Loeb, "Shaman and Seer," p. 67.

71 Jeanne Cuisinier, *Danses magiques de Kelantan*, pp. 5 ff.

72 And the list could easily be extended; cf. Webster, *Magic*, pp. 157 ff. Cf. also T. K. Oesterreich's lengthy analyses, *Possession*, pp. 132 ff., 236 ff.

and infidelity." [73] Sometimes, as among the Jivaro,[74] the future shaman is only reserved and taciturn in temperament or, as among the Selk'nam and the Yamana of Tierra del Fuego, predisposed to meditation and asceticism.[75] Paul Radin brings out the epileptoid or hysteroid psychic structure of most medicine men, citing it to support his thesis of the psychopathological origin of the class of sorcerers and priests. And he adds, precisely in the sense of Wilken, Layard, or Ohlmarks: "What was thus originally due to psychical necessity became the prescribed and mechanical formulae to be employed by anyone who desired to enter the priestly profession or for any successful approach to the supernatural." [76] Ohlmarks declares that nowhere in the world are psychomental maladies as intense and as prevalent as in the Arctic, and he cites a remark of the Russian ethnologist D. Zelenin: "In the North, these psychoses were far more widespread than elsewhere." [77] But similar observations have been made in respect to numerous other primitive peoples, and it does not appear in what way they help us to understand a religious phenomenon.[78]

Regarded in the horizon of *homo religiosus*—the only horizon with which we are concerned in the present study—the mentally

73 *Une Épopée indienne. Les Araucans du Chili*, p. 98.

74 R. Karsten, cited by Métraux, "Le Shamanisme chez les Indiens de l'Amérique du Sud tropicale," p. 201.

75 M. Gusinde, *Die Feuerland Indianern. I: Die Selk'nam*, pp. 779 ff.; *II: Die Yamana*, pp. 1394 ff.

76 *Primitive Religion*, p. 132.

77 *Studien*, p. 15.

78 Even Ohlmarks admits (ibid., pp. 24, 35) that shamanism is not to be regarded solely as a mental malady, the phenomenon being more complex. Métraux saw the crux of the problem better when he wrote, in regard to the South American shamans, that temperamentally neuropathic or religious individuals "feel drawn to a kind of life that gives them intimate contact with the supernatural world and allows them to expend their nervous force freely. In shamanism the uneasy, the unstable, or the merely thoughtful find a propitious atmosphere" ("Le Shamanisme chez les Indiens de l'Amérique du Sud tropicale," p. 200). For Nadel, the problem of the stabilization of psychoneurotics by shamanism remains open ("A Study of Shamanism in the Nuba Mountains," p. 36); but see below, p. 31, his conclusions concerning the mental soundness of the Sudanese shamans.

ill patient proves to be an unsuccessful mystic or, better, the caricature of a mystic. His experience is without religious content, even
if it appears to resemble a religious experience, just as an act of
autoeroticism arrives at the same physiological result as a sexual
act properly speaking (seminal emission), yet at the same time is
but a caricature of the latter because it is without the concrete
presence of the partner. Then too, it is quite possible that the assimilation of a neurotic subject to an individual possessed by spirits
—an assimilation supposed to be quite frequent in the archaic
world—is in many cases only the result of imperfect observations
on the part of the earliest ethnologists. Among the Sudanese tribes
recently studied by Nadel epilepsy is quite common; but the tribesmen consider neither epilepsy nor any other mental maladies to be
genuine possession.[79] However this may be, we are forced to conclude that the alleged Arctic origin of shamanism does not necessarily arise from the nervous instability of peoples living too near
to the Pole and from epidemics peculiar to the north above a certain latitude. As we have just seen, similar psychopathic phenomena
are found almost throughout the world.

That such maladies nearly always appear in relation to the vocation of medicine men is not at all surprising. Like the sick man, the
religious man is projected onto a vital plane that shows him the
fundamental data of human existence, that is, solitude, danger,
hostility of the surrounding world. But the primitive magician, the
medicine man, or the shaman is not only a sick man; he is, above
all, a sick man who has been cured, who has succeeded in curing
himself. Often when the shaman's or medicine man's vocation is
revealed through an illness or an epileptoid attack, the initiation of
the candidate is equivalent to a cure.[80] The famous Yakut shaman
Tüspüt (that is, "fallen from the sky") had been ill at the age of
twenty; he began to sing, and felt better. When Sieroszewski met

---

79 "A Study of Shamanism," p. 36; see also below, p. 31.

80 Cuisinier, p. 5; J. W. Layard, "Malekula: Flying Tricksters, Ghosts,
Gods and Epileptics," cited by Paul Radin, *Primitive Religion*, pp. 65–66;
Nadel, p. 36; Harva, *Die religiösen Vorstellungen*, p. 457.

him, he was sixty and displayed tireless energy. "If necessary, he can drum, dance, jump all night." In addition, he was a man who had traveled; he had even worked in the Siberian gold mines. But he needed to shamanize; if he went for a long time without doing so, he did not feel well.[81]

A shaman of the Goldi (Amur region) told Leo Sternberg: "The old folks say that some generations back there were three great Shamans of my gens. No Shamans were known amongst my nearest forefathers. My father and mother enjoyed perfect health. I am now forty years old. I am married, but have no children. Up to the age of twenty I was quite well. Then I felt ill, my whole body ailed me, I had bad headaches. Shamans tried to cure me, but it was all of no avail. When I began shamaning myself, I got better and better. It is now ten years that I have been a shaman, but at first I used to practice for myself only, and it is three years ago only that I took to curing other people. A shaman's practice is very, very fatiguing." [82]

Sandschejew had come to know a Buryat who, in his youth, had been an "anti-shamanist." But he fell ill and, after vainly seeking a cure (he even traveled to Irkutsk in search of a good doctor), he tried shamanizing. He was immediately cured, and became a shaman for the rest of his life.[83] Sternberg also observes that the election of a shaman is manifested by a comparatively serious illness, usually coincidental with the onset of sexual maturity. But the future shaman is cured in the end, with the help of the same spirits that will later become his tutelaries and helpers. Sometimes these are ancestors who wish to pass on to him their now unemployed helping spirits. In these cases there is a sort of hereditary transmission; the illness is only a sign of election, and proves to be temporary.[84]

81 Sieroszewski, p. 310.

82 "Divine Election in Primitive Religion," pp. 476 f. The remainder of this important autobiography of a Goldi shaman will be found below, pp. 71 ff.

83 "Weltanschauung und Schamanismus," p. 977.

84 "Divine Election," p. 474.

There is always a cure, a control, an equilibrium brought about by the actual practice of shamanism. It is not to the fact that he is subject to epileptic attacks that the Eskimo or Indonesian shaman, for example, owes his power and prestige; it is to the fact that he can control his epilepsy. Externally, it is very easy to note numerous resemblances between the phenomenology of *meryak* or *menerik* and the Siberian shaman's trance, but the essential fact remains the latter's ability to bring on his epileptoid trance at will. Still more significantly, the shamans, for all their apparent likeness to epileptics and hysterics, show proof of a more than normal nervous constitution; they achieve a degree of concentration beyond the capacity of the profane; they sustain exhausting efforts; they control their ecstatic movements, and so on.

According to the testimony of Belyavsky and others, collected by Karjalainen, the Vogul shaman displays keen intelligence, a perfectly supple body, and an energy that appears unbounded. His very preparation for his future work leads the neophyte to strengthen his body and perfect his intellectual qualities.[85] Mytchyll, a Yakut shaman known to Sieroszewski, though an old man, during a performance outdid the youngest by the height of his leaps and the energy of his gestures. "He became animated, bubbled over with intelligence and vitality. He gashed himself with a knife, swallowed sticks, ate burning coals." [86] For the Yakut, the perfect shaman "must be serious, possess tact, be able to convince his neighbors; above all, he must not be presumptuous, proud, ill-tempered. One must feel an inner force in him that does not offend yet is conscious of its power." [87] In such a portrait it is difficult to find the epileptoid who has been conjured up from other descriptions.

Although shamans of the Reindeer Tungus of Manchuria perform their ecstatic dance in a yurt crowded with onlookers, in a very limited space, and wearing costumes that carry more than thirty pounds of iron in the form of disks and other objects, they

---

85 Karjalainen, *Die Religion der Jugra-Völker*, III, 247–48.
86 "Du chamanisme," p. 317.   87 Ibid., p. 318.

never touch anyone in the audience.[88] And the Kazak Kirgiz *baqça*, when in trance, "though he flings himself in all directions with his eyes shut, nevertheless finds all the objects that he needs." [89] This astonishing capacity to control even ecstatic movements testifies to an excellent nervous constitution. In general, the Siberian and North Asian shaman shows no sign of mental disintegration.[90] His memory and his power of self-control are distinctly above the average. According to Kai Donner,[91] "it can be maintained that among the Samoyed, the Ostyak, and certain other tribes, the shaman is usually healthy and that, intellectually, he is often above his milieu." Among the Buryat the shamans are the principal guardians of the rich oral heroic literature.[92] The poetic vocabulary of a Yakut shaman contains 12,000 words, whereas the ordinary language—the only language known to the rest of the community —has only 4,000.[93] Among the Kazak Kirgiz the *baqça*, "singer, poet, musician, diviner, priest, and doctor, appears to be the guardian of religious and popular traditions, preserver of legends several centuries old." [94]

The shamans of other regions have given rise to similar observations. According to T. Koch-Grünberg, "the Taulipang shamans [of Venezuela] are generally intelligent individuals, sometimes wily but always of great strength of character, for in their training and the practice of their functions they are obliged to display energy and self-control." [95] Métraux remarks concerning the Amazonian shamans: "No physical or physiological anomaly or peculiarity seems to have been selected as the symptom of a special predisposition for the practice of shamanism." [96]

88 E. J. Lindgren, "The Reindeer Tungus of Manchuria," cited by N. K. Chadwick, *Poetry and Prophecy*, p. 17.

89 Castagné, "Magie et exorcisme," p. 99.

90 Cf. H. M. and N. K. Chadwick, *The Growth of Literature*, III, 214; N. K. Chadwick, *Poetry and Prophecy*, pp. 17 f. The Lapp shaman must be perfectly healthy (Itkonen, *Heidnische Religion*, p. 116).

91 *La Sibérie*, p. 223.   92 Sandschejew, p. 983.

93 H. M. and N. K. Chadwick, *The Growth of Literature*, III, 199.

94 Castagné, p. 60.

95 Cited by Métraux, "Le Shamanisme chez les Indiens de l'Amérique du Sud tropicale," p. 201.   96 Ibid., p. 202.

Among the Wintu of California the transmission and perfecting of speculative thought are in the hands of the shamans.[97] The intellectual effort of the Dyak prophet-shaman is immense and denotes a mental capacity well above that of the collectivity.[98] The same observation has been made concerning African shamans in general.[99] As for the Sudanese tribes studied by Nadel: "No shaman is, in everyday life, an 'abnormal' individual, a neurotic, or a paranoiac; if he were, he would be classed as a lunatic, not respected as a priest. Nor finally can shamanism be correlated with incipient or latent abnormality; I recorded no case of a shaman whose professional hysteria deteriorated into serious mental disorders." [100] In Australia matters are even clearer: medicine men are expected to be, and usually are, perfectly healthy and normal.[101]

And we must also consider the fact that the shamanic initiation proper includes not only an ecstatic experience but, as we shall soon see, a course of theoretical and practical instruction too complicated to be within the grasp of a neurotic. Whether they still are or are not subject to real attacks of epilepsy or hysteria, shamans, sorcerers, and medicine men in general cannot be regarded as merely sick; their psychopathic experience has a theoretical content. For if they have cured themselves and are able to cure others, it is, among other things, because they know the mechanism, or rather, the *theory* of illness.

All these examples bring out, in one way or another, the exceptional character of the medicine man within society. Whether he is chosen by gods or spirits to be their mouthpiece, or is predisposed to this function by physical defects, or has a heredity that is equivalent to a magico-religious vocation, the medicine man

97 Cora A. du Bois, *Wintu Ethnography*, p. 118.

98 N. K. Chadwick, *Poetry and Prophecy*, pp. 28 ff.; H. M. and N. K. Chadwick, *The Growth of Literature*, III, 476 f.

99 N. K. Chadwick, *Poetry and Prophecy*, p. 30.

100 "A Study," p. 36. One cannot, then, say that "shamanism . . . absorbs mental abnormality at large" or that it "rests on uncommonly widespread psychopathic predispositions; it certainly cannot be explained merely as a cultural mechanism designed either to achieve the former or to exploit the latter" (ibid.).

101 A. P. Elkin, *Aboriginal Men of High Degree*, pp. 22–25.

stands apart from the world of the profane precisely because he has more direct relations with the sacred and manipulates its manifestations more effectively. Infirmity, nervous disorder, spontaneous vocation, or heredity are so many external signs of a "choice," an "election." Sometimes these signs are physical (an innate or acquired infirmity); sometimes an accident, even of the commonest type, is involved (e.g., falling from a tree or being bitten by a snake); ordinarily, as we shall see in greater detail in the following chapter, election is announced by an unusual accident or event—lightning, apparition, dream, and so on.

It is important to bring out this notion of peculiarity conferred by an unusual or abnormal experience. For, properly considered, singularization as such depends upon the very dialectic of the sacred. The most elementary hierophanies, that is, are nothing but a radical ontological separation of some object from the surrounding cosmic zone; some tree, some stone, some place, by the mere fact that *it reveals that it is sacred*, that it has been, as it were, "chosen" as the receptacle for a manifestation of the sacred, is thereby ontologically separated from all other stones, trees, places, and occupies a different, a supernatural plane. We have elsewhere [102] analyzed the structures and the dialectic of hierophanies and kratophanies—in a word, of the manifestations of the magico-religious realities. What it is important to note now is the parallel between the singularization of objects, beings, and sacred signs, and the singularization by "election," by "choice," of those who experience the sacred with greater intensity than the rest of the community—those who, as it were, incarnate the sacred, because they live it abundantly, or rather "are lived" by the religious "form" that has chosen them (gods, spirits, ancestors, etc.). These few preliminary observations will find their application after we have studied the various methods of training and initiating future shamans.

[102] See Eliade, *Patterns*, passim.

CHAPTER TWO

Initiatory Sicknesses
and Dreams

Sickness-Initiation

MORE or less pathological sicknesses, dreams, and ecstasies are, as we have seen, so many means of reaching the condition of shaman. Sometimes these singular experiences signify no more than a "choice" from above and merely prepare the candidate for new revelations. But usually sicknesses, dreams, and ecstasies in themselves constitute an initiation; that is, they transform the profane, pre-"choice" individual into a technician of the sacred.[1] Naturally, this ecstatic type of experience is always and everywhere followed by theoretical and practical instruction at the hands of the old masters; but that does not make it any the less determinative, for it is the ecstatic experience that radically changes the religious status of the "chosen" person.

We shall soon see that all the ecstatic experiences that determine the future shaman's vocation involve the traditional schema of an initiation ceremony: suffering, death, resurrection. Viewed from this angle, any "sickness-vocation" fills the role of an initiation; for the sufferings that it brings on correspond to initiatory tortures, the psychic isolation of "the elected" is the counterpart to the isolation and ritual solitude of initiation ceremonies, and the imminence of death felt by the sick man (pain, unconsciousness, etc.) recalls the symbolic death represented in almost all initiation ceremonies. The examples that follow will show how far the

1 Cf. Eliade, *Myths, Dreams and Mysteries*, pp. 79 f.

33

assimilation between sickness and initiation is carried. Certain physical sufferings find their exact counterparts in terms of a (symbolic) initiatory death—for example, the dismemberment of the candidate's (the sick man's) body, an ecstatic experience that can equally well be brought on by the sufferings of a "sickness-vocation" or by certain ritual ceremonies or, finally, in dreams.

The content of these first ecstatic experiences, although comparatively rich, almost always includes one or more of the following themes: dismemberment of the body, followed by a renewal of the internal organs and viscera; ascent to the sky and dialogue with the gods or spirits; descent to the underworld and conversations with spirits and the souls of dead shamans; various revelations, both religious and shamanic (secrets of the profession). All these themes are clearly initiatory. In some documents all are attested; in others only one or two are mentioned (bodily dismemberment, celestial ascent). However, it is possible that the absence of certain initiatory themes is due, at least in part, to the inadequacy of our information, since the earliest ethnologists were usually content with summary data.

However this may be, the presence or absence of these themes also indicates a particular religious orientation of the corresponding shamanic techniques. There is certainly a difference between a "celestial" shamanic initiation and one that, with certain reservations, we might call "infernal." The role that a celestial Supreme Being plays in granting the ecstatic trance, or, on the contrary, the importance accorded to the spirits of dead shamans or to "demons," reveal different orientations. Probably these differences are due to divergent and even hostile religious conceptions. In any case, they imply a long evolution and certainly a history, which, in the present stage of research, can only be outlined hypothetically and provisionally. For the moment we need not concern ourselves with the history of these types of initiation. And in order not to complicate our exposition we will present each of these great mythico-ritual themes by itself: dismemberment of the candidate's body, ascent to the sky, descent to the underworld. But it should never

e forgotten that such a separation rarely corresponds to the
eality; that, as we shall presently see is the case among the Si-
erian shamans, the three chief initiatory themes sometimes co-
xist in the experience of the same individual; and that, in any
vent, they are usually found together in any one religion. Finally,
t should be borne in mind that these ecstatic experiences, while
hey constitute the initiation proper, always form part of a com-
lex system of traditional instruction.

We will begin our description of shamanic initiation with the
cstatic type, for the twofold reason that it seems to us the earliest
nd that it is the most complete, in the sense that it includes all
he mythico-ritual themes enumerated above. Following this, we
ill give examples of the same type of initiation in regions other
han Siberia and adjacent parts of Northeast Asia.

Initiatory Ecstasies and Visions of the Yakut Shamans

n the preceding chapter we cited some examples of shamanic vo-
ation manifested in the form of illness. Sometimes there is not
xactly an illness but rather a progressive change in behavior. The
andidate becomes meditative, seeks solitude, sleeps a great deal,
eems absent-minded, has prophetic dreams and sometimes sei-
ures.[2] All these symptoms are only the prelude to the new life
hat awaits the unwitting candidate. His behavior, we may add,
uggests the first signs of a mystical vocation, which are the same
n all religions and too well known to dwell upon.

But there are also "sicknesses," attacks, dreams, and hallucina-
ons that determine a shaman's career in a very short time. We are
ot concerned with whether these pathogenic ecstasies have really
een experienced, or have been imagined, or at least later en-
ched by folkloric motifs, to end by being integrated into the
ame of the traditional shamanic mythology. Essential is the fact
hat these experiences justify the vocation and the magico-religious

2 See some Chukchee and Buryat examples in M. A. Czaplicka, *Aboriginal
Siberia*, pp. 179, 185, etc., and in our preceding chapter.

power of a shaman, that they are invoked as the one possible valida tion for a radical change in religious practice.

For example, a Yakut shaman, Sofron Zateyev, states that as rule the future shaman "dies" and lies in the yurt for three day without eating or drinking. Formerly the candidate went throug the ceremony three times, during which he was cut to pieces. An other shaman, Pyotr Ivanov, gives further details. The candidate' limbs are removed and disjointed with an iron hook; the bones ar cleaned, the flesh scraped, the body fluids thrown away, and th eyes torn from their sockets. After this operation all the bones ar gathered up and fastened together with iron. According to a thir shaman, Timofei Romanov, the ceremony of dismemberment last from three to seven days; [3] during all that time the candidate re mains like a dead man, scarcely breathing, in a solitary place.

The Yakut Gavril Alekseyev states that each shaman has Bird-of-Prey-Mother, which is like a great bird with an iron bea hooked claws, and a long tail. This mythical bird shows itself onl twice: at the shaman's spiritual birth, and at his death. It takes h soul, carries it to the underworld, and leaves it to ripen on a branc of a pitch pine. When the soul has reached maturity the bird carrie it back to earth, cuts the candidate's body into bits, and distribut them among the evil spirits of disease and death. Each spir devours the part of the body that is his share; this gives the futur shaman power to cure the corresponding diseases. After devourin the whole body the evil spirits depart. The Bird-Mother restor the bones to their places and the candidate wakes as from a dee sleep.

According to another Yakut account, the evil spirits carry th future shaman's soul to the underworld and there shut it up in house for three years (only one year for those who will becom lesser shamans). Here the shaman undergoes his initiation. Th

---

3 These mystical numbers play an important part in the Central Asi religions and mythologies (see below, pp. 274 ff.). That is, there is here a trad tional theoretical framework in which the shaman's ecstatic experience put, in order to be validated.

pirits cut off his head, which they set aside (for the candidate must watch his dismemberment with his own eyes), and cut him into small pieces, which are then distributed to the spirits of the various diseases. Only by undergoing such an ordeal will the future shaman gain the power to cure. His bones are then covered with new flesh, and in some cases he is also given new blood.[4]

Another Yakut legend, also collected by Ksenofontov,[5] relates that shamans are born in the north. There a giant fir grows, with nests in its branches. The great shamans are in the highest branches, the middling ones in the middle branches, the least are low in the tree.[6] Some informants say that the Bird-of-Prey-Mother, which has the head of an eagle and iron feathers, lights on the tree, lays eggs, and sits on them; great, middling, and lesser shamans are hatched in respectively three years, two years, and one year. When the soul comes out of the egg, the Bird-Mother entrusts it to a devil-shamaness, with only one eye, one arm, and one bone,[7] to be taught. She rocks the future shaman's soul in an iron cradle and feeds him on clotted blood. Then three black "devils" come

4 G. V. Ksenofontov, *Legendy i rasskazy o shamanakh u yakutov, buryat i tungusov* (2nd edn.), pp. 44 ff. (see also the German tr. in Adolf Friedrich and Georg Buddruss, *Schamanengeschichten aus Sibirien*, pp. 136 ff.); T. Lehtisalo, "Der Tod und die Wiedergeburt des künftigen Schamanen," p. 13 ff.

5 *Legendy i rasskazy*, pp. 60 f. (*Schamanengeschichten*, pp. 156 f.).

6 Another Yakut legend (*Legendy i rasskazy*, p. 63; *Schamanengeschichten*, p. 159) describes the souls of shamans as born in a fir on Mount Dzokuo. Another belief tells of the Tree Yjyk-Mas, whose summit reaches the Ninth Heaven. This tree has no branches, but the souls of shamans are in its knots (ibid.). Obviously, this is an example of the Universal Tree that grows at the "Center of the World" and connects the three cosmic zones—underworld, earth, heaven. This symbol plays a considerable role in all the North and Central Asian mythologies. See below, pp. 269 ff.

7 This is a demonic figure of fairly frequent occurrence in Siberian and Central Asian mythologies; cf. Anakhai, the one-eyed demon of the Buryat (U. Harva, *Die religiösen Vorstellungen der altaischen Völker*, p. 378), Arsari of the Chuvash (one eye, one arm, one foot, etc.; ibid., p. 39), the Tibetan goddess Ral gcing ma (one foot, one emaciated breast, one tooth, one eye, etc.), the gods Li byin ha ra, etc. (René de Nebesky-Wojkowitz, *Oracles and Demons of Tibet*, p. 122).

and cut his body to pieces, thrust a lance into his head, and throw bits of his flesh in different directions as offerings. Three other "devils" cut up his jawbone—a piece for each of the diseases that he will be called on to cure. If one of his bones is missing, a member of his family must die to replace it. Sometimes as many as nine of his relatives die.[8]

According to another account, the "devils" keep the candidate's soul until he has learned all of their wisdom. During all this time the candidate lies sick. His soul is transformed into a bird or some other animal or even into a man. His "strength" is kept safe in nest hidden among the leaves of a tree, and when the shamans fight one another—in animal form—they try to destroy their adversary's soul.[9]

In all these examples we find the central theme of an initiation ceremony: dismemberment of the neophyte's body and renewal of his organs; ritual death followed by resurrection. We may also note the motif of the giant bird that hatches shamans in the branches of the World Tree; it has wide application in North Asian mythologies, especially in shamanic mythology.

Initiatory Dreams of the Samoyed Shamans

According to Lehtisalo's Yurak-Samoyed informants, initiation proper begins with learning to drum; it is on this occasion that the candidate is able to see the spirits. The shaman Ganykka told him that once when he was beating his drum the spirits came down and cut him in pieces, also chopping off his hands. For seven days and nights he remained unconscious, stretched on the ground. During this time his soul was in the sky, journeying with the Spirit of Thunder and visiting the god Mikkulai.[10]

A. A. Popov gives the following account concerning a shaman

8 Cf. Ksenofontov, *Legendy*, pp. 60–61 (*Schamanengeschichten*, pp. 156–57).

9 Lehtisalo, "Der Tod und die Wiedergeburt," pp. 29–30.

10 Id.: *Entwurf einer Mythologie der Jurak-Samojeden*, p. 146; "Der Tod und die Wiedergeburt," p. 3.

of the Avam Samoyed.[11] Sick with smallpox, the future shaman remained unconscious for three days and so nearly dead that on the third day he was almost buried. His initiation took place during this time. He remembered having been carried into the middle of a sea. There he heard his Sickness (that is, smallpox) speak, saying to him: "From the Lords of the Water you will receive the gift of shamanizing. Your name as a shaman will be *Huottarie* (Diver)." Then the Sickness troubled the water of the sea. The candidate came out and climbed a mountain. There he met a naked woman and began to suckle at her breast. The woman, who was probably the Lady of the Water, said to him: "You are my child; that is why I let you suckle at my breast. You will meet many hardships and be greatly wearied." The husband of the Lady of the Water, the Lord of the Underworld, then gave him two guides, an ermine and a mouse, to lead him to the underworld. When they came to a high place, the guides showed him seven tents with torn roofs. He entered the first and there found the inhabitants of the underworld and the men of the Great Sickness (syphilis). These men tore out his heart and threw it into a pot. In other tents he met the Lord of Madness and the Lords of all the nervous disorders, as well as the evil shamans. Thus he learned the various diseases that torment mankind.[12]

Still preceded by his guides, the candidate then came to the Land of the Shamanesses, who strengthened his throat and his voice.[13] He was then carried to the shores of the Nine Seas. In the middle of one of them was an island, and in the middle of the island a young birch tree rose to the sky. It was the Tree of the Lord of the Earth. Beside it grew nine herbs, the ancestors of all the plants on earth. The tree was surrounded by seas, and in each of these swam a species of bird with its young. There were several kinds of ducks, a swan, and a sparrow-hawk. The candidate visited all

11 *Tavgytsy. Materialy po etnografii avamskikh i vedeyevskikh tavgytsev*, p. 84 ff. See also Lehtisalo, "Der Tod und die Wiedergeburt," pp. 3 ff.; . Emsheimer, "Schamanentrommel und Trommelbaum," pp. 173 ff.

12 That is, he learned to know and cure them.

13 Probably, taught him to sing.

these seas; some of them were salt, others so hot he could not go near the shore. After visiting the seas, the candidate raised his head and, in the top of the tree, saw men [14] of various nations Tavgi Samoyed, Russians, Dolgan, Yakut, and Tungus. He heard voices: "It has been decided that you shall have a drum (that is the body of a drum) from the branches of this tree." [15] He began to fly with the birds of the seas. As he left the shore, the Lord of the Tree called to him: "My branch has just fallen; take it and make a drum of it that will serve you all your life." The branch had three forks, and the Lord of the Tree bade him make three drums from it to be kept by three women, each drum being for a special ceremony —the first for shamanizing women in childbirth, the second for curing the sick, the third for finding men lost in the snow.

The Lord of the Tree also gave branches to all the men who were in the top of the tree. But, appearing from the tree up to the chest in human form, he added: "One branch only I give not to the shamans, for I keep it for the rest of mankind. They can make dwellings from it and so use it for their needs. I am the Tree that gives life to all men." Clasping the branch, the candidate was ready to resume his flight when again he heard a human voice, this time revealing to him the medicinal virtues of the seven plants and giving him certain instructions concerning the art of shamanizing. But, the voice added, he must marry three women (which, in fact, he later did by marrying three orphan girls whom he had cured of smallpox).

After that he came to an endless sea and there he found trees and seven stones. The stones spoke to him one after the other. The first had teeth like bears' teeth and a basket-shaped cavity, and revealed to him that it was the earth's holding stone; it pressed on the fields with its weight, so that they should not be carried

---

14 These are the ancestors of the nations, stationed in the branches the World Tree, a myth which we shall also come upon elsewhere (see below, pp. 272 f.).

15 On the symbolism of the drum = World Tree, and on its consequence for shamanic technique, see below, pp. 168 ff.

away by the wind. The second served to melt iron. He remained with these stones for seven days and so learned how they could be of use to men.

Then his two guides, the ermine and the mouse, led him to a high, rounded mountain. He saw an opening before him and entered a bright cave, covered with mirrors, in the middle of which there was something like a fire. He saw two women, naked but covered with hair, like reindeer.[16] Then he saw that there was no fire burning but that the light came from above, through an opening. One of the women told him that she was pregnant and would give birth to two reindeer; one would be the sacrificial animal [17] of the Dolgan and Evenki, the other that of the Tavgi. She also gave him a hair, which was to be useful to him when he shamanized for reindeer. The other woman also gave birth to two reindeer, symbols of the animals that would aid man in all his works and also supply his food. The cave had two openings, toward the north and toward the south; through each of them the young women sent a reindeer to serve the forest people (Dolgan and Evenki). The second woman, too, gave him a hair. When he shamanizes, he mentally turns toward the cave.

Then the candidate came to a desert and saw a distant mountain. After three days' travel he reached it, entered an opening, and came upon a naked man working a bellows. On the fire was a caldron "as big as half the earth." The naked man saw him and caught him with a huge pair of tongs. The novice had time to think, "I am dead!" The man cut off his head, chopped his body into bits, and put everything in the caldron. There he boiled his body for three years. There were also three anvils, and the naked man forged the candidate's head on the third, which was the one on which the best shamans were forged. Then he threw the head into one of three pots that stood there, the one in which the water was the coldest. He now revealed to the candidate that, when he

16 These are personifications of the Mother of the Animals, a mythical being that plays a great part in Arctic and Siberian religions.
17 That is, it would be set free by the sick man.

was called to cure someone, if the water in the ritual pot was very hot, it would be useless to shamanize, for the man was already lost; if the water was warm, he was sick but would recover; cold water denoted a healthy man.

The blacksmith then fished the candidate's bones out of a river, in which they were floating, put them together, and covered them with flesh again. He counted them and told him that he had three too many; he was therefore to procure three shaman's costumes. He forged his head and taught him how to read the letters that are inside it. He changed his eyes; and that is why, when he shamanizes, he does not see with his bodily eyes but with these mystical eyes. He pierced his ears, making him able to understand the language of plants. Then the candidate found himself on the summit of a mountain, and finally he woke in the yurt, among his family. Now he can sing and shamanize indefinitely, without ever growing tired.[18]

We have reproduced this account because it is so astonishingly rich mythologically and religiously. If the same care had been taken to collect the confessions of other Siberian shamans, probably no one would ever have been reduced to the meager common formula: the candidate remained unconscious for a certain number of days, dreamed that he was cut to pieces by spirits and carried into the sky, and so on. It is clearly apparent that the initiatory ecstasy very closely follows certain exemplary themes: the novice encounters several divine figures (the Lady of the Waters, the Lord of the Underworld, the Lady of the Animals) before being led by his animal guides to the "Center of the World," on the summit of the Cosmic Mountain, where are the World Tree and the Universal Lord; from the Cosmic Tree and by the will of the Universal Lord himself, he receives the wood to make his drum; sem-

18 Lehtisalo thinks that the role of the blacksmith is secondary in the Samoyed legends and, especially in *mises en scène* such as the one just cited, shows a foreign influence ("Der Tod und die Wiedergeburt," p. 13). And it is true that the relations between metallurgy and shamanism are far more important in Buryat beliefs and mythology. See below, pp. 470 ff.

demonic beings teach him the nature of all diseases and their cures; finally, other demonic beings cut his body to pieces, boil it, and exchange it for better organs. Each of these elements in the initiatory story is consistent and has its place in a symbolic or ritual system well known to the history of religions. To each of them we shall have to return. Taken together, they represent a well-organized variant of the universal theme of the death and mystical resurrection of the candidate by means of a descent to the underworld and an ascent to the sky.

Initiation among the Tungus, the Buryat, and Others

The same initiatory schema is also found among other Siberian peoples. The Tungus shaman Ivan Cholko states that a future shaman must fall ill and have his body cut in pieces and his blood drunk by the evil spirits (*saargi*). These—which are really the souls of dead shamans—throw his head into a caldron, where it is melted with certain metal pieces that will later form part of his ritual costume.[19] Another Tungus shaman relates that he was sick for a whole year. During that time he sang to feel better. His shaman ancestors came and initiated him. They pierced him with arrows until he lost consciousness and fell to the ground; they cut off his flesh, tore out his bones and counted them; if one had been missing, he could not have become a shaman. During this operation he went for a whole summer without eating or drinking.[20]

Although the Buryat have very complex public ceremonies for consecrating shamans, they also know the "sickness-dream" of the initiatory type. Ksenofontov reports the experiences of Mikhail Stepanov. Stepanov learned that before becoming a shaman the candidate must be sick for a long time; the souls of his shaman ancestors then surround him, torture him, strike him, cut his body with knives, and so on. During this operation the future shaman remains inanimate; his face and hands are blue, his heart scarcely

19 Ksenofontov, *Legendy*, p. 102 (*Schamanengeschichten*, p. 211).
20 *Legendy*, p. 103 (*Schamanengeschichten*, pp. 212–13).

beats.[21] According to another Buryat shaman, Bulagat Bucha
cheyev, the ancestral spirits carry the candidate's soul before th
"Assembly of the Saaytani" in the sky, and there he is instructed
After his initiation his flesh is cooked to teach him the art c
shamanizing. It is during this initiatory torture that the shama
remains for seven days and nights as if dead. On this occasion hi
relatives (except women) come to him and sing: "Our shaman i
returning to life and he will help us!" While his body is being cu
to pieces and cooked by his ancestors, no stranger may touch it.

The same experiences are found elsewhere.[23] A Teleut woma
became a shamaness after having a vision in which unknown me
cut her body to bits and cooked it in a pot.[24] According to th
traditions of the Altaian shamans, the spirits of their ancestors ea
their flesh, drink their blood, open their bellies, and so on.[25] Th
Kazak Kirgiz *baqça* says: "I have fivẹ spirits in heaven who cut m
with forty knives, prick me with forty nails," [26] and so forth.

The ecstatic experience of dismemberment of the body followe
by a renewal of the organs is also known to the Eskimo. The
speak of an animal (bear, walrus, etc.) that wounds the candidat
tears him to pieces or devours him; then new flesh grows arour
his bones.[27] Sometimes the animal that tortures him becomes th
future shaman's helping spirit.[28] Usually these cases of spontaneo

21 *Legendy*, p. 101 (*Schamanengeschichten*, p. 208).

22 *Legendy*, p. 101 (*Schamanengeschichten*, pp. 209–10).

23 Cf. H. Findeisen, *Schamanentum*, pp. 36 ff.

24 N. P. Dyrenkova, cited by V. I. Propp, *Le radici storiche dei racconti
fate*, p. 154. Among the Bhaiga and the Gond the primordial shaman instru
his sons, brothers, and disciple to boil his body in a caldron for twelve yea
cf. Rudolf Rahmann, "Shamanistic and Related Phenomena in Northern a
Middle India," pp. 726–27.

25 A. V. Anokhin, *Materialy po shamanstvu u altaitsev*, p. 131; Lehtisa
"Der Tod und die Wiedergeburt," p. 18.

26 W. Radlov: *Proben der Volksliteratur der türkischen Stämme St
Sibiriens und der tsungarishen Steppe*, IV, 60; *Aus Sibirien*, II, 65; Lehtisa
"Der Tod und die Wiedergeburt," p. 18.

27 Lehtisalo, pp. 20 ff.

28 Ibid., pp. 21–22.

vocation are manifested, if not by a sickness, at least by an unusual accident (fight with a sea beast, fall under ice, etc.) that seriously injures the future shaman. But the majority of Eskimo shamans themselves seek out ecstasic initiation and in the course of it undergo many ordeals, sometimes very close to the Siberian and Central Asian shaman's dismemberment. In these cases there is a mystical experience of death and resurrection induced by contemplating one's own skeleton; we shall return to it presently. For the moment we shall cite some initiatory experiences that parallel the documents just reviewed.

Initiation of Australian Magicians

The earliest observers long ago recorded that certain initiations of Australian medicine men involve the candidate's ritual death and removal of his organs, an act performed either by spirits or by the souls of the dead. Thus Colonel Collins (who published his impressions in 1798) reports that among the Port Jackson tribes one became a medicine man if one slept on a grave. "The spirit of the deceased would visit him, seize him by the throat, and opening him, take out his bowels, which he replaced, and the wound closed up." [29]

Recent studies have fully confirmed and supplemented these accounts. According to Howitt, the Wotjobaluk tribesmen believe that a supernatural being, Nagatya, consecrates the medicine man; he opens his belly and inserts the rock crystals that confer magical power.[30] To make a medicine man, the Euahlayi have the following procedure. They carry the chosen young man to a cemetery and leave him there, bound, for several nights. As soon as he is alone, several animals appear and touch and lick him. Then comes a man with a stick; he thrusts the stick into the neophyte's head and puts

[29] Cited by A. W. Howitt, *The Native Tribes of South-East Australia*, p. 405; see also M. Mauss, "L'Origine des pouvoirs magiques dans les sociétés australiennes."

[30] "On Australian Medicine Men," p. 48; *The Native Tribes*, p. 404.

a magical stone the size of a lemon into the wound. Then the spirits appear and intone magical and initiatory songs to teach him the art of healing.[31]

Among the Warburton Ranges aborigines (West Australia) initiation takes place as follows. The aspirant enters a cave, and two totemic heroes (wildcat and emu) kill him, open his body, remove the organs, and replace them with magical substances. They also remove the shoulder bone and tibia, which they dry, and before putting them back, stuff them with the same substances. During this ordeal the aspirant is supervised by his initiator, master, who keeps the fires lighted and observes his ecstatic experiences.[32]

The Aranda (Arunta) of Central Australia know three ways of making medicine men: (1) by the *Iruntarinia*, or "spirits"; (2) by the *Eruncha* (that is, the spirits of the *Eruncha* men of the mythical Alchera [Alcheringa] times); (3) by other medicine men. In the first case the candidate goes to the mouth of a cave and falls asleep. An *Iruntarinia* comes and "throws an invisible lance at him, which pierces the neck from behind, passes through the tongue, making therein a large hole, and then comes out through the mouth. The candidate's tongue remains perforated; one can easily put one's little finger through it. A second lance cuts off his head, and the victim succumbs. The *Iruntarinia* carries him into the cave, which is said to be very deep and where it is believed that the *Iruntarinia* live in perpetual light and near to cool springs (that is, in fact, the paradise of the Aranda). In the cave the spirit tears out his internal organs and gives him others, which are completely new. The candidate returns to life, but for some time behaves like a lunatic. The *Iruntarinia*, which are invisible to other human beings except medicine men, then carry him to his village. Etiquette forbids him to practice for a year; if during that time the opening in his tongue closes, the candidate gives up, for his magical virtues are held to have disappeared. During this year he

31 K. Langloh Parker, *The Euahlayi Tribe*, pp. 25–26.
32 A. P. Elkin, *The Australian Aborigines*, p. 223.

learns the secrets of the profession from other medicine men, especially the use of the fragments of quartz (*atnongara*) [33] that the *Iruntarinia* placed in his body.[34]

The second way of making a medicine man resembles the first, except that, instead of carrying the candidate into a cave, the *Eruncha* take him underground with them. Finally, the third method involves a long ritual in a solitary place, where the candidate must silently submit to an operation performed by two old medicine men. They rub his body with rock crystals to the point of abrading the skin, press rock crystals into his scalp, pierce a hole under a fingernail of his right hand, and make an incision in his tongue. Finally his forehead is marked with a design called *runchilda*, literally, "the devil's hand," *Eruncha* being the evil spirit of the Aranda. His body is decorated with another design, with a black line in the center representing *Eruncha* and lines around it apparently symbolizing the magical crystals in his body. After this initiation the candidate is subjected to a special regime involving countless taboos.[35]

Ilpailurkna, a famous magician of the Unmatjera tribe, told Spencer and Gillen that

when he was made into a medicine man, a very old doctor came one day and threw some of his *atnongara* stones [36] at him with a spear-thrower. Some hit him on the chest, others went right through his head, from ear to ear, killing him. The old man then cut out all of his insides, intestines, liver, heart, lungs—everything in fact, and left him lying all night long on the ground. In the morning the old man came and looked at him and placed some more *atnongara* stones inside his body and in his arms and legs, and covered over his face with leaves. Then he sang over him until

33 On these magical stones, see below, n. 36.

34 B. Spencer and F. J. Gillen: *The Native Tribes of Central Australia*, p. 522 ff.; *The Arunta: a Study of a Stone Age People*, II, 391 ff.

35 Id.: *The Native Tribes*, pp. 526 ff.: *The Arunta*, II, 394 ff.

36 "These *atnongara* stones are small crystalline structures which every medicine man is supposed to be able to produce at will from his body, through which it is believed that they are distributed. In fact it is the possession of these stones which gives his virtue to the medicine man" (Spencer and Gillen, *The Northern Tribes of Central Australia*, p. 480, n. 1).

his body was all swollen up. When this was so he provided him with a complete set of new inside parts, placed a lot more *atnongara* stones in him, and patted him on the head, which caused him to jump up alive. The old medicine man then made him drink water and eat meat containing *atnongara* stones. When he awoke he had no idea as to where he was, and said, "*Tju, tju, tju*"—"I think I am lost." But when he looked round he saw the old medicine man standing beside him, and the old man said, "No, you are not lost; I killed you a long time ago." Ilpailurkna had completely forgotten who he was and all about his past life. After a time the old man led him back to his camp and showed it to him, and told him that the woman there was his lubra, for he had forgotten all about her. His coming back this way and his strange behaviour at once showed the other natives that he had been made into a medicine man.[37]

Among the Warramunga initiation is performed by the *puntidi* spirits, which are equivalent to the *Iruntarinia* of the Aranda. A medicine man told Spencer and Gillen that he had been pursued for two days by two spirits which told him that they were "his father and his brother." On the second night these spirits came to him again and killed him. "While he was lying dead they cut him open and took all his insides out, providing him, however, with a new set, and, finally, they put a little snake inside his body, which endowed him with the powers of a medicine man."[38]

A similar experience occurs during the second initiation among the Warramunga, which, according to Spencer and Gillen,[39] even more mysterious. The candidates are obliged to walk or stand continuously until they fall exhausted and unconscious. Then "their sides are cut open, and, as usual, their internal organs are removed and they are provided with a new set." A snake is put in their head and their noses are pierced by a magical object (*kupitja*) that will later serve them in curing the sick. These objects are believed to have been made in the mythical Alcheringa times by certain very powerful snakes.[40]

The Binbinga hold that medicine men are consecrated by the

37 Spencer and Gillen, pp. 480–81.   38 Ibid., p. 484.
39 Ibid., p. 485.   40 Ibid., p. 486.

spirits Mundadji and Munkaninji (father and son). The magician Kurkutji told how, entering a cave one day, he came upon the old Mundadji, who caught him by the neck and killed him.

Mundadji cut him open, right down the middle line, took out all of his insides and exchanged them for those of himself, which he placed in the body of Kurkutji. At the same time he put a number of sacred stones in his body. After it was all over the younger spirit, Munkaninji, came up and restored him to life, told him that he was now a medicine man, and showed him how to extract bones and other forms of evil magic out of men. Then he took him away up into the sky and brought him down to earth close to his own camp, where he heard the natives mourning for him, thinking that he was dead. For a long time he remained in a more or less dazed condition, but gradually he recovered and the natives knew that he had been made into a medicine man. When he operates the spirit Munkaninji is supposed to be near at hand watching him, unseen of course by ordinary people. When taking a bone out, an operation usually conducted under the cover of darkness, Kurkutji first of all sucks very hard at the stomach of the patient and removes a certain amount of blood. Then he makes passes over the body, punches, pounds and sucks, until at last the bone comes out and is then immediately, before it can be seen by the onlookers, thrown in the direction of the spot at which Munkaninji is sitting down quietly watching. Kurkutji then tells the natives that he must go and ask Munkaninji if he will be so kind as to allow him, Kurkutji, to show the bone to them, and permission having been granted, he goes to the spot at which he has, presumably, previously deposited one, and returns with it.[41]

In the Mara tribe the technique is almost exactly the same. One who wishes to become a medicine man lights a fire and burns fat, thus attracting two spirits called Minnungarra. These approach and encourage the candidate, assuring him that they will not completely kill him. "First of all they make him insensible, and in the usual way cut him open and take out all his organs, which are then replaced by those of one of the spirits. Then he is brought to life again, told that he is now a doctor, shown how to take bones and evil magic out of men, and carried up into the sky. Finally he

41 Ibid., pp. 487–88.

49

is brought down and placed near to his own camp, where he is
found by his friends, who have been mourning for him. . . .
Amongst the powers possessed by a Mara medicine man is that of
climbing at night-time by means of a rope, invisible to ordinary
mortals, into the sky, where he can hold converse with the star
people." [42]

Australian–Siberian–South American and Other Parallels

As we have just seen, the similarity between the initiations of
Siberian shamans and those of Australian medicine men is quite
close. In both cases the candidate is subjected to an operation by
semidivine beings or ancestors, in which his body is dismembered
and his internal organs and bones are renewed. In both cases this
operation takes place in an "inferno" or involves a descent to the
underworld. As for the pieces of quartz or other magical objects
that the spirits are believed to place in the Australian candidate's
body,[43] this practice is of little importance among the Siberians.
As we have seen, there is only rarely some reference to pieces of
iron set to melt in the same caldron in which the future shaman's
flesh and bones have been put. There is a further difference between
the two areas: in Siberia the majority of shamans are "chosen" by
the spirits and gods, while in Australia the career of medicine man
seems to result from a voluntary quest on the candidate's part as
well as from a spontaneous "election" by spirits and divine beings.

We must add, too, that the methods of initiating Australian
magicians cannot be reduced to the types we have cited.[44] Although
the important element of an initiation appears to be dismemberment of the body and replacing of the internal organs, there are

42 Ibid., p. 488. For other aspects of Australian medicine men's initiation,
see below, pp. 135 ff.

43 On the importance that the Australian medicine men attach to rock
crystals, see below, pp. 137 ff. These crystals are believed to have been thrown
from the sky by Supreme Beings or to have fallen from these divinities'
celestial thrones; hence they share in a uranian magico-religious power.

44 See below, pp. 135 ff.

also other ways of consecrating a medicine man, especially the ecstatic experience of an ascent to the sky, including instruction given by celestial beings. Sometimes initiation includes both the candidate's dismemberment and his ascent to the sky (we have just seen that this is the case among the Binbinga and the Mara). Elsewhere, initiation takes place during a mystical descent to the underworld. All these types of initiation are also found among the Siberian and Central Asian shamans. Such a parallelism between two groups of mystical techniques belonging to archaic peoples so far removed in space is not without bearing on the place to be accorded to shamanism in the general history of religions.

In any case, this likeness between Australia and Siberia markedly confirms the authenticity and antiquity of shamanic initiation rites. The importance of the cave in the initiation of the Australian medicine man adds weight to this presumption of antiquity. The role of the cave in paleolithic religions appears to have been decidedly important.[45] Then too, the cave and the labyrinth continue to have a function of the first importance in the initiation rites of other archaic cultures (as, for example, in Malekula); both, indeed, are concrete symbols of passage into another world, of a descent to the underworld. According to the earliest accounts of the Araucanian shamans of Chile, they too received their initiation in caves, which were often decorated with animal heads.[46]

Among the Smith Sound Eskimo the aspirant must go at night to a cliff containing caves and walk straight ahead in the darkness. If he is predestined to become a shaman, he will enter a cave; if not, he will bump into the cliff. As soon as he has entered the cave, it closes behind him and does not open again until some time later.

45 See, most recently, Gertrude R. Levy, *The Gate of Horn: a Study of the Religious Conceptions of the Stone Age, and Their Influence upon European Thought*, especially pp. 46 ff., 50 ff., 151 ff.; Johannes Maringer, *Vorgeschichtliche Religion*, pp. 148 ff.

46 A. Métraux, "Le Shamanisme araucan," p. 313. In Australia, too, painted caves exist, but they are used for other rites. In the present state of our knowledge it is difficult to determine if the painted caves in South Africa were once used for shamanic initiations; see Levy, pp. 38–39.

The candidate must seize the moment when it reopens and hasten out; otherwise he may remain shut up in the cave forever.[47] Caves play an important part in the initiation of North American shamans; it is in caves that aspirants have their dreams and meet their helping spirits.[48]

It should be noted at this point that parallels for the belief that spirits and initiators introduce rock crystals into the candidate's body are to be found elsewhere—among the Semang of the Malay Peninsula, for example.[49] But it is one of the most striking characteristics of South American shamanism. "The Cobeno shaman introduces rock crystals into the novice's head; these eat out his brain and his eyes, then take the place of those organs and become his 'strength.'"[50] Elsewhere the rock crystals symbolize the shaman's helping spirits.[51] In general, for the shamans of tropical South America magical power is concretized in an invisible substance that the masters transfer to the novices, sometimes from mouth to mouth.[52] "Between the magical substance, an invisible but tangible mass, and the arrows, thorns, rock crystals with which the shaman is stuffed there is no difference in nature. These objects materialize the shaman's power, which, among numerous tribes, is conceived in the vaguer and rather abstract form of a magical substance."[53]

47 A. L. Kroeber, "The Eskimo of Smith Sound," p. 307. The motif of doors that open only for the initiated and remain open only a short time is quite frequent in shamanic and other legends; see below, pp. 485 f.

48 Willard Z. Park, *Shamanism in Western North America*, pp. 27 ff.

49 P. Schebesta, *Les Pygmées*, p. 154. Cf. also Ivor H. N. Evans, "Schebesta on the Sacerdo-Therapy of the Semang," p. 119; the hala, the Semang medicine man, cures with the help of quartz crystals, which may be obtained directly from the Cenoi (Chenoi, Chinoi, Cinoi). The Cenoi are celestial spirits. Sometimes they also live in the crystals, in which case they are at the hala's orders; with their help the hala sees in the crystals the disease that afflicts the patient and the means of curing it. Note the celestial origin of these crystals (cenoi); it already indicates the source of the medicine man's powers. See below, pp. 137 ff.

50 Métraux, "Le Shamanisme chez les Indiens de l'Amérique du Sud tropicale," p. 216.

51 Ibid., p. 210.   52 Ibid., p. 214.

53 Ibid., p. 215; cf. H. Webster, *Magic*, pp. 20 ff.

This archaic characteristic, which connects South American shamanism with Australian magic, is important. We shall see in a
moment that it is not the only such connection.[54]

Initiatory Dismemberment in North and South America, Africa, and Indonesia

Then too, in South America as in Australia or Siberia both spontaneous vocation and the quest for initiation involve either a mysterious illness or a more or less symbolic ritual of mystical death,
sometimes suggested by a dismemberment of the body and renewal
of the organs.

Among the Araucanians the choice is usually manifested by a
sudden illness; the young woman falls "as if dead," and on recovering declares her intention to become a *machi* (shamaness).[55]
A fisherman's daughter told Father Housse: "I was gathering
shells from the reefs, when I felt something like a blow on the
breast, and a very clear voice inside me said: 'Become a *machi*! It
is my will!' At the same time violent pains in my entrails made me
lose consciousness. It was certainly the *Ngenechen*, the master of
men, coming down into me." [56]

In general, as Métraux rightly observes, the shaman's symbolic
death is suggested by the long fainting spells and lethargic sleep of
the candidate.[57] The Yamana neophytes of Tierra del Fuego rub
their faces until a second and even a third skin appears, "the new
skin," visible only to initiates.[58] Among the Bakairi, the Tupi-

---

54 On the problem of the cultural relations between Australia and South
America, see W. Koppers, "Die Frage der eventueller alter Kulturbeziehung-
en zwischen südlichsten Südamerika und Südostaustralien." Cf. also Paul
Rivet, "Les Mélano-Polynésiens et les Australiens en Amérique," pp. 51–54
linguistic similarities between Patagonians and Australians, p. 52). Cf.
also below, pp. 135 ff.

55 Métraux, "Le Shamanisme araucan," p. 315.

56 Cited in ibid., p. 316.

57 "Le Shamanisme chez les Indiens de l'Amérique du Sud tropicale,"
. 339.

58 M. Gusinde, "Une École d'hommes-médecine chez les Yamanas de la
Terre de Feu," p. 2162: "The old skin must disappear and make room for a

Imba, and the Carib, the "death" (by tobacco juice) and "resurrection" of the candidate are formally documented.[59] During the Araucanian shaman's consecration festival the masters and neophytes walk barefoot on fire without burning themselves and without their clothes catching fire. They were also seen to tear off their noses or tear out their eyes. "The initiator made the profane audience believe that he tore out his tongue and eyes and exchanged them with those of the initiate. He also pierced him with a rod which, entering at his stomach, emerged by his spine without drawing blood or causing pain (Rosales, *Historia general del Regno de Chile*, I, 168). The Toba shamans receive full in the chest a rod which pierces them like a rifle ball." [60]

Similar practices are attested in North American shamanism. The Maidu initiators put candidates in a hole full of "medicine" and "kill" them with a "medicine-poison"; after this initiation the neophytes are able to hold red-hot stones in their hands without hurting themselves.[61] Initiation into the shamanic "Ghost Ceremony" society of the Pomo involves the torture, death, and resurrection of the neophytes; they lie on the ground like corpses and are covered with straw. The same ritual is found among the Yuki the Huchnom, and the Coast Miwok.[62] The complete series of initiatory ceremonies for the Coast Pomo shamans has the signifi-

---

new translucent and delicate layer. If the first weeks of rubbing and painting have made it visible—at least according to the imaginations and hallucinations of the experienced *yékamush* (= medicine man)—the old initiates feel no more doubt of the candidate's capabilities. From then on he must redoubl his efforts and keep delicately rubbing his cheeks until a third even finer an more delicate skin appears; it is then so sensitive that it cannot be touche without causing him intense pain. When the pupil has finally reached thi stage the usual teaching, such as the Loima-Yékamush can offer, is finished.

59 Ida Lublinski, "Der Medizinmann bei den Naturvölkern Südamerikas, pp. 248 ff.

60 Métraux, "Le Shamanisme araucan," pp. 313–14. When the Warra shaman was initiated, his "death" was announced with loud cries ("I Shamanisme chez les Indiens de l'Amérique du Sud tropicale," p. 339

61 E. W. Gifford, "Southern Maidu Religious Ceremonies," p. 244.

62 E. M. Loeb, *Tribal Initiations and Secret Societies*, p. 267.

cant name "cutting." [63] Among the River Patwin the aspirant to the Kuksu Society is believed to have his navel pierced with a lance and an arrow by Kuksu himself; he dies and is resuscitated by a shaman.[64] The Luiseno shamans "kill" one another with arrows. Among the Tlingit the candidate-shaman's first possession is manifested by a trance that prostrates him. The Menomini neophyte is "stoned" with magical objects by the initiator and is then resuscitated.[65] And, of course, almost everywhere in North America, initiation rites into the secret societies (shamanic or other) involve the ritual of the candidate's death and resurrection.[66]

The same symbolism of death and mystical resurrection, whether in the form of mysterious sicknesses or of shamanic initiation ceremonies, is also found elsewhere. Among the Sudanese of the Nuba Mountains the first initiatory consecration is called "head," and is said "to open the [novice's] head for the spirit to enter." [67] But initiations through shamanic dreams or unusual accidents also occur. For example, at about the age of thirty a shaman had a series of significant dreams: he dreamed of a white horse with a red belly, of a leopard that put its paw on his shoulder, of a snake that bit him —and all these animals play an important part in shamanic dreams. Soon afterward he suddenly began shaking, lost consciousness, and fell to prophesying. It was the first sign of "election," but he waited twelve years before being consecrated a *kujur*. Another shaman had no dreams, but one night his hut was struck by lightning and "as he put it, 'he was dead for two days.' " [68]

An Amazulu sorcerer told his friends "that he has dreamt that he is being carried away by a river. He dreams of many things, and his body is muddled and he becomes a house of dreams. And he dreams constantly of many things, and on awaking says to his

63 Ibid., p. 268.   64 Ibid., p. 269.

65 Constance Goddard DuBois, *The Religion of the Luiseño Indians*, p. 81; John R. Swanton, "Social Conditions, Beliefs, and Linguistic Relationship of the Tlingit Indians," p. 466; Loeb, pp. 270–78. Cf. also below, pp. 317 ff.

66 Loeb, pp. 266 ff.

67 S. F. Nadel, "A Study of Shamanism in the Nuba Mountains," p. 28.

68 Ibid., pp. 28–29.

friends: 'My body is muddled to-day; I dreamt many men were killing me; I escaped I know not how. And on waking, one part of my body felt different from other parts; it was no longer alike all over.' " [69]

Dream, sickness, or initiation ceremony, the central element is always the same: death and symbolic resurrection of the neophyte, involving a cutting up of the body performed in various ways (dismemberment, gashing, opening the abdomen, etc.). In the examples to follow, the candidate's being killed by the initiatory masters is even more clearly indicated.

Here is the first phase of a medicine man's initiation in Malekula: [70]

There was a Bwili of Lol-narong, whose sister's son came to him and said: "I want you to give me something." The Bwili said: "Have you fulfilled the conditions?" "Yes, I have fulfilled them." Again he said: "You have not been lying with a woman?" and his nephew said: "No!" So the Bwili said: "All right."

Then he said to his nephew: "Come here. Lie down on this leaf," and the youth lay down on it. Then the Bwili made himself a bamboo knife and cutting off one of the young man's arms, placed it on two of the leaves. And he laughed at his nephew and the youth laughed back. Then he cut off the other arm and placed it on the leaves beside the first. And he came back and they both laughed again. Then he cut off his leg from the thigh and laid it alongside the arms. And he came and laughed and the youth laughed too. Then he cut off the other leg and laid it beside the first. And he came back and laughed, and saw that his nephew was still laughing. Lastly, he cut off the head, held it out before him. And he laughed, and the head laughed, too.

Then he put the head back in its place and took the arms and legs that he had taken off and put them all back in their places.

The remainder of this initiatory ceremony includes the magical transformation of master and disciple into hens, a well-known

69 Rev. Canon [Henry] Callaway, *The Religious System of the Amazulu* pp. 259 f., cited by Paul Radin, *Primitive Religion*, pp. 123–24.

70 J. W. Layard, "Malekula: Flying Tricksters, Ghosts, Gods and Epileptics," cited by Radin, *Primitive Religion*, pp. 65–66.

symbol of the shaman's and sorcerer's "power of flight" in general, to which we shall return.

According to a tradition of the Kiwai Papuans, one night someone was killed by an *óboro* (spirit of a dead person); the spirit took out all the man's bones and replaced them with *óboro* bones. When the man came back to life, he was like the spirits, that is, he had become a shaman. The *óboro* gave him a bone with which he could summon the spirits.[71]

Among the Dyak of Borneo the *manang*'s (shaman's) initiation requires three different ceremonies, corresponding to the three degrees of Dyak shamanism. The first degree, *besudi* (a word that, it seems, means "to feel, to touch"), is also the most elementary and is obtained for very little money. The candidate lies on the veranda as if ill, and the other *manang* make passes over him through the night. It is believed that this teaches the future shaman to discover sicknesses and remedies by palpating the patient. During this time the old shamans may also introduce magical "power" into the candidate's body in the form of pebbles or other objects.

The second ceremony, *bekliti* (opening), is more complicated and assumes a clearly shamanic character. After a night of incantations the old shamans take the neophyte to a room shut off by curtains. "And there, as they assert, they cut his head open, take out his brains, wash and restore them, to give him a clear mind to penetrate into the mysteries of evil spirits, and the intricacies of disease; they insert gold dust into his eyes to give him keenness and strength of sight powerful enough to see the soul wherever it may have wandered; they plant barbed hooks on the tips of his fingers to enable him to seize the soul and hold it fast; and lastly they pierce his heart with an arrow to make him tender-hearted, and full of sympathy with the sick and suffering." [72] Of course, the

71 G. Landtman, *The Kiwai Papuans of British New Guinea*, p. 325.

72 H. Ling Roth, *The Natives of Sarawak and British North Borneo*, I, 280–81, citing observations published by Archdeacon J. Perham in the *JRAS Straits Branch*, No. 19 (1887). Cf. also L. Nyuak, "Religious Rites and Customs of the Iban or Dyaks of Sarawak," pp. 173 ff.; E. H. Gomes, *Seven-*

ceremony is symbolic; a coconut is put on the neophyte's head and then broken, and so on. A third ceremony, which completes the shaman's initiation, includes an ecstatic journey to the sky on a ritual ladder. We shall return to this last ceremony in a later chapter.[73]

Clearly, in the *bekliti* we again have a ceremony symbolizing the candidate's death and resurrection. The replacement of the viscera is performed ritually, which does not necessarily imply the ecstatic experiences—dream, sickness, or temporary insanity—of Australian or Siberian candidates. If the alleged reason for the renewal of the organs (conferring better sight, tenderheartedness, etc.) is authentic, it indicates that the original meaning of the rite has been forgotten.

Initiation of Eskimo Shamans

Among the Ammasalik Eskimo the disciple does not go to the old *angakok* (plural, *angakut*) to be initiated; the shaman himself chooses the candidate in his early childhood.[74] From among boys from six to eight the shaman selects those whom he considers most gifted for initiation, "in order that a knowledge of the highest powers in existence may be preserved for the coming generation." [75] "Only certain especially gifted souls, dreamers, visionaries of hysterical temperament, can be chosen. An old *angakok* finds a pupil, and the teaching is conducted in the deepest secrecy, far from the hut, in the mountains." [76] The *angakok* teaches him to isolate himself in a lonely place—beside an old grave, by a lake—

---

teen Years among the Sea Dyaks of Borneo, pp. 178 ff.; and the myth of the dismemberment of the primordial shaman among the Nodora Gond, in Verrier Elwin, *Myths of Middle India*, p. 450.

73 Below, pp. 125 ff.

74 W. Thalbitzer, "The Heathen Priests of East Greenland (Angakut)," pp. 452 ff.

75 Ibid., p. 454.

76 Id., "Les Magiciens esquimaux, leur conceptions du monde, de l'âme et de la vie," p. 77. Cf. also E. M. Weyer, Jr., *The Eskimos: Their Environment and Folkways*, p. 428.

and there to rub two stones together while waiting for the significant event. "Then the bear of the lake or the inland glacier will
come out, he will devour all your flesh and make you a skeleton,
and you will die. But you will recover your flesh, you will awaken,
and your clothes will come rushing to you." [77] Among the Labrador
Eskimo it is the Great Spirit himself, Tongársoak, who appears in
the form of a huge white bear and devours the aspirant.[78] In western Greenland, when the spirit appears the candidate remains
"dead" for three days.[79]

These experiences of ritual death and resurrection, during which
the boy loses consciousness for some time, are, of course, ecstatic.
As to the disciple's being reduced to a skeleton and later being re-
clothed in new flesh, this is a specific characteristic of Eskimo
initiation, and we shall come upon it again presently, in connection
with another mystical technique. The neophyte rubs his stones all
through the summer, and even through several consecutive summers, until the time comes when he obtains his helping spirits;[80]
but every season he finds a new master, in order to broaden his
experience (for each *angakok* is a specialist in a particular technique) and to collect a troop of spirits.[81] While he rubs his stones he
is subject to certain taboos.[82] An *angakok* teaches five or six disciples at once [83] and is paid for their instruction.[84]

77 Thalbitzer: "Les Magiciens esquimaux," p. 78; "The Heathen
Priests," p. 454.
78 Weyer, p. 429.   79 Ibid.
80 Thalbitzer, "The Heathen Priests," p. 454; Weyer, p. 429.
81 Thalbitzer, "Les Magiciens esquimaux," p. 78.
82 Id., "The Heathen Priests," p. 454. Everywhere in the world, and of
whatever category, initiation includes a certain number of taboos. It would
be tiresome to rehearse the immense morphology of these prohibitions,
which, all in all, possess no direct interest for our investigation. See
I. Webster, *Taboo: a Sociological Study*, especially pp. 273–76.
83 Thalbitzer, "Les Magiciens esquimaux," p. 79.
84 Id., "The Heathen Priests," p. 454; Weyer, pp. 433–34. Concerning
the teaching of aspirants, see also V. Stefánsson, "The Mackenzie Eskimo."
p. 367 ff.; F. Boas, "The Central Eskimo," pp. 591 ff.; J. W. Bilby, *Among
Unknown Eskimos*, pp. 196 ff. (Baffinland). Knud Rasmussen (*Across Arctic
America*, pp. 82 ff.) tells the story of the shaman Ingjugarjuk who, during

Among the Iglulik Eskimo things appear to be different. A young man or woman who wishes to become a shaman goes with a gift to the master selected and says: "I come to you because I desire to see." That evening the shaman questions his spirits, "in order to 'remove all obstacles.'" Then the candidate and his family proceed to confess their sins (violations of taboos, etc.), thus purifying themselves before the spirits. The instruction period is not long, especially in the case of males. It may even be as short as five days. But it is understood that the candidate will continue training in solitude. Instruction is given in the morning, at noon, in the evening, and at night. During this period the candidate eats very little, and his family does not join in hunting.[85]

The initiation proper begins with an operation of which we have only inadequate accounts. The old *angakok* extracts the disciple's "soul" from his eyes, brain, and intestines, so that the spirits may know what is best in him.[86] After this "extraction of the soul" the future shaman himself becomes able to draw his soul from his body and undertake long mystical journeys through space and the depths of the sea.[87] It is possible that this mysterious operation somewhat resembles the Australian techniques studied above. In any case, extracting the soul from the intestines obviously conceals a "renewal" of the internal organs.

Then the master obtains the *angákoq* for him, also called *qaumaneq*, that is, the disciple's "lighting" or "enlightenment," for the *angákoq* consists "of a mysterious light which the shaman suddenly feels in his body, inside his head, within the brain, an inexplicable searchlight, a luminous fire, which enables him to see in the dark both literally and metaphorically speaking, for he can now, even with closed eyes, see through darkness and perceive things and

his initiatory retreat into solitude, felt that he "sometimes died a little." Later, he himself initiated his sister-in-law by firing a cartridge at her (the lead of which he had replaced by a stone). A third case of initiation mentions five days spent in icy water without the candidate's clothes becoming wet

85 Rasmussen, *Intellectual Culture of the Iglulik Eskimos*, pp. 111 ff.

86 Ibid., p. 112.   87 Ibid., p. 113.

coming events which are hidden from others; thus they look into the future and into the secrets of others."[88]

The candidate obtains this mystical light after long hours of waiting, sitting on a bench in his hut and invoking the spirits. When he experiences it for the first time "it is as if the house in which he is suddenly rises; he sees far ahead of him, through mountains, exactly as if the earth were one great plain, and his eyes could reach to the end of the earth. Nothing is hidden from him any longer; not only can he see things far, far away, but he can also discover souls, stolen souls, which are either kept concealed in far, strange lands or have been taken up or down to the Land of the Dead."[89]

Here too, we find the experience of height and ascent, and even of levitation, which characterizes Siberian shamanism, but which is also found elsewhere and which can be regarded as a typical feature of shamanic techniques in general. We shall have occasion to return more than once to these techniques of ascent and to their religious implications. For the moment let us observe that the experience of inner light that determines the career of the Iglulik shaman is familiar to a number of higher mysticisms. To confine ourselves to a few examples: In the Upaniṣads the "inner light" (*antar jyotih*) defines the essence of the *ātman*.[90] In yogic techniques, especially those of the Buddhist schools, light of different colors indicates the success of particular meditations.[91] Similarly, the Tibetan Book of the Dead accords great importance to the light in which, it appears, the dying man's soul is bathed during his mortal throes and immediately after death; a man's destiny after death (deliverance or reincarnation) depends on the firmness with which he chooses the immaculate light.[92] Finally, we must not forget the immense role played by the inner light in Christian mysticism and theology.[93] All this invites us to a more understanding judgment of the Eskimo

88 Ibid., p. 112.   89 Ibid., p. 113.
90 Cf. Eliade, "Significations de la 'lumière intérieure,'" pp. 196 ff.
91 Cf. id., *Yoga: Immortality and Freedom*, pp. 195 ff.
92 W. Y. Evans-Wentz, ed., *The Tibetan Book of the Dead*, pp. 102 ff.
93 Cf. Eliade, "Significations," pp. 222 ff.

shaman's experiences; there is reason to believe that such mystical experiences were in some manner accessible to archaic humanity from the most distant ages.

Contemplating One's Own Skeleton

Qaumaneq is a mystical faculty that the master sometimes obtains for the disciple from the Spirit of the Moon. It can also be obtained by the disciple directly, with the help of the spirits of the dead, or the Mother of the Caribou, or of bears.[94] But there is always a personal experience; these mythical beings are only the sources from which the neophyte knows he is entitled to expect the revelation when he has prepared himself sufficiently.

Even before setting out to acquire one or more helping spirits, which are like new "mystical organs" for any shaman, the Eskimo neophyte must undergo a great initiatory ordeal. Success in obtaining this experience requires his making a long effort of physical privation and mental contemplation directed to gaining *the ability to see himself as a skeleton*. The shamans whom Rasmussen interrogated about this spiritual exercise gave rather vague answers which the famous explorer summarizes as follows: "Though no shaman can explain to himself how and why, he can, by the power his brain derives from the supernatural, as it were by thought alone divest his body of its flesh and blood, so that nothing remains but his bones. And he must then name all the parts of his body, mentioning every single bone by name; and in so doing, he must not use ordinary human speech, but only the special and sacred shaman's language which he has learned from his instructor. By thus seeing himself naked, altogether freed from the perishable and transient flesh and blood, he consecrates himself, in the sacred tongue of the shamans, to his great task, through that part of his body which will longest withstand the action of the sun, wind and weather, after he is dead." [95]

94 Rasmussen, *Intellectual Culture of the Iglulik Eskimos*, p. 113.
95 Ibid., p. 114.

This important exercise in meditation, which is also equivalent to an initiation (for the granting of helping spirits is strictly dependent upon its success) is strangely reminiscent of the dreams of Siberian shamans—with the difference that, in Siberia, reduction to the state of a skeleton is an operation performed by the shaman-ancestors or other mythical beings, while among the Eskimo the operation is mental, attained by asceticism and deliberate personal efforts to establish concentration. In both regions alike the essential elements of this mystical vision are the being divested of flesh and the numbering and naming of the bones. The Eskimo shaman obtains the vision after a long, arduous preparation. The Siberian shamans are, in most instances, "chosen," and passively witness their dismemberment by mythical beings. But in all these cases reduction to the skeleton indicates a passing beyond the profane human condition and, hence, a deliverance from it.

It must be added that this transcendence does not always lead to the same mystical results. As we shall see when we come to study the shaman's costume,[96] in the spiritual horizon of hunters and herdsmen bone represents the very source of life, both human and animal. To reduce oneself to the skeleton condition is equivalent to re-entering the womb of this primordial life, that is, to a complete renewal, a mystical rebirth. On the other hand, in certain Central Asian meditations that are Buddhistic and tantric in origin or at least in structure, reduction to the skeleton condition has, rather, an ascetic and metaphysical value—anticipating the work of time, reducing life by thought to what it really is, an ephemeral illusion in perpetual transformation.[97]

Such contemplations, it should be noted, have remained alive even within Christian mysticism—which once again shows that the ultimates attained by the earliest conscious awarenesses of archaic man remain unalterable. To be sure, these religious experiences are separated by a difference in content, as we shall see in connection with the process of reduction to a skeleton in use among Central Asian Buddhist monks. But from a certain point of view all

96 Below, pp. 145 ff.   97 See below, pp. 434 ff.

these contemplative experiences are equivalent; everywhere, we find the will to transcend the profane, individual condition and to attain a transtemporal perspective. Whether there is a reimmersion in primordial life in order to obtain a spiritual renewal of the entire being, or (as in Buddhist mysticism and Eskimo shamanism) a deliverance from the illusions of the flesh, the result is the same—a certain recovery of the very source of spiritual existence, which is at once "truth" and "life."

Tribal Initiations and Secret Societies

We have several times observed the *initiatory* essence of the candidate's "death" followed by his "resurrection," in whatever form this takes place—ecstatic dreams, sickness, unusual events, or ritual proper. Indeed, ceremonies implying passage from one age group to another, or admission into some "secret society," always presuppose a series of rites that can be summarized in the convenient formula: death and resurrection of the candidate. We will enumerate the commonest of these rites: [98]

(a) Period of seclusion in the bush (symbol of the beyond) and larval existence, like that of the dead; prohibitions imposed on the candidates by the fact that they are assimilated to the dead (a dead man cannot eat certain dishes, or cannot use his fingers, etc.);

(b) Face and body daubed with ashes or certain calcareous substances, to obtain the pallid hue of ghosts; funerary masks;

(c) Symbolic burial in the temple or fetish house;

(d) Symbolic descent to the underworld;

(e) Hypnotic sleep; drinks that make the candidate unconscious;

(f) Difficult ordeals: beatings, feet held close to a fire, suspension in the air, amputations of fingers, and various other cruelties.

All these rituals and ordeals are designed to make the candidate

[98] Cf. Heinrich Schurtz, *Altersklassen und Männerbünde;* Webster, *Primitive Secret Societies: a Study in Early Politics and Religion* (2nd edn.); A. v. Gennep, *The Rites of Passage;* Loeb, *Tribal Initiations and Secret Societies;* Eliade, *Birth and Rebirth.* We shall return to this problem in a later volume, *Death and Initiation.*

forget his past life. This is why, in many places, when the novice returns to the village he acts as if he had lost his memory and has to be taught all over again to walk, eat, dress. Usually the novices learn a new language and have a new name. During their stay in the bush the rest of the community considers the candidates dead and buried, or devoured by a monster or a god, and upon their return to the village regards them as ghosts.

Morphologically the future shaman's initiatory ordeals are of the same order as this great class of passage rites and ceremonies for entering secret societies. It is sometimes difficult to distinguish between tribal initiation rites and those of a secret society (as is the case in New Guinea),[99] or between rites for admission to a secret society and those of shamanic initiation (especially in North America).[100] In any case, in all these instances there is a "quest" for powers by the candidate.

There are no rites for passage from one age group to another in Siberia and Central Asia. But it would be wrong to attribute too much importance to this fact and to deduce certain consequences from it in regard to the possible origin of Siberian rites of shamanic initiation. For the two great groups of rituals (tribal initiation and shamanic initiation) coexist elsewhere—in Australia, for example, in Oceania, in both Americas. Indeed, in Australia the situation seems comparatively clear: though all males are supposed to be initiated in order to obtain the status of members of the tribe, there is another initiation reserved for medicine men. This latter initiation gives the candidate powers different from those conferred by the tribal initiation. It already represents a high degree of specialization in manipulating the sacred. The great difference observable between these two types of initiation is the fundamental importance of the inner, ecstatic experience in the case of aspirants to the profession of medicine man. Not anyone who wants to do so can become a medicine man; vocation is indispensable. And this vocation is manifested above all by an unusual capacity for ecstatic experience. We shall return to this aspect of shamanism, which we con-

99 Cf. Loeb, *Tribal Initiations*, p. 254.   100 Ibid., pp. 269 f.

sider characteristic and which, in the last analysis, differentiates the type of tribal initiation or initiation into secret societies from a shamanic initiation proper.

Finally, let us note that the myth of renewal by fire, cooking, or dismemberment has continued to haunt men even outside the spiritual horizon of shamanism. Medea succeeds in having Pelias murdered by his own daughters by convincing them that she will restore him to life rejuvenated, as she did a ram.[101] And when Tantalus kills his son Pelops and serves him at the banquet of the gods, they resuscitate him by boiling him in a pot; [102] only his shoulder is missing, Demeter having inadvertently eaten it.[103] The myth of rejuvenation by dismemberment and cooking has also been handed down in Siberian, Central Asian, and European folklore, the role of the blacksmith being played by Jesus Christ or certain saints.[104]

101 Apollodorus *Bibliotheke* I. IX. 27.

102 Pindar *Olymp.* I. 26(40) ff.

103 On this motif, see below, pp. 160 ff.

104 See Oskar Dähnhardt, *Natursagen*, II, 154; J. Bolte and G. Polívka *Anmerkungen zu den Kinder- und Hausmärchen der Brüder Grimm*, III, 198 n. 3; Stith Thompson, *Motif-Index of Folk-Literature*, II, 294; C. M. Eds man, *Ignis divinus: le feu comme moyen de rajeunissement et d'immortalité* pp. 30 ff., 151 ff. Edsman also makes use of C. Marstrander's well-docu mented article, "Deux contes irlandais," which escaped the attention of Bolte and Polívka as well as of Thompson.

CHAPTER THREE

Obtaining Shamanic Powers

W E   H A V E seen that one of the commonest forms of the future shaman's election is his encountering a divine or semidivine being, who appears to him through a dream, sickness, or some other circumstance, tells him that he has been "chosen," and incites him thenceforth to follow a new rule of life. More often it is the souls of his shaman ancestors who bring him the tidings. It has even been supposed that shamanic election was connected with the ancestor cult. But as L. Sternberg rightly remarks,[1] the ancestors themselves had to be "chosen," at the dawn of time, by a divine being. According to Buryat tradition,[2] in olden times the shamans received their *utcha* (the shamanic divine right) directly from the celestial spirits; it is only in our day that they obtain it merely from their ancestors. This belief forms part of the general conception of the decadence of shamans, documented both in the Arctic and in Central Asia; according to this view, the "first shamans" *really* flew through the clouds on their horses and performed miracles that their present-day descendants are incapable of repeating.[3]

---

1 "Divine Election in Primitive Religion," pp. 474 ff.

2 Ibid., p. 475.

3 Cf., among other works, K. Rasmussen, *Intellectual Culture of the I'ulik Eskimos*, p. 131; Mehmed Fuad Köprülüzadé, *Influence du chamanisme turco-mongol sur les ordres mystiques musulmans*, p. 17.

Siberian Myths concerning the Origin of Shamans

Certain legends explain the present decadence of shamans by th
pride of the "first shaman," who is believed to have entered int
competition with God. According to the Buryat version, the "fir
shaman," Khara-Gyrgän, having declared that his power wa
boundless, God put him to the test. God took a girl's soul an
shut it up in a bottle. To make sure that it would not escap
God put his finger into the neck of the bottle. The shaman fle
through the sky, sitting on his drum, discovered the girl's sou
and, to set it free, changed into a spider and stung God in the fac
God instantly pulled out his finger and the girl's soul escape
Furious, God curtailed Khara-Gyrgän's power, and after that th
magical abilities of shamans markedly diminished.[4]

According to Yakut tradition, the "first shaman" possesse
extraordinary power and, in his pride, refused to recognize th
Supreme God of the Yakut. This shaman's body was made of
mass of snakes. God sent down fire to burn him, but a toad emerg
from the flames; from this creature came the "demons" who,
their turn, supplied the Yakut with their outstanding shamans an
shamanesses.[5] The Tungus of Turukhansk have a different legen
The "first shaman" created himself, by his own powers and wi
the help of the devil. He flew out of the hole in his yurt and cam
back later accompanied by swans.[6]

Here we have a dualistic conception, probably deriving fro
Iranian influences. It may well be, too, that this class of legen

4 S. Shashkov, *Shamanstvo v Sibirii*, p. 81, cited by V. M. Mikhailows
"Shamanism in Siberia and European Russia," p. 63; other varian
U. Harva, *Die religiösen Vorstellungen der altaischen Völker*, pp. 543–44. T
mythical theme of the conflict between the shaman-magician and the S
preme Being is also found among the Andamans and the Semang;
R. Pettazzoni, *L'onniscienza di Dio*, pp. 441 ff., 458 ff.

5 N. V. Pripuzov, cited by Mikhailowski, p. 64.

6 P. I. Tretyakov, *Turukhansky krai, evo priroda i zhiteli*, pp. 210–1
Mikhailowski, p. 64. Certain details in these legends (flight through
aperture in the yurt, swans, etc.) will engage our attention later.

deals rather with the origin of the "black" shamans, who are reputed to have relations only with the underworld and the "devil." But the majority of myths concerning the origin of shamans posit the direct intervention of God, or of his representative the eagle, the bird of the sun.

Here is the story the Buryat tell: In the beginning there were only the gods *(tengri)* in the west and the evil spirits in the east. The gods created man, and he lived happily until the time when the evil spirits spread sickness and death over the earth. The gods decided to give mankind a shaman to combat disease and death, and they sent the eagle. But men did not understand its language; besides, they had no confidence in a mere bird. The eagle returned to the gods and asked them to give him the gift of speech, or else to send a Buryat shaman to men. The gods sent him back with an order to grant the gift of shamanizing to the first person he should meet on earth. Returned to earth, the eagle saw a woman asleep under a tree, and had intercourse with her. Some time later the woman gave birth to a son, who became the "first shaman." According to another variant, the woman, after her connection with the eagle, saw spirits and herself became a shamaness.[7]

This is why, in other legends, the appearance of an eagle is interpreted as a sign of shamanic vocation. The story is told that a Buryat girl, seeing an eagle carrying off sheep, understood the sign and was obliged to become a shamaness. Her initiation lasted seven years and after her death, having become a *sayan* ("spirit," "idol"), she continued to protect children from evil spirits.[8]

Among the Yakut of Turukhansk the eagle is likewise considered to be the creator of the "first shaman." But the eagle also bears the name of the Supreme Being, Ai (the "Creator") or Ai

---

7 N. N. Agapitov and M. N. Khangalov, "Materialy dlya izuchenia shamanstva v Sibirii," pp. 41–42; Mikhailowski, p. 64; Harva, *Die religiösen Vorstellungen*, pp. 465–66. Another variant will be found in J. Curtin, *A Journey in Southern Siberia*, p. 105. A similar myth is documented among the Mondo of South Africa; see W. J. Perry, *The Primordial Ocean*, pp. 143–44.

8 Garma Sandschejew, "Weltanschauung und Schamanismus der Alaren-urjaten," p. 605.

Toyon (the "Creator of Light"). Ai Toyon's children are represented as bird-spirits perching in the branches of the World Tree
in the top of it is the two-headed eagle, Toyon Kötör (the "Lord o
the Birds"), probably personifying Ai Toyon himself.[9] Like
number of other Siberian peoples, the Yakut establish a relatio
between the eagle and sacred trees, especially the birch. When A
Toyon created the shaman he also planted in his celestial dwellin
a birch tree with eight branches, on which were nests containin
the Creator's children. In addition, he planted three trees on eart
it is in memory of them that the shaman, too, has a tree on whos
life he is in a manner dependent.[10] It will be remembered that, i
his initiatory dreams, the shaman is carried to the Cosmic Tree
in whose top is the Lord of the World. Sometimes the Suprem
Being is represented in the form of an eagle, and in the branche
of the Tree are the souls of future shamans.[11] The likelihood is tha
this mythical image has a paleo-Oriental prototype.

Among the Yakut, again, the eagle is also related to smith
and these are supposed to have the same origin as shamans.[12] Ac
cording to the Yenisei Ostyak, the Teleut, the Orochon, and othe
Siberian peoples, the "first shaman" was born of an eagle or, a
least, was taught his art by the eagle.[13]

9 Leo Sternberg, "Der Adlerkult bei den Völkern Sibiriens," p. 13
Cf. similar conceptions among the Ket or the Yenisei Ostyak; B. D. Shimki
"A Sketch of the Ket, or Yenisei 'Ostyak,' " pp. 160 ff.

10 Sternberg, "Der Adlerkult," p. 134. On the relations among th
Cosmic Tree, the soul, and birth in Mongol and Siberian beliefs, o
U. Pestalozza, "Il manicheismo presso i Turchi occidentali ed orientali
pp. 487 ff.

11 Cf. E. Emsheimer, "Schamanentrommel und Trommelbaum," p. 17

12 Sternberg, "Der Adlerkult," p. 141.

13 Ibid., pp. 143–44. On the eagle in Yakut beliefs, see W. Sieroszews
"Du chamanisme d'après les croyances de Yakoutes," pp. 218–19; on th
importance of the eagle in the religion and mythology of the Siberian people
cf. Harva, Die religiösen Vorstellungen, pp. 465 ff.; H. Findeisen, "Der Adl
als Kulturbringer im nordasiatischen Raum und in der amerikanisch
Arktis"; on the symbolism of the eagle, F. Altheim and Hans-Wilhe
Haussig, Die Hunnen in Osteuropa, pp. 54 ff. Certain tribes sometimes fe
eagles on raw meat (cf. D. Zelenin, Kult ongonov v Sibiri, pp. 182 ff.), b
this custom appears to be sporadic and late. Among the Tungus the "cu

We may also recall the role played by the eagle in the stories of shamanic initiation [14] and the ornithomorphic elements in the shamanic costume, which magically transform the shamans into eagles.[15] This group of facts reveals a complex symbolism, crystallized around a celestial Divine Being and the idea of magical flight to the Center of the World (World Tree), a symbolism that we shall encounter more than once later on. But it must be emphasized now that the role played by the ancestral souls in a shaman's election is really less important than one would be inclined to think. The ancestors are only the descendants of the mythical "first shaman" created directly by the Supreme Being polarized in the form of an eagle. The shamanic vocation determined by the ancestral souls is sometimes only the transmission of supernatural message inherited from a mythical *illud tempus.*

Shamanic Election among the Goldi and the Yakut

The Goldi clearly distinguish between the tutelary spirit (*ayami*), which chooses the shaman, and the helping spirits (*syvén*), which are subordinate to it and are granted to the shaman by the *ayami* itself.[16] According to Sternberg the Goldi explain the relations between the shaman and his *ayami* by a complex sexual emotion. Here is the report of a Goldi shaman: [17]

---

the eagle has little importance (see S. M. Shirokogoroff, *Psychomental Complex of the Tungus*, p. 298). Sternberg ("Der Adlerkult," p. 131) recalls that Väinämöinen, the "first shaman" of Finnish mythological tradition, also descended from an eagle; see *Kalevala*, Rune I, vv. 270 f. (cf. the analysis this motif in Kaarle Krohn, *Kalevalastudien. V: Väinämöinen*, pp. 15 ff.). The celestial Supreme God of the Finns, Ukko, is also named Aïjä (Lapp Aijo, Aije), a name that Sternberg connects with Ajy (Ai). Like the Yakut Ajy, the Finnish Aïjä is the ancestor of shamans. The Yakut call the "white" shaman Ajy Ojuna (Ai Oyuna), which, according to Sternberg, is very close the Finnish Aïjä Ukko. We should recall the motif of the eagle and the Cosmic Tree (Yggdrasil) in Germanic mythology; Odin is sometimes called Eagle" (cf., for example, E. Mogk, *Germanische Mythologie*, pp. 342, 343).

14 Above, pp. 36 f.   15 Below, pp. 156 ff.

16 Sternberg, "Divine Election," p. 475.

17 The beginning of his confession was quoted in our first chapter, 28.

Once I was asleep on my sick-bed, when a spirit approached me. It wa a very beautiful woman. Her figure was very slight, she was no more that half an arshin (71 cm.) tall. Her face and attire were quite as those of on of our Gold women. Her hair fell down to her shoulders in short blac tresses. Other shamans say they have had the vision of a woman with one half of her face black, and the other half red. She said: "I am the 'ayami' c your ancestors, the Shamans. I taught them shamaning. Now I am goin; to teach you. The old shamans have died off, and there is no one to hea people. You are to become a shaman."

Next she said: "I love you, I have no husband now, you will be m husband and I shall be a wife unto you. I shall give you assistant spirit You are to heal with their aid, and I shall teach and help you mysel Food will come to us from the people."

I felt dismayed and tried to resist. Then she said: "If you will not obe me, so much the worse for you. I shall kill you."

She has been coming to me ever since, and I sleep with her as with m own wife, but we have no children. She lives quite by herself without an relatives in a hut, on a mountain, but she often changes her abode. Some times she comes under the aspect of an old woman, and sometimes und that of a wolf, so she is terrible to look at. Sometimes she comes as winged tiger. I mount it and she takes me to show me different countrie I have seen mountains, where only old men and women live, and village where you see nothing but young people, men and women: they look li Golds and speak Goldish, sometimes those people are turned into tigers.

Now my ayami does not come to me as frequently as before. Formerl when teaching me, she used to come every night. She has given me thr assistants—the "jarga" (the panther), the "doonto" (the bear) and t "amba" (the tiger). They come to me in my dreams, and appear whe ever I summon them while shamaning. If one of them refuses to con the "ayami" makes them obey, but, they say, there are some who do n obey even the "ayami." When I am shamaning, the "ayami" and t assistant spirits are possessing me: whether big or small, they penetra

18 All these details of ecstatic journeys are most important. In North a Southeast Asia the Spirit-Instructor of young candidates for initiati appears in the form of a bear or a tiger. Sometimes the candidate is carri off into the jungle (symbol of the beyond) on the back of such an anim spirit. People who turn themselves into tigers are initiates or "dead me (which, in myths, is sometimes the same thing).

me, as smoke or vapour would. When the "ayami" is within me, it is she who speaks through my mouth, and she does everything herself. When I am eating the "sukdu" (the offerings) and drinking pig's blood (the blood of pigs is drunk by shamans alone, lay people are forbidden to touch it), it is not I who eat and drink, it is my "ayami" alone.[19]

There is no doubt that the sexual elements play an important part in this shamanic autobiography. But it should be noted that the *ayami* does not make her "husband" able to shamanize simply by maintaining sexual relations with him; it is the secret teaching that she gives him over the years, and his ecstatic journeys, that change the "husband's" religious practice, gradually preparing him for his shamanic function. As we shall presently see, anyone can have sexual relations with female spirits, yet without thereby acquiring the magico-religious powers of shamans.

Sternberg, on the contrary, considers that the primary element in shamanism is sexual emotion, to which the idea of hereditary transmission of spirits was added later.[20] He cites a number of other data, all of which, in his view, support his interpretation: a shamaness, observed by Shirokogoroff, experienced sexual feelings during initiatory ordeals; the Goldi shaman's ritual dance as he feeds his *ayami* (who is believed to enter him during the course of it) is interpreted by Sternberg as having a sexual meaning; in the Yakut folklore studied by V. F. Troshchansky there is constant reference to young celestial spirits (children of the Sun, the Moon, the Pleiades, etc.) descending to earth and marrying mortal women, and so on. None of these facts seems to us decisive. In the case of the shamaness observed by Shirokogoroff and that of the Goldi shaman the sexual feelings are distinctly secondary, if not aberrant, for many other records make no mention of this kind of erotic trance; as to the Yakut folklore, it accounts for a general popular belief that simply does not solve the problem with which

19 Sternberg, "Divine Election," pp. 476 ff. Some autobiographies of Savara (Saora) shamans and shamanesses, whose marriages to spirits of the subterranean world are in striking parallel to the documents collected by Sternberg, will be found below, pp. 421 ff.

20 Ibid., p. 480.

we are concerned—namely, why, from among a great number of subjects "possessed" by celestial spirits, are only a few called to be shamans? So it does not seem that sexual relations with spirits constitute the essential and determining element in shamanic vocation. But Sternberg also adduces unpublished information concerning the Yakut, Buryat, and Teleut, information of great interest in itself and which we must consider for a moment.

According to his Yakut informant, N. M. Sliepzova, the *abassy* (spirits), youths or girls, enter the bodies of young people of the opposite sex, put them to sleep, and make love to them. A lad visited by an *abassy* no longer approaches girls, and some of them remain bachelors the rest of their lives. If an *abassy* loves a married man he becomes impotent with his wife. All this, Sliepzova concluded, is of general occurrence among the Yakut; *a fortiori*, the same thing must happen among shamans.

But in the case of the latter, spirits of a different kind are also involved. "The masters and mistresses of the upper and under world, 'abassy,'" Sliepzova stated, "in appearing to the shaman in his dream, do not personally enter upon sexual intercourse with him. This is done by their sons and daughters." [21] This detail important and goes against Sternberg's hypothesis of the erotic origin of shamanism. For, by Sliepzova's own testimony, the shaman's vocation is determined by the appearance of celestial or infernal spirits, and not by the sexual emotion aroused by the *abassy*. Sexual relations with the latter come after the shaman's consecration by an ecstatic vision of the spirits.

Then too, as Sliepzova herself says, sexual relations between young people and spirits are quite frequent among the Yakut; they are equally frequent among a great many other peoples, without warranting any affirmation that they constitute the primary experience generating so complex a religious phenomenon as shamanism. In fact, the *abassy* play a secondary role in Yakut shamanism; according to Sliepzova's account, if the shaman dreams of an *abassy* and has sexual relations with her, he wakes feeling

21 Sternberg, "Divine Election," p. 482.

well, certain that he will be summoned in consultation the same day and no less certain that he will be successful; if, on the contrary, he dreams that he sees the *abassy* full of blood and swallowing the sick person's soul, he knows that the patient will not live, and, if summoned the next day to attend him, he makes every effort to avoid the duty. Finally, if he is summoned without having had any dream, he is disconcerted and does not know what to do.[22]

Election among the Buryat and the Teleut

For Buryat shamanism, Sternberg relies on information supplied by one of his pupils, A. N. Mikhailof, himself a Buryat and a former participant in shamanic ceremonies.[23] According to Mikhailof, the shaman's career begins with a message from a shaman ancestor, who then takes his soul to the sky to teach him. On the way they stop to visit the gods of the Center of the World, especially Tekha Shara Matzkala, the god of the dance, fecundity, and wealth, who lives with the nine daughters of Solboni, god of dawn. These divinities are peculiar to shamans, and only shamans make offerings to them. The young candidate's soul enters into amorous relations with Tekha's nine wives. When his shamanic instruction is finished, his soul meets his future celestial wife in the sky; with her too his soul has sexual relations. Two or three years after this ecstatic experience the initiation ceremony proper takes place; it includes an ascent to the sky and is followed by a three-day feast of somewhat licentious nature. Before this ceremony the candidate travels through all the neighboring villages and is given presents that have a nuptial significance. The tree that is used in the initiation, and that also resembles the one put in the house of a newly married couple, represents, Mikhailof says, the life of the celestial wife; and the cord that connects this tree (planted in the yurt) with the shaman's tree (in the courtyard) is the emblem of the nuptial union between the shaman and his spirit wife. Further according to Mikhailof, the initiation rite of the Buryat shaman

22 Ibid., p. 483.   23 Ibid., pp. 485 f.

signifies his marriage to his celestial fiancée. And Sternberg cite[s]
the fact that during the initiation people dance, drink, and sing
exactly as they do at weddings.[24]

All this is perhaps true, but it does not explain Buryat sha[-]
manism. We have seen that the choice of the shaman, among th[e]
Buryat as everywhere else, involves a quite complex ecstatic ex[-]
perience, during which the candidate is believed to be tortured, c[ut]
to pieces, put to death, and then to return to life. *It is only th[e]
initiatory death and resurrection that consecrates a shaman.* Teachin[g]
by spirits and the old masters later supplements this first conse[-]
cration. The initiation proper—to which we shall return in th[e]
following chapter—consists in the candidate's triumphant journe[y]
to the sky. It is natural that the popular festivities on this occasio[n]
should resemble those at a wedding, for the possible patterns [of]
collective rejoicing are, of course, few. But the role of the celesti[al]
bride appears to be secondary; it is no more than that of the sha[-]
man's helper and inspirer. We shall see that this role must b[e]
interpreted in the light of yet other facts.

Using A. V. Anokhin's data on shamanism among the Teleu[t]
Sternberg states [25] that every Teleut shaman has a celestial wi[fe]
who lives in the seventh heaven. During his ecstatic journey [to]
Bai Ülgän, the shaman meets his wife, and she asks him to rema[in]
with her; she has prepared an exquisite banquet for them. "/ M[y]
darling young kam! [she sings] / We shall sit together at the bl[ue]
table . . . / My darling husband, my young kam, / Let us hi[de]
in the shadow of the curtains / And let us make love to one anoth[er]
and have fun, / My husband, my young kam!" [26] She assures hi[m]
that the road to the sky has been blocked. But the shaman refus[es]
to believe her, and repeats his determination to continue h[is]
ascent: "We shall go up the 'tapti' (the spiral groove cut in t[he]
shaman tree) / And give praise to the full moon" / [27] (an allusi[on]
to the stop that the shaman makes on his celestial journey [to]
venerate the Moon and the Sun). He will touch no food until [he]

24 Sternberg, p. 487. 25 Ibid.
26 Ibid. 27 Ibid., p. 488.

has returned to earth. He calls her "My darling, my wife," and adds: "My wife on earth / Is not fit to pour water on thy hands." [28] The shaman is assisted in his labors not only by his celestial wife but also by feminine spirits. In the fourteenth heaven dwell the nine daughters of Ülgän; it is they who confer his magical powers on the shaman (swallowing hot coals, etc.). When a man dies they come down to earth, take his soul, and carry it to the heavens.

Several details in this Teleut account are interesting. The episode of the shaman's celestial wife inviting her husband to eat is reminiscent of the well-known mythical theme of the meal that the feminine spirits of the beyond offer to every mortal who reaches their domain, in order that he shall forget his earthly life and remain forever in their power. This is true both of the demigoddesses and the fairies of the beyond. The shaman's dialogue with his wife during his ascent forms part of a long and complex dramatic scenario, to which we will return; in any case, it cannot be regarded as essential. As we shall see later, the essential element in every shamanic ascent is the final dialogue with Ülgän. Hence the dialogue with the wife is to be considered a lively dramatic element well suited to interest the audience during a séance that sometimes tends to become monotonous. Nevertheless, it preserves all its initiatory bearing; the fact that the shaman has a celestial wife who prepares meals for him in the seventh heaven and sleeps with him is another proof that he shares to some extent in the condition of semidivine beings, that he is a hero who has experienced death and resurrection and who therefore enjoys a second life, in the heavens.

Sternberg also cites [29] a Uriankhai legend of the "first shaman," Bö-Khân. Bö-Khân loved a celestial maiden. Discovering that he was married, the fairy caused the earth to swallow him and his wife. She then gave birth to a boy, whom she abandoned under a larch tree to be fed by its sap. From this child comes the race of shamans (Bö-Khâ-näkn).

The motif of the fairy wife who leaves her mortal husband after

28 Ibid.   29 Ibid.

giving him a son is universally disseminated. The incidents of th
husband's search for the fairy sometimes reflect initiation scenaric
(ascent to the sky, descent to the underworld, etc.).[30] The fairy
jealousy of the mortal wife is also a frequent theme in folklor
nymphs, fairies, demigoddesses envy the happiness of earthly wive
and steal or kill their children.[31] On the other hand, they are re
garded as the mothers, wives, or teachers of heroes, that is,
those among mankind who succeed in transcending the human co
dition and obtain, if not a divine immortality, at least a sort
privileged afterlife. A large number of myths and legends sho
the essential role played by a fairy, a nymph, or a semidivir
woman in the adventures of heroes; it is she who teaches the
helps them in their difficulties (which are often initiatory ordeals
and shows them how to gain possession of the symbol of in
mortality or long life (the miraculous herb, the magical apple
the fountain of youth, etc.). An important division of the "m
thology of woman" is devoted to showing that it is always
feminine being who helps the hero to conquer immortality or
emerge victorious from his initiatory ordeals.

This is not the place to enter on a discussion of this mythic
motif, but it is certain that it preserves traces of a late "mat
archal" mythology, in which signs of the "masculine" (heroi
reaction against the omnipotence of Woman (= Mother)
already discernible. In some variants the role of the fairy in t
heroic quest is almost negligible; thus the nymph Siduri, of who
in the archaic versions of the Gilgamesh legend, the hero had ask

30 The Maori hero Tawhaki's wife, a fairy come down from the s
remains with him only until the birth of their first child; then she climbs
onto a hut and disappears. Tawhaki goes up into the sky by climbing a v
and, later, succeeds in returning to earth (Sir George Grey, Polynes
Mythology, pp. 42 ff.). According to other variants the hero reaches
sky by climbing a coconut palm, or by a rope, a spider web, or a kite.
the Hawaiian Islands he is said to climb the rainbow; in Tahiti he climb
high mountain and meets his wife on the road; cf. H. M. and N. K. Chadwi
The Growth of Literature, III, 273.

31 Cf. Stith Thompson, Motif-Index of Folk-Literature, III, 44
(F 320 f.).

mmortality directly, goes unnoticed in the classical text. Sometimes the hero, though invited to share in the semidivine woman's
beatific condition and hence in her immortality, accepts unwillingly
nd tries to escape as soon as possible to rejoin his earthly wife
nd his companions (the case of Ulysses and the nymph Calypso).
The love of such a semidivine woman becomes an obstacle rather
han a help for the hero.

The Shaman's Female Tutelary Spirits

t is in such a mythical horizon that we must place the relations of
hamans with their "celestial wives"; it is not they who, properly
peaking, consecrate the shaman; they help him either in his
nstruction or in his ecstatic experience. It is natural that the
celestial wife's" intervention in the shaman's mystical experience
hould be accompanied by sexual emotion; every ecstatic experi-
nce is subject to such deviations, and the close relations between
ystical and carnal love are too well known for the mechanism of
his shift in plane to be misunderstood. Then too, it must not be
verlooked that the erotic elements present in shamanic rites
xceed the mere relationship of the shaman with his "celestial
ife." Among the Kumandin of the Tomsk region the horse sacri-
ce includes an exhibition of wooden masks and phalli, carried by
ree young men; they gallop with the phallus between their legs
like a stallion" and touch the spectators. The song sung on this
ccasion is distinctly erotic.[32] Among the Teleut when the shaman,
limbing the tree, reaches the third *tapty*, the women, girls, and
hildren leave and the shaman begins an obscene song resembling
at of the Kumandin; its purpose is to strengthen the men sexu-
lly.[33] This rite has parallels elsewhere,[34] and its meaning is the
ore explicit because it forms part of the horse sacrifice, whose

32 D. Zelenin, "Ein erotischer Ritus in den Opferungen der altaischen
uerken," pp. 88–89.
33 Ibid., p. 91.
34 Caucasus, ancient China, America, etc.; cf. ibid., pp. 94 ff.

cosmological function (renewal of the world and life) is wel
known.[35]

To return to the role of the "celestial wife": it is remarkabl
that, exactly as in the late versions of myths to which we referrec
the shaman too seems to be both helped and hindered by hi
ayami. For, though she protects him, she tries to keep him fo
herself in the seventh heaven, and opposes his continuing hi
ascent. She also tempts him with a celestial repast, which cou
keep him from his earthly wife and the society of human being:

To conclude: The tutelary spirit (*ayami*, etc.), also conceived i
the form of a celestial wife (or husband), plays an important bu
not decisive role in Siberian shamanism. The decisive element i:
as we have seen, the initiatory drama of ritual death and resurrec
tion (sickness, dismemberment, descent to the underworld, ascer
to the sky, etc.). The sexual relations that the shaman is believe
to have with his *ayami* are not basic to his shamanic vocation. Fo
on the one hand, sexual possession by spirits in dream is not cor
fined to shamans; on the other hand, the sexual elements preser
in certain shamanic ceremonies go beyond the relations betwee

[35] On the sexual elements in the *aśvamedha* and other similar rites, s
P. É. Dumont, *L'Aśvamedha*, pp. 276 ff.; W. Koppers, "Pferdeopfer u
Pferdekult der Indogermanen," pp. 344 ff., 401 ff. In this connection w
might mention another shamanic fertility rite that is performed on an e
tirely different religious plane. The Yakut worship a goddess of fertility a
procreation, Aisyt, who dwells in the east, in the part of the sky in which t
sun rises in summer. Her festivals are held in spring and summer, and a
under the jurisdiction of special shamans, called "summer shamans" (*saing*
or "white shamans." Aisyt is invoked to obtain children, especially ma
children. Singing and drumming, the shaman heads the procession, leadir
nine virgin lads and girls, who follow him holding each other by the ha
and singing in chorus. "In this fashion the shaman ascends to the sky, leadir
the young couples; but Aisyt's servants stand at the gates, armed with silv
whips: they turn back all who are corrupt, evil, dangerous; entrance is al
forbidden to those who have lost their innocence too early" (W. Sieroszewsl
"Du chamanisme d'après les croyances des Yakoutes," pp. 336–37). B
Aisyt is a complex goddess; cf. G. Ränk, "Lapp Female Deities of t
Madder-Akka Group," pp. 56 ff.

he shaman and his *ayami* and form part of well-known rituals in-ended to increase the sexual vigor of the community.

The protection given the Siberian shaman by his *ayami* resembles, as we saw, the role given to fairies and demigoddesses in the eaching and initiation of heroes. This protection undoubtedly reflects "matriarchal" conceptions. The Great Mother of the Animals—with whom the Siberian and Arctic shaman is on the best of terms—is an even clearer image of the ancient matriarchy. There s good reason to believe that at a certain moment this Great Mother of the Animals took over the function of a uranian Supreme Being, but the problem goes beyond our subject.[36] We will only observe that, just as the Great Mother of the Animals grants men —and particularly shamans—the right to hunt and to sustain hemselves on the flesh of beasts, the "feminine" tutelary spirits give shamans the helping spirits that are in some sort indispensable o them in their ecstatic journeys.

Role of the Souls of the Dead

We have seen that the future shaman's vocation can be precipitated —in dreams, ecstasy, or during an illness—by a chance encounter with a semidivine being, the soul of an ancestor or of an animal, or as the result of some extraordinary event (lightning, mortal accident, etc.). Usually such an encounter begins a "familiarity" etween the future shaman and the "spirit" that has determined is career; and this familiarity will occupy our attention later. For

36 Cf. A. Gahs, "Kopf-, Schädel- und Langknochenopfer bei Rentier-ölkern," pp. 241 (Samoyed, etc.), 249 (Ainu), 255 (Eskimo). Cf. also U. Holmberg (later Harva), "Über die Jagdriten der nördlichen Völker siens und Europas,"; E. Lot-Falck, *Les Rites de chasse chez les peuples bériens*; Ivar Paulson, *Schutzgeister und Gottheiten des Wildes (der Jagdtiere nd Fische) in Nordeurasien*; B. Bonnerjea, "Hunting Superstitions of the merican Aborigines"; Otto Zerries, *Wild- und Buschgeister in Südamerika.* he Mother of the Animals is also found in the Caucasus; cf. A. Dirr, "Der aukasische Wild- und Jagdgott," p. 146. The African realm has been ex-lored by H. Baumann, "Afrikanische Wild- und Buschgeister."

the moment let us look more closely into the role of the souls of the dead in recruiting future shamans. As we saw, the souls of ancestors often take a sort of "possession" of a young man and then initiate him. Resistance is unavailing. This phenomenon of pre-election is general in North and Arctic Asia.[37]

Once he has been consecrated by this first "possession" and the initiation that follows, the shaman becomes a receptacle that can be entered indefinitely by other spirits, too; but these are always the souls of dead shamans or other spirits who served the old shamans. The celebrated Yakut shaman Tüspüt told Sieroszewski: "One day when I was wandering in the mountains, up there in the north, I stopped by a pile of wood to cook my food. I set fire to it. Now, a Tungus shaman was buried under the pyre. His spirit took possession of me." [38] This is why Tüspüt uttered Tungusic words during séances. But he received other spirits too —Russians, Mongols, and so on—and spoke their languages.[39]

The role of the souls of the dead in choosing the future shaman is important in places outside Siberia as well. Eskimo, Australians and others too, who wish to become medicine men lie by graves this custom survived even among some historical peoples (e.g. the Celts). In South America initiation by dead shamans, though not the only method, is quite frequent. "The Bororo shamans whether belonging to the class of the *aroettawaraare* or that of the *bari*, are chosen by the soul of a dead person or by a spirit. In the case of the *aroettawaraare* the revelation takes place as follows: The future shaman walks in the forest and suddenly sees a bird perch within reach of his hand, then vanish. Flocks of parrots fly down toward him and disappear as if by magic. The future shaman goes

37 The same phenomenon, of course, is found elsewhere. Among the Batak of Sumatra, for example, refusal to become a shaman after being "chosen" by the spirits is followed by death. No Batak becomes a shaman of his own volition (E. M. Loeb, *Sumatra*, p. 81).

38 "Du chamanisme," p. 314.

39 The same beliefs prevail among the Tungus and the Goldi; see Harva, *Die religiösen Vorstellungen*, p. 463. A Haida shaman, if he is possessed by a Tlingit spirit, speaks Tlingit, even though he does not know the language at other times (J. R. Swanton, cited by H. Webster, *Magic*, p. 213).

home shaking and uttering unintelligible words. An odor of decay [40] and annatto emanates from his body. Suddenly a gust of wind makes him totter; he falls like a dead man. At this moment he has become the receptacle of a spirit that speaks through his mouth. From now on he is a shaman." [41]

Among the Apinaye shamans are appointed by the soul of a relative, which puts them in relation with the spirits; but it is the latter that impart shamanic knowledge and techniques to them. Among other tribes one becomes a shaman through a spontaneous ecstatic experience—for example, by having a vision of the planet Mars, and so on.[42] Among the Campa and the Amahuaca candidates are instructed by a living or dead shaman.[43] "The apprentice shaman of the Conibo of the Ucayali receives his medical knowledge from a spirit. To enter into relations with the spirit the shaman drinks a decoction of tobacco and smokes as much as possible in a hermetically closed hut." [44] The Cashinawa candidate is taught in the bush; souls give him the requisite magical substances and also inoculate his body with them. The Yaruro shamans are taught by their gods, although they learn technique proper from other shamans. But they do not consider themselves able to practice until they have met a spirit in dream.[45] "In the Apapocuva Guarani tribe, the prerequisite for becoming a shaman is learning magical songs, which are taught by a dead relative in dreams." [46] But whatever the source of their revelation, all these shamans practice in accordance with the traditional norms of their tribe. "In other words, they conform to rules and a technique that they can have acquired only by going to school to men of experience," Métraux concludes.[47] This is equally true of any other shamanism.

As we see, if the dead shaman's soul plays an important role in the development of shamanic vocation, it only prepares the

40 Ritually, that is, he is already a "dead man."
41 A. Métraux, "Le Shamanisme chez les Indiens de l'Amérique du Sud tropicale," p. 203. (Cf. below, pp. 90 ff.)

42 Ibid.   43 Ibid.
44 Ibid., p. 204.   45 Ibid., pp. 204–05.
46 Ibid., p. 205.   47 Ibid.

candidate for later revelations. The souls of dead shamans put him in relation with spirits, or carry him to the sky (cf. Siberia, the Altai, Australia, etc.). These first ecstatic experiences are followed by teaching received from the old shamans.[48] Among the Selk'nam spontaneous vocation is manifested by the young man's strange behavior: he sings in his sleep, and so on.[49] But such a state can also be obtained voluntarily; all that is necessary is to see the spirits.[50]

"Seeing spirits," in dream or awake, is the determining sign of the shamanic vocation, whether spontaneous or voluntary. For, in a manner, having contact with the souls of the dead signifies *being dead oneself*. This is why, throughout South America, the shaman must so die that he may meet the souls of the dead and receive their teaching; for the dead know everything.[52]

As we said, shamanic election or initiation in South America sometimes preserves the perfect schema of a ritual death and resurrection. But the death can also be suggested by other means: extreme fatigue, tortures, fasting, blows, and so on. When a young Jivaro decides to become a shaman, he looks for a master, pays him the proper fee, and then embarks on an extremely severe regime; for days he does not touch food and drinks narcotic beverages, especially tobacco juice (which is well known to play an essential part in the initiations of South American shamans). Finally a spirit, Pasuka, appears to the candidate in the form of a warrior. The master immediately begins to strike the apprentice until he falls to the ground unconscious. When he comes to himself, his whole body is sore. This proves that the spirit has taken possession of him; and in fact, the sufferings, intoxications, and blows

48 Cf. ibid., pp. 206 ff.; M. Gusinde: "Der Medizinmann bei den süd-amerikanischen Indianern," p. 293; *Die Feuerland Indianern. I: Die Selk'nam*, pp. 782–86, etc.

49 Gusinde, *Die Selk'nam*, p. 779.   50 Ibid., pp. 781–82.

51 Cf. Ida Lublinski, "Der Medizinmann bei den Naturvölkern Süd-amerikas," p. 249; see also our preceding chapter, pp. 52 f.

52 Lublinski, p. 250. The belief that mantic gifts are explained by dealing with the dead is universal.

that have brought on his loss of consciousness are in a manner assimilated to a ritual death.[53]

It follows that the souls of the dead, whatever the part they have played in precipitating the vocation or initiation of future shamans, do not create the vocation by their mere presence (possession or not), but serve the candidate as a means of entering into contact with divine or semidivine beings (through ecstatic journeys to the sky and the underworld, etc.) or enable the future shaman to share in the mode of being of the dead. This has been very well brought out by Marcel Mauss in connection with magical powers being conferred on Australian sorcerers by supernatural revelation.[54] Here too, the role of the dead often overlaps that of "pure spirits." And indeed, even when it is the spirit of a dead man that directly grants the revelation, the latter implies either the initiatory rite of the killing of the candidate followed by his rebirth,[55] or ecstatic journeys to the sky, a peculiarly shamanic theme in which the ancestral spirit plays the role of psychopomp and which, by its very structure, excludes "possession." It certainly seems that the chief function of the dead in the granting of shamanic powers is less a matter of taking "possession" of the subject than of helping him to become a "dead man"—in short, of helping him to become a "spirit" too.

"Seeing the Spirits"

This explains the extreme importance of "spirit visions" in all varieties of shamanic initiations. "Seeing" a spirit, either in dream or awake, is a certain sign that one has in some sort obtained a "spiritual condition," that is, that one has transcended the profane condition of humanity. This is why, among the Mentaveians, the "vision" (of spirits), whether occurring spontaneously or obtained by effort, immediately confers magical power (*kerei*)

53 M. W. Stirling, "Jivaro Shamanism"; Webster, *Magic*, p. 213.
54 Cf. "L'Origine des pouvoirs magiques dans les sociétés australiennes," p. 144 ff.
55 See our preceding chapter.

on shamans.[56] The Andaman magicians withdraw to the jungle to obtain this "vision"; those who have had only dreams obtain lesser magical powers.[57] Among the Menangkabau of Sumatra the *dukun* complete their shamanic instruction in solitude, on a mountain; there they learn to become invisible and, at night, see the souls of the dead [58]—which means that they *become* spirits, that they *are* dead.

An Australian shaman, of the Yaralde tribe (Lower Murray), admirably describes the initiatory terrors that accompany the vision of the spirits and the dead: "When you lie down to see the prescribed visions, and you do see them, do not be frightened, because they will be horrible. They are hard to describe, though they are in my mind and my *miwi* (i.e., psychic force), and though I could project the experience into you after you had been well trained.

"However, some of them are evil spirits, some are like snakes, some are like horses with men's heads, and some are spirits of evil men which resemble burning fires. You see your camp burning and the blood waters rising, and thunder, lightning and rain, the earth rocking, the hills moving, the waters whirling, and the trees which still stand, swaying about. Do not be frightened. If you get up, you will not see these scenes, but when you lie down again you will see them, unless you get too frightened. If you do, you will break the web (or thread) on which the scenes are hung. You may see dead persons walking towards you, and you will hear their bones rattle. If you hear and see these things without fear, you will never be frightened of anything. These dead people will not show themselves to you again, because your *miwi* is now strong. You are now powerful because you have seen these dead people." [59] And in fact medicine men are able to see the spirits of the dead

56 E. M. Loeb, "Shaman and Seer," p. 66.

57 A. R. Brown, *The Andaman Islanders*, p. 177; cf. some other example (Sea Dyak, etc.) in Loeb, "Shaman and Seer," p. 64.

58 Loeb, *Sumatra*, p. 125.

59 A. P. Elkin, *Aboriginal Men of High Degree*, pp. 70–71.

about their graves, and can easily capture them. These spirits then become their helpers, and during shamanic healing the medicine men send them to great distances to bring back the strayed soul of the sick man they are treating.[60]

Among the Mentaweians, again, "a man or woman may be made a seer by being bodily abducted by the spirits. According to the story of Sitakigagailau, the youth was taken up to heaven by the sky-spirits and given a beautiful body such as theirs. When he returned to earth he was a seer and the sky-spirits served him in his cures. . . . The usual manner, however, in which boys and girls become seers is by being summoned through sickness, dreams, or temporary insanity. The sickness or dreams are sent by the sky-spirits or the jungle-spirits. . . . The dreamer may imagine that he ascends to heaven or that he goes to the woods looking for monkeys. In either case, dreams or sickness, there is a temporary loss of soul." [61]

The master seer then proceeds to initiate the young man. The two go to the forest together to gather magical plants; the master chants: "Spirits of the talisman, reveal yourselves. Make clear the eyes of the body that he may see the spirits." As they return to the master seer's house he invokes the spirits: "Let your eyes be clear, let your eyes be clear, so that we may see our fathers and mothers of the lower heaven." After this invocation "the instructor rubs the herbs on the eyes of the boy. For three days and nights the two men sit opposite each other, singing and ringing their bells. Until the eyes of the boy are clear, neither of the two men obtains any sleep. At the end of the three days the two again go to the woods and obtain more herbs. . . . If at the end of seven days the boy sees the wood-spirits, the ceremony is at an end. Otherwise the entire seven-day ceremony must be repeated." [62]

All this long and tiring ceremony has as its object transforming the apprentice magician's initial and momentary ecstatic experience

60 Ibid., p. 117.   61 Loeb, "Shaman and Seer," pp. 67 ff.
62 Ibid.

(the experience of "election") into a permanent condition—that in which it is possible to "see the spirits," that is, to share in their "spiritual" nature.

The Helping Spirits

This appears even more clearly from an examination of the other categories of "spirits" that also play a role either in the shaman's initiation or in bringing on his ecstatic experiences. We said above that a relation of "familiarity" is established between the shaman and his "spirits." And in fact, in ethnological literature they are known as "familiars," "helping," "assistant," or "guardian" spirits. But we must distinguish carefully between familiar spirits proper and another and more powerful category of spirits known as tutelary spirits; so too, a distinction must be made between these last and the divine or semidivine beings whom the shamans summon up during séances. A shaman is a man who has immediate, concrete experiences with gods and spirits; he sees them face to face, he talks with them, prays to them, implores them—but he does not "control" more than a limited number of them. Any god or spirit invoked during a shamanic séance is not by that fact one of the shaman's "familiars" or "helpers." The great gods are often invoked. This is the case, for example, among the Altaians; before setting out on his ecstatic journey the shaman invites the attendance of Jajyk (Yaik) Kan (the Lord of the Sea), Kaira Kan, Bai Ülgän and his daughters, and other mythical figures.[63] The shaman invokes them, and the gods, demigods, and spirits arrive—just as the Vedic divinities descend and attend the priest when he invokes them during the sacrifice. The shamans also have divinities peculiar to them, unknown to the rest of the people, and to whom they alone offer sacrifices. But all this pantheon is not at the shaman's disposition, as his familiar spirits are; and the divine or semidivine beings who help him must not be classed among these familiar or helping or guardian spirits.

[63] W. Radlov, *Aus Sibirien*, II, 30 ff.

Yet these play an important part in shamanism; we shall see their functions when we come to study shamanic séances. Meanwhile, we must note that the majority of these familiar and helping spirits have animal forms. Thus among the Siberians and the Altaians they can appear in the form of bears, wolves, stags, hares, all kinds of birds (especially the goose, eagle, owl, crow, etc.), of great worms, but also as phantoms, wood spirits, earth spirits, hearth spirits, and so on; there is no need to give the whole list.[64] Their forms, names, and numbers differ from region to region. According to Karjalainen, the number of a Vasyugan shaman's helping spirits may vary, but usually they are seven. In addition to these "familiars," the shaman also enjoys the protection of a "spirit of the head," which defends him during his ecstatic journeys; of a "spirit in the shape of a bear," which accompanies him on his descents to the underworld; of a gray horse, which he rides when he ascends to the sky; and others still. Elsewhere this troop of spirits that attend the Vasyugan shaman is replaced by a single spirit—a bear among the northern Ostyak, a "messenger" among the Tremyugan and other peoples—which brings the gods' answer; this spirit suggests the "messengers" of the celestial spirits (birds, etc.).[65] The shamans summon them from every quarter, and they come, one after the other, and speak through the shaman's voices.[66]

The difference between a familiar spirit in animal form and the strictly shamanic tutelary spirit is clearly apparent among the Yakut. The shamans each have an *ié-kyla* (animal mother), a sort of mythical image of an animal helper, which they conceal. The

64 See, among others, G. Nioradze, *Der Schamanismus bei den sibirischen Völkern*, pp. 26 ff.; Harva, *Die religiösen Vorstellungen*, pp. 334 ff.; Å. Ohlmarks (*Studien zum Problem des Schamanismus*, pp. 170 ff.), who gives a detailed but rather prolix description of the assistant spirits and their functions in shamanic séances; W. Schmidt, *Der Ursprung der Gottesidee*, XII, 669–80, 705–06, 709.

65 K. F. Karjalainen, *Die Religion der Jugra-Völker*, III, 282–83.

66 Ibid., p. 311. The spirits are usually summoned by the drum (ibid., p. 318). The shamans can give their helping spirits to colleagues (ibid., p. 82); they can even sell them (among the Yurak and Ostyak, for example; see Mikhailowski, "Shamanism in Siberia," pp. 137–38).

weaker shamans are those whose *ié-kyla* is a dog; the more power-ful have a bull, a colt, an eagle, an elk, or a brown bear; those who have wolves or dogs are the least favored. The *ämägät* (tutelary spirit) is a completely different being. Usually it is the soul of a dead shaman or a minor celestial spirit. The Yakut shaman Tüs-püt told Sieroszewski, "a shaman sees and hears only through his *ämägät*; I see and hear over a distance of three *nosleg*, but there are some who see and hear much farther." [67]

We have seen that, after he is illuminated, an Eskimo shaman must obtain his helping spirits by his unaided efforts. Usually these are animals appearing in human form; they come of their own volition if the apprentice shows talent. The fox, the owl, the bear, the dog, the shark, and all kinds of mountain spirits are powerful and effective helpers.[68] Among the Alaskan Eskimo the more helping spirits a shaman has, the more powerful he is. In northern Greenland an *angakok* has as many as fifteen.[69]

Rasmussen gives several accounts of shamans receiving their illumination, which he took down from their own lips. The shaman Aua felt a celestial light in his body and brain, which, as it were, proceeded from his whole being; although unobserved by men, it was visible to all the spirits of earth, sky, and sea, and they came to him and became his helpers. "My first helping spirit was my namesake, a little aua," he told Rasmussen. "When it came to me it was as if the passage and roof of the house were lifted up, and I felt such a power of vision, that I could see right through the house, in through the earth and up into the sky; it was the little Aua that brought me all this inward light, hovering over me as long as I was singing. Then it placed itself in a corner of the

67 "Du Chamanisme," pp. 312–13; cf. M. A. Czaplicka, *Aboriginal Siberia*, pp. 182, 213, etc.

68 Rasmussen, *Intellectual Culture of the Iglulik Eskimos*, p. 113; cf. also Weyer, *The Eskimos*, pp. 425–28.

69 Webster, *Magic*, p. 231, n. 36. The spirits all manifest themselves through the shaman, making strange noises, unintelligible sounds, etc.; cf. Thalbitzer, "The Heathen Priests of East Greenland (Angakut)," p. 460. On helping spirits among the Lapps, see Mikhailowski, p. 149; Itkonen, *Heidnische Religion und späterer Aberglaube bei den finnischen Lappen*, p. 15

passage, invisible to others, but always ready if I should call it." [70]
A second spirit, a shark, came one day when he was at sea in his
kayak; it swam up to him and called him by name. Aua summons
his two helping spirits with a monotonous song:

> Joy, joy,
> Joy, joy!
> I see a little shore spirit,
> A little aua,
> I myself am also aua,
> The shore spirit's namesake,
> Joy, joy!

He repeats this song until he bursts into tears; then he feels a
boundless joy.[71] As we see, in this case the ecstatic experience of
illumination is in a manner connected with the appearance of the
helping spirit. But this ecstasy is not without its ingredient of
mystical fear. Rasmussen [72] stresses the feeling of "inexplicable
terror" experienced when "one is attacked by a helping spirit";
he connects this terrible fear with the mortal danger of initiation.

All categories of shamans have their helping and tutelary spirits,
though the latter may differ considerably in nature and potency
from one category to another. The Jakun *poyang* has a familiar
spirit that comes to him in dream or that he inherits from another
shaman.[73] In tropical South America guardian spirits are obtained
at the end of initiation; they "enter" the shaman, "either directly
or in the form of rock crystals that fall into his bag. . . . Among
the Barama Carib each class of spirits with which the shaman enters
into relations is represented by pebbles of different kinds. The
iai [shaman] puts them in his rattle and thus can invoke them at
will." [74] In South America, as everywhere else, helping spirits can

70 *Intellectual Culture of the Iglulik Eskimos*, p. 119.

71 Ibid., pp. 119–20.   72 Ibid., p. 121.

73 Ivor H. N. Evans, *Studies in Religion, Folk-lore, & Custom in British
North Borneo and the Malay Peninsula*, p. 264.

74 Métraux, "Le Shamanisme chez les Indiens de l'Amérique du Sud
tropicale," pp. 210–11. The celestial meaning of rock crystals in Australian
religion has been noted above; this meaning is, of course, obscured in

be of various kinds: souls of ancestral shamans, spirits of plants or animals. The Bororo have two classes of shamans, whom they distinguish according to the spirits from which they receive their power: nature demons or souls of dead shamans on the one hand, ancestral souls on the other.[75] But in this case it is less a matter of helping spirits than of tutelaries, though the distinction between the two categories of spirits is not always easy to make.

The relations between the magician or sorcerer and his spirits run the gamut from those of benefactor and protégé to those of servant and master, but they are always intimate.[76] The spirits are rarely the recipients of prayer or sacrifices, but if they are offended the magician suffers too.[77] In Australia and North America, as well as elsewhere, animal forms of familiar and tutelary spirits preponderate; they could in some sense be compared to the "bush soul" of West Africa and the *nagual* of Central America and Mexico.[78]

These helping spirits in animal form play an important role in the preliminaries to the shamanic séance, that is, in the preparation for the ecstatic journey to the sky and the underworld. Usually their presence is manifested by the shaman imitating animal cries or behavior. The Tungus shaman who has a snake as a helping spirit attempts to imitate the reptile's motions during the séance; another, having the whirlwind as *syvén*, behaves accordingly.[79]

present-day South American shamanism, but it nevertheless points to the origin of shamanic powers.

75 Métraux, p. 211.

76 Webster, *Magic*, p. 215; cf. also ibid., pp. 39–44, 388–91. On helping spirits in European medieval sorcery, cf. Margaret Alice Murray, *The God of the Witches*, pp. 80 ff.; G. L. Kittredge, *Witchcraft in Old and New England*, p. 613, s.v. "familiars"; S. Thompson, *Motif-Index*, III, 60 (F 403), 21 (G 225).

77 See, for example, Webster, *Magic*, p. 232, n. 41.

78 Cf. ibid., p. 215. On guardian spirits in North America, cf. Frazer, *Totemism and Exogamy*, III, 370–456; Ruth Benedict, *The Concept of the Guardian Spirit in North America*. See also below, pp. 99 ff., 305 ff.

79 Harva, *Die religiösen Vorstellungen*, p. 462.

Chukchee and Eskimo shamans turn themselves into wolves; [80] Lapp shamans become wolves, bears, reindeer, fish; [81] the Semang *hala* can change into a tiger, [82] as can the Sakai *halak* [83] and the *bomor* of Kelantan. [84]

In appearance, this shamanic imitation of the actions and voices of animals can pass as "possession." But it would perhaps be more accurate to term it a *taking possession of his helping spirits by a shaman*. It is the shaman who *turns himself* into an animal, just as he achieves a similar result by putting on an animal mask. Or, again, we might speak of a *new identity* for the shaman, who becomes an animal-spirit, and "speaks," sings, or flies like the animals and birds. "Animal language" is only a variant of "spirit language," the secret shamanic tongue to which we shall shortly return.

But first we would call attention to the following point: The presence of a helping spirit in animal form, dialogue with it in a secret language, or incarnation of such an animal spirit by the shaman (masks, actions, dances, etc.) is another way of showing that the shaman can forsake his human condition, is able, in a word, to "die." From the most distant times almost all animals have been conceived either as psychopomps that accompany the soul into the beyond or as the dead person's new form. Whether it is the "ancestor" or the "initiatory master," the animal symbolizes a

80 Waldemar G. Bogoras (V. G. Bogoraz), *The Chukchee*, p. 437; Rasmussen, *Intellectual Culture of the Copper Eskimos*, p. 35.

81 Lehtisalo, *Entwurf einer Mythologie der Jurak-Samojeden*, pp. 114, 159; tkonen, *Heidnische Religion*, pp. 116, 120 ff.

82 Ivor H. N. Evans, "Schebesta on the Sacerdo-Therapy of the Semang,"). 120.

83 Id., *Studies in Religion*, p. 210. On the fourteenth day after death the oul is changed into a tiger (ibid., p. 211).

84 J. Cuisinier, *Danses magiques de Kelantan*, pp. 38 ff. This belief is universally disseminated. For ancient and modern Europe, see Kittredge, *Witchcraft in Old and New England*, pp. 174–84; Thompson, *Motif-Index*, II, 212–13; Lily Weisser-Aall, "Hexe"; Arne Runeberg, *Witches, Demons and Fertility Magic*, pp. 212–13. Cf. also the confused but copiously documented book by Montague Summers, *The Werewolf*.

real and direct connection with the beyond. In a considerable number of myths and legends all over the world the hero is carried into the beyond [85] by an animal. It is always an animal that carries the neophyte into the bush (the underworld) on its back, or holds him in its jaws, or "swallows" him to "kill and resuscitate him," and so on.[86] Finally, we must take into account the mystical solidarity between man and animal, which is a dominant characteristic of the religion of the paleo-hunters. By virtue of this, certain human beings are able to change into animals, or to understand their language, or to share in their prescience and occult powers. Each time a shaman succeeds in sharing in the animal mode of being, he in a manner re-establishes the situation that existed *in illo tempore*, in mythical times, when the divorce between man and the animal world had not yet occurred.[87]

The tutelary animal of the Buryat shamans is called *khubilgan*, a term that can be interpreted as "metamorphosis" (from *khubilkhu* "to change oneself," "to take on another form").[88] In other words the tutelary animal not only enables the shaman to transform himself; it is in a manner his "double," his alter ego.[89] This alter ego is one of the shaman's "souls," the "soul in animal form" [90] or more precisely, the "life soul." [91] Shamans challenge one another

85 Sky, subterranean or submarine underworld, impenetrable forest mountain, wilderness, jungle, etc., etc.

86 Cf. C. Hentze, *Die Sakralbronzen und ihre Bedeutung in den frühchinesischen Kulturen*, pp. 46 ff., 67 ff., 71 ff., etc.

87 See below, p. 99.

88 Cf. Holmberg, *Finno-Ugric [and] Siberian [Mythology]*, pp. 406, 506

89 On the relations between the tutelary animal, the shaman, and the "Tiermutter" of the clan among the Evenki, cf. A. F. Anisimov: "Predstavlenia evenkov o dushe i problema proiskhozhdenia animizma," pp. 110 ff. "Shamanskiye dukhi po vossreniam evenkov i totemicheskiye istoki ideolog shamanstva," pp. 196 ff. Cf. also A. Friedrich, "Das Bewusstsein eine Naturvolkes von Haushalt und Ursprung des Lebens," pp. 48 ff.; Friedric and G. Buddruss, *Schamanengeschichten aus Sibirien*, pp. 44 ff.

90 Harva, *Die religiösen Vorstellungen*, p. 478.

91 V. Diószegi, "K voprosu o borbe shamanov v obraze zhivotnykh, pp. 312 ff.

in animal form, and if his alter ego is killed in the fight, the shaman very soon dies himself.[92]

Hence the guardian and helping spirits without which no shamanic séance is possible can be regarded as the authenticating signs of the shaman's ecstatic journeys in the beyond.[93] This is as much as to say that the animal spirits play the same role as the ancestral spirits; these, too, carry the shaman to the beyond (sky, underworld), reveal the mysteries to him, teach him, and so on. The role of the animal spirit in initiation rites and in myths and legends of the hero's travels in the beyond parallels that of the dead man's soul in (shamanic) initiatory "possession." But it is clear that it is *the shaman himself who becomes the dead man* (or the animal spirit, or the god, etc.), in order to demonstrate his real ability to ascend to the sky or descend to the underworld. In this light, a common explanation for all these groups of facts seems possible: in a sense, they represent the periodical repetition (that is, begun over again at each new séance) of the shaman's death and resurrection. The ecstasy is only the concrete experience of ritual death; in other words, of transcending the profane human condition. And, as we shall see, the shaman is able to attain this "death" by all kinds of means, from narcotics and the drum to "possession" by spirits.

92 On this extremely frequent theme in shamanic beliefs and folklore, cf. Friedrich and Buddruss, *Schamanengeschichten*, pp. 160 ff., 164 ff.; W. Schmidt, *Der Ursprung*, XII, 634; Diószegi: "A viaskodó táltosbika és a samán állataluků életlelke," passim; "K voprosu o borbe," passim. In this last article the author considers himself justified in stating that the shamans' battle animal was originally the reindeer. This appears to be confirmed by the fact that the cave drawings of Saymali Taš, in Kirgiz, dating from the first millennium before our era, represent shamans challenging each other in the form of reindeer; cf. especially p. 308, n. and fig. 1. On the Hungarian *áltos*, cf. ibid., p. 306, and the bibliography given in n. 19.

93 For Dominik Schröder, the tutelary spirits, being inhabitants of the other world, ensure the shaman's existence in the beyond (cf. "Zur Struktur des Schamanismus," pp. 863 ff.).

"Secret Language"—"Animal Language"

In the course of his initiation the future shaman has to learn the secret language that he will use during his séances to communicate with the spirits and animal spirits. He learns this secret language either from a teacher or by his own efforts, that is, directly from the "spirits"; both methods coexist among the Eskimo, for example.[94] The existence of a specific secret language has been verified among the Lapps,[95] the Ostyak, the Chukchee, the Yakut, and the Tungus.[96] During his trance the Tungus shaman is believed to understand the language of all nature.[97] The secret shamanic language is highly elaborated among the Eskimo and used as a means of communication between the *angakut* and their spirits.[98] Each shaman has his particular song, which he intones to invoke the spirits.[99] Even where a secret language is not directly concerned, traces of it are to be found in the incomprehensible refrains that are repeated during séances, as, for example, among the Altaians.[100]

This phenomenon is not exclusively North Asian and Arctic; it occurs almost everywhere. During the séance the Semang Pygmy *hala* talks with the Cenoi (celestial spirits) in their language; as soon as he leaves the ceremonial hut he pretends to have forgotten everything.[101] Among the Mentaweians (Sumatra) the initiatory master blows into the apprentice's ear through a bamboo tube to enable him to hear the voices of the spirits.[102] The Batak shaman

94 Cf. Rasmussen, *Intellectual Culture of the Iglulik Eskimos*, p. 114.

95 Cf. Eliel Lagercrantz, "Die Geheimsprachen der Lappen."

96 Lehtisalo, "Beobachtungen über die Jodler," pp. 12 f.

97 Ibid., p. 13.

98 Thalbitzer: "The Heathen Priests of East Greenland," pp. 448, 454 ff. "Les Magiciens esquimaux," p. 75; Weyer, *The Eskimos*, pp. 435–36.

99 Rasmussen, *Intellectual Culture of the Iglulik Eskimos*, pp. 111, 122. See the texts in "secret language," ibid., pp. 125, 131, etc.

100 Lehtisalo, "Beobachtungen," p. 22.

101 Schebesta, *Les Pygmées*, p. 153; Evans: "Schebesta on the Sacerdo Therapy of the Semang," pp. 118 ff.; *Studies*, pp. 156 ff., 160, etc.

102 Loeb, "Shaman and Seer," p. 71.

uses the "language of the spirits" during séances; [103] and the shamanic chants of the Dusun (North Borneo) are in secret language.[104] "According to Carib tradition, the first *piai* [shaman]
was a man who, hearing a song rise from a stream, dived boldly in
and did not come out again until he had memorized the song of the
spirit women and received the implements of his profession from
them." [105]

Very often this secret language is actually the "animal language"
or originates in animal cries. In South America the neophyte must
learn, during his initiation period, to imitate the voices of animals.[106] The same is true of North America. The Pomo and the
Menomini shamans, among others, imitate bird songs.[107] During
séances among the Yakut, the Yukagir, the Chukchee, the Goldi,
the Eskimo, and others, wild animal cries and bird calls are heard.[108]
Castagné describes the Kirgiz-Tatar *baqça* running around the tent,
springing, roaring, leaping; he "barks like a dog, sniffs at the audience, lows like an ox, bellows, cries, bleats like a lamb, grunts like
a pig, whinnies, coos, imitating with remarkable accuracy the cries
of animals, the songs of birds, the sound of their flight, and so on,
all of which greatly impresses his audience." [109] The "descent of
the spirits" often takes place in this fashion. Among the Indians of
Guiana "suddenly the silence was broken by a burst of indescrib-
able and really terrible yells and roars and shouts, which filled the
house, shaking walls and roof, sometimes sinking to a low distant-
sounding growl, which never ceased for six hours." [110]

103 Id., *Sumatra*, p. 81.

104 Evans, *Studies*, p. 4. Cf. also H. L. Roth, *The Natives of Sarawak*, I,
270.

105 Métraux, "Le Shamanisme chez les Indiens de l'Amérique du Sud
tropicale," p. 210.

106 Ibid., pp. 206, 210, etc.; Ida Lublinski, "Der Medizinmann," pp. 246
f.

107 Loeb, *Tribal Initiations and Secret Societies*, p. 278.

108 Lehtisalo, "Beobachtungen," pp. 23 ff.

109 "Magie et exorcisme chez les Kazak-Kirghizes et autres peuples turcs
orientaux," p. 93.

110 Everard F. Im Thurn, *Among the Indians of Guiana*, p. 336, cited in

Such cries proclaim the presence of the spirits, also proclaimed by animal-like behavior.[111] Many words used during the séance have their origin in the cries of birds and other animals.[112] As Lehtisalo noted,[113] the shaman falls into ecstasy using his drum and "yodel," and magical texts are everywhere sung. "Magic" and "song"—especially song like that of birds—are frequently expressed by the same term. The Germanic word for magic formula is *galdr*, derived from the verb *galan*, "to sing," a term applied especially to bird calls.[114]

All over the world learning the language of animals, especially of birds, is equivalent to knowing the secrets of nature and hence to being able to prophesy.[115] Bird language is usually learned by eating snake or some other reputedly magical animal.[116] These animals can reveal the secrets of the future because they are thought to be receptacles for the souls of the dead or epiphanies of the gods. Learning their language, imitating their voice, is equivalent to ability to communicate with the beyond and the heavens. We shall again come upon this same identification with an animal, especially a bird, when we discuss the shaman's costume and magical flight. Birds are psychopomps. Becoming a bird oneself or being accompanied by a bird indicates the capacity, while still alive, to undertake the ecstatic journey to the sky and the beyond.

Métraux, "Le Shamanisme chez les Indiens de l'Amérique du Sud tropicale," p. 326.

111 See above, p. 89.   112 Lehtisalo, "Beobachtungen," p. 25.

113 Ibid., p. 26.

114 Jan de Vries, *Altgermanische Religionsgeschichte* (2nd edn.), I, 304 ff. Lehtisalo, "Beobachtungen," pp. 27 ff.; cf. *carmen*, magical song; *incantare* enchant; Romanian *descântare* (lit. dis-enchant), exorcise, *descântec*, incantation, exorcism.

115 See Antti Aarne, *Der tiersprachenkundige Mann und seine neugierig Frau*; N. M. Penzer, ed., and C. H. Tawney, tr., *Somadeva's Kathā-sarit sāgara* (or *Ocean of Streams of Story*), I, 48; II, 107 n.; Thompson, *Motif Index*, I, 314 ff. (B 215).

116 Philostratus *Life of Apollonius of Tyana* 1. 20, etc. See L. Thorndike *A History of Magic and Experimental Science*, I, 261; Penzer and Tawney *Somadeva's Kathā-sarit-sāgara*, II, 108, n. 1.

Imitating animal voices, using this secret language during the séance, is yet another sign that the shaman can move freely through the three cosmic zones: underworld, earth, sky. This is as much as to say that he can make his way safely where only the dead or the gods have access. Embodying an animal during the séance is less a possession than a magical transformation of the shaman into that animal. A similar transformation can also be obtained by other means—by donning the shamanic costume, for example, or concealing the face under a mask.

But this is not all. In numerous traditions friendship with animals and understanding their language represent paradisal syndromes. In the beginning, that is, in mythical times, man lived at peace with the animals and understood their speech. It was not until after a primordial catastrophe, comparable to the "Fall" of Biblical tradition, that man became what he is today—mortal, sexed, obliged to work to feed himself, and at enmity with the animals. While preparing for his ecstasy and during it, the shaman abolishes the present human condition and, for the time being, recovers the situation as it was at the beginning. Friendship with animals, knowledge of their language, transformation into an animal are so many signs that the shaman has re-established the "paradisal" situation lost at the dawn of time.[117]

The Quest for Shamanic Powers in North America

We have already referred to the various modes of obtaining shamanic powers in North America. There the source of those powers resides either in divine beings or in the souls of ancestral shamans or in mythical animals or, finally, in certain objects or cosmic zones. Obtaining the powers occurs either spontaneously or after a deliberate quest; in both cases alike, the future shaman must undergo certain ordeals of an initiatory nature.[118]

117 Cf. Eliade, *Myths, Dreams and Mysteries*, pp. 59 ff.
118 Cf. Josef Haekel, "Schutzgeistsuche und Jugendweihe im westlichen Nordamerika."

The procedure among the Shuswap, a tribe of the Salish family in the interior of British Columbia, is as follows:

The shaman is initiated by animals, who become his guardian spirits. The initiation ceremonies for warriors and shamans seem to be identical, the object of the initiation ceremonies being merely to obtain supernatural help for any object that appeared desirable. The young man, on reaching puberty, and before he had ever touched a woman, had to go out on the mountains and pass through a number of performances. He had to build a sweat-house, in which he stayed every night. In the morning he was allowed to return to the village. He had to clean himself in the sweat-house, to dance and to sing during the night. This was continued, sometimes for years, until he dreamt that the animal he desired for his guardian spirit appeared to him and promised him its help. As soon as it appeared the novice fell down in a swoon. "He feels as though he were drunk, and does not know whether it is day or night nor what he is doing." [119] The animal tells him to think of it if he should be in need of help, and gives him a certain song with which to summon him up. Therefore every shaman has his own song, which none else is allowed to sing, except when the attempt is made to discover a sorcerer. . . . Sometimes the spirit comes down to the novice in the shape of a stroke of lightning.[120] If an animal initiates the novice it teaches him its language.

One shaman in Nicola Valley is said to speak "coyote language" in his incantations. . . .

After a man has obtained a guardian spirit he is bullet and arrow proof. If an arrow or a bullet should strike him he does not bleed from the wound, but the blood all flows into his stomach. He spits it out, and is well again. . . .

119 This is the well-known sign of a genuine ecstatic experience; cf. the "inexplicable terror" of Eskimo apprentices upon the appearance of their helping spirits (above, pp. 90 ff.).

120 We have seen (p. 19) that among the Buryat a person struck by lightning is buried like a shaman and his close relatives have the right to become shamans; for he has, in a manner, been "chosen" by the Sky God (Mikhailowski, "Shamanism in Siberia," p. 86). Among others, the Soyot and the Kamchadal believe that one becomes a shaman when lightning flashes during a storm (ibid., p. 68). An Eskimo shaman obtained his power after being struck by a "ball of fire" (Rasmussen, *Intellectual Culture of the Iglulik Eskimos*, pp. 122 ff.).

Men could acquire more than one guardian spirit, and powerful shamans had always more than one helper. . . .[121]

In this example the grant of shamanic powers occurs after a
deliberate quest. Elsewhere in North America candidates withdraw to mountain caves or solitary places and seek, by intense
concentration, to obtain the visions that can alone determine a
shamanic career. The candidate is usually obliged to define the
kind of "power" he seeks.[122] This is an important detail, for it
shows that what is involved is a general technique for procuring
magico-religious powers, not merely shamanic powers.

Here is the story of a Paviotso shaman, collected and published
by Park. At fifty, the man decided to become a "doctor." He
entered a cave and prayed, "My people are sick, I want to save
them. . . ." He tried to go to sleep, but was prevented by
strange noises; he heard the grunts and howls of animals (bears,
mountain lions, deer, etc.). Finally he fell asleep and in his sleep
saw a shamanic healing séance. "They were down at the foot of
the mountain. I could hear their voices and the songs. Then I
heard the patient groan. A doctor was singing and doctoring for
him." Finally the patient died and the candidate heard his family
lamenting. The rock began to split. "A man appeared in the
crack. He was tall and thin. He had the tail-feather of an eagle in
his hand." The man ordered the candidate to obtain' similar
feathers and taught him how to cure. When the candidate woke in
the morning, no one was there.[123]

If a candidate does not follow the instructions received in his
dreams, or the traditional patterns, he is doomed to fail.[124] In
some cases the spirit of the dead shaman appears in his heir's

121 F. Boas, "The Shushwap" (offprint), pp. 93 ff. We shall return to the
shamanic value of the sweat house.
122 Willard Z. Park, *Shamanism in Western North America*, p. 27. Cf. also
Marcelle Bouteiller: "Don chamanistique et adaptation à la vie chez les
Indiens de l'Amérique du Nord," passim; *Chamanisme et guérison magique*,
p. 57 ff.
123 *Shamanism in Western North America*, pp. 27–28.
124 Ibid., p. 29.

first dream; but in the following dreams the higher spirits that grant him the "power" make their appearance. If the heir does not take the "power," he falls ill.[125] We have found the same situation, it will be remembered, almost everywhere.

The souls of the dead are regarded as a source of shamanic powers among the Paviotso, the Shoshone, the Seed Eaters, and farther north, among the Lillooet and the Thompson Indians.[126] In Northern California this method of bestowing shamanic powers is widespread. The Yurok shamans dream of a dead man, usually though not always, a shaman. Among the Sinkyone the power is sometimes received in dreams in which the candidate's dead relatives appear. The Wintu become shamans after such dreams, especially if they dream of their own dead children. In the Shasta tribe the first indication of a shamanic power follows dreams of a dead mother, father, or ancestor.[127]

But in North America there are also other "sources of power" for shamans and likewise other kinds of teachers than the souls of the dead and guardian animals. In the Great Basin we hear of a "little green man," only two feet tall, who carries a bow and arrows. He lives in the mountains and shoots his arrows into those who speak ill of him. The "little green man" is the guardian spirit of medicine men, of those who have become magicians solely by supernatural aid.[128] The idea of a dwarf who grants power or serves as guardian spirit is extremely widespread west of the Rocky Mountains, in the tribes of the Plateau Groups (Thompson, Shuswap, etc.) and in Northern California (Shasta, Atsugewi,

125 Park, *Shamanism*, p. 30.

126 Ibid., p. 79; J. Teit: *The Lillooet Indians*, pp. 287 f.; "The Thompson Indians of British Columbia," p. 353. The Lillooet apprentices sleep on graves, sometimes for several years (id., *The Lillooet Indians*, p. 287

127 Park, p. 80. The same tradition is found among the Atsugewi, the Northern Maidu, the Crow, Arapaho, Gros Ventre, etc. Among some of these tribes, and elsewhere too, powers are sought by sleeping beside graves; sometimes (among the Tlingit, for example) an even more impressive method is used; the apprentice spends the night with the dead shaman's body; cf. Frazer, *Totemism and Exogamy*, III, 439.

128 Park, p. 77.

Northern Maidu, and Yuki).[129] Sometimes shamanic power is derived directly from the Supreme Being or other divine entities. Thus, for example, among the Cahuilla of Southern California (Cahuilla Desert), shamans are considered to obtain their power from Mukat, the Creator, but this power is transmitted through guardian spirits (the owl, fox, coyote, bear, etc.), which act as the god's messengers to shamans.[130] Among the Mohave and the Yuma power comes from the mythical beings who transmitted it to shamans at the beginning of the world.[131] Transmission takes place in dreams and includes an initiatory scenario. In his dreams the Yuma shaman witnesses the beginnings of the world and lives in mythical times.[132] Among the Maricopa initiatory dreams follow a traditional schema: a spirit takes the future shaman's soul and leads him from mountain to mountain, each time revealing songs and cures to him.[133] Among the Walapai the journey under the guidance of spirits is an essential characteristic of shamanic dreams.[134]

As we have already seen more than once, the shaman's instruction often takes place in dreams. It is in dreams that the pure sacred life is entered and direct relations with the gods, spirits, and ancestral souls are re-established. It is always in dreams that historical time is abolished and the mythical time regained—which allows the future shaman to witness the beginnings of the world and hence to become contemporary not only with the cosmogony but also with the primordial mythical revelations. Sometimes

129 See the full list of tribes in ibid., pp. 77 f. Cf. ibid., p. 111, the "little green man" who appears to future shamans in their adolescence.

130 Ibid., p. 82.   131 Ibid., p. 83.

132 A. L. Kroeber, *Handbook of the Indians of California*, pp. 754 ff., 775; . D. Forde, *Ethnography of the Yuma Indians*, pp. 201 ff. Initiation into the shamanic secret society, the Midē'wiwin, also involves a return to the mythical times of the beginnings of the world, when the Great Spirit revealed the mysteries to the first "great doctors." We shall see that these initiatory rituals include the same communication between earth and heaven as was established at the creation of the world.

133 L. Spier, *Yuman Tribes of the Gila River*, p. 247; Park, p. 115.
134 Park, p. 116.

initiatory dreams are involuntary and begin even in childhood, as, for example, among the Great Basin tribes.[135] Even if they do not follow a strict scenario, the dreams are nevertheless stereotyped; the candidate dreams of spirits and ancestors, or hears their voices (songs and teaching). It is always in dream that the candidate receives the initiatory regulations (regime, taboos, etc.) and learns what objects he will need in shamanic cures.[136] Among the Maidu of the Northeast, too, one becomes a shaman by dreaming of spirits. Although shamanism is hereditary, one does not receive the qualification until after seeing the spirits in dream; yet these are in a manner inherited from generation to generation. The spirits sometimes show themselves in animal forms (and in this case the shaman must not eat the particular animal), but they also live, without definite forms, in rocks, lakes, and so on.[137]

The belief that animal spirits or natural phenomena are sources of shamanic powers is widespread throughout North America.[138] Among the Salish tribes of interior British Columbia only a few shamans inherit their relatives' guardian spirits. Almost all animals can become spirits, as can a large number of objects— anything that has any relation to death (e.g., graves, bones, teeth, etc.) and any natural phenomenon (blue sky, east, west, etc.). But here, as in many other cases, we touch upon a magico-religious experience that extends beyond the sphere of shamanism; for warriors, too, have their guardian spirits, in their armor and in wild beasts, hunters collect their guardian spirits from the water, the mountains, the animals they hunt, and so on.[139]

According to some Paviotso shamans power comes to them from the "spirit of the night." This spirit "is everywhere. It has

135 Cf. Park, p. 110.

136 Paviotso, ibid., p. 23; Southern Californian tribes, ibid., p. 82; auditor dreams, ibid., p. 23, etc. Among the Southern Okanagon the future shaman does not see the guardian spirits, he only hears their songs and teaching (ibid., p. 118).

137 R. Dixon, *The Northern Maidu*, pp. 274 ff.

138 See the list of tribes and bibliographical references in Park, pp. 76

139 F. Boas, "The Salish Tribes of the Interior of British Columbia," pp. 222 ff.

no name. There is no word for it." The eagle and owl are only the messengers that bring instruction from the spirit of the night. "Water-babies" or some other animal can also be its messengers. "At the time that the spirit of the night gives power for doctoring, it tells the shaman to ask for help from the water-babies, eagle, owl, deer, antelope, bear or some other bird or animal." [140] The coyote is never a source of power for the Paviotso, though it figures prominently in their tales.[141] The spirits that confer power are invisible; only shamans can perceive them.[142]

There are also the "pains," which are thought of both as sources of power and as causes of illnesses. These "pains" appear to be animated and sometimes even have a certain personality. They do not have human forms, but they are thought of as concrete.[143] Among the Hupa, for example, there are "pains" of every color; one is like a piece of raw flesh, others resemble crabs, small deer, arrowheads, and so on.[144] Belief in these "pains" is general among the tribes of Northern California,[145] but is rare or unknown in other parts of North America.[146]

The *damagomi* of the Achomawi are at once guardian spirits and "pains." A shamaness, Old Dixie, relates how she received the call. She was already married when, one day, "my first *damagomi* came to find me. I still have it. It is a little black thing, you can hardly see it. When it came the first time it made a great noise. It was at night. It told me that I must go to see it in the mountains. So I went. I was very frightened. I hardly dared go. Later I had others. I caught them." [147] They were *damagomi* that had belonged to other shamans and that had been sent to poison people or on

---

140 Paviotso informant cited by Park, p. 17. The "spirit of the night" is probably a late mythological formula for the Supreme Being, which has become partly a *deus otiosus* and helps men through "messengers."

141 Ibid., p. 19. 142 Ibid.

143 Kroeber, *Handbook*, pp. 63 ff., 111, 852; Dixon, *The Shasta*, pp. 472 ff.

144 Park, p. 81. 145 Ibid., p. 80.

146 Ibid., p. 81.

147 Jaime de Angulo, "La Psychologie religieuse des Achumawi. IV: Le Shamanisme," p. 565.

other shamanic errands. Old Dixie sent out one of her own *damagomi* and caught them. In this way she had come to have over fifty *damagomi*, whereas a young shaman has only three or four.[148] The shamans feed them on the blood that they suck during cures.[149] According to Jaime de Angulo [150] these *damagomi* are at once real (bone and flesh) and fantasies. When the shaman wants to poison someone he sends a *damagomi*: "Go find So-and-so. Enter him. Make him sick. Don't kill him at once. Make him die in a month." [151]

As we have already seen in the case of the Salish tribes, any animal or cosmic object can become a source of power or a guardian spirit. Among the Thompson Indians, for example, water is regarded as the guardian spirit of shamans, warriors, hunters and fishers; the sun, thunder or the thunderbird, mountain peaks the bear, wolf, eagle, and crow are the guardian spirits of shaman and warriors. Other guardian spirits are common to shamans an hunters or to shamans and fishers. There are also guardian spirit reserved only for shamans: night, mist, the blue sky, east, west woman, adolescent girls, men's hands and feet, the sexual organs of men and women, the bat, the land of souls, ghosts, graves, the bones, hair, and teeth of the dead, and so on.[152] But the list of the shaman's "sources of power" is far from exhausted.[153]

As we have just seen, any spiritual, animal, or physical entit can become a source of power or guardian spirit, whether for th shaman or for an ordinary individual. This seems to us to have important bearing on the problem of the origins of shaman powers: in no case is their particular quality of shamanic power due to their *sources* (which are often the same for all other magico religious powers) or to the fact that shamanic powers are in carnated in certain animal guardians. Any Indian can obtain h guardian spirit if he is prepared to make a certain effort of will an

---

148 Ibid.

149 Ibid., p. 563.

150 Ibid., p. 580.

151 Ibid.

152 Teit, "The Thompson Indians," pp. 354 ff.

153 Cf. Park, pp. 18, 76 ff.

concentration.[154] Then too, tribal initiation concludes with acquiring a guardian spirit. From this point of view, the quest for shamanic powers becomes part of the far more general quest for magico-religious powers. As we have already seen in a previous chapter, shamans do not differ from other members of the collectivity by their quest for the sacred—which is normal and universal human behavior—but by their capacity for ecstatic experience, which, for the most part, is equivalent to a vocation.

Consequently we may conclude that guardian spirits and mythical animal helpers are not a specific and exclusive characteristic of shamanism. These tutelary and helping spirits are collected almost anywhere in the entire cosmos, and they are accessible to any individual who is willing to undergo certain ordeals to obtain them. This means that everywhere in the cosmos archaic man recognizes a source of the magico-religious sacred, that any fragment of the cosmos can give rise to a hierophany, in accordance with the dialectic of the sacred.[155] What differentiates a shaman from any other individual in the clan is not his possessing a power or a guardian spirit, but his ecstatic experience. But as we have already seen, and shall see even more fully later, guardian or helping spirits are not the direct authors of this ecstatic experience. They are only the messengers of a divine being or the assistants in an experience that implies many other presences besides theirs.

On the other hand, we know that "power" is often revealed by the souls of ancestral shamans (who, in their turn, received it at the dawn of time, in the mythical age), by divine and semidivine personages, sometimes by a Supreme Being. Here, too, we receive the impression that the guardian and helping spirits are only indispensable instruments for the shamanic experience, something like new organs that the shaman receives upon completing his initiation, so that he can better orient himself in the new magico-

154 H. Haeberlin and E. Gunther, "Ethnographische Notizen über die Indianerstämme des Puget-Sundes," pp. 56 ff. On the spirits peculiar to shamans, see ibid., pp. 65, 69 ff.

155 Cf. Eliade, *Patterns in Comparative Religion*, pp. 2 ff.

religious universe that is thenceforth accessible to him. In the following chapters the role of guardian and helping spirits as "mystical organs" will become still more apparent.

As everywhere else, in North America obtaining these guardian and helping spirits is either spontaneous or deliberate. It has been sought to distinguish between the initiations of North American and Siberian shamans by asserting that, for the former, there is always a *deliberate quest*, whereas in Asia the shamanic vocation is always in some sort *inflicted* by the spirits.[156] Bogoras, using the findings of Ruth Benedict,[157] sums up the acquiring of shamanic powers in North America as follows: To enter into contact with the spirits or to obtain guardian spirits, the aspirant withdraws into solitude and subjects himself to a strict regime of self-torture. When the spirits manifest themselves in animal form, the aspirant is believed to give them his own flesh to eat.[158] But offering oneself as food for animal spirits, an act accomplished by dismemberment of one's own body,[159] is only a parallel formula to the ecstatic rite of dismembering the apprentice's body, a rite that we analyzed in the preceding chapter and that involves an initiatory schema (death and resurrection). It is, moreover, found in other regions too—as for example, in Australia [160] or Tibet [161]—and is to be regarded as a substitute for, or a formula paralleling, the ecstatic dismemberment of the candidate by demonic spirits; where it no longer exists, or is comparatively rare, the spontaneous ecstatic experience of dismemberment of the body and renewal of the organs is sometimes

156 Waldemar G. Bogoras, "The Shamanistic Call and the Period Initiation in Northern Asia and Northern America," especially p. 443.

157 Cf. "The Vision in Plains Culture."

158 "The Shamanistic Call," p. 442.

159 As, for example, among the Assiniboin (ibid.).

160 Among the Lunga and Djara tribes in Australia the aspirant to the profession of medicine man enters a pond supposed to be inhabited by monstrous snakes. They "kill" him, and after this initiatory death he obtains his magical powers; see A. P. Elkin, "The Rainbow-Serpent Myth in North West Australia," p. 350; cf. id., *The Australian Aborigines*, p. 223.

161 In the Tantric-Bon rite *chöd* (*gchod*).

replaced by offering one's own body to animal spirits (as among the Assiniboin) or to demonic spirits (Tibet).

If it is true that the "quest" is the dominant note of North American shamanism, it is far from being the only method for obtaining powers. We have seen several examples of spontaneous vocation,[162] but their number is considerably greater. We need only remember the hereditary transmission of shamanic powers, where the decision lies, in the last analysis, with the spirits and the ancestral souls. We may remember, too, the premonitory dreams of future shamans, dreams that, according to Park, become mortal illnesses if they are not rightly understood and piously obeyed. An old shaman is called in to interpret them; he orders the patient to follow the injunctions of the spirits that provoked the dreams. "Usually a person is reluctant to become a shaman, and assumes his powers and follows the spirit's bidding only when he is told by other shamans that otherwise death will result." [163] This is exactly the case of the Siberian and Central Asian shamans, and of others as well. This resistance to "divine election" is explained, as we have said, by mankind's ambivalent attitude toward the sacred.

The voluntary quest for shamanic powers is found in Asia too, though less frequently. In North America, and especially in Southern California, obtaining shamanic powers is often associated with initiation ceremonies. Among the Kawaiisu, the Luiseno, the Juaneno, and the Gabrielino, as among the Diegueno, the Cocopa, and the Akwaala, the aspirant awaits the vision of the tutelary animal after becoming intoxicated by jimson weed.[164] Here we have a rite of initiation into a secret society rather than a shamanic experience. The aspirants' self-inflicted tortures, to which Bogoras refers, belong rather to the terrible ordeals that a candidate must endure for admission to a secret society than to shamanism proper, though in North America it is always difficult to define the boundaries of these two religious forms precisely.

162 E.g., the case of Old Dixie, above, pp. 105 f.   163 Park, p. 26.
164 Kroeber, *Handbook*, pp. 604 ff., 712 ff.; Park, p. 84.

CHAPTER FOUR

Shamanic Initiation

Initiation among the Tungus and the Manchu

BOTH in North Asia and elsewhere in the world ecstatic election is usually followed by a period of instruction, during which the neophyte is duly initiated by an old shaman. At this time the future shaman is supposed to master his mystical technique and to learn the religious and mythological traditions of his tribe. Often, but not always, the preparatory stage culminates in a series of ceremonies that are commonly referred to as the initiation of the new shaman.[1] But as Shirokogoroff rightly remarks in respect to the Tungus and the Manchu, we cannot properly speak of an initiation, since the candidates have actually been "initiated" long before their formal recognition by the master shamans and the community.[2] Moreover, the same thing is true almost everywhere in Siberia and Central Asia; even where there is a public ceremony (e.g., among the Buryat), it only confirms and validates the real ecstatic and secret initiation, which, as we saw, is the work of the spirits (sicknesses, dreams, etc.), completed by apprenticeship to master shaman.[3]

There is, however, a formal recognition by the master shamans. Among the Transbaikal Tungus a child is selected and brought up to be a shaman. After a certain amount of preparation he undergoes

[1] For a synopsis of the instruction and initiation of Siberian and Central Asian shamans, see W. Schmidt, *Der Ursprung der Gottesidee*, XII, 653–6.

[2] *Psychomental Complex of the Tungus*, p. 350.

[3] Cf., for example, E. J. Lindgren, "The Reindeer Tungus of Manchuria," pp. 221 f.; N. K. Chadwick, *Poetry and Prophecy*, p. 53.

the first trials; he has to interpret dreams, demonstrate his ability in divination, and so on. The most dramatic moment comes when the candidate, in ecstasy, describes just what animals the spirits will send him so that he can make a costume from their pelts. Long afterward, when the animals have been hunted and the costume made, there is a new assembly; a reindeer is sacrificed to the dead shaman, the candidate puts on his costume and performs a "great shamanizing." [4]

Among the Tungus of Manchuria the process is somewhat different. The child is selected and taught, but it is his ecstatic capacity that determines his career.[5] After the period of training described above comes the ceremony of "initiation" proper.

Two *turö* (trees of which the large branches have been cut off but whose crowns are preserved) are set up in front of a house.

These two *turö* are connected by cross beams, about 90 or 100 centimetres long, in an odd number, namely, 5, 7, or 9. A third *turö* is erected in a southern direction at the distance of several metres and connected with the eastern *turö* by a string, or narrow thong—*s'ij'im* ["rope"] supplied at a distance of about thirty centimetres with bunches of ribbons and feathers of various birds. It may be made of Chinese red silk or of sinews coloured red. This is the "road" along which the spirits will move. On the strings a wooden ring is put that moves freely from one *turö* to another. When sent by the "teacher" the spirit is located in the plane of the ring (*jŭldu*). Three wooden anthropomorphic placings—*an'akan*, of an unusually large size, about 30 centimetres long—are put near each *turö*.

The candidate sits down between two *turö*, and drums. The old shaman calls one by one the spirits down the southern *turö*, and with the ring sends them to the candidate. Each time the teacher takes back the ring and sends off a spirit. If this were not done, the spirits would enter the candidate and would not leave him. . . .

During the entering of the spirits the elders examine the candidate who . . . must tell the whole history ("biography") of the spirit, with all details, such as who it had been before, where it had lived (in which "rivers" it had been), what it had done, with which shamans it had

4 Shirokogoroff, *Psychomental Complex*, p. 351.   5 See above, pp. 18 f.

been and when the shamans had died . . . in order to convince the audience that the spirit is really in the candidate. . . . After every night of performance the shaman climbs up to the upper beam and remains there for some time. The costume is hung up on the beams of the *turö*. . . .[6]

The ceremony continues for three, five, seven, or nine days. If the candidate succeeds, sacrifice is offered to the clan spirits.

For the moment, we will leave aside the role of the "spirits" in the future shaman's consecration; actually, Tungus shamanism appears to be dominated by spirit guides. Let us consider only two details: (1) the rope called the "road"; (2) the climbing rite. The importance of these two features will become apparent presently: the rope symbolizes the "road" connecting earth and sky (although among the Tungus today the "road" serves rather to permit communication with the spirits); climbing the tree originally signified the shaman's ascent to the sky. If, as is probable, the Tungus received these initiation rites from the Buryat, it is quite possible that they adapted them to their own ideology, at the same time depriving them of their original meaning; this loss of meaning could have taken place quite recently, under the influence of other ideologies (e.g., Lamaism). However that may be, this initiation rite, even if borrowed, was more or less consonant with the general conception of Tungus shamanism; for, as we have seen and shall see more fully later on, the Tungus were at one with all the other North Asian and Arctic peoples in believing that shamans ascended to the sky.

Among the Manchu the public initiation ceremony formerly included the candidate's walking over burning coals; if the apprentice had at his command the spirits that he claimed to possess, he could walk on fire without injury. Today the ceremony has become quite rare; it is said that the shamans' powers have diminished,[7] which is in harmony with the general North Asian idea of the present decadence of shamanism.

The Manchu also have another initiatory ordeal. In winter nine

6 Shirokogoroff, p. 352.   7 Ibid., p. 353.

holes are made in the ice; the candidate has to dive into the first hole and come out through the second, and so on to the ninth hole. The Manchu assert that the extreme severity of this ordeal is due to Chinese influence.[8] And in fact it resembles some Tibetan Yogico-tantric ordeals, in which, on a snowy winter night, the aspirant must dry a certain number of wet sheets on his naked body. The apprentice yogin thus gives proof of the "physical heat" that he is capable of producing in his own body. It will be remembered that among the Eskimo a similar proof of resistance to cold is regarded as the certain sign of shamanic election. And in fact, producing heat at will is one of the essential feats of the primitive magician and medicine man; we shall return to it later.[9]

Yakut, Samoyed, and Ostyak Initiations

We have only dubious and outdated information concerning initiation ceremonies among the Yakut, the Samoyed, and the Ostyak. It is highly probable that the descriptions given are superficial and inaccurate, for the nineteenth-century observers and ethnographers often saw shamanism as demonic; for them, the future shaman undergoing initiation could only be putting himself at the disposition of the "devil." Here is how N. V. Pripuzov describes the initiation ceremony among the Yakut: After the "election" by the spirits [10] the old shaman takes his disciple up on a hill or into a plain, gives him the shamanic costume, invests him with the drum and stick, and places nine chaste young men at his right and nine virgin girls at his left. Then, putting on his own costume, he passes behind the neophyte and makes him repeat certain formulas. He first adjures him to renounce God and all that he holds dear, and makes him promise to devote his whole life to the "devil," in return for which the latter will fulfill all his wishes. Then the master shaman teaches him the places where the demon lives, the sick-

8 Ibid., p. 352.
9 Cf. above, p. 59, n. 84; below, pp. 472 ff.
10 See above, pp. 74 f.

nesses that he cures, and the way to pacify him. Finally the candidate kills the sacrificial animal; his costume is sprinkled with blood, and the flesh is eaten by the participants.[11]

According to the information collected by Ksenofontov from Yakut shamans, the master takes the novice's soul on a long ecstatic journey. They begin by climbing a mountain. From it the master shows the novice the forks in the road from which other paths ascend to the peaks; it is there that the sicknesses that harry men have their dwellings. After this the master takes his disciple into a house. There they don shamanic costumes and shamanize together. The master reveals to the novice how to recognize and cure the sicknesses that attack the various parts of the body. Each time that he names a part of the body, he spits in the disciple's mouth, and the disciple must swallow the spittle so that he may know "the roads of the evils of Hell." Finally the shaman takes his disciple to the upper world, among the celestial spirits. The shaman henceforth possesses a "consecrated body" and can practice his profession.[12]

According to P. I. Tretyakov, the Samoyed and Ostyak of the Turukhansk region go about initiating the new shaman as follows: The candidate turns to face the west, and the master prays the Spirit of Darkness to help the novice and give him a guide. He then intones a hymn to the Spirit of Darkness, and the candidate repeats it. Finally come the ordeals that the Spirit inflicts on the novice demanding his wife, his son, his goods, etc.[13]

Among the Goldi initiation takes place in public, as among the

11 *Svedenia dlya izuchenia shamanstva u yakutov*, pp. 64–65; cf. Mikhailowski, "Shamanism in Siberia and European Russia," pp. 85–86; U. Harva *Die religiösen Vorstellungen der altaischen Völker*, pp. 485–86; V. L. Priklonsky in W. Schmidt, *Der Ursprung*, XI, 179, 286–88. We probably have here an initiation of "black" shamans who devote themselves exclusively to infernal spirits and divinities and who are also found among other Siberian peoples cf. Harva, *Die religiösen Vorstellungen*, pp. 482 ff.

12 G. V. Ksenofontov, in A. Friedrich and G. Buddruss, *Schamanen geschichten aus Sibirien*, pp. 169 ff.; H. Findeisen, *Schamanentum*, pp. 68 ff.

13 *Turukhansky krai, evo priroda i zhiteli*, pp. 210–11; cf. Mikhailowsky p. 86.

Tungus and the Buryat. The candidate's family and numerous guests participate. There is singing and dancing (there must be at least nine dancers), and nine pigs are sacrificed; the shamans drink their blood, go into ecstasy, and shamanize for a long time. The festival continues for several days [14] and becomes a sort of public celebration.

Obviously such an event concerns the whole tribe directly and it is clear that the expense cannot always be borne by the candidate's family alone. In this respect initiation plays an important part in the sociology of shamanism.

Buryat Initiation

The most complex initiation ceremony is that of the Buryat; thanks especially to Khangalov and to the "Manual" published by A. M. Pozdneyev and translated by J. Partanen, it is also the best known.[15] Even here, the real initiation takes place before the new shaman's public consecration. For many years after his first ecstatic experiences (dreams, visions, dialogues with the spirits, etc.) the apprentice prepares himself in solitude, taught by old masters and especially by the one who will be his initiator and who is called the "father shaman." During all this period he shamanizes,

14 Harva, *Die religiösen Vorstellungen*, pp. 486–87, citing I. A. Lopatin.
15 N. N. Agapitov and M. N. Khangalov, "Materialy dlya izuchenia shamanstva v Sibirii. Shamanstvo u buryat Irkutskoi gubernii," pp. 46–52, r. and summarized by L. Stieda, "Das Schamanenthum unter den Burjäten," p. 250 ff. (initiation ceremony, pp. 287–88); Mikhailowski, pp. 87–90; Harva, *Die religiösen Vorstellungen*, pp. 487–96; W. Schmidt, *Der Ursprung*, X, 399–422. A schoolteacher at Irkutsk and himself descended from Buryat, Khangalov supplied Agapitov with a very copious first-hand documentation concerning numerous shamanic rites and beliefs. See also Jorma Partanen, *A Description of Buriat Shamanism*. The "Manual" is a manuscript found by A. M. Pozdneyev in a Buryat village in 1879 and published by him in his *Mongolskaya khrestomatia* (Mongolian Chrestomathy), pp. 293–311. The text is written in literary Mongolian, with traces of modern Buryat. The author seems to have been a half-Lamaist Buryat (Partanen, p. 3). Unfortunately, this document reports only the external side of the ritual. Several details recorded by Khangalov are lacking in it.

invokes the gods and spirits, learns the secrets of his profession. Among the Buryat, too, the "initiation" is rather a public demonstration of the candidate's mystical capacities, followed by his consecration by the master, than a real revelation of mysteries.

When the date for consecration has been determined, there is a purification ceremony, which theoretically should be repeated from three to nine times but which in practice is performed only twice. The "father shaman" and nine young men, called his "sons," fetch water from three springs and offer libations of *tarasun* to the spring spirits. On the way back they pull up young birches and bring them to the house. The water is boiled and, to purify it, wild thyme, juniper, and pine bark are thrown into the pot; a few hairs cut from a he-goat's ear are also added. The animal is then killed and some drops of its blood are allowed to fall into the pot. The flesh is given to the women to prepare. After divining by means of a sheep's shoulder bone, the "father shaman" invokes the candidate's shaman ancestors and offers them wine and *tarasun*. Dipping a broom made of birch twigs into the pot, he touches the apprentice's bare back. The "shaman's sons" repeat this ritual gesture in turn, while the "father" says: "When a poor man has need of you, ask him for little and take what he gives you. Think of the poor, help them, and pray God to protect them from evil spirits and their powers. When a rich man summons you, do not ask him much for your services. If a rich man and a poor man summon you at the same time, go to the poor man and afterward to the rich man." [16] The apprentice promises to obey the rules, and repeats the prayer recited by the master. After the ablution libations of *tarasun* are again offered to the guardian spirits, and the preparatory ceremony is finished. This purification by water is obligatory for shamans at least once a year, if not every month at the time of the new moon.

16 Harva (*Die religiösen Vorstellungen*, p. 493) describes this purification rite as following the initiation proper. As we shall see presently, a similar rite does take place immediately after the ceremonial climbing of the birches. In any case, it is probable that the initiatory scenario has varied considerably in the course of time; there are also marked variations from tribe to tribe.

In addition, the shaman purifies himself in the same fashion each time that he incurs contamination; if the contamination is especially grave, purification is also performed with blood.

Some time after the initiation the first consecration ceremony, *khäragä-khulkhä*, takes place, the whole community sharing the expense. The offerings are collected by the shaman and his assistants (the "sons"), who go in procession on horseback from village to village. The offerings are usually kerchiefs and ribbons, rarely money. In addition, wooden cups, bells for the "horse-sticks," silk, wine, and other objects are bought. In the Balagansk district the candidate, the "father shaman," and the nine "shaman's sons" retire to a tent and fast for nine days, subsisting on nothing but tea and boiled flour. A rope made of horsehair, with small animal pelts fastened to it, is stretched around the tent three times.

On the eve of the ceremony a sufficient number of strong, straight birches is cut by the shaman and his nine "sons." The cutting takes place in the forest where the inhabitants of the village are buried, and to appease the forest spirit offerings of sheep's flesh and *tarasun* are made. On the morning of the festival the trees are put in their places. First a stout birch tree is set up in the yurt, with its roots in the hearth and its top protruding through the smoke hole. This birch is called *udeši-burkhan*, "the guardian of the door" (or "porter god"), for it opens the entrance to the sky for the shaman. It remains in the tent permanently, as a mark to distinguish the shaman's dwelling.

The other birches are set up far from the yurt, in the place where the initiation ceremony is to be performed, and they are planted in a particular order: (1) a birch under which *tarasun* and other offerings are placed and to whose branches ribbons are tied (red and yellow in the case of a "black" shaman, white and blue in the case of a "white" shaman, and of four colors if the new shaman intends to serve all kinds of spirits, good and bad); (2) another birch, to which a bell and the hide of a sacrificed horse are fastened; (3) a third birch, stout and firmly set in the ground, on which the novice will have to climb. These three birches, usually taken up

117

with their roots, are called "pillars" (*särgä*). Then follow: (4) nine birches, grouped in threes, tied together by a rope of white horsehair and with ribbons of various colors fastened to them in a particular order—white, blue, red, yellow (the colors perhaps signify the various levels of the sky); on these birches the hides of the nine animals to be sacrificed and various foods will be displayed; (5) nine stakes to which the animals to be sacrificed are tied; (6) large birches set in order, from which the bones of the sacrificed animals, wrapped in straw, will later be hung.[17] The chief birch—the one inside the yurt—is connected with all the others outside by two ribbons, one red, the other blue; these symbolize the "rainbow," the road by which the shaman will reach the realm of the spirits, the sky.

When these various preparations are completed, the neophyte and the "shaman's sons," all dressed in white, proceed to consecrate the shamanic instruments: a sheep is sacrificed in honor of the Lord and Lady of the Horse-stick, and *tarasun* is offered. Sometimes the stick is daubed with blood from the sacrificed animal; thereupon the "horse-stick" takes on life and becomes a real horse.

This consecration of the shamanic instruments is followed by a long ceremony that consists in offering *tarasun* to the tutelary divinities—the western Khans and their nine sons—and the an-

17 The text translated by Partanen gives many details concerning the ritual birches and posts (§ 10–15). "The tree on the northern side is called Mother Tree. At the top of it a bird's nest is tied with strips of silk and cotton; into it, on cotton, or soft white sheep's wool, nine eggs are put, and also the image of the moon made out of white velvet and glued on a round piece of birch-bark. . . . The stout tree on the southern side is called Father Tree. At its top [a piece of] birch-bark with red velvet glued on it is attached and called Sun" (§ 10). "Seven birch trees are dug into the ground on the northern side of the Mother Tree, towards the yurt; on four sides of the yurt four trees are put, and at the lower end of each a ledge is made for burning juniper and thyme [as incense]. This is called the Ladder [*šita*], or the Stairs [*geskigür*]" (§ 15). A detailed analysis of all the sources for these birches (except the text translated by Partanen) will be found in W. Schmidt, *Der Ursprung*, X, 405–08.

cestors of the "father shaman," to the local spirits and the tutelary spirits of the new shaman, to a number of famous dead shamans, to the *burkhan* and other minor divinities.[18] The "father shaman" again offers a prayer to the different gods and spirits, and the candidate repeats his words; according to certain traditions, the candidate holds a sword in his hand and, thus armed, climbs the birch that is set inside the yurt, reaches its top, and, emerging through the smoke hole, shouts to invoke the aid of the gods. During this time the persons and objects in the yurt are constantly purified. After this, four "sons of the shaman" carry the candidate out of the yurt on a felt carpet, singing.

Headed by the "father shaman" leading the candidate and the nine "sons," the whole group of relatives and spectators sets out in procession for the place where the row of birches has been set up. At a certain point, near a birch, the procession halts; a he-goat is sacrificed and the candidate, stripped to the waist, is anointed with blood on the head, eyes, and ears, while the other shamans drum. The nine "sons" dip their brooms in water, strike the candidate's bare back, and shamanize.

Then nine or more animals are sacrificed, and while the meat is being prepared, the ritual ascent into the sky takes place. The "father shaman" climbs a birch and makes nine notches at the top of it. He comes down and takes up his position on a carpet that his "sons" have brought to the foot of the birch. The candidate ascends in his turn, followed by the other shamans. As they climb, they all fall into ecstasy. Among the Buryat of Balagansk the candidate, seated on a felt carpet, is carried nine times around the

18 On the Khans and the quite complex pantheon of the Buryat, see Sandschejew, "Weltanschauung und Schamanismus der Alaren-Burjaten," p. 939; W. Schmidt, *Der Ursprung*, X, 250 ff. On the *burkhan*, see Shirokogoroff's long note (in Mironov and Shirokogoroff, "Śramaṇa-Shaman," p. 120–21) against the views of B. Laufer ("Burkhan," pp. 390–95), who denies Buddhistic vestiges among the Tungus of Amur. As to the later meanings of the term *burkhan* among the Turks (where it is applied in turn to Buddha, Mani, Zarathustra, etc.), see U. Pestallozza, "Il manicheismo presso i Turchi occidentali ed orientali," p. 456, n. 3.

birches; he climbs each of them and makes nine notches at their summits. While at the top of each birch he shamanizes; meanwhile, the "father shaman" shamanizes on the ground, walking around the trees. According to Potanin, the nine birches are planted close to one another and the candidate, who is being carried on the carpet, jumps down before the last of them, climbs it to the top, and repeats the same ritual for each of the nine trees, which, like the nine notches, symbolize the nine heavens.

By this time the meat is ready and, after offerings are made to the gods (by throwing pieces into the fire and into the air), the banquet begins. The shaman and his "sons" then withdraw into the yurt, but the guests continue to feast for a long time. The bones of the animals are wrapped in straw and hung on the nine birches.

In earlier times there were several initiations. Khangalov and Sandschejew [19] each mention nine, B. E. Petri five.[20] According to the text published by Pozdneyev, a second and third initiation took place after three and six years respectively.[21] Similar ceremonies are attested among the Sibo (a people related to the Tungus), the Tatars of the Altai, and, to some extent, also among the Yakut and the Goldi.[22]

But even where an initiation of this type is not known, we find shamanic rituals of ascent into the sky that depend upon similar conceptions. This fundamental unity of Central and North Asian shamanism will appear when we study the technique of séances. The cosmological structure of all these shamanic rites will then be elucidated. It is, for example, clear that the birch symbolizes the Cosmic Tree or the Axis of the World, and that it is therefore conceived as occupying the Center of the World; by climbing it, the shaman undertakes an ecstatic journey to the Center. We have already come upon this important mythical motif in connection with initiatory dreams, and it will become even more obvious in rela

19 "Weltanschauung," p. 979.
20 Harva, *Die religiösen Vorstellungen*, p. 495.
21 Partanen, p. 24, § 37.
22 Harva, *Die religiösen Vorstellungen*, p. 498.

tion to the séances of Altaic shamans and the symbolism of shamanic drums.

In addition, we shall see that ascent by means of a tree or post
plays an important part in other initiations of the shamanic type;
it is to be regarded as one variation on the mythico-ritual theme of
ascent to heaven (a theme that also includes "magical flight," the
myth of the "chain of arrows," of the rope, the bridge, etc.). The
same symbolism of ascent is attested by the rope (bridge) that
connects the birches and is hung with ribbons of different colors
(the strata of the rainbow, the different celestial regions). These
mythical themes and rituals, although distinctive of the Siberian
and Altaic religions, are not peculiar to these cultures exclusively,
since their area of dissemination far exceeds Central and Northeast
Asia. It is even questionable if a ritual so complex as the initiation
of the Buryat shaman can be an independent creation. For, as
Harva noted over a quarter of a century ago, the Buryat initiation
is strangely reminiscent of certain ceremonies of the Mithraic
mysteries. The candidate, stripped to the waist, is purified by the
blood of a goat, which is sometimes killed above his head; in some
places he must even drink the blood of the sacrificed animal.[23] This
ceremony resembles the *taurobolion*, the chief rite in the Mithraic
mysteries.[24] And the same mysteries made use of a ladder (*klimax*)
with seven rungs, each rung made of a different metal. According to
Celsus,[25] the first rung was lead (corresponding to the "heaven"
of the planet Saturn), the second tin (Venus), the third bronze
(Jupiter), the fourth iron (Mercury), the fifth "monetary alloy"
(Mars), the sixth silver (the moon), the seventh gold (the sun).
The eighth rung, Celsus says, represents the sphere of the fixed

23 Cf. Holmberg (Harva): *Der Baum des Lebens*, pp. 140 ff.; *Die religiösen
Vorstellungen*, pp. 492 ff.

24 In the second century of our era Prudentius (*Peristeph.* X. 1011 ff.)
described this ritual in connection with the mysteries of the Magna Mater,
but there is reason to believe that the Phrygian *taurobolion* was borrowed
from the Persians; cf. Franz Cumont, *Les Religions orientales dans le paganisme
romain* (3rd edn.), pp. 63 ff., 229 ff.

25 Origen *Contra Celsum* VI. 22.

stars. By climbing this ceremonial ladder, the initiate passed through the "seven heavens," reaching the Empyrean.[26] If we consider the other Iranian elements that are present, in more or less distorted form, in the Central Asian mythologies,[27] and remember the important role that the Sogdians played during the first millennium of our era as intermediaries between China and Central Asia in one direction and, in the other, between Iran and the Near East,[28] the Finnish scholar's hypothesis seems tenable.

For the present, we can stop with having indicated these few probabilities of Iranian influence on the Buryat ritual. All this will reveal its importance when we come to discuss the South and West Asian contributions to Siberian shamanism.

Initiation of the Araucanian Shamaness

It is not within the scope of our intention to seek out all the possible parallels to this Buryat shamanic initiation ritual. We shall refer only to the most striking among them, and especially to those that

26 On ascent to heaven by steps, ladders, mountains, etc., cf. A. Dieterich, *Eine Mithrasliturgie* (2nd edn.), pp. 183, 254; see below, pp. 487 ff. We may also recall that the number 7 plays an important role among the Altaians and the Samoyed. The World Pillar had seven stories (Holmberg [Harva], *Finno-Ugric [and] Siberian [Mythology]*, pp. 338 ff.), the Cosmic Tree seven branches (id., *Der Baum des Lebens*, p. 137; *Die religiösen Vorstellungen*, pp. 51 ff.), etc. The number 7, which dominates Mithraic symbolism (seven celestial spheres; seven stars, or seven knives, or seven trees, or seven altars, etc., in the figured monuments), is due to Babylonian influences that early affected the Iranian mystery (cf., for example, R. Pettazzoni, *I Misteri*, pp. 231, 247, etc.). On the symbolism of these numbers, see below, pp. 274 ff.

27 We will mention a few: the myth of the miraculous tree Gaokĕrĕn that grows on an island in the lake (or sea) Vourukasha, and beside which lurks the monster lizard created by Ahriman (*Vidēvdat*, XX, 4; *Bundahišn*, XVIII, 2; XXVII, 4; etc.), a myth that is also found among the Kalmyk (dragon in the ocean, near the miraculous tree Zambu), the Buryat (the snake Abyrga by the tree in the "lake of milk"), and elsewhere (Holmberg [Harva], *Finno-Ugric [and] Siberian [Mythology]*, pp. 356 ff.). But the possibility of Indian influence must also be considered; cf. below, pp. 266 ff.

28 See Kai Donner, "Über soghdisch *nōm* 'Gesetz' und samojedisch *nōm* 'Himmel, Gott,'" pp. 1–8.

involve, as an essential rite, climbing a tree or some other more or less symbolic means of ascending to the sky. We shall begin with a South American consecration, that of the *machi*, the Araucanian shamaness.[29] This initiation ceremony centers upon the ritual climbing of a tree or rather of a tree trunk stripped of bark, called *rewe*. The *rewe* is also the particular symbol of the shamanic profession, and every *machi* keeps it in front of her hut indefinitely.

A nine-foot tree is barked, notched to form a ladder, and solidly set in the ground in front of the future shamaness's house, "tilted slightly backward to make it easier to climb." Sometimes "tall branches are stuck in the ground all around the *rewe*, forming an enclosure for it of 15 by 4 meters." [30] When this sacred ladder has been set up, the candidate undresses and, wearing only her shift, lies down on a couch made of sheepskins and blankets. The old shamanesses rub her body with canelo leaves and make magical passes. Meanwhile the women attending the ceremony sing in chorus and ring bells. This ritual massage is repeated several times. Then "the older women bend over her and suck her breast, belly, and head with such force that blood spurts out." [31] After this first preparation the candidate gets up, dresses, and sits on a chair. The songs and dances continue all day.

The following day, the celebration is at its height. A crowd of guests arrives. The old *machi* form a circle, drumming and dancing one after the other. Finally they and the candidate go to the tree-ladder and begin the ascent, following one another. (According to Moesbach's informant, the candidate goes up first.) The ceremony is terminated by the sacrifice of a sheep.

We have summarized the description by Robles Rodriguez, as cited by Métraux. Father Housse gives additional details. The company forms a circle around the altar, at which lambs provided by the shamaness's family are sacrificed. An old *machi* invokes

29 We shall follow the description by Métraux ("Le Shamanisme arau-can"), who makes use of all the previous documentation, especially E. Robles Rodriguez, "Guillatunes, costumbres y creencias araucanas," and Father Housse, *Une Épopée indienne. Les Araucans du Chili.*

30 Métraux, "Le Shamanisme araucan," p. 319.

31 Ibid., p. 321.

God: "O Lord and Father of mankind, I sprinkle thee with the blood of these animals that thou hast created. Be favorable to us!" etc. An animal is killed and its heart hung from one of the branches of the canelo. Music begins, and all gather around the *rewe*. Feasting and dancing follow, and are continued all night.

At dawn the candidate reappears and the *machi*, accompanied by the drums, begin to dance again. Several of them fall into ecstasy. One of them blindfolds herself and, groping with a knife of white quartz, makes several cuts in the candidate's fingers and lips; she then makes similar cuts in her own body and mixes her blood with the candidate's. After other rites the young initiate "climbs the *rewe*, dancing and drumming. The older women follow her, and steady themselves on the steps; her two sponsors stand on either side of her on the platform. They strip her of the necklace of greenery and the blood-stained fleece (n.b., with which she had been ornamented shortly before) and hang them on the branches of the shrubs. Time alone may destroy them, for they are sacred. Then the college of sorceresses comes down again, their new colleague last, but moving backwards and keeping time. As soon as her feet touch the ground she is greeted by an immense uproar; it is triumph, frenzy, a real scuffle, for everyone wants to see her close to, touch her hands, kiss her." [32] The feast follows, with all those who have attended taking part. The wounds heal in a week.

According to the texts collected by Moesbach, the new *machi's* prayer appears to be addressed to the Father God ("Padre dios rey anciano," etc.). She asks him for the gift of second sight (to see the sickness in the patient's body) and the art of drumming. In addition she asks for a "horse," a "bull," and a "knife"—symbols of certain spiritual powers—and, finally, for a "striped or colored" stone. (This is a magical stone that can be projected into the patient's body to purify him; if it comes out covered with blood, it is a sign that the patient is in danger of death. It is with this stone that the sick are rubbed.) The old *machi* promise the audience that the young initiate will not practice black magic. Robles Rodri-

32 Housse, cited in ibid., p. 325.

guez' text does not mention the Father God but uses the term *vileo*, which means the *machi* of the sky, that is, the celestial Great Shaman. (*Vileos* live in "the middle of the sky.")

As is true wherever there is an initiatory ascent, this one is repeated on the occasion of a shamanic cure.[33]

Let us note the dominant themes of this initiation: ecstatic ascent of a tree-ladder, symbolizing the journey to heaven; prayer addressed from the platform to the Supreme God or the celestial Great Shaman, who are believed to grant the *machi* both curative powers (clairvoyance, etc.) and the magical objects necessary for healing (the striped stone, etc.). The divine, or at least celestial, origin of medical powers is attested among a number of archaic peoples—for example, the Semang Pygmies, where the *hala* treats patients with the help of the Cenoi (intermediaries between Ta Pedn, the Supreme God, and human beings) or with quartz stones in which these celestial spirits are often supposed to reside, but also with the help of God.[34] As for the "striped or colored stone," it too is of celestial origin; we have already cited a number of South American and other examples [35] and shall return to the subject.[36]

Ritual Tree Climbing

Ritually ascending a tree is a shamanic initiation rite in North America too. Among the Pomo the ceremony for entrance into the secret societies lasts four days, one day being devoted entirely to the climbing of a tree-pole from twenty to thirty feet long and six

---

33 Métraux, "Le Shamanisme araucan," p. 336.

34 See below, pp. 337 f. 35 Above, pp. 45 ff.

36 It must also be noted that, among the Araucanians, shamanism is practiced by women; in earlier times, it was the prerogative of sexual inverts. A like situation is found among the Chukchee: the majority of shamans are inverts and sometimes even take husbands; but even when they are sexually normal their spirit guides oblige them to dress as women; cf. W. G. Bogoras, *The Chukchee*, pp. 450 ff. Is there a genetic relation between these two shamanisms? The question seems difficult to decide.

inches in diameter.[37] It will be remembered that future Siberian shamans climb trees during or before their consecration. As we shall see,[38] the Vedic sacrificer also climbs a ritual post to reach heaven and the gods. Ascent by a tree, a liana, or a rope is an extremely widespread mythical motif; examples will be found in a later chapter.[39]

To cite a final example: Initiation into the third and highest shamanic degree of the Sarawak *manang* [40] includes a ritual climb. A great jar is set on the veranda with two small ladders leaning against its sides. Facing each other, the two initiatory masters make the candidate climb up one of the ladders and down the other throughout a whole night. One of the first to observe this initiation, Archdeacon J. Perham, writing about 1885, admitted that he was unable to obtain any explanation of the rite.[41] Yet its meaning seems clear enough; it must represent a symbolic ascent to the sky followed by a return to earth. Similar rituals are found in Malekula: one of the higher degrees of the Maki initiation ceremony is called "ladder," [42] and mounting a platform constitutes the essential act of the rite.[43] But this is not all. Shamans and medicine men, to say nothing of certain types of mystics, are able to fly like birds and perch on the branches of trees. The Hungarian shaman (*táltos*) "could jump up in a willow tree and sit on a branch that would have been too weak for a bird." [44] The Iranian saint Qutb ud-dīn Haydar was frequently seen in the tops of trees.[45] St. Joseph of

37 E. M. Loeb, *Pomo Folkways*, pp. 372–74. Cf. other North and South American examples in Eliade, *Birth and Rebirth*, p. 77. See also Josef Haekel, "Kosmischer Baum und Pfahl im Mythus und Kult der Stämme Nordwestamerikas," pp. 77 ff.

38 Below, pp. 403 f.   39 Below, pp. 487 ff.

40 Cf. above, pp. 57 f.

41 Text quoted by H. Ling Roth, *The Natives of Sarawak and British North Borneo*, I, 281. See also E. H. Gomes, *Seventeen Years among the Sea Dyaks*, pp. 178 ff.

42 On this ceremony, see J. Layard, *Stone Men of Malekula*, ch. xiv.

43 Cf. also A. B. Deacon, *Malekula: a Vanishing People in the New Hebrides*, pp. 379 ff.; A. Riesenfeld, *The Megalithic Culture of Melanesia*, pp. 59 ff., et

44 G. Róheim, "Hungarian Shamanism," p. 134.

45 See below, p. 401, n. 117.

Cupertino flew into a tree and remained half an hour on a branch that "was seen to sway as if a bird had perched on it." [46]

The experiences of Australian medicine men are no less interesting. They claim to possess a sort of magical rope with which they can climb to the tops of trees. "The doctor lies on his back under a tree, sends his cord up and climbs up on it to a nest on top of the tree, then across to other trees, and at sunset down to the tree again." [47] According to the information collected by R. M. Berndt and A. P. Elkin, "a Wongaibon clever man, lying on his back at the foot of a tree, sent his cord directly up, and 'climbed' up with his head well back, body outstretched, legs apart, and arms to his sides. Arriving at the top, 40 feet up, he waved his arms to those below, and then came down in the same manner, and while still on his back the cord re-entered his body." [48] This magical cord cannot fail to suggest the Indian "rope trick," whose shamanic structure we shall study later.[49]

Celestial Journey of the Carib Shaman

Though also centering on the neophyte's ecstatic journey to the sky, the initiation of the Carib shamans of Dutch Guiana makes use of different means.[50] A youth cannot become a *pujai* without succeeding in seeing the spirits and establishing direct and lasting relations with them.[51] There is less a "possession" than an

46 See below, pp. 481 f.

47 Elkin, *Aboriginal Men of High Degree*, pp. 64–65.

48 Ibid., p. 64.   49 Cf. below, pp. 428 ff.

50 We follow Friedrich Andres's study, "Die Himmelsreise der caraïbichen Medizinmänner," which makes use of the researches of the Dutch thnologists F. P. and A. P. Penard, W. Ahlbrinck, and C. H. de Goeje. Cf. W. E. Roth, "An Inquiry into the Animism and Folk-Lore of the Guiana ndians"; Métraux, "Le Shamanisme chez les Indiens de l'Amérique du ud tropicale," pp. 208–09. See also C. H. de Goeje, "Philosophy, Initiation nd Myths of the Indians of Guiana and Adjacent Countries," especially p. 60 ff. (initiation of the medicine man), 72 (trance brought on as a means f traveling to the sky), 82 (ladder to the sky).

51 Ahlbrinck calls him *püyéi* and translates the term as "spirit exorciser" Andres, p. 333). Cf. W. E. Roth, pp. 326 ff.

ecstatic vision making communication and conversation with the spirits possible. This ecstatic experience can take place only in the course of a celestial journey. But the novice cannot undertake the journey unless he has been both taught the traditional ideology and prepared, physically and psychologically, for trance. As we shall see, his apprenticeship is extremely rigorous.

Usually six youths are initiated at once. They live in complete isolation in a hut built especially for the purpose and covered with palm fronds. They are required to do a certain amount of manual work; they tend the master initiator's tobacco field and make a bench in the shape of an alligator from the trunk of a cedar and set it in front of their hut. On this bench they sit every evening to listen to the master or to wait for visions. In addition, each of them makes his own bells and a "magical staff" six feet long. Six girls, under the supervision of an old woman teacher, serve the candidates. They furnish the daily supply of tobacco juice, which the candidates are obliged to drink in large quantities, and every evening each of them rubs the entire body of one of the candidates with a red liquid; this is to make him handsome and worthy to enter the presence of the spirits.

The initiation takes twenty-four days and twenty-four nights and is divided into four parts; each series of three days and night of instruction is followed by three days of rest. Teaching takes place at night, in the hut; there is dancing in a circle and singing, after which the candidates sit on the alligator bench and listen to the master discourse on the spirits, good and evil, and especially on "Grandfather Vulture," who plays an essential role in the initiation. He has the appearance of a naked Indian; it is he who helps the shamans to reach the sky by a spiral ladder. This spirit is the mouthpiece of the "Indian Grandfather," that is, the Creator, the Supreme Being.[52] The dances imitate the movements of the

[52] Andres, p. 336. It is to be noted that, among the Carib too, shaman power finally derives from the sky and the Supreme Being. We may also recall the role of the eagle in the Siberian shamanic mythologies: father of the First Shaman, bird of the sun, messenger of the Celestial God, intercessor between God and mankind.

animals of which the master has spoken during his teaching. By day the candidates remain in their hammocks, in the hut. During the rest period they lie on the bench, their eyes rubbed with red-pepper juice, thinking of the master's lessons and trying to see the spirits.[53]

Throughout the instruction period fasting is almost absolute; the apprentices constantly smoke cigarettes, chew tobacco leaves, and drink tobacco juice. After the exhausting night dances, with fasting and intoxication superadded, the apprentices are ready for their ecstatic journey. The first night of the second period they are taught to turn into jaguars and bats.[54] On the fifth night, after a complete fast (even tobacco juice is forbidden), the master stretches several ropes at different heights, the apprentices dance on them in turn or swing in the air, holding on with their hands.[55] At this time they have their first ecstatic experience; they meet an Indian, who is really a benevolent spirit (*Tukajana*). "Come, novice. You shall go up to the sky by Grandfather Vulture's ladder. It is not far." The apprentice "climbs a sort of spiral ladder and thus reaches the first storey of the sky, where he passes through Indian villages and cities inhabited by Whites. Then the novice meets a Water Spirit (*Amana*), a woman of great beauty, who urges him to dive into the stream with her. There she imparts charms and magical formulas to him. The novice and his guide land on the farther bank and reach the crossroads of 'Life and Death.' The future shaman may choose between going to the 'Land without Evening' or the 'Land without Dawn.' The spirit guiding him now tells him of the destiny of souls after death. The candidate is suddenly brought back to earth by an intense feeling of pain. The master has applied the *maraque* to his skin, a sort of woven mat in whose interstices large poisonous ants have been inserted."[56]

53 Ibid., pp. 336–37.　　54 Ibid., p. 337.　　55 Ibid., p. 338.

56 Métraux, "Le Shamanisme chez les Indiens de l'Amérique du Sud tropicale," p. 208, summarizing Andres, pp. 338–39. See also Alain Gheerant, *Journey to the Far Amazon*, pp. 115, 128, with the accompanying pictures of the *maraque*.

On the second night of the fourth period of instruction the master puts the apprentices in turn on "a platform suspended from the ceiling of the hut by a number of cords twisted together, which as they unwind, make the platform revolve with increasing speed." [57] The novice sings: "The platform of the *pujai* will carry me to the sky. I shall see the village of Tukajana." And he enters the various celestial spheres one after the other and sees the spirits in a vision.[58] Intoxication by the *takini* plant, which produces a high fever, is also employed. The novice shakes in every limb, and evil spirits are believed to have entered him and to be tearing his body. (The well-known initiatory motif of dismemberment by demons is easily recognizable here.) Finally, the apprentice feels that he is carried into the sky and enjoys celestial visions.[59]

Carib folklore preserves the memory of a time when shamans had great powers; they are said to have been able to see the spirits with their bodily eyes and could even bring the dead back to life. Once a *pujai* went up into the sky and threatened God; seizing a saber, God drove the insolent mortal away; since that time shamans can go to heaven only during ecstasy.[60] We must emphasize the resemblance between these legends and North Asian beliefs concerning the original greatness of shamans and their subsequent decadence, which the present has only increased. We can read in it, as it were in filigree, the myth of a primordial age when communication between the shamans and God was more direct and took place concretely. Following some act of pride or revolt by the first shamans, God forbade them direct access to spiritual realities; they can no longer see spirits with their bodily eyes, and ascent to heaven can be accomplished only in ecstasy. As we shall see before long, this mythical motif is still richer.

---

57 Métraux, "Le Shamanisme chez les Indiens de l'Amérique du Sud tropicale," p. 208.

58 Andres, p. 340. In ibid., n. 3, the author cites H. Fühner, "Solanazeen als Berauschungsmittel," on the ecstasy provoked by laurel. On the role of narcotics in Siberian and other shamanisms, see below, pp. 399 ff.

59 Andres, p. 341.   60 Ibid., pp. 341–42.

Métraux [61] cites the observations of early travelers on the initiation of the West Indian Carib. For instance, Laborde reported that the masters "also rub his (the neophyte's) body with gum and cover it with feathers to make him able to fly and go to the house of the *zemeen* (spirits)." There is nothing surprising in this, for the ornithomorphic costume and other symbols of magical flight are an integral part of Siberian, North American, and Indonesian shamanism.

Several elements of the Carib initiation are found elsewhere in South America. Intoxication by tobacco is characteristic of South American shamanism; the ritual seclusion in the hut and the stern ordeals to which the apprentices are subjected are one of the essential aspects of Fuegian initiation (Selk'nam and Yamana); instruction by a master and "visualization" of the spirits are likewise constituent elements of South American shamanism. But the technique of preparation for the ecstatic celestial journey appears to be peculiar to the Carib *pujai*. It should be noted that we here have a complete scenario for the typical initiation: ascent, encounter with a spirit-woman, immersion in water, revelation of secrets (most importantly, of human destiny after death), journey into the regions of the beyond. But the *pujai* makes every effort to gain an ecstatic experience of this initiatory schema, even if ecstasy is to be obtained only at the cost of aberrant methods. We receive the impression that the Carib shaman uses any means to gain a concrete experience of a spiritual condition that, by its very nature, refuses to be "experienced" in the way in which certain human situations are "experienced." This observation should be borne in mind; we will return to and complete it in connection with other shamanic techniques.

Ascent by the Rainbow

The initiation of the Australian medicine man of the Forrest River region includes both the symbolic death and resurrection of the

[61] "Le Shamanisme chez les Indiens de l'Amérique du Sud tropicale," , 209.

candidate and an ascent to the sky. The usual method is as follows: The master assumes the form of a skeleton and equips himself with a small bag, in which he puts the candidate, whom his magic has reduced to the size of an infant. Then, seating himself astride the Rainbow-Serpent, he begins to pull himself up by his arms, as if climbing a rope. When near the top, he throws the candidate into the sky, "killing" him. Once they are in the sky, the master inserts into the candidate's body small rainbow-serpents, *brimures* (i.e., small fresh-water snakes), and quartz crystals (which have the same name as the mythical Rainbow-Serpent). After this operation the candidate is brought back to earth, still on the Rainbow-Serpent's back. The master again introduces magical objects into his body, this time through the navel, and wakens him by touching him with a magical stone. The candidate returns to normal size. On the following day the ascent by the Rainbow-Serpent is repeated in the same way.[62]

Some features of this Australian initiation are already familiar to us: the candidate's death and resurrection, the insertion of magical objects into his body. It is interesting to note that the initiatory master, magically changing himself into a skeleton, reduces the apprentice's stature to that of a newborn infant; both these feats symbolize the abolition of profane time and the restoration of a mythical time, the Australian "Dream Time." The ascent is made by way of the rainbow, mythically imagined as a huge snake, on whose back the master climbs as on a rope. We have already referred to the celestial ascents of Australian medicine men, and we shall soon encounter still clearer examples.

As to the rainbow, a considerable number of peoples are known to see in it the bridge connecting earth and sky, and especially the

<hr/>

62 A. P. Elkin: "The Rainbow-Serpent Myth in North-West Australia," pp. 349–50; *The Australian Aborigines*, pp. 223–24; *Aboriginal Men of High Degree*, pp. 139–40. Cf. Eliade, *Birth and Rebirth*, p. 160. On the Rainbow Serpent and its role in the initiations of Australian medicine men, cf. V. Lanternari, "Il Serpente Arcobaleno e il complesso religioso degli Esseri pluviali in Australia," pp. 120 ff.

bridge of the gods.[63] This is why its appearance after a storm is regarded as a sign of God's appeasement.[64] It is always by way of the rainbow that mythical heroes reach the sky.[65] Thus, for example, in Polynesia the Maori hero Tawhaki and his family, and the Hawaiian hero Aukelenuiaiku, regularly visit the upper regions by climbing the rainbow or by means of a kite, to deliver the souls of the dead or to meet their spirit-wives.[66] The same mythical function of the rainbow is found in Indonesia, Melanesia, and Japan.[67]

Though indirectly, these myths refer to a time when communication between heaven and earth was possible; in consequence of a certain event or a ritual fault, the communication was broken off; but heroes and medicine men are nevertheless able to reestablish it. This myth of a paradisal period brutally abolished by the "fall" of man will engage our attention more than once in the course of our study; it is in one way or another bound up with certain shamanic conceptions. The Australian medicine men, like

---

63 Cf., for example, L. Frobenius, *Die Weltanschauung der Naturvölker*, p. 131 ff.; P. Ehrenreich, *Die allgemeine Mythologie und ihre ethnologischen Grundlagen*, p. 141; R. T. Christiansen, "Myth, Metaphor, and Simile," p. 42 ff. For Finno-Ugric and Tatar data, see Holmberg, *Finno-Ugric and] Siberian [Mythology]*, pp. 443 ff.; for the Mediterranean world, cf. . Renel's rather disappointing study, "L'Arc-en-ciel dans la tradition religieuse de l'antiquité," pp. 58–80.

64 For example, among the Pygmies; see Eliade, *Patterns in Comparative Religion*, p. 49.

65 Ehrenreich, pp. 133 ff.

66 Cf. H. M. and N. K. Chadwick, *The Growth of Literature*, III, 273 ff., 98, etc.; N. K. Chadwick, "Notes on Polynesian Mythology"; id., "The Kite: a Study in Polynesian Tradition." On the kite in China, see B. Laufer, *The Prehistory of Aviation*, pp. 31–43. Polynesian traditions usually mention n superimposed skies; in New Zealand the number is twelve. (The Indian igin of these cosmologies is more than probable.) The hero passes from ne to another, as we have seen the Buryat shaman doing. He meets spirit-omen (often his own ancestresses) who help him find his way; cf. the role spirit-women in the initiation of the Carib *pujai*, the role of the "celestial fe" among Siberian shamans, etc.

67 H. T. Fischer, "Indonesische Paradiesmythen," pp. 208, 238 ff.; K. Numazawa, *Die Weltanfänge in der japanischen Mythologie*, p. 155.

numerous other shamans and magicians elsewhere, simply re
store—temporarily and for themselves alone—this "bridge" be
tween sky and earth, which was once accessible to all mortals.

The myth of the rainbow as road of the gods and bridge between
sky and earth is also found in Japanese tradition,[69] and doubtless
existed in the religious conceptions of Mesopotamia.[70] Further
the seven colors of the rainbow have been assimilated to the seven
heavens, a symbolism found not only in India and Mesopotamia
but also in Judaism. In the Bamiyan frescoes the Buddha is rep
resented seated on a rainbow of seven bands; [71] that is, he tran
scends the cosmos, just as in the myth of his Nativity he transcend
the seven heavens by taking seven strides toward the north an
reaching the Center of the World, the culminating peak of th
universe.

The throne of the Supreme Being is surrounded by a rainbow,
and the same symbolism persists into the Christian art of th
Renaissance.[73] The Babylonian ziggurat was sometimes repre
sented with seven colors, symbolizing the seven celestial region
he who climbed its storeys attained the summit of the cosm
world.[74] Similar ideas are found in India [75] and, what is mor
important, in Australian mythology. The Supreme God of th
Kamilaroi, the Wiradjuri, and the Euahlayi dwells in the upper
sky, seated on a crystal throne; Bundjil, the Supreme God of th
Kulin, remains above the clouds.[76] Mythical heroes and medicir
men ascend to these celestial beings by using, among other thing
the rainbow.

68 On the rainbow in folklore, see S. Thompson, *Motif-Index*, III,
(F 152).

69 Cf. R. Pettazzoni, *Mitologia giapponese*, p. 42, n. 1; Numazaw
pp. 154–55.

70 A. Jeremias, *Handbuch* (2nd edn.), pp. 139 ff.

71 Benjamin Rowland, Jr., "Studies in the Buddhist Art of Bāmiyān: t
Bodhisattva of Group E"; cf. Eliade, *Myths, Dreams and Mysteries*, pp. 110

72 Rev. 4:3.   73 Rowland, p. 46, n. 1.

74 Eliade, *Patterns*, p. 101.   75 Rowland, p. 48.

76 Eliade, *Patterns*, pp. 41 ff.

It will be remembered that the ribbons employed in Buryat initiations are called "rainbows"; in general, they symbolize the shaman's journey to the sky.[77] Shamanic drums are decorated with drawings of the rainbow represented as a bridge to the sky.[78] Indeed, in the Turkic languages the word for rainbow also means bridge.[79] Among the Yurak-Samoyed the shamanic drum is called "bow"; the shaman's magic projects him to the sky like an arrow. Furthermore, there are reasons to believe that the Turks and the Uigur regarded the drum as a "celestial bridge" (rainbow) over which the shaman made his ascent.[80] This idea forms part of the complex symbolism of the drum and the bridge, each of which represents a different formula for the same ecstatic experience: celestial ascent. It is through the musical magic of the drum that the shaman can reach the highest heaven.

Australian Initiations

It will be remembered that several of the Australian medicine men's accounts of initiation, though centered on the symbolic killing and resurrection of the candidate, referred to his rising to the sky.[81] But there are other forms of initiation in which ascent plays the essential role. Among the Wiradjuri the initiatory master introduces rock crystals into the apprentice's body and makes him drink water in which such crystals have been placed; after this the apprentice succeeds in seeing the spirits. The master then leads him to a grave, and the dead in turn give him magical stones. The candidate also encounters a snake, which becomes his totem and guides him into the bowels of the earth, where there are many other snakes; they infuse magical powers into him by rubbing themselves against him. After this symbolic descent to the underworld the master prepares to lead him to the camp of Baiame, the

77 Holmberg (Harva): *Der Baum des Lebens*, pp. 144 ff.; *Die religiösen Vorstellungen*, p. 489.
78 *Die religiösen Vorstellungen*, p. 351; Martti Räsänen, *Regenbogen-Himmelsbrücke*, pp. 7–8.
79 Räsänen, p. 6.   80 Ibid., p. 8.   81 Cf. above, pp. 50 f.

Supreme Being. To reach it, they climb a cord until they mee Wombu, Baiame's bird. "We went through the clouds," an apprentice related, "and on the other side was the sky. We wen through the place where the Doctors go through, and it kep opening and shutting very quickly." Anyone whom the door touched lost his magical power and was certain to die as soon as h had returned to earth.[82]

Here we have an almost complete schema of initiation: descen to the lower regions followed by ascent to the sky, where th Supreme Being grants shamanic power.[83] Access to the uppe regions is difficult and dangerous; it is necessary to enter in twinkling, before the gates shut. (This is a specifically initiator motif, which we have already encountered elsewhere.)

In another account recorded by Howitt there is a cord by whic the blindfolded candidate is conveyed onto a rock, where he find the same magical door that opens and shuts with great rapidity The candidate and his initiatory masters enter the rock, and ther the blindfold is taken from his eyes. He finds himself in a place light with rock crystals glittering from the walls. He is give several of these crystals and told how to use them. Then, sti hanging from the rope, he is carried back to camp through the a and deposited in the top of a tree.[84]

These initiatory rites and myths form part of a more gener belief regarding the medicine man's ability to reach the sky means of a rope,[85] a scarf,[86] or simply by flying [87] or climbing spiral stairway. Several myths mention that the first men mounte

82 A. W. Howitt: "On Australian Medicine Men," pp. 50 ff.; *The Nat Tribes of South-East Australia*, pp. 404–13.

83 On Australian medicine men's initiations, cf. Elkin, *Aboriginal Men High Degree;* Helmut Petri, "Der australische Medizinmann"; Eliade, *Bir and Rebirth*, pp. 96 ff. See also E. Stiglmayr, "Schamanismus in Australien

84 Howitt: "On Australian Medicine Men," pp. 51–52; *The Nat Tribes*, pp. 400 f.; Marcel Mauss, "L'Origine des pouvoirs magiques dans sociétés australiennes," p. 159. The reader will recall the initiatory cave the Samoyed and of the North and South American shamans.

85 See, for example, Mauss, p. 149, n. 1.

86 R. Pettazzoni, *Miti e leggende. I: Africa, Australia*, p. 413.

87 Mauss, p. 148. Medicine men change into vultures and fly (B. Spenc and F. J. Gillen, *The Arunta*, II, 430).

o the sky by climbing a tree; thus the ancestors of the Mara were accustomed to climb a certain tree up to the sky and come down again.[88] Among the Wiradjuri the first man, created by Baiame, the Supreme Being, could reach the sky by a path on a mountain and then by climbing a stairway to Baiame, just as the medicine men still do down to our day among the Wurundjeri and the Wotjoba-luk.[89] The Yuin medicine men go up to the dwelling of Daramulun, the Supreme God, who gives them remedies.[90]

A Euahlayi myth tells how the medicine men reached Baiame. They walked northeastward for several days until they reached the foot of the great mountain Ubi-Ubi, whose peaks were lost in the clouds. They climbed it by a spiral stone stairway and at the end of the fourth day came to the top. There they met Baiame's Spirit Messenger; he summoned Spirit Servants, who carried the medicine men through a hole into the sky.[91]

Thus the medicine men can, when they please, repeat what the first (mythical) men once did in the dawn of time—go up to the sky and return to the earth. Since the ability to ascend (or to fly magically) is essential to the career of medicine men, shamanic initiation includes an ascensional rite. Even when there is no direct reference to such a rite, it is in a manner implicit. The rock crystals that play an important part in the initiation of the Australian medicine man are of celestial origin, or at least related—even sometimes only indirectly—to the sky. Baiame sits on a throne of transparent crystal.[92] And among the Euahlayi it is Baiame himself (= Boyerb) who throws the fragments of crystal, doubtless detached from his throne, down to earth.[93] Baiame's throne the celestial vault. The crystals detached from his throne are solidified light."[94] The medicine men imagine Baiame as a being in all ways like other doctors, "except for the light which

---

88 A. van Gennep, *Mythes et légendes d'Australie*, nos. 32, 49; cf. also p. 44.

89 Howitt, *The Native Tribes*, pp. 501 ff.

90 Pettazzoni, *Miti*, p. 416. 91 Gennep, no. 66, pp. 92 ff.

92 Howitt, *The Native Tribes*, p. 501.

93 K. L. Parker, *The Euahlayi Tribe*, p. 7.

94 Cf. Eliade, "Significations de la 'lumière intérieure,' " p. 195.

radiated from his eyes." [95] In other words, they feel a relatio
between the condition of a supernatural being and a superabun
dance of light. Baiame performs the initiation of young medicin
men by sprinkling them with a "sacred powerful water," which i
supposed to be liquefied quartz.[96] All this is as much as to say tha
one becomes a shaman when one is stuffed with "solidified light,
that is, with quartz crystals; this operation changes the initiand'
mode of being by making him mystically akin to the sky. He wh
swallows one of these crystals flies up to the sky.[97]

Similar beliefs are found among the Negritos of the Mala
Peninsula.[98] In his therapy the *hala* uses quartz crystals obtaine
either from spirits of the air (Cenoi) or produced by the shama
himself with water that is magically "solidified" or, finally, c
from the fragments that the Supreme Being lets fall from the sky.
This is why these crystals are able to reflect what happens c
earth.[100] The shamans among the Sea Dyak of Sarawak (Borne
have "light stones" that reflect whatever happens to the patient
soul and so reveal where it has strayed.[101] A young chief of t
Ehatisaht Nootka tribe (Vancouver Island) one day came up
some rock crystals that were moving and striking against ea
other. He threw his coat over some of them and took four.[102] T
Kwakiutl shamans receive their power through quartz crystals.

We have seen that rock crystals—in close relation to t
Rainbow-Serpent—bestow the power to rise to the sky. Elsewhe
the same stones bestow the power to fly—as, for example, in
American myth recorded by Boas,[104] in which a young ma

95 Elkin, *Aboriginal Men*, p. 96.   96 Ibid.
97 Howitt, *The Native Tribes*, p. 583.
98 Cf. above, p. 52, n. 49.
99 Cf. Pettazzoni, *L'onniscienza di Dio*, p. 469, n. 86 (after Evans a
Schebesta).
100 Cf. below, pp. 337 ff.
101 Pettazzoni, *Essays on the History of Religions*, p. 42.
102 P. Drucker, *The Northern and Central Nootkan Tribes*, p. 160.
103 Werner Müller, *Weltbild und Kult der Kwakiutl Indianer*, p. 29, n.
(after Boas).
104 *Indianische Sagen von der nord-pacifischen Küste Amerikas*, p. 152.

limbing a shining mountain, becomes covered with rock crystals
nd immediately begins to fly. The same conception of a solid
elestial vault explains the virtues of meteorites and thunderstones.
'allen from the sky, they are impregnated with a magico-religious
irtue that can be used, communicated, disseminated; they form,
s it were, a new center of uranian sacrality on earth.[105]

In further connection with this uranian symbolism, we must
lso mention the motif of the crystal mountains or palaces that
eroes come upon in their mythical adventures, a motif that has
lso been preserved in European folklore. Finally, a late creation
f the same symbolism presents Lucifer and the fallen angels with
:ones in their foreheads (in certain variants the stones were
etached when they fell), diamonds in the heads or jaws of
erpents, and so forth. Here, of course, we have extremely complex
eliefs, worked over and revalorized many times, but whose
indamental structure remains clearly discernible: there is always a
rystal or magical stone detached from the sky and which, although
llen to earth, continues to dispense uranian sacrality—that is,
airvoyance, wisdom, power of divination, ability to fly, and so on.

Rock crystals play an essential role in Australian magic and
·ligion, and they are no less important throughout Oceania and
ie two Americas. Their uranian origin is not always distinctly
.tested in the respective beliefs, but forgetting original meanings
a common phenomenon in the history of religions. What is
gnificant for us is to have shown that Australian and other
edicine men in some obscure way connect their powers with the
·esence of these rock crystals in their own bodies. This means that
ey feel that they differ from other human beings by their assimi-
tion—in the most concrete sense—of a sacred substance whose
·igin is uranian.

Other Forms of the Rite of Ascent

)r a full understanding of the complex of religious ideas and
smologies that underlie the shamanic ideology, we should have

105 Cf. Eliade: *The Forge and the Crucible*, p. 20 ff.; *Patterns*, pp. 53, 225 ff.

to review a whole series of myths and rituals of ascent. In the following chapters we shall study some of the most important, but the entire problem cannot be fully discussed here and we shall have to return to it in a later work. For the time being, we shall content ourselves with adding some further aspects of the ascensional morphology of shamanic initiations, without claiming to have exhausted the subject.

Among the Niassans (Sumatra) he who is destined to become a prophet-priest suddenly disappears, carried off by the spirits (probably the youth is taken into the sky); he returns to the village three or four days later; if not, a search is made for him and he is usually found in the top of a tree, conversing with spirits. He seems to have lost his mind, and sacrifices must be offered to restore him to sanity. The initiation also includes a ritual procession to the graves, to a watercourse, and to a mountain. Among the Mentaweians the future shaman is carried to the sky by celestial spirits and there receives a marvelous body like their. Usually he falls ill and imagines that he ascends to the sky. After these first symptoms the initiation by a master takes place. Sometimes, during or immediately after this initiation, the apprentice loses consciousness and his spirit ascends to the sky in a boat carried by eagles; there it converses with the celestial spirits and asks them for remedies.[108]

As we shall presently see, the initiatory ascent gives the future magician the power to fly. All over the world, indeed, shamans and sorcerers are credited with power to fly, to cover immense distances in a twinkling, and to become invisible. It is difficult to determine if all magicians who believe that they can travel through the air have had an ecstatic experience, or been exposed to a ritual ascent, during their period of apprenticeship—that is, if they obtained their magical power of flight as the result of an initiation or of an ecstatic experience that announced their shamanic vocation. It may be supposed that at least some of them did

106 E. M. Loeb, *Sumatra*, p. 155.
107 Id.: "Shaman and Seer," p. 66; *Sumatra*, p. 195.
108 Id., "Shaman and Seer," p. 78.

btain this magical power after and through an initiation. Many of
ne documents attesting the ability of shamans and sorcerers to
y fail to state how these powers were obtained; but it is quite
ossible that this silence is due to the incompleteness of our
ources.

However this may be, in many cases shamanic vocation or
itiation is directly connected with an ascent to the sky. Thus, to
te but a few examples, a great Basuto prophet received his
ocation after an ecstasy during which he saw the roof of his hut
oen above his head and felt himself carried off to the sky, where
: met a multitude of spirits.[109] Many more such cases have been
corded in Africa.[110] Among the Nuba the future shaman has the
npression that the spirit " 'seizes his head from above,' or
nters his head.' "[111] The majority of these spirits are celestial,[112]
d it may be assumed that "possession" finds expression in an
censional trance.

In South America the initiatory journey to the sky or on very
gh mountains plays an essential role.[113] Among the Araucanians,
· example, the illness that determines the career of a *machi* is
lowed by an ecstatic crisis during which the future shamaness
cends to the sky and meets God himself. In the course of this
lestial visit supernatural beings show her the remedies necessary
· cures.[114] The shamanic ceremony of the Manasi includes the
d's descent into the hut, followed by an ascent; the god carries
e shaman to heaven with him. "His departure was accompanied
shocks that made the walls of the sanctuary shake. A few
nutes later the divinity brought the shaman back to earth or
him fall, head first, into the temple."[115]

Finally, we will give a North American example of initiatory

109 N. K. Chadwick, *Poetry and Prophecy*, pp. 50–51.
110 Ibid., pp. 94–95.
111 S. F. Nadel, "A Study of Shamanism in the Nuba Mountains," p. 26.
112 Ibid., p. 27.
113 Ida Lublinski, "Der Medizinmann bei den Naturvölkern Südamerikas,"
248.
114 Métraux, "Le Shamanisme araucan," p. 316.
115 Id., "Le Shamanisme chez les Indiens de l'Amérique du Sud tropicale,"
338.

ascent. A Winnebago medicine man felt that he was killed and, after many adventures, was carried into the sky, where he conversed with the Supreme Being. The celestial spirits put him to the test: he succeeded in killing a supposedly invulnerable bear and then restored it to life by breathing on it. Finally he returned to earth and was born a second time.[116]

The founder of the Ghost-Dance Religion, like all the principal prophets of that mystical movement, had an ecstatic experience that determined his career. He climbed a mountain in trance and met a beautiful woman dressed in white, who revealed to him that the Master of Life was on the summit of the mountain. Following her counsel, the prophet took off his clothes, plunged into a stream, and, in a state of ritual nudity, appeared before the Master of Life. The latter laid various injunctions on him—no longer to allow white men in the territory, to combat drunkenness, to renounce war and polygamy, and so on, and then gave him prayer to be communicated to men.[117]

Wovoka, the most remarkable prophet of the Ghost-Dance Religion, had his revelation at the age of eighteen. He fell asleep in broad daylight and felt himself carried into the beyond. He saw God and the dead, all happy and eternally young. God gave him message to men, bidding them be honest, industrious, charitable, and so on.[118] Another prophet, John Slocum of Puget Sound, "died" and saw his soul leave his body. " 'All at once I saw shining light—a great light— . . . I looked and saw my body had no soul—looked at my own body—it was dead. . . . My soul left body and went up to judgment place of God. . . . I have seen a great light in my soul from that good land . . .' "[119]

116 P. Radin, *Primitive Religion*, pp. 115–16. In this case we have a complete initiation: death and resurrection (= rebirth), ascent, ordeals, etc.

117 J. Mooney, "The Ghost-Dance Religion and the Sioux Outbreak of 1890," pp. 663 ff.

118 Ibid., pp. 771 ff.

119 Ibid., p. 752. Cf. the light of the Eskimo shaman. For the "judgment place of God," cf. the visions of the Ascension of Isaiah, the *Book of Artâ Virâf*, etc.

These first ecstatic experiences of the prophets serve as the model for all the adepts of the Ghost-Dance Religion. These, too, after long continued dancing and singing, fall into trance and visit the regions of the beyond, where they meet the souls of the dead, angels, and sometimes God himself. Thus the first revelations of the founder and the prophets become the pattern for all later conversions and ecstasies.

Ascents to the sky are also typical of the Ojibwa secret society Midē′wiwin, which is strongly shamanistic. As a characteristic example, we may cite the vision of a girl who heard a voice calling her, followed it, climbed a narrow path, and finally reached the sky. There she met the celestial God, who entrusted her with a message for mankind.[120] The goal of the Midē′wiwin society is to restore the road between heaven and earth as it was established by the Creation; [121] it is for this reason that the members of the society periodically undertake the ecstatic journey to the sky; by doing so, they in a manner abolish the present fallen state of the universe and humanity and re-establish the primordial situation, when heaven was easily accessible to all men.

Shamanism in the strict sense is not present here, for both the Ghost-Dance Religion and the Midē′wiwin society are secret societies that anyone may join if he will undergo certain ordeals or shows a certain predisposition to ecstasy. Nevertheless, these North American religious movements exhibit a number of specifically shamanistic features: techniques of ecstasy, mystical journey to the sky, descent to the underworld, conversations with God, semidivine beings, and the souls of the dead, and so on.

As we have just seen, ascent to the sky plays an essential role in shamanic initiations. Tree- or pole-climbing rites, myths of ascent or magical flight, ecstatic experiences of levitation, of flight, of mystical journeys to the heavens, and so on—all these elements have a determinative function in shamanic vocations or conse-

120 H. R. Schoolcraft, cited by Pettazzoni, *Dio*, pp. 299 f.
121 See below, pp. 315 ff.

crations. Sometimes this complex of religious practices and ideas appears to be related to the myth of an ancient time when communication between sky and earth was much easier. Regarded from this point of view, the shamanic experience is equivalent to a restoration of that primordial mythical time and the shaman figures as a privileged being who individually returns to the fortunate condition of humanity at the dawn of time. Many myths some of which will be recounted or referred to in the following chapters, illustrate this paradisal state of a beatific *illud tempus* to which shamans intermittently return during their ecstasies

CHAPTER FIVE

Symbolism of the Shaman's Costume and Drum

Preliminary Remarks

THE shaman's costume itself constitutes a religious hierophany and cosmography; it discloses not only a sacred presence but also cosmic symbols and metapsychic itineraries. Properly studied, it reveals the system of shamanism as clearly as do the shamanic myths and techniques.[1]

1 General studies of the shaman's costume: V. N. Vasilyev, *Shamansky styum i buben u yakutov;* Kai Donner, "Ornements de la tête et de la chevere," especially pp. 10–20; Georg Nioradze, *Der Schamanismus bei den irischen Völkern,* pp. 60–78; K. F. Karjalainen, *Die Religion der Jugra-ölker,* II, 255–59; Hans Findeisen, "Der Mensch und seine Teile in der unst der Jennissejer (Keto)," especially pp. 311–13; E. J. Lindgren, "The aman Dress of the Dagurs, Solons and Numinchens in N. W. Manchuria"; . Harva (Holmberg), *The Shaman Costume and Its Significance;* id., *Die igiösen Vorstellungen der altaischen Völker,* pp. 499–525; Jorma Partanen, *Description of Buriat Shamanism,* pp. 18 ff.
See also L. Stieda, "Das Schamanenthum unter den Burjäten," p. 286; M. Mikhailowski, "Shamanism in Siberia and European Russia," pp. 81–; T. Lehtisalo, *Entwurf einer Mythologie der Jurak-Samojeden,* pp. 147 ff.; Sandschejew, "Weltanschauung und Schamanismus der Alaren-Burjaten," . 979–80; Å. Ohlmarks, *Studien zum Problem des Schamanismus,* pp. 211–; Donner, *La Sibérie,* pp. 226–27; id., *Ethnological Notes about the Yenisey-tyak (in the Turukhansk Region),* especially pp. 78–84; W. I. Jochelson, e *Yukhagir and the Yukaghirized Tungus,* pp. 169 f., 176–86 (Yakut), 6–91 (Tungus); id., *The Yakut,* pp. 107–18; S. M. Shirokogoroff, *Psychontal Complex of the Tungus,* pp. 287–303; W. Schmidt, *Der Ursprung der ttesidee,* XI, 616–26; XII, 720–33; L. Vajda, "Zur phaseologischen ellung des Schamanismus," p. 473, n. 2 (bibliography).
An abundant documentation on the costumes, ritual objects, and drums of

In winter the Altaic shaman puts on his costume over a shirt, in summer directly on his bare body. The Tungus use only the second method, in summer and winter alike. The same thing occurs among other Arctic peoples,[2] though in Northeast Siberia and among most Eskimo tribes there is no shamanic costume in the strict sense. The shaman bares his torso and (among the Eskimo, for example) retains a belt as his only garment. This quasi-nudity probably has a religious meaning, even if the warmth prevalent in Arctic dwellings would apparently suffice by itself to explain the custom. In any case, whether there is ritual nudity (as in the case of the Eskimo shamans) or a particular dress for the shamanic experience the important point is that the experience does not take place with the shaman wearing his profane, everyday dress. Even where a costume does not exist, it is replaced by the cap, the belt, the drum and other magical objects, which form part of the shaman's sacred wardrobe and which substitute for a costume proper. Thus, for example, Radlov[4] states that the Black Tatars, the Shor, and the Teleut have no shamanic costume; yet it often happens (as, for example, among the Lebed Tatars[5]) that use is made of a cloth

---

Siberian shamans will be found in S. V. Ivanov's comprehensive study *Materialy po izobrazitelnomu iskusstvu narodov Sibiri XIX—nachala XX v.* C especially pp. 66 ff., on the costumes and drums of Samoyed shamans (fig 47–57, 61–64, 67); 98 ff., on the Dolgan, Tungus, and Manchu (figs. 36–69 costumes, objects, and designs on shamanic drums among the Evenki 407 ff., on the Chukchee and Eskimo, etc. Chapters IV and V are devoted t the Turkic peoples (pp. 533 ff.) and the Buryat (pp. 691 ff.). Of outstanding interest are the Yakut drawings (figs. 15 ff.), the figures on shamanic drum (e.g., fig. 31), the Altaic drums (pp. 607 ff., fig. 89, etc.), and especially th numerous representations of Buryat *ongons* (idols) (figs. 5–8, 11–12, 19–26 on the *ongons*, cf. pp. 701 ff.).

2 Cf. Harva, *Die religiösen Vorstellungen*, p. 500.

3 It is reduced to a leather belt to which numerous fringes of caribou hide and small bone figures are attached; cf. K. Rasmussen, *Intellectual Culture the Iglulik Eskimos*, p. 114. The essential ritual instrument of the Eskimo shaman remains the drum.

4 *Aus Sibirien*, II, 17.

5 Harva, *Die religiösen Vorstellungen*, p. 501.

which is wound around the head and without which it would be impossible to shamanize.

In itself, the costume represents a religious microcosm qualitatively different from the surrounding profane space. For one thing, it constitutes an almost complete symbolic system; for another, its consecration has impregnated it with various spiritual forces and especially with "spirits." By the mere fact of donning it—or manipulating the objects that deputize for it—the shaman transcends profane space and prepares to enter into contact with the spiritual world. Usually this preparation is almost a concrete introduction into that world; for the costume is donned after many preliminaries and just on the eve of a shamanic trance.

The candidate is expected to see in dream the exact place where he will find his future costume, and he himself goes to look for it.[6] Then he buys it from the relatives of the dead shaman, paying (for example, among the Birartchen) a horse for it. But the costume is not allowed to leave the clan.[7] For in a certain sense it concerns the clan as a whole—not only because it was made or bought by contributions from the entire clan, but primarily because, being impregnated with "spirits," it must not be worn by anyone who cannot control them, for the result would be that they would trouble the whole community.[8]

The costume inspires the same feelings of fear and apprehension as any other object in which "spirits" reside.[9] When it becomes too worn, it is hung up in a tree in the forest; the "spirits" that inhabit leave it and attach themselves to the new costume.[10]

Among the sedentary Tungus, after the shaman's death his costume is kept in his house; the "spirits" that impregnate it show signs of life by making it shake, move, and so on. The nomadic

---

6 There are cases of progressive degeneration in the ritual making of the costume; formerly the Yeniseian shaman himself killed the reindeer from whose hide he would make his costume; today he buys the hide from the Russians (Nioradze, *Der Schamanismus*, p. 62).

7 Shirokogoroff, *Psychomental Complex*, p. 302.

8 Ibid.   9 Ibid., p. 301.

10 Ibid., p. 302.

Tungus, like most of the Siberian tribes, put the costume near the shaman's grave.[11] In many places the costume becomes unclean if, after it has been used in ministering to a sick person, he dies. The same is true of drums that have shown their inability to cure.[12]

The Siberian Costume

According to S. Shashkov (who wrote almost a century ago), every Siberian shaman was obliged to possess: (1) a caftan hung with iron disks and figures representing mythical animals; (2) a mask (among the Tadibei Samoyed, a kerchief, with which the shaman blindfolds his eyes so that he can enter the spirit world by his own inner light); (3) an iron or copper pectoral; (4) a cap, which the author considered to be one of the shaman's chief attributes. In the case of the Yakut, in the center of the back of the caftan, among the disks representing "the sun," there is a pierced disk; according to W. Sieroszewski,[13] it is called "the orifice of the sun" (*oïbonküngätä*), but usually it is supposed to represent the earth with its central opening, through which the shaman enters the underworld.[14] The back of the caftan also bears a lunar crescent, as well as an iron chain symbolizing the shaman's power and resistance.[15] According to the shamans, the iron disks serve as protection against the blows of the evil spirits. Tufts sewn to the fur of the caftan signify feathers.[16]

A fine Yakut shaman's costume, Sieroszewski states,[17] must have from thirty to fifty pounds of metal ornaments. It is princi-

11 Shirokogoroff, p. 301; Harva, *Die religiösen Vorstellungen*, p. 499, etc.

12 Donner, "Ornements," p. 10.

13 "Du chamanisme d'après les croyances des Yakoutes," p. 302.

14 See Nioradze, fig. 16; Harva, *Die religiösen Vorstellungen*, fig. 1. We shall see (pp. 261 ff.) what a consistent cosmology such a symbol implies. On the Yakut shaman's costume, see also W. Schmidt, *Der Ursprung*, X, 292–305 (after V. N. Vasilyev, E. K. Pekarsky, and M. A. Czaplicka). On the "moon" and the "sun," cf. ibid., pp. 300–04.

15 Mikhailowski, p. 81. The twofold symbolism of "iron" and "chain" is, of course, far more complex.

16 Ibid., p. 81 (after N. V. Pripuzov).

17 "Du chamanisme," p. 320.

pally the noise from the ornaments that transforms the shaman's dance into an infernal saraband. These metallic objects have a "soul"; they do not rust. "Along the arms are arranged bars representing the arm bones (*tabytala*). On the sides of the chest are sewn small leaves representing the ribs (*oïgos timir*); a little higher up, large round disks represent a woman's breasts, the liver, heart, and other internal organs. Representations of sacred animals and birds are often added. Finally, a small metal *ämägät* (the 'spirit of Madness') is also attached, in the form of a little canoe containing the image of a man." [18]

Among the Northern Tungus and those of Transbaikal two kinds of costume predominate—one in the form of a duck, the other in that of a reindeer.[19] The staff is carved at one end to resemble the head of a horse. From the back of the caftan hang ribbons a foot wide and three feet long, called *kulin* ("snakes").[20] Both the "horses" and the "snakes" are used in the shaman's journeys to the underworld. According to Shirokogoroff,[21] the iron objects of the Tungus—"moon," "sun," "stars," and so on—are borrowed from the Yakut. The "snakes" are taken from the Buryat and the Turks, the "horses" from the Buryat. (These details should be borne in mind for their bearing on the problem of southern influences on North Asian and Siberian shamanism.)

The Buryat Costume

P. S. Pallas, who wrote in the second half of the eighteenth century, describes the appearance of a Buryat shamaness: she had two sticks

18 Ibid., p. 321. The meanings and roles of these objects will become clearer later. On the *ämägät*, cf. E. Lot-Falck, "À propos d'Ätügän," p. 190 ff.

19 On the Tungus costume, cf. Shirokogoroff, *Psychomental Complex*, p. 288–97.

20 Among the Birartchen, the caftan is called *tabjan* (*tabyan*), the "boa constrictor" (ibid., p. 301). Since this reptile is unknown in northern countries, we here have an important proof of Central Asian influence on the Siberian shamanic complex.

21 Ibid., p. 290.

ending in horseheads and encircled by bells; thirty "snakes" made of black and white pelts hung from her shoulders to the ground; her cap was an iron casque with three points resembling deer horns.[22] But it is N. N. Agapitov and M. N. Khangalov [23] who have given the fullest description of the Buryat shaman. He must have: (1) a fur (*orgoï*), white for a "white" shaman (who is helped by the good spirits), black for a "black" shaman (who has evil spirits as helpers); on the fur are sewn a number of metallic figures representing horses, birds, and so on; (2) a cap in the shape of a lynx; after his fifth ablution (which takes place some time after his initiation) the shaman receives an iron casque [24] with its two ends bent to represent two horns; (3) a "stick-horse" of wood or iron; the wooden one is prepared on the eve of his first initiation, care being taken that the birch from which it is cut does not die; the other, of iron, received only after the fifth initiation, has its end sculptured into a horsehead and is decorated with numerous bells.

Here is the description given by the Buryat shaman's "Manual" translated from the Mongolian by Partanen:

An iron cap of which the crown consists of many iron bands and is furnished with two horns; behind there is an iron chain of nine links, and at its lower end a spear-like piece of iron; this is called the Backbone (*nigurasun*; cf. Tungus *nikima*, *nikama*, vertebra). On both sides of the iron cap, by the temples, there is an iron ring with three one *verša* (= 4.445 cm.) long pieces of iron, twisted by forging and called *qolbuga* (= union, being in couples or pairs; band, tie, bond). Silk, cotton, broadcloth, and velvet ribbons of the colours of various game and domestic animals, twisted into the likeness of the snake, are suspended on both sides of the cap and behind it; with them, cotton clippings of the colours of

22 *Reise durch verschiedene Provinzen des russischen Reiches*, III, 181–89. See the description of the costume of another Buryat shamaness, near Telenginsk, given by J. G. Gmelin, *Reise durch Sibirien, von dem Jahr 1738 bis 1743*, II, 11–13.

23 *Materialy dlya izuchenia shamanstva v Sibirii. Shamanstvo u buryat Irkutskoy gubernii*, pp. 42–44; cf. Mikhailowski, p. 82; Nioradze, *Der Schamanismus*, p. 77; W. Schmidt, *Der Ursprung*, X, 424–32.

24 See Agapitov and Khangalov, *Materialy*, fig. 3, Pl. II.

the skins of the *körüne*, the squirrel, and the yellow weasel are attached. This [headdress] is called *maiqabči* ("covering").

On a piece of cotton of the breadth of one span and a half, which is attached as a band to the collar of the coat, various figures of snakes, and game skins, are fastened. This is called *dalabči* ("wing") or *žiber* ("fin," also "wing"). . . .[25]

Two crutch-like staves of the length of about two ells, [roughly carved] to represent a horse's head at their upper ends; to the necks of these a ring with three *qolbugas* is attached, and this is called the horse's Mane; at their lower ends similar *qolbugas* are attached and called the horse's Tail; to the front part of these staves, in like manner, a *qolbuga* ring, and [in miniature] a stirrup, a spear, a sword, an axe, a sledge-hammer, a boat, an oar, a harpoon-head, etc. all made of iron, are fastened; below them, as before, three *qolbugas* rings are attached. These four [*qolbugas* rings] are called the Feet, and the two staves are called by the name of *sorbi*.

A whip of *suqai* rod, covered with musk-rat skin wound eight times about it, with an iron ring with three *qolbugas*, and with a sledge-hammer, a sword, a spear, a spiked club [all in miniature], and, in addition, with coloured strips of cotton and silk tied to it; this is called by the name of the Whip of the "living things." When shamanizing, [the *böge*] holds it with [a] *sorbi* in his hands; when he has to shamanize in yurts, he may use it alone.[26]

Several of these details will reappear later. For the moment, let us note the importance accorded to the Buryat shaman's "horse"; this is one of the characteristically Central and North Asian means of accomplishing the shamanic journey, and we shall find it elsewhere.[27] The shamans of the Olkhonsk Buryat have in addition a chest in which they keep their magical objects (drums, stick-horse, furs, bells, etc.) and which is usually decorated with images of the sun and moon. Nil, the Archbishop of Yaroslavl, mentions two further pieces of the Buryat shaman's equipment: *bagaldei*, a monstrous mask of hide, wood, or metal, on which is painted an enormous beard, and *toli*, a metal mirror with the

25 *A Description of Buriat Shamanism*, p. 18, § 19–20.

26 Ibid., p. 19, § 23–24.   27 Cf. below, pp. 325 f., 467 ff.

figures of twelve animals, hung on the chest or the back or sometimes sewn directly to the caftan. But according to Agapitov and
Khangalov,[28] these last two objects have practically disappeared
from use.[29] We shall soon come back to their occurrence elsewhere and their complex religious significance.

The Altaic Costume

Potanin's description of the Altaic shaman gives the impression
that his costume is more complete and better preserved than the
costumes of other Siberian shamans. His caftan is made of a goat
or reindeer skin. A quantity of ribbons and kerchiefs sewn to its
frock represent snakes, some of them being shaped into snakes'
heads with two eyes and open jaws. The tails of the larger snakes
are forked and sometimes three snakes have only one head. It is
said that a wealthy shaman should have 1,070 snakes on his
costume.[30] There are also a number of iron objects, among them
a miniature bow and arrows, to frighten the spirits.[31] On the

28 *Materialy*, p. 44.

29 For the Buryat shaman's mirror, bells, and other magical objects, see
also Partanen, § 26.

30 Farther north, the ophidian meaning of these ribbons is vanishing in
favor of a new magico-religious evaluation. Thus, for example, certain
Ostyak shamans told Kai Donner that the ribbons have the same properties
as hair ("Ornements de la tête et de la chevelure," p. 12; ibid., p. 14, fig.
[costume of an Ostyak shaman with a quantity of ribbons hanging to his
feet]; cf. Harva, *Die religiösen Vorstellungen*, fig. 78). The Yakut shamans
call the ribbons "hairs" (ibid., p. 516). We are in the presence of a transfer
of meaning, a frequent process in the history of religions; the magico-
religious value of snakes—a value unknown to most Siberian peoples—is
replaced, in the same object that elsewhere represents the "snakes," by the
magico-religious value of "hair." For long hair similarly signifies a strong
magico-religious power, concentrated, as we should expect, in sorcerers (for
example, the *muni* of *Ṛg-Veda*, X, 136, 7), kings (for example, the Babylonian kings), heroes (Samson), etc. But the testimony of the shamans
questioned by Donner stands more or less alone.

31 Another example of change in meaning, the bow and arrows being
first of all a symbol of magical flight and, as such, forming part of the shaman's apparatus for ascent.

back of the skirt are sewn animal pelts and two copper disks. The collar is decorated with a fringe of black and brown owl feathers. One shaman also had seven dolls sewn to his collar, each with a brown owl's feather for a head. These, he said, were the seven celestial virgins and the seven bells were the seven virgins' voices calling the spirits.[32] Elsewhere the virgins number nine and are believed to be the daughters of Bai Ülgän.[33]

Still other objects are attached to the shaman's costume, each of them having religious meaning. Among the Altaians, for instance, there are two little monsters, inhabitants of the kingdom of Erlik Khan, *jutpa* and *arba,* the one made of black or brown cloth, the other of green, with two pairs of feet, a tail, and with open jaws.[34] Among the peoples of the Siberian Far North, we find certain images of water birds, such as the gull and the swan, which symbolize the shaman's immersion in the submarine underworld, a conception to which we shall return when we study Eskimo beliefs; a number of mythical animals (the bear, the dog, the eagle with a ring around its neck, symbolizing—according to the Yeniseians [35]—that the imperial bird is at the shaman's service); and even drawings of the human sexual organs,[36] which also help to sanctify the costume.[37]

The Shaman's Mirrors and Caps

Among the different Tungusic groups of northern Manchuria (Tungus, Khingan, Birartchen, etc.) copper mirrors play an im-

32 G. N. Potanin, *Ocherki severo-zapadnoi Mongolii,* IV, 49–54; cf. Mikhailowski, p. 84; Harva, *Die religiösen Vorstellungen,* p. 595; W. Schmidt, *Der Ursprung,* IX, 254 f. On the shamanic costume used among the Altaians and the Abakan Tatars, see also ibid., pp. 251–57, 694–96.

33 See, for example, Harva, *Die religiösen Vorstellungen,* p. 505.

34 Ibid., figs. 69–70 (after A. V. Anokhin).

35 Cf. Nioradze, p. 70.   36 Ibid.

37 One wonders if the coappearance of the two sexual symbols (see, for example, Nioradze, fig. 32, after V. I. Anuchin) on the same ornament does not imply a vague memory of ritual androgynization. Cf. also B. D. Shimkin, "A Sketch of the Ket, or Yenisei 'Ostyak,' " p. 161.

portant role.[38] Their origin is clearly Sino-Manchurian,[39] but their magical meaning varies from tribe to tribe; the mirror is said to help the shaman to "see the world" (that is, to concentrate), or to "place the spirits," or to reflect the needs of mankind, and so on. V. Diószegi has shown that the Manchu-Tungusic term designating the mirror, *pañaptu*, is derived from *paña*, "soul, spirit," more precisely the "soul-shade." Hence the mirror is a receptacle (*-ptu*) for the "soul-shade." Looking into the mirror, the shaman is able to see the dead person's soul.[40] Some Mongol shamans see in the mirror the "white horse of the shamans." [41] The courser is pre-eminently the shamanic animal; the gallop and dizzying speed are traditional expressions of "flight," that is, of ecstasy.[42]

As to the cap, in certain tribes (for example, the Yurak-Samoyed) it is considered the most important part of the shamanic dress. "According to these shamans, then, a great part of their power is hidden in these caps." [43] "This is why usually, when a shamanic exhibition is given at the request of Russians, the shaman performs without his cap." [44] "When I questioned them about this, they told me that, shamanizing without a cap, they were deprived of all real power and that hence the whole ceremony was only a parody principally intended to amuse the audience." [45]

---

38 Cf. Shirokogoroff, *Psychomental Complex*, p. 296.

39 Ibid., p. 299.

40 Cf. "Tunguso-manchzhurskoye zerkalo shamana," especially pp. 367 ff. On the mirror of the Tungus shamans, cf. also Shirokogoroff, pp. 278, 299 ff.

41 W. Heissig, "Schamanen und Geisterbeschwörer im Küriye-Banner," p. 46.

42 See below, pp. 467 ff.   43 Donner, "Les Ornements," p. 11.

44 Id., *La Sibérie*, p. 227.

45 Id., "Les Ornements," p. 11. "The importance accorded to the cap also appears from ancient rock drawings of the Bronze Age, in which the shaman is equipped with a cap that is clearly apparent but in which all the other attributes indicative of his dignity may be lacking" (id., *La Sibérie*, p. 277). But Karjalainen does not credit the autochthonous character of the shamanic cap among the Ostyak and the Vogul; he is more inclined to see a Samoyed influence (cf. *Die Religion der Jugra-Völker*, III, 256 f.). In any

In western Siberia the cap consists of a broad strip wound around the head, with lizards or other tutelary animals and innumerable ribbons hanging from it. East of the Ket, the caps "sometimes resemble crowns furnished with reindeer horns made of iron, sometimes they are made of a bear's head with the principal parts of the skin of the beast's head attached." [46] The commonest type is the one representing reindeer horns,[47] although among the eastern Tungus some shamans insist that the iron horns with which their caps are decorated imitate stag horns.[48] Elsewhere, both in the north (as among the Samoyed) and the south (as among the Altaians), the shamanic cap is decorated with feathers—swan, eagle, owl. Thus, for example, feathers of the golden eagle or the brown owl are used among the Altaians,[49] owl feathers among the Soyot, Karagas, and others.[50] Certain Teleut shamans make their caps from the skin of a brown owl, leaving the wings, and sometimes the head, as decorations.[51]

---

case, the question has not been settled. The Kazak-Kirgiz *baqça* "wears the traditional *malakhaï*, a sort of pointed cap of sheepskin or foxskin, which hangs far down the back. Certain *baqças* wear a no less strange headgear of felt, covered with red camel's-hair cloth; others, more especially in the steppes near the Syr Darya, the Chu, the Aral Sea, wear a turban that is almost always blue in color" (J. Castagné, "Magie et exorcisme chez les Kazak-Kirghizes et autres peuples turcs orientaux," pp. 66–67). Cf. also R. A. Stein, *Recherches sur l'épopée et le barde au Tibet*, pp. 342 ff.

46 Donner, *La Sibérie*, p. 228; see also Harva, *Die religiösen Vorstellungen*, pp. 514 f., figs. 82, 83, 86.

47 Ibid., pp. 516 ff.

48 On the shamanic cap with stag horns, see Diószegi, "Golovnoi ubor nanaiskikh (goldskikh) shamanov," pp. 87 ff. and figs. 1, 3–4, 6, 9, 11, 22–23.

49 Potanin, *Ocherki*, IV, 49 ff. See also the exhaustive study of the Altaic cap in Anokhin, *Materialy po shamanstvu u altaitsev*, pp. 46 ff.

50 Harva, *Die religiösen Vorstellungen*, pp. 508 ff.

51 Mikhailowski, p. 84. In some regions the brown owl cap cannot be worn by a shaman immediately after his consecration. In the course of the *kamlanie* (séance) the spirits reveal at what time the cap and other higher insignia can be donned by the new shaman without danger (ibid., pp. 84–85).

Ornithological Symbolism

It is clear that, through all these ornaments, the shamanic costume tends to give the shaman a new, magical body in animal form. The three chief types are that of the bird, the reindeer (stag), and the bear—but especially the bird. We will return to the meaning of the bodies in the form of the reindeer and the bear. For the moment we will consider the ornithomorphic costume.[52] Feathers are mentioned more or less everywhere in the descriptions of shamanic costumes. More significantly, the very structure of the costumes seeks to imitate as faithfully as possible the shape of a bird. Thus the Altaic shamans, those of the Minusinsk Tatars, of the Teleut, Soyot, and Karagas, try to make their costumes resemble an owl.[53] The Soyot costume may even be considered a perfect ornithophany.[54] The bird most often imitated is the eagle.[55] Among the Goldi the predominating costume is also that in the form of a bird.[56] The same is true of the Siberian peoples living farther north, the Dolgan, the Yakut, and the Tungus. Among the Yukagir the costume includes feathers.[57] A Tungus shaman's boot imitates the foot of a bird.[58] The most complicated form of the ornithomorphic costume is found among the Yakut shamans; their costume displays a complete bird skeleton of iron.[59] Indeed, according to Shirokogoroff, the center of dissemination for the bird-form costume appears to be the region today occupied by the Yakut.

52 On the relations between shaman and bird and the ornithological symbolism of the costume, cf. H. Kirchner, "Ein archäologischer Beitrag zur Urgeschichte der Schamanismus," pp. 255 ff.

53 Harva, *Die religiösen Vorstellungen*, pp. 504 f.

54 Ibid., figs. 71–73, 87–88, pp. 507–08, 519–20. Cf. also W. Schmidt, *Der Ursprung*, XI, 430–31.

55 Cf. Leo Sternberg, "Der Adlerkult bei den Völkern Sibiriens," p. 145.

56 Shirokogoroff, p. 296.

57 Jochelson, *The Yukaghir*, pp. 169–76.

58 Harva, *Die religiösen Vorstellungen*, p. 511, fig. 76.

59 Shirokogoroff, p. 296.

Even where the costume presents no visible ornithomorphic structure—as, for example, among the Manchu, who have been strongly influenced by successive waves of Sino-Buddhist culture [60] —the headgear is made of feathers and imitates a bird.[61] The Mongol shaman has "wings" on his shoulders and feels that he is changed into a bird as soon as he dons his costume.[62] Probably, in former times, the ornithomorphic appearance was still more accentuated among the Altaians in general.[63] Today owl feathers decorate only the staff of the Kazak-Kirgiz *baqça*.[64]

On the authority of his Tungus informants, Shirokogoroff adds that the bird costume is indispensable to flight to the other world: "They say that it is easier to go, when the costume is light." [65] It is for the same reason that, in the legends, a shamaness flies into the air as soon as she acquires her magical plumage.[66] Ohlmarks [67] believes that this complex is Arctic in origin and should be directly connected with the beliefs in "helping spirits" who aid the shaman to perform his aerial journey. But as we have already seen, and shall see again later, the same aerial symbolism is found more or less all over the world, precisely in connection with shamans, sorcerers, and the mythical beings that the latter sometimes personify.

But we must also consider the mythical relations that exist between the eagle and the shaman. The eagle, it will be remembered, is held to be the father of the first shaman, plays a consider-

60 Ibid.   61 Ibid., p. 295.

62 Ohlmarks, *Studien*, p. 211.

63 Harva, *Die religiösen Vorstellungen*, p. 504.

64 Castagné, "Magie et exorcisme," p. 67.

65 *Psychomental Complex*, p. 296.

66 Ohlmarks, p. 212. The folklore motif of flight by the aid of birds' feathers is quite widespread, especially in North America; see Stith Thompson, *Motif-Index*, III, 10, 381. Still more frequent is the motif of a bird-fairy, who, married to a mortal, flies away as soon as she is able to get possession of the plumage that her husband has long kept from her. Cf., for example, U. Holmberg, *Finno-Ugric [and] Siberian [Mythology]*, p. 501. See also the legend of the Buryat shamaness who rises on her magical eight-legged horse, below, p. 469.

67 *Studien*, p. 211.

able role in the shaman's initiation, and, finally, is at the center of a mythical complex that includes the World Tree and the shaman's ecstatic journey. Nor must we forget that the eagle in a manner represents the Supreme Being, even if in strongly solarized form. All these elements, it would seem, concur to define the religious meaning of the shaman's costume with considerable precision: to don it is to return to the mystical state revealed and established during the protracted experiences and ceremonies of the shaman's initiation.

Symbolism of the Skeleton

This is further substantiated by the fact that the shaman's costume bears certain iron objects imitating bones and also tending to give it, at least partially, the appearance of a skeleton.[68] Certain authors, among them Holmberg (Harva),[69] have considered that it is the skeleton of a bird. But as early as 1902 Troshchansky showed that, at least in the case of the Yakut shaman, these iron "bones" seek to imitate a human skeleton. A Yenisean told Kai Donner that the bones were the shaman's own skeleton.[70] Harva himself[7] became a convert to the idea that it is a human skeleton, although meanwhile (1910) E. K. Pekarsky had put forward another hypothesis: that it is, rather, a combination of human and bird skeleton. Among the Manchu the "bones" are made of iron and steel, and the shamans state (at least in our day) that they represent wings.[72] However, there is no longer any possible doubt that in many cases, they were seen as representing a human skeleton

68 See, for example, H. Findeisen, "Der Mensch und seine Teile in der Kunst der Jennissejer (Keto)," figs. 37–38 (after Anuchin, figs. 16 and 37). Cf. also Findeisen, *Schamanentum*, pp. 86 ff.

69 *The Shaman Costume*, pp. 14 f.

70 Donner: "Beiträge zur Frage nach dem Ursprung der Jenissei Ostjaken," p. 15; *Ethnological Notes about the Yenissey-Ostyak*, p. 80. More recently, this author seems to have changed his opinion: cf. *La Sibérie*, p. 228.

71 *Die religiösen Vorstellungen*, p. 514.   72 Shirokogoroff, p. 294.

Findeisen reproduces [73] an iron object that admirably imitates the human tibia.[74]

However this may be, basically the two hypotheses come down to the same fundamental idea: by attempting to imitate a skeleton, be it a man's or a bird's, the shamanic costume proclaims the special status of its wearer, who is in some sort one who has been dead and has returned to life. We have seen that, among the Yakut, the Buryat, and other Siberian peoples, shamans are believed to have been killed by the spirits of their ancestors, who, after "cooking" their bodies, counted their bones and replaced them, fastening them together with iron and covering them with new flesh.[75] Now, among hunting peoples bones represent the final source of life, both human and animal, the source from which the species is reconstituted at will. This is why the bones of game are not broken, but carefully gathered up and disposed of according to custom, that is, buried, placed on platforms or in trees, thrown into the sea, and so on.[76] From this point of view the burial of animals exactly follows the method used for disposing of human remains.[77] For, in both cases alike, the "soul" is presumed to reside in the bones and hence the resurrection of the individual from its bones can be expected.

Now, the skeleton present in the shaman's costume summarizes and reactualizes the drama of his initiation, that is, the drama of

73 "Der Mensch und seine Teile," fig. 39.

74 In the Berliner Museum für Völkerkunde.

75 Cf. H. Nachtigall, "Die kulturhistorische Wurzel der Schamanenske-ttierung," passim. On the North Eurasian people's concept of bone as the seat of the soul, cf. Ivar Paulson, *Die primitiven Seelenvorstellungen der nordeurasischen Völker*, pp. 137 ff., 202 ff., 236 ff.

76 Cf. Holmberg (Harva): "Über die Jagdriten der nördlichen Völker Asiens und Europas," pp. 34 ff.; *Die religiösen Vorstellungen*, pp. 434 f.; Adolf Friedrich, "Knochen und Skelett in der Vorstellungswelt Nordasiens," p. 194 f.; K. Meuli, "Griechische Opferbräuche," pp. 234 ff., containing a very copious documentation; Nachtigall, "Die erhöhte Bestattung in Nord- und Hochasien," passim.

77 Harva, *Die religiösen Vorstellungen*, pp. 440–41.

death and resurrection. It is of small importance whether it is supposed to represent a human or an animal skeleton. In either case what is involved is the life-substance, the primal matter preserved by the mythical ancestors. The human skeleton in a manner represents the archetype of the shaman, since it is believed to represent the family from which the ancestral shamans were successively born. (Family stock is designated as "bones"; "from N's bone" is used to express "descendant of N.") [78] The bird skeleton is a variant of the same conception: on the one hand, the first shaman is born from the union between an eagle and a woman; on the other, the shaman himself attempts to turn into a bird and fly, and, indeed, *he is* a bird in so far as, like the bird, he has access to the higher regions. A similar theory underlies the cases in which the skeleton—or the mask—transforms the shaman into some other animal (stag, etc.).[79] For the mythical animal ancestor is conceived as the inexhaustible matrix of the life of the species, and this matrix is found in these animals' bones. One hesitates to speak of totemism. Rather, it is a matter of mystical relations between man and his prey, relations that are fundamental for hunting societies and that both Friedrich and Meuli have recently elucidated.

Rebirth from the Bones

That the hunted or domesticated animal can be reborn from its bones is a belief also found in regions outside Siberia. Frazer had already recorded some American examples.[80] According to Fro-

78 Cf. A. Friedrich and G. Buddruss, *Schamanengeschichten aus Sibirien*, pp. 36 f.

79 For example, the Tungus shaman's costume represents a stag, whose skeleton is suggested by pieces of iron. Its horns are also of iron. According to Yakut legends, the shamans fight one another in the form of bulls, etc. Cf. ibid., p. 212; see above, pp. 94 f.

80 Many Minitari Indians "believe that the bones of those bisons which they have slain and divested of flesh rise again clothed with renewed flesh and quickened with life, and become fat, and fit for slaughter the succeeding June" (*Spirits of the Corn and of the Wild*, II, 256). The same custom i.

benius, this mythico-ritual motif is still alive among the Aranda, the tribes of interior South America, the African Bushmen and Hamites.[81] Friedrich has added to and integrated the African data,[82] rightly regarding them as an expression of pastoral spirituality. The same mythico-ritual complex has, in addition, been preserved in more developed cultures, whether in the religious tradition itself or in the form of tales.[83] A legend of the Gagauzi (South Bessarabia and North Dobrudja) relates that, to supply wives for his sons, Adam gathered up the bones of various animals and prayed to God to animate them.[84] In an Armenian tale a hunter witnessed a wedding of wood spirits. Invited to the banquet, he abstained from eating but kept the ox rib that he was served. Later, when the spirits gathered up all the animal's bones to bring it back to life, they had to replace the missing rib by a walnut tree branch.[85]

In this connection an incident from the *Prose Edda* may be cited—the accident that befell one of Thor's goats. On a journey

---

found among the Dakota, the Eskimo of Baffinland and Hudson Bay, the Yuracare of Bolivia, the Lapps, etc. See ibid., II, 247 f.; O. Zerries, *Wild- und Buschgeister in Südamerika*, pp. 174 ff., 303–04; L. Schmidt, "Der 'Herr der Tiere' in einigen Sagenlandschaften Europas und Eurasiens," pp. 525 ff. Cf. also Émile Nourry (P. Saintyves, pseud.), *Les Contes de Perrault*, pp. 39 f.; C. M. Edsman, *Ignis divinus: le feu comme moyen de rajeunissement et d'immortalité*, pp. 151 ff.

81 *Kulturgeschichte Afrikas*, pp. 183–85.

82 *Afrikanische Priestertümer*, pp. 184–89.

83 Waldemar Liungman (*Traditionswanderungen, Euphrat-Rhein*, II, 1078 f.) cites the fact that the interdict against breaking the bones of animals is found in the tales of the Jews and the ancient Germans, in the Caucasus, Transylvania, Austria, the Alpine countries, France, Belgium, England, and Sweden. But, bound to his Orientalo-disseminationist theories, the Swedish scholar holds all these beliefs to be comparatively recent and of Oriental origin.

84 C. Fillingham Coxwell, comp. and ed., *Siberian and Other Folk-Tales*, p. 422.

85 Ibid., p. 1020. T. Lehtisalo ("Der Tod und die Wiedergeburt des künftigen Schamanen," p. 19) cites the similar adventure of the Bogdan hero Gesser Khan: a calf killed and eaten is reborn from its bones, but one is missing.

with his carriage and goats, Thor lodged in a peasant's house. "About evening, Thor took his he-goats and slaughtered them both; after that they were flayed and borne to the caldron. When the cooking was done, then Thor and his companion sat down to supper. Thor invited to meat with him the husbandman and his wife, and their children. . . . Then Thor laid the goat-hides farther away from the fire, and said that the husbandman and his servants should cast the bones on the goat-hides. Thjálfi, the husbandman's son, was holding a thigh-bone of the goat; and split it with his knife and broke it for the marrow.

"Thor tarried there overnight; and in the interval before day he rose up and clothed himself, took the hammer Mjöllnir, swung it up, and hallowed the goat-hides; straightway the he-goats rose up and then one of them was lame in a hind leg." [86]

This episode bears witness to the survival, among the ancient Germans, of the archaic conception held by the hunting and nomadic peoples. It is not necessarily a characteristic of the "shamanistic" spirituality. We have, however, cited it now, while deferring our examination of the vestiges of Indo-Aryan shamanism until we have obtained a general view of shamanic theories and practices.

Further in connection with resurrection from bones, we might cite the famous vision of Ezekiel, although it belongs to an entirely different religious horizon from that of the examples already given. "The hand of the Lord was upon me, and carried me out in the spirit of the Lord, and set me down in the midst of the valley which was full of bones. . . . And he said unto me, Son of man, can these bones live? And I answered, O Lord God, thou knowest. Again he said unto me, Prophesy upon these bones, and say unto them, O ye dry bones, hear the word of the Lord. Thus saith the Lord God unto these bones; Behold, I will cause breath to enter into you, and ye shall live: . . . and ye shall know

---

86 *Prose Edda*, ch. xxvi (tr. A. G. Brodeur, p. 57). This episode is the subject of a richly documented study by C. W. von Sydow, "Tors färd till Utgard. I: Tors bockslaktning," used by Edsman, *Ignis divinus*, pp. 52 ff. Cf. also J. W. E. Mannhardt, *Germanische Mythen*, pp. 57–75.

that I am the Lord. So I prophesied, as I was commanded: and as I prophesied, there was a noise, and behold a shaking, and the bones came together, bone to his bone. And when I beheld, lo, the sinews and the flesh came up upon them. . . ." [87]

Friedrich also cites a painting, discovered by Grünwedel in the ruins of a temple at Sängimäghiz, which represents a man being resurrected from his bones by the blessing of a Buddhist monk.[88] This is not the place to go into the details of Iranian influence on Buddhist India nor to broach the still scarcely studied problem of the similarities between the Tibetan and Iranian traditions. As J. J. Modi [89] observed some time ago, there is a striking resemblance between the Tibetan and Iranian customs of exposing corpses. Both leave the body to be devoured by dogs and vultures; to the Tibetans, it is of the utmost importance that the body should be transformed into a skeleton as quickly as possible. The Iranians put the bones in the *astodan*, the "place of bones," where they await resurrection.[90] We may consider this custom a survival of pastoral spirituality.

In the magical folklore of India certain saints and yogins are believed to be able to raise the dead from their bones or ashes; Gorakhnāth does so,[91] for example, and it is worth noting at this point that this famous magician is regarded as the founder of a

---

87 Ez. 37:1–8 ff. See also the Book of the Dead, ch. cxxv; in Egypt too, the bones were to be preserved for resurrection. Cf. Koran 2:259. In an Aztec legend mankind is born from bones brought from the nether region; cf. H. B. Alexander, *Latin-American* [*Mythology*], p. 90.

88 A. Grünwedel, *Die Teufel des Avesta und ihre Beziehungen zur Ikonographie des Buddhismus Zentral-Asiens*, II, 68–69, fig. 62; A. Friedrich, Knochen und Skelett," p. 230.

89 Cf. "The Tibetan Mode of the Disposal of the Dead," pp. 1 f.; Friedrich, p. 227. Cf. *Yašt*, 13, 11; *Bundahišn*, 220 (rebirth from the bones).

90 Cf. the house of bones in a Great Russian legend (Coxwell, *Siberian and Other Folk-Tales*, p. 682). It would be interesting, in the light of these facts, to re-examine Iranian dualism, which, to express the opposite of "spiritual," uses the term *uštāna*, "bony." In addition, as Friedrich remarks (pp. 245 f.), the demon Aštôvidatu, which means "bone-breaker," is not unrelated to the evil spirits that torment Yakut, Tungus, and Buryat shamans.

91 See, for example, George W. Briggs, *Gorakhnāth and the Kānphaṭā Yogis*, pp. 189, 190.

Yogic-tantric sect, the Kānphaṭā Yogis, among whom we shall find several other shamanic survivals. Finally, it will be enlightening to cite certain Buddhistic meditations directed to obtaining a vision of the body becoming a skeleton; [92] the important role of human skulls and bones in Lamaism and tantrism; [93] the skeleton dance in Tibet and Mongolia; [94] the part played by the *brāhma-randhra* (= *sutura frontalis*) in Tibetan-Indian ecstatic techniques and in Lamaism; [95] and so on. All these rites and concepts seem to us to show that, despite their present incorporation into very diverse systems, the archaic traditions that find the vital principle in the bones have not completely disappeared from the Asian spiritual horizon.

But bone also plays other roles in shamanic myths and rites. Thus, for example, when the Vasyugan-Ostyak shaman sets out in search of the patient's soul, he travels to the other world in a boat made of a chest and uses a shoulder bone as oar.[96] We should also cite in this connection divination by the shoulder bone of a ram or sheep, extensively practiced among the Kalmyk, the Kirgiz, the Mongols; by a seal's shoulder blade among the Koryak.[97]

92 Cf. A. M. Pozdneyev, *Dhyāna und Samādhi im mongolischen Lamaismus*, pp. 24 f. On the "meditations on death" in Taoism, cf. Rousselle, "Die Typen der Meditation in China," especially pp. 30 ff.

93 Cf. Robert Bleichsteiner, *L'Église jaune*, p. 222; Friedrich, p. 211.

94 Bleichsteiner, p. 222; Friedrich, p. 225.

95 Eliade, *Yoga: Immortality and Freedom*, pp. 321 ff., 419 f.; Friedrich, p. 236.

96 Karjalainen, *Die Religion der Jugra-Völker*, II, 335.

97 The essential details have already been given by R. Andree, "Scapulimantia." See also Friedrich, pp. 214 f.; add to his bibliography: G. I. Kitiredge, *Witchcraft in Old and New England*, pp. 144, 462, n. 44. The center of gravity for this technique of divination appears to be Central Asia (cf. B. Laufer, "Columbus and Cathay, and the Meaning of America to the Orientalist," p. 99); it was frequently used in protohistorical China from the Shang period (see H. G. Creel, *The Birth of China*, pp. 21 ff., 185 ff.). The same technique prevails among the Lolo; cf. L. Vannicelli, *La religion dei Lolo*, p. 151. North American scapulimancy, which is confined to the tribes of Labrador and Quebec, is of Asian origin; cf. John M. Cooper, "Northern Algonkian Scrying and Scapulimancy," and Laufer, p. 99. See also E. J. Eisenberger, "Das Wahrsagen aus dem Schulterblatt," passim.

Divination itself is a technique particularly adapted to actualizing the spiritual realities that are the basis of shamanism or to facilitating contact with them. Here again the animal's bone symbolizes the mystery of life in continual regeneration and hence includes in itself, if only virtually, everything that pertains to the past and future of life.

We do not believe that we have strayed too far from our subject—the skeleton represented by the shamanic costume—in citing all these practices and concepts. Nearly all of them belong to similar or homologizable levels of culture, and, by enumerating them, we have indicated certain datum points in the vast field of the culture of hunters and herders. Let us make it clear, however, that all these vestiges do not equally denote a "shamanic" structure. And let us add that, in regard to the parallels established among certain Tibetan, Mongol, North Asian, and even Arctic customs, it is necessary to take into consideration influences from South Asia and especially from India. To these we shall have to return.

Shamanic Masks

It will be remembered that among the objects possessed by the Buryat shaman, Nil, the Archbishop of Yaroslavl, listed a monstrous mask.[98] In our day its use has disappeared among the Buryat. In fact, shamanic masks occur rather infrequently in Siberia and North Asia. Shirokogoroff cites a single case in which a Tungus shaman had improvised a mask "to show that the spirit of *malu* in him." [99] Among the Chukchee, Koryak, Kamchadal, Yukagir, and Yakut the mask plays no part in shamanism; rather, it is used, sporadically, to frighten children (as among the Chukchee)

, Hoffmann, *Quellen zur Geschichte der tibetischen Bon-Religion*, pp. 193 ff.; Leopold Schmidt, "Pelops und die Haselhexe," p. 72, n. 28; Fritz Boehm, "Spatulimantie," passim; F. Altheim, *Geschichte der Hunnen*, I, 268 ff.; R. Bawden, "On the Practice of Scapulimancy among the Mongols."
98 See above, pp. 151 f.   99 *Psychomental Complex*, p. 152, n. 2.

and, at funerals, to avoid recognition by the souls of the dead (Yukagir). Of the Eskimo peoples, it is principally among the Eskimo of Alaska, who have been strongly influenced by American Indian culture, that the shaman uses a mask.[100]

In Asia the few attested cases come almost exclusively from southern tribes. Among the Black Tatars shamans sometimes use a birch-bark mask, with mustache and eyebrows made of squirrels' tails.[101] The same is true of the Tatars of Tomsk.[102] In the Altai and among the Goldi, when the shaman leads the dead person's soul to the Kingdom of Shades, he daubs his face with suet in order not to be recognized by the spirits.[103] The same custom is found elsewhere, and used for the same purpose, in the bear sacrifice.[104] In this connection it would be well to remember that the custom of anointing the face with fat is fairly widespread among "primitives" and that its meaning is not always as simple as it seems. A disguise or defense against spirits is not always in question, but, rather, an elementary technique for magical participation in the world of spirits. So we find that, in many parts of the world, masks represent ancestors and their wearers are believed to incarnate these.[105] Daubing the face with fat is one of the simplest ways of masking oneself, that is, of incarnating the souls of the dead. Elsewhere masks are connected with men's secret societies and the cult of ancestors. Historico-cultural research considers that the complex made up of masks, ancestor cult, and initiatory secret societies belongs to the cultural cycle of matri-

100 See Ohlmarks, pp. 65 f.

101 G. N. Potanin, *Ocherki severo-zapadnoi Mongolii*, IV, 54; Harva, *Die religiösen Vorstellungen*, p. 524.

102 D. Zelenin, "Ein erotischer Ritus in den Opferungen der altaischen Tuerken," pp. 84 f.

103 Radlov, *Aus Sibirien*, II, 55; Harva, *Die religiösen Vorstellungen*, p. 525.

104 Nioradze, *Der Schamanismus*, p. 77.

105 K. Meuli: "Maske"; *Schweizer Masken*, pp. 44 ff.; A. Slawik, "Kultische Geheimbünde der Japaner und Germanen," pp. 717 ff.; K. Ranke, *Indogermanische Totenverehrung*, I, 117 ff.

archy, secret societies being, according to this interpretation, a reaction against the domination of women.[106]

The rarity of shamanic masks should not surprise us. As Harva has rightly observed,[107] the shaman's costume is itself a mask and may be regarded as derived from a mask originally. An attempt has been made to prove the Oriental—and hence recent—origin of Siberian shamanism by citing, among other things, the fact that masks are more frequent in southern Asia and become increasingly rare and finally disappear in the Far North.[108] We cannot here enter upon a discussion of the "origin" of Siberian shamanism. Yet we may note that, in North Asian and Arctic shamanism, the costume and mask have been variously evaluated. In some places [109] the mask is believed to aid concentration. We have seen that the kerchief covering the shaman's eyes or even his whole face plays a similar role in certain instances. Sometimes, too, even if there is no mention of a mask properly speaking, an object of such a nature is present—for example, the furs and kerchiefs that, among the Goldi and the Soyot, almost cover the shaman's head.[110]

For these reasons, and taking into consideration the various valuations given them in the rituals and techniques of ecstasy, we may conclude that the mask plays the same role as the shaman's costume and the two elements can be considered interchangeable. For wherever it is used (and outside of the shamanic ideology properly speaking), the mask manifestly announces the incarnation

---

106 Cf., for example, Georges Montandon, *Traité d'ethnologie culturelle*, p. 723 ff. See the reservations, for America, expressed by A. L. Kroeber and Catharine Holt, "Masks and Moieties as a Culture Complex," and W. Schmidt's reply, "Die kulturhistorische Methode und die nordamerikanische Ethnologie," pp. 553 ff.

107 *Die religiösen Vorstellungen*, pp. 524 f.

108 Cf. A. Gahs in W. Schmidt, *Der Ursprung*, III, 336 ff.; for the opposite opinion, Ohlmarks, pp. 65 f. See below, pp. 496 ff.

109 For example, among the Samoyed (Castrén, cited by Ohlmarks, p. 67).

110 Harva, figs. 86–88.

of a mythical personage (ancestor, mythical animal, god).[111] For its part, the costume transubstantiates the shaman, it transforms him, before all eyes, into a superhuman being. And this is equally true whether the predominant attribute that it seeks to display is the prestige of a dead man returned to life (skeleton) or ability to fly (bird), or the condition of husband to a "celestial spouse" (women's dress, feminine attributes), and so forth.

The Shamanic Drum

The drum has a role of the first importance in shamanic ceremonies.[112] Its symbolism is complex, its magical functions many and various. It is indispensable in conducting the shamanic séance, whether it carries the shaman to the "Center of the World," or enables him to fly through the air, or summons and "imprisons" the spirits, or, finally, if the drumming enables the shaman to concentrate and regain contact with the spiritual world through which he is preparing to travel.

It will be remembered that several initiatory dreams of future shamans included a mystical journey to the "Center of the World," to the seat of the Cosmic Tree and the Universal Lord. It is from a branch of this Tree, which the Lord causes to fall for the purpose

111 On the masks of prehistoric magicians and their religious meaning cf. J. Maringer, *Vorgeschichtliche Religion: Religionen im Steinzeitlichen Europa*, pp. 184 ff.

112 In addition to the bibliography given in n. 1, p. 145, see A. A. Popov, *Seremonia ozhivlenia bubna u ostyak-samoyedov*; J. Partanen, *A Description of Buriat Shamanism*, p. 20; W. Schmidt, *Der Ursprung*, IX, 258 ff., 696 (Altaians, Abakan Tatars); XI, 306 f. (Yakut), 541 (Yeniseians); XI 733–45 (synopsis); E. Emsheimer, "Schamanentrommel und Trommelbaum"; id., "Zur Ideologie der lappischen Zaubertrommel"; id., "Eine sibirische Parallele zur lappischen Zaubertrommel"; Ernst Manker, *Die lappische Zaubertrommel. II: Die Trommel als Urkunde geistigen Lebens*, especially pp. 61 ff.; H. Findeisen, *Schamanentum*, pp. 148–61; Lászó Vajda, "Zur phaseologischen Stellung des Schamanismus," p. 475, n. V. Diószegi, "Die Typen und interethnischen Beziehungen der Schamanentrommeln bei den Selkupen (Ostjak-Samojeden)"; E. Lot-Falck, "L'Animation du tambour"; id., "À propos d'un tambour de chaman toungouse

that the shaman makes the shell of his drum.[113] The meaning of this symbolism seems sufficiently apparent from the complex of which it is a part: communication between sky and earth by means of the World Tree, that is, by the Axis that passes through the "Center of the World." *By the fact that the shell of his drum is derived from the actual wood of the Cosmic Tree, the shaman, through his drumming, is magically projected into the vicinity of the Tree;* he is projected to the "Center of the World," and thus can ascend to the sky.

Seen in this light, the drum can be assimilated to the shamanic tree with its notches, up which the shaman symbolically climbs to the sky. Climbing the birch or playing his drum, the shaman approaches the World Tree and then ascends it. The Siberian shamans also have their personal trees, which are simply representatives of the Cosmic Tree; some shamans also use "inverted trees," [114] that is, trees planted with their roots in the air, which, as is well known, are among the most archaic symbols of the World Tree. This whole series of facts, combined with the relations already noted between the shaman and the ceremonial birches, shows the intimate connection between the Cosmic Tree, the shaman's drum, and ascending to the sky.

Even the choice of the wood from which the shaman will make the shell of his drum depends entirely on the "spirits" or a transhuman will. The Ostyak-Samoyed shaman takes his ax and, closing his eyes, enters a forest and touches a tree at random; from this tree his comrades will take the wood for his drum on the following day.[115] At the other end of Siberia, among the Altaians, the spirits themselves tell the shaman of the forest and the exact spot where the tree grows, and he sends his assistants to find it

---

113 Cf. above, p. 42.

114 Cf. E. Kagarow, "Der umgekehrte Schamanenbaum." See also Holmberg: *Der Baum des Lebens*, pp. 17, 59, and elsewhere; *Finno-Ugric [and] Siberian [Mythology]*, pp. 349 ff.; R. Karsten, *The Religion of the Samek*, p. 48; A. Coomaraswamy, "The Inverted Tree"; Eliade, *Patterns in Comparative Religion*, pp. 294 ff.

115 Popov, *Seremonia*, p. 94; Emsheimer, "Schamanentrommel," p. 167.

and cut the wood for his drum from it.[116] In other regions the shaman himself gathers up all the splinters. Elsewhere sacrifices are offered to the tree by daubing it with blood and vodka. The next step is "animating the drum" by sprinkling its shell with alcoholic spirits.[117] Among the Yakut it is considered best to choose a tree that has been struck by lightning.[118] All these ritual customs and precautions clearly show that the concrete tree has been transfigured by the superhuman revelation, that it has ceased to be a profane tree and represents the actual World Tree.

The ceremony for "animating the drum" is of the highest interest. When the Altaic shaman sprinkles it with beer, the shell of the drum "comes to life" and, through the shaman, relates how the tree of which it was part grew in the forest, how it was cut, brought to the village, and so on. The shaman then sprinkles the skin of the drum and, "coming to life," it too narrates its past. Through the shaman's voice, the animal whose skin has been used for the drum tells of its birth, its parents, its childhood, and its whole life to the moment when it was brought down by the hunter. It ends by promising the shaman that it will perform many services for him. In one of the Altaic tribes, the Tubalares, the shaman imitates both the voice and behavior of the resuscitated animal.

As both L. P. Potapov and G. Buddruss[119] have shown, the animal that the shaman "reanimates" is his alter ego, his most powerful helping spirit; when it enters the shaman he changes into the mythical theriomorphic ancestor. This makes it clearer why, during the "animation" rite, the shaman has to relate the life history of the drum-animal: he sings of his exemplary model, the primordial animal that is the origin of his tribe. In mythical times every member of the tribe could turn into an animal, that is,

116 Emsheimer, p. 168 (after L. P. Potapov and Menges, *Materialien zur Volkskunde der Türkvölker der Altaj*).

117 Ibid., p. 172.

118 W. Sieroszewski, "Du chamanisme d'après les croyances des Yakoutes," p. 322.

119 *Schamanengeschichten aus Sibirien*, pp. 74 ff.

e was able to share in the condition of the ancestor. In our day uch intimate relations with mythical ancestors are the prerogative nly of shamans.

During the séance the shaman re-establishes, for himself alone, situation that was once general. The deeper meaning of this ecovery of the primordial human condition will become clearer fter we have examined other examples. For the moment, it s enough to have shown that both the shell and the skin of the rum constitute magico-religious implements by virtue of which ne shaman is able to undertake the ecstatic journey to the "Center f the World." In numerous traditions the mythical theriomorphic ncestor lives in the subterranean world, close to the root of the osmic Tree, whose top touches the sky.[120] Separate but related leas are present here. On the one hand, by drumming, the haman flies away to the Cosmic Tree; we shall see in a moment aat the drum harbors a large number of ascensional symbols.[121] n the other hand, by virtue of his mystical relations with the reanimated" skin of the drum, the shaman is able to share in the ature of the theriomorphic ancestor; in other words, he can bolish time and re-establish the primordial condition of which ne myths tell. In either case we are in the presence of a mystical xperience that allows the shaman to transcend time and space. oth metamorphosis into the animal ancestor and the shaman's scensional ecstasy represent different but homologizable expres- ons of one and the same experience—transcendence of the profane ondition, re-establishment of a "paradisal" existence lost in the epths of mythical time.

Usually the drum is oval in shape; its skin is of reindeer, elk, r horse hide. Among the Ostyak and the Samoyed of eastern beria, the outer surface bears no design.[122] According to J. G.

120 Friedrich, "Das Bewusstsein eines Naturvolkes von Haushalt und rsprung des Lebens," p. 52.
121 Below, pp. 173 f.
122 Kai Donner, *La Sibérie*, p. 230; Harva, *Die religiösen Vorstellungen*,). 526 ff.

Georgi,[123] the Tungus drums are ornamented with representa
tions of birds, snakes, and other animals. Shirokogoroff thus de
scribes the representations that he saw on the drums of th
Transbaikal Tungus: the symbol of *terra firma* (for the shama
uses his drum as a boat to cross the sea, hence he indicates i
shores); several groups of anthropomorphic figures, to left an
right; and a number of animals. No image is painted in th
center of the drum; the eight double lines drawn there symboli
the eight feet that hold the earth above the sea.[124] Among th
Yakut there are mysterious signs painted in red and black an
representing men and animals.[125] Various images are also atteste
on the drums of the Yenisei Ostyak.[126]

"At the back of the drum there is a vertical wooden and iro
handle, which the shaman grasps in his left hand. Horizontal wir
or wooden wedges hold innumerable bits of tinkling meta
rattles, bells, iron images representing spirits, various animal
etc., and frequently weapons, such as an arrow, a bow, or
knife." [127] Each of these magical objects has its own symbolis
and plays its part in the shaman's preparing or performing h
ecstatic journey or in his other mystical experiences.

Designs ornamenting the skin of the drum are characteristic
all the Tatar tribes and the Lapps. Among the Lapps both fac
of the skin are covered with images. They are of the greate
variety, although among them are always the most importa
symbols, as, for example, the World Tree, the sun and moon, th
rainbow, and others. In short, the drums constitute a microcos
a boundary line separates sky from earth, and, in some plac
earth from the underworld. The World Tree (that is, the sacrifici
birch climbed by the shaman), the horse, the sacrificed animal, t
shaman's helping spirits, the sun and moon, which he reaches

---

123 *Bemerkungen auf einer Reise im russischen Reiche im Jahre 1772*, I,
124 *Psychomental Complex*, p. 297.   125 Sieroszewski, p. 322.
126 Donner, *La Sibérie*, p. 230.
127 Ibid., p. 230; cf. Harva, *Die religiösen Vorstellungen*, pp. 527, 5
W. Schmidt, *Der Ursprung*, IX, 260, etc.

the course of his celestial journey, the underworld of Erlik Khan (including the Seven Sons and Seven Daughters of the Lord of the Dead, etc.), into which he makes his way when he descends to the realm of the dead—all these elements, which in a manner summarize the shaman's itinerary and adventures, are found represented on his drum. We have not space to record all the signs and images and to comment on their symbolism.[128] We will only note that the drum depicts a microcosm with its three zones—sky, earth, underworld—at the same time that it indicates the means by which the shaman accomplishes the break-through from plane to plane and establishes communication with the world above and the world below. For, as we have just seen, the image of the sacrificial birch (= World Tree) is not the only one. We also find the rainbow; the shaman mounts to the higher spheres by climbing it.[129] We find, too, the image of the bridge, over which the shaman passes from one cosmic region to another.[130]

The iconography of the drums is dominated by the symbolism of the ecstatic journey, that is, by journeys that imply a breakthrough in plane and hence a "Center of the World." The drumming at the beginning of the séance, intended to summon the spirits and "shut them up" in the shaman's drum, constitutes the preliminaries for the ecstatic journey. This is why the drum is called the "shaman's horse" (Yakut, Buryat). The Altaic drum bears a representation of a horse; when the shaman drums, he is believed to go to the sky on his horse.[131] Among the Buryat, too, the drum made with a horse's hide represents that animal.[132] According to O. Mänchen-Helfen, the Soyot shaman's drum is re-

128 Cf. Potanin, *Ocherki*, IV, 43 ff.; Anokhin, *Materialy po shamanstvu u altaitsev*, pp. 55 ff.; Harva, *Die religiösen Vorstellungen*, pp. 530 ff. (and figs. 89–100, etc.); W. Schmidt, *Der Ursprung*, IX, 262 ff., 697 ff.; and especially E. Manker, *Die lappische Zaubertrommel*, II, 19 ff., 61 ff., 124 ff.

129 Cf. Martti Räsänen, "Regenbogen-Himmelsbrücke."

130 H. von Lankenau, "Die Schamanen und das Schamanenwesen," pp. 279 ff.

131 Radlov, *Aus Sibirien*, II, 18, 28, 30, and passim.

132 Mikhailowski, "Shamanism in Siberia and European Russia," p. 80.

garded as a horse and is called *khamu-at*, literally "shaman-horse." [133] Among certain Mongol tribes the shamanic drum is called the "black stag." [134] Where the skin is from a roebuck, the drum is "the shaman's roebuck" (Karagas, Soyot). Yakut legends tell in detail of the shaman flying through the seven skies with his drum. "I am traveling with a wild roebuck!" the Karagas and Soyot shamans sing. And the stick with which the drum is beaten is called "whip" among the Altaians.[135] Miraculous speed is one of the characteristics of the *táltos*, the Hungarian shaman.[136] A *táltos* "put a reed between his legs and galloped away and was there before a man on horseback." [137] All these beliefs, images, and symbols in relation to the "flight," the "riding," or the "speed" of shamans are figurative expressions for ecstasy, that is, for mystical journeys undertaken by superhuman means and in regions inaccessible to mankind.

The idea of the ecstatic journey is also found in the name that the shamans of the tundra Yurak give their drum: *bow* or *singing bow*. According to Lehtisalo as well as Harva,[138] the shamanic drum was originally used to drive away evil spirits, a result that could also be obtained by the use of a bow. It is quite true that the drum is sometimes employed to drive away evil spirits,[139] but in such cases its special use is forgotten and we have an instance of the "magic of noise" by which demons are expelled. Such examples of alteration in function are fairly frequent in the history of religions. But we do not believe that the original function of the drum was to drive away spirits. The shamanic drum is distinguished from all other instruments of the "magic of noise" precisely by the fact that it makes possible an ecstatic experience. Whether this experience was prepared, in the beginning, by the charm of the sounds of the drum, a charm that was evaluated as "voice of the spirits," or as

133 *Reise ins asiatische Tuwa*, p. 117.

134 W. Heissig, "Schamanen und Geisterbeschwörer im Küriye-Banner," p. 47.

135 Harva, *Die religiösen Vorstellungen*, p. 536.

136 G. Róheim, "Hungarian Shamanism," p. 142.

137 Ibid., p. 135.

138 *Die religiösen Vorstellungen*, p. 538.   139 Ibid., p. 537.

ecstatic experience was attained through the extreme concentration provoked by a long period of drumming, is a problem that does not concern us at present. But one fact is certain: it was *musical magic* that determined the shamanic function of the drum, and not the antidemonic *magic of noise*.[140]

The proof is that, even where the drum is replaced by a bow—as among the Lebed Tatars and certain Altaians—what we have is always an instrument of magical music, not an antidemonic weapon; there are no arrows, and the bow is used as a one-stringed instrument. The Kirgiz *baqça* does not use the drum to prepare the trance, but the *kobuz*, which is a stringed instrument.[141] And the trance, as among the Siberian shamans, is induced by dancing to the magical melody of the *kobuz*. The dance, as we shall see more fully later, reproduces the shaman's ecstatic journey to the sky. This is as much as to say that the magical music, like the symbolism of the shamanic drum and costume and the shaman's own dance, is one of many ways of undertaking the ecstatic journey or ensuring its success. The horse-headed sticks that the Buryat call "horses" attest the same symbolism.[142]

Among the Ugrian peoples shamanic drums bear no decoration. On the other hand, the Lapp shamans ornament their drums even more freely than the Tatars. Manker's extensive study of the Lapp magical drum reproduces and analyzes a large number of designs.[143] It is not always easy to identify the mythological figures and the

140 Arrows likewise play a part in some shamanic séances (cf., for example, ibid., p. 555). The arrow embodies a twofold magico-religious significance; on the one hand, it is an exemplary image of speed, of "flight"; on the other, it is the magical weapon par excellence (the arrow kills at a distance). Used in purification ceremonies or ceremonies to eject demons, the arrow "kills" as well as "drives away" and "expels" evil spirits. Cf. also René de Nebesky-Wojkowitz, *Oracles and Demons of Tibet*, p. 543. For the arrow as a symbol at once of "flight" and "purification," see below, p. 388.

141 Castagné, "Magie et exorcisme," pp. 67 ff.

142 Harva, *Die religiösen Vorstellungen*, pp. 538 ff. and fig. 65.

143 *Die lappische Zaubertrommel. I: Die Trommel als Denkmal materieller Kultur; II: Die Trommel als Urkunde geistigen Lebens*. See also T. I. Itkonen, *Heidnische Religion und späterer Aberglaube bei den finnischen Lappen*, pp. 39 ff. and figs. 24–27.

meaning of all the images, which are sometimes quite mysterious. In general, the Lapp drums represent the three cosmic zones separated by boundary lines. In the sky, the sun and moon are discernible, as are gods and goddesses (probably influenced by Scandinavian mythology),[144] birds (swan, cuckoo, etc.), the drum, the sacrificial animals, and so forth; the Cosmic Tree, a number of mythical personages, boats, shamans, the god of the chase, horsemen, etc., people the intermediate space (the earth); the infernal gods, shamans and the dead, snakes and birds are found, with other images, in the lower zone.

The Lapp shamans also use their drums in divination.[145] This custom is unknown among the Turkic tribes.[146] The Tungus practice a sort of limited divination, which consists in throwing the shamanic drumstick into the air; its position after falling answers the question asked.[147]

The problem of the origin and dissemination of the shaman's drum in North Asia is extremely complex and far from being solved. Several things point to its having been originally disseminated from South Asia. It is indubitable that the Lamaist drum influenced the shape not only of the Siberian but also of the Chukchee and Eskimo drums.[148] These facts are not without importance for the formation of present-day shamanism in Central Asia and Siberia, and we shall have to return to them when we attempt to sketch the evolution of Asiatic shamanism.

Ritual Costumes and Magical Drums throughout the World

We cannot possibly consider presenting a comparative picture of the costumes and drums or other ritual instruments employed by

144 Manker, *Die lappische Zaubertrommel*, I, 17.

145 Itkonen, pp. 121 f.; Harva, *Die religiösen Vorstellungen*, p. 538; Karsten, *The Religion of the Samek*, p. 74.

146 With the possible exception of the Kumandin of the Altai. Cf. Buddruss, in Friedrich and Buddruss, *Schamanengeschichten*, p. 82.

147 Harva, *Die religiösen Vorstellungen*, p. 539.

148 Cf. Shirokogoroff, *Psychomental Complex*, p. 299.

orcerers, medicine men, and priests all over the world.[149] The
ubject pertains rather to ethnology and is only of subsidiary
iterest to the history of religions. Let us mention, however, that
ie same symbolism that we have deciphered in the costume of the
iberian shaman also appears elsewhere. We find masks (from the
implest to the most elaborate), animal skins and furs, and espe-
ally bird feathers, whose ascensional symbolism requires no
ressing. We also find magical sticks, bells, and very many kinds of
rums.

H. Hoffmann has usefully studied the resemblances between the
on priests' costume and drum and those of the Siberian shamans.[150]
he costume of the Tibetan oracle-priests includes, among other
iings, eagle feathers, a helmet with broad ribbons of silk, a shield,
id a lance.[151] V. Goloubew had already compared the bronze
rums excavated at Dongson with the drums of the Mongol sha-
ians.[152] Recently H. G. Quaritch Wales has worked out the sha-
.anic structure of the Dongson drums in greater detail; he com-
ares the procession wearing feather headdresses in the ritual
:ene on the tympanum to the Sea Dyak shamans decorated with
athers and pretending to be birds.[153] Although today the drum-
iing of the Indonesian shaman is given various interpretations, it
›metimes signifies the celestial journey or is thought to prepare

149 Cf., for example, E. Crawley, *Dress, Drinks and Drums: Further Studies
Savages and Sex*, pp. 159 ff., 233 ff.; J. L. Maddox, *The Medicine Man*,
›. 95 ff.; H. Webster, *Magic*, pp. 252 ff. On the drum among the Bhil, see
'ilhelm Koppers, *Die Bhil in Zentralindien*, p. 223; among the Jakun, Ivor
. N. Evans, *Studies in Religion*, p. 265; among the Malays, W. W. Skeat,
alay Magic, pp. 25 ff., 40 ff., 512 ff.; in Africa, Heinz Wieschoff, *Die
rikanischen Trommeln und ihre ausserafrikanischen Beziehungen*; A. Friedrich,
frikanische Priestertümer*, pp. 194 ff., 324, etc. Cf. also A. Schaefner, *Origine
s instruments de musique*, pp. 166 ff. (skin drum).

150 *Quellen zur Geschichte der tibetischen Bon-Religion*, pp. 201 ff.

151 Nebesky-Wojkowitz, *Oracles and Demons of Tibet*, pp. 410 ff. Cf.
so Dominik Schröder, "Zur Religion der Tujen des Sininggebietes
:ukunor)," last art., pp. 235 ff., 243 ff.

152 Cf. his "Les Tambours magiques en Mongolie" and "Sur l'origine et
diffusion des tambours métalliques."

153 *Prehistory and Religion in South-East Asia*, pp. 82 ff.

the shaman's ecstatic ascent.[154] The Dusun (Borneo) sorcerer put on some sacred ornaments and feathers when he undertakes a cure; [155] the Mentaweian (Sumatra) shaman uses a ceremonial costume that includes feathers and bells; [156] the African sorcerer and healers cover themselves with the skins of wild beasts, with animal bones and teeth, and similar objects.[157] Although the ritual costume is comparatively rare in tropical South America, some of the shaman's accessories take its place. Such, for example, is the *maraca*, or rattle, "made from a gourd containing seeds or stones and fitted with a handle." This instrument is considered sacred and the Tupinamba even bring it offerings of food.[158] The Yaruro shamans perform on their rattles "highly stylized representations of the chief divinities whom they visit during their trances." [159]

The North American shamans have a ceremonial costume that tends to be symbolic; it consists of eagle or other feathers, a sort of rattle or a drum, small bags with rock crystals, stones, and other magical objects. The eagle from which the feathers are taken is regarded as sacred and is left free.[160] The bag with the accessories never leaves the shaman; at night he hides it under his pillow or his bed.[161] The Tlingit and the Haida use what can even be called a real ceremonial costume (a robe, a blanket, a hat, etc.), which the shaman makes for himself in accordance with the instructions of his tutelary spirit.[162] Among the Apache, besides eagle feathers, the shaman has a rhomb, a magical cord (which makes him invulnerable and also enables him to foresee future events, etc.), and

154 Cf. some examples in ibid., p. 86.

155 Evans, *Studies*, p. 21.

156 E. M. Loeb, "Shaman and Seer," pp. 69 ff.

157 Webster, *Magic*, pp. 253 f.

158 A. Métraux, *La Religion des Tupinamba et ses rapports avec celle des autres tribus Tupi-Guarani*, pp. 72 ff.

159 Id., "Le Shamanisme chez les Indiens de l'Amérique du Sud tropicale, p. 218.

160 W. Z. Park, *Shamanism in Western North America*, p. 34.

161 Ibid.

162 J. R. Swanton, cited by M. Bouteiller, *Chamanisme et guérison magique, p. 88.

ritual hat.[163] Elsewhere, as among the Sanpoil and the Nespelem, the magical power of the costume is embodied in a mere red cloth wound around the arm.[164] Eagle feathers are attested among all the North American tribes.[165] In addition, they are used, fastened to sticks, in initiation ceremonies (for example, among the Maidu), and these sticks are placed on shamans' graves.[166] This betokens the direction that the dead shaman's soul has taken.

In North America,[167] as in most other regions, the shaman uses a drum or a rattle. Where the ceremonial drum is missing, it is replaced by the gong or the shell (especially in Ceylon,[168] South Asia, China, etc.). But there is always some instrument that, in one way or another, is able to establish contact with the "world of the spirits." This last expression must be taken in its broadest sense, embracing not only gods, spirits, and demons, but also the souls of ancestors, the dead, and mythical animals. This contact with the suprasensible world necessarily implies a previous concentration, facilitated by the shaman's or magician's "entering" his ceremonial costume and hastened by ritual music.

The same symbolism of the sacred costume survives in more developed religions: wolf or bear furs in China,[169] the bird feathers of the Irish prophet,[170] and so on. We find the macrocosmic symbolism on the robes of the priests and sovereigns of the ancient Orient. This series of facts falls under a "law" well known to the history of religions: *one becomes what one displays.* The wearers of masks *are* really the mythical ancestors portrayed by their masks. But the same results—that is, total transformation of the individual into something *other*—are to be expected from the various

---

163 J. G. Bourke, "The Medicine-Men of the Apache," pp. 476 ff. (the rhomb; cf. figs. 430–31), 533 ff. (feathers), 550 ff. and figs. 435–39 (the "medicine-cord"), 589 ff. and Pl. V (the "medicine-hat").

164 Park, p. 129. 165 Ibid., p. 134.

166 Ibid. 167 Ibid., pp. 34 ff., 131 ff.

168 Cf. Paul Wirz, *Exorzismus und Heilkunde auf Ceylon.*

169 Cf. Carl Hentze, *Die Sakralbronzen und ihre Bedeutung in den frühchinesischen Kulturen*, pp. 34 ff.

170 Cf. N. K. Chadwick, *Poetry and Prophecy*, p. 58.

signs and symbols that are sometimes merely indicated on the costume or directly on the body: one assumes the power of magical flight by wearing an eagle feather, or even a highly stylized drawing of such a feather; and so on. However, the use of drums and other instruments of magical music is not confined to séances. Many shamans also drum and sing for their own pleasure; yet the implications of these actions remain the same: that is, ascending to the sky or descending to the underworld to visit the dead. This "autonomy" to which instruments of magico-religious music finally attain has led to the constitution of a music that, if not yet "profane," is certainly freer and more vivid than a purely religious music. The same phenomenon is observable in connection with the shamanic songs that narrate ecstatic journeys to the sky and dangerous descents to the underworld. After a time adventures of this kind pass into the folklore of the respective peoples and enrich popular oral literature with new themes and characters.[171]

171 Cf. K. Meuli, "Scythica," pp. 151 ff.

CHAPTER SIX

Shamanism
in Central and North Asia:
I. CELESTIAL ASCENTS. DESCENTS
TO THE UNDERWORLD

The Shaman's Functions

H OWEVER important the role of shamans in the religious life of Central and North Asia, it yet has its limits.[1] The shaman is not a sacrificer; "it is not among his functions to attend to the sacrifices that are to be offered, at particular dates, to the gods of water, the forest, and the family." [2] As W. Radlov already observed, in the Altai the shaman has nothing to do with the ceremonies of birth, marriage, and death—unless, that is, something unusual occurs; for example, the shaman is summoned in cases of sterility or difficult childbirth.[3] Farther north the shaman is sometimes invited to funerals, in order to prevent the soul of the deceased from returning; he is also present at weddings, to protect

1 So too, the social position of the Siberian shamans is of the highest, with the exception of the Chukchee, among whom the shamans seem not to enjoy much respect; cf. V. M. Mikhailowski, "Shamanism in Siberia and European Russia," pp. 131–32. Among the Buryat shamans are said to have been the first political leaders (G. Sandschejew, "Weltanschauung und Schamanismus der Alaren-Burjaten," pp. 981 ff.).

2 Kai Donner, *La Sibérie*, p. 222.

3 *Aus Sibirien*, II, 55.

the newly married couple from the evil spirits.[4] But, clearly, his role in such cases is confined to that of magical defense.

On the other hand, the shaman is indispensable in any ceremony that concerns the experiences of the human soul as such, that is, as a precarious psychic unit, inclined to forsake the body and an easy prey for demons and sorcerers. This is why, all through Asia and North America, and elsewhere as well (e.g., Indonesia), the shaman performs the function of doctor and healer; he announces the diagnosis, goes in search of the patient's fugitive soul, captures it, and makes it return to animate the body that it has left. It is always the shaman who conducts the dead person's soul to the underworld, for he is the psychopomp par excellence.

Healer and psychopomp, the shaman is these because he commands the techniques of ecstasy—that is, because his soul can safely abandon his body and roam at vast distances, can penetrate the underworld and rise to the sky. Through his own ecstatic experience he knows the roads of the extraterrestrial regions. He can go below and above because he has already been there. The danger of losing his way in these forbidden regions is still great; but sanctified by his initiation and furnished with his guardian spirits, the shaman is the only human being able to challenge the danger and venture into a mystical geography.

It is this same ecstatic faculty that, as we shall soon see, enables the shaman to accompany the soul of the horse offered to God in the periodic sacrifices of the Altaians. In this case, it is the shaman himself who sacrifices the horse, but he does so because it is his task to conduct the animal's soul on its celestial journey to the throne of Bai Ülgän and not because his function is that of a sacrificial priest. On the contrary, it appears that among the Tatars of

---

4 K. F. Karjalainen, *Die Religion der Jugra-Völker*, III, 295. According to W. Sieroszewski, the Yakut shaman is present at all important events ("Du chamanisme d'après les croyances des Yakoutes," p. 322); but it does not follow that he dominates "normal" religious life; it is essentially in cases of illness that he becomes indispensable (ibid.). Among the Buryat, children up to the age of fifteen are protected from the evil spirits by shamans (Sandschejew, p. 594).

the Altai the shaman has taken the place of the sacrificial priest; for in the horse sacrifices to the celestial Supreme God among the Proto-Turks (Hiung-Nu, Tukue), the Katshina, and the Beltir, the shamans play no role, whereas they take an active part in other sacrifices.[5]

The same situation obtains among the Ugrian peoples. Among the Vogul and the Ostyak of the Irtysh shamans sacrifice in cases of sickness and before undertaking a cure, but this sacrifice seems to be a late innovation; apparently, only the search for the patient's strayed soul is original and important in these cases.[6] Among the same peoples the shamans are present at expiatory sacrifices, and in the Irtysh region, for example, they may even sacrifice; but nothing is to be concluded from this fact, for anyone at all may sacrifice to the gods.[7] Even when he takes part in sacrifices, the Ugrian shaman does not kill the animal but, as it were, takes over the "spiritual" side of the rite; he performs fumigations, prays, and so on.[8] In the sacrifice of the Tremyugan the shaman is called "the man who prays," but he is not indispensable.[9] Among the Vasyugan, after the shaman is consulted concerning an illness, a sacrifice is performed in accordance with his instructions, but the victim is killed by the master of the house. In the collective sacrifices of the Ugrian peoples the shaman confines himself to praying and guiding the victims' souls to the respective divinities.[10] To conclude: even when he takes part in sacrifices, the shaman plays more of a "spiritual" role; [11] he is concerned only with the mystical itinerary of the sacrificed animal. The reason is plain: the shaman knows the road and, in addition, he has the ability to control and escort a "soul," whether that of a man or of a sacrificial victim.

Northward the religious role of the shaman appears to increase

---

5 Cf. W. Schmidt, *Der Ursprung der Gottesidee*, IX, 14, 31, 63 (Hiung-Nu, Tukue, etc.), 686 (Katshina, Beltir), 771 ff.

6 Karjalainen, III, 286.   7 Ibid., pp. 287 f.

8 Ibid., p. 288.   9 Ibid.

10 Ibid., p. 289.

11 Observe the analogy to the function of the brahman in the Vedic ritual.

in importance and complexity. In the Far North of Asia, when game becomes scarce, the shaman's intervention is sometimes sought.[12] The same is true among the Eskimo [13] and some North American tribes,[14] but these hunting rites cannot be regarded as properly shamanic. If the shaman appears to play a certain role under these circumstances, it is still always due to his ecstatic abilities: he foresees changes in the atmosphere, enjoys clairvoyance and vision at a distance (hence he can find game); in addition, he has closer relations, of a magico-religious nature, with animals.

Divination and clairvoyance are part of the shaman's mystical techniques. Thus a shaman will be consulted to find men or animals gone astray in the tundra or the snow, to recover a lost object, and so forth. But these minor exploits are rather the prerogative of shamanesses or of other classes of sorcerers and sorceresses. Similarly, it is not one of the shaman's specialties to harm his clients' enemies, although sometimes he will undertake to do so. But North Asian shamanism is an extremely complex phenomenon, burdened with a long history, and it has come to absorb a number of magical techniques, especially as a result of the prestige that shamans have accumulated in the course of time.

"Black" and "White" Shamans. "Dualistic" Mythologies

The most marked specialization, at least among certain peoples, is that of "black" and "white" shamans, although it is not always easy to define the distinction. M. A. Czaplicka [15] mentions, for the Yakut, the class of *ajy ojuna* (*ai oyuna*), who sacrifice to the gods and the class of *abassy ojuna* (*oyuna*), who have relations with the "evil spirits." But, as Harva observes,[16] the *ajy ojuna* is not neces-

12 U. Harva, *Die religiösen Vorstellungen der altaischen Völker*, p. 542.
13 See, for example, K. Rasmussen, *Intellectual Culture of the Igluli Eskimos*, pp. 109 ff.; E. M. Weyer, *The Eskimos*, p. 422, etc.
14 For example, the "antelope-charming" of the Paviotso; cf. W. Z. Park, *Shamanism in Western North America*, pp. 62 ff., 139 ff.
15 *Aboriginal Siberia*, pp. 247 ff.; cf. also W. Schmidt, *Der Ursprung*, XI, 273–78, 287–90.
16 *Die religiösen Vorstellungen*, p. 483.

sarily a shaman; he can also be a sacrificing priest. According to N. V. Pripuzov, the same Yakut shaman can invoke both the higher (celestial) spirits and those of the lower regions.[17] Among the Tungus of Turukhansk the shamans are not differentiated into "black" and "white"; but they do not sacrifice to the celestial god, whose rites are always performed by day, whereas the shamanic rites take place at night.[18]

The distinction is clearly marked among the Buryat, who speak of "white" shamans (*sagani bö*) and "black" shamans (*karain bö*), the former having relations with the gods, the latter with the spirits.[19] Their costumes differ, being white for the former and blue for the latter. Buryat mythology itself shows a marked dualism that has become celebrated: the innumerable class of demigods is divided into black Khans and white Khans, separated by fierce enmity.[20] The black Khans are served by the "black" shamans; these are not liked, though they have their use, since only they can fill the role of intermediaries to the black Khans.[21] However, this situation is not primitive; according to the myths, the first shaman was "white," the "black" shaman appeared only later.[22] We have seen, too,[23] that it was the gods who sent the eagle to bestow sha-

17 Cited by Harva, ibid. W. Sieroszewski classifies the Yakut shamans according to their power and distinguishes: (*a*) the "last" (*kennikî oyuna*), who are rather diviners and interpreters of dreams and who treat only minor illnesses; (*b*) the "common" shamans (*orto oyuna*), who are the usual healers; *c*) the "great" shamans, the powerful magicians, to whom the Great Lord Ūlū-Toyon himself has sent a tutelary spirit ("Du chamanisme," p. 315). As we shall see presently, the Yakut pantheon is distinguished by a bipartition, but this does not appear to have a counterpart in the differentiation in the class of shamans. The opposition is, rather, between the sacrificing priests and the shamans. However, there is mention of "white" shamans or "summer" shamans, specializing in the ceremonies of the goddess Aisyt; see above, p. 80, n. 35.

18 Harva, *Die religiösen Vorstellungen*, p. 483.

19 N. N. Agapitov and M. N. Khangalov, "Materialy dlya izuchenia shamanstva v Sibirii. Shamanstvo u buryat Irkutskoi gubernii," p. 46; Mikhailowski, p. 130; Harva, *Die religiösen Vorstellungen*, p. 484.

20 Sandschejew, pp. 952 ff.; cf. W. Schmidt, *Der Ursprung*, X, 250 ff.

21 Sandschejew, p. 952.　　　　　　22 Ibid., p. 976.

23 Above, pp. 69 ff.

manic gifts on the first human being it should meet on earth. This bipartition of shamans may well be a secondary and even rather late phenomenon, due either to Iranian influences or to a negative evaluation of the chthonic and "infernal" hierophanies, which in course of time came to designate "demonic" powers.[24]

We must not forget that many of the divinities and powers of the earth and the underworld are not necessarily "evil" or "demonic." They generally represent autochthonous and even local hierophanies that have fallen in rank as the result of changes within the pantheon. Sometimes the bipartition of gods into celestial and chthonic-infernal is only a convenient classification without any pejorative implication for the latter. We have just seen a quite marked opposition between the white Khans and black Khan of the Buryat. The Yakut, too, know two great classes (*bis*) of gods: those "above" and those "below," the *tangara* ("celestial") and the "subterranean," [25] though there is no clear opposition between them; [26] rather, it is a matter of classification and specialization among various religious forms and powers.

Benevolent as the gods and spirits "above" may be, they are unfortunately passive and hence of almost no help in the drama of human existence. They inhabit "the upper spheres of the sky, scarcely mingle in human affairs, and have relatively less influence on the course of life than the spirits of the '*bis* below,' who are vindictive, closer to the earth, allied to men by ties of blood and a much stricter organization into clans." [27] The chief of the celestial gods and spirits is Art Toyon Aga, the "Lord Father Chief of the World," who resides "in the nine spheres of the sky. Powerful, he remains inactive; he shines like the sun, which is his emblem, he

24 On the relations between the dualistic organization of the spiritual world and a possible dual social organization, cf. Lawrence Krader, "Buryat Religion and Society," pp. 338 ff.

25 "Above" and "below" are, in any case, rather vague terms; they can also designate regions situated upstream and downstream along a river (Sieroszewski, p. 300). Cf. also W. I. Jochelson, *The Yakut*, pp. 107 ff. B. D. Shimkin, "A Sketch of the Ket or Yenisei 'Ostyak,'" pp. 161 ff.

26 Sieroszewski, pp. 300 ff.   27 Ibid., p. 301.

speaks through the voice of the thunder, but he mingles little in human affairs. We should address prayers to him for our daily needs in vain; we may trouble his rest only in extraordinary cases, and even then he grudges mingling in human affairs." [28]

Besides Art Toyon Aga there are seven other great gods "above" and a multitude of lesser gods. But their celestial habitat does not necessarily imply a uranian structure. Side by side with the "White Lord Creator," Ürün (Ürüng) Ai (Toyon), who lives in the fourth heaven, we find, for example, "The Gentle Mother Creatress," "The Gentle Lady of Birth," and "The Lady of the Earth" (An Alaï Chotoun). The god of the chase, Bai Baianai, inhabits both the eastern part of the sky and the fields and forests. But black buffaloes are sacrificed to him—an indication of his telluric origin.[29]

The "*bis* below" comprises eight great gods, headed by "The All-Powerful Lord of the Infinite" Ulū-tūyer Ulū-Toyon, and an unlimited number of "evil spirits." But Ulū-Toyon is not ill-disposed; "he is only extremely close to the earth, the affairs of which excite his lively interest. . . . Ulū-Toyon personifies active existence, full of suffering, desires, struggles. . . . He is to be sought in the West, in the third heaven. But his name must not be invoked in vain; the earth shakes and trembles when he sets down his foot; the heart of the mortal who dares to look on his face bursts with terror. Hence none has seen him. Yet he is the only one of the powerful inhabitants of the sky who descends into this tear-filled human vale. . . . It is he who gave men fire, who

---

28 Ibid., p. 302 (after I. A. Chudyakov). On the passivity of uranian Supreme Beings, see Eliade, *Patterns in Comparative Religion*, pp. 46 ff.

29 "When the hunters are unsuccessful or one of them falls ill, a black buffalo is sacrificed, the shaman burning its flesh, entrails, and fat. During the ceremony a wooden figure of Baianai, covered with a hare skin, is washed in blood. When the thaw frees the waters, stakes connected by a hair rope (*sëty*) from which hang particolored cloths and heads of hair are set up along the waterside; in addition, butter, cakes, sugar, and silver are thrown into the water" (Sieroszewski, p. 303). This is the very type of a hybridized sacrifice; cf. A. Gahs, "Kopf-, Schädel- und Langknochenopfer bei Rentiervölkern," passim.

created the shaman and taight him to combat misfortune. . . . He is the creator of the birds, of the woodland animals, of the forests themselves." [30] Ulū-Toyon does not obey Art Toyon Aga, who treats him as an equal.[31]

Significantly enough, several of these divinities "below" are offered white or roan animals as sacrifices. Kahtyr-Kaghtan Bouraï-Toyon, a powerful god who bows only to Ulū-Toyon, receives in sacrifice a gray horse with a white face; for the "Lady of the White Colt," the sacrifice is a white colt; the rest of the gods and spirits "below" receive sacrifices of roan mares with white hocks or white heads, dapple-gray mares, and so forth.[32] Naturally, the spirits "below" include several famous shamans. The most celebrated is the "prince of shamans" of the Yakut; he lives in the western part of the sky and belongs to the family of Ulū-Toyon. "He was once a shaman of the *ulus* of Nam, of the *nosleg* of Botiugne, of the Tchaky race. . . . The sacrifice to him is a hunting dog, steel-colored with white spots and with head white between eyes and muzzle." [33]

These few examples suffice to show how difficult it is to draw a clear line of demarcation between the "uranian" and the "telluric" gods, between the supposedly "good" and the supposedly "evil" religious powers. What comes out clearly is that the celestial Supreme God is a *deus otiosus* and that in the Yakut pantheon the situations and hierarchies have changed, not to say been usurped, more than once. Given this complex yet vague "dualism," we understand how the Yakut shaman can serve both the gods "above" and the gods "below," for the "*bis* below" does not always mean "evil spirits." The difference between the shamans and other priests (the "sacrificers") is not ritual in nature, but

30 Sieroszewski, pp. 306 ff.

31 The description shows how inadequate it is to classify Ulū-Toyon among the "lesser" divinities "below." Actually, he combines the attribute of a Lord of the Animals, a demiurge, and even a fertility god.

32 Sieroszewski, pp. 303 ff.   33 Ibid., p. 305.

ecstatic; what characterizes the shaman and defines his peculiar situation within the religious community (including both priests and laymen) is not the fact that he can offer one or another sacrifice, but the particular nature of his relations to the divinities, both those "above" and those "below." These relations—as we shall see more clearly later—are more "familiar," more "concrete" than those of others, the sacrificing priests or the laymen; for, in the shaman's case, religious experiences are always ecstatic in structure, whatever divinity it may be that provokes the ecstatic experience.

Though with a less marked differentiation than among the Buryat, the same bipartition is found among the Altaic shamans. A. V. Anokhin [34] speaks of "white shamans" (*ak kam*) and "black shamans" (*kara kam*). Neither Radlov nor Potapov records this difference; according to their information, the same shaman can equally well ascend to the sky and descend to the underworld. But these statements are not irreconcilable. Anokhin [35] notes that there are also "black-white" shamans, who can perform both journeys; the Russian ethnologist found six "white" shamans, three "black," and five "white-black." Probably Radlov and Potapov happened to encounter only shamans of the last category.

The costume of the "white" shamans is less elaborate; the caftan (*manyak*) appears not to be indispensable. But they have a hat of white lambskin and other insignia.[36] The shamanesses are always "black," for they never undertake the journey to the sky. To sum up: the Altaians appear to know three groups of shamans—those who concern themselves with the celestial gods and powers, those who specialize in the (ecstatic) cult of the gods of the underworld, and, finally, those who have mystical relations with both classes of gods. The last group of shamans appears to comprise a considerable number.

34 *Materialy po shamanstvu u altaitsev*, p. 33.

35 Ibid., pp. 108 ff.

36 Ibid., p. 34; Harva, *Die religiösen Vorstellungen*, p. 482; W. Schmidt, *Der Ursprung*, IX, 244.

Horse Sacrifice and the Shaman's Ascent to the Sky (*Altaic*)

All this will become clearer when we have described several shamanic séances, held for various purposes: horse sacrifice and ascent to the sky, search for the causes of an illness and its treatment, escorting the soul of a deceased person to the underworld and purification of the house, and so on. For the present, we shall confine ourselves to descriptions of séances, without studying the shaman's trance proper and limiting ourselves to only a few references to the religious and mythological conceptions that validate these ecstatic journeys. This last problem—that of the mythical and theological foundation for the shamanic ecstasy—will be discussed later. It must also be added that the phenomenology of the séance varies from tribe to tribe, although its structure is always the same. It has not been thought necessary to mention all these differences, which chiefly affect details. In this chapter we have first of all attempted as complete a description as possible of the most important types of shamanic séances. We begin with Radlov's classic description of the Altaic ritual, based not only on his own observations but also on the texts of the songs and invocation recorded, at the beginning of the nineteenth century, by missionaries to the Altai and later edited by the priest V. L. Verbitsky.[37] This sacrifice is celebrated from time to time by every family, and the ceremony continues for two or three consecutive evenings.

The first evening is devoted to preparation for the rite. The *kam* having chosen a spot in a meadow, erects a new yurt there, setting

37 Radlov, *Aus Sibirien*, II, 20–50. Verbitsky printed the Tatar text in a journal published at Tomsk in 1870; he had given a description of the ceremony in 1858. The translation of the Tatar songs and invocations, as well as their incorporation into the presentation of the ritual, is the work of Radlov. A summary of this classic description has been given by Mikhailowski, pp. 74–78; cf. also Harva, *Die religiösen Vorstellungen*, pp. 553–56. Recently W. Schmidt devoted a whole chapter of Vol. IX of his *Der Ursprung der Gottesidee* (pp. 278–341) to a presentation and analysis of Radlov's text.

nside it a young birch stripped of its lower branches and with nine
teps (*tapty*) notched into its trunk. The higher foliage of the
irch, with a flag at the top, protrudes through the upper opening
f the yurt. A small palisade of birch sticks is erected around the
urt and a birch stick with a knot of horsehair is set at the en-
rance.[38] Then a light-colored horse is chosen, and after having
ade sure that the animal is pleasing to the divinity, the shaman
ntrusts it to one of the people present, called, for this reason,
iš-tut-kan-kiši, that is, "head-holder." The shaman shakes a birch
ranch over the animal's back to force its soul to leave and prepare
s flight to Bai Ülgän. He repeats the same gesture over the
head-holder," for his "soul" is to accompany the horse's soul
roughout its celestial journey and hence must be at the *kam*'s
isposition.

The shaman re-enters the yurt, throws branches on the fire, and
migates his drum. He begins to invoke the spirits, bidding them
ter his drum; he will need each one of them in the course of his
cent. At each summons by name, the spirit replies, "I am here,
m!" and the shaman moves his drum as if he were catching the
irit. After assembling his spirit helpers (which are all celestial
irits) the shaman comes out of the yurt. At a few steps' distance
ere is a scarecrow in the shape of a goose; he straddles it, rapidly
aving his hands as if to fly, and sings:

> Under the white sky,
> Over the white cloud;
> Under the blue sky,
> Over the blue cloud:
> Rise up to the sky, bird!

38 According to Potanin (*Ocherki severo-zapadnoi Mongolii*, IV, 79), two
les with wooden birds at their tops are set up near the sacrificial table,
d they are connected by a cord from which hang green branches and a
re skin. Among the Dolgan poles with wooden birds at the top represent
 cosmic pillars; cf. Holmberg (Harva): *Der Baum des Lebens*, p. 16, figs.
6; *Die religiösen Vorstellungen*, p. 44. As for the bird, it of course symbol-
s the shaman's magical power of flight.

To this invocation, the goose replies, cackling: "Ungaigakgak, ungaigak, kaigaigakgak, kaigaigak." It is, of course, the shaman himself who imitates the bird's cry. Sitting astride the goose, the *kam* pursues the soul of the horse (*pûra*)—which is supposed to have fled—and neighs like a charger.

With the help of those present, he drives the animal's soul into the palisade and laboriously mimes its capture; he whinnies, rears, and pretends that the noose that has been thrown to catch the animal is tightening around his own throat. Sometimes he lets his drum fall to show that the animal's soul has escaped. Finally it is recaptured, the shaman fumigates it with juniper and dismisses the goose. Then he blesses the horse and, with the help of several of the audience, kills it in a cruel way, breaking its backbone in such a manner that not a drop of its blood falls to the ground or touches the sacrificers. The skin and bones are exposed, hung from a long pole.[39] After offerings are made to the ancestors and the tutelary spirits of the yurt, the flesh is prepared and eaten ceremonially, the shaman receiving the best pieces.

The second and most important part of the ceremony takes place on the following evening. It is now that the shaman exhibits his shamanic abilities during his ecstatic journey to the celestial abode of Bai Ülgän. The fire is burning in the yurt. The shaman offers horse meat to the Masters of the Drum, that is, the spirits that personify the shamanic powers of his family, and sings:

> Take it, O Kaira Kan,
> Host of the drum with six bosses!
> Come tinkling here to me!
> If I cry: "Cok!" bow thyself!
> If I cry: "Mä!" take it to thee! . . .

[39] The same method of sacrificing the horse and sheep prevails among other Altaic tribes and the Teleut; cf. Potanin, IV, 78 ff. This is the special sacrifice of the head and long bones, the purest forms of which are found among the Arctic peoples; cf. A. Gahs, "Kopf-, Schädel- und Langknochenopfer bei Rentiervölkern"; W. Schmidt, *Der Ursprung*, III, 334, 367 f., 462 and passim; VI, 70-75, 274-81, and passim; IX, 287-92; id., "Das Himmelsopfer bei den innerasiatischen Pferdezüchtervölkern." See also K. Meuli, "Griechische Opferbräuche," pp. 283 ff.

He makes a similar address to the Master of the Fire, symbolizing the sacred power of the owner of the yurt, organizer of the festival. Raising a cup, the shaman imitates with his lips the noise of a gathering of invisible guests busily drinking; then he cuts up pieces of the horse and distributes them among those present (who represent the spirits), who noisily eat them.[40] He next fumigates the nine garments hung on a rope as an offering from the master of the house to Bai Ülgän, and sings:

> Gifts that no horse can carry,
> Alás, alás, alás!
> That no man can lift,
> Alás, alás, alás!
> Garments with triple collars,
> Thrice turning look upon them!
> Be they blankets for the courser,
> Alás, alás, alás!
> Prince Ülgän, thou joyous one!
> Alás, alás, alás!

Putting on his shamanic costume, the *kam* sits down on a bench, and while he fumigates his drum, begins to invoke a multitude of spirits, great and small, who answer, in turn: "I am here, *kam!*" In this way he invokes: Yaik Kan, the Lord of the Sea, Kaira Kan, Paisyn Kan, then the family of Bai Ülgän (Mother Tasygan with nine daughters at her right and seven daughters at her left), and finally the Masters and Heroes of the Abakan and the Altai (Mordo Kan, Altai Kan, Oktu Kan, etc.). After this long invocation, he addresses the Märküt, the Birds of Heaven:

> Birds of Heaven, five Märküt,
> Ye with mighty copper talons,
> Copper is the moon's talon,
> And of ice the moon's beak;
> Broad thy wings, of mighty sweep,
> Like a fan thy long tail,

40 On the paleoethnological and religious implications of this rite, cf. Meuli, pp. 224 ff. and passim.

> Hides the moon thy left wing,
> And the sun thy right wing,
>   Thou, the mother of the nine eagles,
> Who strayest not, flying through the Yaik,
> Who weariest not about Edil,
>   Come to me, singing!
> Come, playing, to my right eye,
> Perch on my right shoulder! . . .

The shaman imitates the bird's cry to announce its presence: "Kazak, kak, kak! I am here, *kam!*" And as he does so, he drops his shoulder, as if sinking under the weight of a huge bird.

The summons to the spirits continues, and the drum becomes heavy. Provided with these numerous and powerful protectors, the shaman several times circles the birch that stands inside the yurt,[41] and kneels before the door to pray the Porter Spirit for a guide. Receiving a favorable reply, he returns to the center of the yurt, beating his drum, convulsing his body, and muttering unintelligible words. Then he purifies the whole gathering with his drum, beginning with the master of the house. It is a long and complex ceremony, at the end of which the shaman is in a state of exaltation. It is also the signal for the ascent proper, for soon afterward the *kam* suddenly takes his place on the first notch (*tapty*) in the birch, beating his drum violently and crying "Čok, čok!" He also makes motions to indicate that he is mounting into the sky. In "ecstasy" (?!) he circles the birch and the fire, imitating the sound of thunder, and then hurries to a bench covered with horsehide. This represents the soul of the *pûra*, the sacrificed horse. The shaman mounts it and cries:

41 This birch symbolizes the World Tree, which stands at the Center of the Universe, the Cosmic Axis that connects sky, earth, and underworld; the seven, nine, or twelve notches (*tapty*) represent the "heavens," the celestial planes. It should be noted that the shaman's ecstatic journey always takes place near the "Center of the World." We have seen (p. 117) that among the Buryat the shamanic birch is called *udeši-burkhan*, "the guardian of the door," for it opens the entrance to the sky for the shaman.

> I have climbed a step,
>> Aihai, aihai!
> I have reached a plane,
>> Šagarbata!
> I have climbed to the *tapty*'s head,
>> Šagarbata!
> I have risen to the full moon,
>> Šagarbata! [42]

The shaman becomes increasingly excited and, continuing to [be]at his drum, orders the *baš-tut-kan-kiši* to hurry. For the soul of [th]e "head-holder" abandons his body at the same time as the soul [of] the sacrificed horse. The *baš-tut-kan-kiši* complains of the diffi-[cu]lty of the road, and the shaman encourages him. Then, mounting [to] the second *tapty*, he symbolically enters the second heaven, [an]d cries:

> I have broken through the second ground,
> I have climbed the second level,
>> See, the ground lies in splinters.

[An]d, again imitating thunder and lightning, he proclaims:

>> Šagarbata! Šagarbata!
>> Now I have climbed up two levels . . .

In the third heaven the *pûra* becomes extremely tired, and, [to] relieve it, the shaman summons the goose. The bird presents [its]elf: "Kagak! Kagak! I am here, *kam!*" The shaman mounts it and [co]ntinues his celestial journey. He describes the ascent and imi[tat]es the cackling of the goose, which, in its turn, complains of the [dif]ficulties of the journey. In the third heaven there is a halt. The [sha]man now tells of his horse's weariness and his own. He also [giv]es information concerning the coming weather, the epidemics

[4]2 All this is clearly an exaggeration, due to intoxication at having [bro]ken through the first cosmic plane. For actually, the shaman has reached [onl]y the first heaven; he has not climbed to the highest *tapty*; he has not [the]n risen to the full moon (which is in the sixth heaven).

and misfortunes that threaten, and the sacrifices that the collectivit
should offer. After the *baš-tut-kan-kiši* has had a good rest, th
journey continues. The shaman climbs the notches in the birc
one after the other, thus successively entering the other celesti
regions. To enliven the performance, various episodes are intro
duced, some of them quite grotesque: the *kam* offers tobacco t
Karakuš, the Black Bird, in the shaman's service, and Karaku
drives away the cuckoo; he waters the *pûra*, imitating the sound c
a horse drinking; the sixth heaven is the scene of the last com
episode: a hare hunt.[43] In the fifth heaven the shaman has a lor
conversation with the powerful Yayutši (the "Supreme Creator"
who reveals several secrets of the future to him; some of these th
shaman communicates aloud, others are murmured. In the six
heaven the shaman bows to the Moon, and to the Sun in t
seventh. He passes through heaven after heaven to the ninth an
if he is really powerful, to the twelfth and even higher; the asce
depends entirely on the shaman's abilities. When he has gone
high as his power permits, he stops and humbly addresses B
Ülgän in the following terms:

> Prince, to whom three ladders lead,
> Bai Ülgän with the three flocks,
> Blue slope that has appeared,
> Blue sky that shows itself!
> Blue cloud, drifting away,
> Blue sky unattainable,
> White sky unattainable,
> Watering place a year away!
> Father Ülgän, thrice exalted,
> Whom the moon's ax-edge spares,
> Who uses the horse's hoof!
> Thou didst create all men, Ülgän,
> All that make a noise around us.
> All cattle thou hast forsaken, Ülgän!
> Deliver us not to misfortune

43 The hare being the lunar animal, it is natural that it should be hunte
the sixth heaven, that of the Moon.

Let us withstand the Evil One!
　　Show us not Körmös [the evil spirit]
Give us not into his hand!
　　Thou who the starry heaven
Hast turned a thousand, thousand times,
Condemn not my sins!

The shaman learns from Bai Ülgän if the sacrifice has been accepted and receives predictions concerning the weather and the coming harvest; he also learns what other sacrifice the divinity expects. This episode is the culminating point of the "ecstasy": the shaman collapses, exhausted. The *baš-tut-kan-kiši* approaches and takes the drum and stick from his hands. The shaman remains motionless and dumb. After a time he rubs his eyes, appears to wake from a deep sleep, and greets those present as if after a long absence.

Sometimes the festival ends with this ceremony; more often, especially for rich people, it continues for another day, spent in libations to the gods and in banquets at which immense quantities of alcoholic beverages are consumed.[44]

---

44 Harva (*Die religiösen Vorstellungen*, p. 557, fig. 105) reproduces a drawing by an Altaic shaman representing the celestial ascent on the occasion of a horse sacrifice. Anokhin publishes texts (poems and prayers) uttered during the shaman's ascent to the sky with the soul of the sacrificed colt, in the setting of the sacrifice to Karšüt, the most popular of Bai Ülgän's sons *Materialy po shamanstvu u altaitsev*, pp. 101–04; cf. tr. and comments in W. Schmidt, *Der Ursprung*, IX, 357–63). W. Amschler reproduces Verbitsky's observations on the horse sacrifice among the Telengit of the Altai; cf. Über die Tieropfer (besonders Pferdeopfer) der Telingiten im sibirischen Altai." D. Zelenin describes the horse sacrifice among the Kumandin of the Altai, a rite that closely follows the one described by Radlov, except that it lacks the shaman's celestial journey to present the soul of the horse to Sultan-man (= Bai Ülgän); see "Ein erotischer Ritus in den Opferungen der altaischen Tuerken," pp. 84–86. Among the Lebed Tatars a horse is sacrificed the full moon following the summer solstice; the purpose is agrarian ("that the wheat may grow") and it is highly possible that a late substitution is involved (Harva, p. 577, after K. Hilden). The same "agrarianization" of the horse sacrifice is found among the Teleut (sacrifice of July 20, "in the fields," ibid.). The Buryat also practice the horse sacrifice, but the shaman

Bai Ülgän and the Altaic Shaman

We will add some observations on the ritual just analyzed. It is clearly made up of two different parts, which are by no means inseparable: (a) the sacrifice to the celestial being; (b) the shaman's symbolic ascent [45] and his appearance, with the sacrificed animal before Bai Ülgän. In the form that was still attested in the nineteenth century, the Altaic horse sacrifice resembled the sacrifice offered to celestial Supreme Beings in the Far North of Asia, a rite that is also known elsewhere in the most archaic regions and that in no way demands the presence of a shaman-sacrificer. For as we said, several Turkic peoples practice the same horse sacrifice to the celestial being without having recourse to a shaman. Beside the Turko-Tatars, the horse sacrifice was practiced by the majority of Indo-European peoples,[46] and always offered to a god of the sky or the storm. So it is a legitimate conjecture that the role of the shaman in the Altaic rite is recent and is directed to different ends from the offering of the animal to the Supreme Being.

The second observation concerns Bai Ülgän himself. Although his attributes are celestial, there is good reason to believe that he is not distinctly, and was not always, a uranian Supreme God. Rather, he displays the character of a god of the "atmosphere" and of fertility, for he has a consort and numerous offspring and he presides over the fertility of flocks and the abundance of harvests. The real celestial Supreme God of the Altaians appears to be Tengere Kaira Kan [47] ("Merciful Emperor Heaven"), to judge

takes no part in it; theirs is a ceremony characteristic of horse-raising people. The most elaborate description of the sacrifice is the one given by Jeremi Curtin, *A Journey in Southern Siberia*, pp. 44–52. Other details are given Harva, pp. 574 ff. (after S. Shashkov) and W. Schmidt, *Der Ursprung*, 226 ff.

45 On this motif, cf. also W. Schmidt, XI, 651–58.

46 Cf. W. Koppers: "Pferdeopfer und Pferdekult der Indogermanen "Urtürkentum und Urindogermanentum im Lichte der völkerkundlich Universalgeschichte."

47 On this name, see Paul Pelliot, "Tängrim>tärim": "the name of 'Sky' is the earliest name attested in the Altaic languages, since it is alrea known in [the] Hiong-nou [language] about the Christian era" (p. 16

from his structure, which is closer to the Samoyed Num and the Turko-Mongol Tengri, "Sky." [48] It is Tengere Kaira Kan who plays the principal role in the myths concerning the cosmogony and the end of the world, whereas Bai Ülgän never appears in them. It is remarkable that no sacrifice is appointed for him, while those offered to Bai Ülgän and Erlik Khan are beyond counting. [49] But Tengere Kaira Kan's withdrawal from the cult is the destiny of almost all uranian gods. [50] It is probable that, in the beginning, the horse sacrifice was addressed to Tengere Kaira Kan; for, as we have seen, the Altaic rite falls in the class of sacrifices of the head and long bones, which are characteristic of the Arctic and North Asian celestial divinities. [51] We may recall, in this connection, that in Vedic India the horse sacrifice (*aśvamedha*), originally offered to Varuṇa and probably to Dyaus, was finally addressed to Prajāpati and even to Indra. [52] This phenomenon of the progressive substitution of a god of the atmosphere (and, in agricultural religions, of a fertility god) for a celestial god is comparatively frequent in the history of religions. [53]

Bai Ülgän, like gods of the atmosphere and fertility in general, is less distant, less passive than the pure uranian deities; he is interested in the fate of human beings and helps them in their daily needs. His "presence" is more concrete, the "dialogue" with him is more "human" and "dramatic." It is legitimate to assume that it was by virtue of a more concrete and morphologically richer religious experience that the shaman succeeded in ousting the earlier sacrificer from the horse sacrifice, just as Bai Ülgän ousted the earlier celestial god. The sacrifice became a sort of "psychophoria" leading to a dramatic encounter between the god and the shaman and to a concrete dialogue (the shaman sometimes going so far as to imitate the god's voice).

48 Cf. Eliade, *Patterns*, p. 60. See also J.-P. Roux, "Tängri. Essai sur le ciel-dieu des peuples altaïques," passim; N. Pallisen, "Die alte Religion der Mongolen und der Kultus Tchingis-Chans," especially pp. 185 ff.

49 W. Schmidt, *Der Ursprung*, IX, 143.

50 Cf. Eliade, *Patterns*, pp. 46 ff.

51 See Gahs, "Kopf-, Schädel- und Langknochenopfer."

52 Eliade, *Patterns*, p. 96.   53 See ibid., pp. 96 f.

It is easy to understand why the shaman, who, among all the varieties of religious experience, is especially drawn by the "ecstatic" forms, succeeded in usurping the principal function in the Altaic horse sacrifice. His technique of ecstasy enabled him to abandon his body and undertake the journey to the sky. Hence it was easy for him to repeat the celestial journey, taking with him the soul of the sacrificed animal to present it *directly and concretely* to Bai Ülgän. That a substitution occurred, probably quite late, is further shown by the slight intensity of the "trance." In the sacrifice described by Radlov, the "ecstasy" is obviously an imitation. The shaman laboriously mimes an ascent (after the traditional canon: bird flight, riding, etc.) and the interest of the rite is dramatic rather than ecstatic. This certainly does not mean that the Altaic shamans are incapable of trances; it is only that these occur at other shamanic séances than the horse sacrifice.

Descent to the Underworld (*Altaic*)

The Altaic shaman's celestial ascent has its counterpart in his descent to the underworld. This ceremony is far more difficult, and though it can be undertaken by shamans who are both "white" and "black," it is naturally the specialty of the latter. Radlov could not arrange to be present at any shamanic séance of the descent to the underworld. Anokhin, who collected the texts of five ascensional ceremonies, found only one shaman (Mampüi) who was willing to repeat to him the formulas for a séance of descent to the underworld. Mampüi, his informant, was a "black and white" shaman; this is perhaps why, in his invocation to Erlik Khan, he also mentioned Bai Ülgän. Anokhin [54] gives only the texts for the ceremony, without any information regarding the ritual proper.

According to these texts, it seems that the shaman makes a vertical descent down the seven successive "levels," or subterra-

54 *Materialy po shamanstvu u altaitsev*, pp. 84–91; cf. W. Schmidt's commentary, *Der Ursprung*, IX, 384–93.

nean regions, called *pudak*, "obstacles." He is accompanied by his ancestors and his helping spirits. As each "obstacle" is passed, he sees a new subterranean epiphany; the word *black* recurs in almost every verse. At the second "obstacle" he apparently hears metallic sounds; at the fifth, waves and the wind whistling; finally, at the seventh, where the nine subterranean rivers have their mouths, he sees Erlik Khan's palace, built of stone and black clay and defended in every direction. The shaman utters a long prayer to Erlik (in which he also mentions Bai Ülgän, "him above"), then he returns to the yurt and tells the audience the results of his journey.

Potanin has given a good description of the ritual of descent (but without the texts), based on the data supplied by an orthodox priest, Chivalkov, who in his youth had attended several ceremonies and had even joined in the chorus.[55] There are some differences between the ritual described by Potanin and the texts collected by Anokhin—differences due, no doubt, to materials coming from different tribes, but also to the fact that Anokhin gave only the texts of the invocations and prayers, without any explanation of the ritual. The most marked difference is in direction—vertical in Anokhin, horizontal and then twice vertical (ascent followed by descent) in Potanin.

The "black" shaman begins his journey from his own yurt. He takes the road to the south, crosses the nearby regions, climbs the Altai mountains and, in passing, describes the Chinese desert of red sand. Then he rides over a yellow steppe that a magpie could not fly across. "By the power of songs we cross it!" the shaman cries to the audience, and then intones a song which the audience carry on in chorus. Another steppe, of a pale color, which a crow could not fly across, stretches before him. Again the shaman appeals to the magic power of songs, and the audience accompany him in chorus. Finally he reaches the Mountain of Iron, *Temir taixa*, whose peaks touch the sky. It is a dangerous climb; the

---

55 *Ocherki*, IV, 64–68; summary in Mikhailowski, "Shamanism in Siberia," pp. 72–73; Harva, *Die religiösen Vorstellungen*, pp. 558–59; commentary in W. Schmidt, *Der Ursprung*, IX, 393–98.

shaman mimes the difficult ascent, and breathes deeply, exhausted, when he reaches the top.

The mountain is sown with the whitened bones of other shamans, whose strength did not suffice them to gain the summit, and of their horses. Once he is across the mountain, another ride takes the shaman to a hole that is the entrance to the other world, *yer mesi*, the "jaws of the earth," or *yer tunigi*, the "smoke hole of the earth." Entering it, the shaman first reaches a plain and finds a sea crossed by a bridge the breadth of a hair; he sets foot on it and, to give a striking image of his crossing this dangerous bridge, he totters and almost falls. At the bottom of the sea he sees the bones of countless shamans who have fallen into it, for a sinner could not cross the bridge. He passes by the places where sinners are tormented; he has time to see a man who, having listened at doors in his lifetime, is now nailed to a post by one ear; another, who had slandered, is hung up by the tongue; a glutton is surrounded by the choicest dishes without being able to reach them; and so on.

Having crossed the bridge, the shaman rides on toward the dwelling of Erlik Khan. He succeeds in entering it, despite the dogs that guard it and the porter who, finally, lets himself be persuaded by gifts (for beer, boiled beef, and polecat skins were prepared for this eventuality before the shaman set out for the underworld). After accepting the gifts, the porter allows the shaman to enter Erlik's yurt. The most dramatic scene now begins. The shaman goes to the door of the tent in which the ceremony is taking place, and pretends that he is approaching Erlik. He bows before the King of the Dead and touching his forehead with his drum and repeating "Mergu! mergu!" he attempts to attract Erlik's attention. Now the shaman begins to shout, to indicate that the god has noticed him and is very angry. The shaman flees to the tent door, and the ceremony is repeated three times. Finally Erlik Khan addresses him:

> Winged creatures wing not here,
> Crawling creatures crawl not here,

> You black, stinking beetle,
> Where did you come from?

The shaman tells him his name and the names of his ancestors and invites Erlik to drink; he pretends to pour wine into his drum and offers it to the King of the Underworld. Erlik accepts, begins to drink, and the shaman imitates everything, even the god's hiccups. He then offers Erlik an ox (killed earlier) and several garments and furs that are hanging from a cord. As he offers these things, the shaman touches each of them. But the furs and garments remain the property of their owner.

Meanwhile, Erlik has become completely drunk and the shaman laboriously mimes the phases of his drunkenness. The god becomes benevolent, blesses him, promises that the cattle will multiply, etc. The shaman joyously returns to earth, riding not a horse but a goose, and he walks about the yurt on tiptoe as if flying and imitates the bird's cry: "Naingak! naingak!" The séance ends, the shaman sits down, someone takes the drum from his hands and strikes it three times. The shaman rubs his eyes as if waking. Asked: "How was your journey? What success did you have?" he answers: "The journey was successful. I was well received!"

These descents to the underworld are undertaken especially to find and bring back a sick person's soul. A number of Siberian accounts of the journey will be found further on. Naturally, the shaman's descent also takes place for the opposite reason, that is, to escort the soul of the deceased to Erlik's realm.

We shall later compare these two types of ecstatic journeys—to the sky and the underworld—and point out the cosmographic schemas that they imply. For the moment, let us more closely examine the ritual of descent described by Potanin. Certain details are specifically characteristic of infernal descents—for example, the dog and the porter who guard the entrance to the realm of the dead. This is a well-known motif of infernal mythologies, and we shall encounter it more than once later. Less specifically infernal is the motif of the bridge as narrow as a hair. The bridge

symbolizes passage to the beyond, but not necessarily to th
underworld; only the guilty cannot cross it and are precipitate
into the abyss. Crossing an extremely narrow bridge that connect
two cosmic regions also signifies passing from one mode of bein;
to another—from uninitiate to initiate, or from "living" t
"dead." [56]

Potanin's account contains several incongruities. The shama
sets off on horseback, heads south, climbs a mountain, and the
descends through a hole to the underworld, from which he returr
not on his horse but on a goose. This last detail is somewh;
suspicious. Not because it is difficult to imagine a flight throug
the hole that leads to the underworld,[57] but because a flight c
goose-back suggests the shaman's celestial ascent. Probably the;
is contamination between the themes of ascent and descent.

As for the fact that the shaman first rides south, climbs a mour
tain, and only then descends into the mouth of the underworld, th
itinerary has been thought to contain a vague memory of a journe
to India and there has even been an attempt to identify the infern
visions with images that could be found in the cave temples
Turkestan or Tibet.[58] Southern, and finally Indian, influences ce.
tainly exist in Central Asian mythologies and folklores. Howeve
these influences conveyed a mythical geography, not vague mem
ories of a real geography (orography, itineraries, temples, cave
etc.). Probably Erlik's underworld had Irano-Indian models; b
the discussion of this problem would lead us too far and we reser
it for a later study.

---

56 Cf. below, pp. 482 ff.

57 In Siberian folklore the hero is often carried by an eagle or some oth
bird from the depths of the underworld to the surface of the earth. Amo;
the Goldi the shaman cannot undertake the ecstatic journey to the unde
world without the help of a bird-spirit (*koori*) which ensures his return to t
surface; the shaman makes the most difficult part of the return journey on t
back of his *koori* (Harva, *Die religiösen Vorstellungen*, p. 338).

58 N. K. Chadwick: "Shamanism among the Tatars of Central Asi;
p. 111; *Poetry and Prophecy*, pp. 82, 101; H. M. and N. K. Chadwick, *7
Growth of Literature*, III, 217.

The Shaman as Psychopomp (Altaians, Goldi, Yurak)

The peoples of North Asia conceive the otherworld as an inverted image of this world. Everything takes place as it does here, but in reverse. When it is day on earth, it is night in the beyond (this is why festivals of the dead are held after sunset; that is when they wake and begin their day); the summer of the living corresponds to winter in the land of the dead; a scarcity of game or fish on earth means that it is plentiful in the otherworld; and so forth. The Beltir put the reins and a bottle of wine in the corpse's left hand, for the left hand corresponds to the right hand on earth. In the underworld rivers flow backward to their sources. And everything that is inverted on earth is in its normal position among the dead; this is why objects offered on the grave for the use of the dead are turned upside down, unless, that is, they are broken, for what is broken here below is whole in the otherworld and vice versa.[59]

The inverted image is also found in the conception of the levels below (the "obstacles," *pudak*, which the shaman traverses in his descent). The Siberian Tatars know of seven or nine underground regions; the Samoyed speak of six levels under the sea. But since the Tungus and the Yakut know nothing of these infernal levels, probably the Tatar concept has an exotic origin.[60]

The funerary geography of the Central and North Asian peoples is quite complex, since it has been constantly contaminated by the invasion of religious ideas of southern origin. The dead set out either to the north or to the west.[61] But we also find the conception that the good go up to the sky and the wicked descend underground (for example, among the Tatars of the Altai [62]); however, this moral evaluation of post-mortem itineraries appears to be a fairly

---

59 Cf. Harva, *Die religiösen Vorstellungen*, pp. 343 ff. On all this, see our work in preparation, *Mythologies of Death.*

60 Harva, p. 350; see below, pp. 275 ff.   61 Harva, p. 346.

62 Radlov, *Aus Sibirien*, II, 12.

late innovation.[63] The Yakut believe that at death both good and bad go up to the sky, where the soul (*kut*) takes the form of a bird.[64] Presumably the "soul-birds" perch on the branches of the World Tree, a mythical image that we shall also find elsewhere. But since the Yakut likewise hold that evil spirits (*abassy*), which are also souls of the dead, dwell underground, we are obviously in the presence of a twofold religious tradition.[65]

According to another conception, certain privileged persons, whose bodies are burned, rise to the sky with the smoke, there to lead a life like that of men on earth. The Buryat believe this to be true of their shamans, and the same conception is found among the Chukchee and the Koryak.[66] The idea that fire ensures a celestial destiny after death is also confirmed by the belief that those who are struck by lightning fly up to the sky. "Fire," of whatever kind, transforms man into "spirit"; this is why shamans are held to be "masters over fire" and become insensitive to the touch of hot coals. "Mastery over fire" or being burned are in a manner equivalent to an initiation. A similar idea underlies the conception that heroes and all who die a violent death mount to the sky;[67] their death is considered an initiation. On the contrary, death from disease can only lead the deceased to the underworld; for disease is provoked by the evil spirits of the dead. When someone falls ill, the Altaians and the Teleut say that "he is being eaten by the *körmös*" (the dead). And of one who has just died they say, "he has been eaten by the *körmös*."[68]

63 Harva, pp. 360 f.   64 Ibid.

65 According to Sieroszewski, some Yakut place the realm of the dead "beyond the eighth heaven, to the north, in a country where eternal night reigns, where an icy wind blows forever, the pale sun of the north shines, the moon shows itself upside down, where girls and youths remain eternally virgin"; while, according to others, there is another world underground exactly like ours, which can be entered through the opening that the inhabitants of the subterranean regions have left as an air hole ("Du chamanisme," pp. 206 ff.). Cf. also B. D. Shimkin, "A Sketch of the Ket, or Yenisei 'Ostyak,'" pp. 166 ff.

66 See below, pp. 249 ff.

67 Harva, *Die religiösen Vorstellungen*, p. 362.   68 Ibid., p. 367.

This is why, in taking leave of a dead man after his burial, the Goldi beg him not to take his wife and children with him. The Yellow Uigur address him as follows: "Take not your child with you, take not your cattle, nor your goods!" And if a man's widow or children or friends die soon after his decease, the Teleut believe that he has taken their souls with him.[69] Feelings toward the dead are ambivalent. On the one hand, they are revered, are invited to funerary banquets, in time they come to be regarded as tutelary spirits of the family; on the other hand, they are feared, and all kinds of precautions are taken to prevent their reappearance among the living. Actually, this ambivalence can be reduced to two opposite and successive behaviors: the recently dead are feared, the long dead are revered and are expected to act as protectors. The fear of the dead is due to the fact that, at first, no dead person accepts his new mode of being; he cannot renounce "living" and he returns to his family. And it is this tendency that upsets the equilibrium of the society. Not yet having entered into the world of the dead, the newly deceased man tries to take his family and friends and even his flocks with him; he wants to continue his suddenly interrupted existence, that is, to "live" among his kin. So what is feared is far less any malice on the part of the dead man than his ignorance of his new condition, his refusal to forsake "his world."

Hence all the precautions taken to prevent the dead man from returning to his village: the funeral party take another road back from the cemetery to confuse the dead man, they hasten away from the grave and purify themselves as soon as they reach home; means of transportation (sled, cart, etc.—all of which will also serve the dead in their new country) are destroyed in the cemetery; finally the roads to the village are guarded for several nights and fires are lighted.[70] All these measures do not prevent the souls of the dead from prowling about their houses for three or seven days.[71] Another idea can be seen in connection with this belief: that the dead do not finally take the road to the beyond until after

69 Ibid., p. 281; cf. also p. 309. 70 Ibid., pp. 282 ff.
71 Ibid., pp. 287 ff.

the funerary banquet that is held in their honor three, seven, or forty days after their decease.[72] On this occasion they are offered food and drink, which are thrown into the fire, the participants visit the cemetery, and the dead man's favorite horse is sacrificed, eaten beside his grave, and its head suspended from a stake planted directly in the grave (Abakan Tatars, Beltir, Sagai, Karginz, etc.[73]). This is followed by a "purification" of the house of the deceased by a shaman. The ceremony includes, among other things, a dramatic search for the deceased's soul and its final expulsion by the shaman (Teleut [74]). Some Altaic shamans even escort the soul to the underworld, and, in order not to be recognized by the inhabitants of the nether regions, they daub their faces with soot.[75] Among the Tungus of Turukhansk the shaman is called in only if the dead person continues to haunt his former home long after the funeral.[76]

The role of the shaman in the Altaic and Siberian funerary complex is clearly shown by the customs just described. The shaman becomes indispensable when the dead person is slow to forsake the

72 Probably these Altaic beliefs have been influenced by Christianity and Islamism. The Teleut call the funerary banquet held seven or forty days or a year after death *üzüt pairamy*; the word *pairam* itself betrays a southern origin (Persian *bairam*, "festival"; ibid., p. 323). The custom of honoring the dead forty-nine days after decease, which is also found among many peoples of Central Asia, attests a Lamaist influence (ibid., p. 332). But there is reason to suppose that these southern influences have been grafted on a ancient festival of the dead, changing its meaning to some extent. For the "death watch" is a widespread custom, its primary purpose being a symbolic accompanying of the dead person into the beyond, or rehearsing the infernal itinerary that he must follow in order not to become lost. In this sense, the Tibetan Book of the Dead denotes a state of affairs far earlier than Lamaism instead of escorting the deceased on his otherworld journey (like the Siberian or Indonesian shaman), the lama reminds him of all the possible itineraries for a dead man (like the Indonesian female mourners, etc.; cf. below pp. 438 ff.). On the mystical number 49 (7 × 7) in China, Tibet, and among the Mongols, see R. A. Stein, "Leao-Tche," pp. 118 ff.

73 Harva, *Die religiösen Vorstellungen*, pp. 322 ff.

74 Ibid., p. 324; Anokhin, *Materialy*, pp. 20 ff.

75 Radlov, *Aus Sibirien*, II, 55.

76 Harva, *Die religiösen Vorstellungen*, p. 541.

world of the living. In such a case, only the shaman possesses the power of the psychopomp. For one thing, because he has traveled it many times himself, he is thoroughly familiar with the road to the underworld; then too, only he can capture the intangible soul and carry it to its new dwelling place. The fact that the psychopompic journey takes place on the occasion of the funerary banquet and the "purification" ceremony, and not immediately after death, seems to indicate that for three, seven, or forty days the soul lives in the cemetery, and only after that period is it believed to take its departure for the underworld.[77] However this may be, among certain peoples (such as the Altaians, the Goldi, the Yurak) the shaman escorts the deceased to the beyond at the end of the funeral banquet, while among others (Tungus) he is summoned to fill his role of psychopomp only if the dead man continues to haunt the land of the living beyond the usual period. If we consider that among other peoples who practice a kind of shamanism (as, for example, among the Lolo) the shaman is obliged to lead all the dead, without exception, to their final abode, we have reason to conclude that, originally, this situation prevailed throughout North Asia, and that certain innovations (such as that of the Tungus) are late.

Here is Radlov's description of a séance organized to escort the soul of a woman forty days after her death. The ceremony takes place in the evening. The shaman begins by circling the yurt, beating his drum; then he enters the tent and, going to the fire, invokes the deceased. Suddenly the shaman's voice changes; he begins to speak on a high pitch, in falsetto, for it is really the dead woman who is speaking. She complains that she does not know the road, that she is afraid to leave her relatives, and so on, but finally consents to the shaman's leading her, and the two set off

77 It must be borne in mind, however, that for the majority of Turko-Tatar and Siberian peoples, a man has three souls, of which at least one always remains in the grave. Cf. Ivar Paulson, *Die primitiven Seelenvorstellungen der nordeurasischen Völker*, especially pp. 223 ff.; A. Friedrich, "Das Bewusstsein eines Naturvolkes von Haushalt und Ursprung des Lebens," p. 47 f.

together for the subterranean realm. When they arrive, the shaman finds that the dead refuse to permit the newcomer to enter. Prayers proving ineffectual, brandy is offered; the séance gradually becomes more lively, even to the point of the grotesque, for the souls of the dead, through the shaman's voice, begin quarreling and singing together; finally they consent to receive the dead woman. The second part of the ritual represents the return journey; the shaman dances and shouts until he falls to the ground unconscious.[78]

The Goldi have two funerary ceremonies: the *nimgan*, which takes place seven days or even longer (two months) after the death, and the *kazatauri*, the great ceremony celebrated some time after the former and at the end of which the soul is conducted to the underworld. During the *nimgan* the shaman enters the dead person's house with his drum, searches for the soul, captures it, and makes it enter a sort of cushion (*fanya*).[79] The banquet follows, participated in by all the relatives and friends of the dead person present in the *fanya*; the shaman offers the latter brandy. The *kazatauri* begins in the same way. The shaman dons his costume takes his drum, and goes to search for the soul in the vicinity of the yurt. During all this time he dances and recounts the difficulties of the road to the underworld. Finally he captures the soul and brings it into the house, where he makes it enter the *fanya* The banquet continues late into the night, and the food that is left over is thrown into the fire by the shaman. The women bring a bed into the yurt, the shaman puts the *fanya* in it, covers it with a blanket, and tells the dead person to sleep. He then lies down in the yurt and goes to sleep himself.

The following day he again dons his costume and wakes the deceased by drumming. Another banquet follows and at night (for

78 *Aus Sibirien*, II, 52–55.

79 The word *fanya* originally meant "shade," but finally came to mean the soul's material receptacle as well; cf. Paulson, *Die primitiven Seelenvorstellungen*, pp. 120 ff. (after I. A. Lopatin, *Goldy amurskiye, ussuriskiye i sungariskiye*). Cf. also G. Ränk, *Die heilige Hinterecke im Hauskult der Völker Nordosteuropas und Nordasiens*, pp. 179 ff.

the ceremony may continue for several days) he puts the *fanya* to bed again and covers it up. Finally one morning the shaman begins his song and, addressing the deceased, advises him to eat well but to drink sparingly, for the journey to the underworld is extremely difficult for a drunken person. At sunset preparations for the departure are made. The shaman sings, dances, and daubs his face with soot. He invokes his helping spirits and begs them to guide him and the dead man in the beyond. He leaves the yurt for a few minutes and climbs a notched tree that has been set up in readiness; from here he sees the road to the underworld. (He has, in fact, climbed the World Tree and is at the summit of the world.) At the same time he sees many other things: plentiful snow, successful hunting and fishing, and so on.

Returning to the yurt, he summons two powerful tutelary spirits to help him: *butchu*, a kind of one-legged monster with a human face and feathers, and *koori*, a long-necked bird.[80] Without the help of these two spirits, the shaman could not come back from the underworld; he makes the most difficult part of the return journey sitting on the *koori's* back.

After shamanizing until he is exhausted, he sits down, facing the west, on a board that represents a Siberian sled. The *fanya*, containing the dead person's soul, and a basket of food are set beside him. The shaman asks the spirits to harness the dogs to the sled and for a "servant" to keep him company during the journey. A few moments later he "sets off" for the land of the dead.

The songs he intones and the words he exchanges with the "servant" make it possible to follow his route. At first the road is easy, but the difficulties increase as the land of the dead is approached. A great river bars the way, and only a good shaman can get his team and sled across to the other bank. Some time later, he sees signs of human activity: footprints, ashes, bits of wood—the village of the dead is not far away. Now, indeed, dogs are heard

80 Wooden figurines of these mythical beings exist; cf. Harva, *Die religiösen Vorstellungen*, figs. 39–40, p. 339. The shaman takes them with him on his descent to the underworld.

barking at no great distance, the smoke from the yurts is seen, the first reindeer appear. The shaman and the deceased have reached the underworld. At once the dead gather and ask the shaman to tell them his name and that of the newcomer. The shaman is careful not to give his real name; he searches through the crowd of spirits for the close relatives of the soul he is conducting, so that he may entrust it to them. Having done so, he hastens to return to earth and, arriving, gives a long account of all that he has seen in the land of the dead and the impressions of the dead man whom he escorted. He brings each of the audience greetings from their dead relatives and even distributes little gifts from them. At the close of the ceremony the shaman throws the *fanya* into the fire. The strict obligations of the living to the dead are now terminated.[81]

A similar ceremony is held among the forest Yurak, in Central Siberia, at a great distance from the Goldi. The shaman seeks the soul of the deceased and takes it with him to the underworld. The ritual occupies two sessions: on the first day the descent to the land of the dead is accomplished; on the second the shaman returns to earth alone. His songs make it possible to follow his adventures. He comes to a river full of pieces of wood; his bird-spirit, *yorra*, opens the way for him through these obstacles (which are presumably the old, worn-out skis of the spirits). A second river is full of the remains of old shamanic drums, a third is made impassable by the cervical vertebrae of dead shamans. With *yorra* opening the way for him, the shaman comes to the Great Water beyond which stretches the land of the shades. There the dead continue to lead the same life that they did on earth; the rich are still rich, the poor still poor. But all become young again, and

81 Harva, *Die religiösen Vorstellungen*, pp. 334–40, 345 (after Lopatin, *Goldy*, and P. P. Shimkevich, *Materialy dlya izucheniya shamanstva u goldov*). The essential information in Shimkevich's book had already been condensed in W. Grube, "Das Schamanentum bei den Golden." A similar ceremony prevails among the Tungus; cf. Shirokogoroff, *Psychomental Complex*, p. 309. On the Tibetan ceremony for "projecting" the dead person's soul into an effigy, in order to save it from reincarnation in the lower worlds, see below pp. 439 f.

await their rebirth on earth. The shaman leads the soul to the group of its relatives. When he comes to the dead man's father, the latter cries, "Look! here is my son!" The shaman returns by another road, which is full of adventures. The narrative of his return journey takes a whole day. One after the other, he comes upon a pike, a reindeer, a hare, and other animals; he pursues them and brings back to earth good luck in hunting.[82]

Some of these themes of shamanic descents to the underworld have passed into the oral literature of the Siberian peoples. Thus we find the adventures of the Buryat hero Mu-monto narrated; he descends to the underworld in his father's stead and, on his return to earth, describes the torments of sinners.[83] Among the Tatars of the Sayan Steppe A. Castrén obtained the story of Kubaiko, the brave girl who goes down to the underworld to bring back the head of her brother, decapitated by a monster. After many adventures and after witnessing the torments by which various sins are punished, Kubaiko finds herself in the presence of the King of the Underworld himself, Irle Kan. He consents to her carrying back her brother's head if she can emerge triumphant from an ordeal: she must draw out of the ground a seven-horned ram buried so deep that only its horns can be seen. Kubaiko successfully performs the feat and returns to earth with her brother's head and the miraculous water that the god has given her to restore him to life.[84]

The Tatars have a considerable literature on the subject; but it consists rather of heroic cycles in which the protagonist, among

---

82 T. Lehtisalo, *Entwurf einer Mythologie der Jurak-Samojeden*, pp. 33–35; ibid., pp. 135–37 (the ritual songs of the Samoyed shamans). The Jurak believe that certain human beings ascend to the sky after death, but they are very few, their number being limited to those who have been pious and pure during their life on earth (ibid., p. 138). Ascent to the sky after death is also attested in tales: An old man, Vyriirje Seerradeetta, tells his two young wives that the god (Num) has summoned him and that the next day a wire will come down from the sky; he will climb up the wire to the abode of God (ibid., p. 139). Cf. the motif of ascent by a vine, a tree, a scarf, etc., below, pp. 487 ff.

83 Harva, *Die religiösen Vorstellungen*, pp. 354–55.

84 *Nordische Reisen und Forschungen*, III, 147 ff.

many other ordeals, must also go down to the underworld.[85] Such descents are not always shamanic in structure—that is, based on the shaman's power to consort with the dead with impunity, search for the soul of a sick person in the underworld, or accompany a dead person there. The Tatar heroes must emerge victorious from certain ordeals which, as we have just seen in the case of Kubaiko, constitute a schema of heroic initiation, challenging the daring, courage, and strength of the protagonist. In the legend of Kubaiko however, certain elements are shamanic: the girl goes down to the underworld to bring back her brother's head,[86] that is, his "soul," just as the shaman brings the sick person's soul back from there; she sees the infernal torments, which she describes and which, even though influenced by ideas from South Asia or the ancient Near East, contain certain descriptions of infernal topography which, all over the world, shamans were the first to communicate to the living. As we shall see more clearly later, several of the most famous journeys to the underworld, undertaken to learn the fate of men after death, are "shamanic" in structure, in the sense that they employ the ecstatic technique of shamans. All this is not without importance for an understanding of the "origins" of epic literature. When we attempt to evaluate the cultural contribution of shamanism, we shall show to what an extent shamanic experiences contributed toward crystallizing the first great epic themes.[87]

85 See the excellent summary (after Radlov's and Castrén's texts) in H. M. and N. K. Chadwick, *The Growth of Literature*, III, 81 ff. Cf. also N. Poppe, "Zum khalkhamongolischen Heldenepos," especially pp. 202 ff (the exploits of Bolot Khan).

86 The same "Orpheus motif" is found among the Manchu, the Polynesians, and the North American Indians; cf. below, pp. 238, 310 ff., 367 ff

87 Cf. below, pp. 507 ff.

CHAPTER SEVEN

Shamanism
in Central and North Asia:
II. MAGICAL CURES. THE
SHAMAN AS PSYCHOPOMP

T H E principal function of the shaman in Central and North Asia is magical healing. Several conceptions of the cause of illness are found in the area, but that of the "rape of the soul" is by far the most widespread.[1] Disease is attributed to the soul's having strayed away or been stolen, and treatment is in principle reduced to finding it, capturing it, and obliging it to resume its place in the patient's body. In some parts of Asia the cause of illness can be the intrusion of a magical object into the patient's body or his "possession" by evil spirits; in this case, cure consists in extracting the harmful object or expelling the demons. Sometimes disease has a twofold cause—theft of the soul aggravated by "possession" by evil spirits—and the shamanic cure includes both searching for the soul and expelling the demons.

Obviously all this is complicated by the fact of the multiplicity of souls. Like so many other "primitive" peoples, and especially the Indonesians, the North Asian peoples believe that man can have

---

1 Cf. Forrest E. Clements, *Primitive Concepts of Disease*, pp. 190 ff. See also Ivar Paulson, *Die primitiven Seelenvorstellungen der nordeurasischen Völker*, pp. 337 ff.; Lauri Honko, *Krankheitsprojectile: Untersuchung über eine urtümliche Krankheitserklärung*, pp. 27.

as many as three or even seven souls.[2] At death one of them remains in the grave, another descends to the realm of shades, and a third ascends to the sky. But this same conception—attested, for example, among the Chukchee and the Yukagir [3]—is but one of the many ideas concerning the destiny of the three souls after death. Among other peoples at least one soul disappears at death, or is eaten by demons, or the like.[4] In the case of these latter conceptions, the soul that, at death, is eaten by evil spirits or descends to the land of the dead is the one that, during earthly life, causes illnesses by its flight.

Only the shaman can undertake a cure of this kind. For only he "sees" the spirits and knows how to exorcise them; only he recognizes that the soul has fled, and is able to overtake it, in ecstasy, and return it to its body. Often the cure involves various sacrifices, and it is always the shaman who decides if they are needed and what form they shall take; the recovery of physical health is closely dependent on restoring the balance of spiritual forces, for it is often the case that the illness is due to a neglect or an omission in respect to the infernal powers, which also belong to the sphere of the sacred. Everything that concerns the soul and its adventure, here on earth and in the beyond, is the exclusive province of the shaman. Through his own preinitiatory and initiatory experiences, he knows the drama of the human soul, its instability, its precariousness; in addition, he knows the forces that threaten it and the regions to which it can be carried away. If shamanic cure in-

2 On all this, see Paulson, passim.

3 Cf. W. G. Bogoras, *The Chukchee*, p. 332; W. I. Jochelson, *The Yukaghir and the Yukaghirized Tungus*, p. 157.

4 On the three souls of the Buryat, see G. Sandschejew, "Weltanschauung und Schamanismus der Alaren-Burjaten," pp. 578 ff., 933, and passim; the first soul resides in the bones, the second—which probably resides in the blood—can leave the body and move about in the form of a wasp or a bee; the third, which resembles the man in every particular, is a kind of ghost. At death the first soul remains in the skeleton, the second is eaten by the spirits, and the third appears to humans in the form of a ghost (ibid., p. 585). On the seven souls of the Ket, cf. B. D. Shimkin, "A Sketch of the Ket, or Yenisei 'Ostyak,' " p. 166.

volves ecstasy, it is precisely because illness is regarded as a corruption or alienation of the soul.

In what follows we shall describe a number of healing séances, without any pretension to exhausting the abundant documentation that has been collected and published to date. To lessen the monotony (for in general the majority of the descriptions are much alike), we have taken the liberty of grouping the data without always taking geographic or cultural continuity into account.

Summoning and Searching for the Soul: Tatars, Buryat, Kazak-Kirgiz

The Teleut shaman calls back the soul of a sick child in these words: 'Come back to your country! . . . to the yurt, by the bright fire! . . . Come back to your father . . . to your mother! . . .'' [5] Among some peoples calling back the soul constitutes a stage in the shamanic cure. It is only if the soul refuses or is unable to return to its place in the body that the shaman goes to look for it and finally descends to the realm of the dead to bring it back. The Buryat, for example, have both the invocation of the soul and the shaman's search for it.

Among the Buryat of the Alarsk region the shaman seats himself on a rug beside the patient, surrounded by several objects, among them an arrow. From its point a red silk thread leads to the birch set up outside the yurt, in the court. Along this thread the patient's soul is supposed to re-enter its body; hence the door of the yurt is left open. Near the tree, someone holds a horse; the Buryat believe that the horse is the first to perceive the return of the soul and shows it by quivering. On a table in the yurt are cakes, *arasun*, brandy, tobacco. If the patient is old, chiefly old people are invited to the séance; if an adult, grown men; if a child, children. The shaman begins by invoking the soul: "Your father is A, your mother B, your own name is C. Where are you lingering, whither have you gone? . . . Sad sit those in the yurt. . . ."

5 U. Harva, *Die religiösen Vorstellungen*, p. 268.

Those present burst into tears. The shaman expatiates on the grief of the family and the sadness of the house. "Your wife and your dear children, so unexpectedly orphaned, call you, hopelessly weeping and wailing, and cry to you, 'Father, where are you?' Hear and have pity on them, come back to them. . . . Your herd of countless horses longs for you, whinnying loudly and crying pitifully, 'Where art thou, our master? Come back to us!' " and so on.[6]

Usually this is only a first ceremony. If it does not succeed, the shaman renews his efforts in another direction. According to G. N. Potanin, the Buryat shaman holds a preliminary séance to determine if the patient's soul has strayed away or if it has been stolen from him and is a captive in Erlik's prison. The shaman begins to search for the soul; if he finds it near the village, its reinstallation in the body is easy. If not, he searches the forests, the steppes, and even the bottom of the sea. Failure to find it indicates that it is a prisoner of Erlik, and the only recourse is costly sacrifices. Erlik sometimes demands another soul in place of the one he has imprisoned; the problem then is to find one that is available. With the patient's consent, the shaman decides who the victim shall be. While the latter is asleep the shaman, taking the form of an eagle, descends on him and, tearing out his soul, goes down with it to the realm of the dead and presents it to Erlik, who then allows him to take away the patient's. The victim dies soon afterward, and the patient recovers. But he has gained only a respite, for he too will die three, seven, or nine years later.[7]

---

6 Harva, pp. 268–72 (after P. P. Batarov); cf. Sandschejew, pp. 582–83. On the shamanic séance among the Buryat, see also L. Stieda, "Das Schamanenthum unter den Burjäten," especially pp. 299 ff., 316 ff.; N. Melnikow "Die ehemaligen Menschenopfer und der Schamanismus bei den Burjaten des irkutskischen Gouvernements"; W. Schmidt, *Der Ursprung der Gottesidee,* X, 375–85; L. Krader, "Buryat Religion and Society," pp. 330–33.

7 *Ocherki severo-zapadnoi Mongolii,* IV, 86–87; cf. V. M. Mikhailowski "Shamanism in Siberia and European Russia," pp. 69–70; Sandschejew pp. 580 ff. See also Mikhailowski, pp. 127 ff., on the various Buryat healing techniques.

Among the Abakan Tatars the séance may continue up to five or six hours and includes, among other elements, the shaman's ecstatic journey to distant regions. But the journey is on the whole figurative. After spending a long time shamanizing and praying to the god for the patient's health, the *kam* leaves the yurt. On his return he lights a pipe and relates that he has gone as far as China, has crossed mountains and seas, to find the remedy needed for a cure.[8] Here we have a hybrid type of shamanic séance, in which the search for the patient's strayed soul is transformed into an ecstatic pseudo-journey in search of remedies. The same procedure is found in extreme northeastern Siberia, among the Chukchee, where the shaman simulates a trance for a quarter of an hour, during which he is believed to journey ecstatically to ask advice from the spirits.[9] Recourse to ritual sleep to enter into communication with the spirits in order to cure an illness is also found among the Ugrian peoples.[10] But among the Chukchee there is, rather, a recent decadence of the shamanic technique. As we shall see presently, the "old shamans" undertook real ecstatic journeys in search of the soul.

A hybrid method, in which the shamanic cure is already transformed into a ceremony of exorcism, is that of the Kazak-Kirgiz *baqça*. The séance begins with an invocation to Allah and the Moslem saints, and continues with an appeal to the jinni and threats to the evil spirits. The *baqça* sings on and on. At a certain moment the spirits take possession of him, and during this trance he "walks barefoot over red-hot iron" and several times introduces a lighted wick into his mouth. He touches the red-hot iron with his tongue and "with his knife, sharp as a razor, strikes at his face, leaving no visible mark." After these shamanic exploits he again invokes Allah: "O God, bestow happiness! Oh, deign to look on my tears! I implore thy help! . . ."[11] Invocation of the

---

8 H. von Lankenau, "Die Schamanen und das Schamanenwesen," pp. 81 ff. For ritual songs among the Teleut, see Mikhailowski, p. 98.

9 Bogoras, *The Chukchee*, p. 441.   10 See below, pp. 220 f.

11 J. Castagné, "Magie et exorcisme chez les Kazak-Kirghizes et autres peuples turcs orientaux," pp. 68 ff., 90 ff., 101 ff., 125 ff. Cf. Mikhailowski,

Supreme God is not incompatible with shamanic healing, and we shall find it again among some peoples of extreme northeastern Siberia. But among the Kazak-Kirgiz first place is given to expelling the evil spirits that have taken possession of the patient. To accomplish this, the *baqça* puts himself in the shamanic state, that is, obtains insensibility to fire and knife cuts, in other words, assumes the condition of a "spirit"; as such, he has the power to frighten and expel the demons of disease.

The Shamanic Séance among the Ugrians and Lapps

When he is called to perform a cure, the Tremyugan shaman begins beating his drum and playing the guitar until he falls into ecstasy. Abandoning his body, his soul enters the underworld and goes in search of the patient's soul. He persuades the dead to let him bring it back to earth by promising them the gift of a shirt or other things; sometimes, however, he is obliged to use more forcible means. When he wakes from his ecstasy the shaman has the patient's soul in his closed right hand and replaces it in the body through the right ear.[12]

Among the Ostyak shamans of the Irtysh the technique is markedly different. Summoned to a house, the shaman performs fumigations and dedicates a piece of cloth to Sänke, the celestial Supreme Being.[13] After fasting all day, at nightfall he takes a bath, eats three or seven mushrooms, and goes to sleep. Some hours later he suddenly wakes and, trembling all over, communicates what the spirits, through their "messenger," have revealed to him: the spirit to which sacrifice must be made, the man who made the

---

p. 98: the shaman rides over the steppe for a long time and, on his return, strikes the patient with his whip.

12 K. F. Karjalainen, *Die Religion der Jugra-Völker*, III, 305. The same means of inducing ecstasy (drum, guitar) are employed when the shamanic séance is held for the hunt or to determine what sacrifices the gods desire (ibid., p. 306) On the search for the soul, see ibid., I, 31.

13 The original meaning of *sänke* was "luminous, shining, light" (ibid. II, 260).

hunt fail, and so on. The shaman then relapses into deep sleep and on the following day the specified sacrifices are offered.[14]

Ecstasy through intoxication by mushrooms is known throughout Siberia. In other parts of the world it has its counterpart in ecstasy induced by narcotics or tobacco, and we shall return to the problem of the mystical powers of toxins. Meanwhile, we may note anomalies in the rite just described. A piece of cloth is offered to the Supreme Being, but communication is with the spirits and it is to them that sacrifices are offered; shamanic ecstasy proper is obtained by intoxication with mushrooms—a method, by the way, which allows shamanesses, too, to fall into similar trances, with the difference that they address the celestial god Sänke directly. These contradictions show that there is a certain hybridism in the ideology underlying these techniques of ecstasy. As Karjalainen already observed,[15] this type of Ugrian shamanism appears to be comparatively recent and derivative.

Among the Ostyak-Vasyugan shamanic technique is considerably more complicated. If the patient's soul has been carried off by one of the dead, the shaman sends one of his helping spirits to seek it. The spirit assumes the appearance of a dead man and goes down to the underworld. When it finds the thief it suddenly produces from its breast a spirit in the shape of a bear; the thief is frightened and lets the patient's soul escape through his throat or his fist. The helping spirit catches it and brings it back to the shaman on earth. During all this time the shaman plays the guitar and recounts his messenger's adventures. If the patient's soul has been carried off by an evil spirit, the shaman himself is obliged to undertake the journey of recovery, which is far more difficult.[16]

The Vasyugan have another method of shamanizing. The sha-

---

14 Ibid., III, 306. A similar custom is attested among the Tsingala (Ostyak). Sacrifices are offered to Sänke, the shaman eats three mushrooms and falls into trance. Shamanesses employ similar methods; achieving ecstasy by mushroom intoxication, they visit Sänke and then sing songs in which they reveal what they have learned from the Supreme Being himself (ibid., p. 307). Cf. also Jochelson, *The Koryak*, II, 582–83.

15 *Die Religion der Jugra-Völker*, III, 315 ff.   16 Ibid., pp. 308 ff.

man seats himself in the darkest corner of the house and begins playing the guitar. In his left hand he holds a sort of spoon, which also serves as a means of divination. He now invokes his helping spirits, which are seven in number. He has a powerful messenger, the "Stern Woman with the Handled Stick," whom he sends off through the air to summon his helpers. One after the other, they present themselves, and the shaman relates their journeys in songs. "From the Sky Quarter of May-junk-kān, May-junk-kān's little daughter has been granted me; I perceive her arrival from under the six layers of the earth, I hear 'the hairy beast of the great earth' (= the bear) coming from under the first layer of the earth to the water of the second." (At this moment the shaman begins to move the spoon.) In the same way he describes the arrival of the spirits from the second and third underground regions and so on to the sixth, and each new arrival is announced by the spoon. After this the spirits from the different celestial regions present themselves. They are summoned, one by one, from all directions: "From the Sky Quarter of the Reindeer Samoyed, from the Sky Quarter of the northern people, from the city of the spirit princes of the Samoyed with their wives . . ." Then follows a dialogue between all these spirits (speaking through the shaman's mouth) and the shaman himself. This operation continues through a whole evening.

The second evening the shaman makes his ecstatic journey accompanied by his helping spirits. The audience is told at length of the vicissitudes of this difficult and dangerous expedition; it is exactly like the journey that the shaman makes to conduct the soul of the sacrificed horse to heaven.[17] The shaman is in no sense "possessed" by his helping spirits. As Karjalainen observes,[18] they whisper into his ear in just the same way in which "birds" inspire the epic bards. "The breath of the spirit comes to the magician," the northern Ostyak say; it "touches" the shaman, say the Vogul.[19]

Among the Ugrians shamanic ecstasy is less a trance than a "state of inspiration"; the shaman sees and hears spirits; he is

17 Karjalainen, *Die Religion der Jugra-Völker*, pp. 310–17.
18 Ibid., p. 318.   19 Ibid.

"carried out of himself" because he is journeying in ecstasy through distant regions, but he is not unconscious. He is a visionary and inspired. However, the basic experience is ecstatic, and the principal means of obtaining it is, as in other regions, magico-religious music. Intoxication by mushrooms also produces contact with the spirits, but in a passive and crude way. But, as we have already said, this shamanic technique appears to be late and derivative. Intoxication is a mechanical and corrupt method of reproducing "ecstasy," being "carried out of oneself"; it tries to imitate a model that is earlier and that belongs to another plane of reference.

Among the Yenisei Ostyak healing requires two ecstatic journeys. The first is more of a rapid survey; it is during the second, which ends in trance, that the shaman enters deep into the beyond. The séance begins, as usual, with invoking the spirits and putting them in the drum one after the other. During all this time the shaman sings and dances. When the spirits have come he begins to leap; this means that he has left the earth and is rising toward the clouds. At a certain moment he cries: "I am high in the air, I see the Yenisei a hundred versts away." On his way he meets other spirits and tells the audience whatever he sees. Then, addressing the spirit helper who is carrying him through the air, he cries: "O my little fly, rise still higher, I want to see farther! . . ." Soon afterward he returns to the yurt, surrounded by his spirits. It seems that he has not found the patient's soul, or he has seen it at a great distance, in the land of the dead. To reach it, he begins dancing again, until trance supervenes. Still carried by his spirits, he leaves his body and enters the beyond, from which he finally returns with the patient's soul.[20]

So far as Lapp shamanism is concerned, we shall confine our-

20 Å. Ohlmarks, *Studien zum Problem des Schamanismus*, p. 184, citing . I. Anuchin, *Ocherk shamanstva u yeniseiskikh ostyakov*, pp. 28–31; cf. also imkin, "A Sketch of the Ket," pp. 169 ff. On the cultural history of this ople, cf. the comprehensive study by Kai Donner, "Beiträge zur Frage ch dem Ursprung der Jenissei-Ostjaken." On shamanism among the yot inhabiting the Yenisei region, see V. Diószegi, "Der Werdegang zum hamanen bei den nordöstlichen Sojoten"; id., "Tuva Shamanism."

selves to a mere reference, for it disappeared in the eighteenth century and, in addition, the influences from Scandinavian mythology and from Christianity to be found in the Lapp religious traditions would oblige us to study it in the frame of the religious history of Europe. According to the seventeenth-century authors, confirmed by folklore, the Lapp shamans held their séances entirely naked, like many other Arctic peoples, and attained genuine cataleptic trances during which their souls were believed to descend to the underworld to escort the dead or to seek the souls of the sick.[21] This descent to the land of shades began by an ecstatic journey to a mountain,[22] as among the Altaians; the mountain, as we know, symbolizes the Cosmic Axis and hence is at the "Center of the World." The Lapp magicians of our day still remember the miracles of their ancestors, who could fly through the air, and so on.[23] The séance included songs and invocations of the spirits; the drum—which, it has been noted, bore drawings similar to those on Altaic drums—played a great part in producing the trance.[24] There have been attempts to explain the Scandinavian *seidhr* as a borrowing from Lapp shamanism.[25] But, as we shall see, the religion of the ancient Germans preserved enough elements that can be considered "shamanic" to make it unnecessary to postulate an influence from Lapp magic.[26]

21 Cf. Ohlmarks, pp. 34, 50, 51, 176 ff. (descent to the underworld) 302 ff., 312 ff.

22 Hilda R. Ellis, *The Road to Hel: a Study of the Conception of the Dead i Old Norse Literature*, p. 90.

23 Ohlmarks, pp. 57, 75.

24 Cf. Mikhailowski, pp. 144 ff. On divination by means of the drum, se ibid., pp. 148–49; on the Lapp magician of our day and his folklore, T. I. Itko nen, *Heidnische Religion und späterer Aberglaube bei den finnischen Lappe* pp. 116 ff.; on the rites of magical healing, J. Quigstad, *Lappische Heilkund* R. Karsten, *The Religion of the Samek*, pp. 68 ff.

25 By Johan Fritzner (*Lappernes Hedenskap og Inolddomskunst*), as early 1877, and, more recently (1935), by Dag Strömbäck (*Sejd. Textstudier nordisk religionshistoria*); cf. the discussion of this thesis in Ohlmarks, p 310–50.

26 Hungarian shamanism had aroused the interest of the psychoanalys ethnologist Géza Róheim, and two years before his death he published "Hu

Séances among the Ostyak, the Yurak, and the Samoyed

In the ritual songs of the Ostyak and Yurak-Samoyed shamans, recorded by Tretyakov during healing séances, the ecstatic journey undertaken for the patient's benefit is recounted at length. But these songs have already acquired a certain autonomy in relation to the cure proper; the shaman boasts of his own adventures in the highest sky, and we get the impression that the search for the patient's soul—the primary reason for such an ecstatic journey—

---

garian Shamanism." The problem is also approached in his posthumous book, *Hungarian and Vogul Mythology* (see especially pp. 8 ff., 48 ff., 61 ff.). Róheim considers the Asiatic origin of Magyar shamanism obvious. "Curiously enough, the most striking parallels are among the Samojed and Mongoloid (Buriat) and Eastern Turc tribes and the Lapps, and not with the Ugrian first cousins (Vogul and Ostjak) of the Magyars" ("Hungarian Shamanism," p. 162). As a good psychoanalyst, Róheim could not resist the temptation to explain shamanic flight and ascent in Freudian terms; ". . . a flying dream is an erection dream, [i.e.], in these dreams the body represents the penis. *Our hypothetical conclusion would be that the flying dream is the nucleus of shamanism*" [Róheim's italics] (ibid., p. 154).

Róheim held that "there is no direct evidence that the táltos [i.e., the Hungarian shaman] falls into a trance" (ibid., p. 147). This statement is directly contradicted by Diószegi, "Die Überreste des Schamanismus in der ungarischen Volkskultur," pp. 122 ff. In this study the author summarizes the abundantly documented volume, treating the same problem, which he published in Hungarian (*A sámánhit emléki a magyar népi müveltségben*). Diószegi shows how greatly the Hungarian *táltos* differs from apparently similar figures attested in countries near Hungary, i.e., the Romanian *solomoar*, the Polish *planetnik*, and the *garabancias* of the Serbs and Croats. Only the *táltos* experiences a sort of "shamanic sickness" ("Die Überreste," pp. 98 ff.) or the "long sleep" (i.e., a ritual death) or "initiatory dismemberment" (ibid., pp. 103 ff., 106 ff.); only the *táltos* undergoes an initiation, has a particular costume and a drum, and goes into ecstasy (ibid., pp. 112 ff., 115 ff., 122 ff.). Since all these elements are also found among the Turkic, Finno-Ugric, and Siberian peoples, the author concludes that shamanism represents a magico-religious element belonging to the original culture of the Magyars. The Hungarians brought in shamanism when they came from Asia to the territory that they inhabit today. (In a study of the Hungarian shaman's ecstasy, "A magyar samán réülete," János Balázs stresses the experience of "magical heat.")

has receded into the background and even been forgotten. For the subject of the song is more the shaman's own ecstatic experiences, and it is not hard to see in these exploits the repetition of an exemplary model—that, particularly, of the shaman's initiatory journey to the underworld and his ascent to the sky.

He relates how he mounts to the sky by the help of a rope especially let down for him and how he shoulders aside the stars that block his way. In the sky he rides in a boat and then descends to earth at such a speed that the wind passes through him. With the help of winged demons he makes his way underground; it is so cold there that he asks the spirit of darkness, *Ama*, or the spirit of his own mother, for a coat. (At this point in the shaman's narrative, someone in the audience throws a coat over his shoulders.) Finally he returns to earth and, after prophesying the future for each of the gathering, tells the patient that the demon that had caused his illness has been driven away.[27]

Clearly there is here no more question of a shamanic ecstasy implying concrete ascent and descent; there is a narration full of mythical reminiscences and with its point of departure in an experience that definitely precedes the moment of the cure. The Ostyak and Yurak shamans of the Taz River region speak of their marvelous flight among flowering roses; they go so high in the sky that they see the tundra for a distance of seven versts; very far away, they see the place where their masters long ago made their drums. (Actually, they see the "Center of the World.") They finally reach the sky and, after many adventures, enter an iron hut where they fall asleep among purple clouds. They return to earth by a river. And the song ends with a hymn of adoration to all the divinities, beginning with the Sky God.[28]

Often the ecstatic journey is made in a vision. The shaman sees his helping spirits, in the form of reindeer, entering other worlds, and he sings their adventures.[29] Among the Samoyed shamans the

27 P. I. Tretyakov, *Turukhansky krai, evo priroda i zhiteli*, pp. 217 ff.; Mikhailowski, pp. 67 ff.; Shimkin, pp. 169 ff.

28 Mikhailowski, p. 67.

29 T. Lehtisalo, *Entwurf einer Mythologie der Jurak-Samojeden*, pp. 153 f

helping spirits perform a more "religious" function than they do among other Siberian peoples. Before undertaking a cure the shaman enters into contact with his spirits to learn the cause of the illness; if it has been sent by Num, the Supreme God, the shaman refuses to treat it. And it is his spirits who then ascend to the sky to ask Num's help.[30] This does not mean that all Samoyed shamans are "good"; although they have no distinction between "black" and "white," some of them are known to practice black magic and to do harm.[31]

The descriptions of Samoyed séances available to us leave the impression that the ecstatic journey is either "sung" or performed by the shaman's helping spirits in his name. Sometimes his dialogue with the spirits serves to tell the shaman the "will of the gods." This is sufficiently apparent from the séance that Castrén attended among the Samoyed of Tomsk, and which he described as follows: The audience gathers about the shaman, being careful to avoid the door, at which he stares. In his left hand he holds a stick, one end of which bears mysterious signs and figurines. In his right hand he holds two arrows, points upward; the point of each arrow bears a bell. The séance begins with a song intoned by the shaman alone, accompanying himself by striking the two belled arrows rhythmically against the stick. This is the summons to the spirits. As soon as they arrive the shaman rises and begins to dance, with motions that are as difficult as they are ingenious. But he continues singing and striking the stick. In his song he reproduces his dialogue with the spirits, and its intensity follows the dramatic interest of the conversation. When the song reaches its paroxysmic point, the audience begins to sing in chorus. After obtaining answers from the spirits to all his questions, the shaman stops and announces the will of the gods.[32]

There are, of course, great shamans who go into trance and thus undertake the ecstatic journey in search of the patient's soul; such

30 A. M. Castrén, *Nordische Reisen und Forschungen. II: Reiseberichte und Briefe aus den Jahren 1845–1849*, pp. 194 ff.; on Samoyed shamanism, cf. also P. Schmidt, *Der Ursprung*, III, 364–66.

31 Mikhailowski, p. 144.   32 Castrén, pp. 172 ff.

was the Yurak-Samoyed shaman Ganjkka (Ganykka), observed by Lehtisalo.[33] But, together with such masters, we find a considerable proportion of "visionaries," who receive the commands of the gods and spirits in dream,[34] or who have recourse to intoxication by mushrooms to learn, for example, the means to be employed for a cure.[35] In any case, it is plain that real shamanic trances are comparatively rare, and the majority of séances involve only an ecstatic journey undertaken by the spirits or the fabulous account of adventures whose mythological prototypes are already known.[36]

The Samoyed shamans also practice divination by means of stick, marked with certain signs, which they throw into the air; the future is read from the position of the stick when it returns to the ground. They also exhibit specifically shamanic feats. They let themselves be tied up, then invoke the spirits (whose animal voices are soon heard in the yurt), and at the end of the séance they are found free from their bonds. They cut themselves with knives, strike themselves violent blows on the head, and so on.[37] In dealing with the shamans of other Siberian peoples, and even of peoples outside of Asia, we shall constantly come upon the same feats, which have much in common with fakirism. All this is not merely a boastful display or a play for prestige on the shaman's part. The "miracles" have an organic affinity with the shamanic séance; there is the realization of a second state defined by the abolition of the profane condition. The shaman justifies the genuineness of his experience by the "miracles" that it makes possible.

Shamanism among the Yakut and the Dolgan

Among the Yakut and the Dolgan the shamanic séance usually includes four stages: (1) evocation of the helping spirits; (2) di

33 *Entwurf*, pp. 153 ff. 34 Ibid., p. 145. 35 Ibid., pp. 164 ff.

36 For the Samoyed cultural complex, cf. Kai Donner, "Zu der ältesten Berührung zwischen Samojeden und Türken"; A. Gahs, "Kopf-, Schädel- und Langknochenopfer bei Rentiervölkern," pp. 238 ff.; W. Schmidt, *Ursprung*, III, 334 ff.

37 Cf., for example, Mikhailowski, p. 66.

covery of the cause of the illness, usually an evil spirit that has stolen the patient's soul or entered his body; (3) expulsion of the evil spirit by threats, noise, etc.; and finally (4) the shaman's ascent to the sky.[38] "The most difficult problem is discovering the causes of the illness, learning what spirit is tormenting the patient, determining its origin, its hierarchic situation, its power. Hence the ceremony always has two parts: first the tutelary spirits are summoned from the sky, and their help is invoked in finding the causes of the illness; then comes the struggle against the enemy spirit or against the *üör* [ghosts]." The obligatory journey to the sky follows.[39]

The struggle against the evil spirits is dangerous and finally exhausts the shaman. "We are all destined to fall before the power of the spirits," the shaman Tüspüt told Sieroszewski, "the spirits hate us because we defend men . . ."[40] And in fact, in order to extract the evil spirits from the patient, the shaman is often obliged to take them into his own body; in doing so, he struggles and suffers more than the patient himself.[41]

We now give Sieroszewski's classic description of a séance among the Yakut. It takes place in the evening, in the yurt, and the neighbors are invited to attend. "Sometimes the master of the house prepares two nooses from strong thongs; the shaman secures them to his shoulders and the others present grasp their ends to hold him back in case the spirits should try to carry him off."[42]

38 Harva, *Die religiösen Vorstellungen*, p. 545 (after N. Y. Vitashevsky); Jochelson, *The Yakut*, pp. 120 ff.

39 W. Sieroszewski, "Du chamanisme d'après les croyances des Yakoutes," p. 324. There is only a seeming contradiction between Vitashevsky's statement (séance in four stages) and Sieroszewski's ("two parts," followed by the celestial journey); actually the two observers say the same thing.   40 Ibid., p. 325.

41 Harva, *Die religiösen Vorstellungen*, pp. 545–46.

42 Sieroszewski, p. 326. This practice is found among several Siberian and Arctic peoples, although with different meanings. Sometimes the shaman tied so that he will not fly away; among the Samoyed and the Eskimo, on the contrary, the shaman allows himself to be tied to show his magical powers, for, during the séance, he always succeeds in untying himself "with the help of the spirits."

The shaman stares into the fire on the hearth; he yawns, hiccups spasmodically, from time to time he is shaken by nervous tremors He puts on his shamanic costume and begins to smoke. Soon afterward his face grows pale, his head falls on his breast, his eyes half close. A white mare's hide is spread in the middle of the yurt. The shaman drinks cold water and genuflects to the four cardinal points spitting water to right and left. Silence reigns in the yurt. The shaman's assistant throws some horsehairs on the fire, then covers it over completely with ashes. The darkness now becomes total The shaman sits down on the mare's hide and dreams, facing south All hold their breath.

"Suddenly a succession of shrill cries, piercing as the screech o steel, sounds from no one knows where; then all is silent again Another cry; and now from above, now from below, now before now behind the shaman rise mysterious sounds: nervous, terrifying yawns, hysterical hiccups; it is as if one heard the plaintive cry c the lapwing mingled with the crowing of a falcon and interrupte by the whistling of the woodcock; it is the shaman making thes sounds by changing the tone of his voice."

Suddenly he stops; again silence reigns, except for a faint humming, like that of a mosquito. The shaman begins to beat his drum He murmurs a song. The song and the drumming rise in crescendo Soon the shaman is bellowing. "We hear the croaking of eagles mixed with the lamenting of lapwings, the piercing cries of wood cocks and the refrain of cuckoos." The music grows louder t the point of paroxysm, then stops abruptly, so that again nothin is heard but the hum of mosquitoes. The alternation between bir cries and silence recurs several times. Finally the shaman change the rhythm of his drumming and chants his hymn:

> The strong bull of the earth, the horse of the steppe,
> The strong bull has bellowed!
> The horse of the steppe has trembled!
> I am above you all, I am a man!
> I am the man who has all gifts!
> I am the man created by the Lord of Infinity!

Come, then, O horse of the steppe, and teach!
Appear, then, marvelous bull of the Universe, and answer!
O Lord of Power, command! . . .
O Lady my Mother, show me my faults and the roads
That I must follow! Fly before me, following a broad road;
Prepare my way for me!
O Spirits of the Sun who dwell in the South on the nine wooded
  hills, O Mothers of Light, you who know jealousy, I implore
  you: may your three shadows remain high, very high! And thou
  in the West, on thy mountain, O Lord my Ancestor of fearful
  powers, strong-necked, be with me! . . .

The music resumes furiously and reaches its highest intensity.
The shaman then invokes the help of the *ämägät* and his familiar
spirits. They do not accede at once; the shaman implores them,
they equivocate. Sometimes they arrive so suddenly and violently
that the shaman falls over backward. Then the audience clash iron
over him, murmuring: "The strong iron sounds—the capricious
clouds swirl, many mists have risen!"

On the arrival of the *ämägät* the shaman begins leaping, makes
swift, violent gestures. Finally he takes his place in the center of
the yurt, the fire is rekindled, and he begins to drum and dance
again. He flings himself into the air, sometimes as high as four
feet.[43] He cries out wildly. This is followed by another pause; then
in a low, serious voice he intones a solemn hymn. Next comes a
light dance, during which his song becomes ironic or else diaboli-
cal, depending on the beings whose voices he is imitating. Finally
he goes to the patient and summons the cause of the illness to
depart; "or he lays hold of the trouble, carries it to the middle of
the room and, never stopping his imprecations, chases it away,

---

43 This is clearly an ecstatic "ascent" to the sky; the Habakuk Eskimo
shamans likewise attempt to reach the sky by ritual leaps into the air (K. Ras-
sussen, cited by Ohlmarks, *Studien*, p. 131). Among the Menri of Kelantan
the medicine men spring into the air singing and throwing a mirror or necklace toward Karei, the Supreme God (Ivor H. N. Evans, "Schebesta on the
Sacerdo-Therapy of the Semang," p. 120).

spits it from his mouth, kicks it, drives it with his hands and breath." [44]

Now the shaman begins his ecstatic journey to escort the soul of a sacrificed animal to the sky. Three trees stripped of their branches are set up outside the yurt; the middle one is a birch, to whose top is fastened a dead kingfisher. East of the birch a stake is set up, bearing the skull of a horse. The three trees are connected by a rope with handfuls of horsehair. Between the trees and the yurt is a small table on which stands a jug containing brandy. The shaman begins making motions imitating a bird flying. Little by little he rises to the sky. The road has nine halting places, and at each of them he makes offerings to the local spirit. On returning from his ecstatic journey the shaman asks to be "purified" by fire (burning coals) on some part of his body (foot, thigh, etc.). [45]

Naturally, the Yakut shamanic séance presents a number of variants. Here is Sieroszewski's description of the celestial journey: "Then a row of small firs, chosen in advance, is carefully placed and decorated with garlands of white horsehair (the only kind that the shamans use); then they set up three stakes in a line, their tops bearing representations of birds: on the first is the two-headed *öksökjou*; on the second the *grana nour* (*kougos*) or else crow; on the third a cuckoo (*kögö*). To the last stake the sacrificial beast is tied. A rope stretched above represents the way to heaven 'by which the birds will fly and which the animal will follow.' "

At each halting place (*oloh*) the shaman sits down and rests; his rising again shows that he is resuming his journey. He represents

44 Sieroszewski, pp. 326–30. Some scholars have expressed doubts regarding the genuineness of the liturgical texts recorded by Sieroszewski; cf. Jochelson, *The Yakut*, p. 122.

45 Harva, *Die religiösen Vorstellungen*, p. 547. The meaning of this rite is obscure. Kai Donner states that the Samoyed likewise purify their shaman with burning coals at the end of the séance (Harva, ibid.). Presumably the purification is applied to the part of the body through which the evil spirit that troubled the patient were "absorbed"; but, in that case, why is the shaman purified on his return from his celestial journey? Is this not, rather, the ancient shamanic rite of "playing with fire"? (See below, pp. 472 ff.)

46 "Du chamanisme," p. 332.

the journey by dance movements and gestures imitating the flight of a bird. "The dance always depicts a journey through the air in company with spirits; when the expiatory beast is escorted, dancing is also obligatory. According to legend, not long ago there were shamans who really flew into the sky, and the audience saw an animal sailing through the clouds, followed by the shamanic drum; the shaman himself, dressed entirely in iron, closed the procession." " 'The drum is our horse,' the shamans say." [47]

The skin, horns, and hoofs of the sacrificed animal are exposed on a dead tree. Sieroszewski often found remains of such sacrifices in deserted places. Nearby, sometimes on the same tree, "one may see a *kotchaï*, a long wooden arrow, planted in the sapless trunk. It has the same function as the rope with the handfuls of horsehair in the preceding ceremony. It indicates the part of the sky to which the victim is to go." [48] Still according to the same author, the shaman used to tear out the sacrificial animal's heart with his own hands and raise it skyward. He then daubed blood on his face and costume, the image of his *ämägät*, and the small wooden figurines of the spirits.[49]

Elsewhere nine trees are set up, close to a stake bearing a bird at its top. The trees and the stake are connected by an ascending rope, sign of the ascent to the sky.[50] The Dolgan also use the nine trees, each with a wooden bird at the top and with the same meaning—the road to the sky for the shaman and the soul of the sacrificed animal. For the Dolgan shamans likewise scale the nine heavens in performing a cure. According to them, before each new heaven there are guardian spirits whose office is to watch over the shaman's journey and at the same time to prevent the evil spirits from mounting.[51]

---

47 Ibid., p. 331; cf. above pp. 173 f.   48 Ibid., pp. 332–33.

49 Ibid., p. 333. We here have a strongly hybridized sacrifice: symbolic offering of the heart to the Celestial Being and libation of blood to the powers "below" (*sjaadai*, etc.). The same cruel ritual is found among the Araucanians; see below, p. 330.

50 Harva, *Die religiösen Vorstellungen*, p. 548.

51 Ibid., p. 549. See other descriptions of the Yakut shamanic séance in

In the long and animated shamanic séance of the Yakut one point only remains obscure. If the patient's soul was carried off by demons, why must the Yakut shaman make the journey to the sky? V. N. Vasilyev proposed the following explanation: the shaman carries the patient's soul to the sky to cleanse it from the defilement inflicted on it by the evil spirits.[52] Troshchansky, however, insists that among the shamans of his acquaintance none undertook the journey to the underworld; without exception, they all used only the journey to the sky in their cures.[53] This testifies to the variety in shamanic techniques and the uncertainty of our information; very probably descents to the underworld, being more dangerous and more secret, were less easily accessible to European observers. But it is beyond doubt that journeys to the underworld were also familiar to the Yakut shamans, at least to some of them. For their costume bears a symbol of the "Opening into the Earth," which has precisely the name "Hole of the Spirits" (*abassy-oibono*) and by which shamans could descend into the nether regions. In addition on his ecstatic journeys the shaman is accompanied by an aquatic bird (gull, grebe), whose symbolism is precisely immersion in the water, that is, a descent to the underworld.[54] Finally, the technical vocabulary of the Yakut shamans uses two different terms to designate the directions of the mystical journey: *allara kyrar* (to the "spirits below") and *üsä kyrar* (to the "spirits above").[55] Then too, Vasilyev had also observed that among the Yakut and the Dolgan the shaman searching for a patient's soul

---

J. G. Gmelin, *Reise durch Sibirien, von dem Jahr 1733 bis 1743*, II, 349 ff. V. L. Priklonsky, "Das Schamanenthum der Jakuten" (German tr. of "O shamanstve u yakutov"). There is also a long English summary of Sieroszewski's bulky volume, *Yakuty*, by William G. Sumner, "The Yakuts. Abridged from the Russian of Sieroszewski," with pp. 102–08 devoted to shamanism (after *Yakuty*, pp. 621 ff.). Cf. Jochelson, *The Yakut*, pp. 120 ff. (after Vitashevsky). See the discussion in W. Schmidt, *Der Ursprung*, XI, 322–29; cf. ibid., pp. 329–32, on the shamanic cure for sterility in women.

52 Cf. Harva, *Die religiösen Vorstellungen*, p. 550.

53 Ibid., p. 551.　　　　　　　　54 Ibid.

55 Ibid., p. 552.

arried off by demons acts as if he were diving, and the Tungus, the Chukchee, and the Lapps refer to the shamanic trance as an immersion.'' [56] We shall find the same behavior and the same cstatic technique among the Eskimo shamans; for a number of eoples, and more especially of maritime peoples, situate the beond in the depths of the sea.[57]

To understand the necessity for the Yakut shamans' celestial ourney in healing, we must consider two things: (1) the comlexity and even confusion of their religious and mythological conptions, and (2) the prestige of shamanic celestial ascents roughout Siberia and Central Asia. As we have seen, this restige explains why, in his ecstatic descent to the underworld o deliver the patient's soul from the power of Erlik Khan), e Altaic shaman finally borrows certain characteristic features ' the ascensional technique.

Hence in the case of the Yakut we may conceive the situation ore or less as follows: the fact that animals were sacrificed to e celestial beings and that the direction taken by the victim's ul was indicated by visible symbols (arrows, wooden birds, cending rope, etc.) finally led to the shaman's being employed to iide the animal's soul on its celestial journey; and because he companied the soul of the sacrificed animal on the occasion of a re, it came to be believed that the principal object of his ascent as to "purify" the patient's soul. In any case, in its present form e ritual of shamanic healing is hybrid; it gives the impression of ving been built up under the influence of two different techques: (1) search for the strayed soul of the patient or expulsion the evil spirits, and (2) ascent to the sky.

But we must also take into consideration another fact: aside m the rare cases of "infernal specialization" (confined to scents to the underworld), the Siberian shamans are equally pable of celestial ascents and descents to the nether regions. We

[56] Ibid.

[57] But as we shall see later, never exclusively; certain "elect" and "privi-ed" persons ascend to the sky after death.

have seen that this twofold technique derives in a manner from their initiation itself; for the initiatory dreams of future shaman include both descents (= ritual sufferings and death) and ascent (= resurrection). In this context we can understand that, after battling the evil spirits or descending to the underworld to re cover the patient's soul, the Yakut shaman feels the need to re establish his own spiritual equilibrium by repeating the ascen to the sky.

We must note again here that the Yakut shaman's power an prestige derive exclusively from his capacity for ecstasy. He ha taken the place of the priest in sacrifices offered to the Suprem Being; but just as in the case of the Altaic shamans, the substitu tion has brought about a change in the very structure of the rite the offering has been transformed into a psychophoria, that is, int a dramatic ceremony based on an ecstatic experience. It is still t his mystical capacities that the shaman owes his ability to discove and combat the evil spirits that have seized the patient's soul; h does not confine himself to exorcising them, he takes them int his own body, "possesses" them, tortures and expels them. A this is because he shares their nature, that is, he is free to leave h body, to transport himself to great distances, to descend to th underworld, to scale the sky, and so on. This "spiritual" mobili and freedom, which are fostered by the shaman's ecstatic exper ences, at the same time make him vulnerable, and frequentl through his constant struggling with evil spirits, he falls into the power, that is, he ends by being really "possessed."

Shamanic Séances among the Tungus and the Orochi

Shamanism occupies a considerable place in the religious life the Tungus.[58] It will be remembered that the term "shaman

58 Cf. J. G. Gmelin, *Reise durch Sibirien*, II, 44–46, 193–95, etc.; Mikha lowski, pp. 64–65, 97, etc.; S. M. Shirokogoroff: "General Theory of Sh manism among the Tungus"; "Northern Tungus Migrations in the F East (Goldi and Their Ethnical Affinities)"; "Versuch einer Erforschung Grundlagen des Schamanentums bei den Tungusen"; and especially t

itself is Tungusic (*šaman*), whatever the origin of the word may be.[59] As Shirokogoroff has shown, and as we shall have occasion to repeat, it is highly probable that Tungus shamanism, at least in its present form, has been strongly influenced by Sino-Lamaist ideas and techniques. Then too, as we have several times pointed out, influences from the south are attested for Central Asian and Siberian shamanism in general. We shall see elsewhere in what way we may conceive southern cultural complexes to have expanded into North and Northeast Asia.[60] In any case, Tungus shamanism today displays a complex physiognomy; several different traditions can be detected in it, their coalescence having sometimes produced distinctly hybrid forms. Here, too, we observe a certain "decadence" of shamanism, a condition attested almost everywhere in North Asia. The Tungus compare especially the strength and courage of the "old shamans" with the cowardice of shamans today, who in some districts no longer dare to undertake the dangerous journey to the underworld.

The Tungus shaman is called on to exercise his powers on many and various occasions. Indispensable in cures—whether he seeks the patient's soul or exorcises the demons—he is also a psychopomp; he conveys sacrifices to the sky or the underworld; and, in particular, it is his mission to ensure that the spiritual equilibrium of the entire society is maintained. If diseases, misfortune, or sterility threaten the clan, it is the shaman's task to diagnose the cause and correct the situation. The Tungus are more inclined than their neighbors to accord considerable importance to the spirits—not only to the spirits of the infernal world but also to those of this earthly world, the virtual authors of all kinds of disorders. This is why—in addition to the classic reasons for shamanic séances (disease, death, sacrifices to the gods)—the Tungus shamans undertake séances, and especially the preliminary

---

author's inclusive study, *Psychomental Complex of the Tungus*. Cf. also W. Schmidt, *Der Ursprung*, X, 578-623.

59 See below, pp. 495 f.   60 See below, pp. 499 f.

"little séances," for a great number of reasons, though all implying the need to know and master the "spirits."

The Tungus shamans also take part in a certain number o sacrifices. In addition, the annual sacrifice offered to a shaman' spirits is also a great religious event for the entire tribe.[61] And of course, shamans are indispensable in hunting and fishing rites.[6]

Séances that include a descent to the world below may be under taken for the following reasons: (1) sacrifices to be conveyed t ancestors and the dead in the nether regions; (2) search for th soul of a patient and its return; (3) escorting the dead who ar unwilling to leave this world and settling them in the land o shades.[63] Despite the number of these occasions, the ceremony i quite uncommon, for it is considered dangerous and few shaman dare to brave its perils.[64] Its technical name is *örgiski*, literally "i the direction of *örgi*" (lower or "western" region). Recourse i had to the *örgiski* only after a preliminary séance of "little sha manism." For example, a series of troubles, illnesses, or misfor tunes is observed in the tribe; the shaman, bidden to determin the cause, incarnates a spirit and learns the reasons why the spirit of the nether regions or the dead and the ancestral souls are causin the disequilibrium; he also learns what sacrifice can placate them The community then decides to undertake the sacrifice, includin the shaman's descent to the underworld.

One day before the *örgiski* the objects that the shaman will us in his ecstatic journey are assembled; among them are a smal raft on which he will cross the sea (Lake Baikal); a sort of lanc to break rocks; small objects representing two bears and tw boars, which will hold up the boat in case of shipwreck and open path through the dense forest of the beyond; four small fish t swim ahead of the boat; an "idol" representing the shaman helping spirit, which will help him to carry the sacrifice; variou instruments for purification; and other objects. On the evening

---

61 Shirokogoroff, *Psychomental Complex*, pp. 322 ff.
62 Ibid.   63 Ibid., p. 307.
64 Ibid., p. 306.

the séance the shaman dons his costume, drums, chants, and invokes "fire," "Mother Earth," and the "ancestors" to whom the sacrifice is offered. Fumigations are followed by divination; with his eyes shut, the shaman throws his drumstick into the air; if it falls with the convex side up, it is a good sign.

The second part of the ceremony begins with the sacrifice of the animal, usually a reindeer. The objects displayed are daubed with its blood; the meat is prepared later. Poles are brought into the *wigwan*, their tops protruding through the smoke hole. A long string connects the poles to the objects displayed outside on the platform; this cord is the "road" for the spirits.[65] When all these things have been done, the audience gather in the *wigwan*. The shaman begins drumming, singing, and dancing. He leaps higher and higher into the air.[66] His assistants repeat the refrain of his song in chorus with the spectators. He stops for a moment, drinks a glass of vodka, smokes a few pipes, and resumes dancing. Little by little he excites himself to the point where he falls to the ground inanimate, in ecstasy. If he does not return to his senses, he is thrice sprinkled with blood. He rises and begins to talk in a high voice, answering the sung questions addressed to him by two or three interlocutors. The shaman's body is now inhabited by a spirit, and it is the spirit that answers in his stead. For the shaman himself is now in the lower regions. When he comes back everyone utters joyful cries to greet his return from the world of the dead.

This second part of the ceremony lasts about two hours. After an interval of two or three hours, that is, at dawn, comes the last phase, which resembles the first and during which the shaman thanks the spirits.[67]

Among the Tungus of Manchuria sacrifices can be made without

65 Clearly there is contamination here with the shamanic journey to the sky, examples of which will be given later, for, as we have seen, the poles emerging through the smoke hole symbolize the *axis mundi* along which sacrifices are sent to the highest sky.

66 Another indication of confusion with the celestial ascent: leaps into the air signify "magical flight."

67 Shirokogoroff, *Psychomental Complex*, pp. 304 ff.

any assistance from a shaman. But only the shaman can descend to the lower regions and bring back the patient's soul. This ceremony, too, is in three sections. When a preliminary session of "little shamanism" has shown that the patient's soul is really imprisoned in the underworld, sacrifice is made to the spirits (*séven*) so that they will help the shaman descend to the lower regions. The shaman drinks blood and eats flesh from the sacrificed animal, and having thus taken its spirit into himself, he goes into ecstasy. This first phase accomplished, the second begins; it is the shaman's mystical journey. He reaches a mountain in the northwest and descends it to the otherworld. The perils increase as he approaches the nether regions. He meets spirits and other shamans, and wards off their arrows with his drum. He sings all the vicissitudes of his journey, so that the audience can follow him step by step. He goes down through a narrow hole and crosses three streams before he comes upon the spirits of the infernal regions. Finally he reaches the world of darkness, and the audience strike sparks from gunflints; these are the "lightning flashes" by which the shaman is able to see his way. He finds the patient's soul and, after a long struggle or negotiations with the spirits, brings it back to earth through a thousand difficulties and makes it resume its place in the patient's body. The last part of the ceremony, which takes place the next day or some days later, is a thanksgiving to the shaman's spirits.[68]

The Reindeer Tungus of Manchuria still remember a "time long ago" when shamans "shamanized toward the earth," but no shaman any longer dares do so. Among the nomadic Tungus of Mankova the ceremony is different. At night, a black he-goat is sacrificed; its flesh is not eaten. When the shaman reaches the lower regions he falls to the ground and lies motionless for half an hour. During this time the audience jump three times over the fire.[69] Among the Manchu, too, the ceremony of "descent to the world of the dead" is comparatively rare. During his long stay with them Shirokogoroff was able to attend only three such

68 *Psychomental Complex*, p. 307.   69 Ibid., p. 308.

séances. The shaman invokes all the spirits (Chinese, Manchu, and Tungus), tells them the reason for the séance (in the case analyzed by Shirokogoroff, the illness of an eight-year-old child), and asks their help. He then begins beating his drum; when his particular spirit has entered him, he falls to the floor. His assistants ask him questions, and his answers show that he is already in the nether regions. Since the spirit "possessing" him is a wolf, he acts accordingly. His language is difficult to understand. Nevertheless, the questioners gather that the cause of the illness is not the soul of a dead person, as had been thought before the séance, but a certain spirit, which, in return for a cure, demands that a small temple (*m'ao*) be built for it and sacrifices offered to it regularly.[70]

A similar descent to the "world of the dead" is recounted in the Manchu poem *Nišan šaman*, which Shirokogoroff considers to be the only written document for Manchu shamanism. Its story is as follows: In the time of the Ming dynasty a young man, the son of wealthy parents, goes hunting in the mountains and is killed in an accident. A shamaness, Nišan, resolves to bring back his soul and goes down to the "world of the dead." She meets a number of spirits, among them that of her dead husband, and, after many vicissitudes, succeeds in returning to earth with the young man's soul; he revives. The poem—which all Manchu shamans know—unfortunately gives very few details concerning the ritual side of the séance.[71] It finally became a "literary" text, differing from similar Tatar poems by the fact that it was long ago recorded and circulated in written form. Yet its importance is considerable, for it shows how close the "descent-of-Orpheus" theme is to the shamanic descents to the underworld.[72]

For the same therapeutic purpose, there are also ecstatic journeys in the opposite direction, that is, involving an ascent to the

---

70 Ibid., p. 309. 71 Ibid., p. 308.

72 Cf. also Owen Lattimore, "Wulakai Tales from Manchuria," pp. 273 ff.; Å. Hultkrantz, *The North American Indian Orpheus Tradition*, pp. 91 ff.

sky. In this case the shaman sets up 27 (9 × 3) young trees and a symbolic ladder by which he will begin his ascent. Among the ritual objects present are numerous figurines of birds, examples of the well-known ascensional symbolism. The celestial journey may be undertaken for many reasons, but the séance described by Shirokogoroff was directed to curing a sick child. The first part resembles the preparation for a séance of descent to the lower regions. A session of "little shamanism" reveals the precise moment when the god Dayachan, who is being besought to return the sick child's soul, is inclined to receive the sacrifice. The animal—in this case a lamb—is ritually slaughtered; its heart is plucked out and the blood collected in special vessels, not a drop being allowed to fall to the ground. The skin is then hung up. The second part of the séance is entirely devoted to bringing on ecstasy. The shaman sings, drums, dances, and leaps, from time to time going close to the sick child. He then hands his drum to his assistant, drinks vodka, smokes, and resumes dancing until he falls to the ground exhausted. This is the sign that he has left his body and is flying to the sky. All crowd around him, and his assistant, as in the case of descents to the underworld, produces sparks with a gunflint. Such a séance can be held by day as well as by night. The costume used by the shaman is not at all elaborate, and Shirokogoroff believes that this type of séance involving ascent to the sky was borrowed by the Tungus from the Buryat.[73]

The hybrid nature of this séance seems clear. Although celestial symbolism is duly represented by the trees, the ladder, and the bird figurines, the shaman's ecstatic journey shows a contrary direction (the "darkness" that must be lighted by sparks). Then too, the shaman does not carry the sacrificed animal to Buga, the Supreme Being, but to the spirits of the upper regions. This type of séance is found among the Reindeer Tungus of the Transbaikal and Manchuria, but is not known among the Tungus groups in North Manchuria,[74] which confirms the hypothesis of Buryat origin.

Aside from these two great types of shamanic séance, the

73 *Psychomental Complex*, pp. 310–11.   74 Ibid., p. 325.

Tungus also know several forms that have no particular relation with the worlds above or below but concern the spirits of this earth. Their purpose is to control these spirits, to drive away the evil ones, to sacrifice to those that might become hostile, and so on. Obviously, the cause of many séances is illness, for certain spirits are believed to provoke diseases. To identify the author of the trouble, the shaman incarnates his familiar spirit and pretends to sleep (a poor imitation of the shamanic trance) or attempts to evoke and embody the spirit that is troubling the patient.[75] For the multiplicity of souls [76] and their instability sometimes make the shaman's task difficult. He must determine which of the souls has left the body and go in search of it; in this case, the shaman calls back the soul in stereotyped phrases or songs and attempts to make it re-enter the body by gesturing rhythmically. But sometimes spirits have entered the patient; then the shaman expels them with the help of his familiar spirits.[77]

Ecstasy plays a great part in Tungus shamanism proper; dancing and singing [78] are the methods most often employed to induce it. And the phenomenology of the Tungus séance suggests throughout the séances of other Siberian peoples: voices of spirits are heard; the shaman becomes "light" and can spring into the air with a costume that may weigh as much as sixty-five pounds, yet the patient scarcely feels the shaman tread on his body; [79] the sha-

75 Ibid., p. 313.

76 There are three souls (ibid., pp. 134 f.; I. Paulson, *Die primitiven Seelenvorstellungen*, pp. 107 f.).

77 Shirokogoroff, *Psychomental Complex*, p. 318. The Tungus shamans also practice suction: cf. Mikhailowski, p. 97; Shirokogoroff, p. 313.

78 According to J. Yasser ("Musical Moments in the Shamanistic Rites of the Siberian Pagan Tribes," pp. 4–15, cited by Shirokogoroff, *Psychomental Complex*, p. 327), the Tungus melodies show a Chinese origin, which confirms Shirokogoroff's theories of strong Sino-Lamaist influence on Tungus shamanism. Cf. also H. Haslund-Christensen, K. Grønbech, and E. Emsheimer, *The Music of the Mongols. I: Eastern Mongolia*, pp. 13–38, 69–100. On certain "southern" complexes among the Tungus, see also W. Koppers, "Tungusen und Miao."

79 Shirokogoroff, *Psychomental Complex*, p. 364. This is explained by the magical power of levitation and "flight" (ibid., p. 332).

man feels an intense heat during his trance, and hence can play with burning coals and red-hot iron, and becomes completely insensible (for example, he stabs himself deeply but no blood flows); and so on.[80] All this, as we shall see more clearly later, forms part of an ancient magical inheritance, which still survives in the most distant parts of the world and which preceded the southern influences that have so greatly contributed to the present physiognomy of Tungus shamanism. For the moment, it is enough to have briefly indicated the two magical traditions to be detected in Tungus shamanism: the substratum that we may call "archaic," and the Sino-Buddhist contribution from the south. Their importance will become manifest when we attempt to outline the history of shamanism in Central and North Asia.

A similar form of shamanism is found among the Orochi and Ude (Udekhe) tribes. I. A. Lopatin gives a long description of the healing séance among the Orochi of Ulka (on the Tumnin River).[81] The shaman begins by a prayer to his guardian spirit—for he, the shaman, is weak, but his spirit is all-powerful and nothing can resist it. He dances nine times around the fire, then addresses his spirit in a song: "Thou wilt come. Oh yes, thou wilt be here. Thou wilt have pity on these poor people . . ." He promises it fresh blood; from the few allusions he makes, his spirit appears to be the Great Thunder Bird: "Stretch out thine iron wings! . . : Thine iron feathers jingle when thou art flying . . . thy mighty claws are in readiness to seize thine enemies!" This invocation continues for some half an hour and the shaman ends it in a state of exhaustion.

Suddenly he cries in a different voice: "I am here; I have come to help these poor people. I will look at the child." The shaman is close to ecstasy; he dances about the fire, spreads his arms, still holding his stick and drum, and cries again: "I am flying; I am flying; I will overtake you. I will catch you. You have no place of

80 Shirokogoroff, *Psychomental Complex*, p. 365.

81 "A Shamanistic Performance for a Sick Boy"; cf. id., "A Shamanistic Performance to Regain the Favor of the Spirit." Cf. also Bronislav Pilsudski, "Der Schamanismus bei den Ainu-Stämmen von Sachalin."

escape." As Lopatin was told later, this dance represents the shaman's flight to the world of spirits, where he hunts the evil spirit that has carried off the sick boy's soul. Then comes a dialogue among several voices, studded with incomprehensible words. Finally the shaman cries: "I have it, I have it!" and, closing his hands as if he had caught something, he goes to the bed on which the sick boy is lying and gives him back his soul. For, as the shaman explained to Lopatin the following day, he had captured the boy's soul in the form of a sparrow.

The interest of this séance lies in the fact that the shaman's ecstasy is not expressed in trance but is achieved and continued during the dance that symbolizes magical flight. The tutelary spirit appears to be the Thunder Bird or Eagle, which plays such a large part in the mythologies and religions of North Asia. Hence, although the patient's soul had been carried off by an evil spirit, the spirit is hunted not, as one would have expected, in the lower regions but high in the sky.

Yukagir Shamanism

The Yukagir have two terms to designate the shaman: *a'lma* (from the verb "to do") and *i'rkeye*, literally "the trembling one." [82] *A'lma* treats sicknesses, offers sacrifices, prays to the gods for good luck in hunting, and maintains relations both with the supernatural world and the Kingdom of Shadows. In ancient times his role was indubitably more important, for all the Yukagir tribes trace their origin to a shaman. Until the last century the skulls of dead shamans were still venerated; each was set in a wooden figurine, which was kept in a box. Nothing was undertaken without recourse to divination by these skulls. The method most usual in the Arctic was employed—if the skull seems light to the diviner when he questions it, the answer is "yes," if heavy, "no." And the oracle's answer was obeyed to the letter. The rest of the dead shamans' bones were divided among the relatives, and the flesh

82 Jochelson, *The Yukaghir and the Yukaghirized Tungus*, pp. 162 ff.

was dried to preserve it. "Wooden men" were also erected to the memory of the ancestral shamans.[83]

According to Yukagir belief, when a man dies, his three souls separate: one remains with the corpse, the second goes to the Kingdom of Shadows, the third ascends to the sky.[84] The last, it seems, finds its way to the Supreme God, whose name is Pon, literally "Something." [85] In any case, the most important soul appears to be the one that becomes a shadow. On its way it meets an old woman, guardian of the threshold of the beyond, then comes to a river, which it crosses in a boat. (In the Kingdom of Shadows the dead person continues to lead the same life that he had known on earth, in company with his relatives, hunting "animal shadows.") It is to this Kingdom of Shadows that the shaman descends to seek the patient's soul.

But he goes there on another occasion too: to "steal" a soul from there and cause it to be born here on earth by introducing it into a woman's womb. For the dead return to earth and begin a new life. But sometimes, when the living forget their duties toward them, the dead refuse to send their souls—and women no longer conceive. Then the shaman goes down to the Kingdom of Shadows, and, if he fails to persuade the dead, steals a soul and forcibly introduces it into a woman's body. But in such cases the children do not live long. Their souls are in haste to return to the Kingdom of Shadows.[86]

Some vague references to a former division of shamans into "good" and "evil" persist, together with references to "shamanesses," who have disappeared today. Among the Yukagir there is

83 Jochelson, *The Yukaghir*, p. 165.

84 Ibid., p. 157. ["Shadow" is Jochelson's term.—Tr.]

85 Ibid., p. 140.

86 Ibid., p. 160. (The same conception of an "eternal return" of the souls of the dead is found in Indonesia and elsewhere.) To learn what ancestor had reincarnated himself, the Yukagir used to practice divination by the bones of shamans. The names of the dead were spoken, and the bone became light when the name of the ancestor who had become reincarnated was hit on. In our day the names are recited before the newborn infant, and he smiles when he hears the right one (ibid., p. 161).

no sign that women take part in what has been called "family shamanism" or "domestic shamanism," which still survives among
the Koryak and the Chukchee and which allows the heads of families among these people to keep family drums.[87] But in former
times every Yukagir family had its own drum,[88] which shows that
at least certain "shamanic" ceremonies were periodically practiced
by members of the household.

Among the various séances described by Jochelson—not all of
which are interesting [89]—we shall confine ourselves to summarizing the most important of those directed to obtaining a cure.
The shaman sits down on the ground and, after drumming for a
long time, invokes his tutelary spirits, imitating the voices of
animals: "My fore-father, my ancestors, stand near by me. In
order to help me, stand near me, my girl-spirits. . . ." He begins
drumming again and, rising with the help of his assistant, goes to
the door and breathes deeply, in order to swallow the souls of his
ancestors and other spirits that he has summoned. "The soul of
the patient, it seems, has travelled along the road to the Kingdom
of Shadows," the spirits of the ancestors announce through the
shaman's voice. The patient's relatives encourage him: "Be
strong, strength do not spare!" The shaman drops his drum and
lies face down on the reindeer skin; he remains motionless, the
sign that he has left his body and is journeying in the beyond. He
has descended into the Kingdom of Shadows "through the drum
as through a lake." [90] For a long time he does not stir and all those
present patiently wait for him to wake. His return is indicated by a
few motions. Two girls massage his legs, and, now completely
restored to himself, he replaces the soul in the patient's body.
He then goes to the door and dismisses his helping spirits.[91]

87 See below, p. 252.   88 Jochelson, *The Yukaghir*, pp. 192 ff.
89 See, for example, ibid., pp. 200 ff.
90 Ibid., p. 197. In addition, the drum is called *yálgil*, "sea" (ibid., p. 195).
91 Ibid., pp. 196–99. The reader will have recognized the classic scenario
of a descent to the underworld: the guardian of the threshold, the dog, crossing the stream. There is no need to cite all the parallels, shamanic and otherwise; we shall return to some of these motifs later.

At the end of such a séance the shaman gave Jochelson the particulars of his ecstatic journey. Accompanied by his helping spirits, he had followed the road that leads to the Kingdom of Shadows. He came to a little house and found a dog that began to bark. An old woman, who guarded the road, came out of the house and asked him if he had come for ever or for a short time. The shaman did not answer her; instead, he addressed his spirits: "Do not listen to the old woman's words, walk on without stopping." Soon they came to a stream. There was a boat, and on the other bank the shaman saw tents and men. Still accompanied by his spirits, he entered the boat and crossed the stream. He met the souls of the patient's dead relatives, and entering their tent, found the patient's soul there too. As the relatives refused to give it to him, he had to take it by force. To carry it safely back to earth, he inhaled the patient's soul and stuffed his ears to prevent it from escaping.

The Yukagir shaman does not necessarily cure by descending to the underworld to steal a soul. He may hold a séance without mentioning the souls of the dead shamans, and, though invoking his helping spirits and imitating their voices, he addresses himself to the Creator of Light and other celestial powers.[92] This fact shows the plurivalence of his ecstatic capacities. For he also serves as intermediary between man and the gods, and for this reason plays a role of the first importance in the hunt; it is alway he who can intercede with the divinities that, in one way or another, rule over the animal world. Thus, when famine threaten the clan, the shaman holds a séance that in every way resemble one for healing. Only, instead of addressing the Creator of Light or descending to seek the patient's soul in the underworld, he flie up to Earth-Owner. Coming before him, he begs: "Your childre sent me to you for some food for the future." Earth-Owner give him the "soul" of a reindeer, and the next day the shaman goes t a certain place near a stream and waits; a reindeer passes, and th

92 Jochelson, *The Yukaghir*, pp. 205 ff.

shaman kills it with an arrow. This is the sign that game will no longer be scarce.[93]

Aside from performing all these rituals, the shaman is also employed as a master of divination. This is practiced either by oracular bones or by a shamanic séance.[94] This gift comes to him from his relations with the spirits. But it may be supposed that the importance of spirits in the beliefs of the Yukagir is greatly indebted to Yakut and Tungus influences. Two facts seem to us significant in this respect: the Yukagir's awareness that a decadence had overtaken their ancestral shamanism, and the strong Yakut and Tungus influences discernible in the present practices of the Yukagir shamans.[95]

Religion and Shamanism among the Koryak

The Koryak know a celestial Supreme Being, "He Above," to whom they sacrifice dogs. But, as everywhere else, this Supreme Being tends to be passive; men are open to the attacks of the evil spirit, Kalau, and "He Above" seldom comes to their aid. Nevertheless, while among the Yakut and the Buryat the importance of evil spirits has become considerable, the religion of the Koryak still gives a large place to the Supreme Being and the beneficent spirits.[96] Kalau constantly tries to intercept the sacrifices offered to "Him Above," and he often succeeds. Thus when the shaman, during a cure, sacrifices a dog to the Supreme Being, Kalau may intercept the offering, and then the patient dies; if, on the contrary, the sacrifice reaches the sky, a cure is certain.[97] Kalau is the Evil

93 Ibid., pp. 210 ff.   94 Ibid., pp. 208 ff.

95 Ibid., p. 162.   96 Jochelson, *The Koryak*, pp. 92, 117.

97 Cf. ibid., p. 93, figs. 40–41, the naïve drawings of a Koryak representing two shamanic sacrifices. In the first, Kalau intercepts the offering, with the result already stated; in the second, the sacrificed dog rises to the sky, and the patient is saved. In sacrificing to the Supreme Being, one faces east, whereas one faces west when sacrificing to Kalau. (The same directions for sacrifice are found among the Yakut, the Samoyed, and the Altaians. The

Wizard, Death, and probably the First of the Dead. In any case, it is he who causes death in human beings, by eating their flesh and especially the liver.[98] Now, it is known that in Australia and elsewhere sorcerers kill their victims by eating their livers and internal organs while they sleep.

Shamanism still plays a considerable role in the religion of the Koryak. But here too we find the motif of the "decadence of the shaman." And, what seems to us still more important, in Koryak belief the decadence of the shaman follows the decadence of mankind in general, a spiritual tragedy that took place very long ago. In the mythical days of the hero Great Crow men could easily go up to the sky and no less easily descend to the underworld; today only the shamans can do these things.[99] In the myths the sky was reached by climbing through the central opening through which the Creator of the Earth looked down here below; [100] or one could ascend there along the path traced by an arrow shot upward.[101] But, as we have already learned in our analysis of other religious traditions, these easy communications with sky and underworld were violently interrupted (the Koryak do not say as the result of what event), and since then only shamans can re-establish them.

But in our day even the shamans have lost their miraculous powers. Not so long ago very powerful shamans were able to capture the soul of a person who had just died and restore him to life; Jochelson heard such feats related of the "old shamans," but they had all been dead for a long time.[102] Indeed, the shamanic profession itself was falling off. Jochelson could find only two young shamans, who were quite poor and enjoyed little consideration. The séances that he attended were of small interest. Sound

directions are reversed only among the Buryat: east for the evil Tengr, west for the good; cf. N. N. Agapitov and M. N. Khangalov, "Material dlya izuchenia shamanstva v Sibirii. Shamanstvo u buryat Irkutskoi gubernii," p. 4; Jochelson, *The Koryak*, p. 93.)

98 Jochelson, *The Koryak*, p. 102.

99 Ibid., pp. 103, 121.   100 Ibid., pp. 301 ff.

101 Ibid., pp. 293, 304; on this mythical motif, see below, pp. 490 f.

102 *The Koryak*, p. 48.

were heard, and strange voices came from every direction (the helping spirits), then suddenly ceased; when the lights were re-kindled the shaman was found lying on the ground, exhausted. And he announced, awkwardly, that the spirits had assured him that the "sickness" would leave the village.[103] At another séance, which had begun, as usual, with songs, drumming, and evoking the spirits, the shaman asked Jochelson for his knife; the spirits, he said, had ordered him to cut himself. But he did nothing of the sort. It is true that other shamans were said to open the patient's body, look for the cause of the illness, and eat the piece of flesh that repre-sented it—and the wound instantly closed.[104]

The name of the Koryak shaman is *eñeñalan*, that is, a "man in-spired by spirits." [105] And it is the spirits who determine a sha-man's career; no one would become an *eñeñalan* of his own free will. The spirits manifest themselves in the form of birds and other ani-mals. There is every reason to believe that the "old shamans" made use of these spirits in order to descend to the underworld scatheless, as we have seen the Yukagir and other shamans do. Presumably they gained the good will of Kalau and other infernal figures. For at death the soul mounts to the sky, to the Supreme Being—but the shadow and the dead man himself descend to the lower regions. The entrance is guarded by dogs. The underworld proper consists of villages like those on earth, each family having its house. The road to the underworld begins directly under the funeral pyre, and remains open only long enough for the dead person to pass through.[106]

103 Ibid., p. 49. 104 Ibid., p. 51.
105 Ibid., p. 47.

106 Ibid., p. 103. The "opening" in the sky has its counterpart in the opening in the earth, which permits passage to the underworld, in accord-ance with a schema characteristic of North Asia; see below, pp. 260 ff. The road that rapidly opens and closes is a frequent symbol for the "break-through in planes" and it often appears in initiatory stories. Cf., in ibid., p. 302 ff., a Koryak tale (no. 112) in which a girl lets a cannibal monster at her so that she can quickly descend to the underworld and return to earth, with all the rest of the cannibal's victims, before the "road of the dead" closes. This tale preserves, with astonishing consistency, several

The decadence of Koryak shamanism is also apparent in the fact that the shaman no longer uses a special costume.[107] Nor has he a drum of his own. Each family has a drum that serves it for what Jochelson and Bogoras, and other writers after them, have called "family shamanism." And it is true that each family practices a kind of shamanism on the occasion of its domestic rituals—the sacrifices and ceremonies, periodical or otherwise, that make up the religious duties of the community. According to Jochelson [108] and Bogoras, "family shamanism" preceded professional shamanism. A number of facts, which we shall soon cite, speak against this view. As everywhere else in the history of religions, Siberian shamanism confirms the observation that it is the laymen who attempt to imitate the ecstatic experiences of certain privileged individuals, and not vice versa.

Shamanism among the Chukchee

"Family shamanism" is also found among the Chukchee, in the sense that, during the ceremonies celebrated by the head of the family, everyone, even the children, takes a try at the drum. This is the case, for example, on the occasion of the "autumn slaughter," when animals are immolated to ensure a supply of game throughout the year. The drum is beaten—for each family has its own drum— and attempts are made to incarnate the "spirits" and to shamanize.[109] But, in Bogoras' own opinion, this is obviously only a poor imitation of the shamanic séance. The ceremony is held in the outer tent and by day, whereas shamanic séances take place in the sleeping room, at night, and in complete darkness. One after the other the members of the family imitate "possession by the spirits" in shamanic fashion, writhing, leaping into the air, and trying to emi

initiatory motifs: passage to the underworld by the stomach of a monster; search for innocent victims and their rescue; the road to the beyond that opens and shuts in a few seconds.

107 Jochelson, *The Koryak*, p. 48.   108 Ibid.

109 Waldemar G. Bogoras, *The Chukchee*, pp. 374, 413.

inarticulate sounds, which are supposed to be the voice and language of the "spirits." Sometimes even, shamanic cures are attempted and prophecies are uttered, to which no one pays any attention.[110] All these features prove that, with the help of a temporary religious exaltation, laymen try to attain the shamanic state by aping all the shaman's gestures. The model is certainly the trance of the real shaman, but the imitation is largely confined to its external aspects: the "spirit voices" and the "secret language," the pseudo-prophesying, and so on. "Family shamanism," at least in its present form, is only a plagiaristic aping of the ecstatic technique of the professional shaman.

Then too, shamanic séances proper take place in the evening, at the end of the religious ceremonies just described; they are executed by professional shamans. "Family shamanism" has every appearance of being a hybrid phenomenon, presumably arising from two causes: (1) a great many Chukchee claim to be shamans [111] and, since each house has its drum, there are many who, on winter evenings, set themselves to drumming and singing, and sometimes even attain a parashamanic ecstasy; (2) the religious tension of the periodical festivals encourages any latent exaltation and produces a certain contagion. But we repeat: in both cases there is attempted imitation of a pre-existing model—the professional shaman's ecstatic technique.

Among the Chukchee, as throughout Asia, the shamanic vocation is usually manifested by a spiritual crisis, brought on either by an "initiatory illness" or by a supernatural apparition (a wolf, a walrus, etc., appearing at a moment of great danger and saving the future shaman). In any case, the crisis brought on by the "sign" (illness, apparition, etc.) is basically resolved in the shamanic experience itself; the Chukchee assimilate the period of preparation to a serious illness, and "inspiration" (that is, accomplished initiation) to cure.[112] Most of the shamans Bogoras encountered

110 Ibid., p. 413.
111 Nearly a third of the population, according to Bogoras, ibid.
112 Ibid., p. 421.

claimed to have had no masters,[113] but this does not mean that they did not have superhuman teachers. The meeting with "shamanic animals" itself indicates the kind of teaching that an apprentice may receive. A shaman told Bogoras [114] that, while still a youth, he heard a voice of command: "Go into the wilderness: there you will find a tiny drum. Try it and prove its qualities!" He obeyed the voice, and found himself able to see the whole world, to mount to the sky, and even to set up his tent in the clouds.[115] For, whatever the general tendency of Chukchee shamanism in its present phase (that is, as observed by ethnographers at the beginning of this century), the Chukchee shaman is no less able than others to fly through the air and traverse the heavens one after the other, passing through the orifice of the Pole Star.[116]

But, as we have already noted in connection with other Siberian peoples, the Chukchee are aware of a decadence in their shamans. For example, they often have recourse to tobacco as a stimulant, a practice borrowed from the Tungus.[117] And whereas Chukchee folklore dwells on the trances and ecstatic journeys of the old shamans in search of patients' souls, today the Chukchee shaman is satisfied with a pseudo-trance.[118] We receive the impression that ecstatic technique is in decadence, shamanic séances being generally reduced to evocation of the spirits and fakiristic feats.

Yet the shamanic vocabulary itself reveals the ecstatic value of the trance. The drum is called "canoe" and a shaman in trance is said to "sink." [119] All this proves that the séance was regarded as a journey through the submarine beyond (as among the Eskimo, for example), which, however, did not prevent the shaman from rising to the highest sky if he wished. But the search for the strayed soul

113 Bogoras, *The Chukchee*, p. 425.   114 Ibid., p. 426.

115 The tradition of celestial ascents is also especially alive in the Chukchee myths. See, for example, the story of the young man who, marrying "sky-girl," went up into the sky by climbing a vertical mountain (Bogoras, *Chukchee Mythology*, pp. 107 ff.).

116 Id., *The Chukchee*, p. 331.   117 Ibid., p. 434.
118 Ibid., p. 441.   119 Ibid., p. 438.

implied a descent to the underworld, as Chukchee folklore also attests. In our day the healing séance is conducted as follows: The shaman takes off his shirt and, bare to the waist, smokes his pipe and begins to drum and sing. It is a simple melody, without words; each shaman has his own songs, and he often improvises. Suddenly the voices of the "spirits" are heard from every direction; they seem to rise out of the ground or to come from very far away. A *ké'let* (spirit) enters the shaman's body, whereupon, moving his head rapidly, the shaman begins to cry out and speak in falsetto, the voice of the spirit.[120] During this time, in the darkness of the tent, all sorts of strange phenomena occur: levitation of objects, the tent shaking, rain of stones and bits of wood, and so on.[121] Through the shaman's voice the spirits of the dead converse with the audience.[122]

If the séances abound in parapsychological phenomena, the shamanic trance proper has become increasingly rare. Sometimes the shaman falls to the ground unconscious, and his soul is believed to leave his body to go and seek counsel from the spirits. But this ecstasy occurs only if the patient is rich enough to pay a handsome price for it. And even in such cases, according to Bogoras' observations, there is simulation. Suddenly breaking off his drumming, the shaman lies on the ground motionless; his wife covers his face with

120 Bogoras (ibid., pp. 435 ff.) believes that he can explain the "separate voices" of the Chukchee shamans by ventriloquism. But his phonograph recorded all the "voices" exactly as they were heard by the audience, that is, as coming from the doors or rising from the corners of the room, and not as emitted by the shaman. The recordings "show a very marked difference between the voice of the shaman himself, which sounds from afar, and the voices of the 'spirits,' who seemed to be talking directly into the funnel" (p. 436). We shall later cite some other examples of the Chukchee shamans' magical powers. As we have already said, the problem of the "genuineness" of all these shamanic phenomena lies beyond the scope of the present book. See an analysis and a bold interpretation of such phenomena in E. de Martino, *Il mondo magico*, passim (the Chukchee data, pp. 46 ff.). On "shamanistic tricks," see Mikhailowski, "Shamanism in Siberia," pp. 137 ff.

121 Bogoras, *The Chukchee*, pp. 438 ff.

122 Cf. ibid., p. 440 (the revelations of the soul of an old spinster).

a cloth, rekindles the lights, and begins to drum. After a quarter o
an hour the shaman wakes and gives the patient "advice." [123] The
genuine search for the patient's soul used to take place in trance
today it is replaced by pseudo-trance or by sleep. For the Chukchee
regard dreams as contacts with spirits; and after a night of deep
sleep, the shaman wakes with the patient's soul in his hand and at
once proceeds to restore it to its place in the body.[124]

From these few examples we can gauge the decadence of Chukchee shamanism today. Although the schemas of classic shamanism
still survive in traditional folklore and in the techniques of cure
(ascent, descent to the underworld, search for the soul, etc.), the
shamanic experience proper is reduced to a sort of spiritualistic
"corporealization" and to performances of a fakiristic nature. The
Chukchee shamans also know another classic method of cure: suc
tion. After performing it, they display the cause of the illness—an
insect, a pebble, a thorn, or similar objects.[125] Often they undertake
an "operation" that still preserves all its shamanic character. With
a ritual knife, duly "heated" by certain magical exercises, the sha
man professes to open the patient's body to examine his internal
organs and remove the cause of the illness.[126] Bogoras even wit
nessed an "operation" of this kind. A boy of fourteen lay naked on
the ground, and his mother, a celebrated shamaness, opened hi
abdomen; the blood and the gaping flesh were visible; the sha
maness thrust her hand deep into the wound. During all this time
the shamaness felt as if she were on fire and constantly drank water
A few moments later the wound had closed, and Bogoras could de

123 Bogoras, *The Chukchee*, p. 441.

124 Ibid., p. 463. The shaman is believed to open the patient's skull an
replace the soul, which he has just captured in the form of a fly; but the sou
can also be introduced through the mouth, the fingers, or the great toe
cf. ibid., p. 333. The human soul usually manifests itself in the form of a fl
or bee. But, like other Siberian peoples, the Chukchee know several souls
after death one flies into the sky with the smoke of the pyre, another descend
to the underworld, where it continues an existence exactly like its life o
earth (ibid., pp. 334 ff.).

125 Ibid., p. 465.   126 Ibid., pp. 475 ff.

tect no trace of it.[127] Another shaman, after drumming for a long time to "heat" his body and his knife to the point at which, he said, the cut would not be felt, opened his own abdomen.[128] Such feats are frequent throughout North Asia, and they are connected with the "mastery over fire," for the same shamans who gash their bodies are able to swallow burning coals and to touch white-hot iron. The majority of these "tricks" are performed in broad daylight. Among the performances that Bogoras witnessed was the following: A shamaness rubbed a small stone, and a quantity of pebbles dropped from her fingers and piled up in her drum. At the end of the experiment the pebbles formed a sizeable heap, while the stone that the woman had rubbed between her fingers remained intact.[129] All this forms part of the competition in magical performances in which the shamans indulge, with intense rivalry, on the occasion of the periodic religious ceremonies. Chukchee folklore constantly refers to such feats,[130] which seems to indicate even more astonishing magical powers among the "old shamans." [131]

Chukchee shamanism has another interesting aspect. There is a special class of Chukchee shamans who "undergo a change of sex." They are the "soft men" or men "similar to a woman," who, receiving a command from the *ké'let*, have exchanged their male

---

127 Ibid., p. 445.   128 Ibid.
129 Ibid., p. 444.   130 Ibid., p. 443.

131 As for divination, it is practiced both by shamans and laymen. The commonest method is by suspending an object on the end of a thread, as among the Eskimo. Divination is also practiced by the human head or foot; this system is employed especially by women, as among the Kamchadal and the American Eskimo (cf. ibid., pp. 484 ff.; F. Boas, *The Eskimo of Baffin Land and Hudson Bay*, pp. 135, 363). On divination by the shoulder bone of a reindeer, cf. Bogoras, *The Chukchee*, pp. 487 ff. It will be remembered that this method of divination is common to all Central Asia and is also attested in the protohistory of China (cf. above, pp. 163 ff.). It has not been considered necessary to describe the respective divinatory methods practiced by each of the peoples whose shamanic traditions and techniques we have examined. In general, they are much alike. But it is pertinent to state that the ideological foundations for divination throughout Central Asia are to be sought in the belief in an "incorporation" of spirits, as is the case for a great part of Oceania.

clothing and behavior for those of women and have even finally married other men. Usually, the *ké'let*'s bidding is obeyed only in part: the shaman dresses as a woman, but he continues to cohabit with his wife and to have children. Some, rather than carry out the command, have chosen suicide, although pederasty is not unknown among the Chukchee.[132] Ritual transformation into a woman also occurs among the Kamchadal, the Asiatic Eskimo, and the Koryak; but in the latter case Jochelson found only a recollection of such a transformation.[133] Though rare, the phenomenon is not confined to northeastern Asia; transvestitism and ritual change of sex are found, for example, in Indonesia (the *manang bali* of the Sea Dyak), in South America (Patagonians and Araucanians), and among certain North American tribes (Arapaho, Cheyenne, Ute, etc.). Ritual and symbolic transformation into a woman is probably explained by an ideology derived from the archaic matriarchy; but as we shall show, it does not appear to indicate any priority of women in the earliest shamanism. In any case, the presence of this special class of men "similar to a woman"—which plays a minor role in Chukchee shamanism—cannot be laid to the "decadence of the shaman," a phenomenon that extends far beyond the North Asian area.

132 Bogoras, *The Chukchee*, pp. 448 ff.
133 Cf. *The Koryak*, p. 52.

CHAPTER EIGHT

Shamanism and Cosmology

The Three Cosmic Zones and the World Pillar

THE pre-eminently shamanic technique is the passage from one cosmic region to another—from earth to the sky or from earth to the underworld. The shaman knows the mystery of the break-through in plane. This communication among the cosmic zones is made possible by the very structure of the universe. As we shall see presently, the universe in general is conceived as having three levels—sky, earth, underworld—connected by a central axis. The symbolism employed to express the interconnection and intercommunication among the three cosmic zones is quite complex and not without contradictions. For it has had a "history" and has been frequently contaminated and modified, in the course of time, by other more recent cosmological symbols. But the essential schema is always to be seen, even after the numerous influences to which it has been subjected; there are three great cosmic regions, which can be successively traversed because they are linked together by a central axis. This axis, of course, passes through an "opening," a "hole"; it is through this hole that the gods descend to earth and the dead to the subterranean regions; it is through the same hole that the soul of the shaman in ecstasy can fly up or down in the course of his celestial or infernal journeys.

Before examples of this cosmic topography are cited, a preliminary remark is in place. The symbolism of the "Center" is not necessarily a cosmological idea. In the beginning, "Center," or site of a possible break-through in plane, was applied to any sacred space, that is, any space that had been the scene of a hierophany and

so manifested realities (or forces, figures, etc.) that were not o
our world, that came from elsewhere and primarily from the sky
The idea of a "Center" followed from the experience of a sacrec
space, impregnated by a transhuman presence: at this particula
point something from above (or from below) had manifested itsel
Later, it was supposed that manifestation of the sacred in itself im
plied a break-through in plane.[1]

The Turko-Tatars, like a number of other peoples, imagine th
sky as a tent; the Milky Way is the "seam"; the stars, the "holes
for light.[2] According to the Yakut, the stars are the "windows c
the world"; they are openings provided for ventilating the variou
celestial spheres (usually 9 in number, but sometimes also 12, $
or 7).[3] From time to time the gods open the tent to look at th
earth, which accounts for meteors.[4] The sky is also conceived as
lid; sometimes it is not perfectly fitted to the edges of the earth
and then the great winds blow in through the crack. It is likewis
through this narrow crack that heroes and other privileged being
can squirm to enter the sky.[5]

In the middle of the sky shines the Pole Star, holding the celesti
tent like a stake. The Samoyed call it the "Sky Nail"; the Chukche

1 On this whole problem of the sacred space and the "Center," se
Eliade: *Patterns in Comparative Religion*, pp. 367 ff.; *Images and·Symbols*, p
27 ff.; "Centre du Monde, Temple, Maison."

2 U. Harva, *Die religiösen Vorstellungen der altaischen Völker*, pp. 178 f
189 ff.

3 W. Sieroszewski, "Du chamanisme d'après les croyances des Yakoutes
p. 215.

4 Harva, *Die religiösen Vorstellungen*, pp. 34 ff. Similar ideas prevail
among the Hebrews (Isa. 40), etc.; cf. Robert Eisler, *Weltenmantel u*
Himmelszelt, II, 601 ff., 619 ff.

5 Holmberg (Harva): *Der Baum des Lebens*, p. 11; *Die religiösen Vo*
stellungen, p. 35. P. Ehrenreich (*Die allgemeine Mythologie und ihre e*
nologischen Grundlagen, p. 205) remarks that this mythico-religious id
dominates the whole of the Northern Hemisphere. It is yet another expressi
of the widespread symbolism of ascent to the sky through a "strait gate
the aperture between the two cosmic planes widens for only a moment a
the hero (or the initiate,, the shaman, etc.) must take advantage of t
paradoxical instant to enter the beyond.

nd the Koryak the "Nail Star." The same image and terminology re found among the Lapps, the Finns, and the Estonians. The Turko-Altaians conceive the Pole Star as a pillar; it is the "Golden Pillar" of the Mongols, the Kalmyk, the Buryat, the "Iron Pillar" of the Kirgiz, the Bashkir, the Siberian Tatars, the "Solar Pillar" of the Teleut, and so on.[6] A complementary mythical image is that of the stars as invisibly linked to the Pole Star. The Buryat picture he stars as a herd of horses, and the Pole Star (the "Pillar of the World") is the stake to which they are tethered.[7]

As we should expect, this cosmology has found an exact replica n the microcosm inhabited by mankind. The Axis of the World has een concretely represented, either by the pillars that support the ouse, or in the form of isolated stakes, called "World Pillars." or the Eskimo, for example, the Pillar of the Sky is identical with he pole at the center of their dwellings.[8] The Tatars of the Altai, he Buryat, and the Soyot assimilate the tent pole to the Sky Pillar. among the Soyot the pole rises above the top of the yurt and its end s decorated with blue, white, and yellow cloths, representing the olors of the celestial regions. This pole is sacred; it is regarded lmost as a god. At its foot stands a small stone altar, on which offerings are placed.[9]

6 Cf. Holmberg (Harva): *Der Baum des Lebens*, pp. 12 ff.; *Die religiösen Vorstellungen*, pp. 38 ff. The *Irminsūl* of the Saxons is termed by Rudolf of ulda (*Translatio S. Alexandri*) "universalis columna, quasi sustinens mnia." The Lapps of Scandinavia received this idea from the ancient Germans; they call the Pole Star the "Pillar of the Sky" or "Pillar of the World." he *Irminsūl* has been compared to the pillars of Jupiter. Similar ideas till survive in Southeast European folklore; cf., for example, *Coloana Ceriului* (the Sky Pillar) of the Romanians (see A. Rosetti, *Colindele Românilor*, pp. 70 ff.).

7 The idea is common to the Ugrian and Turko-Mongol peoples; cf. Holmberg (Harva): *Der Baum des Lebens*, pp. 23 ff.; *Die religiösen Vorstellungen*, pp. 40 ff. Cf. also Job 38:31; the Indian *skambha* (*Atharva Veda*, X, 7, 35; etc.).

8 W. Thalbitzer, "Cultic Games and Festivals in Greenland," pp. 239 f.

9 Harva, *Die religiösen Vorstellungen*, p. 46. Cf. the cloths of various olors, used in shamanic ceremonies or sacrifices, which always indicate the ymbolic traversal of the celestial regions.

The central pillar is a characteristic element in the dwellings c the primitive peoples [10] of the Arctic and North America; it is foun among the Samoyed and the Ainu, among the tribes of Norther and Central California (Maidu, Eastern Pomo, Patwin) and amon the Algonkin. Sacrifice and prayer are conducted at the foot of th pillar, for it opens the road to the celestial Supreme Being.[11] Th same microcosmic symbolism has been preserved among the herds men-breeders of Central Asia, but since the form of the dwellin has changed (there is a transition from the conical-roofed hut wit central pillar to the yurt), the mythico-religious function of th pillar has passed to the upper opening, through which the smok escapes. Among the Ostyak this opening corresponds to the simila orifice in the "Sky House," and the Chukchee have assimilated to the "hole" made in the celestial vault by the Pole Star. Th Ostyak also speak of the "golden flues of the Sky House" or th "seven flues of the Sky God." [12] The Altaians also believe that it through these "flues" that the shaman passes from one cosm zone to another. So too the tent put up for the Altaic shaman ascension ceremony is assimilated to the celestial vault, and like i has a smoke hole.[13] The Chukchee hold that the "hole in the sky" the Pole Star; that the three worlds are connected by simila "holes," and that it is through them that the shaman and th mythical heroes communicate with the sky.[14] And among th

10 The "Urkultur" of the school of Graebner–Schmidt.

11 Cf. the material assembled by W. Schmidt, *Der Ursprung der Gottesid* VI, pp. 67 ff., and the same author's remarks, "Der heilige Mittelpfahl d Hauses," p. 966; id., *Der Ursprung*, XII, 471 ff.

12 Cf., for example, K. F. Karjalainen, *Die Religion der Jugra-Völker*, 48 ff. The entrance to the subterranean world is, of course, directly belc the "Center of the World"; cf. Holmberg, *Der Baum des Lebens*, pp. 30– and fig. 13 (Yakut disk with central hole). The same symbolism is found the ancient East, India, the Greco-Roman world, etc.; cf. Eliade, *Cosmolog și alchimie babiloniană*, pp. 35 ff.; A. K. Coomaraswamy, "Svayamātṛṇṇ Janua Coeli."

13 Harva, *Die religiösen Vorstellungen*, p. 53.

14 W. G. Bogoras, *The Chukchee*, p. 331; W. I. Jochelson, *The Koryc* p. 301. The same idea is found among the Blackfoot Indians; cf. H. B. Ale ander, *North American [Mythology]*, pp. 95 ff. See also the comparati data for North Asia and North America in Jochelson, *The Koryak*, p. 371.

Altaians—as among the Chukchee—the road to the sky runs through the Pole Star.[15] The *udeši-burkhan* of the Buryat open the road to the shaman as one opens doors.[16]

This symbolism, of course, is not confined to the Arctic and North Asian regions. The sacred pillar, rising in the center of the house, is also found among the Hamitic Galla and Hadia herdsmen, the Hamitoid Nandi, and the Khasi (Assam).[17] Everywhere, sacrificial offerings are brought to the foot of this pillar. Sometimes they are oblations of milk to the celestial God (as among the African tribes cited above); in some cases, even, blood sacrifices are offered (for example, among the Galla of Kenya).[18] The World Pillar is sometimes represented apart from the house—as among the ancient Germans (*Irminsūl*, an image of which Charlemagne destroyed in 772), the Lapps, the Ugrian peoples. The Ostyak call these ritual posts "The Powerful Posts of the Center of the City"; the Ostyak of Tsingala know them under the name of "Man-Pillar of Iron," invoke them in their prayers as "Man" and "Father," and offer them blood sacrifices.[19]

15 A. V. Anokhin, *Materialy po shamanstvu u altaitsev*, p. 9.

16 Harva, *Die religiösen Vorstellungen*, p. 54.

17 W. Schmidt, "Der heilige Mittelpfahl," p. 967, citing his *Der Ursprung*, II, 53, 85, 165, 449, 590 ff.

18 The question of the empirical "origin" of such conceptions (for example, the structure of the cosmos conceived in accordance with certain material elements of the dwelling, which in turn are explicable by the necessity of adaptation to the milieu, etc.) is wrongly posed and hence fruitless. For, for "primitives" in general, there is no clear difference between "natural" and "supernatural," between empirical object and symbol. An object becomes "itself" (that is, the carrier of a value) in so far as it participates in a "symbol"; an act acquires meaning in so far as it repeats an archetype, etc. In any case, this problem of the "origin" of values belongs rather to philosophy than to history. For, to cite but one example, it scarcely seems that the fact that the first discovery of geometrical laws was due to the empirical necessities of irrigating the Nile delta can have any bearing on the validity or invalidity of those laws.

19 Karjalainen (*Die Religion der Jugra-Völker*, II, 42 ff.) supposes, erroneously, that the role of these posts is to hold the sacrificial victim. Actually, as Holmberg (Harva) has shown, this pillar is called the "Seven-divided high man-father," just as Sänke, the celestial god, is invoked as "Seven-visioned high man, Sänke, my father, my three-directions-watching man

The symbolism of the World Pillar is also familiar to more de
veloped cultures—Egypt, India,[20] China, Greece, Mesopotamia
Among the Babylonians, for example, the link between heaven and
earth—a link symbolized by a Cosmic Mountain or its replica
(ziggurat, temple, royal city, palace)—was sometimes imagine
as a celestial column. We shall see before long that the same idea i
also expressed in other images: Tree, Bridge, Stair, and so or
This whole complex forms part of what we have called the sym
bolism of the "Center," which appears to be of considerable an
tiquity, for it is found in the most "primitive" cultures.

At this point we wish to emphasize the following fact: Althoug
the shamanic experience proper could be evaluated as a mystica
experience by virtue of the cosmological concept of the three com
municating zones, this cosmological concept does not belong ex
clusively to the ideology of Siberian and Central Asian shamanism
nor, in fact, of any other shamanism. It is a universally dissem
nated idea connected with the belief in the possibility of direct com
munication with the sky. On the macrocosmic plane this commun
cation is figured by the Axis (Tree, Mountain, Pillar, etc.); on th

---

father," etc. (*Finno-Ugric* [*and*] *Siberian* [*Mythology*], p. 338). The pill
was sometimes marked with seven notches; the Ostyak of Salym, when the
offer blood sacrifices, make seven incisions in a post (ibid., p. 339). Th
ritual post corresponds to the "Seven-divided pure silver holy pillar"
Vogul tales, to which the sons of the god tie their horses when they vi
their father (ibid., pp. 339–40). The Yurak also offer blood sacrifices
wooden idols (*sjaadai*) with seven faces or seven gashes; according
Lehtisalo (*Entwurf einer Mythologie der Jurak-Samojeden*, pp. 67, 102, etc
these idols are related to "sacred trees" (that is, to a degradation of t
Cosmic Tree with seven branches). Here we see a process of substituti
well known in the history of religions and which is also confirmed by oth
cases in the Siberian religious complex. So, for example, the pillar th
originally served as the offering place for the celestial god Num becom
among the Yurak-Samoyed, a sacred object to which blood sacrifices a
offered; cf. A. Gahs, "Kopf-, Schädel- und Langknochenopfer bei Renti
völkern," p. 240. On the cosmological meaning of the number 7 and its r
in shamanic rituals, see below, pp. 274 ff.

20 See, for example, *Ṛg-Veda*, X, 89, 4; etc.

microcosmic plane it is signified by the central pillar of the house or the upper opening of the tent—which means that *every human habitation is projected to the "Center of the World,"* [21] or that every altar, tent, or house makes possible a break-through in plane and hence ascent to the sky.

In the archaic cultures communication between sky and earth is ordinarily used to send offerings to the celestial gods and not for a concrete and personal ascent; the latter remains the prerogative of shamans. Only they know how to make an ascent through the "central opening"; only they transform a cosmo-theological concept into a *concrete mystical experience*. This point is important. It explains the difference between, for example, the religious life of a North Asian people and the religious experience of its shamans; the latter is a *personal and ecstatic experience*. In other words, what for the rest of the community remains a cosmological ideogram, for the shamans (and the heroes, etc.) becomes a mystical itinerary. For the former, the "Center of the World" is a site that permits them to send their prayers and offerings to the celestial gods, whereas for the latter it is the place for beginning a flight in the strictest sense of the word. Only for the latter is *real communication* among the three cosmic zones a possibility.

In this connection the reader will remember the previously cited myth of a paradisal age in which human beings could easily go up to the sky and maintained familiar relations with the gods. The cosmological symbolism of the dwelling and the experience of shamanic ascent confirm, though in another aspect, this archaic myth. They do so in this way: After the interruption of the *easy communications* that, at the dawn of time, existed between mankind and the gods, certain privileged beings (and first of all the shamans) reserved the power to actualize, for their own persons, the connection with the upper regions; similarly, the shamans have the power to fly and to reach the sky through the "central opening," whereas for the rest of mankind the opening serves only for the

21 See Eliade: *Patterns in Comparative Religion*, pp. 379 ff.; *The Myth of the Eternal Return*, pp. 76 ff.

265

transmission of offerings. In both cases alike, the shaman's privileged status is due to his faculty for ecstatic experiences.

We have had to emphasize this point—of primary importance,
in our view—a number of times in order to bring out the universal
character of the ideology implied in shamanism. The shamans did
not create the cosmology, the mythology, and the theology of their
respective tribes; they only interiorized it, "experienced" it, and
used it as the itinerary for their ecstatic journeys.

The Cosmic Mountain

Another mythical image of the "Center of the World" that makes
connection between earth and sky possible is that of the Cosmic
Mountain. The Tatars of the Altai imagine Bai Ülgän in the middle of the sky, seated on a golden mountain.[22] The Abakan Tatar
call it "The Iron Mountain"; the Mongols, the Buryat, the Kalmyk
know it under the names of Sumbur, Sumur, or Sumer, which
clearly show Indian influence (= Mount Meru). The Mongol
and the Kalmyk picture it with three or four storeys; the Siberian
Tatars, with seven; in his mystical journey the Yakut shaman, too,
climbs a mountain with seven storeys. Its summit is in the Pole
Star, in the "Navel of the Sky." The Buryat say that the Pole Star
is fastened to its summit.[23]

The idea of a Cosmic Mountain as Center of the World is not
necessarily of Oriental origin, for, as we have seen, the symbolism
of the "Center" seems to have preceded the rise of the paleo-
Oriental civilizations. But the ancient traditions of the peoples of
Central and North Asia—who doubtless knew the image of the
"Center of the World" and of the Cosmic Axis—were modified by
the continual influx of Oriental religious ideas, whether Mesopotamian in origin (and disseminated through Iran) or Indian
(disseminated through Lamaism). In Indian cosmology Mount
Meru rises at the "Center of the World" and above it shines the

22 W. Radlov, *Aus Sibirien*, II, 6.
23 Holmberg (Harva): *Der Baum des Lebens*, pp. 41, 57; *Finno-Ugric*
[*and*] *Siberian* [*Mythology*], p. 341; *Die religiösen Vorstellungen*, pp. 58

Pole Star.[24] Just as the Indian gods grasped this Cosmic Mountain (= World Axis) and stirred the primordial ocean with it, thus giving birth to the universe, so a Kalmyk myth relates that the gods used Sumer as a stick to stir the ocean, thus creating the sun, moon, and stars.[25] Another Central Asian myth shows the penetration achieved by Indian elements: the Mongolian god Ochirvani (= Indra), taking the form of the eagle Garide (= Garuda), attacked the snake Losun in the primordial ocean, wound it three times around Mount Sumeru, and finally crushed its head.[26]

There is no need to cite all the other Cosmic Mountains of Oriental or European mythologies—Haraberezaiti (Elbruz) of the Iranians, for example, Himingbjörg of the ancient Germans, and so on. In Mesopotamian beliefs a Central Mountain joins heaven and earth; it is the "Mount of the Lands," which connects the territories.[27] But the very names of the Babylonian temples and sacred towers bear witness to their assimilation to the Cosmic Mountain: "Mount of the House," "Mount of the Mountains of All Lands," "Mount of Storms," "Link between Heaven and Earth," and the like.[28] The ziggurat was, properly speaking, a Cosmic Mountain, a symbolic image of the Cosmos; its seven storeys represented the seven planetary heavens (as at Borsippa) or bore the colors of the world (as at Ur).[29] The temple of Borobudur, a veritable *imago mundi*, was built in the form of a mountain.[30] Artificial mountains are attested in India, and are also

24 W. Kirfel, *Die Kosmographie der Inder*, p. *15.

25 Harva, *Die religiösen Vorstellungen*, p. 63.

26 G. N. Potanin, *Ocherki severo-zapadnoi Mongolii*, IV, 228; Harva, *Die religiösen Vorstellungen*, p. 62. On Greek coins a snake twines three times round the omphalos (ibid., p. 63).

27 A. Jeremias, *Handbuch*, p. 130; cf. Eliade, *The Myth of the Eternal Return*, pp. 13 ff. For the Iranian data, see A. Christensen, *Les Types du premier homme et du premier roi dans l'histoire légendaire des Iraniens*, II, 42.

28 T. Dombart, *Der Sakralturm. I: Ziqqurat*, p. 34.

29 Id., *Der babylonische Turm*, pp. 5 ff.; Eliade, *Cosmologie și alchimie biloniană*, pp. 31 ff. On the symbolism of the ziggurat, cf. A. Parrot, *Ziggurats et Tour de Babel*.

30 P. Mus, *Barabuḍur. Esquisse d'une histoire du Bouddhisme fondée sur la critique archéologique des textes*, I, 356.

found among the Mongols and in Southeast Asia.[31] It seems probable that Mesopotamian influences reached India and the Indian
Ocean, although the symbolism of the "Center" (Mountain, Pillar,
Tree, Giant) is an organic part of the most ancient Indian spirituality.[32]

Mount Tabor, in Palestine, might signify *ṭabbūr*, that is,
"navel," omphalos. Mount Gerizim, at the center of Palestine, was
doubtless invested with the prestige of the "Center," for it is called
"navel of the earth." [33] A tradition preserved by Petrus Comestor
says that at the summer solstice the sun casts no shadow on "Jacob's Fountain" (close to Gerizim). And he goes on: "Sunt qui
dicunt locum illum esse umbilicum terrae nostrae habitabilis"
("Some say that place is the navel of our habitable earth").[34]
Palestine, being the highest land—since it lay close to the summit
of the Cosmic Mountain—was not covered by the Flood. A rab-
binical text says: "The land of Israel was not submerged by the
Deluge." [35] For the early Christians, Golgotha was at the "Center
of the World," for it was the summit of the Cosmic Mountain and
at the same time the place where Adam was created and buried.
Thus the Saviour's blood falls on Adam's skull, buried exactly at
the foot of the Cross, and redeems him.[36]

31 Cf. W. Foy, "Indische Kultbauten als Symbole des Götterbergs,"
pp. 213–16; Harva, *Die religiösen Vorstellungen*, p. 68; R. von Heine-Geldern,
"Weltbild und Bauform in Südostasien," pp. 48 ff.; cf. also H. G. Quaritch
Wales, *The Mountain of God: a Study in Early Religion and Kingship*,
passim.

32 Cf. Mus, *Barabuḍur*, I, 117 ff., 292 ff., 351 ff., 385 ff., etc.; J. Przyl-
ski, "Les Sept Terrasses de Barabuḍur," pp. 251–56; Coomaraswamy, *Elements of Buddhist Iconography*, passim; Eliade, *Cosmologie*, pp. 43 ff.

33 *Ṭabbūr ereṣ*; cf. Judges 9:37: ". . . See there come people down by the
middle [Heb., navel] of the land . . ."

34 Eric Burrows, "Some Cosmological Patterns in Babylonian Religion,"
pp. 51, 62, n. 1.

35 Cited by A. J. Wensinck, *The Ideas of the Western Semites concerning
the Navel of the Earth*, p. 15; Burrows (p. 54) mentions other texts.

36 Wensinck, p. 22; Eliade, *Cosmologie*, pp. 34 ff. The belief that Golgotha
is at the "Center of the World" has been preserved in the folklore of the
eastern Christians (for example, among the Little Russians; cf. Holmberg,
Der Baum des Lebens, p. 72).

We have shown elsewhere how frequent and essential this symbolism of the "Center" is both in the archaic ("primitive") cultures and in all the great civilizations of the East.[37] To summarize very briefly: palaces, royal cities,[38] and even simple houses were believed to stand at the "Center of the World," on the summit of the Cosmic Mountain. We have already seen the deeper meaning of this symbolism; it is at the "Center" that the break-through in plane, that is, communication with the sky, becomes possible.

It is such a Cosmic Mountain that the future shaman climbs in dream during his initiatory illness and that he later visits on his ecstatic journeys. Ascending a mountain always signifies a journey to the "Center of the World." As we have seen, this "Center" is made present in many ways, even in the structure of the human dwelling place—but it is only the shamans and the heroes who *actually scale* the Cosmic Mountain, just as it is primarily the shaman who, climbing his ritual tree, is really climbing a World Tree and thus reaches the summit of the universe, in the highest sky. For the symbolism of the World Tree is complementary to that of the Central Mountain. Sometimes the two symbols coincide; usually they complete each other. But both are merely more developed mythical formulations of the Cosmic Axis (World Pillar, etc.).

The World Tree

There is no occasion to review the extensive documentation on the World Tree here.[39] We will confine ourselves to citing the themes most frequently found in Central and North Asia, and indicating

37 Eliade: *Cosmologie*, pp. 31 ff.; *Patterns*, pp. 367 ff.; *The Myth of the Eternal Return*, pp. 12 ff.

38 Cf. Mus, *Barabuḍur*, I, 354 ff. and passim; Jeremias, *Handbuch*, pp. 113, 142, etc.; M. Granet, *La Pensée chinoise*, pp. 323 ff.; Wensinck, *Tree and Bird as Cosmological Symbols in Western Asia*, pp. 25 ff.; Birger Pering, "Die geflügelte Scheibe"; Burrows, "Some Cosmological Patterns," pp. 48 ff.

39 The essential elements and bibliographies will be found in Eliade, *Patterns*, pp. 273 ff., 327 ff.

their role in the shamanic ideology and experience. The Cosmic Tree is essential to the shaman. From its wood he makes his drum;[40] climbing the ritual birch, he effectually reaches the summit of the Cosmic Tree; in front of his yurt and inside it are replicas of the Tree, and he depicts it on his drum.[41] Cosmologically, the World Tree rises at the center of the earth, the place of earth's "umbilicus," and its upper branches touch the palace of Bai Ülgän.[42] In the legends of the Abakan Tatars a white birch with seven branches grows on the summit of the Iron Mountain. The Mongols imagine the Cosmic Mountain as a four-sided pyramid with a Tree in the center; the gods use it as a hitching post for their horses, as they do the Pillar of the World.[43]

The Tree connects the three cosmic regions.[44] The Vasyugan Ostyak believe that its branches touch the sky and its roots go down to the underworld. According to the Siberian Tatars, a replica of the Celestial Tree stands in the underworld; a fir with nine roots (or, in other variants, nine firs) rises before the palace of Irle Kan; the King of the Dead and his sons hitch their horses to its trunk. The Goldi reckon three Cosmic Trees: the first is in the sky (and the souls of men perch on its branches like birds, waiting

40 See above, pp. 169 f.

41 See, for example, the drawing on the drum of an Altaic shaman, in Harva, *Die religiösen Vorstellungen*, fig. 15. The shamans sometimes use an "inverted tree," which they set up near their house, which it is believed to protect; cf. E. Kagarow, "Der umgekehrte Schamanenbaum." The "inverted tree" is, of course, a mythical image of the cosmos; cf. Coomaraswamy, "The Inverted Tree," which contains an abundant Indian documentation; Eliade, *Patterns*, pp. 274 ff., 327. The same symbolism is preserved in Christian and Islamic traditions: cf. ibid., p. 274; A. Jacoby, "Der Baum mit den Wurzeln nach oben und den Zweigen nach unten"; Carl Martin Edsman, "Arbor inversa."

42 Radlov, *Aus Sibirien*, II, 7.

43 Cf. Holmberg (Harva): *Der Baum des Lebens*, p. 52; *Die religiösen Vorstellungen*, p. 70. In the same way, Odin hitches his horse to Yggdrasil (Eliade, *Patterns*, p. 277). On the mythical complex horse–tree (post) in China, see C. Hentze, *Frühchinesische Bronzen und Kultdarstellungen*, pp. 128–30.

44 Cf. H. Bergema, *De Boom des Levens in Schrift en Historie*, pp. 539

to be carried down to earth to bring infants to birth), the second on earth, and the third in the underworld.[45] The Mongols know the tree *Zambu* whose roots plunge to the base of Mount Sumer and whose crown spreads over its summit; the gods (*Tengeri*) feed on the fruits of the Tree, and the demons (*asuras*), hidden in the gorges of the Mountain, watch them enviously. A similar myth is found among the Kalmyk and the Buryat.[46]

Several religious ideas are implied in the symbolism of the World Tree. On the one hand, it represents the universe in continual regeneration,[47] the inexhaustible spring of cosmic life, the paramount reservoir of the sacred (because it is the "Center" for the reception of the celestial sacred, etc.); on the other, it symbolizes the sky or the planetary heavens.[48] We shall return later to the Tree as symbol of the planetary heavens, since this symbolism plays an essential role in Central Asian and Siberian shamanism. But it is important to remember at this point that in a number of archaic traditions the Cosmic Tree, expressing the sacrality of the world, its fertility and perenniality, is related to the ideas of creation, fecundity, and initiation, and finally to the idea of absolute reality and immortality. Thus the World Tree becomes a Tree of Life and Immortality as well. Enriched by innumerable mythical doublets and complementary symbols (Woman, the Wellspring, Milk, Animals, Fruits, etc.), the Cosmic Tree always presents itself as the very reservoir of life and the master of destinies.

45 Harva, *Die religiösen Vorstellungen*, p. 71.

46 Holmberg (Harva): *Finno-Ugric [and] Siberian [Mythology]*, pp. 356 ff.; *Die religiösen Vorstellungen*, pp. 72 ff. We have already referred to a possible Iranian model: the tree Gaokērēna which grows on an island in Lake Vourukasha and beside which lurks the monstrous lizard created by Ahriman (cf. above, p. 122, n. 27). As for the Mongol myth, it is, of course, Indian in origin: *Zambu = Jambū*. Cf. also the Tree of Life (Cosmic Tree) of Chinese tradition, growing on a mountain and sending its roots down to the underworld (Hentze: "Le Culte de l'ours et du tigre et le t'ao-t'ié," p. 57; *Die Sakralbronzen und ihre Bedeutung in den frühchinesischen Kulturen*, pp. 24 ff.).

47 Cf. Eliade, *Patterns*, pp. 273 ff.

48 Or sometimes the Milky Way; cf., for example, Y. H. Toivonen, "Le Gros Chêne des chants populaires finnois."

These ideas are sufficiently old, for they are found among numerous "primitive" peoples, incorporated in a lunar and initiatory symbolism.[49] But they have been frequently altered and developed, the symbolism of the Cosmic Tree being almost inexhaustible. There is no doubt that southeastern influences contributed greatly toward the present physiognomy of the mythologies of the Central and North Asian peoples. In particular, the idea of the Cosmic Tree, reservoir of souls and "Book of Fate," seems to have been imported from more developed civilizations. For the World Tree is a Tree that *lives and gives life*. The Yakut believe that at the "golden navel of the Earth" stands a tree with eight branches; it rises in a sort of primordial paradise, for there the first man was born and he feeds on the milk of a woman who half emerges from the trunk of the tree.[50] As Harva remarks,[51] it is hard to believe that such an image was invented by the Yakut in the bitter climate of northern Siberia. The prototypes are found in the ancient East, as well as in India (where Yama, the first man drinks with the gods beside a miraculous tree [52]) and Iran (where Yima on the Cosmic Mountain imparts immortality to man and animals [53]).

The Goldi, the Dolgan, and the Tungus say that, before birth the souls of children perch like little birds on the branches of the Cosmic Tree and the shamans go there to find them.[54] This mythical motif, which we have already encountered in the initiatory dreams of future shamans,[55] is not confined to Central and North

49 Cf. Eliade, *Patterns*, p. 275.

50 Harva (Holmberg): *Die religiösen Vorstellungen*, pp. 75 ff.; *Der Baum des Lebens*, pp. 57 ff. For the paleo-Oriental prototypes of this mythical motif, see Eliade, *Patterns*, pp. 283 ff. Cf. also Gertrude R. Levy, *The Gate of Horn*, p. 156, n. 3. On the theme Tree–Goddess (= First Woman) in the mythologies of America, China, and Japan, cf. Hentze, *Frühchinesische Bronzen*, pp. 129 f.

51 *Die religiösen Vorstellungen*, p. 77.

52 *Ṛg-Veda*, X, 135, 1.

53 *Yasna*, 9, 4 f.; *Vidēvdat*, 2, 5.

54 Harva, *Die religiösen Vorstellungen*, pp. 84, 166 ff.

55 See above, pp. 39 f.

Asia; it is attested, for example, in Africa and Indonesia.[56] The cosmological schema Tree–Bird (= Eagle), or Tree with a Bird at its top and a Snake at its roots, although typical of the peoples of Central Asia and the ancient Germans, is presumably of Oriental origin,[57] but the same symbolism is already formulated on pre-historic monuments.[58]

Another theme—clearly of exotic origin— is that of the Tree–Book of Fate. Among the Osmanli Turks the Tree of Life has a million leaves, on each of which a human fate is written; each time a man dies, a leaf falls.[59] The Ostyak believe that a goddess, seated on a seven-storey celestial mountain, writes a man's fate, as soon as he is born, on a tree with seven branches.[60] The same belief is found among the Batak; [61] but as both the Turks and the Batak acquired writing only comparatively late, the Oriental origin of the myth is obvious.[62] The Ostyak also believe that the gods look for the child's future in a Book of Fate; according to the legends of the Siberian Tatars, seven gods write the destiny of newborn infants in a "Book of Life." [63] But all these images derive from the Meso-

56 In the sky there is a tree on which there are children; God picks them and throws them down to earth (H. Baumann, *Lunda. Bei Bauern und Jägern in Inner-Angola*, p. 95). On the African myth of the origin of man from trees, cf. id., *Schöpfung und Urzeit des Menschen im Mythus der afrikanischen Völker*, pp. 224 f.; for comparative material, see Eliade, *Patterns*, pp. 300 ff. The Dyak believe that the first pair of ancestors was born from the Tree of Life (H. Schärer, *Die Gottesidee der Ngadju Dajak in Süd-Borneo*, p. 57; see also below, pp. 352 f.). But it should be noted that the image of soul (child)-bird–World Tree is peculiar to Central and North Asia.

57 Harva, *Die religiösen Vorstellungen*, p. 85. On the meaning of this symbolism, see Eliade, *Patterns*, pp. 290 ff. Documentation: A. J. Wensinck, *Tree and Bird as Cosmological Symbols in Western Asia*. Cf. also Hentze, *Frühchinesische Bronzen*, p. 129.

58 See Georg Wilke, "Der Weltenbaum und die beiden kosmischen Vögel in der vorgeschichtlichen Kunst."

59 Harva, *Die religiösen Vorstellungen*, p. 72.   60 Ibid., p. 172.

61 J. Warneck, *Die Religion der Batak*, pp. 49 ff. On the symbolism of the tree in Indonesia, see below, pp. 284 ff., 357 f.

62 Cf. G. Widengren: *The Ascension of the Apostle of God and the Heavenly Book; The King and the Tree of Life in Ancient Near Eastern Religion.*

63 Harva, *Die religiösen Vorstellungen*, pp. 160 ff.

potamian concept of the seven planetary heavens regarded as a Book of Fate. We have mentioned them in this context because the shaman, when he reaches the summit of the Cosmic Tree, in the last heaven, also in a manner asks the "future" of the community and the "fate" of the "soul."

The Mystical Numbers 7 and 9

The identification of the seven-branched Cosmic Tree with the seven planetary heavens is certainly due to influences originally from Mesopotamia. But, to repeat, this does not mean that the idea of the Cosmic Tree = Axis of the World was conveyed to the Turko-Tatars and other Siberian peoples by Oriental influences. Ascent to the sky along the Axis of the World is a universal and archaic idea, much earlier than the idea of traversing the seven celestial regions (= seven planetary heavens), which could only have spread through Central-Asia long after the Mesopotamian speculations on the seven planets. It is known that the religious value of the number 3—symbolizing the three cosmic regions—preceded the value of the number 7. We also hear of 9 heavens (and of 9 gods, 9 branches of the Cosmic Tree, etc.), a mystical number probably explicable as 3×3 and hence to be regarded as forming part of a more archaic symbolism than that depending on the number 7, of Mesopotamian origin.[65]

64 On the antiquity, consistency, and importance of cosmological conceptions based on a tripartite schema, see Coomaraswamy, "Svayamātṛṇṇā Janua Coeli," passim.

65 On the religious and cosmological implications of the numbers 7 and 9 cf. W. Schmidt, *Der Ursprung*, IX, 91 ff., 423, etc. Harva (*Die religiöse Vorstellungen*, pp. 51 f., etc.), on the contrary, considers the number 9 more recent. He also thinks that the nine heavens are a late idea explained by the concept of the nine planets, which, though also attested in India, is of Iranian origin (ibid., p. 56). In any case, two different religious complexes are involved. Obviously, in contexts where the number 9 clearly shows multiplication of the number 3, one is justified in considering it earlier than the number 7. See also F. Röck, "Neunmalneun und Siebenmalsieben," passim; H. Hoffmann, *Quellen zur Geschichte der tibetischen Bon-Religion*

The Altaic shaman climbs a tree or a post notched with seven or nine *tapty*, representing the seven or nine celestial levels. The "obstacles" (*pudak*) that he must overcome are really, as Anokhin remarked,[66] the heavens that he must enter. When the Yakut make blood sacrifices, their shamans set up a tree with nine notches outdoors and climb it to carry the offering to the celestial god Ai Toyon. The initiation of shamans among the Sibo (related to the Tungus) includes, as we have seen, the presence of a tree with steps; another, smaller tree notched with nine *tapty* is kept in his yurt by the shaman.[67] It is one more indication of his ability to journey ecstatically through the celestial regions.

We have seen that the Cosmic Pillars of the Ostyak have seven incisions.[68] The Vogul believe that the sky is reached by climbing a stairway of seven stairs. The conception of seven heavens is general throughout southeastern Siberia. But it is not the only one found; the image of nine celestial levels, or of sixteen, seventeen, and even thirty-three heavens, is not less widespread. As we shall see presently, the number of heavens does not correspond to the number of gods; the correlations between the pantheon and the number of heavens sometimes seem quite forced.

Thus the Altaians speak of seven heavens, but also of twelve, sixteen, or seventeen; [69] among the Teleut the shamanic tree has sixteen incisions, representing as many celestial levels.[70] In the highest heaven dwells Tengere Kaira Kan, "The Merciful Emperor Heaven," on the three lower levels are the three principal gods brought forth by Tengere Kaira Kan through a sort of emanation: Bai Ülgän sits in the sixteenth on a golden throne on top of a golden mountain; Kysugan Tengere, "The Very Strong," in the ninth (no information is given as to the inhabitants of the fifteenth

---

p. 150, 153, 245; A. Friedrich and G. Buddruss, *Schamanengeschichten aus Sibirien*, pp. 21 ff., 96 ff., 101 ff., etc.; W. Schmidt, *Der Ursprung*, XI, 13–16.

66 *Materialy po shamanstvu u altaitsev*, p. 9.
67 Harva, *Die religiösen Vorstellungen*, p. 50.
68 Above, pp. 263–64, n. 19.   69 W. Radlov, *Aus Sibirien*, II, 6 ff.
70 Harva, *Die religiösen Vorstellungen*, p. 52.

to tenth heavens); Mergen Tengere, "The All-Knowing," in the seventh, where the Sun also resides. The other lower levels are populated by the rest of the gods and a number of semidivine figures.[71]

Among the same Tatars of the Altai Anokhin found an entirely different tradition.[72] Bai Ülgän, the Supreme God, inhabits the highest heaven—the seventh; Tengere Kaira Kan does not figure at all (we have already observed that he is in the process of disappearing from the current religion); Ülgän's seven Sons and nine Daughters live in heavens, but in which ones is not stated.[73]

The group of seven or nine Sons (or Servants) of the celestial god is frequently found in Central and North Asia, both among the Ugrians and the Turko-Tatars. The Vogul know seven Sons of God, the Vasyugan-Ostyak speak of seven Gods inhabiting the seven levels: in the highest is Num-tôrem, the other gods are called the "Guardians of the Sky" (Tôrem-karevel) or the "Interpreters of the Sky." [74] A group of seven Supreme Gods is also found among the Yakut.[75] Mongolian mythology, on the contrary, speaks of "nine Sons of the God" or "Servants of the God," which are at once tutelary gods (sulde-tengri) and warrior gods. The Buryat even know the names of these nine Sons of the Supreme God, but they vary from one region to another. The number 9 also appears in the rituals of the Chuvash of the Volga and of the Cheremis.[76]

In addition to these groups of seven or nine gods, and the respective images of seven or nine heavens, more numerous groups are found in Central Asia—such as the thirty-three gods (tengri,

71 Radlov, pp. 7 f.   72 Materialy, pp. 9 ff.

73 See the analysis of these two cosmological conceptions in W. Schmidt, Der Ursprung, IX, 84 ff., 135 ff., 172 ff., 449 ff., 480 ff., etc.

74 In all probability, as Karjalainen has shown (Die Religion der Jugra Völker, II, 305 ff.), these names were borrowed from the Tatars, together with the conception of seven heavens.

75 Harva, Die religiösen Vorstellungen, p. 162 (after V. L. Priklonsky and N. V. Pripuzov). Sieroszewski says that Bai Baianai, Yakut god of the chase, has seven companions, of whom three are favorable and two unfavorable to hunters ("Du chamanisme," p. 303).

76 Harva, Die religiösen Vorstellungen, pp. 162 f.

who inhabit Sumeru and whose number may be of Indian origin.[77] V. L. Verbitsky found among the Altaians the idea of thirty-three heavens, and N. V. Katanov found the same conception among the Soyot.[78] This number, however, appears very infrequently, and it may be considered a recent importation, presumably of Indian origin. Among the Buryat the number of gods is three times as great: ninety-nine gods, divided into good and evil and distributed by regions—fifty-five good gods in the southwestern regions and forty-four evil ones in the northeastern. These two groups of gods have been fighting each other for a very long time.[79] The Mongols, too, knew ninety-nine *tengri* in times past.[80] But neither the Buryat nor the Mongols can say anything definite about these gods, whose names are obscure and artificial.

It should, however, be remembered that belief in a celestial Supreme God is autochthonous and very ancient in Central Asia and the Arctic.[81] No less ancient is the belief in the Sons of God, though the number 7 represents an Oriental, and hence recent, influence. It is probable that the shamanic ideology has played a part in the dissemination of the number 7. A. Gahs considers the mythico-cultural complex of the lunar Ancestor related to the idol with seven gashes and the Tree-Mankind with seven branches, as well as to the periodical and "shamanistic" blood sacrifices, of southern origin, that have taken the place of the bloodless sacrifices (offerings of the head and bones to the celestial Supreme Gods).[82] However this may be, among the Yurak-Samoyed the Earth Spirit has seven sons and the idols (*sjaadai*) have seven faces, or a face with seven gashes, or simply seven incisions; and these *sjaadai* are related to the sacred trees.[83] We have seen that the

---

77 Ibid., p. 164. 78 Ibid., p. 52.

79 G. Sandschejew, "Weltanschauung und Schamanismus der Alaren-Burjaten," pp. 939 ff.

80 Harva, *Die religiösen Vorstellungen*, p. 165.

81 Eliade, *Patterns*, pp. 60 ff.

82 "Kopf-, Schädel- und Langknochenopfer bei Rentiervölkern," p. 237; "Blutige und unblutige Opfer bei den altaischen Hirtenvölkern," pp. 220 ff.

83 T. Lehtisalo, *Entwurf einer Mythologie der Jurak-Samojeden*, pp. 67, 77 ff., 102. On these seven-faced idols, see also Kai Donner, *La Sibérie*, p. 222 ff.

shaman has seven bells on his costume, representing the voices of the seven celestial maidens.[84] Among the Ostyak of the Yenisei the future shaman withdraws into solitude, cooks a flying squirrel, divides it into eight parts, eats seven, and throws away the eighth. After seven days he returns to the same place and receives a sign that determines his vocation.[85] The mystical number 7 apparently plays an important role in the shaman's technique and ecstasy, for among the Yurak-Samoyed the future shaman lies unconscious for seven days and seven nights, while the spirits dismember and initiate him; [86] the Ostyak and Lapp shamans eat mushrooms with seven spots to enter into trance; [87] the Lapp shaman is given a mushroom with seven spots by his master; [88] the Yurak-Samoyed shaman has a glove with seven fingers; [89] the Ugrian shaman has seven helping spirits; [90] and so on. In the case of the Ostyak and the Vogul it has been shown that the importance of the number 7 is due to definite influences from the ancient East [91]—and it is beyond doubt that the same phenomenon has occurred in the rest of Central and North Asia.

What is significant for our study is that the shaman appears to have more direct knowledge of all these heavens, and hence, of all the gods and demigods inhabiting them. For his ability to enter the celestial regions one after the other is due in part to the help their inhabitants give him; before he can address Bai Ülgän, he converses with the other celestial figures and asks their support and protection. The shaman displays a like experiential knowledge of the subterranean regions. The Altaians conceive the entrance to the underworld as a "smoke hole" of the earth, located, of course

84 Cf. Mikhailowski, "Shamanism in Siberia," p. 84.

85 Donner, p. 223.   86 Lehtisalo, *Entwurf*, p. 147.

87 Karjalainen, *Die Religion der Jugra-Völker*, II, 278; III, 306; T. I Itkonen, *Heidnische Religion und späterer Aberglaube bei den finnischen Lappen* p. 149. Among the Ostyak of Tsingala the patient sets a loaf of bread with seven gashes on a table and sacrifices to Sänke (Karjalainen, III, 307).

88 Itkonen, p. 159.   89 Lehtisalo, p. 147.

90 Karjalainen, III, 311.

91 Josef Haekel, "Idolkult und Dualsystem bei den Ugriern (zum Problem des eurasiatischen Totemismus)," p. 136.

at the "Center" (situated, according to the myths of Central Asia, in the North, which corresponds to the Center of the Sky; [92] for, as we know, the "North" is assimilated to the "Center" through the whole Asian area, from India to Siberia). By a sort of symmetry, the underworld has been imagined to have the same number of levels as the sky: three, among the Karagas and the Soyot, who reckon three heavens; seven or nine for most of the Central and North Asian peoples.[93] We have seen that the Altaic shaman successively passes through the seven underworld "obstacles" (*pudak*). Indeed it is he, and he alone, who commands experiential knowledge of the underworld, for he enters it as a living man, just as he mounts and descends through the seven or nine heavens.

Shamanism and Cosmology in the Oceanian Region

Without undertaking to compare two phenomena as complex as Central and North Asian shamanism on the one hand and the shamanism of Indonesia and Oceania on the other, we will rapidly review certain data from the Southeast Asian area in order to demonstrate two points: (1) the presence, in these regions, of the archaic symbolism of the three cosmic zones and the World Axis; (2) the Indian influences (recognizable especially from the cosmological and religious role of the number 7) that have been superimposed on the substratum of the autochthonous religion. For, in our opinion, the two cultural units, Central and North Asia on the one hand and Indonesia and Oceania on the other, display common characteristics in this respect, due to the fact that both have seen their religious traditions definitely modified by the radiation of higher cultures. It is not our intention to enter upon a historico-cultural analysis of the Indonesian and Oceanian area; such a study would go far beyond the limits of this book.[94] We wish

92 Harva, *Die religiösen Vorstellungen*, p. 54.

93 Among the Ugrians the underworld always has seven levels, but the idea seems not to be native; cf. Karjalainen, II, 318.

94 The essentials will be found in Pia Laviosa-Zambotti's brief and daring synthesis, *Les Origines et la diffusion de la civilisation*, pp. 337 ff. On the

only to set up a few signposts to show from what ideologies and by virtue of what techniques shamanism could develop there.

Among one of the most archaic peoples of the Malay Peninsula, the Semang Pygmies, we find the symbol of the World Axis; an immense rock, Batu Ribn, rises at the "Center of the World"; below it is the underworld. Formerly, a tree trunk rose from Batu Ribn into the sky.[95] According to the data collected by Evans, a stone pillar, Batu Herem, supports the sky; its top passes through the celestial vault and comes out above the heaven of Tapern, in a region called Ligoi, where the Chinoi live and amuse themselves.[96] The underworld, the center of the earth, and the "gate" of the sky are situated on the same axis, and in past times it was by this axis that passage from one cosmic region to another was effected. One would hesitate to credit the genuineness of this cosmological schema among the Semang Pygmies, if there were not reason to believe that a similar theory had already been outlined in prehistoric times.[97]

---

earliest history of Indonesia, see G. Coèdes, *Les États hindouisés d'Indochine et d'Indonésie*, pp. 67 ff.; cf. also H. G. Quaritch Wales, *Prehistory and Religion in South-East Asia*, especially pp. 48 ff., 109 ff.

95 P. Schebesta, *Les Pygmées*, pp. 156 ff.

96 Ivor H. N. Evans, *Studies in Religion, Folk-Lore, & Custom in British North Borneo and the Malay Peninsula*, p. 156. The Chinoi (Schebesta: cenoï) are at once souls and nature spirits, which serve as intermediaries between God (Tata Ta Pedn) and men (Schebesta, pp. 152 ff.; Evans, pp. 148 ff.) On their role in healing, see below, pp. 337 ff.

97 Cf., for example, W. Gaerte, "Kosmische Vorstellungen im Bilde prähistorischer Zeit: Erdberg, Himmelsberg, Erdnabel und Weltströme." As for the problem of the authenticity and archaism of the Pygmies' culture, stoutly maintained by W. Schmidt and O. Menghin, it is not yet solved; for a contrary view, cf. Laviosa-Zambotti, *Les Origines*, pp. 132 ff. However this may be, there is no doubt that the Pygmies of the present day, though affected by the higher culture of their neighbors, still preserve many archaic characteristics; this conservatism is found especially in their religious beliefs, so different from those of their neighbors, which are more developed. Hence we believe we are justified in classing the cosmological schema and the myth of the World Axis among the genuine survivals of the Pygmies' religious tradition.

When we come to examine the beliefs held regarding the Semang healers and their magical techniques, we shall note certain Malayan influences (for example, the power to take the form of a tiger). Such influences can also be discerned in these Pygmies' ideas (given below) concerning the destiny of the soul in the beyond. At death the soul leaves the body through the heel and sets off eastward to the sea. For seven days the dead souls can return to their village; after that, those who have led a good life are guided by Mampes to a miraculous island, Belet; to reach it they go over a switchbacked bridge, which crosses the sea. The bridge is called Balan Bacham; Bacham is a kind of fern that grows at the further end of the bridge; there they encounter a Chinoi woman, Chinoi-Sagar, who decks her head with Bacham ferns, and the dead must do likewise before setting foot on the island of Belet. Mampes is the guardian of the bridge, and he is imagined as a gigantic Negrito; it is he who eats the offerings for the dead. Arrived in the island, the dead go to the Mapic Tree (presumably the tree stands in the center of the island), where all the other dead are assembled. But the new arrivals may not wear flowers from the tree or taste its fruits until the dead who have preceded them have broken all their bones and reversed their eyes in the sockets, so that they look inward. When these conditions have been duly fulfilled, the newly deceased become real spirits (*kemoit*) and may eat the fruits of the tree.[98] This, of course, is a miraculous tree and the source of life; for at its roots are breasts heavy with milk, and there too are the spirits of infants [99]—presumably the souls of the yet unborn. Although the myth obtained by Evans is silent on this point, probably the dead become infants again, thus preparing themselves for another life on earth.

98 The breaking of bones and reversal of the eyes suggest the initiatory rites intended to transform the candidate into a "spirit." On the paradisal Fruit Island of the Semang, Sakai, and Jakun, cf. W. W. Skeat and C. O. Blagden, *Pagan Races of the Malay Peninsula*, II, 207, 209, 321. See also below, pp. 282–83, n. 102.

99 Evans, *Studies*, p. 157; Schebesta: *Les Pygmées*, pp. 157–58; "Jenseitsglaube der Semang auf Malakka."

Here we find the idea of the Tree of Life, in whose branches the souls of infants are perched, which seems to be a very old myth, although belonging to a different religious complex from that which centers on the god Ta Pedn and the symbolism of the World Axis. For in this myth we discern, on the one hand, the mystical solidarity between man and plant and, on the other, some traces of a matriarchal ideology, both of which are foreign to the archaic complex: uranian Supreme God, symbolism of the three cosmic zones, myth of a primordial time when there were direct and easy communications between earth and heaven (myth of the "Lost Paradise"). In addition, the detail that the dead can return to their village for *seven* days shows an Indo-Malayan influence that is still more recent.

Among the Sakai such influences become still more marked. They believe that the soul leaves the body through the back of the head and sets off westward. The dead man attempts to enter the sky through the same gate by which the souls of Malays go in, but, failing, starts over a bridge, Menteg, across a caldron of boiling water (this idea is of Malayan origin [100]). The bridge is really a tree trunk stripped of its bark. The souls of the wicked fall into the caldron. Yenang seizes them and burns them to dust; then he weighs them; if the souls have become light, he sends them to the sky; otherwise, he continues burning them to purify them by fire.[101]

The Besisi of the Kuala Langat district of Selangan, like those of Bebrang, speak of a Fruit Island to which the souls of the dead go. The island is comparable to the Mapic Tree of the Semang. There, when men reach old age they can become children and begin to grow again.[102] According to the Besisi conception, the universe is

100 Evans, *Studies*, p. 209, n. 1.

101 Ibid., p. 208. The weighing of the soul and its purification by fire are Oriental ideas. The underworld of the Sakai shows strong and probably recent influences that have replaced the autochthonous conceptions of the beyond.

102 This is the widespread myth of the "paradise" where life flows on endlessly, in an eternal recapitulation. Cf. Tuma, the island of spirits (= the dead) of the Melanesians of the Trobriands: ". . . when they [the spirits] find themselves old, they slough off the loose, wrinkled skin, and

divided into six upper regions, the earth, and six underground regions; [103] this shows a mixture of the old tripartite conception with Indo-Malayan cosmological ideas.

Among the Jakun [104] a post five feet high is set up on the grave; it has fourteen notches, seven running up one side and seven down the other; the post is called the "soul ladder." [105] We shall return to this ladder symbolism; [106] for the present, we may note the presence of the seven incisions, which, whether the Jakun are aware of it or not, represent the seven celestial levels that the soul must pass through—which proves the penetration of ideas of Oriental origin even among peoples as "primitive" as the Jakun.

The Dusun [107] of North Borneo picture the road of the dead as mounting a hill and crossing a stream.[108] The role of the mountain in funerary mythologies is always explained by the symbolism of ascent and implies a belief in a celestial dwelling place for the dead. We shall see elsewhere that the dead "cling to the mountains," just as the shamans or heroes do in their initiatory ascents. What it is important to note at this point is that, among all the peoples whom we are passing in review, shamanism shows the closest dependence on funerary beliefs (mountain, paradisal island, Tree of Life) and cosmological concepts (World Axis, Cosmic Tree, three cosmic regions, seven heavens, etc.). In exercising his profession of healer or psychopomp, the shaman employs the traditional details of infernal topography (be it celestial, marine, or subterranean), details that are finally based on an archaic cosmology,

---

merge with a smooth body, dark locks, sound teeth, and full of vigor. Thus life with them is an eternal recapitulation of youth with its accompaniment of love and pleasure." (B. Malinowski, *The Sexual Life of Savages in NW Melanesia*, p. 435.) The same idea is expressed in id., *Myth in Primitive Psychology*, pp. 80 ff. ("Myth of Death and the Recurrent Cycle of Life").

103 Evans, *Studies*, pp. 209–10.

104 According to Evans (ibid., p. 264), they are of Malay race but represent an earlier wave (coming from Sumatra) than the Malays proper.

105 Ibid., pp. 266–67.   106 Cf. below, pp. 487 ff.

107 Of Proto-Malayan race and the aboriginal inhabitants of the island Evans, *Studies*, p. 3).

108 Ibid., pp. 33 ff.

though one that has frequently been enriched or altered by exotic influences.

The Ngadju Dyak of South Borneo have a peculiar conception of the universe: although they know an upper and a lower world, they do not regard our world as a third one but as the sum of the two others, for it at once reflects and represents them.[109] All this, however, forms part of the archaic idea that the things of the earth are only a replica of the exemplary models that exist in the sky or the beyond. We may add that the concept of three cosmic zones does not contradict the idea of the unity of the world. The numerous symbolisms that express the likeness between the three worlds and the means of communication between them are at the same time an expression of their *unity*, their integration in a single cosmos. The tripartition of the cosmic zones—a motif that, for reasons set forth above, we must emphasize—excludes neither the profound unity of the universe nor its apparent "dualism."

The mythology of the Ngadju Dyak is quite complicated, but a dominant can be discerned in it; and this is precisely a "cosmological dualism." The World Tree precedes this dualism, for it represents the cosmos in its totality; [110] it even symbolizes the unification of the two supreme divinities.[111] The creation of the world is the result of a conflict between two gods representing two polar principles: feminine (cosmologically lower, represented by the waters and the snake) and masculine (the upper region, the bird). During the struggle between these two antagonists, the World Tree (= the primordial totality) is destroyed.[112] But its destruction is only temporary; archetype of all creative human activity, the

109 Cf. H. Schärer: "Die Vorstellungen der Ober- und Unterwelt bei der Ngadju Dajak von Süd-Borneo," especially p. 78; *Die Gottesidee der Ngadju Dajak in Süd-Borneo*, pp. 31 ff. Cf. also W. Münsterberger, *Ethnologische Studien an Indonesischen Schöpfungsmythen. Ein Beitrag zur Kulturanalyse Südostasiens*, especially pp. 143 ff. (Borneo); J. G. Röder, *Alahatala. Die Religion der Inlandstämme Mittelcerams*, pp. 33 ff., 63 ff., 75 ff., 96 ff. (Ceram).

110 Schärer, *Die Gottesidee*, pp. 35 ff.   111 Ibid., pp. 37 f.
112 Ibid., p. 34.

World Tree is destroyed only that it may be reborn. In this myth we are inclined to see both the ancient cosmological schema of the hierogamy between heaven and earth (a schema also expressed, on another plane, by the symbolism of the complementary opposites bird-snake) and the "dualistic" structure of the ancient lunar mythologies (opposition between contraries, alternate destructions and creations, the eternal return). In any case, it is incontestable that Indian influences were later imposed on the ancient autochthonous material, though they were often confined to the nomenclature of the gods.

What must be noted as of particular importance is the presence of the World Tree in every Dyak village and even in every Dyak house.[113] And the Tree is represented with seven branches. That it symbolizes the World Axis and hence the road to the sky is proved by the fact that a similar World Tree is always found in the Indonesian "ships of the dead," which are believed to transport the deceased to the celestial beyond.[114] This Tree, represented with six branches (seven including the tufted top) and with the sun and moon on either side, sometimes takes the form of a lance decorated with the same symbols that serve to designate the "shaman's ladder," by which he climbs to the sky to bring back the patient's fugitive soul.[115] The tree-lance-ladder represented in the "ships of the dead" is only the replica of the miraculous tree that stands in the beyond and to which souls come on their journey to the god Devata Sangiang. The Indonesian shamans (for example, among the Sakai, the Kubu, and the Dyak) also have a tree that they use as a ladder to reach the world of the spirits in seeking the souls of patients.[116] We shall realize the role played by the tree-lance when we examine the technique of Indonesian shamanism. Let us note in

113 Cf. ibid., pp. 76 f. and Pls. I–II.

114 Alfred Steinmann: "Das kultische Schiff in Indonesien," p. 163; "Eine Geisterschiffmalerei aus Südborneo" (offprint), p. 6.

115 Id., "Das kultische Schiff," p. 163.

116 Ibid. In Japan, too, the mast and the tree are still believed today to be the "road to the gods"; cf. A. Slawik, "Kultische Geheimbünde der Japaner und Germanen," pp. 727–28, n. 10.

passing that the shamanic tree of the Dusun Dyak, which serves in healing ceremonies, has seven branches.[117]

The Batak, most of whose religious ideas derive from India, conceive the universe as divided into three regions: sky, with seven storeys, inhabited by the gods; earth, occupied by mankind; and underworld, the home of the demons and the dead.[118] Here too we find the myth of a paradisal time, when the sky was nearer to earth and there was continuous communication between gods and men; but, because of man's pride, the road to the celestial world was blocked. The Supreme God, Mula djadi na bolon ("He who has his beginning in himself"), the creator of the universe and of the other gods, inhabits the most distant heaven and seems to have become—like all the Supreme Gods of "primitives"—a *deus otiosus*; no sacrifices are offered to him. A cosmic snake lives in the subterranean regions and will finally destroy the world.[119]

The Menangkabau of Sumatra have a hybrid religion, based on animism but strongly influenced by Hinduism and Islamism.[120]

117 Steinmann, "Das kultische Schiff," p. 189.

118 But, as we should expect, many of the dead reach the sky (E. M. Loeb, *Sumatra*, p. 75). On the plurality-of funerary itineraries, see below pp. 355 ff.

119 Loeb, *Sumatra*, pp. 74–78.

120 As we have noted before, and shall show in more detail later, this phenomenon is general throughout the Malay world. Cf., for example, the Mohammedan influence in Toradja, Loeb, "Shaman and Seer," p. 61; complex Indian influences on the Malays, J. Cuisinier, *Danses magiques de Kelantan*, pp. 16, 90, 108, etc.; R. O. Winstedt, *Shaman, Saiva and Sufi: Study of the Evolution of Malay Magic*, especially pp. 8 ff., 55 ff., and passim (Islamic influences, pp. 28 ff. and passim); id., "Indian Influence in the Malay World"; Münsterberger, *Ethnologische Studien*, pp. 83 ff. (Indian influences in Indonesia); Hindu influences in Polynesia, E. S. C. Handy, *Polynesian Religion*, passim; H. M. and N. K. Chadwick, *The Growth of Literature*, III, 303 ff.; W. E. Mühlmann, *Arioi und Mamaia. Eine ethnologische, religionssoziologische und historische Studie über polynesische Kultbünde*, pp. 177 ff. (Hindu and Buddhist influences in Polynesia). But we must not lose sight of the fact that these influences have usually altered only the *expression* of magico-religious life; that, in any case, they have not *created* the great mystico-cosmological schemas with which we are concerned in this study.

The universe has seven levels. After death the soul must cross the edge of a razor that extends over a fiery underworld; sinners fall into the flames, the good go up to the sky, where there is a great tree. There souls remain until the final resurrection.[121] It is easy to perceive the mixture of archaic themes (the bridge, the Tree of Life as receptacle and nurse of souls) with exotic influences (underworld fire, the idea of a final resurrection).

The Niassans know the Cosmic Tree that gave birth to all things. To go up to the sky, the dead pass over a bridge; under the bridge is the abyss of the underworld. A guardian with shield and lance is posted at the entrance to the sky; a cat throws guilty souls into the infernal waters for him.[122]

So much for Indonesian examples. We shall return to all these mythical motifs (funerary bridge, ascent, etc.) and the shamanic techniques that are in one way or another connected with them. For the moment, it is enough to have shown the presence, at least in part of the Oceanian area, of a cosmological and religious complex of very great antiquity, variously modified by successive influences from Indian and Asian ideas.

121 Loeb, *Sumatra*, p. 124.
122 Ibid., pp. 150 ff. The author notes (p. 154) the similarity between his complex of Niassan infernal mythology and the ideas of the Indian Naga peoples. The comparison could be extended to other aboriginal peoples of India; we are dealing with vestiges of what has been called the Austroasiatic civilization, shared by the pre-Aryan and pre-Dravidian peoples of India and the majority of the aboriginal peoples of Indochina and the Indian Archipelago. On some of its characteristics, cf. Eliade, *Yoga: Immortality and Freedom*, pp. 344 ff.

CHAPTER NINE

Shamanism
in North and South America

Shamanism among the Eskimo

WHATEVER the truth may be concerning the historical relations between North Asia and North America, the cultural continuity between the Eskimo and the present Arctic peoples of Asia and even Europe (Chukchee, Yakut, Samoyed, and Lapps) is beyond the shadow of a doubt.[1] One of the chief elements of this cultural continuity is shamanism; in Eskimo religious and social life the shamans play the same leading role that they do among the Eskimo's Asiatic neighbors. We have seen that Eskimo initiation in all cases exhibits the universal schema of initiation into mystical life: vocation, withdrawal into solitude, apprenticeship to a master, acquisition of one or more familiar spirits, symbolic ritual of death and resurrection, secret language. As we shall soon see, the ecstatic experiences of the Eskimo *angakok* include mystical flight and the journey to the depths of the sea, two exploits that are characteristic of North Asian shamanism. We also observe close relations between the Eskimo shaman and the celes-

1 Cf. W. Thalbitzer, "Parallels within the Culture of the Arctic Peoples"; K. Birket-Smith, "Über die Herkunft der Eskimos und ihre Stellung in der zirkumpolaren Kulturentwicklung"; Paul Rivet, *Los origines del hombre americano*, pp. 105 ff. There have even been attempts to demonstrate a linguistic relationship between Eskimo and the languages of Central Asia: cf., for example, Aurélien Sauvageot, "Eskimo et Ouralien." But the hypothesis has not yet obtained the assent of specialists.

tial divinity or the cosmocratic god who was later substituted for him.[2] There are, however, minor differences between Eskimo shamanism and that of Northeast Asia: the Eskimo shaman lacks both the ritual costume proper and the drum.

The Eskimo shaman's principal prerogatives are healing, the undersea journey to the Mother of the Sea Beasts to ensure a plentiful supply of game, fair weather (through his contacts with Sila), and the help that he provides for sterile women.[3] Illness is presumably caused by violation of taboos, that is, disorder in the sacred, or by the theft of the patient's soul by one of the dead. In the former case the shaman attempts to cleanse the impurity by collective confessions;[4] in the latter he undertakes an ecstatic journey to the sky or the depths of the sea to find the patient's soul and bring it back to his body.[5] It is always by ecstatic journeys that the *angakok* approaches Takánakapsâluk (Mother of the Sea Beasts) in the depths of the ocean or Sila in the sky. He is, besides, a specialist in magical flight. Some shamans have visited the moon, others have flown around the earth.[6] According to the traditions, shamans fly like birds, spreading their arms as a bird does its

2 Cf. K. Rasmussen, *Die Thulefahrt*, pp. 145 ff.; the shamans, as the intermediaries between men and Sila (the Cosmocrator, the Master of the Universe), have a special veneration for this Great God and attempt to enter into contact with him by concentration and meditation.

3 Thalbitzer, "The Heathen Priests of East Greenland (Angakut)," p. 457; Rasmussen: *Intellectual Culture of the Iglulik Eskimos*, p. 109; *Intellectual Culture of the Copper Eskimos*, pp. 28 ff.; E. M. Weyer, *The Eskimos: Their Environment and Folkways*, pp. 422, 437 ff.

4 Cf., for example, Rasmussen, *Intellectual Culture of the Iglulik Eskimos*, pp. 133 ff., 144 ff.

5 The patient's soul is believed to travel to regions rich in all kinds of sacrality—the great cosmic regions ("Moon," "Sky"), places haunted by the dead, the sources of life ("the land of bears," as among the Greenland Eskimo; cf. Thalbitzer, "Les Magiciens esquimaux," pp. 80 ff.).

6 Rasmussen, *The Netsilik Eskimos: Social Life and Spiritual Culture*, pp. 299 ff.; G. Holm, "Ethnological Sketch of the Angmagsalik Eskimo," pp. 96 ff. On the Central Eskimo's journey to the moon, see below, p. 292. Surprisingly enough, these traditions of ecstatic journeys of shamans are entirely lacking among the Copper Eskimo; cf. Rasmussen, *Intellectual Culture of the Copper Eskimos*, p. 33.

wings. The *angakut* also know the future, make prophecies, predict atmospheric changes, and excel in magical feats.

However, the Eskimo remember a time when the *angakut* were far more powerful than they are today.[7] "I am a shaman myself," one of them told Rasmussen, "but I am nothing compared with my grandfather Titqatsaq. He lived in the time when a shaman could go down to the mother of the sea beasts, fly up to the moon or make excursions out through space. . . ."[8] It is remarkable to find here, too, this idea of the present decadence of shamans, which we have already observed in other cultures.

The Eskimo shaman can not only pray to Sila for fair weather;[9] he can also end a storm by a complicated ritual involving the aid of his helping spirits and the evocation of the dead as well as a duel with another shaman, during which the latter is "killed" and "resuscitated" several times.[10] Whatever their object, the séances are held in the evening, in the presence of the entire village. The spectators encourage the shaman from time to time by strident songs and cries. The shaman sings for a long time in "secret language" to evoke the spirits. Falling into trance, he speaks in a high, strange voice that seems not to be his.[11] The songs improvised during trance may reveal some of the shaman's mystical experiences.

> My body is all eyes.
> Look at it! Be not afraid!
> I look in all directions!

sings a shaman,[12] no doubt referring to the mystical experience of inner light that he undergoes before entering into trance.

7 Rasmussen: *Intellectual Culture of the Iglulik Eskimos*, pp. 131 ff.; *The Netsilik Eskimos*, p. 295.

8 Id., *The Netsilik Eskimos*, p. 299.

9 Cf. id., *Die Thulefahrt*, pp. 168 ff.

10 See the long description of a séance of this kind in id., *Intellectual Culture of the Copper Eskimos*, pp. 34 ff. Cf. also Ernesto de Martino's penetrating commentary in his *Il mondo magico*, pp. 148–49.

11 Cf., for example, Rasmussen, *The Netsilik Eskimos*, p. 294; Weyer, pp. 437 ff.

12 Thalbitzer, "Les Magiciens esquimaux," p. 102.

But in addition to these séances demanded by collective problems (storms, scarcity of game, weather information, etc.) or by sickness (which, in one way or another, likewise threatens the society's equilibrium), the shaman undertakes ecstatic journeys to the sky, to the land of the dead, "for joy alone." He has himself tied, as is usual when he prepares for an ascent, and flies into the air; there he has long conversations with the dead and, on his return to earth, describes their life in the sky.[13] This fact shows the Eskimo shaman's need of the ecstatic experience for its own sake and also explains his liking for solitude and meditation, his long dialogues with his helping spirits, and his need for quiet.

The Eskimo usually distinguish three dwelling places for the dead: [14] the sky, an underworld immediately below the earth's surface, and another deep underground. In the sky, as in the real underworld (the deep one), the dead lead a happy existence, enjoying a life of pleasure and prosperity. The only great difference from life on earth is that there the seasons are always the opposite of the seasons here; when it is winter here, it is summer in the sky and the underworld, and vice versa. Only in the underworld directly beneath the earth's surface, reserved for those who have been guilty of various violations of taboo and for unskillful hunters, do despair and famine reign.[15] The shamans have perfect knowledge of all these regions, and when a dead person, fearing to take the road to the beyond alone, abducts the soul of a living person, the *angakok* knows where to go to look for it.

Sometimes the shaman's otherworld journey takes place during a cataleptic trance that has every appearance of death. Such was the case with an Alaskan shaman who declared that he had been dead and had followed the road of the dead for two days; it was well trodden by all those who had preceded him. As he walked on, he heard continual weeping and wailing; he learned that it was the living mourning their dead. He came to a big village, which was

13 Rasmussen, *Intellectual Culture of the Iglulik Eskimos*, pp. 129–31.
14 Cf., for example, id., *The Netsilik Eskimos*, pp. 315 ff.
15 Ibid.

exactly like a village of the living; there, two shades took him into a house. A fire was burning in the middle of it, with some pieces of meat broiling on the coals, but they had living eyes that followed the shaman's movements. His companions told him not to touch the meat (a shaman who had once tasted food in the land of the dead would find it hard to return to earth). After resting for a time in the village, the *angakok* pursued his journey, reached the Milky Way, followed it for a long time, and finally came down on his own grave. When he re-entered his body it came back to life, and, leaving the graveyard, he went to his village and narrated his adventures.[16]

Here we have an ecstatic experience whose content extends beyond the sphere of shamanism proper but which, though accessible to other privileged human beings, is very frequent in shamanic circles. The descents to the underworld or ascents to the celestial paradise that figure among the exploits of Polynesian, Turko-Tatar, North American, and other heroes belong in this class of ecstatic journeys in forbidden zones, and the respective funerary mythologies have drawn largely on this type of material.

To return to the Eskimo shamans: their ecstatic capacities enable them to undertake any journey "in spirit" to any region of the cosmos. They always take the precaution of having themselves bound with ropes, so that they will journey only "in spirit"; otherwise they would be carried into the sky and would vanish for good. Securely tied, and sometimes separated from the rest of those present by a curtain, they begin by invoking their familiar spirits; with their help they leave the earth and reach the moon or enter the depths of the earth or the sea. Thus a Baffinland Eskimo shaman was carried to the moon by his helping spirit (in this case, a bear); there he came to a house whose door, made of the jaw of a walrus, threatened to tear the intruder to pieces (the well-known motif of the "difficult entrance," to which we shall return later). Having managed to enter the house, he there found the Man in the Moon and his wife, the Sun. After many adventures he re-

16 E. W. Nelson, "The Eskimo about Bering Strait," pp. 433 ff.

urned to earth, and his body, which had remained inanimate during his ecstasy, showed signs of life. Finally the shaman freed himself from all the ropes that bound him, and told to the audience all the incidents of his voyage.[17]

Such exploits, undertaken for no apparent motive, to some extent repeat the initiatory journey with its many dangers and especially the passage through a "strait gate" that remains open only for an instant. The Eskimo shaman feels the need for these ecstatic journeys because it is above all during trance that he becomes truly himself; the mystical experience is necessary to him as a constituent of his true personality.

But it is not only his journeys "in spirit" that confront him with such initiatory ordeals. The Eskimo are periodically terrorized by evil spirits, and the shamans are summoned to drive them away. In cases of this sort, the séance involves an intense struggle between the shaman's familiar spirits and the evil spirits (these being either nature spirits angered by the violation of taboos, or the souls of some of the dead). Sometimes the shaman leaves the hut and returns with his hands covered with blood.[18]

When on the verge of going into trance, the shaman makes motions as if he were diving. Even when he is supposed to be entering the subterranean regions, he gives the impression that he is diving and returning to the surface of the ocean. Thalbitzer was told that a shaman "comes up a third time, before he goes down for good." [19] The term most commonly used in referring to a shaman is "one who drops down to the bottom of the sea." [20] As we have seen, submarine descents are symbolically represented on the costumes of

17 Franz Boas, "The Central Eskimo," pp. 598 ff. The shaman's deliverance from the ropes with which he is tightly bound constitutes, with many others, a parapsychological problem into which we cannot enter here. From the point of view that we have adopted—that of the history of religions—deliverance from the ropes, like many other shamanic "miracles," signifies the condition of "spirit," which the shaman is considered to have obtained through his initiation.

18 Rasmussen, *Intellectual Culture of the Iglulik Eskimos*, pp. 144 ff.

19 "The Heathen Priests," p. 459.

20 Rasmussen, *Intellectual Culture of the Iglulik Eskimos*, p. 124.

many Siberian shamans (ducks' feet, pictures of diving birds, etc.) For the bottom of the sea is the abode of the Mother of the Sea Beasts, mythical formula for the Great Goddess of the Animals source and matrix of all life, upon whose good will the existence of the tribe depends. This is why the shaman must periodically descend to re-establish spiritual contact with the Mother of the Sea Beasts. But as we have already noted, the position of great importance that she holds in the religious life of the community and the shaman's mystical experience do not affect the veneration of Sila, the Supreme Being, of celestial structure, who also rules the weather by sending hurricanes or snowstorms. This is why the Eskimo shamans do not seem to specialize either in descents to the bottom of the sea or in celestial ascents; their profession involves both in equal measure.

Descent to the abode of Takánakapsâluk, the Mother of the Sea Beasts, is undertaken at an individual's request, sometimes because of illness, sometimes because of bad luck in hunting; only in the latter case is the shaman paid. But it sometimes happens that no game at all is to be found and the village is threatened with famine; then all the villagers gather in the house where the séance is held and the shaman's ecstatic journey is made in the name of the whole community. Those present must unfasten their belts and laces, and remain silent, their eyes closed. For a time the shaman breathes deeply, in silence, before summoning his helping spirits. When they come the shaman begins to murmur, "The way is made ready for me; the way opens before me!" and the audience answer in chorus: "Let it be so." And now the earth opens, and the shaman struggles for a long time with unknown forces before he finally cries: "Now the way is open." And the audience exclaim in chorus: "Let the way be open before him; let there be way for him." Now first under the bed, then farther away, under the passage, is heard the cry, "Halala-he-he-he, Halala-he-he-he"; this is the sign that the shaman has set off. The cry grows more and more distant until it is no longer heard.

During this time the audience sing in chorus, their eyes closed and sometimes the shaman's clothes—which he had taken off before the séance—come to life and start flying about the house, over the heads of the audience. The sighs and deep breathing of people long dead are also heard; they are dead shamans, come to help their colleague on his dangerous journey. And their sighs and their breathing seem to come from very far under water, as if they were sea beasts.

Reaching the bottom of the ocean, the shaman finds himself facing three great stones in constant motion barring his road; he must pass between them at the risk of being crushed. (This is another image of the "strait gate" that forbids access to the plane of higher being to anyone but an "initiate," that is, one who can act like a "spirit.") Successfully passing this obstacle, the shaman follows a path and comes to a sort of bay; on a hill stands Takánakapsâluk's house, made of stone and with a narrow entrance. The shaman hears sea beasts blowing and panting, but does not see them. A dog with bared teeth defends the entrance; the dog is dangerous to anyone who is afraid of it, but the shaman passes over it, and it understands that he is a very powerful magician. (All these obstacles oppose the ordinary shaman, but the really powerful shamans reach the bottom of the sea and the presence of Takánakapsâluk directly, by diving beneath their tent or snow hut, as if slipping through a tube.)

If the goddess is angry with men, a great wall rises before her house. And the shaman has to knock it down with his shoulder. Others say that Takánakapsâluk's house has no roof, so that the goddess can better see men's acts from her place by the fire. All kinds of marine animals are gathered in a pool to the right of the fire, and their cries and breathings are heard. The goddess's hair hangs down over her face and she is dirty and slovenly; this is the effect of men's sins, which have almost made her ill. The shaman must approach her, take her by the shoulder, and comb her hair (for the goddess has no fingers with which to comb herself). Before he can do this, there is another obstacle to be overcome; Takánakapsâluk's father, taking him for a dead man on the way to the land of shades, tries to seize him, but the shaman cries, "I am flesh and blood!" and succeeds in passing.

As he combs Takánakapsâluk's hair, the shaman tells her that men have no more seal. And the goddess answers in the spirit language: "The secret miscarriages of the women and breaches of taboo in eating boiled meat bar the way for the animals." The shaman now has to summon all his powers to appease her anger; finally she opens the pool and sets the animals free. The audience hears their movements at the bottom of the sea, and soon afterward the shaman's gasping breathing, as if he were emerging from the surface of the water. A long silence follows. Finally the shaman speaks: "I have something to say." All answer: "Let us hear, let us hear." And the shaman, in the spirit language, demands the confession of sins. One after another, all confess their miscarriages or their breaches of taboos and repent.[21]

As we see, this ecstatic descent to the bottom of the sea involves a continuous series of obstacles that bear every resemblance to initiatory ordeals; the motif of passing through an aperture that is constantly closing and over a bridge as narrow as a hair, the infernal dog, the appeasing of the angry divinity, return as leitmotif in accounts both of initiations and of mystical journeys into the beyond. In both cases there is the same break-through in ontological plane; these are ordeals meant to prove that he who undertakes such an exploit has transcended the human condition, that is, he is assimilated to the "spirits" (an image that perceptualizes an ontological mutation: having access to the world of the "spirits"); otherwise, if he were not a "spirit," the shaman could never pass through so narrow an aperture.

Besides the shamans, any Eskimo can consult the spirits, by the method called *qilaneq*. The patient is seated on the ground and his head held up by a belt. The spirits are invoked; when the head becomes heavy, it is the sign that they have come. They are then asked questions. If the head becomes still heavier, the answer is

21 Rasmussen, *Intellectual Culture of the Iglulik Eskimos*, pp. 124 ff. Cf. also Erland Ehnmark, *Anthropomorphism and Miracle*, pp. 151 ff.

the affirmative; if, on the contrary, it seems light, the answer is negative. Women frequently employ this easy method of divination by the spirits. The shaman sometimes practices it, using his own foot.[22]

All this is made possible by the general belief in spirits and especially by the communication that is felt to exist with the souls of the dead. A sort of elementary spiritualism in one way or another forms part of the mystical experience of the Eskimo. The dead are not feared, except those among them who, because of various breaches of taboos, become cruel and malicious. With the others, the Eskimo gladly enters into relationship. In addition to the dead, there is the infinite number of nature spirits that render the Eskimo service, each in its fashion. Every Eskimo can obtain the help or protection of a spirit or of one of the dead; but such relationships do not suffice to bestow shamanic powers. Here, as in so many other cultures, he alone is a shaman who, through mystical vocation or voluntary quest, submits himself to the teaching of a master, successfully passes through the initiatory ordeals, and becomes capable of ecstatic experiences that are inaccessible to the rest of mankind.

North American Shamanism

Among many North American tribes shamanism dominates religious life, or at least is its most important aspect. But nowhere does the shaman monopolize all religious experience. Besides him, there are other technicians of the sacred—the priest, the sorcerer (black magician); in addition, as we have seen,[23] every individual seeks to obtain, for his own personal advantage, a number of magico-religious "powers," usually identified with certain tutelary or helping "spirits." The shaman, however, is distinguished from both classes—his colleagues and the lay population—by the intensity of his own magico-religious experiences. Every Indian can

22 Rasmussen, *Intellectual Culture of the Iglulik Eskimos*, pp. 141 ff.
23 Above, pp. 99 ff.

obtain a "tutelary spirit" or a "power" of some sort that makes him capable of "visions" and augments his reserves of the sacred; but only the shaman, by virtue of his relations with the spirits, is able to enter deeply into the supernatural world; in other words, he alone succeeds in acquiring a technique that enables him to undertake ecstatic journeys at will.

The differences that distinguish shamans from other specialists in the sacred (priests and black magicians) are less well defined. John Swanton has proposed the following bipartition: priests work for the entire tribe or nation, or in any case for a society of some sort, while the authority of shamans depends entirely on their personal skill.[24] But Park rightly observes that in a number of cultures (e.g., those of the Northwest Coast) shamans perform certain sacerdotal functions.[25] Clark Wissler favors the traditional distinction between knowing and practicing the rituals, which defines the priesthood, and direct experience of supernatural forces characteristic of the shamanic function.[26] In general, this distinction must be accepted; but we must not forget that—to repeat—the shaman too is obliged to acquire a body of doctrines and traditions and sometimes serves an apprenticeship under an old master, or undergoes an initiation by a "spirit" that imparts the shamanic tradition of the tribe to him.

Park, in turn,[27] defines North American shamanism by the supernatural power that the shaman acquires as the result of a direct personal experience. "This power is generally manipulated in such a way as to be a matter of concern to others in the society. Accordingly, the practice of witchcraft may be as important a part of shamanism as the curing of disease or the charming of game in communal hunt. We will designate by the term of shamanism, then all the practices by which supernatural power may be acquired by mortals, the exercise of that power either for good or evil, and all the concepts and beliefs associated with these practices." The defi-

---

24 "Shamans and Priests," pp. 522 ff.
25 Willard Z. Park, *Shamanism in Western North America*, p. 9.
26 *The American Indian*, pp. 200 ff.   27 *Shamanism*, p. 10.

ition is useful and permits the inclusion of a number of rather disparate phenomena. So far as we are concerned, we should prefer to emphasize the *ecstatic capacity* of the shaman as opposed to the priest, and his *positive* function in comparison with the antisocial activities of the sorcerer, the black magician (although in many cases the North American shaman, like his fellows everywhere, combines the two attitudes).

The shaman's chief function is healing, but he also plays an important role in other magico-religious rites, as, for example, the communal hunt,[28] and, where they exist, in secret societies (Midē'-wiwin type) or mystical sects (Ghost-Dance-Religion type). Like all their fellows, the North American shamans claim to have power over the atmosphere (they bring on or stop rain, etc.), know future events, discover thieves, and so on. They defend men against the harms of sorcerers and, in former times, a Paviotso shaman had only to accuse a sorcerer of crime for the latter to be killed and his house burned.[29] It appears that in the past, at least among some tribes, the shamans' magical power was still greater and more spectacular. The Paviotso still tell of old shamans who put burning coals in their mouths and touched red-hot iron unharmed.[30] In our day shamans have become more largely healers, though their ritual songs and even their own statements claim an omnipotence that is almost divine. "My white brother," an Apache shaman told Reagan, "you probably will not believe it, but I am all powerful. I will never die. If you shoot me, the bullet will not enter my flesh, or if it enters it will not hurt me. . . . If you stick a knife in my throat, thrusting it upwards, it will come out through my skull at the top of my head. . . . I am all powerful. If I wish to kill any one, all I need to do is to thrust out my hand and touch him and he dies. My power is like that of a god."[31]

Possibly this euphoric consciousness of omnipotence is related to

---

28 On this rite, see ibid., pp. 62 ff., 139 ff.   29 Ibid., p. 44.
30 Ibid., p. 57; but see also below, pp. 315–16, n. 74.
31 Albert B. Reagan, *Notes on the Indians of the Fort Apache Region*, 391, cited in Marcelle Bouteiller, *Chamanisme et guérison magique*, p. 160.

initiatory death and resurrection. In any case, the magico-medica
powers enjoyed by the North American shamans exhaust neither
their ecstatic nor their magical capacities. There is every reason
to believe that the secret societies and modern mystical sects have
largely taken over the ecstatic activity that formerly belonged to
shamanism. For example, the ecstatic journeys to the sky by the
founders and prophets of recent mystical movements, to which we
have already referred, belong to the sphere of shamanism. As fo
the shamanic ideology, it has strongly impregnated certain areas o
North American mythology [32] and folklore, especially those con
cerned with life after death and journeys to the underworld.

The Shamanic Séance in North America

Summoned to a sickbed, the North American shaman first turns hi
attention to discovering the cause of the illness. Two principa
kinds of diseases are distinguished; those due to the introduction c
a pathogenic object, and those resulting from "soul loss." [33] Th
treatment in the two cases is essentially different. In the first th
effort is directed to expelling the cause of the trouble, in the secon
to finding and restoring the patient's fugitive soul. In the latte
situation the shaman is absolutely necessary, for only he can se
and capture souls. In the societies that, in addition to shamans, hav
medicine men and healers, these can treat certain maladies, bu
"soul loss" is always the business of shamans. In cases of illnes
brought on by the introduction of a harmful magical object, it i
always by virtue of his ecstatic capacities, and not by any reason
ing in the realm of secular science, that the shaman is able t
diagnose the cause; he commands a number of helping spirits wh

32 Cf., for example, M. E. Opler, "The Creative Role of Shamanism i
Mescalero Apache Mythology."

33 Cf. F. E. Clements, *Primitive Concepts of Disease*, pp. 191 ff. Cf. al
William W. Elmendorf, "Soul Loss Illness in Western North America
Å. Hultkrantz, *Conceptions of the Soul among North American Indians*, p
449 ff.

seek the cause of the illness for him, and the séance necessarily implies summoning up these spirits.

The flight of the patient's soul may be due to many causes: dreams that frighten it away; dead persons who are reluctant to set out for the land of shades and prowl about the camp, looking for another soul to take with them. Or, finally, the patient's soul strays far from his body of itself. A Paviotso informant told Park: "When someone dies suddenly, there is time to get a shaman. If the soul has not gone far, he can bring it back. He goes into a trance to bring back the soul. When the soul has gone a long way to the afterworld, the shaman cannot do anything. It has too much of a start to the land of the dead and he cannot overtake it." [34] The soul leaves the body during sleep, and one may kill a person by waking him suddenly. A shaman must never be startled awake.

Injurious objects are usually projected by sorcerers. They are pebbles, small animals, insects; the magician does not introduce them *in concreto*, but creates them by the power of his thought.[35] They may also be sent by spirits, who sometimes themselves take up residence in the patient's body.[36] Once he has discovered the cause of the illness, the shaman extracts the magical objects by suction.

The séances are held at night and almost always in the patient's house. The ritual nature of the cure is clearly apparent: the shaman and the patient must observe a certain number of prohibitions (they avoid pregnant or menstruating women and, in general, any source of impurity, do not touch flesh or salt foods, the shaman undertakes radical purifications by using emetics, etc.). Sometimes the patient's family also fast and remain continent. As for the shaman, he bathes at dawn and dusk and devotes himself to meditation and prayers. Since the séances are public, they cause a certain religious tension in the entire community, and, in the absence of other religious ceremonies, shamanic cures constitute the all-important rite. The invitation extended to the shaman by a member

34 Park, *Shamanism*, p. 41.   35 Ibid., p. 43.
36 Bouteiller, p. 106.

of the patient's family and the determination of his fee themselves have a ritual character.[37] If the shaman asks too high a price, or if he asks nothing, he falls ill. In any case, it is not he but his "power" that determines the fee for the cure.[38] Only members of his own family are entitled to gratuitous treatment.

A large number of séances have been described in North American ethnological literature.[39] In their general characteristics they are much alike. It will therefore be best to present in some detail one or two séances from among those most adequately recorded.

Shamanic Healing among the Paviotso [40]

After consenting to undertake a cure, the Paviotso shaman inquires into the patient's actions before his illness in order to divine its cause. He then gives instructions for preparing the stick that is to be placed upright beside the patient's head; it must be three or four feet long, made of willow wood, and decorated at the top with an eagle feather supplied by the shaman. This feather remains beside the patient the first night, and the stick is carefully guarded from impure contacts. (If a dog or coyote should touch it, the shaman would fall ill.) We may note in passing the importance of the eagle feather in North American shamanic healing. This symbol of magical flight is probably related to the shaman's ecstatic experiences.

The shaman arrives at the patient's house about nine o'clock in the evening, accompanied by his interpreter, the "talker," whose office is to repeat aloud all the words that the shaman murmurs (The interpreter also receives a fee, usually amounting to half of

37 Park, p. 46; Bouteiller, pp. 111 ff.   38 Park, pp. 48 ff.

39 Cf., for example, the information assembled by Bouteiller, p. 134, n. 1 See also ibid., pp. 128 ff. Cf. Roland Dixon, "Some Aspects of the American Shaman"; Frederick Johnson, "Notes on Micmac Shamanism"; M. E. Opler "Notes on Chiricahua Apache Culture. I: Supernatural Power and the Shaman."

40 After Park, "Paviotso Shamanism"; id., *Shamanism in Western North America*, pp. 50 ff.

what is paid the shaman.) Sometimes the interpreter utters a prayer before the séance and addresses himself directly to the illness to inform it that the shaman has arrived. He figures again at the middle of the séance, when he ritually implores the shaman to cure the patient. Some shamans also employ a dancer (always a woman). She must be beautiful and virtuous; she dances with the shaman, or alone when the latter executes suction. But the participation of dancers in magical cures appears to be a rather recent innovation, at least among the Paviotso.[41]

The shaman approaches the patient barefoot and naked to the waist and begins singing softly. The audience, who are stationed along the walls, repeat the songs one after the other with the interpreter. These songs are improvised by the shaman and he forgets them after the séance; their purpose is to summon the helping spirits. But in inspiration they are purely ecstatic; some shamans affirm that it is their "power" that inspires them during the period of concentration preceding the séance, others claim that the songs come to them by the agency of the eagle-feather stick.[42]

After some time the shaman rises and walks around the fire in the center of the house. If there is a dancer, she follows him. He returns to his place, lights his pipe, draws a few puffs from it, then passes it to those present, who, at his invitation, smoke one or two puffs in turn. During all this time the songs continue. The next stage is determined by the nature of the illness. If the patient is unconscious, he is obviously suffering from "soul loss"; in this case the shaman must go into trance (*yaíka*) at once. If the illness is due to some other cause, the shaman may go into trance to establish the diagnosis or to discuss the proper treatment with his "powers." But this last type of diagnosis is used only if the shaman is powerful enough.

When the shaman's spirit returns victorious from its ecstatic journey in pursuit of the patient's soul, the audience is so informed by the shaman, who gives a long account of his journey. When the purpose of the trance is to discover the cause of the illness, the

41 Id., *Shamanism*, p. 50.   42 Ibid., p. 52.

images that the shaman sees during his ecstasy reveal the secret to him; if he sees the image of a whirlwind, it is a sign that the illness was caused by a whirlwind; if he sees the patient walking among fresh flowers, a cure is certain; but if the flowers are faded, death is inevitable; and so forth. The shaman returns from trance by singing until he completely recovers consciousness. He hastens to communicate his ecstatic experience and, if he has seen that the cause of the illness is an object introduced into the patient's body, he proceeds to extract it by sucking the part of the body that has appeared to him in trance as the seat of the illness. Usually the shaman sucks the skin directly; some, however, suck it through a bone or a willow-wood tube. During the whole of this operation the interpreter and the audience sing in chorus until the shaman stops them by violently ringing a bell. After sucking the blood the shaman spits it into a small hole and repeats the ceremony—that is, he draws a few puffs from his pipe, dances around the fire, and begins sucking again, until he has succeeded in extracting the magical object (a pebble, a lizard, an insect, or a worm). He shows it round, then throws it into the little hole and covers it with dust. The songs and the ritual pipe-smoking continue until midnight; there is then a recess for half an hour, during which food is served to those present, according to the shaman's instructions, though he himself does not eat. Care is taken that not a crumb falls to the ground; any food left over is buried.

The ceremony ends shortly before dawn. Just before its conclusion, the shaman invites the audience to dance around the fire with him for from five to fifteen minutes. He leads the dance, singing. Then he gives the family instructions as to the patient's diet and decides what designs are to be painted on his body.[43]

The Paviotso shaman extracts bullets and arrow heads in the same fashion.[44] Shamanic ceremonies of clairvoyance and weather control are much less frequent than healing séances. But it is known that the shaman can bring rain, halt the clouds, melt the ice of

43 Park, *Shamanism*, pp. 55 f.   44 Ibid., p. 59.

rivers, simply by singing or shaking a feather.[45] As we said, his magical virtues seem to have been far greater in the past, and he used to enjoy exhibiting them. Some Paviotso shamans make prophecies or interpret dreams. But they have no function in war, and they are subordinated to the military chiefs.[46]

The Shamanic Séance among the Achomawi

Jaime de Angulo has given a very full description of shamanic healing among the Achomawi.[47] As we shall soon see, the séance is in no way mysterious or gloomy. The shaman sometimes loses himself in meditation and talks *sotto voce;* he is conversing with his *damagomi,* his "powers" (helping spirits), to discover the cause of the illness. For it is really the *damagomi* that make the diagnosis.[48] Broadly speaking, illness is divided into six categories: (1) visible accidents; (2) breach of a taboo; (3) terror caused by the apparition of monsters; (4) "bad blood"; (5) poisoning by another shaman; (6) loss of the soul.

The séance takes place in the evening, in the patient's house. The shaman kneels beside the patient, who is lying on the floor, his head to the east.

He sways, chanting, his eyes half closed. First it is a humming in a plaintive tone, as if the shaman wanted to sing despite some inward pain. The chanting becomes louder, takes the form of a real melody, but still hummed. The audience begins to fall silent, to listen, pay attention. The shaman has not yet his *damagomi.* It is somewhere, perhaps far off in the mountains, perhaps in the night air, quite close by. The song is to charm it, invite it to come, even constrain it. . . . These songs, like all those of the Achomawi, comprise only a line or two, making up two, three, or at most four musical phrases. The song is repeated ten, twenty, thirty times in succession, uninterruptedly, the last note being immediately followed by the first of the beginning, with no musical rest. The singing

45 Ibid., pp. 60 ff. 46 Ibid., pp. 61 ff.
47 "La Psychologie religieuse des Achumawi. IV: Le Chamanisme."
48 Ibid., p. 570.

is in unison. As for the measure, it is clapped out. It has nothing to do with the rhythm of the melody. It is in a different rhythm, a perfectly ordinary rhythm, but regular and without accent. Usually at the beginning of a song everyone beats a slightly different measure. But after a few repetitions, they come together. The shaman sings only a few measures by himself. At first he is alone, then there are a few voices, then everyone. Then he stops singing, leaving the task of attracting the *damagomi* to the audience. Naturally, the louder the singing and the more in unison, the better. There is more likelihood of waking the *damagomi* if it is asleep somewhere far away. It is not merely the physical sound that wakens it. Quite as much, and even more, it is the emotional warmth. (This is not my [De Angulo's] interpretation. I am repeating what many Indians told me.) As for the shaman, he meditates deeply. He closes his eyes, listens. Soon he feels his *damagomi* arriving, approaching, fluttering through the night air, in the bush, underground, everywhere, even in his own abdomen. . . . Then suddenly the shaman claps his hands, at any point in the song, and everyone stops singing. There is profound silence (and it is very impressive in the heart of the brush under the stars, by the flickering firelight, this sudden silence after the rapid and slightly hypnotic rhythm of the song). Then the shaman speaks to his *damagomi*. His voice is high, as if he were talking to someone deaf. He speaks in a quick, jerky, monotonous voice, but in the ordinary language, which everyone understands. The sentences are short. And whatever he says, the "interpreter" repeats exactly, word for word. . . . The shaman is so excited that his speech becomes confused. The interpreter, if it is his usual one, knows the kind of confusions into which he habitually falls. . . . As for the shaman, he is more and more in ecstasy, he talks to his *damagomi* and his *damagomi* answers his questions. He is so at one with his *damagomi*, projects himself so fully into it, that he repeats all the *damagomi*'s words, exactly. . . .[49]

The dialogue between the shaman and his "powers" is sometimes amazingly monotonous. The master complains that the *damagomi* has kept him waiting, and the *damagomi* offers excuses: it had fallen asleep beside a stream, etc. The master dismisses and summons another. "The shaman stops. He opens his eyes. H

[49] "La Psychologie religieuse des Achumawi. IV: Le Chamanisme," p 567–68.

seems like someone coming out of deep meditation. He looks a little dazed. He asks for his pipe. The interpreter fills it for him, lights it, and hands it to him. Everyone stretches, cigarettes are lighted, there is talk, joking, someone makes up the fire. The shaman himself joins in the joking, but less and less, as a half hour, an hour, two hours pass. He becomes more and more abstracted, sullen. He begins again, and yet again. . . . This sometimes goes on for hours and hours. Sometimes it lasts little more than an hour. Sometimes the shaman becomes discouraged, gives up the cure. His *damagomi* can find nothing. Or they are afraid. The 'poison' is a very powerful *damagomi*, stronger than themselves. . . . There is no use attacking it.'' [50]

After finding the cause of the illness, the shaman begins the cure. Except in cases of soul loss, treatment consists in extracting the ''trouble'' or in sucking blood. By suction, the shaman draws out with his teeth a small object ''like a bit of black or white thread, sometimes like a nail paring.'' [51] An Achomawi told De Angulo: ''I don't believe those things come out of the sick man's body. The shaman always has them in his mouth before he starts the treatment. But he draws the sickness into them, he uses them to catch the poison. Otherwise how could he catch it?'' [52]

Some shamans suck the blood directly. A shaman explained how he went about it: ''It is black blood, it is bad blood. First I spit it into my hands to see if the sickness is really in it. Then I hear my *damagomi* quarreling. They all want me to give them something to drink. They have worked well for me. They have helped me. Now they are all hot. They're thirsty. They want to drink. They want to drink blood. . . .'' [53] If he does not give them blood, the *damagomi* rush wildly about and protest clamorously. ''Then I drink blood. I swallow it. I give it to them. And that quiets them. That calms them. That refreshes them. . . .'' [54]

According to De Angulo's observations, the ''bad blood'' is not

50 Ibid., p. *569*.
52 Ibid.
54 Ibid.

51 Ibid., p. *563*.
53 Ibid.

sucked from the patient's body; it is "the product of a hemorrhagic extravasation, of hysterical origin, in the shaman's stomach." [55] And in fact the shaman is extremely tired at the end of a séance and after drinking two or three quarts of water, "falls into a heavy sleep." [56]

However this may be, sucking blood appears to be an aberrant form of shamanic healing. It will be recalled that some Siberian shamans likewise drink the blood of the sacrificed animals and claim that it is really their helping spirits that demand and drink it. This extremely complex rite, based on the sacred value of hot blood, is "shamanic" only secondarily and through coalescence with other rites belonging to different magico-religious complexes.

If the case is one of poisoning by another shaman, the healer after sucking the skin for a long time, seizes the magical object with his teeth and displays it. Sometimes the poisoner is among the audience, and the shaman returns the "object" to him: "There is your *damagomi*, I don't want to keep it for myself!" [57] In a case of soul loss, the shaman, always acting on the information supplied by his *damagomi*, goes to look for it and finds it wandering in some wild place, on a rock, etc.[58]

Descent to the Underworld

The Achomawi shaman's séance is distinguished by its moderation. But this is not always the case. The trance, which among the Achomawi seems to be rather weak, is elsewhere accompanied by pronounced ecstatic movements. The shaman of the Shuswap (a tribe of the interior of British Columbia) "acts as if he were mad as soon as he has put on his ritual headgear (made of a mat two yards long by one broad). He begins to sing songs that his tutelary spirit taught him at the time of his initiation. He dances until he sweats profusely and the spirit comes and talks with him. Then he lies down beside the patient and sucks the painful area. Finally he

55 Ibid., p. 574.   56 Ibid.
57 Ibid.   58 Ibid., pp. 575–77.

extracts a thong or a feather, the cause of the illness, and makes it disappear by blowing on it.[59]

As to the search for the soul that has strayed away or been abducted by spirits, it sometimes assumes a dramatic aspect. Among the Thompson Indians (British Columbia) the shaman dons his mask and begins by taking the old path that the ancestors used in times past to reach the land of the dead; if he does not find the patient's soul, he searches the cemeteries where the Indians who have become converts to Christianity are buried. But, in any case, he has to fight the ghosts before he can wrest the patient's soul from them, and when he returns to earth he shows the audience his blood-stained club. Among the Twana Indians of Washington the descent to the underworld is still more realistic; the surface of the ground is often opened; the shaman imitates crossing a stream; he vigorously mimes his struggle with the spirits, and so on.[60] Since the Nootka attribute the "theft of the soul" to marine spirits, the shaman, in ecstasy, dives to the bottom of the ocean and returns wet, "sometimes streaming blood at nose and temples, carrying the stolen soul in a little bunch of eagle down in his hands." [61]

As everywhere else, the shaman's descent to the lower world to bring back the patient's soul follows the underground itinerary of the dead and hence accords with the funerary mythologies of the respective tribes. During a funeral ceremony a Yuma woman lost consciousness. When, several hours later, she was revived, she related what had befallen her. She suddenly found herself riding on horseback behind one of her male relatives, who had been dead for many years. Around her were many riders. Riding south, they came to a village whose inhabitants were Yuma. She recognized

---

59 Boas, "The Shushwap," pp. 95 ff. of offprint.

60 James Teit, "The Thompson Indians of British Columbia," pp. 363 ff.; Rev. Myron Eells, *A Few Facts in Regard to the Twana, Clallam and Cheakum Indians of Washington Territory*, pp. 677 ff., cited by Frazer, *Taboo and the Perils of the Soul*, p. 58. In Vea Island in the Pacific the medicine man also goes to the cemetery, in procession. The same ritual is found in Madagascar; cf. Frazer, ibid., p. 54.

61 Philip Drucker, *The Northern and Central Nootkan Tribes*, pp. 210 ff.

many people whom she had known in their lifetimes. All came to meet her, showing great joy. But soon afterward she saw a thick cloud of smoke, as if the whole village were on fire. She began to run, but stumbling on a piece of wood, fell to the ground. Just at that moment she regained consciousness, and saw a shaman bent over her, treating her.[62] More rarely, the North American shaman is also summoned to call back someone's guardian spirit, which has been carried off by deceased persons to the land of the dead.[63]

But it is principally in searching for a patient's soul that the shaman uses his knowledge of infernal topography and his capacities for ecstatic clairvoyance. There is no need to cite here all the data relating to loss of the soul and the search for it by the North American shaman.[64] It will suffice to observe that this belief is quite common in North America, especially in the West, and that its presence in South America as well excludes the hypothesis of a comparatively recent borrowing from Siberia.[65] As we shall show later, the theory of soul loss as a cause of illness, though probably more recent than that of an injurious agent, nevertheless seems comparatively ancient, and its presence on the American continent is not explicable by a late influence from Siberian shamanism.

Here as everywhere else, the shamanic ideology (or, more precisely, that part of the traditional ideology that was assimilated and largely developed by shamans) is also found in myths and legends in which shamans properly speaking do not figure. Such is

62 C. D. Forde, *Ethnography of the Yuma Indians*, p. 193.

63 Cf., for example, Herman Haeberlin, "SBETETda'q, a Shamanistic Performance of the Coast Salish." At least eight shamans together perform this ceremony, which includes an ecstatic journey to the underworld in an imaginary boat.

64 Cf. Robert H. Lowie, *Notes on Shoshonean Ethnography*, pp. 294 ff. Park, *Shamanism*, p. 137; Clements, *Primitive Concepts of Disease*, pp. 195 ff. Hultkrantz: *Conceptions of the Soul*, pp. 449 ff.; *The North American Indian Orpheus Tradition*, pp. 242 ff.

65 This is R. H. Lowie's hypothesis (*Primitive Religion*, pp. 176 ff.) which he later renounced: cf. his "On the Historical Connection between Certain Old World and New World Beliefs." Cf. also Clements, pp. 196 ff. Park, *Shamanism*, p. 137.

the case, for example, with what has been called the "North American Orpheus Myth," which is attested among most tribes, especially in the western and eastern parts of the continent.[66] Here is the version of the Telumni Yokuts. A man loses his wife. He determines to follow her and watches by her grave. The second night the wife rises and, as if in sleep, sets out walking toward the land of the dead, which lies to the west (or the northwest). Her husband follows her until he comes to a stream crossed by a bridge that constantly shakes and moves. The wife turns to him and says: "What are you doing here? You are alive. You can't cross that bridge. You'll fall in and become a great fish." A bird guards the middle of the bridge; its cries frighten those who pass over, some of whom fall into the abyss. But the man has a talisman, a magical rope; with its help, he succeeds in crossing the stream. On the other side he finds his wife with a crowd of the dead dancing a round dance (the classic form of the Ghost Dance). The man approaches them and they all begin to complain that he has an unpleasant smell. A messenger from Tipiknits, the Lord of the Underworld, invites him to a meal. The messenger's wife herself serves him countless dishes, of which he eats without making them diminish. The Lord of the Underworld asks him the reason for his visit. On learning it, he promises him that he can take his wife back to earth if he is able to stay awake all night. The round dance begins again, but the man, to keep from tiring himself, does not join it but stands and watches. Tipiknits orders him to bathe. Then he summons the woman, to make sure that she is really the man's wife. The couple spend the whole night in a bed, talking. Before dawn the man falls asleep, and on waking finds a rotten log in his arms. Tipiknits sends his messenger to invite him to breakfast. He gives him an-

---

66 Cf. A. H. Gayton, "The Orpheus Myth in North America." See the geographical distribution of the myth on p. 265; now cf. Hultkrantz, *The North American Indian Orpheus Tradition* (the map, p. 7, and the list of tribes, pp. 313–14). The myth is unknown to the Eskimo, which seems to us to exclude the theory of Sibero-Asiatic influence. Cf. also A. L. Kroeber, "A Karok Orpheus Myth"; the heroines are two women who pursue a youth to the underworld, but fail completely in their undertaking.

other chance, and the man sleeps all day so that he will not be tired at night. That evening, everything goes as before. The couple laugh and amuse themselves until dawn, when the man falls asleep again, to wake with the rotten log in his arms. Tipiknits summons him again, gives him some seeds that will enable him to cross the river, and bids him leave the underworld. Returned home, the man tells his adventure to his relatives but asks them not to say anything, for if he cannot remain hidden for six days, he will die. The neighbors, however, learn of his disappearance and return, and the man decides to confess everything, so that he may rejoin his wife. He invites the village to a great feast, and tells all that he saw and heard in the realm of the dead. The next day he dies of a snakebite.

All the recorded versions of this myth display an amazing similarity. The bridge, the rope on which the hero crosses the infernal river, the kindly person (old woman or old man, Lord of the Underworld), the animal guardian of the bridge, and so on— all the classic motifs of the descent to the underworld are present in nearly all the variants. In several versions (Gabrielino, etc.) the ordeal that the hero must undergo is that of chastity; he must remain chaste with his wife for three nights.[67] An Alibamu version concerns two brothers following their dead sister. They walk westward until they reach the horizon; there, the sky is unsteady, constantly moving about. Turning into animals, the two brothers enter the beyond and, with the help of an old man or old woman, emerge victorious from four ordeals. From the heights of the beyond they are shown their earthly house, which is exactly beneath them ("Center of the World" motif). They see the dance of the dead; their sister is present, and, by touching her with a magical object, they make her fall and carry her off in a gourd. But, returned to earth, they hear their sister crying inside the gourd and rashly open it. The girl's soul flees.[68]

We shall see that a similar myth is attested in Polynesia, but the North American myth better preserves a memory of the initiatory ordeal implied in the descent to the underworld. The four ordeal:

67 Gayton, pp. 270, 272.　　　　68 Ibid., p. 273.

mentioned in the Alibamu version, the ordeal of chastity, and especially the ordeal of "keeping awake," are clearly initiatory in character.[69] What is "shamanic" in all these myths is the descent to the underworld to bring back the soul of the beloved woman. For shamans are believed capable not only of bringing back the strayed souls of the sick but also of restoring the dead to life;[70] and they who are thus restored, on their return from the underworld, tell the living what they have seen—exactly like those who have gone down to the land of the dead "in spirit," those who have visited the nether worlds and paradise in ecstasy, and have nourished the multimillenary visionary literature of the entire world. It would be going too far to regard such myths as solely creations of shamanic experiences; but it is certain that they use and interpret such experiences. In the Alibamu variant the heroes capture their sister's soul in the same way in which the shaman captures the patient's soul, to bring it back to this earth from the land of the dead, to which it has been carried off.

Secret Brotherhoods and Shamanism

The problem of the relations between shamanism and the various North American secret societies and mystical movements is decidedly complex and far from being solved.[71] Yet it may be said

69 In the island of the mythical Ancestor Ut-Napishtim, Gilgamesh must likewise watch six successive days and nights to obtain immortality, and, like the North American Orpheus, he fails; cf. Eliade, *Patterns in Comparative Religion*, pp. 289 ff.

70 See, for example, the resurrection of a boy by the Midē'wiwin, a feat the memory of which is preserved in the traditions of that secret society (W. J. Hoffman, "The Midē'wiwin or 'Grand Medicine Society' of the Ojibwa," pp. 241 ff. Cf. also Hultkrantz, *The North American Indian Orpheus Tradition*, pp. 247 ff.).

71 Cf. some general data in Bouteiller, *Chamanisme*, pp. 51 ff. Clark Wissler (*General Discussion of Shamanistic and Dancing Societies*) studies the dissemination of a particular shamanic complex from the Pawnee to other tribes, and shows (especially on pp. 857–62) the process by which mystical techniques are assimilated. Cf. also Werner Müller, *Weltbild und Kult der Kwakiutl-Indianer*, pp. 114 ff.; J. Haekel, "Initiationen und Geheimbünde in der Nordwestküste Nordamerikas."

that all these brotherhoods based on mysteries have a shamanic structure, in the sense that their ideology and techniques share in the great shamanic tradition. We shall soon give some examples drawn from secret societies (Midē'wiwin type) and ecstatic movements (Ghost-Dance-Religion type). They will clearly show the chief elements of the shamanic tradition: initiation involving the candidate's death and resurrection, ecstatic visits to the land of the dead and to the sky, insertion of magical substances in the candidate's body, revelation of secret doctrines, instruction in shamanic healing, and so on. The chief difference between traditional shamanism and the secret societies lies in the fact that the latter are open to anyone who displays some predisposition to ecstasy, who is willing to pay the required fee, and, above all, who consents to submit to the necessary apprenticeship and initiatory ordeals. A certain opposition, and even antagonism, is often observable between the secret brotherhoods and ecstatic movements on the one hand and the shamans on the other. The brotherhoods, like the ecstatic movements, oppose shamanism in so far as it has become assimilated to sorcery and black magic. Another cause for opposition is the exclusivistic attitude of certain shamanic circles; the secret societies and ecstatic movements, on the contrary, display a quite marked spirit of proselytism that, in the last analysis, tends to abolish the special privilege of shamans. All these brotherhoods and mystical sects work toward a religious revolution by the fact that they proclaim the spiritual regeneration of the entire community and even of all North American Indian tribes (cf. the Ghost-Dance Religion). Hence they are conscious of being at the opposite pole from the shamans, who on this point represent both the most conservative elements of the religious tradition and the least generous tendencies of the tribal spirituality.

But actually, things are far more complex. For, if all that we have just said is perfectly true, it is no less true that in North America the differences between "consecrated" men and the "profane" multitude are not so much qualitative as quantitative; they lie in the *amount* of the sacred that the former have assimilated.

We have shown that every Indian seeks religious power, that every Indian commands a guardian spirit acquired by the same techniques that the shaman uses to obtain his own spirits.[72] The difference between layman and shaman is quantitative; the shaman commands a greater number of tutelary or guardian spirits and a stronger magico-religious "power." [73] In this respect we could almost say that every Indian "shamanizes," even if he does not consciously wish to become a shaman.

If the difference between the profane and the shamans is so indefinite, it is no clearer between shamanic circles and the secret brotherhoods or mystical sects. On the one hand, the latter exhibit supposedly "shamanic" techniques and ideologies; on the other, the shamans usually share in the activities of the most important secret mystery societies, and sometimes take them over entirely. These relationships are very clearly demonstrated by the Midē'-wiwin, or, as it has been erroneously called, the "Grand Medicine Society," of the Ojibwa. The Ojibwa have two kinds of shamans: the *Wâbĕnō'* (the "Men of the dawn," the "Eastern men") and the *jĕs'sakkīd'*, prophets and seers, also called "jugglers" and "revealer[s] of hidden truths." Both categories are capable of shamanic exploits; the *Wâbĕnō'* are also called "fire-handlers," and can touch burning coals and remain unhurt; the *jĕs'sakkīd'* perform cures, the gods and spirits speak through their mouths, and they are famous "jugglers," for they can instantly undo the ropes and chains with which they are bound.[74] Yet both voluntarily

72 Above, pp. 99 ff.

73 To the examples already cited (above, pp. 99 ff.) we add the excellent analysis by Leslie Spier, *Klamath Ethnography*, pp. 93 ff. ("The Power Quest"), pp. 107 ff. (quantitative difference in powers), pp. 249 ff. (universality of the quest), etc.

74 W. J. Hoffman, "The Midē'wiwin," pp. 157 ff. Cf. some examples of the magical powers of the *jĕs'sakkīd'* (ibid., pp. 275 ff.). But it should be added that the magical feats of the North American shamans are far from ending here. They are credited with the power to make a grain of wheat germinate and sprout before the eyes of the audience; to cause pine branches to come from distant mountains in the twinkling of an eye; to make rabbits and kids appear, feathers and other objects fly, etc. They can also throw

join the Midē'wiwin—the *Wâbĕnō'* when he has specialized in magical medicine and incantations, the *jĕs'sakkīd'* when he wants to increase his prestige in the tribe. They are, of course, in the minority, for the "Grand Medicine" fraternity is open to any who are interested in spiritual matters and have the means to pay the entrance fees. Among the Menomini, who in Hoffman's time numbered 1,500, the Midē'wiwin had one hundred members, among them two *Wâbĕnō'* and five *jĕs'sakkīd'*.[75] But there could not have been many shamans who were not members.

The important aspect of the case is that the "Grand Medicine" fraternity itself exhibits a shamanic structure. In fact, Hoffman calls its members, the *midē*, "shamans," though other writers call them at once shamans and medicine men, prophets, seers, and even priests. All these terms are partly justified, for the *midē* act both as healing shamans and seers and, to a certain extent, even as priests. The historical origins of the Midē'wiwin are unknown, but its mythological traditions are not far from the Siberian myths of the "first shaman." The myths tell that Mi'nabō'zho, the messenger of the Dzhe Manido (the Great Spirit) and intercessor between him and mankind, seeing the miserable state of sick and enfeebled humanity, revealed the most sublime secrets to the otter and inserted *mīgis* (symbol of the *midē*) in its body so that it should become immortal and be able to initiate and at the same time consecrate men.[76] Thus the otterskin pouch plays an essential

---

themselves from heights into small baskets, produce a living rabbit from a rabbit's skeleton, transform various objects into animals. But above all, shamans are "masters over fire" and perform all sorts of "fire tricks"; they burn a man to ashes in the embers—and a few minutes later the same man is taking part in a dance a great distance away; cf. Elsie Clews Parsons, *Pueblo Indian Religion*, I, 440 ff. Among the Zuni and the Keres there are secret societies that specialize in fire tricks, and their members can swallow coals, walk on fire, touch red-hot iron, etc.; cf. Matilda Coxe Stevenson (*The Zuñi Indians: Their Mythology, Esoteric Fraternities, and Ceremonies*, pp. 503, 506, etc.), who also records personal observations (a shaman holding embers in his mouth for from 30 to 60 seconds, etc.).

75 W. J. Hoffman, "The Midē'wiwin," p. 158.

76 Hoffman: ibid., pp. 166 ff.; "Pictography and Shamanistic Rites of the

part in the initiation of the *midē*; in it are placed the *mīgis*, the small shells that are believed to hold magico-religious power.[77]

The initiation of candidates follows the general pattern of all shamanic initiations. It includes revelation of the mysteries (that is, especially the myth of Mi'nabō'zho and the immortality of the otter), the death and resurrection of the candidate, and the insertion into his body of a large number of *mīgis* (which is strangely reminiscent of the "magical stones" with which the apprentice magician's body is stuffed in Australia and elsewhere). There are four degrees of initiation, but the last three are only a repetition of the first ceremony. The *midēwigan*, the "Great Medicine Lodge," a sort of enclosure twenty-five by eight yards, is constructed, with leafy branches between the posts to obviate eavesdropping. Some thirty yards away the *wigiwam*, or steam bath for the candidate, is built. The chief designates a teacher, who tells the candidate the origins and properties of the drum and rattles and shows him how to use them to invoke the Great God (Manitou) and exorcise demons. He is also taught the magical songs, the medicinal plants, therapy, and especially the elements of the secret doctrine. Beginning with the sixth or fifth day before the initiation the candidate purifies himself daily in the steam bath and then attends the demonstrations of magical power by the *midē*; assembled in the *midēwigan*, they make various wooden figurines and their own pouches move at a distance. The last night he spends alone with his teacher in the steam bath; the following morning, after another purification, and if the sky is clear, the initiation ceremony takes place. All the *midē* are assembled in the "Great Medicine Lodge." After smoking in silence for a long time, they intone ritual songs revealing secret—and, for the most part, unintelligible—aspects of the primordial tradition. At a given moment, all the *midē* rise and, approaching the candidate, "kill" him

---

Ojibwa," pp. 213 ff. See also Werner Müller, *Die blaue Hütte*, pp. 28 ff., 40 ff.; Sister Bernard Coleman, "The Religion of the Ojibwa of Northern Minnesota," pp. 44 ff. (on the Midē'wiwin).

77 Hoffman, "The Midē'wiwin," pp. 217, 220 ff.

by touching him with *mīgis*.[78] The candidate trembles, falls to his knees, and, when a *mīgi* is placed in his mouth, lies lifeless on the ground. He is then touched with the pouch and "revives." Whereupon he is given a magical song, and the chief presents him with an otterskin pouch in which the candidate puts his own *mīgis*. To test the power of these shells, he touches all his fellow members one after the other, and they fall to the ground as if struck by lightning, then are resuscitated by the same touching process. He now has proof that his shells bestow both death and life. At the feast that ends the ceremony, the oldest *midē* narrates the tradition of the Midē'wiwin, and, in conclusion, the new member sings his song and drums.

The second initiation takes place at least a year after the first. The initiate's magical power is now increased by the large number of *mīgis* with which his body is stuffed, especially about the joints and the heart. With the third initiation, the *midē* obtains power enough to become a *jĕs'sakkīd'*; that is, he is able to perform all the various shamanic "juggleries," and, especially, he is now officially a master of healing. The fourth initiation introduces still more *mīgis* into his body.[79]

This example sufficiently shows the close relations between shamanism proper and the North American secret brotherhoods; both share the same archaic magico-religious tradition. But we can also detect in such secret brotherhoods, and especially in the Midē'wiwin, an attempted "return to origins," in the sense that the society seeks to regain contact with the primordial tradition and to eliminate sorcerers. The role of tutelary and helping spirits proves to be rather small, while, on the contrary, much importance is given to the Great Spirit and celestial journeys. There is an effort to re-establish communications between earth and sky as they existed at the dawn of time. But despite its "reforming" aspect, the Midē'wiwin adopts the most archaic techniques of

78 Cf. W. Müller, *Die blaue Hütte*, pp. 52 ff.
79 Hoffman, "The Midē'wiwin," pp. 204–76.

magico-religious initiation (death and resurrection,[80] the body stuffed with "magical stones," etc.). And, as we have seen, the *midē* become medicine men, their initiation also teaching them the various techniques of magical healing (exorcism, magical pharmacopoeia, treatment by suction, etc.).

Somewhat different is the Winnebago "Medicine Rite," whose complete initiation ceremony has been published by Paul Radin.[81] Here, too, we have a secret brotherhood to which admission is granted only after an extremely complex initiation ritual consisting principally in the candidate's "death" and resurrection from being touched by magical shells kept in otterskin pouches.[82] But here the resemblance to the Midē'wiwin of the Ojibwa and Menomini ends. Probably the rite of shooting shells into the candidate's body was incorporated at a late period (toward the end of the seventeenth century) into an earlier Winnebago ceremony rich in shamanic elements.[83] Since the Winnebago Medicine Rite shows various resemblances to the Pawnee "Ceremony of the Medicine Men," and since the distance between the two tribes excludes the possibility of direct borrowing, it may be concluded that both have preserved vestiges of an ancient ritual belonging to a cultural complex of Mexican origin.[84] It is also highly probable that the Ojibwa Midē'wiwin is only a development of such a ritual.

In any case, the point to be emphasized is that the goal of the Winnebago Medicine Rite is the perpetual regeneration of the initiate. The mythical demiurge, the hare, sent to earth by the Creator to help mankind, was much struck by the fact that men died. To remedy the evil, he built an initiation lodge and turned himself into a small child. "If anyone repeats what [I] have done here," he declared, "this is the way he will look."[85] But the Creator interpreted the regeneration he had granted man differ-

---

80 On the shamanic character of the Kwakiutl "Cannibal Societies," cf. W. Müller, *Weltbild und Kult*, pp. 65 ff.; Eliade, *Birth and Rebirth*, pp. 68 ff.
81 *The Road of Life and Death: a Ritual Drama of the American Indians.*
82 Ibid., pp. 5 ff., 283 ff., etc.   83 Ibid., p. 75.
84 Ibid.   85 Ibid., p. 31.

ently: men can become reincarnated as many times as they wish.[8] And, basically, the Medicine Rite communicates the secret of a return to earth ad infinitum by revealing the right road to be taken after death and the words that the dead man must speak to the woman guardian of the beyond and to the Creator himself. Of course, the cosmogony and the origin of the Medicine Rite are also revealed, for in each case there is always a return to the mythical origins, an abolishing of time and thus a reinstatement of the miraculous moment of creation.

A number of shamanic elements are also preserved in the great mystical movements known as the Ghost-Dance Religion, which though already endemic at the beginning of the nineteenth century, did not sweep through the North American tribes until toward its close.[87] Probably Christianity influenced at least some of its "prophets."[88] Messianic tension and the expectation of the imminent "end of the world" proclaimed by the prophets and masters of the Ghost-Dance Religion were easy to harmonize with an elementary and abortive Christian experience. But the actual structure of this important popular mystical movement is none the less autochthonous. Its prophets had their visions in the purest archaic style; they "died" and ascended to the sky and there a celestial woman taught them how to approach the "Master of Life";[89] they received their great revelations in trances during which they journeyed through the beyond, and, after returning to normal consciousness, they told what they had seen;[90] during their voluntary trances they could be cut with knives, burned without feeling anything,[91] and so on.

The Ghost-Dance Religion prophesied the coming of universal

86 Radin, *The Road of Life and Death*, p. 25.

87 Cf. James Mooney, "The Ghost-Dance Religion and the Sioux Outbreak of 1890"; Leslie Spier, *The Prophet Dance of the Northwest and I. Derivatives: the Source of the Ghost Dance*; Cora A. Du Bois, *The 1870 Ghost Dance*.

88 Cf. Mooney, pp. 748 ff., 780, etc.

89 Ibid., pp. 663 ff., 746 ff., 772 ff., etc.

90 Ibid., pp. 672 ff.   91 Ibid., pp. 719 ff.

regeneration: then all Indians, the dead and the living alike, would be called to inhabit a "regenerated earth"; they would reach this paradisal land by flying through the air with the help of magical feathers.[92] Some prophets—such as John Slocum, creator of the Shakers' movement—opposed the old Indian religion and especially the medicine men. This did not prevent the shamans from joining Slocum's movement; for in it they found the ancient tradition of celestial ascents and experiences of mystical light, and, like the shamans, the Shakers could resuscitate the dead.[93] The principal ritual of this sect consisted in prolonged contemplation of the sky and a continuous shaking of the arms, elementary techniques that are also found, in even more aberrant guises, in the ancient and modern Near East, always in connection with "shamanizing" groups. Other prophets also denounced the practice of sorcery and the tribe's medicine men, but did so rather to reform and regenerate them. An example is the prophet Shawano who, at about the age of thirty, was carried up to the sky and received a new revelation from the Master of Life, enabling him to know past and future events, and who, though he denounced shamanism, declared that he had received the power to cure all illnesses and to withstand death itself in the midst of battle.[94] In addition, this prophet regarded himself as the incarnation of Manabozho, the first "Great Demiurge" of the Algonkins, and wanted to reform the Midē'wiwin.[95]

But the astonishing success of the Ghost-Dance Religion was due to the simplicity of its mystical technique. To prepare for the coming of the savior of the race, the members of the fraternity danced continuously for five or six days and so went into trances during which they saw and conversed with the dead. The dances were ring dances around the fires, there was singing but no drumming. The apostle confirmed the new priests by giving them an eagle's feather during the dance. And he had only to touch one of

---

92 Ibid., pp. 777 ff., 781, 786.
93 See, for example, the case of four persons resuscitated, ibid., p. 748.
94 Ibid., p. 672.   95 Ibid., pp. 675–76.

the participants with such a feather for the dancer to fall lifeless; he remained in this state for a long time, during which his soul met the dead and talked with them.[96] No other essential element of shamanism was lacking; the dancers became healers; [97] they wore "ghost shirts," which were ritual costumes with representations of stars, mythological beings, and even of visions obtained during trances; [98] they adorned themselves with eagle feathers; [99] used the steam bath; [100] and so on. Their dancing in itself represented a mystical technique that, if not exclusively shamanic, plays, as we have seen, a decisive role in the shaman's ecstatic preparation.

Of course, the Ghost-Dance Religion reaches beyond shamanism proper in all directions. The lack of an initiation and of a secret traditional teaching, for example, suffices to separate it from shamanism. But we are dealing with a collective religious experience crystallized around the imminence of an "end of the world"; the source of this experience—communication with the dead—in itself implies, for one who obtains it, the abolition of the present world and the reign, even though temporary, of a "confusion" that constitutes both the closing of the present cosmic cycle and the beginning of the glorious restoration of a new, paradisal cycle. The mythical visions of the "beginning" and the "end" of time being homologizable, since eschatology, at least in certain aspects, overlaps cosmology, the *eschaton* of the Ghost-Dance Religion reactualized the mythical *illud tempus* when communications with the sky, the Great God, and the dead were accessible to every human being. Such mystical movements differed from the traditional shamanism by the fact that, while preserving the essential elements of the shamanic ideology and techniques, they held that the time had come for the whole Indian people to obtain the shaman's privileged state, that is, to experience the re-establishment of "easy communication" with the sky, even as it existed at the dawn of time.

96 Mooney, pp. 915 ff.
97 Ibid., p. 786.
98 Ibid., pp. 789 ff., Pl. CIII, p. 895.
99 Ibid., p. 791.
100 Ibid., pp. 823 f.

South American Shamanism: Various Rituals

The shaman appears to play a role of considerable importance among the tribes of South America.[101] Not only is he the healer par excellence, and, in some regions, the guide who leads the souls of the recently dead to their new home, he is also the intermediary between men and the gods or the spirits (for example, among the Mojo and the Manasi of eastern Bolivia, the Taino of the Greater Antilles, etc.),[102] he sees to it that ritual prohibitions are observed, defends the tribe from the evil spirits, indicates the sites for profitable hunting and fishing, increases game,[103] controls atmospheric phenomena,[104] facilitates birth,[105] reveals future events,[106] and so

101 A. Métraux, "Le Shamanisme chez les Indiens de l'Amérique du Sud tropicale," pp. 329 ff. Cf. also id., "Religion and Shamanism," pp. 559–99; E. H. Ackerknecht, "Medical Practices"; J. H. Steward, "Shamanism among the Marginal Tribes"; Métraux, "The Social Organization of the Mojo and Manasi," pp. 9–16 (Mojo shamanism), 22–28 (Manasi shamanism); W. Madsen, "Shamanism in Mexico"; Nils M. Holmer and S. Henry Wassén, eds. and trs., *Nia-Ikala: Canto mágico para curar la locura*; O. Zerries, "Krankheitsdämonen und Hilfsgeister des Medizinmannes in Südamerika." On the problem of cultural cycles in South America, see W. Schmidt, "Kulturkreise und Kulturschichten in Südamerika"; critique by Roland B. Dixon, *The Building of Cultures*, pp. 182 ff., and review by W. Koppers, *Anthropos*, XXIV (1929), 695–99. Cf. also Rafael Karsten, *The Civilization of the South American Indians*; id., "Zur Psychologie des indianischen Medizinmannes"; John M. Cooper, "Areal and Temporal Aspects of Aboriginal South American Culture." On the origin and history of the South American civilizations, see Erland Nordenskiöld, *Origin of the Indian Civilization in South America*, especially pp. 1–76; Paul Rivet, *Les Origines de l'homme américain*, passim.

102 Métraux, "Le Shamanisme chez les Indiens de l'Amérique du Sud tropicale," pp. 337 ff.   103 Ibid., pp. 330 ff.

104 The shamans stop torrential rains (ibid., pp. 331 ff.). "The Ipurina shamans send their doubles into the sky to extinguish the meteors that threaten to burn the universe" (ibid., p. 332).

105 According to the Tapirape, and other tribes as well, a woman cannot conceive and bear a child unless the shaman brings a spirit-child down into her. Among some tribes the shaman is summoned to identify the spirit that has incarnated itself in the child (ibid.).

106 To know the future, the Tupinamba shamans "retired to small huts

forth. Thus he enjoys a considerable degree of prestige and authority in South American societies. Only the shamans can become rich, that is, accumulate knives, combs, hatchets, and other treasures. They are believed to perform miracles (which are strictly shamanic in character: magical flight, swallowing hot coals, etc.[107]). The Guarani so venerated their shamans that their bones were the object of a cult; the remains of especially powerful magicians were preserved in huts, where they were consulted and offerings were sometimes made to them.[108]

Naturally, the South American shaman, like his colleagues everywhere else, can also fill the role of sorcerer; he can, for example, turn into an animal and drink the blood of his enemies. The belief in werewolves is widely disseminated in South America.[109] However, it is rather to his ecstatic capacities than to his exploits as a magician that the South American shaman owes his magico-religious position and his social authority. For his ecstatic capacities enable him, in addition to his usual prerogative of healing, to make mystical journeys to the sky to meet the god directly and convey men's prayers to them. (Sometimes it is the god who descends into the ceremonial hut; such is the case among the Manasi, where the god comes down to earth, converses with the shaman, and finally carries him to the sky with him, letting him fall to earth a few moments later.[110])

As an example of a sacerdotal function taken over by the shaman, we may cite a periodical collective ceremony of the Araucanians, named *ngillatun*, whose purpose is to strengthen the re-

after observing various taboos, among them nine days of continence" (ibid., p. 331). The spirits came down and revealed future events in the spirit language. Cf. also Métraux, *La Religion des Tupinamba*, pp. 86 ff. On the eve of military expeditions the shaman's dreams are especially significant: id., "Le Shamanisme chez les Indiens de l'Amérique du Sud tropicale," p. 33

107 Ibid., p. 334.

108 Id.: *La Religion des Tupinamba*, pp. 81 ff.; "Les Hommes-dieux chez les Chiriguano et dans l'Amérique du Sud," p. 66, etc.; "Le Shamanisme chez les Indiens de l'Amérique du Sud tropicale," p. 334.

109 Ibid., pp. 335-36.   110 Ibid., p. 338.

lations between God and the tribe.[111] The *machi* (shamaness) plays
the principal role in this ceremony. It is she who falls into trance
and sends her soul into the presence of the "Sky Father" to present
the wishes of the community. The ceremony takes place in public.
In former times the *machi* mounted a platform supported by shrubs
(the *rewe*) and there, in prolonged contemplation of the sky, she
had her visions. Among the audience two had a function whose
shamanic nature is obvious: "their heads bound with a white
kerchief, their faces daubed with black, astride a wooden horse,
and grasping a wooden sword and their bauble," the two pages
"make their wooden horses curvet and shake their rattles with
maddening frenzy" [112] as soon as the *machi* goes into trance. (We
may compare the Buryat shaman's "horse" and the Muria dances
on a wooden horse.[113]) During the *machi*'s trance other riders fight
the demons and expel evil spirits.[114] When the *machi* has returned
to her senses, she describes her journey to the sky, and announces
that the Sky Father has granted all the wishes of the community.
Her words are greeted by prolonged cheers and general rejoicing.
When the tumult has subsided a little the *machi* is told of all that
took place while she was away on her journey to the sky—the
battle with the demons, their expulsion, and other events.

There is a striking resemblance between this Araucanian ritual
and the Altaic sacrifice of a horse followed by the shaman's celestial
journey to the palace of Bai Ülgän. In both cases we have a periodical communal ritual intended to present the desires of the tribe to
the celestial god; in both cases it is the shaman who plays the chief
role, and solely because of his ecstatic capacities, which enable him

111 Métraux, "Le Shamanisme araucan," pp. 351 ff. Cf. the Yaruro
shaman, intermediary between man and the gods (Vincenzo Petrullo, "The
Yaruros of the Capanaparo River, Venezuela," pp. 249 ff.).

112 Father Housse, *Une Épopée indienne.*

113 The Yaruro shaman travels to the land of the dead, which is also the
land of the Great Mother, on the back of a "horse" (Petrullo, p. 256).

114 It is probable, too, that the *ngillatun* festival belongs to the complex
of periodical ceremonies for regenerating Time; cf. Eliade, *The Myth of the
Eternal Return*, pp. 51 ff.

to make his mystical journey to the sky and talk to the god face to face. Rarely does the shaman's religious function—intermediary between men and the god—come out more clearly than among the Araucanians and the Altaians.

We have already noted other similarities between shamanism in South America and among the Altaians: ascent by a vegetable ladder (among the Araucanians [115]) or to a platform suspended from the ceiling of the ceremonial hut by several braided ropes (among the Carib of Dutch Guiana [116]), the role of the celestial god, the wooden horse, the frenzied gallops. To conclude, we must note that, as among the Altaians and the Siberians, some South American shamans are psychopomps. Among the Bakairi the journey to the beyond is too difficult for the deceased to undertake alone; he needs someone who knows the road, who has made the journey several times before; now, the shaman reaches the celestial region in the twinkling of an eye; for him, the Bakairi say, the sky is no higher than a house.[117] Among the Manacica the shaman leads the soul of the deceased to the sky as soon as the funeral ceremonies are completed. The road is extremely long and difficult; travelers on it go through a virgin forest, climb a mountain, cross seas, streams, and swamps, until they come to the shore of a great river which they must cross by a bridge guarded by a divinity.[118] Without the shaman's help, the soul could never make the journey.

Shamanic Healing

As everywhere else, the essential and strictly personal function of the South American shaman remains healing.[119] It is not always wholly magical in character. The South American shaman, too,

115 Above, pp. 123 ff.   116 Above, p. 130.

117 Karl von den Steinen, *Unter den Naturvölkern Zentral-Brasiliens*, p. 357.

118 Theodor Koch, "Zum Animismus der südamerikanischen Indianer," pp. 129 ff. (after eighteenth-century sources).

119 Cf. Ida Lublinski, "Der Medizinmann bei den Naturvölkern Südamerikas," pp. 247 ff.

knows the medicinal virtues of plants and animals, employs massage, and so on. But since, in his view, the vast majority of illnesses have a spiritual cause—that is, involve either the flight of the soul or a magical object introduced into the body by spirits or sorcerers—he is obliged to have recourse to shamanic healing.

The conception of disease as a loss of the soul, either strayed away or abducted by a spirit or a ghost, is extremely widespread in the Amazonian and Andean regions,[120] but appears to be rather rare in tropical South America. It has, however, been found among a certain number of tribes there [121] and is even attested among the Yahgan of Tierra del Fuego.[122] Usually this conception is found together with the theory of a magical object introduced into the patient's body,[123] a conception that seems to be more widely disseminated.

When a soul carried off by spirits or the dead is to be sought, the shaman is believed to leave his body and enter the underworld or the regions inhabited by the abductor. Thus, among the Apinaye, he goes to the land of the dead, who are stricken with panic and flee, whereupon the shaman captures the patient's soul and brings it back to the body. A Taulipang myth relates the search for the soul of a child that the moon had carried off and hidden under a pot; the shaman goes up to the moon and, after many adventures, finds the pot and frees the child's soul.[124] The songs of the Araucanian *machi* sometimes tell of the soul's misadventures: an evil spirit has made the patient walk on a bridge or a ghost has frightened him.[125] In some cases the *machi*, instead of

120 Cf. F. E. Clements, *Primitive Concepts of Disease*, pp. 196–97 (table); Métraux, "Le Shamanisme chez les Indiens de l'Amérique du Sud tropicale," p. 325.

121 Among the Caingang, Apinaye, Cocama, Tucuna, Coto, Cobeno, Taulipang, Itonama, and Witoto (ibid., p. 325).

122 Cf., for example, W. Koppers, *Unter Feuerland-Indianern*, pp. 72, 172.

123 As is the case, for example, among the Araucanians; cf. Métraux, Le Shamanisme araucan," p. 331.

124 Id., "Le Shamanisme chez les Indiens de l'Amérique du Sud tropicale," p. 328.

125 Id., "Le Shamanisme araucan," p. 331.

going in search of the soul, merely implores it to return and recognize its relatives,[126] as is also the case elsewhere (cf., for example, Vedic India). The shaman's ecstatic journey to perform a cure sometimes occurs in the aberrant form of a celestial ascent whose purpose has been forgotten. Thus we are told that "for the Taulipang the result of a cure sometimes depends on a battle between the shaman's double and a sorcerer. In order to reach the land of the spirits, the shaman drinks an infusion made from a liana whose form suggests a ladder." [127] The symbolism of the ladder indicates the ascensional meaning of the trance. But usually the sorcerers and spirits that abduct souls do not inhabit the celestial regions. As in so many other cases, the Taulipang shaman shows a confusion of religious ideas whose deep meaning is becoming lost.

The shaman's ecstatic journey is generally indispensable, even if the illness is not due to the theft of the soul by demons or ghosts. The shamanic trance forms part of the cure; whatever interpretation the shaman puts on it, it is always by his ecstasy that he finds the exact cause of the illness and learns the best treatment. The trance sometimes ends in the shaman's "possession" by his familiar spirits (for example, among the Taulipang and the Yecuana [128]). But we have already seen that, for the shaman, "possession" often consists in entering into possession of all his "mystical organs," which in some sort constitute his true and complete spiritual personality. In most cases "possession" merely puts the shaman's own helping spirits at his disposal, realizing their *effective presence* manifested through all perceptible means; and this presence, invoked by the shaman, ends not in trance but in a dialogue between the shaman and his helping spirits. Indeed, the reality is still more complex; for the shaman can turn himself into various animals, and it is sometimes a question to what extent the animal cries uttered

126 Métraux, "Le Shamanisme araucan," p. 331.
127 Id., "Le Shamanisme chez les Indiens de l'Amérique du Sud tropicale, p. 327.
128 Ibid., p. 322.

n the course of the séance belong to the familiar spirits [129] or represent the stages of the shaman's own transformation into an animal, that is, the manifest revelation of his true mystical personality.

The morphology of shamanic cure is the same almost throughout South America. It includes fumigations with tobacco, songs, massage of the affected area of the body, identification of the cause of the illness by the aid of the helping spirits (at this point comes the shaman's "trance," during which the audience sometimes ask him questions not directly connected with the illness), and, finally, extraction of the pathogenic object by suction.[130] Among the Araucanians, for example, the *machi* first addresses "God the Father," who, though Christian influences cannot be excluded, still preserves his archaic structure (for example, androgyny; he is invoked as "Father God, *old woman* who art in Heaven . . ." [131]). The *machi* then addresses Anchimalen, the wife or "sweetheart" of the sun, and the souls of the dead *machi*, "those of whom it is said that they are in the skies and who look down upon their colleague here below"; [132] she prays to them to appeal to God for her.

To be noted is the importance of the motifs of celestial ascent and riding through the air in the technique of the *machi*. For, soon after invoking the help and protection of God and the dead *machi*, the shamaness announces that "she is about to mount on horseback with her helpers, the invisible *machi*." [133] During the trance her soul leaves her body and flies through the air.[134] To achieve ecstasy, the *machi* employs the elementary means: dance, arm movements, accompaniment of rattles. As she dances, she addresses

129 On the South American conception of spirit animals, see R. Karsten, *The Civilization of the South American Indians*, pp. 265 ff. Cf. ibid., pp. 86 ff. the role of feathers as ritual ornaments among medicine men), pp. 365 ff. the magical power of crystals and rocks).

130 See, for example, the description of the séance of the Carib tribes of Guiana (for which there is an abundant documentation) by Métraux, "Le Shamanisme chez les Indiens de l'Amérique du Sud tropicale," pp. 325 ff., and n. 90.

131 Id., "Le Shamanisme araucan," p. 333. 132 Ibid.

133 Ibid., p. 334. 134 Ibid., p. 336.

the celestial *machi*, asking them to help her during her ecstasy. "When the shamaness is on the point of sinking to the ground unconscious, she raises her arms and begins revolving on herself. A man now goes to her and supports her to keep her from falling. Another Indian comes hurrying and performs a dance called *lañkañ* whose purpose is to revive her." [135] Trance is obtained by swinging on the top (*rewe*) of the sacred ladder.

During the whole ceremony much use is made of tobacco. The *machi* draws a puff and sends it skyward, toward God. "I offer thee this smoke!" she says. But, Métraux adds, "in no case are we told that the tobacco helps in obtaining a state of ecstasy." [136]

According to eighteenth-century European travelers, the shamanic cure also included the sacrifice of a sheep; the shaman tore out its still palpitating heart. In our day an incision in the sacrificial animal suffices. But the majority of the earlier and later observers are agreed that, by a trick of illusion, the *machi* makes the audience believe that she opens the patient's belly and exposes his entrails and liver.[137] According to Father Housse, the *machi* "appears to open the sufferer's body, feels about in it, and extracts something from it." She then exhibits the cause of the illness: a pebble, worm, an insect. The "wound" is believed to close of itself. But since the usual cure does not involve an apparent opening of the body but merely suction (sometimes to the point of drawing blood) applied to the part of the body indicated by the spirit,[138] it is highly probable that we here have an aberrant application of a well-known initiatory technique: the neophyte's body is magically opened to give him a new set of inner organs and cause his "rebirth." In the case of the Araucanian cure, exchange of a candidate's inner organs and extraction of a pathogenic object have become confused, doubtless because the initiatory schema (death and resurrection involving renewal of the inner organs) was in the course of disappearing.

135 Métraux, "Le Shamanisme araucan," p. 337.　　136 Ibid., p. 33.
137 Cf. ibid., pp. 339 ff. (after an eighteenth-century author, Nuñes (Pineday Bascuñan), 341 ff. (after Manuel Manquilef and Father Housse).
138 Cf. ibid., p. 341.

However this may be, in the eighteenth century this magical operation was accompanied by a cataleptic trance; the shaman (for at that period shamanism among the Araucanians was the prerogative of men and perverts rather than of women) fell "as if dead." [139] During his trance he was asked the name of the sorcerer who had brought on the illness, etc. In our day the *machi* likewise falls into trance, and the cause of the illness is learned in the same way—but her trance does not occur immediately after the "opening" of the patient's body. In some cases there is no trace of any such magical operation, there is only suction, which is performed after the trance and in accordance with the directions given by the spirits.

Suction and extraction of the pathogenic object, however, remain a magico-religious operation. For in the majority of cases the "object" is supernatural in nature, having been invisibly projected into the body by a sorcerer, a demon, or one of the dead. The "object" is only the sensible manifestation of a "trouble" that is not of this world. As we saw in the case of the Araucanians, the shaman is doubtless helped in his work by his familiar spirits, but also by his dead confreres and even by God. The *machi*'s magical formulas are dictated by God.[140] The Yamana shaman, who also employs suction to extract the *yekush* (the "trouble" magically projected into the patient's body), at the same time has recourse to prayers.[141] He, too, commands a *yefatchel*, a helping spirit, and as long as he is "possessed" by it he is insensible.[142] But this insensibility belongs, rather, to his shamanic condition, for he can lay about barefoot on fire and swallow burning coals,[143] just like his Oceanian, North American, and Siberian colleagues.

To sum up: South American shamanism still displays a number of extremely archaic characteristics: initiation by the ritual death and resurrection of the candidate, insertion of magical substances into his body, celestial ascent to lay the wishes of the whole society

---

139 Ibid., p. 340. 140 Ibid., p. 338.
141 M. Gusinde, *Die Feuerland Indianer. II: Die Yamana*, pp. 1417 ff., 1421. Cf. the Selk'nam séance, ibid., I: *Die Selk'nam*, pp. 757 ff.
142 Ibid., II, 1429 f. 143 Ibid., p. 1426.

before the Supreme God, shamanic healing by suction or search for the patient's soul, the shaman's ecstatic journey as psychopomp, the "secret songs" revealed by God or by animals, more especially birds. It would serve no purpose here to draw up a comparative table of all the cases in which the same complex recurs. We shall merely refer to the resemblances with the Australian medicine men (insertion of magical substances in the candidate's body, celestial initiatory journey, therapy by suction) to show the extreme antiquity of certain techniques and beliefs of the South American shamans. We are not called upon to decide whether these striking resemblances are due to the fact that, like the Australians, the oldest South American peoples represent the remains of an archaic humanity driven to the extreme regions of the habitable globe, or if direct contacts existed, through the Antarctic, between Australia and South America. This latter theory is maintained by such scholars as Mendes Correa, W. Koppers, and Paul Rivet.[144] Others —including Rivet, who holds both—favor the theory of later migrations to South America from the Malayo-Polynesian area.[145]

144 Cf. Koppers, "Die Frage eventueller alter Kulturbeziehungen zwischen dem südlichen Südamerika und Südost-Australien." On the linguistic similarities, see Rivet, "Les Australiens en Amérique"; id., *Les Origines de l'homme américain,* pp. 88 ff. See also W. Schmidt, *Der Ursprung der Gottesidee,* VI, 361 ff.

145 Cf. Rivet, "Les Malayo-Polynésiens en Amérique"; id., *Les Origines,* pp. 103 ff.; Georg Friederici, "Zu den vorkolumbischen Verbindungen der Südsee-Völker mit Amerika"; Walter Lehmann, "Die Frage völkerkundlicher Beziehungen zwischen der Südsee und Amerika"; James Hornell, "Was There Pre-Columbian Contact between the Peoples of Oceania and South America?" Rivet considers it possible, chronologically speaking, to distinguish three migrations that peopled the American continent: Asiatic, Australian, and Melano-Polynesian. He sees the last as decidedly more important than the Australian. Though no sites of paleolithic man have yet been found in South America, it is most probable that migrations and contacts between that continent and Oceania (if their reality is accepted) took place quite early. See also D. S. Davidson, "The Question of Relationship between the Cultures of Australia and Tierra del Fuego"; Carl Schuster, *Joint-Marks: a Possible Index of Cultural Contact between America, Oceania and the Far East.*

Antiquity of Shamanism in the Two Americas

The problem of the "origin" of shamanism in the two Americas is still far from being solved. Probably, in the course of time, a certain number of magico-religious practices were added to the beliefs and practices of their earliest inhabitants. If the Fuegians are taken to be descended from one of the first waves of immigrants to enter the Americas, we are justified in supposing that their religion represents the survival of an archaic ideology, which, from the point of view that concerns us, included belief in a celestial God, shamanic initiation by vocation or voluntary quest, relations with the souls of dead shamans and with familiar spirits (relations that sometimes reached the point of "possession"), the conception of illness as the intrusion of a magical object or as soul loss, and the shaman's insensibility to fire. Now, it seems that the majority of these characteristics are also found not only in the regions where shamanism dominates the religious life of the community (North America, Eskimo, Siberians) but also in regions where it is but one of the constituent phenomena of magico-religious life (Australia, Oceania, Southeast Asia). Hence we may assume that a certain form of shamanism spread through the two American continents with the first waves of immigrants, whatever their "original home" may have been.

Certainly, the prolonged contacts between North Asia and North America made Asian influences possible long after the coming of the first settlers.[146] Following E. B. Tylor, Thalbitzer,

146 There is an extensive bibliography on this problem. See Waldemar
. Bogoras, "The Folklore of Northeastern Asia, as Compared with That of Northwestern America"; Berthold Laufer, "Columbus and Cathay, and the Meaning of America to the Orientalist"; B. Freiherr von Richthofen, "Zur Frage der archäologischen Beziehungen zwischen Nordamerika und Nord-siens"; Diamond Jenness, "Prehistoric Culture Waves from Asia to America"; G. Hatt, *Asiatic Influences in American Folklore*; R. von Heine-eldern, "Cultural Connections between Asia and Pre-Columbian America" on the Congrès International des Américanistes, held at New York in 1949).

A. I. Hallowell, and others, Robert Lowie [147] has noted a number of resemblances between the Lapps and the American tribes, especially those of the Northeast. In particular, the drawings on the Lapp drum are astonishingly reminiscent of the pictographic style of the Eskimo and the eastern Algonkin.[148] The same scholar has drawn attention to the resemblance between the Lapp shaman's song, inspired by an animal and more especially by a bird, and the

---

Heine-Geldern has brought out the Asiatic origin of the art of the American tribes of the Northwest Coast; he considers that he has identified the same stylistic principle among the coastal tribes of British Columbia and southern Alaska, in the north of New Ireland, in Melanesia, and on certain monument and ritual objects in Borneo, Sumatra, and New Guinea, and, finally, i Chinese art of the Shang period. He supposes that this artistic style, c Chinese origin, spread southward to Indonesia and Melanesia and eastward to North America, where it arrived not later than the first part of the firs millennium B.C. It is only just to note that the parallelism between ancien China and America, studied particularly in artistic documents, had alread been drawn by C. Hentze, *Objets rituels, croyances et dieux de la Chine antiqu et de l'Amérique*. On the Siberian and Chinese influences discernible in th prehistoric Ipiutak culture (western Alaska), provisionally dated to th first century of our era, cf. Helge Larsen, "The Ipiutak Culture: Its Origi and Relationship." Cf. also Carl Schuster, "A Survival of the Eurasiati Animal Style in Modern Alaskan Eskimo"; R. von Heine-Geldern, "Da Problem vorkolumbischer Beziehungen zwischen Alter und Neuer Welt un seine Bedeutung für die allgemeine Kulturgeschichte."

147 "Religious Ideas and Practices of the Eurasiatic and North America Areas." Cf. also id., "On the Historical Connection between Certain Ol World and New World Beliefs," especially pp. 547 ff. A traveler at the end the seventeenth century gave the following description of a Finnish custom The peasants heated stones in the middle of a bathhouse, threw water c them, remained inside for some time to open their pores thoroughly, the came out and plunged into an extremely cold stream. The same custom wa attested in the sixteenth century among the Scandinavians. Lowie ("Rel gious Ideas," p. 188) cites the fact that the Tlingit and the Crow likewis plunge into an icy stream after remaining for a long time in a steam bat We shall see later that the steam bath is one of the elementary techniqu for increasing "mystical heat," sweating sometimes having pre-emine creative value; in a number of mythological traditions man was created l God after a period of violent sweating; on this motif, cf. K. Meuli, "Scythica pp. 133 ff., and below, p. 412.

148 Lowie, "Religious Ideas," p. 186.

North American shamans' songs of the same origin.[149] We should add, however, that the same phenomenon is found in South America—which, in our view, excludes a recent Eurasiatic influence. Lowie also notes the resemblances between the theory of soul loss among the North Americans and the Siberians, shamanic playing with fire (common to North Asia and a number of North American tribes, such as the Fox and the Menomini), the shaking of the ceremonial hut [150] and ventriloquism among the Chukchee and the Cree, the Saulteaux and the Cheyenne, and finally certain common features of the initiatory steam bath in North America and North Europe—all of which would lead to supposing not only a Siberian-Western American cultural solidarity but also American-Scandinavian relations.

We should note, however, that all these cultural elements are found not only in South America (search for the soul, movement of the shamanic hut, ventriloquism, steam bath, insensibility to fire) but that the most distinctive among them (playing with fire, steam bath, shaking of the ceremonial hut, search for the soul) are also attested in many other places (Africa, Australia, Oceania, Asia) and precisely in relation with the most archaic forms of magic in general and especially with shamanism. Of particular importance, in our view, is the role of "fire" and "heat" in South American shamanism. Such "fire" and mystical "heat" are always connected with access to a certain ecstatic state—and the same connection is observed in the most archaic strata of magic and universal religion. Mastery over fire, insensibility to heat, and, hence, the "mystical heat" that renders both extreme cold and the temperature of burning coals supportable, is a magico-mystical virtue that, accompanied by no less marvelous qualities (ascent, magical flight, etc.) translates into sensible terms the fact that the shaman has passed beyond the human condition and already shares in the condition of "spirits." [151]

149 Ibid., p. 187.

150 On this cultural complex, see Regina Flannery, "The Gros Ventre Shaking Tent," pp. 82 ff. (comparative study).

151 Cf. below, pp. 474 ff.

These few facts suffice to cast doubt on the theory of the comparatively recent origin of American shamanism. We find the broad outlines of one and the same shamanic complex from Alaska to Tierra del Fuego. North Asian or even Asiatic-Oceanian contributions in all probability merely reinforced, and sometimes modified in details, a shamanic ideology and technique already widely disseminated and, as it were, naturalized, in the two Americas.

CHAPTER TEN

Southeast Asian and Oceanian Shamanism

Shamanic Beliefs and Techniques among the Semang, the Sakai, and the Jakun

THE Negritos are generally agreed to be the earliest inhabitants of the Malay Peninsula. Kari, Karei, or Ta Pedn, the Supreme Being of the Semang, has all the characteristics of a celestial god (indeed, Kari means "thunder," "storm"), but he is not the object of a cult properly speaking; he is invoked only in case of storm by expiatory offerings of blood.[1] The medicine man of the Semang is called *hala* or *halak*, a term also employed by the Sakai.[2] As soon as anyone falls ill, the *hala* and his assistant retire to a leaf hut and begin singing to invoke the *cenoi*, the "nephews of God." [3] After some time, the voices of the *cenoi* themselves rise

---

1 Eliade, *Patterns in Comparative Religion*, pp. 46 ff.

2 W. W. Skeat and C. O. Blagden, *Pagan Races of the Malay Peninsula*, I, 229 ff., 252 ff.; Ivor H. N. Evans, *Studies in Religion, Folk-Lore, & Custom in British North Borneo and the Malay Peninsula*, p. 158. There are two classes of *hala*: the *snahud*, from the verb *sahud*, "to evoke," can only diagnose; the *puteu* can also cure (Evans, "Schebesta on the Sacerdo-Therapy of the Semang," p. 119). On the *halak*, cf. also Fay-Cooper Cole, *The Peoples of Malaysia*, pp. 67, 73, 108; W. Schmidt, *Der Ursprung der Gottesidee*, III, 20 ff.; R. Pettazzoni, *L'onniscienza di Dio*, pp. 453 ff., 468, n. 86; Engelbert Stiglmayr, "Schamanismus bei den Negritos Südostasiens," Pt. 1.

3 "Little celestial beings, amiable and luminous; children and servants of the divinity"—so the *cenoi* are described by Schebesta, *Les Pygmées*, p. 152 f. It is they who serve as intermediaries between man and Ta Pedn. But they are also regarded as the ancestors of the Negritos (Evans: "Schebesta on the Sacerdo-Therapy of the Semang," p. 118; *Studies*, p. 148).

from the hut; the *hala* and his assistant sing and speak in an unknown language, which, when they leave the cabin, they profess to have forgotten.[4] Actually, the *cenoi* have sung through their mouths. The descent of these luminous spirits is manifested by the hut shaking.[5] It is they who reveal the cause of the illness and indicate the treatment; and it is on this occasion that the *hala* is supposed to go into trance.[6]

In reality, the technique is not quite so simple as it might seem. The concrete presence of the *cenoi* implies, in one way or another, a communication between the *hala* and the sky, if not with the celestial god himself. "If Ta Pedn had not told him what medicine to use, the time to give it to the sick man, and the words he must speak, how could the *hala* cure?" a Semang Pygmy asked.[7] For sicknesses are sent by Ta Pedn himself, to punish men's sins.[8] That there are more direct relations between the *hala* and the celestial god than between the same god and other Negritos is further proved by the fact that the Menri of Kelantan hold that the *hala* has divine powers and hence makes no blood oblations during storms.[9] The Menri *hala* springs into the air during the ceremony, sings, and throws a mirror and a necklace toward Karei.[10] Now, we know that the ceremonial leap symbolizes celestial ascent.

But there are still more definite data concerning the Pygmy shaman's relations with the sky. During his séance the *hala* of the Pahang Negritos holds threads made from palm leaves or, according

---

Cf. also id., *Papers on the Ethnology and Archaeology of the Malay Peninsula*, pp. 18, 25; Cole, p. 73.

4 Schebesta, pp. 153 ff. This is, of course, the "spirit language," the secret language peculiar to shamans. Evans (*Studies*, p. 159) gives some invocations and transcribes (pp. 161 f.) texts of songs that are astonishing in their simplicity. According to the same author, during the séance the *hala* is controlled by the *cenoi* (ibid., p. 160), but Schebesta's description gives more the impression of a dialogue between the *hala* and his helping spirits.

5 Cf. the séances of North American shamans, above, p. 335, n. 150.

6 Evans, "Schebesta on the Sacerdo-Therapy of the Semang," p. 118.

7 Schebesta, p. 152.

8 Evans, "Schebesta on the Sacerdo-Therapy of the Semang," p. 115.

9 Ibid., p. 121.   10 Ibid.

ing to other accounts, very fine cords. These threads and cords reach to Bonsu, the celestial god who dwells above the seven levels of the sky. (He lives there with his brother, Teng; the other levels have no inhabitants.) As long as the séance continues, the *hala* is directly connected with the celestial god by these threads or cords, which the god sends down and, after the ceremony, draws back to himself.[11] Finally, an essential element in the cure is quartz crystals (*chebuch*), whose relations with the celestial vault and the sky gods we noted earlier.[12] These crystals can be obtained directly from the *cenoi* or they can be prepared; *cenoi* are believed to live in these magical stones and to be at the *hala's* orders. The healer is said to see the sickness in these crystals; that is, the *cenoi* inside them show him the cause of the sickness and the treatment for it. But in these crystals the *hala* can also see a tiger approaching the camp.[13] The *hala* himself can turn into a tiger,[14] just like the *bomor* of Kelantan and the Malayan shamans and shamanesses.[15] Such a conception indicates Malayan influence. We must not forget, however, that the mythical Tiger Ancestor is regarded throughout Southeast Asia as the initiatory master; it is he who takes the neophytes to the jungle to initiate them (in reality, to "kill" and "revive" them). In other words, the tiger forms part of an extremely archaic religious complex.[16]

11 Evans, *Papers*, p. 20.   12 Above, pp. 137 ff.

13 Evans, "Schebesta on the Sacerdo-Therapy of the Semang," p. 119.

14 Ibid., p. 120; Schebesta, p. 154.

15 Jeanne Cuisinier, *Danses magiques de Kelantan*, pp. 38 ff., 74 ff.; on the role of the tiger in Malayan shamanism, see below, pp. 345 f. The Sungkai Sakai also believe that the shaman can turn into a tiger (Evans, *Studies*, p. 210). In any case, on the fourteenth day after his death the shaman becomes a tiger (ibid., p. 211).

16 A *bomor belian* (that is, a specialist in invocations to the tiger spirit) of the Kelantan region, attempting to recall his period of initiatory insanity, could remember only that he had wandered in the jungle and met a tiger; he had mounted on its back and the tiger had taken him to *Kadang baluk*, the mythical place where tiger-men live. He returned after an absence of three years and thenceforth had no more epileptic seizures (Cuisinier, pp. 5 ff.). *Kadang baluk* is, of course, the "underworld in the bush" where initiation is performed (not necessarily a shamanic initiation).

There is a Negrito legend that, in our opinion, preserves an ancient shamanic initiation scenario. A great snake, Mat Chinoi, lives on the road that leads to the palace of Tapern (Ta Pedn). This snake makes carpets for Tapern; they are beautiful carpets, with many ornaments, hung out over a beam; the snake lives under them. In its belly there are twenty or thirty female Chinoi, of the utmost beauty, and a great quantity of head ornaments, combs, and other objects. A Chinoi named Halak Gihmal ("The Weapon Shaman") lives on the snake's back as the guardian of its treasures. When a Chinoi wants to enter the snake's belly, Halak Ghimal submits him to two ordeals, whose structure and meaning are clearly initiatory. The snake lies stretched out under a beam that holds seven carpets, and these carpets are in motion, constantly approaching and separating. The Chinoi candidate must pass through quickly enough not to fall on the snake's back. The second ordeal consists in entering a tobacco box whose cover opens and closes at great speed. If the candidate emerges from these two ordeals victorious, he may enter the snake and choose a wife among the Chinoi women.[17]

Here we find once again the initiatory motif of the magical door that shuts and opens in an instant, a motif that we have already encountered in Australia, North America, and Asia. We have seen, too, that passage through an ophidian monster is equivalent to an initiation.

Among the Batak of Palawan, another Pygmy people of Malaysia, the shaman, *balian*, obtains his trance by dancing. This is already an indication that the technique has undergone Indo-Malayan influences. These influences are still more perceptible in their funerary beliefs. The dead man's soul remains with his relatives for four days; then it crosses a plain, in the middle of which stands a tree. It climbs the tree and reaches the point where earth touches the sky. There waits a giant spirit that, according to the man's acts in life, determines whether his soul may proceed or

17 Evans, *Studies*, p. 151.

must be cast into the fire. The land of the dead has seven levels—which is as much as to say that it is the sky. The spirit traverses them one after the other. When it reaches the last, it turns into a glowworm.[18] The number 7 and punishment by fire are, as we have seen,[19] ideas of Indian origin.

The two other aboriginal, pre-Malayan peoples of the Malay Peninsula, the Sakai and the Jakun, present numerous problems to the ethnologist.[20] From the point of view of the history of religions, it is certain that shamanism plays a far more important role among them than among the Semang Pygmies, although the technique is essentially the same. We find again the round hut made of leaves, which the *hala* (Sakai) or the *poyang* (Jakun: variant of the Malayan term *pawang*) enters with his assistants; we find them intoning songs, invoking their helping spirits. The increased importance of the latter, which are inherited and obtained as the result of a dream, denotes Malayan influence. The helping spirits are sometimes invoked in Malay. Inside the hut there are two small pyramids with steps,[21] the sign of a symbolic climb into the sky. For the séance the shaman puts on a special headdress decorated with many ribbons,[22] another indication of Malayan influence.

The corpses of the Sakai shamans are left in the houses where they died, without burial.[23] The *puteu* of the Kenta Semang are buried with their heads protruding from the grave; it is believed that their souls set out for the East, instead of for the West like those of other mortals.[24] These particulars show that they are regarded as a class of privileged beings, who therefore enjoy an afterlife different from that of the rest of the tribe. The Jakun

18 Cole, *The Peoples of Malaysia*, pp. 70 ff.   19 Above, pp. 282 ff.
    20 Cf. Cole, pp. 92 ff., 111 ff.; Evans, *Studies*, pp. 208 ff. (Sakai), 264 ff.
 Jakun). An attempt to define the religious beliefs of the three pre-Malayan peoples of the Malay Peninsula—the Pygmies, the Sakai, and the Jakun—is made in Skeat and Blagden, *Pagan Races*, II, 174 ff.
    21 Evans, *Studies*, pp. 211 ff.   22 Ibid., p. 214.
    23 Cf. ibid., p. 217.
    24 Evans, "Schebesta on the Sacerdo-Therapy of the Semang," p. 120.

poyang are placed on platforms after death, for "their souls go up to the sky, while those of ordinary mortals, whose bodies are buried, go to the under-world." [25]

Shamanism in the Andaman Islands and Nicobar

According to the information furnished by Radcliffe-Brown, in the northern Andaman Islands the medicine man (*oko-jumu*, literally "dreamer" or "one who speaks from dreams") obtains his power by contact with the spirits. The spirits are encountered directly, in the jungle, or in dreams. But the most usual means of contact with the spirits is death; when someone dies and returns to life, he is thenceforth an *oko-jumu*. Thus, Radcliffe-Brown saw a man who was seriously ill and who, remaining unconscious for twelve hours, was considered dead. He heard of another who had died and revived three times. This tradition clearly shows the schema of initiatory death followed by resurrection of the candidate. But further details respecting the theory and technique of initiation are lacking; the last *oko-jumus* were already dead when, toward the beginning of this century, it was thought worth while to study them objectively.[26]

The *oko-jumus* maintained their reputation by the efficiency of their cures and their meteorological magic (for it was they who were believed to foresee storms). But treatment proper consisted in prescribing remedies already familiar to, and used by, everyone. Sometimes they also went on to expel the demons that caused the illness; or again, they proimsed to finish the cure directly in dreams. The spirits revealed to them the magical properties of various objects (mineral substances and plants). They did not use quartz crystals.

The medicine men of the Nicobar Islands are acquainted both

25 Id., *Studies*, p. 265. On the cosmologico-religious implications of these funerary customs and beliefs, see above, pp. 139 ff.; on the *poyang* of the Benua-Jakun of Johore, Skeat and Blagden, *Pagan Races*, II, 350 ff.

26 A. R. Radcliffe-Brown, *The Andaman Islanders*, pp. 175 ff.; cf. also Stiglmayr, "Schamanismus bei den Negritos Südostasiens," Pt. 2.

with healing by the "extraction" of the magical object that has brought on the sickness (a bit of charcoal or a pebble, a lizard, etc.) and the search for the soul abducted by evil spirits. In Car Nicobar there is a very interesting ceremony for the initiation of future medicine men. Usually a youth who displays a sickly temperament is destined to become a shaman; the spirits of recently dead relatives or friends mark their choice by leaving certain signs (leaves, hens with their feet tied together, etc.) in the house at night. If such a youth refuses to become a shaman, he dies. After this election there is a public ceremony marking the beginning of the novitiate. The relatives and friends gather in front of the house; inside, the shamans lay the novice on the ground and cover him with leaves and branches, placing the wing feathers of a chicken on his head. (This vegetable burial could be interpreted as a symbolic interment and the feathers as the magical sign of the mystical power to fly.) When the novice rises, those present give him necklaces and various jewels, which he must wear around his neck during his whole novitiate; he will return them to their owners when his apprenticeship ends.

Then a throne is made for him, in which he is carried from village to village, and he is given a sort of scepter and a lance to fight evil spirits. Some days later the master shamans take him into the depths of the jungle, in the middle of the island. Some friends accompany the group at a certain distance; they stop before entering the "land of the spirits," for the souls of the dead might be frightened away. The secret teaching amounts essentially to learning the dances and acquiring the ability to see the spirits. After some time in the jungle (that is, in the land of the dead) the novice and his masters return to the village. The young apprentice continues to dance in front of his house for at least an hour every night during his novitiate. When his initiation is completed, the masters give him a staff. There is certainly another ceremony that consecrates him a shaman, but it has not been possible to collect any precise details concerning it.[27]

27 George Whitehead, *In the Nicobar Islands*, pp. 128 ff., 147 ff.

This extremely interesting shamanic initiation is found only in Car Nicobar; it is unknown in the rest of the Nicobar Archipelago. Certain elements are indubitably archaic (the burial under leaves, the withdrawal to the "land of the spirits"), but many others show Indian influence (the novice's throne, the lance, the scepter, the staff). We here have a typical example of the hybridization of a shamanic tradition as the result of cultural contacts with an advanced civilization that has elaborated a highly complex magical technique.

Malayan Shamanism

What is called Malayan shamanism has as its distinctive characteristics the evocation of the tiger spirit and obtaining the condition of *lupa*. The latter is the state of unconsciousness into which the shaman falls and during which the spirits descend on him, "possess" him, and answer questions put by the audience. Whether the case is one of individual cure or a ceremony of collective defense against epidemics (as, for example, in the *belian* dances of Kelantan), the Malayan séance usually includes the evocation of the tiger. This is because the role of mythical ancestor and, hence, of initiatory master, is given to the tiger throughout this area.

The Proto-Malayan Benua tribe believe that the *poyang* becomes a tiger on the seventh day after his death. If his son wishes to inherit his powers, he must watch by the corpse alone, burning perfumes. On the seventh day the dead shaman appears in the form of a tiger ready to spring on the aspirant. The latter must continue censing, without showing the slightest sign of fear. Then the tiger disappears, to be replaced by two beautiful spirit-women; the aspirant loses consciousness and the initiation takes place during his trance. The women then become his familiar spirits. If the *poyang*'s son did not perform this rite, the dead shaman's spirit would remain in the tiger's body forever and his shamanic "energy" would be irremediably lost to the community.[28] We recog-

28 T. J. Newbold, *Political and Statistical Account of the British Settle*

nize the scenario of a typical initiation: solitude in the bush, the watch beside a corpse, the ordeal of fear, the terrible apparition of the initiatory master (= mythical ancestor), the protection of a beautiful spirit-woman.

The séance proper takes place inside a round hut or a magic circle, and the object of most séances is cure, the discovery of lost or stolen objects, or knowledge of the future. Usually the shaman remains under a covering during the séance. Censing, dancing, music, and drumming are the indispensable preparatory elements in any Malayan séance. The arrival of the spirit is manifested by the quivering of a candle flame. The spirit is believed first of all to enter the candle, and hence the shaman keeps his eyes fixed on the flame for a long time, hoping thus to discover the cause of the illness. Cure usually consists in suction of the affected parts, but when the *poyang* falls into trance he can also drive away demons and he answers whatever questions are asked him.[29]

The evocation of the tiger is performed for the purpose of summoning and securing the incarnation of the mythical ancestor, the first Great Shaman. The *pawang* observed by Skeat did in effect turn himself into a tiger; he ran on all fours, roared, and licked the patient's body for a long time as a tigress licks her cubs.[30] The magical dances of the *belian bomor* of Kelantan must include evocation of the tiger, no matter for what reason the séance has been organized.[31] The dance culminates in the state of *lupa*, "forgetfulness" or "trance" (from Sanskrit *lopa*, "loss," "disappearance"), in which the actor loses consciousness of his own personality and incarnates some spirit.[32] Then come endless dialogues between the dancer in trance and the audience. If the dance was organized for a

ients in the Straits of Malacca, II, 387–89; R. O. Winstedt: *Shaman, Saiva and Sufi: a Study of the Evolution of Malay Magic*, pp. 44–45; "Kingship and Enthronement in Malaya," pp. 135 ff. ("The Malay King as Shaman").

29 Winstedt, *Shaman, Saiva and Sufi*, pp. 96–101.

30 W. W. Skeat, *Malay Magic*, pp. 436 ff.; Winstedt, *Shaman, Saiva and Sufi*, pp. 97 ff.

31 Cuisinier, pp. 38 ff., 74 ff., etc.

32 Ibid., pp. 34 ff., 80 ff., 102 ff.

cure, the healer makes use of the trance to ask questions and discover the causes of the illness and the treatment for it.[33]

It does not seem that such magical dances and cures should be regarded as shamanic phenomena in the strict sense of the term. Evocation of the tiger and trance-possession are not confined to the sphere of the *bomor* and *pawang*. Many other individuals can see the tiger, evoke it, or assume its form. As for the state of *lupa*, elsewhere in Malaya (for example, among the Besisi) it is accessible to all; during the evocation of the spirits, anyone can fall into trance and answer whatever questions may be asked him.[34] It is a mediumistic phenomenon that is also highly characteristic of the Batak of Sumatra. But, according to all that we have tried to show in this book, "possession" must not be confused with shamanism.

Shamans and Priests in Sumatra

The religion of the Batak of Sumatra, which has been strongly influenced by ideas from India,[35] is dominated by the concept of the soul (*tondi*); it enters and leaves the body through the fontanel. Death is, in reality, the abduction of the soul by a spirit (*begu*); if the deceased is a young man, a woman *begu* has taken him for her husband, and vice versa. The dead and the spirits speak through mediums.

Shamans (*sibaso*, "the word") and priests (*datu*), although differing in structure and religious vocation, pursue the same end—defending the soul against being abducted by demons, ensuring the integrity of the human person. Among the northern Batak the *sibaso* is always a woman, and shamanism is usually hereditary. There is no human teaching; one "chosen" by the spirits receives initiation directly from them—that is, becomes able to "see" and prophesy, or to be "possessed" by a spirit,[36] in other words,

33 Cuisinier, p. 69. 34 Skeat and Blagden, *Pagan Races*, II, 307.
35 See above, p. 286.
36 "Possession," spontaneous or deliberately induced, is a frequent

identifies himself with it. The *sibaso* séance takes place at night; the shaman drums and dances around the fire to invoke the spirits. Each spirit has its particular melody and even its special color, and the *sibaso* wears a costume of several colors if he wishes to invoke several spirits. Their presence is manifested by words uttered by the *sibaso* in secret language, the "language of the spirits," which must be interpreted. The dialogue concerns the causes of the illness and the means of curing it; the *begu* promises that it will perform a cure if the patient will offer certain sacrifices.[37]

The Batak priest, *datu*, is always a man and holds the highest social position after the chief. But he, too, is a healer and invokes the spirits in a secret language. The *datu* protects against illnesses and spells; the healing séance consists in searching for the patient's soul. In addition, he can exorcise *begu* that have entered the sick; he can also poison, though he is supposed to be only a "white magician." Unlike the *sibaso*, the *datu* is initiated by a master; in particular, the secrets of magic are revealed to him, written in "books" made of tree bark. The master has the Indian name *guru*; he attaches great importance to his magical staff, encrusted with ancestral figures and with a cavity containing magical substances. With the help of this staff, the *guru* protects the village and can bring rain. But making such a magical staff is extremely complicated; the process even involves the sacrifice of a child, who is killed

---

phenomenon among the Batak. Anyone can become the receptacle of a *begu*, that is, of the spirit of a dead person; it speaks through the medium's mouth and discloses secrets. "Possession" often takes shamanic forms: the medium picks up burning coals and puts them in his mouth, dances and leaps to the point of paroxysm, etc.; cf. J. Warneck, *Die Religion der Batak*, pp. 58 ff.; T. K. Oesterreich, *Possession*, pp. 252 ff. But, unlike the shaman, the Batak medium cannot control his *begu* and is at its mercy or at that of any other dead person who wishes to "possess" him. This spontaneous mediumship, which is characteristic of the Batak religious sensibility, may be regarded as an imitation of certain shamanic techniques. On Indonesian shamanism in general, see also G. A. Wilken, "Het Shamanisme bij de Volken van den Indischen Archipel," pp. 427–97; A. C. Kruyt (Kruijt), *Het Animisme in den Indischen Archipel*, pp. 443 ff.

37 E. M. Loeb, *Sumatra*, pp. 80–81.

with melted lead to drive out its soul and turn it into a spirit at the magician's disposition.[38]

All this shows the influence of Indian magic. We may suppose that the *datu* fills the role of the priest-magician, while the *sibaso* represents only the ecstatic, the "man with spirits." The *datu* does not experience mystical ecstasy; he operates as magician and "ritualist"; he exorcises demons. He, too, must go to seek the patient's soul, but his mystical journey is not ecstatic; his relations with the world of the spirits are those of hostility or superiority—master-servant relations. The *sibaso* is the ecstatic par excellence; he lives familiarly with the spirits, he lets himself be "possessed," he becomes the clairvoyant and prophet. He has been "chosen"—and against divine or semidivine election there is no recourse.

The *dukun* of the Menangkabau of Sumatra is at once healer and medium. The office, which is generally hereditary, is open to both men and women. One becomes a *dukun* after undergoing an initiation, that is, after learning to become invisible and to see the spirits at night. The séance takes place under a blanket; after a quarter of an hour the *dukun* begins to shake, the sign that his soul has left his body and is on its way to the "spirit village." Voices are heard under the blanket. The *dukun* asks his spirits to search for the patient's strayed soul. The trance is simulated; the *dukun* has not the courage to hold the séance in full view of the audience, as his Batak colleague does.[39] The *dukun* is also found in Nias, together with other classes of priests and healers. During the cure he wears a special costume; he adorns his hair and throws a piece of cloth over his shoulders. Here too, sickness is generally due to the theft of the soul by gods, demons, or spirits, and the séance consists in searching for it. Usually it is discovered that the soul has been carried off by the "Sea Serpents" (the sea being the symbol of the beyond). To bring it back, the medicine man appeals to three gods—Ninwa, Falahi, and Upi—and evokes them by whistling continuously until he obtains communication with them; then he falls into trance. But the Niassan *dukun* also uses suction, and, when he succeeds in finding the cause of the illness, he shows the audience small red or white stones.[40]

The Mentaweian shaman also cures by massage, purifications, herbs, and similar means. But the real séance follows the usual Indonesian pattern: the shaman dances for a long time, falls to the ground unconscious, and his soul is carried to the sky in a boat drawn by eagles. There he consults the spirits regarding the causes of the illness (flight of the soul; poisoning by other sorcerers) and receives medicines. The Mentaweian shaman never shows any sign of "possession" and has no knowledge of exorcising evil spirits from the patient's body.[41] He is more a pharmacist who finds his simples after a celestial journey. The trance is not dramatic; the audience does not hear his dialogue with the celestial spirits. He appears to have no relations with demons or "power" over them.

A similar technique is employed by the Kubu shaman (of southern Sumatra): he dances until he falls into trance, then he sees the patient's soul held captive by a spirit or perched like a bird in a tree.[42]

Shamanism in Borneo and Celebes

Among the Dusun of North Borneo, who are of Proto-Malayan race and represent the aboriginal inhabitants of the island, priestesses play a leading role. Their initiation continues for three months. During the ceremony they use a secret language. On this occasion they put on a special costume: the face is covered by a blue cloth and they wear a conical hat decorated with cocks' feathers and shells. The séance consists in dances and songs; the men only supply a musical accompaniment. But the priestess's particular technique is divinatory and belongs to minor magic rather than to shamanism proper. She balances a bamboo stem on one finger and asks: If so-and-so is a thief, may the bamboo make such-and-such a movement, etc.[43]

40 Ibid., pp. 155 ff.
41 Loeb, *Sumatra*, pp. 198 ff.; "Shaman and Seer," pp. 66 ff.
42 Id., *Sumatra*, p. 286.   43 Evans, *Studies*, pp. 4 ff., 21 ff., 26 ff.

Among the Dyak of the interior there are two kinds of magician-healers: *daya beruri*, usually men, whose field is healing, and *barich*, commonly recruited among women, specialists in the "treatment" of paddy harvests. Illness is interpreted either as the presence of an evil spirit in the body or as the absence of the soul. Shamans of both classes have ecstatic power to see the human soul or the soul of the harvest, even if these have fled to great distances. They then pursue the fugitive souls, capture them (in the form of a hair), and restore them to their place in the body (or the crops). When the illness is caused by an evil spirit, the séance is reduced to an expulsion ceremony.[44]

The Sea Dyak shaman is called *manang*. He enjoys high social standing, ranking immediately after the chief. Usually the profession of *manang* is hereditary. But two classes are distinguished: those who obtained their revelation in dreams and so received the protection of one or more spirits, and those who became shamans of their own volition and hence have no familiar spirits. In any case, a *manang* is not qualified as such until he has been initiated by accepted masters.[45] The *manang* can be either a man or a woman, as well as a sexless (impotent) man; the ritual significance of the latter class will be discussed later.

The *manang* has a box containing a quantity of magical objects, the most important of which are quartz crystals, *bata ilau* ("the stones of light"), by help of which the shaman discovers the patient's soul. For, here too, illness is a flight of the soul and the purpose of the séance is to discover it and restore it to its place in the body. The séance takes place at night. The patient's body is rubbed with stones, then the audience begins to intone monotonous songs while the chief *manang* dances to the point of exhaustion; it is thus that he seeks and summons the patient's soul. If the illness is serious, the soul escapes from the *manang*'s hands several times. Once the leading shaman has fallen to the ground, a blanket is

44 H. Ling Roth, *The Natives of Sarawak and British North Borneo*, I, 259-63.

45 See above, pp. 57 f.

thrown over him and the audience await the result of his ecstatic journey. For as soon as he is in ecstasy the *manang* goes down to the underworld in search of the patient's soul. Finally he captures it, and suddenly rises, holding it in his hand, then replaces it through the skull. The séance is called *belian*, and Perham distinguishes as many as fourteen species of it, according to their technical difficulty. The cure ends with the sacrifice of a chicken.[46]

In its present form, the *belian* of the Sea Dyak appears to be a complex and composite magico-religious phenomenon. The initiation of the *manang* (massage with magical stones, ritual of ascent, etc.) and certain elements in the cure (importance of quartz crystals, massage with stones) indicate a shamanic technique of considerable antiquity. But the pseudotrance (which is carefully concealed under a blanket) shows recent influences, of Indo-Malayan origin. In former times, at the end of the initiation every *manang* put on women's clothing, which he continued to wear for the rest of his life. Today such a costume has become extremely rare.[47] However, a special class of *manang*, the *manang bali* of certain sea tribes (a class unknown to the hill Dyak), wear women's dress and devote themselves to the same occupations as women. Sometimes they take a "husband," despite the mockery of the village. This transvestitism, with all the changes that it involves, is accepted after a supernatural command has been thrice received in dreams; to refuse would be to seek death.[48] This combination of elements shows

46 Cf. H. L. Roth, I, 265 ff.; Archdeacon J. Perham, "Manangism in Borneo," quoted by Roth, I, 271 ff. See also Waldemar Stöhr, *Das Totenritual der Dajak*, pp. 152 ff.; cf. also ibid., pp. 48 ff. (the shaman accompanies the dead man's soul to the beyond), 125 ff. (the funerary ritual).

47 H. L. Roth, I, 282. Cf. the disappearance of transvestites and sexual perverts among the Araucanian shamans (A. Métraux, "Le Shamanisme araucan," pp. 315 f.).

48 H. L. Roth, I, 270 f. A young man seldom becomes a *manang bali*. They are generally old or childless men, attracted by the extremely tempting material situation. For transvestitism and change of sex among the Chukchee, cf. W. G. Bogoras, *The Chukchee*, pp. 448 ff. In Ramree Island, off the coast of Burma, some sorcerers adopt women's dress, become the "husband" of a colleague, and then bring him a woman as a "second wife," with whom both men can cohabit (H. Webster, *Magic*, p. 192). This is clearly a ritual

clear traces of a feminine magic and a matriarchal mythology, which must formerly have dominated the shamanism of the Sea Dyak; almost all the spirits are invoked by the *manang* under the name of *Ini* ("Great Mother").[49] However, the fact that this *manang bali* class is unknown in the interior of the island shows that the entire complex (transvestitism, sexual impotence, matriarchy) has come from outside, though in distant times.

Among the Ngadju Dyak of southern Borneo the intermediaries between men and the gods (especially the Sangiang) are the *balian* and the *basir*, priestess-shamaness and asexual priest-shaman (the term *basir* means "unable to procreate, impotent"). The latter are true hermaphrodites, dressing and behaving like women.[50] Both *balian* and *basir* are "chosen" by the Sangiang, and without their summons one cannot become their servant even if one has recourse to the usual techniques of ecstasy, the dance and drumming. The Ngadju Dyak are very clear on this point: no ecstasy is possible except to one called by the divinity. As for the bisexuality and impotence of *basir*, they arise from the fact that these priest-shamans are regarded as the intermediaries between the two cosmological planes—earth and sky—and also from the fact that they combine in their own person the feminine element (earth) and the masculine element (sky).[51] We here have a ritual androgyny, a well-known archaic formula for the divine biunity and the *coincidentia oppositorum*.[52] Like the hermaphroditism of the *basir*, the prostitution of the *balian* is similarly based on the sacred value of the "intermediary," on the need to abolish polarities.

---

transvestitism, accepted either in obedience to a divine command or for the sake of woman's magical prestige.

49 H. L. Roth, I, 282.

50 On this problem, see Justus M. van der Kroef, "Transvestitism and the Religious Hermaphrodite in Indonesia," passim.

51 H. Schärer: "Die Vorstellungen der Ober- und Unterwelt bei den Ngadju Dajak von Süd-Borneo," pp. 78 ff.; *Die Gottesidee der Ngadju Dajak in Süd-Borneo*, pp. 59 ff.

52 Cf. Eliade, *Patterns*, pp. 420 ff.

The gods (Sangiang) incarnate themselves in *balian* and *basir* and speak through them directly. But this phenomenon of incarnation is not a "possession." The souls of the ancestors or the dead never take possession of the *balian* or the *basir*; they are solely instruments of expression for the divinities. The dead make use of another class of sorcerers, the *tukang tawur*. The ecstasy of the *balian* and the *basir* is brought on by the Sangiang or after mystical journeys that they make to the sky to visit the "village of the gods."

Several points here deserve notice: the religious vocation, determined solely by the gods above; the sacred character of sexual behavior (impotence, prostitution); the minor role played by the technique of ecstasy (dance, music, etc.); trance brought on by embodying Sangiang or by the mystical journey to the sky; absence of relations with the souls of the ancestors and hence absence of "possession." All these features contribute to show the religious archaism of such a phenomenon. Although the cosmology and religion of the Ngadju Dyak have probably undergone Asiatic influences, we are justified in assuming that the *balian* and the *basir* represent an ancient and autochthonous form of shamanism.

The Ngadju Dyak *basir* has a counterpart in the *tadu* or *bajasa* of the Bare'e Toradja (Celebes). These are usually women or men who pose as women (*bajasa* had originally meant "deceiver"). Their particular technique consists in ecstatic journeys to the sky and the underworld, which the *bajasa* can perform either in spirit or *in concreto*. An important ceremony is the *mompanrilangka*, an initiation ceremony for girls, which continues for three consecutive days. It also falls to the *bajasa* to seek the wandering souls of the sick; with the help of a *wurake* spirit (belonging to the class of spirits of the atmosphere), the *bajasa* climbs the rainbow to the house of Puë di Songe, Supreme God, and brings back the patient's soul. She also seeks and brings back the "soul of the rice" when it deserts the crops, leaving them to wither and perish. But her ecstatic capacities are not confined to journeys to the sky and about the earth; on the occasion of the great funerary festival, the *mompemate*, *bajasa* lead the souls of the dead to the beyond.[53]

According to R. E. Downs, "The litany described how the dead were waked, dressed themselves and were conducted through the underworld to the *dinang* tree which they climbed to reach the earth, where they came out in Mori (to the east of the Toradja), and finally were led to the temple or feast hut. There they were welcomed by their relatives and entertained by them and the rest of the participants by singing and dancing. . . . The next day the *angga* [i.e., the souls] were conducted by the shamans to their final resting place." [54]

These few data show that the *bajasa* of Celebes are specialists in the great drama of the soul: purifiers, healers, or psychopomps, they exercise their functions only in cases where the welfare or existence of the soul itself is at stake. It is remarkable that their most frequent relations are with the sky and the celestial spirits. The symbolism of magical flight or of ascent by the rainbow, which dominates Australian shamanism, is archaic. In addition, the Toradja, too, know the myth of the vine that once joined earth and sky and remember a paradisal time when men communicated easily with the gods.[55]

53 N. Adriani and A. C. Kruyt, *De Bare'e-sprekende Toradja's van Midden-Celebes*, I–II, especially I, 361 ff.; II, 85–106, 109–46, and passim; and the long summary in H. H. Juynboll, "Religionen der Naturvölker Indonesiens," pp. 583–88. See also R. E. Downs, *The Religion of the Bare'e-speaking Toradja of Central Celebes*, pp. 47 ff., 87 ff. Cf. James Frazer, *Aftermath*, pp. 209–19 (summarizing Adriani and Kruyt, I, 376–93); H. G. Quaritch Wales, *Prehistory and Religion in South-East Asia*, pp. 81 ff. Other descriptions of shamanic séances for bringing back the souls of the sick will be found in Frazer, *Aftermath*, pp. 212–13 (Dyak of South Borneo), 214–16 (Kayan of Sarawak, Borneo).

54 P. 89 (after Kruyt).

55 On shamanic ideology and practices among the inhabitants of Ceram, cf. J. G. Röder, *Alahatala. Die Religion der Inlandstämme Mittelcerams*, pp. 46 ff., 71 ff., 83 ff., 118 ff.

The "Boat of the Dead" and the Shamanic Boat

The "boat of the dead" plays a great role in Malaysia and Indonesia, both in strictly shamanic contexts and in funerary practices and laments. All these beliefs are, of course, connected on the one hand with the custom of loading the dead on canoes or throwing them into the sea, and, on the other, with the funerary mythologies. The practice of exposing the dead in boats might well be explained by vague recollections of ancestral migrations; [56] the boat would carry the dead man's soul back to the original homeland from which the ancestors set forth. But (except, perhaps, for the Polynesians) these possible memories lost their historical meaning; the "original homeland" became a mythical country and the ocean that separates it from inhabited lands was assimilated to the Waters of Death. This phenomenon is, in any case, frequent within the horizon of archaic mentality, where "history" is continually transformed into mythical events.

Similar funerary beliefs and practices are found among the ancient Germans [57] and the Japanese.[58] But in both cases, as also in the Oceanian area, in addition to a marine or submarine beyond ("horizontal" complex), there is also a vertical complex: the mountain as realm of the dead,[59] or even the sky. (It will be remembered that the mountain is "charged" with a celestial symbolism.) Usually only the privileged (chiefs, priests and shamans, initiates,

---

56 Cf. Rosalind Moss, *The Life after Death in Oceania and the Malay Archipelago*, pp. 4 ff., 23 ff., etc. On the relations between forms of burial and conceptions of life after death in Oceania, see also Frazer, *The Fear of Death in Primitive Religion*, I, 181 ff.; Erich Doerr, "Bestattungsformen in Ozeaien"; Carla van Wylick, *Bestattungsbrauch und Jenseitsglaube auf Celebes*; H. G. Quaritch Wales, *Prehistory*, pp. 90 ff.

57 Cf. W. Golther, *Handbuch der germanischen Mythologie*, pp. 90 ff., 90, 315 ff.; O. Almgren, *Nordische Felszeichnungen als religiöse Urkunden*, p. 191, 321, etc.; O. Höfler, *Kultische Geheimbünde der Germanen*, I, 196, etc.

58 Alexander Slawik, "Kultische Geheimbünde der Japaner und Germanen," pp. 704 ff.

59 Höfler, I, pp. 221 ff., etc.; Slawik, pp. 687 ff.

etc.) go up to the sky; [60] other mortals journey "horizontally" or descend to an underground beyond. We should add that the problem of the beyond and its orientations is extremely complex, and that it cannot be solved by ideas of "original homelands" or by forms of interment. In the last analysis, we have to do with mythologies and religious conceptions that, if they are not always independent of material usages and practices, are nevertheless autonomous as spiritual structures.

Aside from the custom of exposing the dead in canoes, there are in Indonesia, and also, in part, in Melanesia, three important categories of magico-religious practices that involve the use (real or symbolic) of a ritual boat: (1) the boat for the expulsion of demons and sicknesses; (2) the boat in which the Indonesian shaman "travels through the air" in search of the patient's soul; (3) the "boat of the spirits," which carries the souls of the dead to the beyond. In the first two categories of rites shamans play the principal if not the only role; the third category, though it consists in an underworld journey of the shamanic type, nevertheless extends beyond the shaman's function. As we shall soon see, these "boats of the dead" are evoked rather than manipulated, and their evocation occurs in the course of funerary laments recited by professional women mourners and not by shamans.

Annually, or on the occasion of epidemics, the demons of sickness are expelled in one of the following ways: they are caught and shut up in a box, or directly in the boat, and the boat is thrown into the sea; or, alternatively, a number of wooden figures, representing sicknesses, are prepared and set in a boat, which is left to the mercy of the waves. This procedure, which is widespread in Malaysia [61]

60 To confine ourselves to the area with which we are concerned, cf. W. Perry, *The Megalithic Culture of Indonesia*, pp. 113 ff. (chiefs, after death go to the sky); Moss, pp. 78 ff., 84 ff. (the sky is a place of rest for certain privileged classes); A. Riesenfeld, *The Megalithic Culture of Melanesia* pp. 654 ff.

61 Cf., for example, Skeat, *Malay Magic*, pp. 427 ff., etc.; Cuisinier, pp. 180 ff. The same custom is found in the Nicobar Islands; cf. Whitehead p. 152 (illustration).

nd Indonesia,[62] is often carried out by shamans and sorcerers. The expulsion of the demons of sickness during an epidemic is probably n imitation of the more archaic and universal ritual of the expulsion of "sins" at the time of the New Year, when the strength and ealth of a society are totally restored.[63]

In addition, the Indonesian shaman uses a boat in the course of is magical cure. That sickness is due to a flight of the soul is the redominant conception throughout the Indonesian area. Most requently the soul is believed to have been abducted by demons or pirits, and to seek it the shaman uses a boat. This is the case, for xample, with the *balian* of the Dusun. If he thinks that the patient's soul has been captured by an aerial spirit, he makes a miniature boat with a wooden bird at one end. In this boat he journeys cstatically through the air, looking to left and right, until he finds ne patient's soul. This technique is known to the Dusun of North, outh, and East Borneo. The Maanyan shaman also has a boat ree to six feet long, which he keeps in his house and which he oards when he wishes to journey to the god Sahor and ask his elp.[64]

The idea of traveling through the air in a boat is only an Indoesian application of the shamanic technique of celestial ascent. rom the fact that the boat played the essential role in ecstatic ourneys into the beyond (land of the dead and of the spirits), unertaken either to escort the deceased to the underworld or to seek ne patient's soul abducted by demons or spirits, it came to be used ven when the shaman was to transport himself to the sky in trance. he fusion or coexistence of these two shamanic symbolisms—the orizontal journeys to the beyond, the vertical ascent to the sky— manifested by the presence of a Cosmic Tree in the shaman's oat. The Tree is sometimes represented as rising from the middle

62 A. Steinmann, "Das kultische Schiff in Indonesien," pp. 184 ff. (North orneo, Sumatra, Java, Moluccas, etc.).

63 Cf. Eliade, *The Myth of the Eternal Return*, pp. 53 ff.

64 Steinmann, pp. 190 ff. The shamanic boat is also found elsewhere; r example, in America (the shaman goes down to the underworld in a boat; , G. Buschan, ed., *Illustrierte Völkerkunde*, I, 134; Steinmann, p. 192).

of the boat in the form of a lance or of a ladder connecting earth and sky.[65] Here we find again the same symbolism of the "Center" by which the shaman can reach the sky.

In Indonesia the shaman conducts the deceased to the beyond and he often uses a boat for this ecstatic journey.[66] We shall soon see that the women mourners of the Dyak of Borneo fill the same role by chanting ritual songs that describe the deceased's journey in a boat. In Melanesia we also find the custom of sleeping near the corpse; in dream, the sleeper accompanies and guides the soul through the beyond, and, on waking, narrates the various incident of the journey.[67] This last practice may be compared, on the one hand, to the ritual accompaniment of the deceased by the shaman or professional woman mourner (Indonesia) and, on the other, to the funeral orations delivered at the grave in Polynesia. On different planes, all these funerary rites and customs pursue the same end: escorting the deceased to the beyond. But only the shaman is a psychopomp in the strict sense, only he escorts and guides the deceased *in concreto*.

---

65 Steinmann, pp. 193 ff.; H. G. Quaritch Wales, *Prehistory*, pp. 101 f According to W. Schmidt (*Grundlinien einer Vergleichung der Religionen und Mythologien der austronesischen Völker*), the Indonesian Cosmic Tree is of lunar origin, for which reason it figures prominently in the mythologies of the western part of Indonesia (that is, in Borneo, southern Sumatra, and Malacca) while it is absent from the eastern parts, where a lunar mythology was replaced by solar myths; cf. Steinmann, pp. 192, 199. But important objections have been raised against this astro-mythological construction cf., for example, F. Speiser, "Melanesien und Indonesien," pp. 464 f It should further be noted that the Cosmic Tree carries a far more complex symbolism and that only some of its aspects (e.g., its periodical renewal) can legitimately be interpreted in terms of a lunar mythology; cf. Eliade *Patterns*, pp. 296 ff.

66 Cf., for example, Krujt (Kruyt), "Indonesians," p. 244; Moss, p. 100 Among the East Toradja, eight or nine days after a death the shaman descends to the lower world to bring back the soul of the deceased and takes to the sky in a boat (H. G. Quaritch Wales, *Prehistory*, pp. 95 ff., after N. Adriani and A. C. Kruyt).

67 Moss, pp. 104 f.

Otherworld Journeys among the Dyak

There is some relation to shamanism in the funerary ceremonies of the Sea Dyak, though they are not performed by shamans. A professional woman mourner, whose vocation has, however, been determined by the appearance of a god in a dream, recounts at great length (sometimes for as long as twelve hours) the vicissitudes of the deceased's journey in the beyond. The ceremony takes place immediately after death. The mourner sits down beside the corpse and recites in a monotonous voice, without the support of any musical instrument. The purpose of the recital is to keep the soul from going astray in its journey in the underworld. Indeed, the mourner plays the role of a psychopomp, although she does not herself escort the soul; but the ritual text provides a quite precise itinerary. First of all, the mourner seeks a messenger who will go to the underworld to carry word of the newcomer's imminent arrival. In vain does she address herself to birds, wild animals, fish; they have not the courage to cross the frontier that divides the living from the dead. Finally the Wind Spirit consents to carry the message to its destination. He starts across an endless plain; he climbs a tree to find his way, for it is dark, and on every side stretch the paths that lead to the underworld; in fact there are 77 × 7 roads to the realm of the dead. From the top of the tree the Wind Spirit discovers the best road; he abandons his human shape and rushes toward the underworld as a hurricane. Frightened by the sudden storm, the dead become apprehensive and ask the reason for his coming. So-and-so has just died, the Wind Spirit answers, and you must hasten to fetch his soul. Joyfully the spirits jump into a boat and row so vigorously that they kill all the fish they meet. They stop the boat before the house of the deceased, rush out and seize the soul, which struggles and cries out. But even before it reaches the shores of the underworld, it seems to be at peace.

The mourner ends her song. Her part is performed; by narrating the vicissitudes of the two ecstatic journeys, she has really

guided the deceased to his new home. The same journey to the be
yond is recounted by the mourner on the occasion of the *pana* cere
mony, when she causes the offerings of food for the dead to pas
over into the underworld; it is only after the *pana* ceremony tha
the dead become conscious of their new condition. Finally th
mourner invites the souls of the dead to the great funeral festiva
the *Gawei antu*, which is celebrated from one to four years after th
decease. A large number of guests gather, and the dead are be
lieved to be present. The mourner's song describes them leavin
the underworld joyfully, boarding their boat, and hastening to th
feast.[68]

Obviously, not all these funerary ceremonies are shamanic i
character; at least in the *pana* and the *Gawei antu*, there is no direc
mystical relation between the dead man and the mourner who d
scribes the journeys in the beyond. All in all, we here have a ritu
literature that preserves the schemas of descents to the underworl
whether shamanic or not. But we must remember that the shama
too, everywhere conducts the souls of the dead to the underworl
and, as we have seen, throughout the Indonesian area the "boat
the dead"—which is constantly referred to in the funerary recita
that we have just summarized—is pre-eminently a shamanic mea
of journeying in ecstasy. The mourner herself, though she perforr
no magico-religious function, is nevertheless not one of the "pr
fane." She was chosen by a god, she received revelations in dream
In one way or another she is "inspired," a "seeress," who, wi
nessing otherworld journeys in vision, knows the beyond with i
topography and roads. Morphologically, the Dyak mourner is

68 Most of the texts and recitations of the Dyak women mourners we
published by Archdeacon Perham in the *JRAS Straits Branch* (1878
and republished, in abridged form, by H. L. Roth, *The Natives of Sarav
and British North Borneo*, I, 203 ff., and by the Rev. W. Howell, "A S
Dayak Dirge" (an article which has been inaccessible to us and which
know through the lengthy extracts in H. M. and N. K. Chadwick, *1
Growth of Literature*, III, 488 ff.). On funerary beliefs and customs amo
the Ngadju Dyak of South Borneo, see H. Schärer, *Die Gottesidee der Nga
Dajak*, pp. 159 ff.

he same plane as the seeresses and poetesses of the archaic Indo-European world; a certain class of traditional literary creations derives from the "visions" and the "inspiration" of such women chosen by the gods, whose dreams and reveries are so many mystical revelations.

Melanesian Shamanism

We cannot review all the various beliefs and mythologies that form the ideological foundation for the practices of the Melanesian medicine men. Here we will merely say that, generally speaking, three types of culture are distinguishable in Melanesia, each disseminated by one of the three ethnic groups that would seem to have colonized (or merely passed through) the area: the aboriginal Papuans, the white-skinned conquerors who brought agriculture, megaliths, and other forms of civilization and then moved on to Polynesia, and the black-skinned Melanesians, the last to reach the islands.[69] The white-skinned immigrants disseminated a very rich mythology, centered about a culture hero (Qat, Ambat, etc.) who has direct relations with the sky, whether by marrying a celestial fairy, whom, after the precaution to steal and hide her wings, he pursues to the sky by climbing a tree, a vine, or a "chain of arrows," or because he is himself a native of the celestial region.[70]

69 A. Riesenfeld, *The Megalithic Culture of Melanesia*, pp. 665 ff., 680, and passim. This work contains a vast bibliography and a critical examination of earlier studies, especially those of Rivers, Deacon, Layard, and Speiser. For the cultural relations between Melanesia and Indonesia, see Speiser, "Melanesien und Indonesien"; for relations with Polynesia (and from an "anti-historicistic" point of view), Ralph Piddington, ed., in R. W. Williamson, *Essays in Polynesian Ethnology*, pp. 302 ff.; for everything concerning the prehistory and first migrations of the Austronesians who disseminated their megalithic culture and a particular ideology (head-hunting, etc.) from southern China to New Guinea, the study by Heine-Geldern, "Urheimat und früheste Wanderungen der Austronesier." According to Riesenfeld's investigations, the authors of the megalithic culture of Melanesia seem to have come from an area bounded by Formosa, the Philippines, and North Celebes (p. 668).

70 Cf. Riesenfeld, pp. 78, 80 ff., 97, 102, and passim.

The myths of Qat correspond to the Polynesian myths of Tagarac and Maui, whose relations with the sky and celestial beings are well known. It is possible that the mythical theme of the "celestial journey" was applied by the Papuan aborigines to the white skinned newcomers, but it would be fruitless to explain the "origin" of such a myth (which, in any case, is found all over the world) by the historical event of the arrival or departure of the immigrants.[71] To repeat, far from "creating" myths, historical events end by being adopted into mythical categories.

In any event, in Melanesia we observe, together with techniques of magical cure whose archaism seems beyond doubt, the absence of a properly shamanic tradition and initiation. Is the disappearance of shamanic initiations to be attributed to the large role played by secret societies based on initiations? Possibly.[72] However this may be, the essential function of the Melanesian medicine men is restricted to healing and divination. Certain other specifically shamanic powers (magical flight, for example) remain the almost exclusive prerogative of black magicians. (Indeed, what is generally called "shamanism" is nowhere so divided up among a multitude of magico-religious groups as it is in Oceania, and especially in Melanesia, where we can distinguish priests, medicine men, sorcerers, diviners, the "possessed," etc.). Finally, and we consider this important, a number of motifs that in one way or another form part of the shamanic ideology survive only in myths or funerary beliefs. We referred above [73] to the motif of the civilizing hero who communicates with the sky by means of a "chain of arrows," a vine, and so on; we shall have occasion to return to it.[74] We may

71 As Riesenfeld seems to try to prove in his otherwise admirable book
72 The problem is too complex for us to enter into here. There is indubitably a striking morphological similarity among all forms of initiation-age-group initiations, initiations into secret societies, or shamanic initiation. To cite but one example, the candidate for entrance into a secret society in Malekula mounts a platform to sacrifice a pig (A. B. Deacon, *Malekula*, pp. 379 ff.); now, we have seen (above, pp. 125 ff.) that mounting a platform or a tree is a rite peculiar to shamanic initiations.

73 P. 361.   74 Pp. 423 ff.

lso note the belief that the deceased, on reaching the land of the ead, is subjected by its guardian to the mutilation of ear piercing.[75] Now, this operation is distinctive of shamanic initiations.

In Dobu, one of the islands to the east of New Guinea, the sorcerer is believed to be "burning," and magic is associated with heat nd fire, an idea that belongs to archaic shamanism and that has urvived even in developed ideologies and techniques.[76] For this eason the sorcerer must keep his body "dry" and "burning"; this e attempts to achieve by drinking salt water and eating highly piced foods.[77] The sorcerers and sorceresses of Dobu fly through ne air, and at night the fiery trails they leave behind them can be een.[78] But it is especially the women who fly; for in Dobu magical echniques are divided between the sexes as follows: the women re the true magicians, they operate directly through their souls, vhile their bodies are sunk in sleep, and attack their victim's soul which they can extract from his body and then destroy); male orcerers operate only through magical charms.[79] The difference in tructure between magician-ritualists and ecstatics here assumes ne aspect of a division based on sex.

In Dobu, as in other parts of Melanesia, illness is brought on ither by magic or by the spirits of the dead. In either case it is the atient's soul that is attacked, even if it is not carried out of the ody but merely harmed. On either theory, the medicine man is ummoned to discover the cause of the illness by gazing into crys-ls or water. He concludes from certain pathological manifesta-ons on the patient's part that the soul has been carried off; the atient is delirious or talks of ships at sea, and so forth; this is the gn that his soul has left his body. In his crystal the healer sees

75 C. G. Seligman, *The Melanesians of British New Guinea*, pp. 158, 3 ff. (Roro), p. 189 (Koita). See also Kira Weinberger-Goebel, "Melasische Jenseitsgedanken," p. 114.

76 See below, pp. 474 ff.

77 R. F. Fortune, *Sorcerers of Dobu*, pp. 295 ff.

78 Ibid., pp. 150 ff., 296, etc. The mythical origin of fire from the vagina an old woman (ibid., pp. 296 f.) seems to indicate that the feminine agic is earlier than the masculine sorcery.

79 Ibid., p. 150.

the person, living or dead, who has brought on the illness. The living author of the charm is paid to cease his hostility, or offerings are made to the dead man who proves to be the cause of the illness.[80] In Dobu divination is practiced by everyone, but without magic; [81] so too everyone possesses volcanic crystals which are supposed to fly by their own power if they are left in sight and which the sorcerers use to "see" the spirits.[82] No esoteric teaching concerning these crystals survives,[83] which shows the decadence of male shamanism in Dobu; for elsewhere there is a whole doctrine of maleficent charms, which is transmitted from master to pupil.[8]

Throughout Melanesia treatment of a disorder begins with sacrifices and prayers addressed to the dead person responsible, so that he will "remove the sickness." But if this approach, which is made by members of the family, fails, a *mane kisu*, "doctor," is summoned. By magical means the latter discovers the particular dead man responsible for the sickness and begs him to remove the cause of the trouble. In case the first "doctor" fails, another is called in. In addition to his strictly magical cure, the *mane kisu* rubs the patient's body and applies various kinds of massage. In Ysabel and Florida of the Solomons the "doctor" hangs some heavy object on a thread and names those who have recently died; when he reaches the name of the dead man who has brought on the illness, the object begins to move. The *mane kisu* then asks what sacrifice is desired—a fish, a pig, a human being—and the dead man replies by making the suspended object move when the desired sacrifice is named.[85] In Santa Cruz (Solomons) the spirits cause sicknesses by shooting magical arrows, which the healer extracts by massage. In the Banks Islands the illness is expelled by massages or by suction; the shaman then shows the patient a bit of bone or wood or leaf, and makes him drink water in which magical stones have been

80 Fortune, pp. 154 ff. On the *vada* method (murder by magic), cf. ibid, pp. 284 ff.; Seligman, pp. 170 ff.

81 Fortune, p. 155. 82 Ibid., pp. 298 ff.

83 Ibid. 84 Ibid., pp. 147 ff.

85 R. H. Codrington, *The Melanesians*, pp. 194 ff.

86 Ibid., p. 197.

placed.[87] The *mane kisu* uses the same method of divination in other cases as well. For example, before the fishermen set out, he asks a *tindalo* (spirit) if the fishing will be successful, and the boat gives the answer by shaking.[88] In Mota Lava and other islands of the Banks Archipelago a thief is discovered by the use of a bamboo stick in which a spirit nests; the stick goes to the thief of itself.[89]

Aside from this class of diviners and healers, any person can be possessed by a spirit or the soul of a dead person; when this occurs he speaks in a strange voice and prophesies. Usually the possession is involuntary. The man is with his neighbors, discussing one matter or another; suddenly he begins to sneeze and shake. "His eyes would glare, his limbs twist, his whole body be convulsed, foam would burst from his lips; then a voice, not his own, would be heard in his throat, allowing or disapproving of what was proposed. Such a man used no means of bringing on the ghost; it came upon him, as he believed himself, at its own will, its *mana* overpowered him, and when it departed it left him quite exhausted." [90]

In other parts of Melanesia, in New Guinea for example, possession by a dead relative is employed voluntarily and under all kinds of circumstances. When someone is ill, or it is wished to discover something unknown, a member of the family takes the image of the dead relative whose counsel is to be asked, sets it on his knees or his shoulder, and lets himself be possessed by the dead

87 Ibid., p. 198. The same technique is found in Fiji (ibid., p. 1). On the magical stones and quartz crystals of the Melanesian sorcerers, see Seligman, p. 284–85.

88 Codrington, p. 210.

89 Ibid. On the medicine man in Koita, see Seligman, pp. 167 ff.; in Roro, ibid., pp. 278 ff.; at Bartle Bay, ibid., p. 591; in Massim, ibid., pp. 638 ff.; in the Trobriands, ibid., p. 682.

90 Codrington, pp. 209 ff. In Lepers Island it is believed that the spirit tagaro infuses his spiritual power into a man to enable him to discover hidden things and reveal them (ibid., p. 210). The Melanesians do not confuse insanity—which is also possession by a *tindalo*—with possession proper, which has a purpose: revealing some particular thing (ibid., p. 219). During possession the man devours a large quantity of food and displays his magical virtues; he eats burning coals, raises enormous weights, and prophesies (ibid., p. 219).

person's soul.[91] But such phenomena of spontaneous mediumship, which are very frequent in Indonesia and Polynesia, are only superficially related to shamanism proper. We have cited them, however, in order to suggest the spiritual climate in which shamanic techniques and ideologies developed.

Polynesian Shamanism

In Polynesia matters are further complicated by the fact that there are several classes of specialists in the sacred, all of them having more or less direct relations with gods and spirits. Broadly speaking, we find three great categories of religious functionaries: the divine chiefs (*ariki*), the prophets (*taula*), and the priests (*tohunga*), but to these we must add healers, sorcerers, necromancers and the spontaneously "possessed," all of whom, in the last analysis, employ more or less the same technique: entry into contact with the gods or spirits, inspiration or possession by them. Probably at least some of the religious ideologies and techniques have been influenced by Asian ideas, but the problem of the cultural relations between Polynesia and South Asia is far from solved; however, it can be ignored here.[92]

91 J. G. Frazer, *The Belief in Immortality and the Worship of the Dead* I, 309.

92 E. S. C. Handy (*Polynesian Religion*) had attempted to define what h calls the two strata of Polynesian religion, one of Indian origin, the othe with its roots in China. But his comparisons were built on rather vagu analogies; see the critique by Piddington in R. W. Williamson, *Essays i Polynesian Ethnology*, pp. 257 ff. (On the Asiatic-Polynesian analogies, se ibid., pp. 268 ff.) But it is beyond doubt that certain cultural sequences ca be established in Polynesia; hence it is possible to write the history of th cultural complexes and even show their probable origin; cf., for exampl Edwin G. Burrows, "Culture-Areas in Polynesia," discussing Piddington criticisms. See above, p. 286, n. 120. However, we do not believe that suc investigations, despite their interest, are destined to solve the problem o shamanic ideologies and the techniques of ecstasy. As for possible contac between Polynesia and America, see the lucid general summary by Jame Hornell, "Was There Pre-Columbian Contact between the Peoples o Oceania and South America?"

We must observe at once that the essentials of shamanic ideology and technique—that is, communication among the three cosmic zones along an axis situated at the "Center" and the faculty of ascension, or magical flight—are abundantly attested in Polynesian mythology and continue to survive in popular beliefs about sorcerers. We will give only a few examples, for we shall later return to this mythical ascension theme. The hero Maui, whose myths are to be found throughout the Polynesian area and even beyond it, is famous for his ascents to the sky and descents to the underworld.[93] He flies in the form of a pigeon; and when he wants to go down to the world below, he removes the central pillar of his house and, through the opening thus left, feels the winds of the lower regions.[94] A number of other myths and legends tell of ascending to the sky by vines, trees, or kites, and the ritual meaning of the latter sport indicates that, all through Polynesia, there is faith in the possibility of such an ascent and the corresponding desire.[95] Finally, as everywhere else, the sorcerers and prophets in Polynesia are believed to be able to fly and to traverse vast distances in the twinkling of an eye.[96]

We must also touch upon another category of myths, which, without belonging to shamanic ideology proper, nevertheless reveal an essential shamanic theme; that of a hero's descent to the underworld to bring back the soul of a beloved woman. Thus the Maori hero Hutu goes down to the underworld in search of the princess Pare who had committed suicide for his sake. Hutu encounters the Great Lady of Night, who reigns over the Land of Shades, and gains her help; she tells him the road to follow and gives him a basket of food so that he need not touch the viands of

93 All the myths and an abundant documentation will be found in Kathaine Luomala, *Maui-of-a-Thousand-Tricks: His Oceanic and European Biographers*. On the ascension theme, see N. K. Chadwick, "Notes on Polynesian Mythology."

94 Handy, *Polynesian Religion*, p. 83. For descent into the underworld in the form of a pigeon, see N. K. Chadwick, "The Kite: a Study in Polynesian Tradition," p. 478.

95 See ibid., passim. See also below, pp. 477 ff.   96 Handy, p. 164.

the underworld. Hutu finds Pare among the shades and succeeds in bringing her back to earth with him. The hero then replaces her soul in her body, and the princess returns to life. In the Marquesas Islands there is the tale of the hero Kena's sweetheart, who had also killed herself because her lover had scolded her. Kena goes down to the underworld, catches her soul in a basket, and returns it to earth. In the Mangaian version Kura kills herself accidentally and is brought back from the underworld by her husband. In Hawaii the roles of the New Zealand Hutu and Pare are taken by Hiku and Kawelu. Forsaken by her lover, Kawelu dies of grief; Hiku goes down to the underworld by a vine, captures Kawelu's soul, shuts it up in a coconut, and returns to earth. The restoration of the soul to the lifeless body is accomplished as follows: Hiku forces it into the great toe of the left foot, then, by massaging the sole of the foot and the calf, finally makes it enter the heart. Before going below, Hiku had taken the precaution to anoint his body with rancid oil, so that he should smell like a corpse; Kena's neglect to do this had caused his instant discovery by the Lady of the Under world.[97]

As we see, these Polynesian myths of descent to the lower regions are closer to the myth of Orpheus than to shamanism proper. And we have found the same myth in North American folklore. We may note, however, that Kawelu's soul is restored to the body in accordance with shamanic procedure. And the capture of the soul in the underworld is reminiscent in itself of the way that shamans seek and catch the souls of the sick, whether they have already entered the land of the dead or have simply strayed far away. As for the "smell of the living," it is a folklore theme that is widely disseminated, whether in connection with myths of the Orpheus type or with shamanic descents.

Nevertheless, the majority of Polynesian shamanic phenomena are of a more special type; for the most part they amount to a possession by gods or spirits, usually sought by a priest or a prophet

97 Handy, pp. 81 ff.   98 Above, pp. 310 ff.

ut which may also occur spontaneously. Possession and inspira-
ion by the gods are the specialty of the *taula*, the prophet, but
re also practiced by priests, and in Samoa and Tahiti are acces-
ible to all heads of families: the patron god of the family commonly
peaks through the mouth of its living head.[99] A *taula atua* claims
he ability to communicate with his dead brothers. He declares that
e can see them clearly, and when they appear he loses conscious-
ess.[100] In his case it is his brother's spirits who reveal the causes
f an illness and the remedies for it, or tell him if the patient is
loomed. But there is the memory of a time when the shaman was
"possessed by the gods" alone and not, as he is today, by "the
pirits." [101] Although chiefly representing the ritualistic tradition
f the religion, the priests (*tohunga*) are not without ecstatic ex-
eriences; they are even obliged to learn the arts of magic and
orcery. A. Fornander mentions ten "colleges of priests" in Ha-
vaii: three specialize in sorcery, two in necromancy, one in divina-
ion, one in medicine and surgery, one in building temples.[102] What
ornander called "colleges" were more nearly different classes of
xperts, but his observation shows that the priests also received a
nagical and medical instruction that, in other regions, was the
rerogative of shamans.

Indeed, magical cures are practiced both by the *taula* and the
ohunga. The Maori priest, summoned to a sickbed, first tries to
iscover the road by which the evil spirit came from the under-
vorld; to do so, he plunges his head into water. The road is usu-
lly the stem of a plant, and the *tohunga* gathers it and puts it on
he patient's head; he then recites incantations to make the spirit
eave its victim and return to the lower regions.[103] In Mangareva,
o, it is the priests who undertake cures. Sickness being usually
rought on through possession by a god of the Viriga family, the
elatives immediately consult a priest; he makes a little canoe of

99 Handy, p. 136.
100 E. M. Loeb, "The Shaman of Niue," pp. 399 ff.
101 Ibid., p. 394.   102 Handy, p. 150.
103 Ibid., p. 244.

wood and carries it to the patient's house, imploring the god-spirit to leave the body and board the boat.[104]

As we said, possession by gods or spirits is a marked characteristic of the Polynesian ecstatic religion. As long as they are possessed, prophets, priests, or mere mediums are considered to be divine incarnations and are treated accordingly. The inspired are like "vessels" into which the gods and spirits enter. The Maori term *waka* clearly indicates that the inspired man carries the god in him as a canoe carries its owner.[105] The manifestations of the incarnation of the god or spirit resemble those observed everywhere else. After a preliminary stage of calm concentration comes a frantic state during which the medium speaks in a falsetto voice interrupted by spasms; his words are oracular and determine the action to be taken. For mediums are consulted not only to learn what kind of sacrifice such-and-such a god desires but also before beginning a war, setting out on a long journey, and other critical undertakings. The same method is employed to discover the cause and cure of an illness or the perpetrator of a theft.

It is not necessary to cite the material accumulated by the early

104 Te Rangi Hiroa (Peter H. Buck), *Ethnology of Mangareva*, pp. 475 f. It should, however, be noted that in Mangareva the priests are called *taura*, a word corresponding to *taula* of Samoa and Tonga, *kaula* of Hawaii, and *tau* of the Marquesas, terms that, as we saw, designate the "prophets" (cf. Handy, pp. 159 ff.). But in Mangareva the religious dichotomy is not expressed by the pair *tohunga* (priest)–*taula* (prophet) but by the pair *taura* (priest) and *akarata* (diviner); cf. Honoré Laval, *Mangareva. L'Histoire ancienne d'un peuple polynésien*, pp. 309 ff. Both are possessed by gods, but the *akarata* obtain their title after a sudden inspiration followed by a short consecration ceremony (cf. Hiroa, pp. 446 ff.), whereas the *taura* undergo a long initiation in a *marae*, a sacred stone enclosure (ibid., p. 443). Laval (p. 309) and other authorities state that there is no initiation for the *akarata*; but Hiroa (pp. 446 ff.) has shown that the installation ceremony (which lasts five days and during which the priest invites the gods to dwell in the neophyte's body) has the structure of an initiation. The great difference between the "priests" and the "diviners" consists in the strong ecstatic vocation of the latter.

105 Handy, p. 160.

travelers and the ethnologists on the phenomenology of inspiration and possession in Polynesia. The classic descriptions will be found in W. Mariner, W. Ellis, C. S. Stewart, and others.[106] We will only note that mediumistic séances for private purposes take place at night [107] and are less frenetic than the great public séance, held in broad daylight, to learn the will of the gods. The difference between a person spontaneously and temporarily "possessed" and a prophet lies in the fact that the latter is always "inspired" by the same god or the same spirit, and that he can incarnate it at will. A new prophet is consecrated only after he has been officially authenticated by the spirit-god who dominates him; he is asked questions and must deliver oracles.[108] He is not recognized as a *taula* or *karata* until he has proved the authenticity of his ecstatic experiences. If he is the representative (or, rather, the incarnation) of a great god, his house and himself become *tapu* and he enjoys high social standing, equaling or even exceeding the political chief in prestige. Becoming the incarnation of a great god is sometimes shown by obtaining supernatural magical powers; the Marquesan prophet, for example, can fast for a month, sleep under water, see things taking place at vast distances, and the like.[109]

To these great classes of magico-religious personages must be added the sorcerers or necromancers (*tahu, kahu,* etc.), whose

---

106 Séances in Tahiti: William Ellis, *Polynesian Researches* (3rd edn.), I, 73–74 (convulsions, cries, incomprehensible words that the priests must interpret, etc.); Society Islands: ibid., I, 370 ff.; J. A. Moerenhout, *Voyages aux îles du Grand Océan,* I, 482; Marquesas: C. S. Stewart, *A Visit to the South Seas,* I, 70; Tonga: W. Mariner, *An Account of the Natives of the Tonga Islands,* I, 86 ff., 101 ff., etc.; Samoa, Hervey Islands: R. W. Williamson, *Religion and Social Organization in Central Polynesia,* pp. 112 ff.; Pukapuka: Ernest and Pearl Beaglehole, *Ethnology of Pukapuka,* pp. 323 ff.; Mangareva: Hiroa, *Ethnology of Mangareva,* pp. 444 ff.

107 See the description of one of these séances in Handy, *The Native Culture in the Marquesas,* pp. 265 ff.

108 In Mangareva: Hiroa, p. 444; Marquesas: Ralph Linton, "Marquesan Culture."

109 Linton, p. 188.

specialty is possessing a familiar spirit, which they obtain by extracting it from the body of a dead friend or relative.[110] Like the prophets and priests, they are healers; they are also consulted to discover thieves (e.g., in the Society Islands), though they often undertake operations in black magic as well. (In Hawaii the *kahu* can destroy his victim's soul by crushing it between his fingers;[111] in Pukapuka the *tangata wotu* has the power to see souls while they wander about during sleep, and he kills them because they may be preparing to cause illness.[112]) The essential difference between the sorcerers and the inspired is that the former are not "possessed" by the gods or spirits, but instead have at command a spirit who works magic (in the full sense) for them. In the Marquesas, for instance a clear distinction is made between (1) the ritualistic priests, (2) the inspired priests, (3) those possessed by spirits, and (4) the sorcerers. The "possessed" also have regular relations with particular spirits, but such relations do not confer magical powers on them. These are the exclusive monopoly of the sorcerers, who may be chosen by spirits or acquire power through study and the murder of a close relative, whose soul becomes their servant.[11]

Finally, it should also be mentioned that certain shamanic powers are transmitted by heredity in certain families. The best-known example is power to walk on burning coals or stones heated white hot, an ability confined to some Fijian families.[114] The genuineness of such feats is beyond doubt; a number of competent observers have described the "miracle" after taking all possible measures to ensure objectivity. What is even more remarkable, the Fijian sha

---

110 On the magicians and their art, see Handy, *Polynesian Religion* (Hawaii, Marquesas), pp. 235 ff.; Williamson, pp. 238 ff. (Society Islands) Hiroa, pp. 473 ff. (Mangareva); Beaglehole, p. 326 (Pukapuka); etc.

111 Handy, *Polynesian Religion*, p. 236.

112 Beaglehole, p. 326.   113 Linton, p. 192.

114 Cf., for example, W. E. Gudgeon, "Te Umu-ti, or Fire-Walking Ceremony," and other accounts excellently analyzed by E. de Martino *Il mondo magico*, pp. 29 ff. On shamanism in Fiji, see B. Thompson, *The Fijians*, pp. 158 ff.

mans can confer insensibility to fire on the entire tribe and even on outsiders. The same phenomenon has been recorded elsewhere—for example, in southern India.[115] If we remember that Siberian shamans are reputed to swallow burning coals, that "heat" and "fire" are magical attributes occurring in the most archaic strata of primitive societies, that similar phenomena are found in the higher systems of magic and contemplative techniques of Asia (Yoga, tantrism, etc.), we may conclude that the "power over fire" exhibited by certain Fijian families belongs to true shamanism. Nor is this power confined to the Fiji Islands. Though to a lesser degree and without such inclusive manifestations, insensibility to fire has been documented in the case of numerous Polynesian prophets and persons subject to inspiration.

The facts that we have reviewed lead to the conclusion that shamanic techniques in the strict sense are found in Polynesia in more or less sporadic fashion ("fire-walking ceremony" in Fiji, magical flight of sorcerers and prophets, etc.) and survive half forgotten in ceremonies that are becoming mere sports (kiteflying). The conception of sickness is not that of shamanism proper (flight of the soul); the Polynesians attribute sickness to an object introduced into the body by a god or a spirit, or to possession. And treatment consists in extracting the magical object or expelling the spirit. The introduction and, correspondingly, the extraction of a magical object form part of a complex that is apparently to be considered archaic. But in Polynesia healing is not the exclusive prerogative of the medicine man, as it is in Australia and elsewhere; the extreme frequency of possession by gods and spirits has made it possible for healers to proliferate. As we have seen, priests, inspired persons, medicine men, sorcerers can all undertake magical cures. In fact, the ease and frequency of quasi-mediumistic possession have finally extended it far beyond the categories and functions of the "specialists in the sacred"; in the face of

115 Cf. Olivier Leroy, *Les Hommes salamandres. Recherches et réflexions sur incombustibilité du corps humain*, passim.

this collective mediumship, the traditionalistic and ritualistic institution of the priesthood has itself been obliged to change its ways. Only the sorcerers have resisted possession, and in all probability any vestiges of the archaic shamanic ideology are to be sought in their secret traditions.[116]

116 We have omitted Africa; to present the shamanic elements that it might be possible to identify in the various African religions and magico-religious techniques would lead us too far. On African shamanism, see Adolf Friedrich, *Afrikanische Priestertümer*, pp. 292–325; S. F. Nadel, "A Study of Shamanism in the Nuba Mountains." On the various magical ideologies and techniques, cf., among others, E. E. Evans-Pritchard, *Witchcraft, Oracles and Magic among the Azande*; H. Baumann, "Likundu, die Sektion der Zauberkraft"; C. M. N. White, "Witchcraft, Divination and Magic among the Balovale Tribes."

CHAPTER ELEVEN

Shamanic
Ideologies and Techniques
AMONG THE INDO-EUROPEANS

Preliminary Remarks

L I K E all other peoples, the Indo-Europeans had their magicians and ecstatics. As everywhere else, these magicians and ecstatics filled a definite function in the total magico-religious life of the society. In addition, both the magician and the ecstatic sometimes had a mythical model. Thus, for example, Varuṇa has been seen as a "great magician" and Odin as (among many other things!) a particular type of ecstatic: "Wodan, id est furor," wrote Adam of Bremen, in which lapidary definition shamanic overtones have inevitably been detected.

But is it possible to speak of an Indo-European shamanism in the sense in which we speak of an Altaic or Siberian shamanism? The answer to this question depends partly on the meaning that we give the word "shamanism." If we understand by it any ecstatic phenomenon and any magical technique whatever, it goes without saying that a number of "shamanic" features will be found among the Indo-Europeans, just as, to repeat, they will be found among any other ethnic or cultural group. To discuss, even with the utmost brevity, the immense documentation on the magico-ecstatic techniques that have been found among all the Indo-European peoples would require a special volume and competence in many disciplines. Fortunately, it is not necessary for us to attack this problem, which far exceeds the scope of the present study. Our role is limited solely to discovering to what extent the various Indo-European peoples preserve vestiges of an ideology and technique that are shamanic in the strict sense of the term, that is, which exhibit one of its essential features: ascent to heaven, descent to the underworld to bring back the patient's soul or to escort the dead, evocation and incarnation of the "spirits" in order to undertake the ecstatic journey, "mastery over fire," and so on.

Such vestiges remain among almost all the European peoples and we shall present them in a moment; there are probably more of them, for we do not pretend to have exhausted the documentation. However, two preliminary remarks are in order. To repeat what we have already said in regard to other peoples and other religions, the presence of one or more shamanic elements in an Indo-European religion does not justify regarding that religion as dominated by shamanism or as having a shamanic structure. Secondly, it must also be remembered that, if care is taken to distinguish shamanism from other "primitive" magics and techniques of ecstasy, the shamanic survivals that may be detected here and there in a "developed" religion in no way imply a negative value judgment in respect to such survivals or to the whole of the religion into which they are incorporated. It is proper to stress this point, because modern ethnographic literature tends to treat shamanism as something of an aberrant phenomenon, whether in confusing it with "possession" or in choosing to emphasize its degenerate aspects. As this study has shown more than once, in many cases shamanism is now found in a state of disintegration, but nothing justifies regarding this late phase as representing *the* shamanic phenomenon as a whole.

Attention must also be drawn to another possible confusion to which the investigator lays himself open as soon as, instead of making his subject of study a "primitive" religion, he approaches the religion of a people whose history is far richer in cultural exchanges, in innovations, in creations. There is the danger that he will fail to recognize what "history" may have done to an archaic magico-religious schema, the extent to which its spiritual content has been transformed and re-evaluated, and will continue to read the same "primitive" meaning into it. A single example will suffice to show the danger of this sort of confusion. It is well known that many shamanic initiations involve "dreams" in which the future shaman sees himself tortured and cut to pieces by demons and ghosts. Now, similar scenarios are found in Christian hagiography, notably in the legend of the temptations of St. Anthony; demons torture, bruise, dismember the saints, carry them high into the air, and so on. In the last analysis, such temptations are equivalent to an "initiation," for it is through them that the saints transcend the human condition, that is, distinguish themselves from the profane masses. But a little perspicacity suffices to recognize the difference in spiritual content that separates the two "initiatory schemas," however close together they may seem to be on the plane of typology. Unfortunately, if it is easy to distinguish the demonic tortures of a Christian saint from those of a shaman, the distinction is less apparent between the latter and a saint of a non-Christian religion. Now, it must always be borne in mind that an archaic schema is able constantly to renew its spiritual content. We have already encountered a considerable number of shamanic ascents to the world above, and shall cite others later; we have also seen that such ascents represent an ecstatic experience that is nowise "aberrant" in itself; that, on the contrary, this very ancient magico-religious schema, documented among all primitives, is perfectly consistent, "noble," "pure," and, in the last analysis, "beautiful." Hence, on the plane on which we have placed the shamanic ascent to the sky, there would be nothing pejorative in saying, for example, that Mohammed's ascension exhibits shamanic content. Nevertheless, despite all the typological similarities, it is impossible to assimilate the ecstatic ascension of Mohammed to the ascension of an Altaic or Buryat shaman. The content, the meaning, and the spiritual orientation of the prophet's ecstatic experience presuppose certain mutations in religious values that make it irreducible to the general type of ascension.[1]

1 On the different evaluations of ascension, cf. Eliade, *Myths, Dreams and Mysteries*, pp. 99–122.

These few preliminary observations were necessary at the beginning of this chapter, which will treat of peoples and civilizations infinitely more complex than those that have engaged our attention so far. We have very little certain knowledge concerning the religious prehistory and protohistory of the Indo-Europeans, that is, concerning the periods during which the spiritual horizon of this ethnic group was presumably comparable to that of a number of the peoples we have discussed. The documents at our disposition bear witness to religions already elaborated, systematized, sometimes even fossilized. It is our task to recognize, in this enormous mass, the myths, rites, or techniques of ecstasy that may have a shamanic structure. As we shall see in a moment, such myths, rites, and techniques of ecstasy are attested, in more or less "pure" form, among all the Indo-European peoples. But we do not believe it possible to find in shamanism the dominant in the magico-religious life of the Indo-Europeans. The fact is the more surprising because, morphologically and in its general outlines, the Indo-European religion resembles that of the Turko-Tatars—supremacy of the celestial God, absence or minor importance of goddesses, cult of fire, and so on.

The difference between the religions of the two groups on this particular point of the predominance or lesser importance of shamanism could be briefly explained by two facts pregnant with consequences. The first is the great innovation of the Indo-Europeans, brilliantly illuminated by the studies of Georges Dumézil: divine tripartition, corresponding both to a particular organization of society and to a systematic conception of magico-religious life, each type of divinity having a particular function and a corresponding mythology. Such a systematic reorganization of magico-religious life in its entirety, already basically accomplished at a period when the Proto-Indo-Europeans had not yet separated, certainly implied an inclusion of the shamanic ideology and experiences. But this inclusion was at the cost of a specialization and, finally, a limitation in shamanic powers; these found their place beside other magico-religious powers and sources of prestige; they were no longer alone in employing the techniques of ecstasy, they no longer dominated the entire horizon of the tribal spirituality. It is in somewhat this way that we conceive the shamanic traditions to have been "put in their place" by the work of organizing magico-religious beliefs, a task that had already been accomplished during the period of Indo-European unity. To employ Georges Dumézil's schemas, the shamanic traditions were principally grouped about the mythical figure of the terrifying Sovereign, whose archetype seems to be Varuṇa, the Master of Magic, the great "Binder." This, of course, implies neither that all shamanic elements crystallized solely around the figure of the terrible Sovereign, nor that, within the Indo-European religion, these shamanic elements exhausted all the magical or ecstatic ideologies and techniques. On the contrary, there were certainly both magics and techniques of ecstasy completely independent of any "shamanic" structure—for example, the magic of warriors or the magic and techniques of ecstasy connected with the Great Mother Goddesses and agricultural mysticism, which were in no way shamanic.

The second factor that, in our opinion, contributed to differentiate the Indo-Europeans from the Turko-Tatars in respect to the importance accorded to shamanism was the influence of the Oriental and Mediterranean civilizations of agrarian and urban type. Directly or indirectly, this influence affected the Indo-European peoples in proportion as they approached the Near East. The transformations undergone by the religious heritage of the various Greek immigrations that swept from the Balkans toward the Aegean are an indication of the extremely complex phenomenon of assimilation and re-evaluation that resulted from contact with a culture of the agrarian and urban type.

Techniques of Ecstasy among the Ancient Germans

In the religion and mythology of the ancient Germans some details are comparable to the conceptions and techniques of North Asian shamanism. We will cite the most striking instances. The figure and the myth of Odin—the Terrible Sovereign and Great Magician [2]—display several strangely "shamanic" features. To acquire the occult knowledge of runes, Odin spends nine days and nights hanging in a tree.[3] Some Germanists have seen an initiation rite in this; Otto Höfler [4] even compares it to the initiatory tree-climbing of Siberian shamans. The tree in which Odin "hanged" himself can only be the Cosmic Tree, Yggdrasil; its name, by the way, means the "steed of Ygg (Odin)." In Nordic tradition the gibbet is called the "hanged man's horse" [5] and certain Germanic initiation rites included the symbolic "hanging" of the candidate, for this custom is abundantly documented elsewhere.[6] But Odin also ties his horse to Yggdrasil, and the occurrence of this mythical theme in North and Central Asia is well known.[7]

Odin's steed, Sleipnir, has eight hooves, and it is he who carries his master, and even other gods (e.g., Hermódhr), to the underworld. Now, the eight-hoofed horse is the shamanic horse par excellence; it is found among the Siberians, as well as elsewhere (e.g., the Muria), always in connection with the shaman's ecstatic experience.[8] It is probable, as Höfler [9] supposes, that Sleipnir is the mythical archetype of a many-footed hobbyhorse that played an important part in the secret cult of the men's society.[10] But this is a magico-religious phenomenon that goes beyond the bounds of shamanism.

Describing Odin's ability to change shape at will, Snorri writes:

2 On this see G. Dumézil, *Mythes et dieux des Germains*, pp. 19 ff., where the essential bibliography will be found. On the shamanism of the ancient Germans, cf. Jan de Vries, *Altgermanische Religionsgeschichte* (2nd edn.) I, 326 ff.

3 *Hávamál*, vv. 138 ff.

4 *Kultische Geheimbünde der Germanen*, I, 234 ff.

5 Ibid., p. 224.

6 Cf. the bibliographical indications given in ibid., p. 225, n. 228.

7 See above, p. 261.   8 See below, pp. 468 f.

9 *Kultische Geheimbünde*, I, 46 ff., 52.

10 On the relations smith–"horse"–secret society, cf. ibid., pp. 52 ff. The same religious complex is found in Japan; cf. Alexander Slawik, "Kultische Geheimbünde der Japaner und Germanen," p. 695.

"His body lay as though he were asleep or dead, and he then became a bird or a beast, a fish or a dragon, and went in an instant to far-off lands. . . ." [11] This ecstatic journey of Odin in animal forms may properly be compared to the transformations of shamans into animals; for, just as the shamans fought one another in the shape of bulls or eagles, Nordic traditions present several combats between magicians in the shape of walruses or other animals; and during the combat their bodies remained inanimate, just as Odin's did during his ecstasy.[12] Of course, such beliefs are also found outside of shamanism proper, but the comparison with the practices of the Siberian shamans is inescapable. And all the more so since other Scandinavian beliefs tell of helping spirits in the shape of animals visible only to the shamans,[13] which is even more clearly reminiscent of shamanic ideas. Indeed, we may ask if Odin's two crows, Huginn ("Thought") and Muninn ("Memory") do not represent, in highly mythicized form, two helping spirits in the shape of birds, which the Great Magician sent (in true shamanic fashion!) to the four corners of the world.[14]

11 *Ynglinga Saga*, VII (trs. E. Monson and A. H. Smith, p. *5*); cf. the commentary by Hilda R. Ellis, *The Road to Hel: a Study of the Conception of the Dead in Old Norse Literature*, pp. 122 ff.

12 *Saga Hjálmthérs ok Olvérs*, XX, cited by Ellis, p. 123. Cf. ibid., p. 124, the story of the two women magicians who, while they remained inanimate on the "incantation platform" (*seidhjallr*), were seen on the sea, at a very great distance, riding a whale; they were pursuing the boat of a hero and trying to wreck it, but the hero succeeded in breaking their spines and at that precise moment the sorceresses fell from the platform and broke their backs. *Sturlaugs Saga Starfsama*, XII, tells of two magicians fighting each other in the shape of dogs and then of eagles (ibid., p. 126).

13 Ibid., p. 128.

14 Ibid., p. 127. Among Odin's shamanic attributes, Alois Closs ("Die Religion des Semnonenstammes," pp. 665 ff., n. 62) further reckons the two wolves, the name "Father," which was given him (*galdrs fadir* = the father of magic; *Baldrs draumar*, 3, 3), the "motif of intoxication," and the Valkyries. N. K. Chadwick had long since seen in the Valkyries mythical creatures far closer to "werewolves" than to celestial fairies; cf. Ellis, p. 77. But all these motifs are not necessarily "shamanic." The Valkyries are psychopomps and sometimes play the role of the "celestial wives" or "spirit wives" of the Siberian shamans; but we have seen that this latter complex extends

Odin is also the institutor of necromancy. On his horse Sleipnir, he enters Hel and bids a long-dead prophetess rise from the grave to answer his questions.[15] Others later practiced this kind of necromancy,[16] which, of course, is not shamanism in the strict sense but belongs to a horizon that is extremely close to it. The scene of divination with the mummified head of Mimir [17] should also be mentioned, suggesting, as it does, the Yukagir method of divination by the skulls of ancestral shamans.[18]

A prophet becomes such by sitting on tombs, a "poet" (that is, one inspired) by sleeping on a poet's grave.[19] The same custom is found among the Celts: the *fili* (poet) ate raw bull's flesh, drank the blood, and then slept wrapped in the hide; during his sleep "invisible friends" gave him the answer to the question that was troubling him.[20] Or again, a man slept on the grave of a relative or an ancestor, and became a prophet.[21] Typologically, these customs come close to the initiation or inspiration of future shamans and magicians who spend the night beside corpses or in graveyards. The underlying idea is the same: the dead know the future, they can reveal hidden things, and so forth. Dream sometimes plays a similar role; the poet of the *Gísla Saga* [22] reports the fate after death of certain privileged persons, of which he has learned in dream.

We cannot here examine the Celtic and Germanic myths and legends devoted to ecstatic journeys in the beyond, and especially to descents to the underworld. We will merely remark that neither the Celtic nor the Germanic ideas concerning life after death were

---

beyond the sphere of shamanism and has elements both of the mythology of Woman and the mythology of Death. On "shamanism" among the ancient Germans, see Closs, "Die Religion der Germanen in ethnologischer Sicht," pp. 296 ff.; Horst Kirchner, "Ein archäologischer Beitrag zur Urgeschichte des Schamanismus," p. 247, n. 25 (bibliography).

15 *Baldrs draumar*, vv. 4 ff.; Ellis, p. 152.   16 Ibid., pp. 154 ff.

17 *Völuspa*, v. 46; *Ynglinga Saga*, IV; Ellis, pp. 156 ff.

18 See above, p. 245.   19 Ellis, pp. 105 ff., 108

20 Thomas F. O'Rahilly, *Early Irish History and Mythology*, pp. 323 ff. See also some bibliographical references on Celtic shamanism in Kirchner, p. 247, n. 24.

21 Cf. the texts in Ellis, p. 109.   22 XXII ff.; Ellis, p. 74

free from inconsistencies. The traditions mention several destinations for the dead, coinciding on this point with the faith of other peoples in a variety of destinies after death. But Hel, the underworld proper, lies, according to the *Grimnismál*, beneath one of the roots of Yggdrasil, that is, at the "Center of the World." We even hear of nine subterranean levels; a giant professes to have obtained his wisdom by descending through "nine worlds below." [23] Here we have the Central Asian cosmological schema of seven or nine hells corresponding to seven or nine heavens. But what seems to us more significant is the giant's claim: he becomes "wise"—that is, clairvoyant—after a descent to the underworld, a descent which, by that fact, we are entitled to regard as an initiation.

In the *Gylfaginning* (*Prose Edda*),[24] Snorri recounts how Hermódhr, riding Odin's steed Sleipnir, descends to Hel to bring back Balder's soul.[25] This type of infernal descent is definitely shamanic. As in the various non-European variants of the Orpheus myth, in Balder's case the descent did not produce the expected result. That such a feat was considered possible, we are further informed by the *Chronicon Norvegiae*: A shaman was trying to bring back the soul of a woman who had died suddenly, when he fell dead himself from a terrible wound in his stomach. A second shaman entered the scene and revived the woman, whereupon she related that she had seen the first shaman's spirit crossing a lake in the form of a walrus, and that someone had hit him with a weapon, the effect of the blow being visible on the corpse.[26]

Odin himself goes down to the underworld on his horse Sleipnir to revive the volva and learn Balder's fate. A third example of such a descent is found in Saxo Grammaticus,[27] with Hadingus as hero.[28] A woman suddenly appears while the latter is at dinner and asks him to follow her. They go underground, traverse a damp and

23 Ellis, p. 83.   24 XLVIII.

25 Hermódhr rides through "dark and deep valleys" for nine nights and crosses the bridge Gjallar, which is paved with gold (Ellis, pp. 85, 171; Dumézil, *Loki*, p. 53).

26 Ellis, p. 126.   27 *Historia Danica*, I, 31.

28 See Dumézil, *La Saga de Hadingus*, passim.

shadowy region, find a beaten path along which well-dressed people are walking, then enter a sunny place where all kinds of flowers grow, and reach a river, which they cross by a bridge. They come upon two armies engaged in a battle, which the woman says goes on forever; they are warriors fallen on the field who are continuing their fight.[29] Finally they come to a wall, which the woman tries to cross; she kills a cock that she had brought and throws it over the wall; the cock comes back to life, for, a moment later, they hear it crowing on the other side of the wall. Unfortunately, Saxo breaks off his account here.[30] But he has said enough for us to find, in this descent of Hadingus under the guidance of a mysterious woman, the familiar mythical motif: the road of the dead, the river, the bridge, the initiatory obstacle (the wall). The cock that revives as soon as it reaches the farther side of the wall seems to indicate the belief that at least certain privileged persons (that is, "initiates") can count on the possibility of a "return to life" after death.[31]

Germanic mythology and folklore preserve yet other accounts of underworld descents, in which "initiatory ordeals" can likewise be found (e.g., crossing a "wall of flame," etc.), but not necessarily the type of the shamanic descent. As the *Chronicon Norvegiae* attests, the latter was known to the Nordic magicians, and if we take their other exploits into consideration we may conclude that there is a quite marked resemblance to the Siberian shamans.

29 This is the "Wütende Heer," a mythical theme on which see Karl Meisen, *Die Sagen vom Wütenden Heer und Wilden Jäger*; Dumézil, *Mythes et dieux*, pp. 79 ff.; Höfler, *Kultische Geheimbünde*, pp. 154 ff.

30 Ellis, p. 172.

31 This detail recorded by Saxo Grammaticus could be compared with the funeral ritual of a Scandinavian ("Rus") chief witnessed by the Arabian traveler Ahmed ibn Fadlan in 921, by the Volga. One of the women slaves before being immolated to follow her master, performed the following rite: the men lifted her up three times so that she could look over the frame of a door, and she told what she saw. The first time, it was her father and mother; the second, all her relatives; and the third, her master "seated in paradise." She was then given a hen and she cut off its head and threw it into the funerary boat (the boat that was soon to become her own pyre). Cf. the texts and bibliography in Ellis, pp. 45 ff.

We shall do no more than mention the "wild beast warriors," the *berserkir* who magically appropriated animal "fury" and transformed themselves into beasts of prey.[32] This technique of martial ecstasy, attested among the other Indo-European peoples and parallels to which have also been found in extra-European cultures,[33] bears only a superficial relation to shamanism in the strict sense. Initiation of the military (heroic) type is distinguished by its very structure from shamanic initiations. Magical transformation into a wild beast belongs to an ideology that extends far beyond the sphere of shamanism. Its roots will be found in the hunting rites of the paleo-Siberian peoples, and we shall see[34] what techniques of ecstasy can develop from a mystical imitation of animal behavior.

Odin, Snorri tells us, knew and used the magic called *seidhr:* by it, he could foresee the future and cause death, misfortune, or sickness. But, Snorri adds, this sorcery implied such "turpitude" that men did not practice it "without shame"; *seidhr* remained the concern of the *gydhjur* ("priestess" or "goddess"). And in the *Lokasenna* Odin is reproached with practicing *seidhr*, which is "unworthy of a man."[35] The sources speak of male magicians (*seidhmenn*) and female magicians (*seidhkonur*), and we know that Odin learned *seidhr* from the goddess Freyja.[36] So there is reason to suppose that this kind of magic was a feminine specialty—which accounts for its being considered "unworthy of a man."

In any case, the *seidhr* séances described in the text are always conducted by a *seidhkona*, a *spákona* ("clairvoyante," prophetess).

32 Dumézil: *Mythes et dieux*, pp. 79 ff.; *Horace et les Curiaces*, pp. 11 ff.

33 Cf. Dumézil, *Horace et les Curiaces*, passim; Stig Wikander, *Der arische Männerbund*, passim; G. Widengren, *Hochgottglaube im alten Iran*, pp. 324 ff.

34 Below, pp. 459 f.

35 Cf. Dag Strömbäck, *Sejd. Textstudier i nordisk religionshistoria*, pp. 33, 31 ff.; Arne Runeberg, *Witches, Demons and Fertility Magic*, p. 7. Strömbäck believes that *sejd* (*seidhr*) was borrowed by the ancient Germans from Lapp shamanism (pp. 110 ff.). Olof Pettersson is of the same opinion; cf. *Jabmek and Jabmeaimo: a Comparative Study of the Dead and the Realm of the Dead in Lappish Religion*, pp. 168 ff.

36 Jan de Vries, *Altgermanische Religionsgeschichte* (2nd edn.), I, 330 ff.

The best description is that in the *Eiriks Saga Rautha*. The *spákona* has a highly elaborated ritual costume: a blue cloak, jewels, a head-piece of black lamb with white catskins; she also carries a staff and, during the séance, sits on a rather high platform, on a cushion of chicken feathers.[37] The *seidhkona* (or volva, *spákona*) goes from farm to farm to reveal men's futures and predict the weather, the quantity of the harvest, and so on. She travels with fifteen girls and fifteen youths singing in chorus. Music plays an essential role in preparing her ecstasy. During the trance the *seidhkona*'s soul leaves her body and travels through space; she usually assumes the form of an animal, as is shown by the episode cited above.[38]

Several features connect *seidhr* with the classic shamanic séance:[39] the ritual costume, the importance of chorus and music, ecstasy. But we do not consider it necessary to regard *seidhr* as shamanism in the strict sense; "mystical flight" is a leitmotiv of

37 Strömbäck, pp. 50 ff.; Runeberg, pp. 9 ff.

38 P. 381, n. 12.

39 Strömbäck sees in *seidhr* a shamanism in the strict sense; cf. Å. Ohl-marks' critique, *Studien zum Problem des Schamanismus*, pp. 310 ff.; id "Arktischer Schamanismus und altnordischer Seidhr." On the vestiges of Nordic shamanism, cf. also Carl Martin Edsman, "Återspeglar Voluspå 2:5–8 ett shamanistik Ritual eller en keltisk Åldersvers?" For everything concerning magical conceptions among the Scandinavians, see Magnus Olsen "Le Prêtre-magicien et le dieu-magicien dans la Norvège ancienne." We may add that certain "shamanic" characteristics, in the broad sense of the term, are discernible in the highly complex figure of Loki; on this god, see Dumézil's excellent study, *Loki*. Transformed into a mare, Loki bred with the stallion Svadhilfari and gave birth to the eight-hoofed horse Sleipnir (see the texts in ibid., pp. 28 ff.). Loki can take various animal shapes: seal salmon, etc. He engenders the wolf and the world snake. He also flies through the air after donning a costume of falcon feathers; but this magical garment belongs not to him but to Freyja (ibid., p. 35; see also pp. 25, 31). Re-membering that Freyja taught Odin *seidhr*, we may compare this tradition of the art of magical flight taught by a goddess (or sorceress) with the similar Chinese legends (see below, pp. 448 f.). Freyja, mistress of *seidhr*, owns a magic feather garment that enables her to fly in the manner of shamans Loki's magic seems to be of a blacker variety, its meaning being clearly indicated by his animal transformations. We could not consult W. Muster's dissertation, "Der Schamanismus und seine Spuren in der Saga, im deutschen Brauch, Märchen und Glauben."

magic everywhere and especially of European sorcery. The specifically shamanic themes—descent to the underworld to bring back a patient's soul or to escort the deceased—although attested, as we have seen, in Nordic magic, are not a primary element in the *seidhr* séance. Instead, the latter seems to concentrate on divination, that is, belongs rather to "minor magic."

Ancient Greece

We shall not here attempt to study the various ecstatic traditions attested in ancient Greece.[40] We will only refer to the documents whose morphology may approximate to shamanism in the strict sense. There is no need to discuss the Dionysian Bacchanalia simply because the classical authors describe the insensibility of the *Bakchai;*[41] nor to discuss *enthousiasmos*, the various oracular techniques,[42] necromancy, or the conception of Hades. In all these things, of course, certain motifs and techniques similar to those employed in shamanism will be found; but such coincidences are explained by the survival, in ancient Greece, of magical conceptions and archaic techniques of ecstasy that are of almost universal occurrence. Nor will we discuss the myths and legends of the centaurs [43]

40 Cf. Erwin Rohde, *Psyche: the Cult of Souls and Belief in Immortality among the Greeks*, pp. 258 ff., 284 ff.; Martin P. Nilsson, *Geschichte der griechischen Religion*, I, especially pp. 578 ff. Recently, E. R. Dodds has seen Scythian shamanism as playing an important part in the history of Greek spirituality; cf. *The Greeks and the Irrational*, ch. v ("The Greek Shamans and the Origin of Puritanism"), pp. 135 ff. Cf. also F. M. Cornford, *Principium Sapientiae: the Origins of Greek Philosophical Thought*, pp. 88 ff.; Walter Burkert, "ΓΟΗΣ. Zum griechischen 'Schamanismus.' "

41 Cf. the texts brought together by Rohde, p. 274, n. 43.

42 There is nothing "shamanic" about the oracle of Delphi and Apollonian manticism; see the recent collection of documents and the commentaries in Pierre Amandry, *La Mantique apollinienne à Delphes. Essai sur le fonctionnement de l'Oracle* (the texts, pp. 241–60). Can the famous Delphic tripod be compared with the platform of the Germanic *seidhkona?* "But normally it is Apollo who sits on his tripod. It is only exceptionally that the Pythoness takes his place, as substitute for her god" (Amandry, p. 140).

43 See Dumézil's fine study, *Le Problème des centaures*, in which certain "shamanic" initiations in the broad sense of the term are cited.

and the first divine healers and doctors, although their traditions sometimes show faint traces of a certain primordial "shamanism." But all these traditions have already been interpreted, elaborated, re-evaluated; they form an integral part of complex mythologies and theologies; they presuppose contacts, contaminations, syntheses with the spiritual world of the Aegean and even of the East, and to study them would require many more pages than those of the present sketch.

We may note that the healers, diviners, or ecstatics who might be connected with shamanism have no relation to Dionysus. The Dionysiac mystical current appears to have an entirely different structure; Bacchic enthusiasm does not resemble shamanic ecstasy. Instead, the few figures of Greek legend who can be compared with shamanism are related to Apollo. And it is from the North, from the land of the Hyperboreans, from Apollo's country of origin, that they are said to have come to Greece.[44] Such a one, for example, is Abaris. "Carrying in his hand the golden arrow, the proof of his Apolline origin and mission, he passed through many lands dispelling sickness and pestilence by sacrifices of a magic kind, giving warning of earthquakes and other disasters."[45] A later legend shows him flying through the air on his arrow, like Musaeus.[46] The arrow, which plays a certain role in Scythian mythology and religion,[47] is a symbol of "magical flight."[48] The occurrence of the arrow in many Siberian shamanic ceremonies will be recalled in this connection.[49]

Aristeas of Proconnesus is similarly related to Apollo; he fell into ecstasy and the god "seized" his soul. He could appear at the same time in places far apart;[50] he accompanied Apollo in the form

44 W. K. C. Guthrie inclines to believe that Apollo's original home was northwestern Asia, perhaps Siberia; cf. *The Greeks and Their Gods*, p. 204.

45 Rohde, p. 300.   46 Ibid., p. 327, n. 108.

47 Cf. Karl Meuli, "Scythica," pp. 161 ff.; Dodds, pp. 140 ff.

48 On other similar legends among the Greeks, see P. Wolters, *Der geflügelte Seher*. On "magical flight," see also below, pp. 477 ff.

49 Cf., for example, above, p. 217.

50 Cf. Rohde, pp. 300 ff.; Nilsson, I, 584. On the *Arimaspeia*, a poem attributed to Aristeas, see Meuli, "Scythica," pp. 154 ff. Cf. also E. D

of a crow,[51] which is reminiscent of shamanic transformations. Hermotimos of Clazomenae had the power of leaving his body "for many years"; during this long ecstasy he journeyed to great distances and brought back "much mantic lore and knowledge of the future. At last, enemies set fire to the tenantless body of Hermotimos when his soul was away, and the latter returned no more." [52] This ecstasy shows all the features of the shamanic trance.

The legend of Epimenides of Crete must also be cited. He "slept" for a long time in the cave of Zeus on Mount Ida; there he fasted and learned prolonged ecstasies. He left the cave a master of "enthusiastic wisdom," that is, of the technique of ecstasy. "Next he journeyed through many lands bringing his health-giving arts with him, prophesying the future as an ecstatic seer, interpreting the hidden meaning of past occurrences, and as Kathartic priest expelling the daimonic evils that arose from specially foul misdeeds of the past." [53] Retirement to a cave (= descent to Hades) is a classic initiatory ordeal, but it is not necessarily "shamanic." It is in his ecstasies, his magical cures, his divinatory and prophetic powers that Epimenides approaches the shaman.

Before discussing Orpheus, we may glance at the Thracians and the Getae, the "bravest and most law-abiding of all Thracians,"

Phillips, "The Legend of Aristeas: Fact and Fancy in Early Greek Notions of East Russia, Siberia and Inner Asia," especially pp. 76–77.

51 Herodotus IV. 15.

52 Rohde, p. 301, with the sources, especially Pliny *Naturalis historia* VII. 174.

53 Rohde, p. 301. Dodds holds that the fragments of Empedocles are "the one first-hand source from which we can still form some notion of what a Greek shaman was really like; he is the last belated example of a species which with his death became extinct in the Greek world, though it still flourishes elsewhere" (*The Greeks and the Irrational*, p. 145). This interpretation has been rejected by Charles H. Kahn: "Empedocles' soul does not leave his body like that of Hermotimus and Epimenides. He does not ride on an arrow like Abaris or appear in the form of a raven like Aristeas. He is never seen in two places at the same time, and does not even descend to the Underworld like Orpheus and Pythagoras" ("Religion and Natural Philosophy in Empedocles' Doctrine of the Soul," especially pp. 30 ff.: "Empedocles among the Shamans").

according to Herodotus.[54] Although several scholars have seen a "shaman" in Zalmoxis,[55] we find no reason to accept this interpretation. The "sending of a messenger" to Zalmoxis, which took place every four years,[56] as well as the "underground chamber" into which he vanished and lived for three years, then reappeared and proved the immortality of man to the Getae,[57] are in no way shamanic. Only one document appears to indicate the existence of a Getic shamanism: it is Strabo's account [58] of the Mysian *kapnobatai*, a name that has been translated,[59] by analogy with Aristophanes' *aerobates*, as "those who walk in the clouds," [60] but which should be translated "those who walk in smoke." [61] Presumably the smoke is hemp smoke, a rudimentary means of ecstasy known to both the Thracians [62] and the Scythians. The *kapnobatai* would seem to be Getic dancers and sorcerers who used hemp smoke for their ecstatic trances.

It is certain that other "shamanic" elements persisted in the Thracian religion, but it is not always easy to identify them. We may, however, cite an example that shows the existence of the ideology and ritual of celestial ascent by means of stairs. According to Polyaenus,[63] Kosingas, priest-king of the Kebrenoi and the

54 IV. 93 (tr. A. D. Godley, p. 93).

55 Cf., for example, Meuli, "Scythica," p. 163; Alois Closs, "Die Religion des Semnonenstammes," pp. 669 ff. On the problem of this god, see Carl Clemen, "Zalmoxis"; Jean Coman, "Zalmoxis"; Ion I. Russu, "Religia Geto-Dacilor." An attempt has recently been made to rehabilitate the etymology of Zalmoxis ("the bear-god" or "the god with the bear-skin") proposed by Porphyry; cf., for example, Rhys Carpenter, *Folk Tale, Fiction and Saga in the Homeric Epics*, pp. 112 ff. ("The Cult of the Sleeping Bear") But see Alfons Nehring, "Studien zur indogermanischen Kultur und Urheimat," pp. 212 ff.

56 Herodotus IV. 94. 57 Ibid., 95.

58 VII. 3. 3; C. 296.

59 Vasile Pârvan, *Getica. O protoistorie a Daciei*, p. 162.

60 *Clouds*, vv. 225, 1503. 61 J. Coman, "Zalmoxis," p. 106

62 Provided that we thus interpret a passage of Pomponius Mela (2. 21) quoted by Rohde, p. 272, n. 39. On the Scythians, see below, pp. 394 ff.

63 *Strategematon* VII. 22.

Sykaiboai (Thracian tribes), threatened his subjects that he would ascend to the goddess Hera by a wooden ladder to complain to her of their conduct. Now, as we have often seen, symbolic ascent to heaven by stairs is typically shamanic. As we shall show later, the symbolism of stairs is also attested in other religions of the ancient Near East and the Mediterranean.

As to Orpheus, his myth displays several elements that can be compared to the shamanic ideology and techniques. The most significant is, of course, his descent to Hades to bring back the soul of his wife, Eurydice. At least one version of the myth has no mention of the final failure.[64] The possibility of wresting someone from Hades is further confirmed by the legend of Alcestis. But Orpheus also displays other characteristics of a "Great Shaman": his healing art, his love for music and animals, his "charms," his power of divination. Even his character of "culture hero" [65] is not in contradiction to the best shamanic tradition—was not the "first shaman" the messenger sent by God to defend humanity against diseases and to civilize it? A final detail of the Orpheus myth is clearly shamanic. Cut off by the bacchantes and thrown into the Hebrus, Orpheus's head floated to Lesbos, singing. It later served as an oracle,[66] like the head of Mimir. Now, the skulls of the Yukagir shamans also play a role in divination.[67]

As for Orphism itself, nothing in it suggests shamanism,[68] except perhaps the gold plates found in tombs and which were long

64 Cf. W. K. C. Guthrie, *Orpheus and Greek Religion*, p. 31.

65 See the texts appropriately brought together in Coman, "Orphée, civilisateur de l'humanité" (music, pp. 146 ff.; poetry, pp. 153 ff.; magic, medicine, pp. 157 ff.).

66 Guthrie, *Orpheus*, pp. 35 ff. On the shamanic elements in the myth of Orpheus, cf. Dodds, *The Greeks and the Irrational*, pp. 147 ff.; Å. Hultkrantz, *The North American Indian Orpheus Tradition*, pp. 236 ff.

67 Cf. above, p. 245.

68 Vittorio Macchioro (*Zagreus. Studi intorno all'orfismo*, pp. 291 ff.) compares the religious atmosphere in which Orphism arose to the Ghost-Dance Religion and other popular ecstatic movements; but in all this there are only superficial resemblances to shamanism proper.

regarded as Orphic. However, it appears that they are Orphico-Pythagorean.[69] In any case, they contain texts telling the deceased what road to take in the beyond;[70] they represent a sort of condensed "book of the dead" and are to be compared with the similar texts used in Tibet and among the Moso.[71] In these latter cases the deathbed recitation of the funerary itineraries is equivalent to mystical escort by the shaman-psychopomp. Without wishing to force the comparison, we can see in the funerary geography of the Orphico-Pythagorean plates the substitute for a soul-guiding of the shamanic type.

We will merely mention Hermes Psychopompos; the god's figure is far too complex to be reduced to a "shamanic" guide to the underworld.[72] As for Hermes' "wings," symbolic of magical flight, vague indications seem to show that certain Greek sorcerers professed to furnish the souls of the deceased with wings to enable them to fly to heaven.[73] But this is only the ancient soul-bird symbolism, complicated and contaminated by many late interpretations of Oriental origin, connected with solar cults and the idea of ascension-apotheosis.[74]

Similarly, the descents to Hades documented in Greek tradition,[75] from the most celebrated (the one that constituted Herakles

69 See Franz Cumont, *Lux perpetua*, pp. 249 ff., 406. On the problem in general, cf. Carl (Charles) Kerényi, *Pythagoras und Orpheus* (3rd edn.)

70 Cf. the texts and commentaries in Guthrie, *Orpheus*, pp. 171 ff.

71 See below, p. 446.

72 P. Raingeard, *Hermès psychagogue. Essai sur les origines du cult d'Hermès*; concerning Hermes' feathers, see pp. 389 ff.

73 Arnobius II. 33; Cumont, p. 294.

74 Cf. E. Bickermann, "Die römische Kaiserapotheose"; Josef Kroll, *Di Himmelfahrt der Seele in der Antike*; D. M. Pippidi, *Recherches sur le cult impérial*, pp. 159 ff.; id., "Apothéoses impériales et apothéose de Péré grinos." This problem goes beyond our subject, but we have touched on it in passing to show once again to what an extent an archaic symbolism (here the "flight of the soul") can be rediscovered and readapted by doctrines that appear to be innovating.

75 On all this, see Kroll, *Gott und Hölle*, pp. 363 ff. This work also examines the Oriental and Judaeo-Christian traditions of descent to the under

initiatory ordeal) to the legendary descents of Pythagoras [76] and Zoroaster,[77] have no shamanic structure whatever. We might rather cite the ecstatic experience of Er the Pamphylian, son of Armenios, recorded by Plato.[78] "Killed" on the battlefield, Er returns to life on the twelfth day, when his body is already on the pyre, and relates what he was shown in the other world. The influence of Oriental ideas and beliefs has been seen in this tale.[79] However that may be, Er's cataleptic trance resembles that of the shamans and his ecstatic journey in the beyond suggests not only the *Book of Artay Virāf* but also numerous "shamanic" experiences. Er sees, among other things, the colors of heaven and the central axis, as well as the fates of men decreed by the stars.[80] This ecstatic vision of astrological destiny can be compared with the myths, of Oriental origin, concerning the Tree of Life or the "heavenly book," on the leaves or pages of which the fates of men were inscribed. The symbolism of a "celestial book" containing fate and communicated by God to sovereigns and prophets, after their ascent to heaven, is very ancient and widely disseminated in the Orient.[81]

We see to what an extent an archaic myth or symbol can be reinterpreted: in Er's vision, the Cosmic Axis becomes the "spindle of

---

world, which show only vague resemblances to shamanism in the strict sense.

76 Cf. Isidore Lévy, *La Légende de Pythagore de Grèce en Palestine*, pp. 9 ff.

77 Cf. Joseph Bidez and Franz Cumont, *Les Mages hellénisés*, I, 113; II, 158 texts).

78 *Republic* 614B ff.

79 See the present position of scholarship and the discussion of the problem n Joseph Bidez, *Eos, ou Platon et l'orient*, pp. 43 ff.

80 *Republic* 617D–618C.

81 Cf. G. Widengren, *The Ascension of the Apostle of God and the Heavenly Book*, passim. In Mesopotamia it was the king (in his quality of anointed) who, after an ascension, received from the god the heavenly tablets or book ibid., pp. 7 ff.); in Israel, Moses received the Tables of the Law from Yahveh (ibid., pp. 22 ff.).

necessity" and astrological destiny takes the place of the "heavenly book." Yet we may note that the "situation of man" remains constant; it is still by an ecstatic journey, exactly as among the shamans and mystics of rudimentary civilizations, that Er the Pamphylian receives the revelation of the laws that govern the cosmos and life; it is by an ecstatic vision that he is brought to understand the mystery of destiny and of existence after death. The enormous gap that separates a shaman's ecstasy from Plato's contemplation, all the difference deepened by history and culture, changes nothing in this gaining consciousness of ultimate reality; it is through ecstasy that man fully realizes his situation in the world and his final destiny. We could almost speak of an archetype of "gaining existential consciousness," present both in the ecstasy of a shaman or a primitive mystic and in the experience of Er the Pamphylian and of all the other visionaries of the ancient world who, even here below, learned the fate of man beyond the grave.[8]

Scythians, Caucasians, Iranians

Herodotus [83] has left us a good description of the funerary custom of the Scythians. The funeral was followed by purifications. Hemp was thrown on heated stones and all inhaled the smoke; "the Scythians howl in joy for the vapour-bath." [84] Karl Meuli [85] has well brought out the shamanic nature of the funerary purification; the cult of the dead, the use of hemp, the vapor bath, and the "howls" compose a specific religious ensemble, the purpose of which could only be ecstasy. In this connection Meuli [86] cites the Altaic séance

82 Wilhelm Muster ("Der Schamanismus bei den Etruskern") has attempted to compare the Etruscan afterlife beliefs and journeys to Hades with shamanism. It does not seem that anything is to be gained from applying the term "shamanic" to ideas and phenomena that belong to magic in general and to the various mythologies of death.

83 IV. 71 ff.   84 IV. 75 (tr. A. D. Godley).

85 "Scythica," pp. 122 ff. Rohde had already remarked on the ecstatic role of hemp among the Scythians and the Massagetae (*Psyche*, p. 272, n. 39)

86 "Scythica," p. 124.

escribed by Radlov,[87] in which the shaman guided to the underworld the soul of a woman who had been dead forty days. The shaman-psychopomp is not found in Herodotus' description; he speaks
only of purifications following a funeral. But among a number of
Turko-Tatar peoples such purifications coincide with the shaman's
escorting the deceased to his new home, the nether regions.

Meuli has also drawn attention to the "shamanic" structure of
Scythian otherworld beliefs; to the mysterious " 'female' sickness"
that, according to a legend transmitted by Herodotus,[88] had transformed certain Scythians into "Enareis," and which this Swiss
scholar compares to the feminization of Siberian and North American shamans; [89] and to the shamanic origin of the *Arimaspeia* and
even of epic poetry in general. We will leave these theories to be
discussed by others more competent than ourselves. One fact, at
least, is certain: shamanism and ecstatic intoxication produced by
hemp smoke were known to the Scythians. As we shall see, the use
of hemp for ecstatic purposes is also attested among the Iranians,
and it is the Iranian word for hemp that is employed to designate
mystical intoxication in Central and North Asia.

It is known that the Caucasian peoples, and especially the Osset,
have preserved a number of the mythological and religious traditions of the Scythians.[90] Now, the conceptions of the afterlife held
by certain Caucasian peoples are close to those of the Iranians,
particularly in regard to the deceased crossing a bridge as narrow
as a hair, the myth of a Cosmic Tree whose top touches the sky and
whose root there is a miraculous spring, and so on.[91] Then too,

---

87 See above, pp. 209 f.   88 I. 105.

89 "Scythica," pp. 127 ff. As Meuli remarks (ibid., p. 131, n. 3), W. R.
Halliday proposed in 1910 to explain the "Enareis" by the Siberian shamans'
magical transformations into women. For another interpretation, see Dumézil, "Les 'Énarées' scythiques et la grossesse du Narte Hamyc."

90 Cf. Dumézil, *Légendes sur les Nartes*, passim, and, in general, the 4 vols.
id., *Jupiter, Mars, Quirinus*.

91 Robert Bleichsteiner, "Rossweihe und Pferderennen im Totenkult der
kaukasischen Völker," pp. 467 ff. Among the Osset "the deceased, after
taking leave of his family, mounts on horseback. On his road he soon comes to
various kinds of sentinels, to whom he must give some cakes, the same that

diviners, seers, and necromancer-psychopomps play a certain ro
among the mountain Georgian tribes. The most important of the
sorcerers are the *messulethe*; their ranks are filled for the most pa
from among women and girls. Their chief office is to escort tl
dead to the other world, but they can also incarnate them, and the
the dead speak through their mouths; psychopomp or necromance
the *messulethe* performs her task by falling into trance.[92] This grou
of characteristics is strangely rèminiscent of Altaic shamanisr
How far this state of affairs reflects beliefs and techniques of tl
"European Iranians," that is, of the Sarmato-Scythians, it is impo
sible to say.[93]

We have observed the striking resemblance between the othe
world ideas of the Caucasians and of the Iranians. For one thin
the Činvat bridge plays an essential role in Iranian funerary m
thology;[94] crossing it largely determines the destiny of the sou
and the crossing is a difficult ordeal, equivalent, in structure, to ir

---

have been placed in his grave. Then he comes to a river, over which, by w
of bridge, there is only a beam. . . . Under the steps of the just, or rath
of the truthful, the beam widens, becomes stronger, turns into a magnifice
bridge. . . ." (Dumézil, *Légendes sur les Nartes*, pp. 220–21). "There is
doubt that the 'bridge' of the beyond comes from Mazdaism, like the 'narr
bridge' of the Armenians, the 'hair bridge' of the Georgians. All the
beams, hairs, etc. have the power to widen generously for the soul of the ju
man and to narrow to the width of a sword blade for the guilty soul" (ibi
p. 202). See also below, pp. 482 ff.

92 Bleichsteiner, "Rossweihe," pp. 470 ff. These facts should be compar
with the functions of the Indonesian "mourners" (above, pp. 359 ff.).

93 Cf. also W. Nölle, "Iranisch-nordasiatische Beziehungen im Sch
manismus"; H. W. Haussig, "Theophylakts Exkurs über die skythisch
Völker," p. 360 and n. 313. On the "shamanizing" horsemen who swept ir
Europe toward the end of the second millennium and the beginning of t
first, cf. F. Altheim, *Römische Geschichte*, I, 37 ff.; H. Kirchner, "Ein arch
logischer Beitrag zur Urgeschichte des Schamanismus," pp. 248 ff. Arn
Kollantz's "Der Schamanismus der Awaren" is made almost unusable by
typographical errors.

94 Cf. N. Söderblom, *La Vie future d'après le mazdéisme*, pp. 92 ff.; H.
Nyberg: "Questions de cosmogonie et de cosmologie mazdéennes," Pt.
pp. 119 ff.; *Die Religionen des alten Iran*, pp. 180 ff.

atory ordeals. The Činvat bridge is like "a beam of many sides" [95] nd it is divided into several passages; for the just it is nine lance-ngths wide, for the ungodly it is as narrow as the edge of a zor.[96] The Činvat bridge is at the "Center." At the "middle of ne world" and "the height of a hundred men," [97] rises Kakâd-i-âitîk, the "Peak of Judgment," and the Činvat bridge runs to the lbruz from the Kakâd-i-Dâitîk—which is as much as to say that ne bridge connects earth and heaven at the "Center." Under the invat bridge is the pit of hell; [98] tradition describes it as "a con-nuation" of the Elbruz.[99]

Here we find a "classic" cosmological schema of the three cos-ic regions connected by a central axis (pillar, tree, bridge, etc.). he shamans travel freely among the three zones; the dead must oss a bridge on their journey to the beyond. We have encoun-red this funerary motif a number of times, and shall do so again. he important feature of the Iranian tradition (at least as it sur-ved after Zarathustra's reform) is that, at the crossing of the idge, there is a sort of struggle between the demons, who try to st the soul down to hell, and the tutelary spirits (whom the rela-ves of the deceased have invoked for the purpose), who resist em: Aristât, "the conductor of heavenly and earthly beings," d the good Vayu.[100] On the bridge, Vayu supports the souls of e pious; the souls of the dead also come to help them cross.[101] The nction of psychopomp assumed by the good Vayu may reflect "shamanistic" ideology.

The Gāthās make three references to this crossing of the Činvat idge.[102] In the first two passages Zarathustra, according to

95 *Dātastān i dēnīk*, 21, 3 ff. (tr. E. W. West, p. 48).
96 *Dīnkart*, IX, 20, 3.
97 *Bundahišn*, 12, 7 (tr. E. W. West, p. 36).
98 *Vidēvdat*, 3, 7.   99 *Bundahišn*, 12, 8 ff.
100 On Vayu, see G. Widengren, *Hochgottglaube im alten Iran*, pp. 188 ff.; ig Wikander, *Vayu*, I; Dumézil, *Tarpeia*, pp. 69 ff. We have cited these ree important works to warn the reader of the summary nature of our esentation; actually, Vayu's function is less clear-cut and his character cidedly more complex.
101 Söderblom, pp. 94 ff.   102 45, 10–11; 51, 13.

H. S. Nyberg's interpretation,[103] refers to himself as a psychopomp
Those who have been united to him in ecstasy will cross the bridg
with ease; the impious, his enemies, will be "for all time . .
dwellers in . . . the House of the Lie." [104] The bridge, then, i
not only the way for the dead; in addition—and we have frequentl
encountered it as such—it is the road of ecstatics. It is likewise i
ecstasy that Artay Virāf crosses the Činvat bridge in the course o
his mystical journey. According to Nyberg's interpretation, Zara
thustra would seem to have been an ecstatic very close to a "sha
man" in his religious experiences. The Swedish scholar consider
that the Gāthic term *maga* is proof that Zarathustra and his dis
ciples induced an ecstatic experience by ritual songs intoned i
chorus in a closed, consecrated space.[105] In this sacred space (*maga*
communication between heaven and earth became possible [106]—
that is, in accordance with a universally disseminated dialectic,[1]
the sacred space became a "Center." Nyberg stresses the fact tha
this communication was ecstatic, and he compares the mystical ex
perience of the "singers" with shamanism proper. This interpreta
tion has been attacked by the majority of Iranists.[108] We may ob

103 *Die Religionen*, pp. 182 ff. Near the bridge the dead man finds
beautiful girl with two dogs (*Vidēvdat*, 19, 30), an Indo-Iranian infern
complex also documented elsewhere.

104 Gāthās, 46, 11 (tr. D. F. A. Bode and P. Nanaiutty, p. 85).

105 *Die Religionen*, pp. 157, 161, 176, etc.   106 Ibid., p. 157.

107 Cf. Eliade, *Patterns in Comparative Religion*, pp. 371 ff.

108 Cf. the only partially convincing observations of Otto Paul, "Z
Geschichte der iranischen Religionen," pp. 227 ff.; Walther Wüst, "Bestar
die zoroastrische Urgemeinde wirklich aus berufsmässigen Ekstatikern ur
schamanisierenden Rinderhirten der Steppe?"; W. B. Henning, *Zoroaste
Politician or Witch-Doctor?*, passim. Recently G. Widengren has re-examine
the documents for shamanic elements in Zoroastrianism; cf. "Stand und Au
gaben der iranischen Religionsgeschichte," Pt. 2, pp. 66 f. Cf. also J. Schmid
"Das Etymon des persischen Schamane"; Jean de Menasce, "The Mysteri
and the Religion of Iran," pp. 135–48, especially pp. 146 ff.; Jacqu
Duchesne-Guillemin, *Zoroastre. Étude critique avec une traduction comment
des Gâthâ*, pp. 140 ff. It should be noted that Stig Wikander (*Der arisc
Männerbund*, pp. 64 ff.) and G. Widengren (*Hochgottglaube*, pp. 328 f
342 ff., etc.) have thoroughly demonstrated the existence of Iranian "mer

serve, however, that the ecstatic and mystical elements in the religion of Zarathustra that bear resemblances to the ideology and techniques of shamanism form part of a larger complex and hence do not imply any "shamanic" structure in Zarathustra's religious experience. The sacred space, the importance of song, mystical or symbolical communication between heaven and earth, the initiatory or funerary bridge—these various elements, although they form an integral part of Asian shamanism, precede it and go beyond it.

In any case, shamanic ecstasy induced by hemp smoke was known in ancient Iran. *Bangha* (hemp) is not referred to in the Gāthās, but the *Fravaši-yašt* mentions a certain *Pouru-bangha*, "possessor of much hemp." [109] In the *Yašt*, Ahura-Mazda is said to be "without trance and without hemp," [110] and in the *Vidēvdat* hemp is demonized. [111] This seems to us to prove complete hostility to shamanic intoxication, which was probably practiced by the Iranians and perhaps to the same extent as by the Scythians. What is certain is that Artay Virāf had his vision after drinking a mixture of wine and "narcotic of Vishtâsp," which put him to sleep for seven days and nights. [112] His sleep is more like a shamanic trance, for, the *Book of Artay Virāf* tells us, "the soul of Vîrâf went, from the body, to the Chinvat bridge of Chakât-i-Dâîtîk, and came back the seventh day, and went into the body." [113] Virāf, like Dante, visited all parts of the Mazdean paradise and Hades, witnessed the tortures of the impious, and saw the rewards of the just. From this point of view his otherworld journey is comparable to the accounts of shamanic descents, some of which, as we have seen,

---

societies" of initiatory and ecstatic structure, counterparts to the Germanic *berserkir* and the Vedic *marya*.

109 Nyberg, *Die Religionen*, p. 177.

110 19, 20; Nyberg, *Die Religionen*, p. 178.

111 Nyberg, *Die Religionen*, p. 177.

112 We follow the tr. by M. A. Barthélemy, *Artâ Vîrâf-Nâmak ou Livre Ardâ Vîrâf*. [The quotations given are from the Eng. tr. by M. Haug and W. West.] Cf. also S. Wikander, *Vayu*, 43 ff.; G. Widengren, "Stand und Aufgaben," Pt. 2, pp. 67 ff.

113 Ch. III (trs. Haug and West).

also contain references to the punishment of sinners. The infernal imagery of the Central Asian shamans would seem to have undergone the influence of Oriental, and principally Iranian, ideas. But this does not mean that the shamanic descent to the underworld derives from an exotic influence. The Oriental contribution only amplified and added color to the dramatic scenarios of punishments; it was the *narratives* of ecstatic journeys to the underworld that were enriched under Oriental influences; the *ecstasy* long preceded them (we have, it will be remembered, found the technique of ecstasy in archaic cultures where it is impossible to suspect any influence from the ancient East).

Thus, though the question of the possible "shamanic" experience of Zarathustra himself must remain open, there is no doubt that the most elementary technique of ecstasy, intoxication by hemp, was known to the ancient Iranians. Nor does anything speak against our believing that the Iranians also knew other constituent elements of shamanism—magical flight, for example (attested among the Scythians?), or celestial ascent. Artay Virāf took "the first footstep" and reached the sphere of the stars, "second footstep" and reached the sphere of the moon, the "third footstep" brought him to the light called "the highest of the highest," the "fourth footstep" to the light of Garôdmân.[114] Whatever the cosmology implied by this ascent may be, it is certain that the symbolism of the "footsteps"—the same that we shall find again when we come to the myth of the Buddha's Nativity—coincides precisely with the symbolism of the "stairs" or notches of the shamanic tree. This complex of symbolisms is closely connected with ritual ascent to the sky. Now, as we have seen many times, these ascents are a constituent part of shamanism.

The importance of the intoxication sought from hemp is further confirmed by the extremely wide dissemination of the Iranian term through Central Asia. In a number of Ugrian languages the Iranian word for hemp, *bangha*, has come to designate both the pre-eminently shamanic mushroom *Agaricus muscarius* (which

114 Chs. VII–X (trs. Haug and West, p. 163).

sed as a means of intoxication before or during the séance) and itoxication; [115] compare, for example, the Vogul *pânkh*, "mush-oom" (*Agaricus muscarius*), Mordvinian *panga, pango*, and Chere-is *pongo*, "mushroom." In northern Vogul, *pânkh* also means intoxication, drunkenness." The hymns to the divinities refer to cstasy induced by intoxication by mushrooms. [116] These facts rove that the magico-religious value of intoxication for achiev-ig ecstasy is of Iranian origin. Added to the other Iranian influ-ices on Central Asia, to which we shall return, *bangha* illus-ates the high degree of religious prestige attained by Iran. It is ossible that, among the Ugrians, the technique of shamanic intoxi-tion is of Iranian origin. But what does this prove concerning the riginal shamanic experience? Narcotics are only a vulgar substi-te for "pure" trance. We have already had occasion to note this ct among several Siberian peoples; the use of intoxicants (alcohol, bacco, etc.) is a recent innovation and points to a decadence in amanic technique. Narcotic intoxication is called on to provide i *imitation* of a state that the shaman is no longer capable of taining otherwise. Decadence or (must we add?) vulgarization a mystical technique—in ancient and modern India, and indeed l through the East, we constantly find this strange mixture of lifficult ways" and "easy ways" of realizing mystical ecstasy or me other decisive experience.

In the case of the mystical traditions of Islamized Iran it is hard make a correct apportionment between what is a national heri-ge and what is due to Islamic or Oriental influences. But there is doubt that a number of legends and miracles found in Persian igiography belong to the universal stock of magic and especially shamanism. We have but to look through the two volumes of Huart's *Saints des derviches tourneurs* to find miracles in the irest shamanic tradition at every turn: ascensions, magical flight, sappearance, cures, etc. [117] Then too, we must remember the role

115 Bernhardt Munkácsi, " 'Pilz' und 'Rausch.' " I owe this reference to e kindness of Stig Wikander.
116 Ibid., p. 344.
117 Cf. C. Huart, *Les Saints des derviches tourneurs. Récits traduits du*

of hashish and other narcotics in Islamic mysticism, although the purest saints never had recourse to such substitutes.[118]

Finally, with the propagation of Islam among the Turks of Central Asia, certain shamanic elements were assimilated by Moslem mystics.[119] Professor Köprülüzadé cites the legend that "Ahmed Yeseví and some of his dervishes could change into birds and so have power to fly." [120] Similar legends were current concerning the Bektashite saints.[121] In the thirteenth century Barak Baba—founder of an order whose distinguishing ritual sign was the "two horned headdress"—appeared in public riding an ostrich, and legend tells that "the ostrich flew a little way under its rider"

---

persan, I–II: events known at a distance (I, 45); light proceeding from the saint's body (I, 37 ff., 80); levitation (I, 209); incombustibility: "listening to the sheik's teaching and discovering the mysteries, the *séyyd* [disciple] became so inflamed that he put his two feet on the fire in the brasier and drew out burning coals with his hands . . ." (I, 56: shamanic "mastery over fire" is clearly present in this anecdote); magicians throw a boy into the air: the sheik keeps him there (I, 65); sudden disappearance (I, 80); invisibility (II, 131); ubiquity (II, 173); ascent and flight (II, 345); etc. Professor Fritz Meier of Basel informs me that according to the still unpublished biographical work of Amīn Ahmad Rāzī, composed in 1594, the saint Qutb ud dīn Haydar (12th cent.) was reputed to be insensible to fire and to the most intense cold; in addition, he was frequently seen on roofs and treetops. We know, of course, the shamanic meaning of tree-climbing (see above, pp. 125 ff.).

118 The influence of narcotics (hashish, opium) becomes discernible in certain Persian mystical orders from the twelfth century on; cf. L. Massignon, *Essai sur les origines du lexique technique de la mystique musulmane*, pp. 86 ff. The *raqs*, ecstatic "dance" of jubilation, *tamzīq*, "tearing of garments" during trance, *nazar ila'l mord*, the "Platonic gaze," a highly suspect form of ecstasy through erotic inhibition, are some indications of the trances induced by narcotics; these elementary recipes for ecstasy can be connected with both pre-Islamic mystical techniques and with certain aberrant Indian techniques that may have influenced Sufism (ibid., p. 87).

119 Cf. Mehmed Fuad Köprülüzadé, *Influence du chamanisme turco-mongol sur les ordres mystiques musulmans*; see also the (French) summary of Köprülüzadé's book on the earliest mystics in Turkish literature (published in Turkish) in L. Bouvat, " 'Les Premiers Mystiques dans la littérature turque de Kieuprilizâdé, analyse critique."

120 *Influence du chamanisme*, p. 9.   121 Ibid.

influence." [122] It is possible that these details are in fact due to influences from Turko-Mongol shamanism, as the learned Turkologist affirms. But ability to turn into a bird is the common property of all kinds of shamanism, not only the Turko-Mongol but also the Arctic, American, Indian, and Oceanian. As to the presence of the ostrich in the legend of Barak Baba, one wonders if it does not rather indicate a southern origin.

Ancient India: Ascensional Rites

The ritual importance of the birch in the Turko-Mongol religion and especially in its shamanism will be remembered. The birch or the post with seven or nine notches symbolizes the Cosmic Tree and hence is believed to stand at the "Center of the World." By climbing it the shaman reaches the highest heaven and stands face to face with Bai Ülgän.

We meet the same symbolism again in Brāhmanic ritual; it too involves a ceremonial ascent to the world of the gods. For the sacrifice, we are told, "there is only one foundation, only one finale . . . even heaven." [123] "The ship fair crossing is the sacrifice"; [124] "every sacrifice is a ship bound heavenwards." [125] The mechanism of the ritual is a *dūrohaṇa*,[126] a "difficult ascent," since it implies ascending the World Tree itself.

For in fact the sacrificial post (*yūpa*) is made from a tree that is assimilated to the Cosmic Tree. The priest himself, accompanied by the woodcutter, chooses it in the forest.[127] While it is being felled, the sacrificing priest apostrophizes it: "Graze not the sky!

122 Ibid., pp. 16–17.

123 *Śatapatha Brāhmaṇa*, VIII, 7, 4, 6 (tr. J. Eggeling, pp. 145–46).

124 *Aitareya Brāhmaṇa*, I, 3, 13 (tr. A. B. Keith).

125 *Śatapatha Brāhmaṇa*, IV, 2, 5, 10 (tr. J. Eggeling, p. 311). Cf. the numerous texts assembled by Sylvain Lévi, *La Doctrine du sacrifice dans les Brāhmaṇas*, pp. 87 ff.

126 On the symbolism of the *dūrohaṇa*, see Eliade, "Dūrohaṇa and the Waking Dream.' "

127 *Śatapatha Brāhmaṇa*, III, 6, 4, 13; etc.

hurt not the air!" [128] The sacrificial post becomes a sort of cosmic pillar: "[Vanaspati,] Lord of the forest, raise thyself up on the loftiest spot of earth"—so the *Ṛg-Veda* [129] invokes it. "With thy crest thou hast touched the sky; with thy middle thou hast filled the air; with thy foot thou hast steadied the earth," proclaims the *Śatapatha Brāhmaṇa*.[130]

Along this cosmic pillar the sacrificer goes up to heaven, alone or with his wife. Setting a ladder against it, he addresses her: "Come, wife, ascend we the sky!" She answers: "Ascend we!" And they exchange these ritual words three times.[131] Reaching the top, the sacrificer touches the capital and, spreading his arms (like a bird its wings!), cries: "We have come to the heaven, to the gods; we have become immortal!" [132] "Verily the sacrificer makes it a ladder and a bridge to attain the world of heaven." [133]

The sacrificial post is an *axis mundi*, and just as the archaic peoples dispatched sacrifices to heaven through the smoke hole or central post of their house, so the Vedic *yūpa* was an "accomplisher of the sacrifice." [134] Prayers were addressed to it as "lord of the forest": "[O Tree,] present this our oblation to the gods!" [135] and so on.

We have observed the ornithological symbolism of the shamanic costume and many examples of magical flight among the Siberian shamans. We find similar ideas in ancient India. "The Sacrificer, having become a bird, soars to the world of heaven," the *Pañcaviṃśa Brāhmaṇa* affirms.[136] Numerous texts speak of the wings that one must possess to attain the top of the sacrificial

---

128 Ibid. (tr. Eggeling, p. 165); *Taittirīya Saṃhitā*, I, 3, 5; etc.

129 III, 8, 3 (tr. R. T. H. Griffith, II, 4).

130 III, 7, 1, 14 (tr. Eggeling, p. 171).

131 *Śatapatha Brāhmaṇa*, V, 2, 1, 10; etc. (tr. Eggeling).

132 *Taittirīya Saṃhitā*, I, 7, 9, e; etc. (tr. Keith, p. 40).

133 Ibid., VI, 6, 4, 2; etc. (tr. Keith, p. 550).

134 *Ṛg-Veda*, III, 8, 3 (tr. Griffith).

135 Ibid., I, 13, 11 (tr. Griffith).

136 V, 3, 5, cited by A. Coomaraswamy, "Svayamātṛṇṇā: Janua Coeli," p. 47.

tree,[137] of the "Gander whose seat is in the Light," [138] of the sacrificial horse that, in the shape of a bird, carries the sacrificer to heaven,[139] and so on.[140] And, as we shall soon see, the tradition of magical flight is more than abundantly documented in ancient and medieval India, always in connection with saints, yogins, and magicians.

In the Brāhmanic texts "climbing a tree" became a frequent image for spiritual ascent.[141] The same symbolism was preserved in folklore traditions, though its meaning is not always apparent at first sight.[142]

Ascent of the shamanic type is also found in the legends of the Nativity of the Buddha. "The moment . . . the Bodhisattva has come to birth," says the *Majjhima-nikāya*,[143] "standing on even feet and facing north, he takes seven strides; and while a white sunshade is being held over him, he scans all the quarters and utters as with the voice of a bull: 'I am highest in the world, I am best in the world, I am eldest in the world. This is the last birth, there is not now again becoming.' " The seven strides carry the Buddha to the summit of the world; like the Altaic shaman, who climbs the seven or nine notches in the ceremonial birch in order finally to reach the furthest heaven, the Buddha symbolically traverses the seven cosmic levels to which the seven planetary heavens correspond. It need hardly be said that the old cosmological schema of shamanic (and Vedic) celestial ascent here appears as it was enriched by the millennial metaphysical speculation of India.

137 *Jaiminīya Upaniṣad Brāhmaṇa*, III, 13, 9.

138 *Kaṭha Upaniṣad*, V, 2.

139 Mahīdhara, ad *Śatapatha Brāhmaṇa*, XIII, 2, 6, 15.

140 Cf. the other texts brought together by Coomaraswamy, "Svayamā-tṛṇṇā," pp. 8, 46, 47, etc.; also S. Lévi, *La Doctrine*, p. 93. The same itinerary is, of course, followed after death (Lévi, pp. 93 ff.; H. Güntert, *Der arische Weltkönig und Heiland*, pp. 401 ff.).

141 See, for example, the texts mentioned by Coomaraswamy, pp. 7, 42, etc. See also Paul Mus, *Barabuḍur*, I, 318.

142 Cf. N. M. Penzer, ed., and C. H. Tawney, tr., *Somadeva's Kathā-sarit-sāgara, or Ocean of Streams of Story*, I, 153; II, 387; VIII, 68 ff.; etc.

143 III, 123 (tr. I. B. Horner [modified]).

It is no longer the Vedic "world of the gods" and "immortality" to which the Buddha's *seven strides* are directed; it is to transcending the human condition. Indeed, the expression "I am highest in the world" (*aggo'ham asmi lokassa*) signifies nothing other than the Buddha's transcendence over space, as the expression "I am eldest in the world" (*jeṭṭho'ham asmi lokassa*) signifies his supra-temporality. For, by reaching the cosmic summit, the Buddha attains the "Center of the World" and, since the creation came forth from a "Center" (= summit), the Buddha becomes *contemporary with the beginning of the world*.[144]

The conception of the seven heavens, to which the *Majjhima-nikāya* alludes, goes back to Brāhmanism, and probably represents the influence of Babylonian cosmology, which (though indirectly) left its mark on Altaic and Siberian cosmological conceptions too. But Buddhism also knows a cosmological schema with nine heavens, though they have been profoundly "interiorized," for the first four heavens correspond to the four *jhānas*, the next four to the four *sattāvāsas*, and the ninth and last heaven symbolizes Nirvāṇa.[145] Each of these heavens contains the projection of a divinity of the Buddhist pantheon, who at the same time represents a particular degree of yogic meditation. Now, we know that among the Altaians the seven or nine heavens are inhabited by various divine and semidivine figures, whom the shaman encounters in the course of his ascent and with whom he converses; in the ninth

144 This is not the place to pursue a more thorough discussion of this detail in the Nativity of the Buddha; but we were obliged to touch on it in passing to show, on the one hand, the plurivalence of archaic symbolism, which leaves it open to new interpretations indefinitely, and, on the other, to stress the fact that the survival of a "shamanic" schema in a developed religion in no way implies preservation of the original content. The same observation applies, of course, to the various ascensional schemas of Christian and Islamic mysticism. Cf. Eliade, "Sapta padāni kramati"; id., "The Seven Steps of Buddha."

145 Cf. W. Kirfel, *Die Kosmographie der Inder*, pp. 190 ff. The nine heavens are also known to the *Bṛhadāraṇyaka Upaniṣad*, III, 6, 1; cf. W. Ruben, "Schamanismus im alten Indien," p. 169. On the relations between cosmological schemas and degrees of meditation, cf. Mus, *Barabuḍur*, passim.

heaven he finds himself in the presence of Bai Ülgän. Of course, in Buddhism it is no longer a question of a symbolic ascent to the heavens, but of degrees of meditation and, at the same time, of "strides" toward final liberation. (It seems that, on his death, the Buddhist monk attains the celestial plane that he has reached by his yogic experiences during life, while the Buddha attains Nirvāṇa.[146])

Ancient India: Magical Flight

The Brāhmanic sacrificer mounts to heaven by ritually climbing a ladder; the Buddha transcends the cosmos by symbolically traversing the seven heavens; the Buddhist yogin, through meditation, realizes an ascent whose nature is completely spiritual. Typologically, all these acts share the same structure; each on its own plane indicates a particular way of transcending the profane world and attaining to the world of the gods, or Being, or the Absolute. We have shown above to what extent such acts can be classified under the shamanic tradition of ascent to the sky; the one great difference lies in the intensity of the shamanic experience, which, as we have seen, includes ecstasy and trance. But ancient India, too, knows the ecstasy that makes ascension and magical flight possible. The long-haired (*keśin*) "ecstatic" (*muni*) of the *Ṛg-Veda* declares in so many words: "Exhilarated by the sanctity of the *Muni* we have mounted upon the wind; behold, mortals, (in them) our forms! . . . The steed of the wind, the friend of Vāyu, the *Muni* is instigated by the deity. . . ."[147] We may remind ourselves that the drum of the Altaic shamans is called "horse" and that among

146 Cf. also Ruben, p. 170.

147 X, 136, 3–5 (tr. H. H. Wilson, V, 364). On this *muni*, see E. Arbman, *Rudra. Untersuchungen zum altindischen Glauben und Kultus*, pp. 298 ff.; on the magico-religious meaning of long hair, ibid., p. 302 (cf. the "snakes" of Siberian shamanic costumes; above, pp. 152 f.). On the earliest Vedic ecstasies, cf. J. Hauer, *Die Anfänge der Yogapraxis*, pp. 116 ff., 120; Eliade, *Yoga*, pp. 101 ff. Cf. also G. Widengren, "Stand und Aufgaben der iranischen Religionsgeschichte," Pt. 2, p. 72, n. 123.

the Buryat, for example, the horse-headed stick (which is also called "horse") plays an important role. Ecstasy induced by the drum or by dancing astride a horse-headed stick (a kind of hobby-horse) is assimilated to a fantastic gallop through the skies. As we shall see, among certain non-Aryan peoples of India the magician still uses a wooden horse or a horse-headed stick in performing his ecstatic dance.[148]

In the same *Ṛg-Veda* hymn it is said: "They [the *muni*] have assumed the (power of) the gods";[149] here we have a kind of mystical possession that retains high spiritual value even in non-ecstatic circles.[150] The *muni* "repairs to both oceans, the eastern and the western. Wandering in the track of the *Apsarasas* and the *Gandharvas* . . . and the wild beasts . . ."[151] The *Atharva Veda* thus praises the disciple filled with the magical power of asceticism (*tapas*): "Swiftly he goes from east to northern ocean."[152] This macranthropic experience, which is rooted in the shamanic ecstasy,[153] persists in Buddhism and has considerable importance in Yogic-tantric techniques.[154]

Ascension and magical flight have a leading place among the popular beliefs and mystical techniques of India. Rising into the air, flying like a bird, traveling immense distances in a flash, disappearing—these are some of the magical powers that Buddhism and Hinduism attribute to arhats, kings, and magicians. There

148 Below, pp. 467 ff.   149 X, 136 (tr. Wilson, p. 364)

150 Witness *Bṛhadāraṇyaka Upaniṣad*, III, 3–7.

151 *Ṛg-Veda*, X, 136 (tr. Wilson).

152 XI, 5, 6 (tr. Griffith, p. 69).

153 Cf., for example, the extremely obscure hymn of the *vrātya* (*Atharva Veda*, XV, 3 ff.). The homologizations between the human body and the cosmos, of course, go beyond the shamanic experience proper, but we see that both the *vrātya* and the *muni* acquire macranthropy during an ecstatic trance.

154 The Buddha sees himself in a dream as a giant holding the two oceans in his arms (*Anguttara-nikāya*, III, 240; cf. also W. Ruben, p. 167). It is impossible to cite here all the traces of "shamanism" found in the earliest Buddhist texts; for example, the magical power to "plunge into the air and shoot up again as if in water" (*Anguttara-nikāya*, I, 254 f. [tr. F. L. Woodward, I, 233]; etc.). See also below, pp. 410 f.

are numerous legends of flying kings and magicians.[155] The miraculous lake Anavatapta could only be reached by those possessing the magical power of flight; Buddha and the Buddhist saints traveled to Anavatapta in an instant, as the rishis of Hindu legend soared through the air to the divine and mysterious land in the north, called Śvetadvīpa.[156] The conception is, of course, one of "pure lands," of a mystical space that has at once the nature of a "paradise" and of an "interior space" accessible only to initiates. The lake Anavatapta, Śvetadvīpa, or the other Buddhist "paradises" are all so many modes of being, attained through Yoga, asceticism, or contemplation. But we would emphasize the *identity in expression* between such superhuman experiences and the archaic symbolism of ascent and flight, so frequent in shamanism.

Buddhist texts speak of four different magical powers of translation (*gamana*), the first being ability to fly like a bird.[157] In his list of *siddhis* obtainable by yogins, Patañjali cites the power to fly through the air (*laghiman*).[158] It is always by the "power of yoga" that, in the *Mahābhārata*, the sage Nārada soars into the sky and reaches the summit of Mount Meru (the "Center of the World"); from there, far away in the Ocean of Milk, he sees Śvetadvīpa.[159] For "with such a [yogic] body, the yogin goes where he will." [160] But another tradition recorded in the *Mahābhārata* already makes a distinction between true mystical ascent—which cannot always be said to be "concrete"—and magical flight, which is only an illusion:

155 Cf., for example, Penzer and Tawney, *Somadeva's Kathā-sarit-sāgara*, I, 62 ff.; III, 27, 35; V, 33, 35, 169 ff.; VIII, 26 ff., 50 ff.; etc.

156 Cf. W. E. Clark, "Śakadvīpa and Śvetadvīpa," passim; Eliade, *Yoga*, pp. 414 f. On Anavatapta, cf. M. W. Visser, *The Arhats in China and Japan*, pp. 24 ff.

157 Cf. *The Visuddhimagga of Buddhagosa*, tr. P. M. Tin, p. 396. On *gamana*, see Sigurd Lindquist, *Siddhi und Abhiññā*, pp. 58 ff. There is a good bibliography of sources on the *abhijñās* in Étienne Lamotte, tr., *Le Traité de la Grande Vertu de sagesse de Nāgārjuna* (*Mahāprajñāpāramitāśāstra*) I, 320, n. 1.

158 *Yoga-sūtras*, III, 45; cf. *Gheraṇḍa Saṃhitā*, III, 78; Eliade, *Yoga*, pp. 326 ff. On similar traditions in the *Mahābhārata* and the *Rāmāyaṇa*, see E. W. Hopkins, "Yoga-Technique in the Great Epic," pp. 337, 361.

159 *Mahābhārata*, XII, 335, 2 f.   160 Ibid., XII, 317, 6.

"We too can fly to the heavens and manifest ourselves under various forms, but through illusion (*māyayā*)." [161]

We see in what direction Yoga and the other Indian techniques of meditation elaborated the ecstatic experiences and magical prowesses belonging to an immemorial spiritual heritage. However this may be, the secret of magical flight is also known to Indian alchemy.[162] And the same miracle is so common among the Buddhist arhats [163] that *arahant* yielded the Singhalese verb *rahatve*, "to disappear," "to pass instantaneously from one place to another." [164] The *ḍākinīs*, fairy sorceresses who play an important role in some tantric schools,[165] are called in Mongolian "they who walk through the air," and in Tibetan "they who go to the sky." [166] Magical flight and ascending to the sky by means of a ladder or rope are also frequent motifs in Tibet, where they are not necessarily borrowed from India, the more so since they are documented in the Bon-po traditions or in traditions deriving from them.[167] In addition, as we shall soon see, the same motifs play a considerable role in Chinese magical beliefs and folklore, and they are also found almost everywhere in the archaic world.[168]

---

161 *Mahābhārata*, V, 160, 55 ff.

162 Eliade, *Yoga*, pp. 274 ff., 414 ff. A Persian author (Emir Khosru) affirms that yogins "can also fly like fowls in the air, however improbable it may seem" (ibid., p. 276).

163 On the flight of arhats, see Visser, *The Arhats*, pp. 172 ff.; Sylvain Lévi and É. Chavannes, "Les Seize Arhats protecteurs de la loi," p. 23 (the arhat Nandimitra "rose into space to the height of seven *tāla* trees," etc.); pp. 262 f. (the arhat Piṇḍola, whose dwelling place is Anavatapta, was punished by the Buddha for having flown through the air with a mountain in his hands, improperly exhibiting his magical powers to the profane: Buddhism, of course, forbade exhibitions of the *siddhis*).

164 A. M. Hocart, "Flying Through the Air," p. 80. Hocart explains all these legends in accordance with his theory of royalty: kings, being gods cannot touch the ground and hence are believed to proceed through the air. But the symbolism of flight is more complex, and in any case it cannot be derived from the conception of god-kings. Cf. Eliade, *Myths, Dreams and Mysteries*, pp. 99 ff.

165 Cf. Eliade, *Yoga*, pp. 324 ff.

166 Cf. P. J. van Durme, "Notes sur le Lamaïsme," p. 374, n. 2.

167 See below, pp. 430 ff.   168 Below, pp. 487 ff.

All these practices and beliefs, which we have had to review rather more hastily than we might wish, are not necessarily "shamanic"; each, in the content from which it has been removed to facilitate our exposition, has its own particular meaning. But our aim was to show the structural equivalences of these Indian magico-religious phenomena. The ecstatic, like the magician, does not appear as a unique figure in Indian religion as a whole, except by the intensity of his mystical experience or his pre-eminence in magic; for the underlying theory—ascent to heaven—is also found, as we saw, even in the symbolism of the Brāhmanic sacrifice.

The thing, that is, which distinguishes the *muni*'s ascent from the ascent realized through the Brāhmanic ritual is precisely its experiential nature; in his case, we have a "trance" comparable to the full ecstatic séance of the Siberian shamans. But the important fact is that this *ecstatic experience* is not in opposition to the general *theory* of Brāhmanic sacrifice, just as the shamans' trance fits perfectly into the cosmo-theological system of the Siberian and Altaic religions. The chief difference between the two types of ascent is the intensity of the experience, that is, it is finally psychological. But whatever its intensity, this ecstatic experience becomes communicable through universally current symbolism, and is validated to the extent to which it can enter into the already existing magico-religious system. The power of flight can, as we have seen, be obtained in many ways (shamanic trance, mystical ecstasy, magical techniques), but also by a severe psychological discipline, such as the Yoga of Patañjali, by vigorous asceticism, as in Buddhism, or by alchemical practices. This variety in techniques doubtless corresponds to a variety of experiences and also, though in lesser degree, to different ideologies (for example, abduction by spirits, "magical" and "mystical" ascent, etc.). But all these techniques and mythologies have a common characteristic—the importance accorded to the ability to fly through the air. This "magical power" is not an isolated element, valid in itself, based entirely on the personal experience of magicians; on the contrary, it is an integral part of a theologico-cosmological complex far more embracing than the various shamanic ideologies.

Tapas *and* Dīkṣā

The same continuity between ritual and ecstasy is also found in connection with another conception, which plays a considerable role in pan-Indian ideology: *tapas*, whose original meaning is "extreme heat" but which came to designate ascetic effort in general. *Tapas* is definitely documented in the *Ṛg-Veda*,[169] and its powers are creative on both the cosmic and the spiritual plane: through *tapas* the ascetic becomes clairvoyant and even incarnates the gods. Prajāpati creates the world by "heating" himself to an extreme degree through asceticism; [170] he creates it, that is, by a sort of magical sweating. The "inner heat" or "mystical heat" is creative: it results in a kind of magical power that, even when not manifested directly as a cosmogony (cf. the myth of Prajāpati) "creates" on a lesser cosmic plane; for example, it creates the countless illusions or miracles of the ascetics and yogins (magical flight, negation of physical laws, disappearance, etc.). Now, "inner heat" forms an integral part of the technique of "primitive" magicians and shamans; [171] everywhere in the world acquisition of "inner heat" is expressed by a "mastery over fire" and, in the last analysis, by the abrogation of physical laws—which is as much as to say that the duly "heated" magician can perform "miracles," can create new conditions of existence in the cosmos, in some measure repeats the cosmogony. Regarded from this point of view, Prajāpati becomes one of the archetypes of "magicians."

This excess of heat was obtained either by meditating close to a fire—and this ascetic method became extraordinarily esteemed in India—or by holding the breath.[172] It is scarcely necessary to say that respiratory technique and holding the breath had a large place

169 Cf., for example, VIII, 59, 6; X, 136, 2; 154, 2, 4; 167, 1; 109, 4; etc.
170 *Aitareya Brāhmaṇa*, V, 32, 1.   171 See below, pp. 474 ff.
172 Cf., for example, *Baudhāyana Dharma Sūtra*, IV, 1, 24; etc.

in organizing the complex of ascetic practices and of magical, mystical, and metaphysical techniques that are included under the general term Yoga.[173] *Tapas*, in the sense of ascetic effort, is an essential part of every form of Yoga, and we consider it important, in passing, to note its "shamanic" implications. We shall later see that "mystical heat," in the proper sense of the term, has great importance in Himalayan and Tibetan tantric Yoga.[174] We will, however, add that the tradition of classic Yoga employs the "power" conferred by *prāṇāyāma* (breath control) as a "cosmogony in reverse," in the sense that, instead of leading to the creation of new universes (that is, of new "mirages" and "miracles"), this power enables the yogin to detach himself from the world and even in some measure to destroy it. Because yogic liberation is equivalent to completely breaking all ties with the cosmos; for a *jīvan-mukta*, the universe no longer exists, and if he projected his own process on the cosmological plane he would witness a total resorption of the cosmic forces in the first substance (*prakṛti*), in other words, a return to the nondifferentiated state that existed before the creation. All this goes very far beyond the horizon of "shamanic" ideology; but it seems to us significant that Indian spirituality, seeking a means of metaphysical liberation, employed a technique of archaic magic reputedly able to abolish physical laws and play a part in the very constitution of the universe.

But *tapas* is not an ascetic exercise exclusively confined to "ecstatics"; it forms part of lay religious experience. For the *soma* sacrifice requires the officiant and his wife to perform the *dīkṣā*, a consecration rite that involves *tapas*.[175] *Dīkṣā* comprises ascetic vigil, meditation in silence, fasting, and also "heat" (*tapas*), and this period of "consecration" could continue for from one or two

173 See Eliade, *Techniques du Yoga*; id., *Yoga*.
174 Below, pp. 437 f.
175 On *dīkṣā* and *tapas*, see H. Oldenberg, *Die Religion des Veda* (2nd edn.), pp. 397 ff.; A. Hillebrandt, *Vedische Mythologie* (2nd edn.), I, 482 ff.; J. W. Hauer, *Die Anfänge der Yogapraxis*, pp. 55 ff.; A. B. Keith, *The Religion and Philosophy of the Veda and Upanishads*, I, 300 ff.; S. Lévi, *La Doctrine du sacrifice dans les Brāhmaṇas*, pp. 103 ff. Cf. also Meuli, "Scythica," pp. 134 ff.

days to a year. Now, the *soma* sacrifice is one of the most important in Vedic and Brāhmanic India; this is as much as to say that asceticism to the end of ecstasy necessarily forms part of the religious life of the entire Indian people. Continuity between ritual and ecstasy, already observed in connection with the rites of ascent performed by lay persons and of the mystical flight of the ecstatics, is also found on the plane of *tapas*. It remains to inquire if Indian religious life, as a whole and with all the symbolisms that it includes, is a creation—"degraded" in a measure, in order to become accessible to the profane—produced by a series of ecstatic experiences on the part of a few privileged persons, or if, on the contrary, the ecstatic experience of the latter is only the result of an effort toward "interiorization" of certain cosmo-theological schemas that precede it. The problem is pregnant with consequences, but it lies beyond the sphere of the history of Indian religions as well as of the subject of the present study.[176]

"Shamanic" Symbolisms and Techniques in India

As for shamanic healing by calling back or searching for the patient's fugitive soul, the *Ṛg-Veda* presents a number of examples. The priest thus addresses the dying man: "Although thy spirit have gone far away to heaven, or to . . . the four-quartered earth, we bring back that (spirit) of thine to dwell here, to live (long)." [177] Again in the *Ṛg-Veda*, the Brahman conjures the patient's soul in these terms: "May (thy) spirit . . . come back again to perform pious acts; to exercise strength; to live; and long to see the sun. May our progenitors, may the host of the gods, restore (thy) spirit; may we obtain (for thee) the aggregate of the functions of life." [178] And in the magico-medical texts of the *Atharva Veda* the magician, to bring the dying man back to life,

---

176 Yet we make bold to hope that the present study will show the manner in which the problem should be posed.

177 X, 58, 2–4 (tr. Wilson, VI, 151).

178 X, 57, 4–5 (tr. Wilson, VI, 150).

summons his breath from the Wind and his eye from the Sun, replaces his soul in his body, and frees the sufferer from the bonds of the death goddess Nirṛti.[179]

These represent, of course, only vestiges of shamanic healing, and if Indian medicine later employed certain traditional magical ideas, they do not belong to shamanic ideology proper.[180] The summoning of the various "organs" from the cosmic regions, as performed by the magician of the *Atharva Veda*,[181] involves a different conception—that of the man-microcosm—and though it seems to be quite old (perhaps Indo-European), it is not "shamanic." Nevertheless, calling back the patient's fugitive soul is documented in a book of the *Ṛg-Veda* (the latest in date), and as the same shamanic ideology and technique dominate the non-Aryan peoples of India, the question arises if an influence from the substratum may not be assumed. The magician of the Oraon in Bengal also seeks the patient's strayed soul through mountains and rivers and on into the land of the dead,[182] exactly like the Altaic and Siberian shamans.

Nor is this all. Ancient India knows the doctrine of the soul's instability, which is so marked a feature in the various cultures dominated by shamanism. In dream the soul wanders far from the body, and the *Śatapatha Brāhmaṇa*[183] advises not wakening a sleeper suddenly, for his soul might go astray on its way back. Yawning also involves the danger of losing one's soul.[184] The legend of Subandhu tells how the soul can be lost and recovered.[185]

Further in connection with the idea that the magician can leave his body at will—a strictly shamanic notion, whose ecstatic founda-

---

179 *Atharva Veda*, VIII, 1, 3, 1; VIII, 2, 3; etc. On calling back the soul, cf. also W. Caland, *Altindischer Ahnenkult*, pp. 179 ff.

180 Cf., for example, Jean Filliozat, *La Doctrine classique de la médecin indienne. Ses origines et ses parallèles grecs.*

181 See also *Ṛg-Veda*, X, 16, 3.

182 Cf. F. E. Clements, *Primitive Concepts of Disease*, p. 197 ("soul loss" among the Garo and the Hinduized peoples of the north).

183 XIV, 7, 1, 12.   184 *Taittirīya Saṃhitā*, II, 5, 2, 4.

185 *Jaiminīya Brāhmaṇa*, III, 168–70; *Pañcaviṃśa Brāhmaṇa*, XII, 12, 5.

tions we have several times observed—we find, both in technical texts and folklore, another magical power: that of "entering another's body" (*parapurakāyapraveśa*).[186] But this magical feat already bears the marks of Indian elaboration; in addition, it figures among the yogic *siddhis*, and Patañjali cites it [187] along with other magical powers.

We cannot consider reviewing all the aspects of Yoga technique that may be in some way related to shamanism. From the fact that the great synthesis that we have termed "baroque Yoga" incorporates a considerable number of elements belonging to the magical and mystical traditions of both Aryan and aboriginal India, it follows that shamanic elements can occasionally be identified here and there in the vast complex. But it is necessary to determine in each instance if the element is strictly shamanic or belongs to a magical tradition that reaches far beyond shamanism. Such an exhaustive comparative study is impossible here.[188] We will simply observe that even Patañjali's classic text cites certain "powers" familiar to shamanism—flying through the air, disappearing, becoming extremely tall or extremely short, and the like. In addition, a reference in the *Yoga-sūtras* [189] to medicinal plants (*auṣadhi*) that, in equal measure with *samādhi*, can give the yogin the "miraculous powers," attests the use of narcotics in yogic circles precisely for the purpose of obtaining ecstatic experiences. On the other hand, the "powers" play but a secondary role in classic and Buddhist Yoga, and numerous texts warn the aspirant against the danger of

---

186 Cf. Eliade, *Yoga*, pp. 393 ff.   187 *Yoga-sūtras*, III, 37.

188 Cf. Eliade: *Yoga*, pp. 311 ff.; *Techniques du Yoga*, pp. 175 ff. However, we would make it clear that, in discussing the "origins" of Yoga, we do not necessarily refer to shamanism. A whole popular mystical tradition, *bhakti*, which invaded Yoga at a certain moment, is not shamanic. The same observation holds, too, for the practices of mystical eroticism or other magical practices, some of them aberrant (involving cannibalism, murder, etc.), which, though of autochthonous pre-Aryan origin, are not shamanic. All these confusions have been made possible by the erroneous identification of "shamanism" with "primitive magic and mysticism."

189 IV, 1.

letting himself be seduced by the magical sense of boundless capability that they produce and that can make the yogin forget his true aim—final liberation. Hence the ecstasy attained by material means cannot be compared with the ecstasy of true *samādhi*. But we have seen that, in shamanism itself, narcotics already represent a decadence and that, in default of true ecstatic methods, recourse is taken to narcotics to induce trance. We will note, in passing, that just as in the case of baroque (popular) Yoga, shamanism itself displays aberrant variants. But let us emphasize once again the structural difference that distinguishes classic Yoga from shamanism. Although the latter is not without certain techniques of concentration (compare, for example, Eskimo initiations, etc.), its final goal is always ecstasy and the soul's ecstatic journey through the various cosmic regions, whereas Yoga pursues enstasis, final concentration of the spirit and "escape" from the cosmos. Of course, the protohistorical origins of classic Yoga in no sense exclude the existence of intermediate forms of shamanic Yoga directed to obtaining particular ecstatic experiences.[190]

Certain "shamanic" elements might also be found in Indian beliefs concerning death and the destiny of the dead.[191] As among so many other Asian peoples, these beliefs show traces of a plurality of souls.[192] But in general, ancient India believed that, after death, the soul went up to heaven, into the presence of Yama (King of the Dead) [193] and the ancestors (*pitaras*). The dead man was counseled not to be deterred by Yama's four-eyed dogs and to continue on his way, that he might reach the ancestors and the god Yama.[194] The *Ṛg-Veda* contains no precise reference to a bridge to be crossed

190 For a dissenting view, see Filliozat, "Les Origines d'une technique mystique indienne," discussing our hypothesis of a pre-Aryan origin for yogic techniques.

191 See a clear general exposition in Keith, *The Religion and Philosophy of the Veda and Upanishads*, II, 403 ff. The world of the dead is an "inverted" world, as it is for the Siberians, among other peoples; cf. Hermann Lommel, "Bhrigu im Jenseits," pp. 101 ff.

192 E.g., *Taittirīya Upaniṣad*, II, 4.   193 *Ṛg-Veda*, X, 58.

194 *Ṛg-Veda*, X, 14, 10–12; *Atharva Veda*, XVIII, 2, 12; VIII, 1, 9; etc.

by the dead.[195] But we hear of a river [196] and a boat,[197] which suggests rather an infernal than a celestial itinerary. In any case, we recognize traces of an ancient ritual in which the dead man was told the road he must follow to reach Yama's realm.[198] And it was also known that the soul of the deceased did not leave the earth immediately; it lingered about the house for a certain period, which might be as much as a year. This explains, too, why it was invoked during the sacrifices and offerings were made in its honor.[199]

But the Vedic and Brāhmanic religion lacks any definite notion of a psychopompic god.[200] Rudra-Śiva sometimes plays such a role, but this conception is late and probably influenced by the beliefs of the pre-Aryan aborigines. In any case, in Vedic India there is nothing resembling the Altaic and northern Siberian guides of the dead; the deceased was merely told the road to follow, rather after the fashion of the Indonesian and Polynesian funerary laments and the Tibetan Book of the Dead. The presence of a psychopomp was probably made unnecessary during the Vedic and Brāhmanic period by the fact that, despite all the exceptions and contradictions found in the texts, the journey of the dead was heavenward and therefore less dangerous than a road that led to the nether world.

In any case, ancient India presents very few "infernal descents." Although the idea of a beyond underground is already documented in the *Ṛg-Veda*,[201] ecstatic otherworld journeys are extremely rare. Naciketas' father does, indeed, give him to "Death," and the lad does go to Yama's dwelling,[202] but this otherworld journey gives no impression of being a "shamanic" experience; it does not imply ecstasy. The only clear case of an ecstatic journey into the

195 Keith, II, 406, n. 9. 196 *Atharva Veda*, XVIII, 4, 7.
197 *Ṛg-Veda*, X, 63, 10.
198 For example, *Ṛg-Veda*, X, 14, 7–12; for the Sūtras, cf. Keith, II, 418, n. 6.
199 Keith, II, 412.
200 In opposition to the thesis maintained by E. Arbman, *Rudra*, passim.
201 Cf. Keith, II, 409. 202 *Taittirīya Brāhmaṇa*, III, 11, 8.

beyond is that of Bhṛgu, the "son" of Varuṇa.[203] The god, having made Bhṛgu unconscious, sends his soul to visit the various cosmic regions and the underworld. He even witnesses the punishments prescribed for those who have committed certain ritual crimes. Bhṛgu's unconsciousness, his ecstatic journey through the cosmos, the punishments he sees, which are explained to him by Varuṇa himself—all this is reminiscent of the *Book of Artāy Virāf*. There is, of course, the difference between an otherworld exploration that gives a complete view of afterdeath retributions, as in the case of the *Book of Artāy Virāf*, and an ecstatic journey that reveals only a small number of situations. But in both cases we can still discern a schema that is based on an otherworld initiatory journey and has been adopted and reinterpreted by ritualistic circles.

To be noted, too, are the "shamanic" motifs that still survive in figures as complex as Varuṇa, Yama, and Nirṛti. Each of these gods is, on his own plane, a "binding" god.[204] Many hymns mention the "laces of Varuṇa." The bonds of Yama (*yamasya paḍbīśa*)[205] are usually called the "bonds of death" (*mṛtyupāśah*).[206] Nirṛti, for her part, chains those whom she would destroy,[207] and the gods are implored to keep away "the bonds of Nirṛti."[208] For sicknesses are "laces" and death is only the supreme "bond." We have elsewhere studied the extremely complex symbolism that forms the background for the magic of "bonds."[209] Suffice it to say here that some aspects of this magic are shamanic. If it is true that "bonds" and "knots" figure among the most characteristic attributes of gods of death, and not only in India and Iran but elsewhere as well (China, Oceania, etc.), the shamans likewise possessed laces and nooses to serve the same purpose—capturing vagabond souls that have left their bodies. The gods and the demons of death capture the souls of the dead with a net; the

203 *Śatapatha Brāhmaṇa*, XI, 6, 1; *Jaiminīya Brāhmaṇa*, I, 42–44.
204 Cf. Eliade, *Images and Symbols*, pp. 95 ff., 99 ff.
205 *Atharva Veda*, VI, 96, 2.
206 Ibid., VII, 112, 2; etc.
207 Ibid., VI, 63, 1–2; etc.
208 Ibid., I, 31, 2.
209 See Eliade, *Images and Symbols*, pp. 92 ff.

Tungus shaman, for example, uses a noose to retrieve a patient's fugitive soul.[210] But the symbolism of "binding" extends far beyond the boundaries of shamanism proper; it is only in the sorcery of "knots" and "bonds" that we find certain similarities to shamanic magic.

Finally, we will also mention Arjuna's ecstatic ascent of the Mountain of Śiva, with all the luminous epiphanies that it involves; [211] though not "shamanic," it falls in the category of mystical ascensions, to which shamanic ascent also belongs. As to the luminous experiences, we may think of the *qaumaneq* of the Eskimo shaman, the "flash" or "illumination" that overwhelms him.[21] Clearly, the "inner light" that suddenly bursts forth after long efforts of concentration and meditation is well known in all religious traditions, and it is amply documented in India, from the Upaniṣads to tantrism.[213] We have mentioned these few examples to indicate the category in which certain shamanic experiences may be placed. For, as we have repeatedly remarked in the course of this study, shamanism as a whole is not always and necessarily an aberrant and sinister mysticism.[214]

In passing, we may also cite the magical drum and its role in Indian magic.[215] Legend sometimes tells of the divine origin of the drum; one tradition records that a *nāga* (snake-spirit) teaches King Kaniṣka the efficacy of the *ghaṇṭa* (drum) in rain rites.[216] Here we suspect the influence of the non-Aryan substratum—the more

210 S. M. Shirokogoroff, *Psychomental Complex of the Tungus*, p. 290.

211 *Mahābhārata*, VII, 80 ff.   212 See above, pp. 60 ff.

213 See above, pp. 61 f.

214 See also W. Nölle, "Schamanistische Vorstellungen im Shaktismus."

215 See E. Crawley, *Dress, Drinks and Drums: Further Studies of Savage and Sex*, pp. 236 ff.; Claudie Marcel-Dubois, *Les Instruments de musique de l'Inde ancienne*, pp. 33 ff. (bells), 41 ff. (frame drum), 46 ff. (two-headed round-bodied drum), 63 ff. (hour-glass drum). On the ritual role of the drum in the *aśvamedha*, cf. P. É. Dumont, *L'Aśvamedha*, pp. 150 ff. J. Przyluski had already drawn attention to the non-Aryan origin of the Indian name of the drum, *ḍamaru*; cf. "Un Ancien Peuple du Punjab: les Udumbara," pp. 34 ff. On the drum in the Vedic cult, cf. J. W. Hauer, *Der Vrātya*, pp. 282 ff.

216 S. Beal, *Si-yu-ki*, I, 66.

o since, in the magic of the aboriginal Indian peoples (a magic hat, though not always shamanic in structure, is nevertheless on he borderline of shamanism) drums have a considerable place.[217] This is also the reason why we shall not undertake to study the drum in non-Aryan India, or the cult of skulls,[218] which is so important in Lamaism and in many Indian sects with tantric leanings. ome details will be given later, but with no attempt at a general iscussion.

Shamanism among the Aboriginal Tribes of India

hanks to the researches of Verrier Elwin, we have an excellent icture of shamanism among the Savara (Saora), an aboriginal Drissan tribe of great ethnological interest. We shall dwell particularly on the autobiographies of Savara shamans and shamanesses; they present astonishing similarities to the "initiatory marriages" f the Siberian shamans, studied above.[219] There are, however, wo differences: (1) since the Savara have both shamans and shamanesses—and sometimes the latter even outnumber the former—both sexes enter into these marriages with an otherworld eing; (2) whereas the "celestial wives" of the Siberian shamans ve in the heavens or, in some cases, in the bush, the spiritual pouses of the Savara all inhabit the underworld, the kingdom of nades.

Kintara, a shaman of Hatibadi, gave Elwin the following account: "When I was about twelve years old, a tutelary girl called angmai came to me in a dream and said, 'I am pleased with you; love you; I love you so much that you must marry me.' But I

217 Cf. some facts concerning the Santal, the Bhil, and the Baiga in ′. Koppers, "Probleme der indischen Religionsgeschichte," p. 805 and 176. Cf. also id., *Die Bhil in Zentralindien*, pp. 178 ff. See also R. Rahann, "Shamanistic and Related Phenomena in Northern and Middle India,"). 735–36.

218 For the cult of skulls in non-Aryan India, see W. Ruden, *Eisenschmiede d Dämonen in Indien*, pp. 168, 204–08, 244, etc.

219 Pp. 72 ff.

refused, and for a whole year she used to come making love to me and trying to win me. But I always rejected her until at last she got angry and sent her dog [a tiger] to bite me. That frightened me and I agreed to marry her. But almost at once another tutelary came and begged me to marry her instead. When the first girl heard about it she said, 'I was the first to love you, and I look on you as my husband. Now your heart is on another woman, but I'll not allow it.' So I said 'No' to the second girl. But the first in her rage and jealousy made me mad and drove me out into the jungle and robbed me of my memory. For a whole year she drove me." Finally the boy's parents called in a shaman from a neighboring village, and the first tutelary spoke through his mouth: "Don't be afraid. I am going to marry him. . . . I will help the boy in all his troubles." The father was satisfied and arranged the marriage. Five years later Kintara married a woman of his village. After the wedding, Jangmai, the tutelary, addressed Dasuni, the bride, in these words, through their husband's mouth: " 'Now you are going to live with my husband. You will fetch his water, husk his rice, cook his food: you will do everything, I can do nothing. I must live below. All I can do is to help when trouble comes. Tell me, will you honour me or no, or are you going to quarrel with me?' Dasuni answered, 'Why should I quarrel with you? You are a good wife and I will give you everything you need.' Jangmai was pleased at that and said, 'That is well. You and I will live together as sisters.' Then she said to me, 'Look! Keep this woman as you have kept me. Do not beat her. Do not abuse her.' So saying, she went away." Kintara had a son and three daughters by his earthly wife and, by his tutelary, a son and two daughters, who lived in the underworld. When the boy was born, the tutelary, Kintara continued, "brought him to me and told me his name; she put him in my lap and asked me to make arrangements for his food. When I said I would, she took him down again to the Under World. I sacrificed a goat for the child and dedicated a pot." [220]

The same pattern—visits by a spirit, marriage proposal, re-

[220] Elwin, *The Religion of an Indian Tribe*, pp. 135–37.

sistance, period of acute crisis, resolved when the proposal is accepted—is found among girls "chosen" to become shamanesses.

The dream which forces a girl into her profession and seals it with supernatural approval takes the form of visits of a suitor from the Under World who proposes marriage with all its ecstatic and numinous consequences. This "husband" is a Hindu, well-dressed and handsome, wealthy, and observant of many customs to which the Saoras are strangers. He comes, according to tradition, in the depth of night; when he enters the room the whole household is laid under a spell and sleeps like the dead. In nearly every case, the girl at first refuses, for the profession of shamanin is both arduous and beset with dangers. The result is that she begins to be plagued with nightmares: her divine lover carries her to the Under World or threatens her with a fall from a great height. She generally falls ill; she may even be out of her wits for a time, and wanders pathetically dishevelled in the fields and woods. The family then takes a hand. Since in most cases the girl has been having training for some time, everyone knows what she is in for, and even if she herself does not tell her parents what is happening they usually have a shrewd idea. But the proper thing is for the girl herself to confess to her parents that she has been "called," that she has refused, and that she is now in danger. This immediately relieves her own mind of its burden of guilt and sets the parents free to act. They at once arrange the girl's marriage with her tutelary. . . .

After the marriage, the shamanin's spirit-husband visits her regularly and lies with her till dawn. He may even take her away into the jungle for days at a time, feeding her there on palm wine. In due course a child is born and the ghostly father brings it every night to be nursed by the girl. But the relationship is not primarily a sexual one; the important thing is that the tutelary husband should inspire and instruct his young wife in her dreams, and when she goes to perform her sacred duties he sits by her and tells her what to do.[221]

A shamaness recalled the first visit made to her—in dream—by a tutelary "dressed in smart Hindu clothes." She refused him, so "he took me up in a whirlwind and carried me away to a very high tree, where he made me sit on a fragile branch. There he began to sing and as he sang he swung me to and fro. I was terrified of falling from the great height and I hastily agreed to marry him." [222] The reader will have recognized some typically initiatory motifs: the whirlwind, the tree, swinging.

Another shamaness was already married and had a child, when she was visited by a tutelary and fell ill. "I sent for a shamanin and Rasuno (i.e., the tutelary) came on her and said, 'I am going to marry her; if she does not agree, she will go mad.' " It was in vain that she and her husband attempted to resist by offering sacrifices for the tutelary. Finally she was obliged to accept, and learned in dreams the art of shamanizing. She had two children in the underworld. [223]

The Savara shamanic séance consists in the shaman being possessed by the spirit of the tutelary or by the god, whichever is invoked, who speaks through his voice at great length. It is the spirit that takes possession of the shaman or shamaness that reveals the cause of the illness and tells them what action is to be taken (usually a sacrifice or offerings). "Shamanism" through possession is also known in other provinces of India. [224]

The "spirit marriage" of the Savara shamans appears to be a unique phenomenon in aboriginal India; in any case, it is not of Kolarian origin. This is one of the conclusions of the richly documented comparative study by Rudolf Rahmann, "Shamanistic and Related Phenomena in Northern and Middle India." [225] We cite some of the conclusions of this important essay.

---

222 Elwin, p. 153.   223 Ibid., pp. 151–52.

224 Cf. Edward B. Harper, "Shamanism in South India," on "shamanic" practices in northwestern Mysore. These are phenomena of possession and do not necessarily imply a shamanic structure or ideology. Other examples— rightly presented as possession by gods or demons—will be found in Louis Dumont's excellent monograph, *Une Sous-Caste de l'Inde du Sud. Organisation sociale et religion des Pramalai Kallar*, pp. 347 ff. (possession by gods) 406 ff. (possession by demons).

225 *Anthropos*, LIV (1959), 681–760; cf. pp. 722, 754. In a first descriptive section (pp. 683–715) the author presents the material relating to the Munda-speaking, or Kolarian, tribes (Santal, Munda, Korku, Savara, Birhor,

1. "Supernatural" election of the future shaman is indispensable among the Savara, the Bondo, the Birhor, and the Baiga. Among the Baiga, the Khond, and the Bondo "supernatural" election is necessary even if the shaman's office is hereditary. Among the Juang, the Birhor, the Oraon, and the Muria the "elect" usually exhibit psychic traits characteristic of shamanism.[226]

2. Systematic instruction of future shamans is obligatory in a considerable number of tribes (Santal, Munda, Savara, Baiga, Oraon, Bhil, etc.).[227] An initiation ceremony is clearly documented among the Santal, the Munda, the Baiga, the Oraon, and the Bhil, but presumably it also exists among the Korku and the Maler.[228]

3. Shamans have personal tutelary spirits among the Santal, the Savara, the Korwa, the Birhor, the Bhuiya, the Baiga, the Oraon, the Khond, and the Maler.[229] "Since the reports on most of these tribes are incomplete and somewhat vague, it is safe to suppose that the features we have spoken of are in reality more numerous and unequivocal than can be shown from the data actually at hand. But the data already presented warrant for now the general statement that in the magic and shamanism of North and Middle India the following elements are to be found: shaman schools or at least some systematic training of the candidates; an initiation; a personal tutelary spirit; a call by a spirit or deity."[230]

4. Among the shamanistic paraphernalia the winnowing fan plays the most important role. "The winnow is an ancient element in the culture of the Munda peoples."[231] Just as the Siberian shaman brings on his trance by beating his drum, the magicians of North and Middle India "try to achieve the same result by shaking rice in the winnow."[232] This explains the almost total absence of

---

tc.), the Aryan-language tribes (Bhuiya, Baiga, Bhil), and the Dravidian-speaking tribes (Oraon, Khond, Gond, etc.). On the shamanism of the Munda, cf. also Rev. J. Hoffmann, *Encyclopaedia Mundarica*, II, 422 ff., and Koppers, "Probleme der indischen Religionsgeschichte," pp. 801 ff.

226 Rahmann, p. 730.
227 Ibid.
228 Ibid.
229 Ibid., p. 731.
230 Ibid.
231 Ibid., p. 733.
232 Ibid.

the drum in Central and North Indian shamanism. "The winnow has almost the same function." [233]

5. Among some peoples ladders play a role in shamanic rituals The Baiga *barua* "erects for himself a small shrine, and plants couple of poles in front of it. Near the shrine he may also have: wooden ladder, a swing, a rope studded with iron spikes, an iron chain with sharp prongs, a flat board bristling with spikes, and shoes pierced with sharp nails. During his trance he sometimes runs up the ladder without touching it with his hands, and scourges himself with the above-mentioned instruments. He replies to question either from the ladder or from the spike-studded board." [234] The shamanic ladder is also attested among the Gond of Mohaghir. [235] William Crooke reports that the shaman of the Dusadh and the Djangar (tribes of the eastern part of the [former] North-Western Province of India) makes a ladder of wooden sword blades, "up which the priest is compelled to climb, resting the soles of his feet on the edges of the weapons. When he reaches the top he decapitates a white cock which is tied to the summit of the ladder." [236] Among the Savara "a bamboo pole is let through the roof of the house where the rite is held, until it stands on the ground in the main room. Elwin calls it the 'heavenly ladder.' . . . The shamanesses spread a new mat before it and made a cock perch on projecting branch of the ladder." [237]

6. Rahmann rightly interprets as representing the Cosmic Tree "the earth mound with the holy Basil shrub, which the Santal *ojh* and the Munda *marang deora* keep in their houses. . . . The same symbolism of the world mountain or the shaman tree may likewise be seen in the lumps of clay that are found in combination with the iron snake and trident in the school of the Oraon snake shaman and in the cylindrical stone used at the preliminary consecration

---

233 Rahmann, p. 733.   234 Ibid., p. 702.
235 Cf. Koppers, *Die Bhil in Zentralindien*, Pl. XIII, 1.
236 W. Crooke, *Popular Religion and Folk-Lore of Northern India*, I, 19 cited by Rahmann, p. 737. See the rituals of the Lolo and the Kachin, below pp. 441 ff.
237 Rahmann, p. 696.

pre-initiation ceremony) of the Santal shamans, also in the rotating seat of the Munda, and finally in the stone which the Oraon *okha* sees in a night-vision as Śiva's likeness." [238]

7. Among a great many tribes [239] the shaman calls back the dead person's soul between the third and tenth day after death.[240] But there is no evidence of the typical Altaic and Siberian shaman's ritual of accompanying the souls of the deceased to the land of the dead.[241]

In conclusion, Rahmann considers that "shamanism essentially consists in a specific relation to a tutelary spirit, which is manifested by the spirit's taking hold of the shaman as its medium, or by its entering into the shaman to invest him with higher knowledge and powers, above all with dominion over (other) spirits." [242] This definition applies admirably to the characteristics of Middle and North Indian shamanism, but it does not seem to fit other forms of shamanism (e.g., Central and North Asian). The "ascensional" elements (ladder, pillar, shaman's tree, *axis mundi*, etc.)—to which, as we have seen, the author has not failed to draw attention—demand a more precise definition of shamanism. From the historical point of view the author concludes that "shamanistic phenomena certainly occurred in India prior to the coming of Śaktism, and we should not suppose that the Munda peoples remained unaffected by them." [243]

238 Ibid., pp. 738–39.
240 Ibid., pp. 748 ff.
242 Rahmann, p. 751.

239 See the list in ibid., p. 748, n. 191.
241 See above, pp. 205 ff.
243 Ibid., p. 753.

CHAPTER TWELVE

Shamanic
Symbolisms and Techniques
IN TIBET, CHINA,
AND THE FAR EAST

Buddhism, Tantrism, Lamaism

W H E N, after his Illumination, the Buddha returned fo the first time to his native city, Kapilavastu, he exhib ited several "miraculous powers." To convince his relatives of hi spiritual capacities and prepare them for conversion, he rose int the air, cut his body to pieces, let his head and limbs fall to th ground, then joined them together again before the amazed eye of the spectators. This miracle is described even by Aśvaghoṣa but it is so essentially a part of the Indian tradition of magic tha it has become the typical prodigy of fakirism. The famous rop trick of the fakirs creates the illusion that a rope rises very hig into the sky; the master makes a young disciple climb it until h disappears from view. The fakir then throws his knife into the ai and the lad's limbs fall to the ground one after the other.[2]

This rope trick has a long history in India, and is to be compare with two shamanic rites—the future shaman's initiatory dismen

1 *Buddhacarita*, vv. 1551 ff.

2 Cf. Eliade, *Yoga*, pp. 321 ff. See also A. Jacoby, "Zum Zerstückelung und Wiederbelebungswunder der indischen Fakire." It is unnecessary to re peat that we are not concerned with the "reality" of this magical exploit. O only interest is to discover to what extent such magical phenomena presu pose a shamanic ideology and technique. Cf. Eliade, "Remarques sur le 'ro trick.' "

erment by "demons" and the shamanic ascent into the sky. The initiatory dreams" of the Siberian shamans will be recalled: the candidate witnesses the dismemberment of his own body by the ancestral or evil spirits. But then his bones are put together again and fastened with iron, his flesh is renewed, and, on returning to life, the future shaman has a "new body" that enables him to gash his flesh with knives, run swords through himself, touch white-hot iron, and so forth. It is remarkable that the Indian fakirs are reputed to perform the same miracles. In the rope trick they as it were subject their assistants to the "initiatory dismemberment" that their Siberian colleagues undergo in dreams. In addition, though the rope trick has become a specialty of Indian fakirism, it is also found in places as distant as China, Java, ancient Mexico, and medieval Europe. The Moroccan traveler Ibn Baṭūṭah [3] observed it in China in the fourteenth century, E. Melton [4] saw it in Batavia in the seventeenth century, and Sahagún [5] attests it, in almost identical terms, in Mexico. As for Europe, numerous texts,

3 *Voyages d'ibn Batoutah*, trs. and eds. C. F. Defrémery and B. R. Sanguinetti, IV, 291–92. (The translation below is from E. Conze, *Buddhism*, 174.) A juggler "took a wooden ball, with several holes in it, through which long ropes were passed, and, laying hold of one of these, slung it into the air. It went so high that we lost sight of it altogether. There now remained only a little of the end of a thong in the conjurer's hand, and he desired one of the boys who assisted him to lay hold of it and to mount. He did so, climbing by the rope, and we lost sight of him also! The conjurer then called to him three times, but getting no answer, he snatched up a knife as if in a great rage, laid hold of the thong, and disappeared also! Bye and bye he threw down one of the boy's hands, then a foot, then the other hand, and the other foot, then the trunk and last of all the head! Then he came down himself, all puffing and panting, and with his clothes all bloody. . . . The Amir gave [him] some order . . . and our friend then took the lad's limbs, laid them together in their places, and gave a kick, when, presto! there was the boy, who got up and stood before us! All this astonished me beyond measure." Ibn Baṭūṭah then recalls how, having seen a like performance in India, he had been similarly astonished. Cf. also H. Yule, tr. and ed., *The Book of Ser Marco Polo*, I, 318 ff. On the rope trick in Moslem hagiographic legends, L. Massignon, *La Passion d'al-Hosayn-ibn-Mansour al-Hallaj, martyr mystique de l'Islam*, I, 80 ff.

4 The passage is quoted in Jacoby, pp. 460 ff.

5 E. Seler, "Zauberei im alten Mexiko," pp. 84–85 (after Sahagún).

at least from the thirteenth century on, mention the very same prodigies, performed by sorcerers and magicians, who also possessed the power to fly and to make themselves invisible, exactly like the shamans and yogins.[6]

The rope trick of the fakirs is only a spectacular variant of the shaman's celestial ascent; the latter is always symbolic, for the shaman's body does not disappear and the journey takes place "in spirit." But the symbolism of the rope, like that of the ladder, necessarily implies communication between sky and earth. It is by means of a rope or a ladder (as, too, by a vine, a bridge, a chain of arrows, etc.) that the gods descend to earth and men go up to the sky. This is an archaic and widespread tradition, found both in India and Tibet. The Buddha descends from the Trayastriṃśa Heaven by a stairway to "tread the human path"; from the top of the stairway all the Brahmalokas are visible above and the depths of hell below,[7] for it is a true *axis mundi*, set at the "Center of the Universe." This miraculous stairway is depicted in the reliefs at Bhārhut and Sanchi, and in Tibetan Buddhist painting it also gives human beings access to heaven.[8]

In Tibet the ritual and mythological function of the rope is even more fully documented, especially in the pre-Buddhist tradition. The first king of Tibet, Gña-k'ri-bstan-po, is said to have come

6 See the numerous examples brought together by Jacoby, pp. 466 f. and in Eliade, "Remarques." Cf. also id., *Yoga*, p. 323. It is still difficult to decide definitely whether the rope trick of European sorcerers is due to an influence from Oriental magic or derives from ancient local shamanic techniques. The fact that, on the one hand, the rope trick is attested in Mexico and, on the other, the magical dismemberment of the sorcerer is also found in Australia, Indonesia, and South America leads us to believe that in Europe it may well be a matter of a survival of local pre-Indo-European magical techniques. On the symbolism of levitation and "magical flight," see Ananda K. Coomaraswamy, *Hinduism and Buddhism*, p. 83, n. 269.

7 Cf. Coomaraswamy, "Svayamātṛṇṇā: Janua Coeli," pp. 27, n. 8; 46, n. 64.

8 Giuseppe Tucci, *Tibetan Painted Scrolls*, II, 348, and tanka no. 127, Pls. XIV–XXII. On the symbolism of stairs, see also below, p. 487.

lown from heaven by a rope named *dmu-t'ag*.[9] This mythical rope was also depicted on royal tombs, a sign that the sovereign ascended to heaven after death. Indeed, for kings, communications between heaven and earth were never altogether broken. And the Tibetans believed that in ancient times their sovereigns did not die but ascended to heaven,[10] a concept that suggests memory of a certain "lost paradise."

Bon traditions further speak of a clan, dMu, a name that at the same time designates a class of gods; these dwell in heaven and the dead go to them there by climbing a ladder or a rope. Long ago on earth there was a class of priests who professed to have power to guide the dead to heaven because they were masters of the rope or ladder; these priests were the dMu.[11] This rope, which in those days connected earth with heaven and by which the dead ascended to the celestial dwelling of the dMu gods, was replaced, among other Bon priests, by the rope of divination.[12] This symbol survives —perhaps—in the piece of cloth that, among the Na-khi, represents the bridge over which the soul passes to the realm of the gods.[13] All these features are an integral part of the shamanic complex of ascent and soul-guiding.

It would be chimerical to attempt in a few pages to list all the other shamanic motifs present in Bon-po myths and rituals.[14] and

9 R. A. Stein, "Leao-Tche," p. 68, n. 1. The author mentions the fact that H. A. Jäschke, in his dictionary, cites the *rgyal·rabs* under this word, and states that it appears to designate certain supernatural means of communication between Tibetan kings and their ancestors dwelling among the gods. See also Helmut Hoffmann: *Quellen zur Geschichte der tibetischen Bon-Religion*, pp. 141, 150, 153, 245; *The Religions of Tibet*, pp. 19–20; M. Hermanns, *Mythen und Mysterien, Magie und Religion der Tibeter*, pp. 35 ff.

10 Tucci, II, 733–34. The author cites the Chinese and Thai myth of a communication between heaven and earth, to which we shall return. At Gilgit, where the Bon religion was very flourishing, the tradition of a golden chain connecting heaven with earth is still found in our day (ibid., p. 734, citing *Folklore*, XXV [1914], 397).

11 Ibid., p. 714.   12 Ibid., p. 716.

13 Ibid., citing J. F. Rock; see below, p. 446.

14 Ever since J. H. Klaproth's "Description du Tubet" (pp. 97, 148, etc.), Western writers, following the lead of the Chinese scholars, have identified

persisting in Indo-Tibetan tantrism. The Bon-po priests differ in no way from real shamans; they are even separated into "white" Bon-po and "black" Bon-po, though they all use the drum in their rites. Some claim to be "possessed by the gods"; the majority of them practice exorcism.[15] One class is called "possessors of the heavenly rope." [16] The *pawo* and the *nyen-jomo* are mediums, male and female, regarded by the Buddhists as typical representatives of Bon. They are not connected with the Bon monasteries of Sikkim and Bhutan, and "they seem to be a remnant of the earliest unorganized Bon as it existed before the so called 'White Bon' (*Bon dtkar*) had developed after the example of Buddhism." [17] It appears that they can be possessed by the spirits of the dead and during their trance, enter into communication with their tutelary divinities.[18] As for the Bon mediums, one of their chief functions is

Taoism with the Bon-po religion; see the history of this confusion (due probably, to an error on the part of Abel Rémusat, who had read the term *tao-chih* as "the taoist") in W. W. Rockhill, *The Land of the Lamas*, pp. 217 ff.; cf. also Yule, *The Book of Ser Marco Polo*, I, 323 ff. On the Bon see Tucci, *Tibetan Painted Scrolls*, II, pp. 711–38; the works by H. Hoffmann already cited and his "Gšen," especially pp. 344 ff.; M. Hermanns, *Mythen*, pp. 232 and passim; Li An-che, "Bon: the Magico-Religious Belief of the Tibetan-Speaking Peoples"; Siegbert Hummel, *Geheimnisse tibetischer Malereien. II: Lamaistische Studien*, pp. 30 ff.; René de Nebesky Wojkowitz, *Oracles and Demons of Tibet*, pp. 425 ff.: "Die tibetische Bön Religion." On the Lamaist pantheon and the divinities of sickness and healing, see Eugen Pander, "Das lamaische Pantheon"; F. G. Reinhold Müller, "Die Krankheits- und Heilgottheiten des Lamaismus." Hummel has attempted a historical analysis of Bon, comparing it not only with the Central and North Asian shamanisms but also with the religious ideas of the ancient Near East and of the Indo-Europeans; cf. "Grundzüge einer Urgeschichte der tibetischen Kultur," especially pp. 96 ff.; "Eurasiatische Traditionen in der tibetischen Bon-Religion," pp. 165–212, especially pp. 198 ff.

15 Tucci, pp. 715 ff.   16 Ibid., p. 717.

17 Nebesky-Wojkowitz, *Oracles*, p. 425.

18 Ibid. Cf. also J. Morris, *Living with the Lepchas*, pp. 123 ff. (description of the trance of a woman medium). According to Hermanns, Lepcha shamanism is not identical with Bon-po but represents a more archaic form of shamanism; cf. *The Indo-Tibetans*, pp. 49–58.

"to serve as the temporary mouthpiece of spirits of the dead, who had later to be conducted to the other world." [19]

The Bon shamans are believed to use their drums as vehicles to convey them through the air. A classic example is the flight of Na-ro bon-č'un on the occasion of his tournament of magic with Mi-la ras-pa.[20] "A remnant of a similar tradition may be the legend which claims that gShen rab mi bo used to fly on a huge wheel, on which he occupied the central position, while his eight disciples sat on the eight spokes." [21] Probably the original vehicle was the shamanic drum, later replaced by the wheel, which is a Buddhist symbol. The Bon shaman's cure includes seeking the patient's soul,[22] a characteristically shamanic technique. A similar ceremony takes place when the Tibetan exorcist is summoned to cure a patient; he undertakes a search for the patient's soul.[23] Calling back the patient's soul sometimes requires an extremely complex ritual involving objects (threads of five different colors, arrows, etc.) and effigies.[24] Nebesky-Wojkowitz has recently demonstrated other shamanic elements in Tibetan Lamaism.[25] In the State-oracle the prophetic trance, indispensable in ceremonial divination, is markedly para-shamanic.[26]

19 Nebesky-Wojkowitz, *Oracles*, p. 428. Among the Lepcha too, the shamaness summons the spirit of the deceased to enter her before being led to the beyond; cf. id., "Ancient Funeral Ceremonies of the Lepchas," p. 33 ff.

20 Text tr. by H. Hoffmann, *Quellen zur Geschichte der tibetischen Bon-Religion*, p. 274.

21 Nebesky-Wojkowitz, *Oracles*, p. 542. On the drum divination of the Bon priests of Sikkim and Bhutan, which is comparable to that of the Siberian shamans, cf. id., "Tibetan Drum Divination, 'Ngamo.' "

22 Cf. H. Hoffmann, *Quellen*, pp. 117 f.

23 Cf. the description of a séance with a Lhasan exorcist in S. H. Ribbach, *Drogpa Namgyal. Ein Tibeterleben*, pp. 187 f.; cf. also H. Hoffmann, *Quellen*, p. 205 f.

24 Cf. the eighteenth-century text tr., with commentary, by F. D. Lessing, "Calling the Soul: a Lamaist Ritual."

25 Cf. *Oracles*, pp. 538 f.

26 Ibid., pp. 428 f.; cf. also Nebesky-Wojkowitz, "Das tibetische Staatsorakel," and, especially, D. Schröder, "Zur Religion der Tujen des Sining-gebietes (Kukunor)," [Pt. 1], pp. 27–33, 846, 850; [Pt. 2], pp. 237–48,

Lamaism has preserved the Bon shamanic tradition almost in it entirety. Even the most famous masters of Tibetan Buddhism ar reputed to have performed cures and worked miracles in the pures tradition of shamanism. Certain elements that contributed to th development of Lamaism are in all probability of tantric, and per haps Indian, origin. But the question cannot always be decided When, according to a Tibetan legend, Vairocana, Padmasaṃ bhava's disciple and coworker, expels the spirit of her illness fron Queen Tshe-spong-bza's body in the form of a black pin,[27] have w an Indian or a Tibetan tradition? Padmasaṃbhava demonstrates th same famous ability to fly that is attributed to the bodhisattva and arhats, for he, too, journeys through the air, ascends to heaver and becomes a bodhisattva. But that is not all. His legend als shows purely shamanic features; he goes up to the roof of hi house and there, clad only in "seven ornaments of bone," [28] dance a mystical dance—which takes us back to the Siberian shaman' costume.

The roles played by human skulls and by women in tantric and Lamaist [30] ceremonies are well known. The so-called skeleto

and "Zur Struktur des Schamanismus," pp. 867–68, 872–73 (on the *gurtu* [shaman] in Kukunor).

27 R. Bleichsteiner, *L'Église jaune*, p. 71.   28 Ibid., p. 67.

29 See Eliade, *Yoga*, pp. 296 ff., on the Aghorīs and Kāpālikas ("wearer of skulls"). It is probable that these simultaneously ascetic and orgiasti sects, which still practiced cannibalism at the end of the nineteenth centur (cf. *Yoga*, ibid.), had assimilated certain aberrant traditions connected wit the cult of skulls (which also frequently implies ritual eating of relatives cf., for example, the custom among the Issedones, recorded by Herodotu IV. 26). On the prehistoric antecedents of the skull cult, cf. H. Breuil an H. Obermaier, "Crânes paléolithiques façonnés en coupe"; P. Werner "L'Anthropophagie rituelle et la chasse aux têtes aux époques actuelle e paléolithique"; id., "Culte des crânes," passim; J. Maringer, *Vorgeschichtlich Religion*, pp. 112 ff., 220 ff., 248 ff.

30 Cf. W. W. Rockhill, "On the Use of Skulls in Lamaist Ceremonies" B. Laufer, *Use of Human Skulls and Bones in Tibet*. The Tibetans used thei fathers' skulls, like the Issedones (ibid., p. 2), but today the family cu has disappeared and, according to Laufer (ibid., p. 5), the magico-religiou role of skulls appears to be a tantric (Śaivite) innovation. But it is possibl

dance has a peculiar importance in the dramatic scenarios named *ǎcham*, one of whose purposes is to familiarize the spectators with the terrible images of the tutelary divinities who appear in the state of *bardo*, that is, the intermediate state between death and a new reincarnation. From this point of view, the *ǎcham* can be considered an initiatory ceremony, for it furnishes certain revelations regarding experiences after death. Now, it is striking to what a degree these Tibetan costumes and masks representing the skeleton recall the costumes of Central and North Asian shamans. In certain cases we indubitably have to do with Lamaist influences, which are, moreover, attested by other ornaments of the Siberian shamanic costume and even by some forms of the drum. But we must not hasten to conclude that the role of the skeleton in the symbolism of the North Asian shamanic costume derives entirely from a Lamaist influence. Such an influence, if it was in fact exerted, only reinforced very ancient autochthonous conceptions regarding the sacredness of animal bones and hence of human bones.[31] As for the role given to the image of one's own skeleton, which is so important in the meditation techniques of Mongolian Buddhism, we must not forget that the Eskimo shaman's initiation also includes contemplating his skeleton; it will be remembered that the future *angakok*, by the force of thought, strips his body of flesh and blood until only the bones remain.[32] Until more data become available, we incline to believe that this type of meditation belongs to an archaic, pre-Buddhistic stratum of spirituality, which was based, in one way or another, on the ideology of the hunting peoples (the sacredness of bones) and whose object was to "withdraw" the soul from the practitioner's own body for a mystical journey—that is, to achieve ecstasy.

---

that Indian influences were superimposed on an ancient stratum of local beliefs; cf. the religious and divinatory role of shamans' skulls among the Yukagir (W. I. Jochelson, *The Yukaghir and the Yukaghirized Tungus*, p. 165). On the protohistorical relations between the cult of skulls and the idea of a renewal of cosmic life, in China and Indonesia, cf. Carl Hentze, "Zur ursprünglichen Bedeutung des chinesischen Zeichens t'oû = Kopf."

31 See above, pp. 158 ff. 32 See above, p. 62.

Tibet has a tantric rite, named *chöd* (*gchod*), which is clearly shamanic in structure. It consists in offering one's own flesh to be eaten by demons—which is curiously reminiscent of the future shaman's initiatory dismemberment by "demons" and ancestral souls. R. Bleichsteiner describes it as follows: "To the sound of the drum made of human skulls and of the thighbone trumpet, the dance is begun and the spirits are invited to come and feast. The power of meditation evokes a goddess brandishing a naked sword; she springs at the head of the sacrificer, decapitates him, and hacks him to pieces; then the demons and wild beasts rush on the still-quivering fragments, eat the flesh, and drink the blood. The words spoken refer to certain *Jātakas*, which tell how the Buddha, in the course of his earlier lives, gave his own flesh to starving animals and man-eating demons. But despite this Buddhist coloring," Bleichsteiner concludes, the rite is but "a sinister mystery going back to the most primitive times." [33]

It will be remembered that a similar initiation rite is found among some North American tribes. In the case of the *chöd*, we are in the presence of a mystical re-evaluation of a shamanic initiation schema. The "sinister" side is the most apparent; we have an experience of death and resurrection which, like all experiences of this category, is "terrifying." Indo-Tibetan tantrism has ever more radically spiritualized the initiation schema of "being killed" by demons. We cite some tantric meditations whose object is the practitioner's stripping his own body of flesh and contemplating his skeleton. The yogin is asked to imagine his body as a corpse and his mind as an angry goddess, with a face and two hands holding a knife and a skull. "Think that she severeth the head from the corpse . . . and cutteth the corpse into bits and flingeth them inside the skull as offerings to the deities." Another exercise consists in his seeing himself as "a radiant white skeleton of enormous size, whence issueth flames, so great that they fill the voidness of

33 *L'Église jaune*, pp. 194–95. On the *chöd*, see also Alexandra David-Neel, *With Mystics and Magicians in Tibet*, pp. 126 ff.; Eliade, *Yoga*, pp. 323 f.

the Universe." Finally, a third meditation sets the yogin the task of contemplating himself as transformed into the raging Ḍākinī, stripping the skin from his own body. The text continues: "Visualize thyself as . . . that thou . . . spreadest it [the skin] out so that it covereth the Third-Void Universe, and upon it heapest up all thy bones and flesh. Then, when the malignant spirits are in the midst of enjoying the feast, imagine that the Wrathful Ḍākinī taketh the hide and rolleth it up . . . and dasheth it down forcibly, reducing it and all its contents to a mass of bony and fleshly pulp, upon which many mentally-produced wild beasts feed." [34]

These few extracts suffice to show the transformation that a shamanic schema can undergo when it is incorporated into a complex philosophical system, such as tantrism. Important for our purpose is the survival of certain shamanic symbols and methods even in highly elaborated techniques of meditation oriented to goals other than ecstasy. All this, in our opinion, sufficiently illustrates the genuineness and the initiatory spiritual value of many shamanic experiences.

Finally, we will briefly point out some other shamanic elements in Yoga and Indo-Tibetan tantrism. "Mystical heat," which is already documented in Vedic texts, holds a considerable place in Yogic-tantric techniques. This "heat" is induced by holding the breath [35] and especially by the "transmutation" of sexual energy,[36] a Yogic-tantric practice which, though quite obscure, is based on *prāṇāyāma* and various "visualizations." Some Indo-Tibetan initiatory ordeals consist precisely in testing a candidate's degree of preparation by his ability, during a winter night snowstorm, to dry a large number of soaked sheets directly on his naked body.[37]

34 Lama Kazi Dawa-Samdup's rendering in W. Y. Evans-Wentz, *Tibetan Yoga and Secret Doctrines*, pp. 311-12, 330-31. Presumably it is meditations of this type that certain Indian yogins pursue in cemeteries.

35 Cf. *Majjhima-nikāya*, I, 244, etc.

36 Cf. Evans-Wentz, *Tibetan Yoga*, pp. 156 ff., 187 ff., 196 ff.

37 This "psychic heat" has in Tibetan the name *gtūm-mō* (pronounced *tūm-mō*). "Sheets are dipped in the icy water. Each man wraps himself in one of them and must dry it on his body. As soon as the sheet has become dry, it is again dipped in the water and placed on the novice's body to be dried as

A similar ordeal is characteristic of the Manchurian shaman's initiation,[38] and probably we here have a Lamaist influence. But "mystical heat" is not necessarily a creation of Indo-Tibetan magic; we have already cited the example of a young Labrador Eskimo who remains five days and nights in the icy sea and, having proved that he was not even wetted, immediately obtains the title of *angakok*. Intense heat produced in the practitioner's own body is directly connected with "mastery over fire," and we are justified in believing that the latter technique is extremely archaic.

Also shamanic in structure is what has been called the Tibetan Book of the Dead.[39] Although strictly speaking it is not a psychopompic guide, we may compare the role of the priest who recites ritual texts concerning the roads in the afterlife in order that the deceased may follow them with the function of the Altaic or Goldi shaman who symbolically escorts the deceased into the beyond. This *Bardo thödol* represents an intermediate stage between the narrative of the shaman-psychopomp and the Orphic plates, which briefly told the deceased the right paths to take in his journey through the beyond; it also has a number of features in common with the Indonesian and Polynesian funerary chants. A Tibetan manuscript from Tun Huang, entitled "Exposition of the Road of Death" and recently translated by Marcelle Lalou,[40] describes the directions to be avoided, first of all the "Great Hell," which lies 8,000 *yojana* underground and whose center is of blazing iron. "Within the house of iron, in hells of all descriptions

---

before. The operation goes on in that way until daybreak. Then he who has dried the largest number of sheets is acknowledged the winner of the competition" (David-Neel, *With Mystics and Magicians in Tibet*, pp. 227 f.). Cf also Hummel, *Geheimnisse tibetischer Malereien. II: Lamaistische Studien* pp. 21 ff.

38 Above, pp. 112 f.

39 Evans-Wentz, ed., and Lama Kazi Dawa-Samdup, tr. *The Tibetan Book of the Dead*, pp. 87 ff. A lama, a brother in belief, or a close friend must read the funerary text into the dead man's ear, but without touching him.

40 "Le Chemin des morts dans les croyances de Haute-Asie."

countless demons (*rākṣasa*) torment and afflict by burning, roasting, and cutting to pieces . . ."[41] Hell (*pretaloka*), the world (*Jambudvīpa*), and Mount Meru lie on the same axis, and the deceased is urged to make his way directly to Mount Meru, on whose summit Indra and thirty-two ministers winnow the "transmigrants."[42] Under the veneer of Buddhist beliefs, it is easy to recognize the old schema of the *axis mundi*, communications among the three cosmic zones, and the guardian who classifies souls. The shamanic elements are still more clearly apparent in the funerary rite for causing the soul of the deceased to enter his effigy.[43] The effigy, or "name-card," represents the deceased kneeling and with arms raised in supplication.[44] His soul is invoked: "Let the deceased come here, whose effigy is fixed to this card. He who has passed from this world and is in process of changing his body, whether he is already born in one of the six spheres or still wanders in the intermediate state, wherever he may be, let his consciousness gather upon this symbol. . . ."[45] If one of his bones is available, it is placed on the name-card.[46] Again the deceased is addressed: "Listen, thou who wanderest amidst the illusions of another world! Come to this most delightful place in our human world! This umbrella shall be your place, your protection, your consecrated shrine. This name-card is the symbol of your body, this bone the symbol of your speech, this jewellery the symbol of your mind. . . . O make these symbols your abode!"[47] Since it is believed that the deceased may be reborn in any of the six spheres of existence, the ritual seeks to liberate him "from each in turn, his name-card being moved around the lotus-petals, so that he progresses from the hells to the sphere of unhappy spirits, thence to the animals, men, titans and gods."[48] The purpose of the ritual is to prevent the

41 Ibid., p. 44. Cf. the Iron Mountain to which the Altaic shaman comes during his descent to the underworld. The tortures inflicted by the *rākṣasa* suggest the initiatory dreams of Siberian shamans in every point.

42 Ibid., p. 45.

43 Cf. above, pp. 210 ff., the description of a similar Goldi ritual.

44 D. L. Snellgrove, *Buddhist Himalaya*, p. 265.

45 Ibid., p. 266.

46 Ibid., p. 267.

47 Ibid.

48 Ibid., p. 268.

soul from becoming incarnated in one of these six worlds and, instead, to cause it to attain the region of Avalokiteśvara.[49] But making the deceased enter an effigy and guiding him through the hells and extrahuman worlds are purely shamanic techniques.

In Tibet a number of other shamanic ideas and techniques have survived in Lamaism. So, for example, the lama-sorcerers fight with one another by magical means, even as the Siberian shamans do.[50] The lamas control the atmosphere, just like the shamans,[51] they fly through the air,[52] perform ecstatic dances,[53] and so forth. Tibetan tantrism has a secret language, called the "tongue of the ḍākinī," just as the various Indian tantric schools use the "twilight language" in which the same term can have as many as three or four different meanings.[54] All this in some measure approaches the "spirit language" or "secret language" of the shamans, both of North Asia and of Malaya and Indonesia. It would even be highly instructive to study to what extent techniques of ecstasy lead to linguistic creations and to determine the mechanisms of the latter. Now, we know that the shamanic "spirit language" not only attempts to imitate animal cries but contains a certain proportion of spontaneous creations presumably explained by pre-ecstatic euphoria and ecstasy itself.

This rapid review of Tibetan material has enabled us to discover, on the one hand, a certain structural likeness between the Bon-po myths and shamanism and, on the other, the survival of shamanic themes and techniques in Buddhism and Lamaism. "Survival" does not, perhaps, clearly express the true state of affairs; rather, we should speak of a re-evaluation of the ancient shamanic motifs and their incorporation into a system of ascetic theology in which even their content has undergone radical change. This is only normal, however, if we consider that the very notion of the "soul"—which is fundamental in shamanic ideology—changes its meaning completely in consequence of the Buddhist critique. To

49 Ibid., p. 274.   50 Bleichsteiner, pp. 187 ff.
51 Ibid., pp. 188 ff.   52 Ibid., p. 189.
53 Ibid., pp. 224 ff.   54 Cf. Eliade, *Yoga*, pp. 249 ff.

whatever extent Lamaism is a regression in comparison with the great Buddhist metaphysical tradition, it was impossible for it to return to the realistic concept of the "soul," and this one point suffices to distinguish the various contents of a Lamaist technique from those of a shamanic technique.

But then too, as we shall soon see, Lamaist ideology and practice made their way deep into Central and North Asia, contributing toward giving a number of Siberian shamanisms their present aspect.

Shamanic Practices among the Lolo

Like the Thai and the Chinese,[55] the Lolo believe that the first men moved freely between earth and heaven; as the result of a "sin," the road was blocked.[56] But at his death man finds the road to heaven again; or at least so it appears from certain funerary rituals in which the *pimo*, priest-shaman, attends the deathbed to read prayers that tell of the various kinds of bliss awaiting the deceased in heaven. [57] To arrive there, he must cross a bridge; to the mingled sounds of the drum and horn, other prayers are recited to guide him. At this time the priest-shaman removes three beams from the roof of the house, so that the sky becomes visible—this is called "opening the bridge to heaven." [58] Among the Lolo of southern Yunnan the funerary ritual is somewhat different. The priest-shaman accompanies the coffin, reciting what is called "the ritual of the road." The text, after describing the places through which the deceased passes between his house and the grave, continues by enumerating the cities, mountains, and rivers that he must traverse before reaching the Taliang mountains, the original home of the Lolo race. From there the deceased goes on to the Tree of Thought

55 H. Maspero, "Légendes mythologiques dans le *Chou king*," pp. 94 ff.; F. Kiichi Numazawa, *Die Weltanfänge in der japanischen Mythologie*, pp. 314 ff.

56 Luigi Vannicelli, *La religione dei Lolo*, p. 44.

57 Ibid., p. 184.   58 Ibid., pp. 179–80.

and the Tree of Speech, and enters hell.[59] Leaving aside the difference between the two religions in respect to the region to which the deceased journeys, we may note the role of psychopomp played by the shaman; the ritual is to be compared with the Tibetan *Bardo thödol* and the funerary laments of Indonesia and Polynesia.

Since sickness is interpreted as a flight of the soul, cure involves calling it back. The shaman reads a long litany in which the patient's soul is implored to return from the distant mountains, valleys, rivers, forests and fields, or wherever it may be wandering.[60] The same summoning back the soul is found among the Karen of Burma, who, in addition, employ a similar treatment for the "sicknesses" of the rice, imploring its "soul" to return to the crop.[61] As we shall presently see, the same ceremony is used by the Chinese.

Lolo shamanism appears to have been influenced by Chinese magic. The Lolo shaman's knife and drum, as well as the "spirits," have Chinese names.[62] Divination is practiced according to the Chinese method.[63] And one of the most important Lolo shamanic rites, the "ladder of knives," is also found in China. This rite is used when there are epidemics. A double ladder is built, made of thirty-six knives, and the shaman, barefoot, climbs it to the top and then goes down on the other side. A number of plowshares are also heated white-hot and the shaman must walk over them. Father

59 A. Henry, "The Lolos and Other Tribes of Western China," p. 103.
60 Ibid., p. 101; Vannicelli, p. 174.
61 Cf. Rev. H. I. Marshall, *The Karen People of Burma*, p. 245; Vannicelli, p. 175; Eliade, *Patterns in Comparative Religion*, p. 339. Calling back the patient's soul is an integral part of the shamanic ceremonials among the Kachin and the Palaung of Burma, and the Lakher, the Garo, and the Lushai of Assam; cf. Frazer, *Aftermath*, pp. 216–20. Cf. also Nguyĕn-vǎn-Khoan, "Le Repêchage de l'âme." On metal drums in the cult of the dead among the Garo, the Karen, and other related peoples, cf. R. Heine-Geldern, "Bedeutung und Herkunft der ältesten hinterindischen Mettalltrommeln (Kesselgongs)."

62 Vannicelli, pp. 169 ff.   63 Ibid., p. 170.

Lietard observes that this rite is strictly Lolo, for the Chinese always call on Lolo shamans to perform it.[64] Probably it is an old shamanic rite modified under the influence of Chinese magic. For the formulas spoken during the ceremony are in the Lolo language, only the names of the spirits being Chinese.

This rite appears to us of great importance. It involves the shaman's symbolic ascent by stairs, a variant of ascent by a tree, post, rope, and so forth. It is performed in case of epidemics, that is, on occasions of extreme danger to the community, and whatever its present significance may be, its original meaning implied the shaman's ascending to heaven to ask the celestial God to put an end to the sickness. Furthermore, the ascensional role of stairs is attested elsewhere in Asia, and we shall return to it. For the moment, we will add that the Chingpaw shaman of Upper Burma ascends a stairway of knives during his initiation.[65] The same initiation rite is found in China, but probably in this case we have a protohistorical heritage common to all these peoples (Lolo, Chinese, Chingpaw, etc.), for the symbolism of shamanic ascent is found in regions too numerous and too far apart to be given a definite historical "origin." Traces of a shamanism of the Central Asian type are found among the shamans of the white Meo in Indochina. The séance consists in imitating a journey on horseback; the shaman is believed to go in search of the patient's soul, which, we may add, he always succeeds in capturing. Occasionally the mystical journey includes a celestial ascent. The shaman makes a series of leaps and is said to be going up to heaven.[66]

64 Ibid., pp. 154–55.

65 Hans J. Wehrli, "Beitrag zur Ethnologie der Chingpaw (Kachin) von Ober-Burma," p. 54 (after Sladen). The Chingpaw shaman (*tumsa*) also uses a "secret language" (ibid., p. 56). Sickness is interpreted as the soul having been abducted or having strayed away (ibid.). Cf. also Yule, *The Book of Ser Marco Polo*, II, 97 ff. On the initiation of the *Mwod Mod* of the Black Thai of Laos, see Pierre-Bernard Lafont, "Pratiques médicales des Thai noirs du Laos de l'ouest," pp. 825–27.

66 Cf. G. Moréchand, "Principaux traits du chamanisme mèo blanc en Indochine," especially pp. 513 ff., 522 ff.

Shamanism among the Moso

Conceptions very close to those of the Tibetan Book of the Dead are found among the Moso or Na-khi, groups belonging to the Tibeto-Burmese family and inhabiting southwestern China, especially Yunnan Province, from the beginning of the Christian era.[67] According to Rock, the latest and best informed authority on the subject, the religion of the Na-khi is pure Bon shamanism.[68] This does not exclude the cult of a celestial Supreme Being, Më, who is structurally very close to the Chinese God of Heaven, T'ien.[69] The periodical sacrifice to heaven is even the most ancient ceremony of the Na-khi; there is reason to believe that it was already practiced when they were leading a nomadic existence on the grassy plains of northeastern Tibet.[70] On this occasion the prayers

67 Cf. Jacques Bacot, *Les Mo-so*; Joseph F. Rock, *The Ancient Na-khi Kingdom of Southwest China*, I–II.

68 Rock, "Studies in Na-khi Literature. I: The Birth and Origin of Dto-mba Shi-lo, the Founder of the Mo-so Shamanism, According to Mo-so Manuscripts; II: The Na-khi ¹Hă ²zhi ¹p'i or the Road the Gods Decide." (References below are to the BEFEO edition.) The same author has recently published "Contributions to the Shamanism of the Tibetan-Chinese Borderland," the first part of which is devoted to the *llü-bu*, the genuine sorcerer of of the Na-khi. In all probability the office of *llü-bu* was held by women in ancient times (p. 797). The office is not hereditary, and vocation is declared by an almost psychopathic crisis: the person destined to become a *llü-bu* dances to the temple of a guardian divinity. Above the image of the god "a number of red scarves are suspended on a rope." If the divinity "approves of the man, one of the red scarves will drop on him." If not, "the man is . . . considered merely an epileptic or insane and taken home" (pp. 797–98—a passage to be added to the documentation already given under "Shamanism and Psychopathology"; cf. above, pp. 23 ff.). During the séance the spirits speak through the *llü-bu*, but he does not embody them, he is not "possessed" (p. 800, etc.). The *llü-bu* exhibits specifically shamanic powers: he walks on fire and touches white-hot iron (p. 801). Rock's study also contains personal observations on the *Nda-pa* or Moso sorcerers of Yunnan, China (pp. 801 ff.) and on the Tibetan *srung-ma* or "guardian of the Faith" (pp. 806 ff.). Cf. also Siegbert Hummel, "Die Bedeutung der Na-khi für die Erforschung der tibetischen Kultur."

69 Bacot, pp. 15 f.

70 Rock, "The Muan bpö Ceremony or the Sacrifice to Heaven as Practiced by the Na-khi," pp. 3 f.

to heaven are followed by prayers to the earth and to the juniper, the Cosmic Tree that supports the universe and rises at the "Center of the World." [71] As we see, the Na-khi have preserved substantially the faith of the herdsmen of Central Asia: the cult of the sky, the conception of the three cosmic zones, the myth of the World Tree planted at the center of the universe and upholding it by its thousand branches.

After death the soul should rise to heaven. But it is necessary to reckon with the demons, who force it down to hell. The number, power, and importance of these demons have given the Moso religion its typical physiognomy, which is so close to Bon shamanism. And in fact Dto-mba Shi-lo, the founder of Na-khi shamanism, passed into myth and the cult as conqueror of the demons. Whatever the case may be in regard to his "historical" personality, his biography is completely mythical. He is born from his mother's left side, like all heroes and saints, he immediately ascends to heaven (like the Buddha), and terrifies the demons. The gods have given him power to exorcise demons and "to send the souls of the dead to the realm of the gods." [72] He is at once psychopomp and savior. As in other Central Asian traditions, the gods sent this First Shaman to defend mankind against the demons. The word *dto-mba*, which is of Tibetan origin and equivalent to the Tibetan *ston-pa*, "master, founder, or promulgator of a particular doctrine," clearly indicates that an innovation is involved: Na-khi "shamanism" is a later phenomenon than the organization of Na-khi religion. It was made necessary by the terrifying multiplication of "demons," and there are a number of reasons for believing that this demonology developed under the influence of Chinese religious ideas.

Dto-mba Shi-lo's mythical biography contains, though with certain adulterations, the typical schema of shamanic initiation. Struck by the newborn infant's extraordinary intelligence, the 360 demons abduct it and take it to the place where "a thousand roads cross" (that is, to the "Center of the World"); there they

71 Ibid., pp. 20 ff. 72 Rock, "Studies," I, 18.

put it to boil in a caldron for three days and nights; but when the demons take off the cover, the child appears unharmed.[73] We are reminded of the "initiatory dreams" of the Siberian shamans; of the demons who cook the future shaman's body for three days. But since this is a case of a master exorcist, who is pre-eminently a demon-slayer, the role of the demons in an initiation is camouflaged; the initiatory ordeal becomes an attempted murder.

Dto-mba Shi-lo "open[s] the road for the soul of the departed." The funerary ceremony is called precisely *Zhi-mä*, the "Road desire," and the numerous texts recited in the presence of the corpse are a counterpart to the Tibetan Book of the Dead.[74] On the day of the funeral the officiants unfurl a long scroll or a piece of cloth on which are painted the various infernal regions that the deceased must pass through before reaching the realm of the gods.[75] This is the map of the complicated and dangerous itinerary along which the deceased will be guided by the shaman (*dto-mba*). Hell contains nine precincts, which are reached after crossing a bridge.[76] The descent is dangerous, for demons block the bridge; the *dto-mba*'s mission is precisely to "open the road." Constantly invoking the First Shaman,[77] Dto-mba Shi-lo, he succeeds in escorting the deceased from precinct to precinct, to the ninth and last. After this descent among the demons the deceased climbs the seven golden mountains, comes to the foot of a tree whose top bears the "medicine of immortality," and finally reaches the realm of the gods.[78]

73 Rock, "Studies," I, 37.

74 See tr., with commentary, in ibid., II, 46 ff., 55 ff. The number of these texts is considerable (ibid., p. 40).

75 Ibid., p. 41. 76 Ibid., p. 49.

77 Indeed, all these funerary rituals in a measure repeat the creation of the world and the biography of Dto-mba Shi-lo; each text begins by picturing the cosmogony and then relates the miraculous birth of Shi-lo and his heroic feats in his battle with the demons. This reactualization of a mythical *illua tempus* and of the primordial event that revealed the efficacy of the First Shaman's acts—acts that later became exemplary and repeatable ad infinitum—is the normal behavior of archaic man; cf. Eliade, *The Myth of the Eternal Return*, pp. 30 ff. and passim.

78 Rock, "Studies," II, 91 ff., 101 ff. See also id., *The Zhi Mä Funera*.

As representative of the First Shaman, Dto-mba Shi-lo, the *dto-mba* succeeds in "opening the road" for the deceased and guiding him through the precincts of hell, where he might otherwise be devoured by demons. The *dto-mba* guides the deceased symbolically, by reading him the ritual texts; but he is always with him "in spirit." He warns him of all dangers: "Oh dead, when crossing the bridge and road you will find them closed by the Lä-ch'ou. Your soul will be unable to arrive in the realm of the gods." [79] Then he tells him how to escape them: the family must sacrifice to the demons, for it is the dead man's sins that bar the road, and the family must redeem his sins by sacrifices.

These few data give an idea of the shaman's function in the Na-khi religion. The shaman was sent by the gods to defend mankind from the demons; such a defense is even more needed after death, for men are great sinners, which makes them the demons' rightful prey. But the gods, moved by pity for mankind, sent the First Shaman to show them the road to their heavenly dwelling. As among the Tibetans, communication between earth, heaven, and hell takes place along a vertical axis, the *axis mundi*. The after-death descent to hell, with the crossing of the bridge and the labyrinthine passage through the nine precincts, still preserves the initiatory schema; no one can reach heaven without having first gone down to hell. The shaman plays the role both of psychopomp and of post-mortem initiatory master. In all probability the shaman's position in the Na-khi religion represents an ancient stage through which the other religions of Central Asia also passed; the Siberian myths of the First Shaman contain allusions not unrelated to the mythical biography of Dto-mba Shi-lo.

Shamanic Symbolisms and Techniques in China

The following custom exists in China: When someone has just died, a fine new garment, for example, is shown to the soul from

---

Ceremony of the Na-khi of Southwest China, pp. 95 ff., 105 ff., 116 ff., 199 ff., and passim.

79 Id., "Studies," II, 50.

the housetop and it is implored to return to the body. This ritual is abundantly attested in classical texts [80] and has continued to our day; [81] it even supplied Sung Yü with the subject of a long poem entitled, precisely, "Calling Back the Soul." [82] Sickness, too, often involves the flight of the soul, and then the sorcerer pursues it in ecstasy, captures it, and replaces it in the patient's body.[83]

Ancient China already reckoned several categories of sorcerers and sorceresses, mediums, exorcisers, rainmakers, and other magicians. One type of magician in particular will engage our attention: the ecstatic, he whose art consisted primarily in "exteriorizing" his soul, in other words, "journeying in spirit." The legendary history and folklore of China abound in examples of "magical flight," and we shall soon see that even in the ancient period well-informed Chinese regarded "flight" as a plastic formula for ecstasy. In any case, if we set aside the ornithological symbolism of proto-historical China, to which we shall return later, it is important to note that the first man whom tradition credited with attaining the power to fly was the Emperor Shun (2258–2208 according to Chinese chronology). The Emperor Yao's daughters, Nü Ying and O Huang, revealed to Shun the art of "flying like a bird." [84] (We observe, in passing, that down to a certain date the source of

80 Cf. S. Couvreur, tr., *Li ki; ou, Mémoires sur les bienséances et les cérémonies* (2nd edn.), I, 85, 181, 199 ff.; II, 11, 125, 204, etc.; J. J. M. de Groot, *The Religious System of China*, I, 245 ff. On Chinese conceptions of the life after death, cf. E. Erkes: "Die alt-chinesischen Jenseitsvorstellungen"; "The God of Death in Ancient China."

81 Cf., for example, Theo Körner, "Das Zurückrufen der Seele in Kuei-chou."

82 Erkes, *Das "Zurückrufen der Seele" (Chao-Hun) des Sung Yüh.* Cf. also Maspero, *Les Religions chinoises*, pp. 50 ff.

83 This type of cure is still practiced today; cf. Groot, VI, 1284, 1319, etc. The sorcerer has the power to call back and replace even the soul of a dead animal; cf. ibid., p. 1214 (the resurrection of a horse). The Thai sorcerer sends some of his souls to search for the strayed soul of the patient, and he does not fail to warn his souls to take the right road when they come back to this world. Cf. Maspero, p. 218.

84 É. Chavannes, tr., *Les Mémoires historiques de Se-ma-Ts'ien*, I, 74. Cf. other texts in B. Laufer, *The Prehistory of Aviation*, pp. 14 ff.

magical power lay in women—a detail that, with some others, might be considered an indication of an ancient Chinese matriarchy.[85]) We may note the fact that a perfect sovereign must have the powers of a "magician." "Ecstasy" was no less necessary to the founder of a state than his political virtues, for this magical ability was equivalent to an authority, a jurisdiction over nature. Marcel Granet has observed that the step of Yü the Great, Shun's successor, "does not differ from the dances that induce trance in the sorcerers (*t'iao-shen*). . . . The ecstatic dance forms part of the procedures for acquiring a power of command over men and nature. We know that this regulating power, in the so-called Taoist as in the so-called Confucian texts, is called Tao." [86]

And so we find that many emperors, sages, alchemists, and sorcerers "went up to heaven." [87] Huang Ti, the Yellow Emperor, was carried to heaven by a bearded dragon, with his wives and councilors who together numbered seventy persons.[88] But his is already an apotheosis and no longer the "magical flight" of which Chinese tradition offers many examples.[89] The obsession with flight found expression in a quantity of legends concerning flying

85 On this problem, see Erkes, "Der Primat des Weibes im alten China." On Yao's daughters and the ordeals for succession to the throne, cf. Marcel Granet, *Danses et légendes de la Chine ancienne*, I, 276 ff. and passim. For criticism of Granet's views, cf. Carl Hentze, *Bronzegerät, Kultbauten, Religion im ältesten China der Shang-Zeit*, pp. 188 ff.

86 Granet, "Remarques sur le taoïsme ancien," p. 149. See also id., *Danses et légendes*, I, 239 ff. and passim. On the archaic elements in the myth of Yü the Great, cf. Hentze, *Mythes et symboles lunaires*, pp. 9 ff. and passim. On Yü's dance, cf. W. Eberhard, *Lokalkulturen im alten China*, Pt. 1, pp. 362 ff.; Pt. 2, pp. 52 ff.

87 In China, as among the Thai, there is a memory of the communication between heaven and earth that existed in mythical times. According to the myths, this communication was broken off so that the gods could no longer come down to oppose men (Chinese versions) or so that man could no longer trouble the gods (Thai versions). Cf. Maspero, *Les Religions chinoises*, pp. 186 ff. See also above, pp. 430 ff. The explanation given by the Chinese versions indicates a late reinterpretation of an archaic mythical theme.

88 Chavannes, *Les Mémoires historiques de Se-ma-Ts'ien*, III, Pt. 2, pp. 488–89.

89 Laufer, *The Prehistory of Aviation*, pp. 19 ff.

chariots and other vehicles.[90] In cases of this sort we have the well-known phenomenon of the degeneration of a symbolism, a phenomenon that, broadly speaking, consists in obtaining on the concrete plane of immediate reality "results" that pertain to an inner reality.

However this may be, the shamanic origin of magical flight is clearly documented in China too. "Flying up to heaven" is expressed in Chinese as follows: "by means of feathers he was transformed and ascended as an immortal"; and the terms "feather scholar" or "feather guest" designate the Taoist priest.[91] Now, we know that the feather is one of the most frequent symbols of "shamanic flight," and its occurrence in protohistorical Chinese iconography is not without significance in estimating the dissemination and antiquity of the symbol, and hence of the ideology presupposed by it.[92] As for the Taoists, whose legends abound with ascensions and every other kind of miracle, it is probable that they elaborated and systematized the shamanic technique and ideology of protohistorical China and hence have a far better right to be regarded as the successors of shamanism than the exorcists, mediums, and "possessed" persons whom we shall discuss later; in China, as elsewhere, these latter rather represent the aberrant shamanic tradition. That is to say: he who does not succeed in mastering the "spirits" will be "possessed" by them, in which case the magical technique of ecstasy becomes a mere mediumistic automatism.

In this connection it is striking to observe the absence of references to "possession" in the Chinese tradition of "magical flight" and of the shamanic dance. Some examples will be given later, in which shamanic technique results in a possession by gods and spirits; but in the legends of the emperors, the Taoist immortals, the alchemists, and even the "sorcerers," although ascents to heaven and other miracles are always mentioned, nothing is said about possession. We are justified in considering that all these

90 Ibid.   91 Ibid., p. 16.

92 On the relations among wings, down, flight, and Taoism, cf. Max Kaltenmark, ed. and tr., *Le Lie-sien tchouan*, pp. 12 ff.

things belong to the "classic" tradition of Chinese spirituality, which includes both a spontaneous self-mastery and a perfect incorporation into all the cosmic rhythms. In any case, the Taoists and alchemists had the power to rise into the air. Liu An, also known as Huai-nan Tse (second century B.C.), ascended to heaven in broad daylight, and Li Shao-kun (140–87 B.C.) boasted that he could rise beyond the ninth heaven.[93] "We rise to heaven and brush away the comets" said a shamaness in her song.[94] A long poem by Ch'ü Yüan mentions numerous ascents to the "gates of heaven," fantastic horseback journeys, ascent by the rainbow—all of them familiar motifs in shamanic folklore.[95] Chinese tales frequently refer to magicians' exploits that are almost exactly like the legends that grew up around the fakirs; they fly to the moon, pass through walls, make a plant sprout and grow in an instant, and so on.[96]

All these mythological and folklore traditions have their point of departure in an ideology and a technique of ecstasy that imply "journeying in spirit." From the earliest times, the classic method of achieving trance was dancing. As everywhere else, ecstasy made possible both the shaman's "magical flight" and the descent of a "spirit." The latter alternative did not necessarily mean "possession"; the spirit could inspire the shaman. That magical flight and fantastic journeys through the universe were, for the Chinese, only plastic formulas to describe the experiences of ecstasy is shown by the following document, among others. The *Kuo yü* relates that King Chao (515–488 B.C.) one day said to his minister: "The writings of the Chen dynasty state that Chung-li was

93 Laufer, *The Prehistory of Aviation*, pp. 26 ff., who also gives other examples. See also ibid., pp. 31 ff., 90 (on the kite in China), 52 ff. (on the legends of magical flight in India).

94 Erkes, "The God of Death in Ancient China," p. 203.

95 P. Franz Biallas, "K'üh Yüan's 'Fahrt in die Ferne' (Yüan-yu)," pp. 10, 215, 217, etc.

96 Cf. the seventeenth–century tales summarized by Vannicelli, *La religione dei Lolo*, pp. 164–66 (after J. Brand, *Introduction to the Literary Chinese* [2nd edn.], pp. 161–75). See also Eberhard, *Lokalkulturen im alten China*, I, 50.

actually sent as an envoy to the inaccessible parts of heaven and earth; how was such a thing possible? . . . Tell me whether there be any possibility for people to ascend to Heaven?" The minister explained that the true meaning of this tradition was spiritual; those who were upright and could concentrate were able "to rise to higher spheres and descend into the lower, and distinguish there the things which it would be proper to do. . . . Being in this condition, intelligent *shen* descended into them; if a *shen* thus settled in a male person, this was called a *hih*, and if it settled in one of the other sex, this was called a *wu*. As functionaries, they regulated the places for the seats of the gods (at sacrifices), the order of their tablets, as also their sacrificial victims and implements, and the ceremonial attires to be worn in connection with the season." [97]

This seems to indicate that ecstasy—which induced the experiences that were expressed as "magical flight," "ascent to heaven," "mystical journey," and so on—was the *cause* of the in-

---

[97] Groot, VI, 1190–91. We may note that the woman possessed by *shen* was called *wu*, the name which later became the general term for shaman in China. This might seem to prove the earlier existence there of shamanesses. However, there are reasons for believing that the *wu*, a woman possessed by *shen*, had been preceded by the shaman hooded with a bearskin, the "dancing shaman," whom L. C. Hopkins believes he has identified in an inscription of the Shang period and in another from the beginning of the Chou dynasty; cf his "The Bearskin, Another Pictographic Reconnaissance from Primitive Prophylactic to Present-Day Panache: a Chinese Epigraphic Puzzle" and "The Shaman or Chinese Wu: His Inspired Dancing and Versatile Character." The bearskin-masked "dancing shaman" belongs to an ideology dominated by the magic of the hunt, in which men play the leading part. The same shaman continues to have an important role in historical times; the chief exorcist was dressed in a bearskin with four golden eyes (É. Biot, tr., *Le Tcheou-li, ou Rites des Tcheou*, II, 225). But if all this appears to confirm the existence of a "male" shamanism in the protohistorical period, it does not necessarily follow that shamanism of the *wu* type—which strongly encourages "possession"—is not a magico-religious phenomenon dominated by woman. See E. Rousselle, in *Sinica*, XVI (1941), 134 ff.; A. Waley, *The Nine Songs, a Study of Shamanism in Ancient China*. Cf. also Erkes, "Der schamanistische Ursprung des chinesischen Ahnenkultus"; H. Kremsmayer, "Schamanismus und Seelenvorstellungen im alten China."

carnation of the *shen* and not its *result*; it was because a man was already able to "rise to higher spheres and descend into the lower" (that is, ascend to heaven and descend to hell) that "intelligent *shen* descended into" him. Such a phenomenon appears to differ considerably from the "possessions" of which we shall see examples later. Of course, the "descent of the *shen*" very soon gave rise to many parallel experiences that finally faded into the mass of "possessions." It is not always easy to distinguish the nature of an ecstasy from the terminology used to express it. According to H. Maspero, the Taoist term for ecstasy, *kuei-ju*, the "coming in of a spirit," can be explained only by deriving the Taoist experience from the "possession of sorcerers." For it was said of a sorceress in trance and speaking in the name of a *shen*: "this body is that of the sorceress, but the spirit is that of the god." In order to incarnate it, the sorceress purified herself with perfumed water, donned the ritual attire, made offerings; "with a flower in her hand, she mimed her journey [in search of the god] by a dance accompanied by music and songs, to the sound of drums and flutes, until she fell exhausted. This was the moment of the presence of the god who answered through her mouth." [98]

To a greater extent than Yoga and Buddhism, Taoism assimilated a number of archaic techniques of ecstasy, especially if we consider late Taoism, so extensively corrupted by magical elements.[99] Nevertheless, the importance of the symbolism of ascent

98 Maspero: *Les Religions chinoises*, 34, 53–54; *La Chine antique*, pp. 195 ff.

99 There was even an attempt to identify Taoism and shamanizing Bon-po; see above, pp. 431–32, n. 14. On the assimilation of shamanic elements by Neo-Taoism, see also Eberhard, *Lokalkulturen*, II, 315 ff. Nor must we forget the influence of Indian magic, which is incontestable for the period following the entrance of Buddhist monks into China. For example, Fo-t'u-têng, a Buddhist monk of Kucha, who had visited Kashmir and other parts of India, arrived in China in 310 and exhibited a number of magical feats; in particular, he prophesied from the sound of bells (cf. A. F. Wright, "Fo-t'u-têng: a Biography," pp. 337 ff., 346, 362). Now, it is known that "mystical sounds" play an important role in certain Yogic techniques, and that for the Buddhists the voices of the Devas and Yakṣas sounded like golden bells (Eliade, *Yoga*, p. 390).

and, in general, the balanced and healthy structure of Taoism differentiate it from the ecstasy-possession so characteristic of sorceresses. Chinese "shamanism" ("*wu*-ism," as Groot calls it) appears to have dominated religious life prior to the pre-eminence of Confucianism and of the state religion. In the first centuries before our era the *wu* priests were the real priests of China.[100] Doubtless the *wu* was not exactly the same as a shaman; but he incarnated the spirits, and, in doing so, served as intermediary between man and the divinity; in addition, he was a healer, again with the help of the spirits.[101] The proportion of women *wu* was overwhelming.[102] And the majority of the *shen* and *kuei* that the *wu* incarnated were souls of the dead.[103] It is with incarnating ghosts that "possession" proper begins.

Wang Ch'ung wrote: "Among men the dead speak through living persons whom they throw into a trance, and the *wu*, thrumming their black chords, call down souls of the dead, which then speak through the mouths of the *wu*. But whatever these people say is always falsehood." [104] This is obviously the judgment of a writer who was adverse to mediumistic phenomena. But the thaumaturgy of the female *wu* did not stop here; they could become invisible, they slashed themselves with knives and swords, cut their tongues, swallowed swords, and spat fire, were carried off on a cloud that shone as if with lightning. The female *wu* danced whirling dances, spoke the language of spirits, and around them objects rose into the air and knocked together.[105] All these fakiristic phenomena are still very common in Chinese magical and mediumistic circles. It is not even necessary to be a *wu* in order to see spirits and utter prophecies; it is enough to be possessed by a *shen*.[106] As everywhere else, mediumship and "possession" sometimes resulted in a spontaneous and aberrant shamanism.

There is no need to multiply examples of Chinese sorcerers

100 Groot, *The Religious System of China*, VI, 1205.
101 Ibid., pp. 1209 ff. 102 Ibid., p. 1209.
103 Ibid., p. 1211. 104 Ibid.
105 Ibid., p. 1212. 106 Ibid., pp. 1166 ff., 1214, etc.

wu, and "possession" to show how closely this phenomenon, taken as a whole, approaches Manchu, Tungus, and Siberian shamanism in general.[107] We would only emphasize the fact that, in the course of the ages, the Chinese ecstatic became more and more confused with sorcerers and "possessed" persons of rudimentary type. At a certain moment, and for a long period of time, the *wu* was so close to the exorcist that he was commonly called *wu-shih*.[108] In our day he is called *sai kung*, and the office is hereditary from father to son. The preponderance of women seems no longer to exist. After preliminary teaching by his father, the apprentice attends the lectures in a "college" and obtains his title of "Chief of the Religion" after an initiation that is definitely shamanic in type. The ceremony is public, and consists in mounting the *to t'ui*, the "sword-ladder." Barefoot, the apprentice climbs the swords to a platform; usually the ladder is made of twelve swords, and sometimes there is another ladder by which he climbs down. A similar initiatory rite has been found among the Karen of Burma, where a class of priests bears the name of *Wee*, a word that may be another form of the Chinese *wu*.[109] (In all probability, there is here a Chinese influence that has contaminated ancient local magical traditions; but it does not seem necessary to consider the initiatory ladder itself a borrowing from China. For similar rites of shamanic ascent have been found in Indonesia and elsewhere.)

The magico-religious activity of the *sai kung* falls within the sphere of Taoist ritual; the *sai kung* himself adopts the title *tao shih*, "Taoist doctor." [110] He has come to be completely identified with the *wu*, particularly because of his fame as an exorcist.[111] His ritual costume is rich in cosmological symbolism; it shows the

107 On the sexual and licentious elements in the ceremonies of the *wu*, see ibid., pp. 1235, 1239.

108 Ibid., p. 1192.

109 Ibid., pp. 1248 ff. Ibid., p. 1250, n. 3, cites A. R. McMahon, *The Karens of the Golden Chersonese*, p. 158, for a similar rite among the Burmese Kakhyen. See other examples (the Ch'uang, a Tai tribe of Kwangsi Province; aborigines of Northern Formosa) in R. Rahmann, "Shamanistic and Related Phenomena in Northern and Middle India," pp. 737, 741, n. 168.

110 Groot, VI, 1254. 111 Ibid., pp. 1256 ff.

cosmic ocean with Mount T'ai in the middle of it, and so on.[112] The *sai kung* generally uses a medium, who goes into "a state of delirium" and, in his turn, exhibits fakiristic powers; he stabs himself with knives, and so on.[113] Here we have another instance of the phenomenon that we noted in Indonesia and Polynesia: spontaneous imitation of shamanism after possession. Like the shaman in Fiji, the *sai kung* directs a fire-walking. The ceremony is called "walking on a path of fire" and takes place before the temple; the *sai kung* walks over the coals first, followed by his junior colleagues and even by the audience. A similar rite consists in walking on a "bridge of swords." It is believed that spiritual preparation before the ceremony makes it possible to walk on swords and fire unharmed.[114] In this case, as in innumerable examples of mediumship, spiritism, or other oracular techniques, we encounter an endemic phenomenon of spontaneous pseudoshamanism, which is difficult to classify but whose most important characteristic is its *easiness*.[115]

We do not profess to have traced the history of shamanic ideas and practices in China. We are not even certain that such a history is possible. It is well known to what an extensive process of elaboration and interpretation, not to say "distillation," Chinese scholars have subjected their archaic traditions for the past two thousand years. Our purpose has been served by merely noting the presence of a considerable number of shamanic techniques throughout the course of Chinese history. Obviously, they are not to be regarded as all belonging to the same ideology or to the same cultural stratum. We have seen, for example, what differences may

112 Groot, VI, 1261 ff.   113 Ibid., pp. 983 ff., 1270 ff., etc
114 Ibid., pp. 1292 ff.

115 On shamanism in modern China, cf. P. H. Doré, *Manuel des superstitions chinoises*, pp. 20, 39 ff., 82, 98, 103, etc.; S. M. Shirokogoroff, *Psychomental Complex of the Tungus*, pp. 388 ff.; on mediumistic cults in Singapore Alan J. A. Elliott, *Chinese Spirit-Medium Cults in Singapore*, especially pp 47 ff., 59 ff., 73 ff., 154 ff.; on shamanism among the aboriginal tribes of Formosa, M. D. Coe, "Shamanism in the Bunun Tribe, Central Formosa. The study by Tcheng-tsu Shang, "Der Schamanismus in China" (diss. Hamburg, 1934), was inaccessible to us.

exist between the ecstasy of sovereigns, alchemists, and Taoists and the ecstasy-possession of the sorceresses or the *sai kung's* assistants. The same differences in content and spiritual orientation are observable in respect to any other shamanic symbolism or technique. Our final impression is always that a shamanic schema can be experienced on different though homologizable planes; and this is a phenomenon that extends far beyond the sphere of shamanism and can be observed in respect to any religious symbolism or idea.

In general, China shows the presence of almost all the constituent elements of shamanism: ascent to heaven, summoning and searching for the soul, incarnation of "spirits," mastery over fire and other fakiristic exploits, and so on. On the other hand, descents to hell appear to be less usual, especially the descent for the purpose of bringing back the soul of a sick person or of one just dead, although all these motifs are documented in Chinese folklore. Thus there is the story of King Mu of Chu, who traveled to the ends of the earth, to Mount Kunlun and even further, until he came to the Queen Mother of the West (= Death) after crossing a river on an improvised bridge of fish and turtles; and the Queen Mother of the West gave him a song and a talisman for long life.[116] There is also the tale of the scholar Hu Ti, who went down to hell by way of the Mountain of the Dead and saw a river that the souls of the righteous crossed by a golden bridge, while sinners crossed it swimming, assailed by demons.[117] Finally, we also find an aberrant variant of the Orpheus myth: the Buddhist saint Mu-lian learns through mystical clairvoyance that his mother, who had failed to to give alms in her life, is suffering from hunger in hell, and goes down to rescue her; he puts her on his back and carries her to heaven.[118] Two other tales in Eberhard's collection [119] show the

116 Richard Wilhelm, tr., *Chinesische Volksmärchen*, pp. 90 ff.

117 Ibid., pp. 116 ff. See also ibid., pp. 184 ff. (the account of another journey to hell).

118 Ibid., pp. 126–27. In comparison with these tales of descent, the number of those referring to ascensions and other magical miracles is markedly greater. Cf. also Eberhard, *Typen chinesischer Volksmärchen*, s.v. "Aufsteigen im Himmel."

119 Nos. 144, 145 II.

Orpheus motif. In the first, a man goes down into the other world to seek his dead wife. He finds her by a spring, but she begs him to go away, for she has become a spirit. However, the husband remains for some time in the realm of shades. Finally the couple flee together, but no sooner have they returned to earth than the wife enters a house and vanishes. At the same moment the mistress of the house gives birth to a daughter. When the child grows up, the husband recognizes his wife in her, and marries her for the second time. In the second tale it is a father who goes down to hell to bring back his dead son, but the son does not recognize him, and the father fails in his attempt.[120] But all these tales belong to the magical folklore of Asia and some of them have been strongly influenced by Buddhism; hence it would be hazardous to infer from them the existence of a definite ritual of descent to the underworld. (For example, in the story of the saint Mu-lian, there is no reference to any shamanic capture of the soul.) In all probability, the shamanic ritual of descent, if it existed in the form in which it is found in Central and North Asia, fell into disuse after the crystallization of the ancestor cult, which gave "hell" a wholly different religious value.

We must stress one more point, which, though it goes beyond the problem of shamanism in the strict sense, is nevertheless important: the relations between the shaman and animals and the contribution of animal mythologies to the elaboration of Chinese shamanism. The "step" of Yü the Great did not differ from the dance of the magicians; but Yü also dressed up as a bear and, in some measure, incarnated the Bear Spirit.[121] The shaman described in the *Chou li* also wore a bearskin, and it would be easy to multiply examples of the rite known to ethnology as "bear ceremonialism," which is documented in North Asia as well as in North America.[122] It has been demonstrated that ancient China felt a

120 Eberhard, *Typen*, pp. 198 ff.

121 Cf. C. Hentze: *Mythes et symboles lunaires*, pp. 6 f.; "Le Culte de l'our et du tigre et le t'ao-t'ié," p. 54; *Die Sakralbronzen und ihre Bedeutung in der frühchinesischen Kulturen*, p. 19; Granet, *Danses et légendes*, II, 563 ff.

122 A. Irving Hallowell, "Bear Ceremonialism in the Northern Hemi

elationship, charged with a highly complex cosmological and initiatory symbolism, between the shamanic dance and an animal. The specialists are opposed to seeing any traces of a Chinese totemism in the mythology and ritual that bound man and animal together.[123] Rather, the relations are cosmological (the animal usually representing night, the moon, the earth, etc.) and initiatory (animal = mythical ancestor = initiator).[124]

How are all these facts to be interpreted, in the light of what we have now learned concerning Chinese shamanism? Let us beware of oversimplifying and explaining everything by a single schema. "Bear ceremonialism" is indubitably connected with the magic and mythology of the hunt. We know that the shaman plays a definite part in ensuring an abundance of game and the good luck of the hunters (meteorological prophecies, changing weather, mystical journeys to the Great Mother of the Animals, etc.). But we must not forget that the relations between the shaman (and, indeed, "primitive man" in general) and animals are spiritual in nature and of a mystical intensity that a modern, desacralized mentality finds it difficult to imagine. For primitive man, donning the skin of an animal was becoming that animal, feeling himself transformed into an animal. We have seen that, even today, shamans believe that they can change themselves into animals. Little would be gained by recording the fact that shamans dressed up in animal skins. The important thing is what they felt when they masqueraded as animals. We have reason to believe that this magical transformation resulted in a "going out of the self" that very often found expression in an ecstatic experience.

---

here"; N. P. Dyrenkova, "Bear Worship among Turkish Tribes of Si-ria," pp. 411–40; Hans Findeisen, "Zur Geschichte der Bärenzeremonie"; . Alföldi, "The Bear Cult and Matriarchy in Eurasia" (in Hungarian; professor Alföldi most kindly supplied us with an English translation of this important article). Cf. also Marius Barbeau, "Bear Mother."

123 Cf. Dyrenkova, p. 453; Hentze: "Le Culte de l'ours et du tigre," p. ; *Die Sakralbronzen*, pp. 45, 161.

124 On all this, see Hentze's studies, especially *Mythes et symboles lunaires; objets rituels, croyances et dieux de la Chine antique et de l'Amérique; Früh-chinesische Bronzen und Kultdarstellungen*.

Imitating the gait of an animal or putting on its skin was ac
quiring a superhuman mode of being. There was no question of
regression into pure "animal life"; the animal with which th
shaman identified himself was already charged with a mythology,
it was, in fact, a mythical animal, the Ancestor or the Demiurg
By becoming this mythical animal, man became something fa
greater and stronger than himself. We are justified in supposin
that this projection into a mythical being, the center at once of th
existence and renewal of the universe, induced the euphoric ex
perience that, before ending in ecstasy, showed the shaman h
power and brought him into communion with cosmic life. We nee
only recall the role of exemplary model played by certain anima
in Taoist mystical techniques in order to realize the spiritual rich
ness of the "shamanic" experience that still haunted the memor
of the ancient Chinese. He who, forgetting the limitations ar
false measurements of humanity, could rightly imitate the behavic
of animals—their gait, breathing, cries, and so on—found a ne
dimension of life: spontaneity, freedom, "sympathy" with all th
cosmic rhythms and, hence, bliss and immortality.

It seems to us that, viewed from this angle, the ancient Chines

125 A number of animal and especially ornithomorphic motifs are found
the earliest Chinese iconography (Hentze, *Die Sakralbronzen*, pp. 115 ff.
Several of these iconographic motifs suggest the designs on shamanic co
tumes, e.g., snakes (ibid., figs. 146–48). The Siberian shaman's costume h
probably been influenced by certain Chinese magico-religious ideas (ibi
p. 156). Cf. also id.: "Schamanenkronen zur Han-Zeit in Korea"; "Ei
Schamanendarstellung auf einem Han-Relief"; "Eine Schamanentracht u
ihre Bedeutung für die altchinesische Kunst und Religion." Alfred Salmon
sees shamans in the figures of two dancers wearing antlers, engraved on
late Chou bronze vessel supposedly found at Changsha; cf. *Antler ai
Tongue: an Essay on Ancient Chinese Symbolism and Its Implications*. Reviev
ing Salmony's book in *Artibus Asiae*, R. Heine-Geldern accepts this i
terpretation and notes that William Watson had already reached the san
conclusion; cf. "A Grave Guardian from Ch'ang-sha." The possible influen
of shamanic dress on military armor could profitably be studied in detail;
K. Meuli, "Scythica," p. 147, n. 8; F. Altheim, *Geschichte der Hunnen*,
311 ff. The Chinese shaman's costume, including a scale cuirass, is alrea
documented in the archaic period; cf. Laufer, *Chinese Clay Figures*, especia
pp. 196 ff. and Pls. XV–XVII.

ites that so closely resemble "bear ceremonialism" disclose their
mystical values and enable us to understand how ecstasy could
equally well be obtained by choreographic imitation of an animal [126]
and by a dance that mimed ascension; in either case, the soul "came
ut of itself" and flew away. The expression of this mystical flight
y the "descent" of a god or spirit was sometimes merely a matter
f terminology.

Mongolia, Korea, Japan

hamanism, strongly hybridized by Lamaism, is characteristic of
he religion of the Monguor of Sining, in Northwest China, a peo-
le whom the Chinese knew by the name of T'u-jen, that is, "folk
f the country." [127] Among the Mongols, as early as the seven-
eenth century Lamaism attempted to wipe out shamanism [123]
ut the old Mongolian religion finally assimilated the Lamaistic
ontributions without losing its peculiar character.[129] Until very
ecently shamans and shamanesses still played an important part
n the religious life of the tribes.[130]

In Korea, where shamanism is documented as early as the Han
eriod,[131] male shamans wear women's dress, and are far out-

---

126 Account must also be taken of the role of metallurgy and its sym-
olism in the constitution of prehistoric Chinese magic and mysticism; see
ranet, *Danses et légendes*, II, 496 ff., 505 ff. The connections between sha-
anism and metal-casters and smiths are well known; see below, pp. 470 ff.
f. also Eliade, *The Forge and the Crucible*, pp. 62 ff.

127 Cf. D. Schröder, "Zur Religion der Tujen," last art., especially pp.
35 ff.; L. M. J. Schram, *The Monguors of the Kansu-Tibetan Border*, Pt. 2,
specially pp. 76 ff., 91 ff.

128 Cf. W. Heissig: "Schamanen und Geisterbeschwörer im Küriye-
anner," pp. 40 f.; "A Mongolian Source to the Lamaist Suppression of
hamanism in the 17th Century," pp. 500 ff. and passim.

129 Cf. J.-P. Roux, "Eléments chamaniques dans les textes pré-mongols."

130 Cf. Heissig, "Schamanen und Geisterbeschwörer," pp. 42 ff. On
Mongolian shamanism, cf. also W. Schmidt, *Der Ursprung der Gottesidee*, X,
4–100, and N. Poppe's remarks in *Anthropos*, XLVIII (1953), 327–28; V.
iószegi, "Problems of Mongolian Shamanism."

131 Cf. Hentze, "Schamanenkronen."

numbered by shamanesses.[132] It is difficult to determine the "origin" of Korean shamanism; it may include southern elements but the presence of stag horns on the shaman's headdress of the Han period indicates relations with the stag cult characteristic of the ancient Turks.[133] In addition, the cult of the stag is typical of hunter and nomad cultures, in which shamanesses do not appear to play much of a role. The present predominance of shamanesses in Korea may be the result either of a deterioration in traditional shamanism or of influences from the south.

The history of shamanism in Japan is likewise obscure, though we have ample data on modern shamanic practices, due especially to the work of Nakayama Tarō and Hori Ichirō. Knowledge of the various aspects and phases of Japanese shamanism must await the publication of Masao Oka's extensive work on the cultural history of ancient Japan.[134] As documented today, Japanese shamanism is rather far from shamanism proper of the North Asian or Siberian type. It is primarily a technique of possession by ghosts and is practiced almost exclusively by women. According to Matthias Eder, the principal functions of the shamanesses are: "1. They summon a dead person's soul from the beyond. In popular parlance this is called *shinikuchi*, i.e., 'dead man's mouth.' When they summon a living person's soul from far away, it is called *ikikuchi*, i.e. 'mouth of a living person.' 2. They prophesy success or failure for the client; the popular term is *kamikuchi*, i.e., 'mouth of the god.' 3. They expel disease and other evils and practice religious purification. 4. They ask their god the name of the medicine to be used against a particular illness. 5. They give information concerning lost objects. The services most often demanded of a shamaness are summoning the ghosts of dead persons and the souls of persons living at a distance, and divining good and bad fortune. Souls sum-

132 Cf. Eberhard, *Lokalkulturen*, II, 313 ff.; M. C. Haguenauer, "Sorciers et sorcières de Corée."

133 Cf. Eberhard, *Lokalkulturen*, II, 501 ff.

134 Cf., for shamanism, the data given, after Masao Oka's unpublished manuscript, by Alexander Slawik, "Kultische Geheimbünde der Japaner und Germanen," pp. 677, 688 ff., 733, 757.

moned from the beyond are in most cases those of parents and relatives, lovers or friends." [135]

Many Japanese shamanesses are blind from birth. In our day their "ecstasy" is factitious and crudely simulated.[136] While the soul of the deceased is supposed to be speaking through her mouth, the shamaness plays with a pearl necklace or a bow.[137] A candidate is taught for from three to seven years by an accredited shamaness, after which the girl is married to her tutelary god.[138] In some districts initiation also involves an exhausting physical ordeal, at the end of which the novice falls to the ground unconscious. Her reanimation is assimilated to "birth" (*tanjō*), and she dons wedding garments. The mystical marriage of the shamaness to her tutelary god appears to be an archaic custom. The "spirit-women gods" (*mikogami*) already documented in the *Kojiki*, the *Nihongi*, and other ancient sources are gods "in whom a spirit-woman [i.e., shamaness] is herself venerated as divine; later, gods born of a marriage between a spirit-woman and a god. Such spirit-women are also called 'Divine Mothers' or 'Holy Mothers.' The list in the *Engishiki* of gods venerated in shrines includes a whole series of these spirit-women gods (*mikogami*). In addition to these spirit-women (*miko*) officially serving their god at shrines, there were also private so-called 'one-night spouses' (*ichiya-tsuma*), whose partner was a wandering god (*marebito*) who came to visit them. As an emblem of this special role, such women put a white-feathered arrow on the roof tree of their house. When a god summoned a woman to serve him at his shrine, she brought with her a rice pot (*meshibitsu*, for keeping cooked rice hot; from this container the rice is served into the rice bowls at table) and a pan, that is, implements such as are brought with her by a bride. Until recent times, coitus between a spirit-woman and a priest of the shrine was part of her program of initiation. The god had himself represented." [139]

---

135 "Schamanismus in Japan," p. 368.   136 Ibid., p. 371.
137 Ibid., p. 377.   138 Ibid., pp. 372 f.
139 Ibid., p. 374. Cf. W. P. Fairchild, "Shamanism in Japan."

This marriage with a god suggests the customs of the Savara shamanesses—with the difference, however, that in Japan we do not find the intense personal ecstatic experience that is so striking in the case of the Savara girl. In Japan marriage with the tutelary god appears to be a result of the institution rather than a personal destiny. In addition, there are certain elements that do not fit into the structure of feminine magic: for example, the bow and the horse.[140] All this leads us to think that we here have a hybrid and late phase of shamanism. On the other hand, the "spirit-women gods" and certain rituals pertaining to them can be compared with the characteristic features of matriarchy: female rulers of territorial states, female heads of families, matrilocal marriage, visitor marriage, matriarchal clan with clan exogamy, and so on.[141]

M. Eder appears not to have known the important study by Charles Haguenauer, *Origines de la civilisation japonaise; Introduction à l'étude de la préhistoire du Japon* (Vol. I, Paris, 1956). Although in this first part the author does not actually discuss the origin of Japanese shamanism, he cites a number of facts which, in his view, point to similarities with Altaic shamanism:

What we know, for example, concerning the behavior and role of the sorceress in ancient Japan—despite the effort made by the compilers of the Imperial Annals to pass her over in silence and mention only her rival, the priestess-vestal, the *miko*, who had attained a place among the ritualists at the court of the Yamato—permits her identification both with her Korean colleague, the *muday*, . . . and with the Altaic shamanesses. The essential function of all these sorceresses consisted in causing a soul to descend (Japanese *or.o-s.u*) into a support (sacred post or any other substitute) or incarnating a soul in order to serve as intermediary between it and the living, and then to send it back. That a sacred post was used in connection with these practices would follow from the fact that the word *haśira* (column) served in Japanese as the specific term used in enumerating sacred beings (cf. *JA*, 1934, p. 122). In addition the Japanese sorceress's professional instruments were the same as those used by her colleagues on the mainland, that is, the drum . . . rattle

140 On the horse-headed figurines, cf. ibid., p. 378.
141 Ibid., p. 379.

. . the mirror . . . and the saber called *katā.na* (another word of Altaic origin) whose antidemonic virtues are illustrated by more than one aspect of Japanese folklore.[142]

We must wait for the continuation of Haguenauer's book to learn at what stage, and by what means, Altaic shamanism—an almost exclusively masculine institution—became the constituent element of a specifically feminine religious tradition. Neither the saber nor the drum are instruments originally belonging to feminine magic. The fact that they are used by shamanesses indicates that they were already part of the paraphernalia of sorcerers and shamans.[143]

142 *Origines*, pp. 178–79.
143 The attraction exercised by the magical powers of the opposite sex is well known; cf. Eliade, *Birth and Rebirth*, pp. 79 ff.

CHAPTER THIRTEEN

Parallel Myths, Symbols, and Rites

T HE various shamanic ideologies have assimilated a certai
number of mythical themes and magico-religious symbolism
Without any intention of enumerating them all, still less of stud
ing them exhaustively, we consider it of interest to cite some
these myths and symbols, to show how they were adapted or r
evaluated in shamanism.

Dog and Horse

The mythology of the dog is fully treated in the work by Fre
Kretschmar.[1] Shamanism proper introduced no innovations in th
direction. The shaman encounters the funerary dog in the cour
of his descent to the underworld, as it is encountered by the d

1 *Hundestammvater und Kerberos*, I–II; cf. especially II, 222 ff., 258 f. S
also W. Koppers, "Der Hund in der Mythologie der zirkumpazifisch
Völker," and Paul Pelliot's remarks in his review of the above (*T'oung P*
XXVIII [1931], 463–70). On the dog-ancestor among the Turco-Mongo
cf. Pelliot, ibid., and Rolf A. Stein, "Leao-Tche," pp. 24 ff. On the mytholog
cal role of the dog in ancient China, see E. Erkes, "Der Hund im alten China
pp. 221 ff. On the infernal dog in Indian conceptions, cf. E. Arbman, *Rud*
pp. 257 ff.; B. Schlerath, "Der Hund bei den Indogermanen"; in Germa
mythology, H. Güntert, *Kalypso*, pp. 40 ff., 55 ff.; in Japan—where it is no
funerary animal—A. Slawik, "Kultische Geheimbünde der Japaner u
Germanen," pp. 700 ff.; in Tibet, S. Hummel, "Der Hund in der religiös
Vorstellungswelt des Tibeters."

ceased or by heroes undergoing an initiatory ordeal. It is especially the secret societies based on a martial initiation—in so far as their ecstasies and frantic ceremonies can be termed "shamanic"—that developed and reinterpreted the mythology and magic of the dog and the wolf. Certain cannibal secret societies and, in a general way, lycanthropy, involve the member's magical transformation into a dog or a wolf. Shamans, too, can turn themselves into wolves, but in a sense different from lycanthropy; as we saw, they can assume a number of other animal forms.

Quite different is the place taken by the horse in shamanic mythology and ritual. Pre-eminently the funerary animal and psychopomp,[2] the "horse" is employed by the shaman, in various contexts, as a means of achieving ecstasy, that is, the "coming out of oneself" that makes the mystical journey possible. This mystical journey—to repeat—is not necessarily in the infernal direction. The "horse" enables the shaman to fly through the air, to reach the heavens. The dominant aspect of the mythology of the horse is not infernal but funerary; the horse is a mythical image of death and hence is incorporated into the ideologies and techniques of ecstasy. The horse carries the deceased into the beyond; it produces the "break-through in plane," the passage from this world to other worlds. And this is why it also plays a role of the first importance in certain types of masculine initiation (the *Männerbünde*).[3]

The "horse"—that is, the horse-headed stick—is used by the Buryat shamans in their ecstatic dances. We have noted a similar dance in connection with the Araucanian *machi*'s séance.[4] But the ecstatic dance on a stick-horse is far more widely disseminated. We will confine ourselves to a few examples. Among the Batak, in the course of the horse sacrifice in honor of the ancestors, four dancers dance on sticks carved in the shape of horses.[5] In Java and

2 See L. Malten, "Das Pferd im Totenglauben." Cf. also V. I. Propp, *Le radici storiche dei racconti di fate* (tr. from Russ.), pp. 274 ff.

3 Cf. O. Höfler, *Kultische Geheimbünde der Germanen*, I, 46 ff.; Slawik, 'Kultische Geheimbünde der Japaner und Germanen," pp. 692 ff.

4 Above, p. 325.

5 Cf. J. Warneck, *Die Religion der Batak*, p. 88.

Bali the horse is likewise associated with the ecstatic dance.[6] Among the Garo the "horse" forms part of the harvest ritual. The body of the horse is made from banana stems, its head and hoofs from bamboo. The head is mounted on a stick, held so that it reaches the height of the chest. With shuffling steps the man performs a wild dance while, facing him, the priest dances, pretending to beckon the "horse." [7]

V. Elwin has recorded a similar ritual among the Muria of Bastar. In his sanctuary at Semurgaon the great Gond god Lingo Pen has several wooden "horses." At the time of the god's festival these "horses" are carried by mediums and used both to induce ecstatic trance and for divination. "At Metawand I watched for several hours the antics of a medium who was carrying on his shoulders the wooden horse of his clan god and at Bandopal a medium carrying an imaginary horse on his shoulders 'ambled, caracoled, pranced and plunged' for two miles before my slow-moving car as we made our way into the jungle for the Marka Pandum (ceremonial eating of mangoes). 'The god rides upon him,' they told me, 'and he cannot stop dancing for days at a time.' At a wedding in Malakot, I saw a medium riding on a characteristic hobby-horse, and again in the Dhurwa country to the south, I saw a man dancing astride a similar wooden hobby-horse. In both cases the rider would fall into trance if anything went wrong with the proceedings and would be able to diagnose the supernatural cause of the trouble." [8]

At another ceremony, the Laru Kaj of the Gond-Pardhan, the "horses of the god" perform an ecstatic dance.[9] We may also mention that several aboriginal peoples of India represent their dead on horseback—the Bhil, for example, or the Korku, who carve

6 Cf. B. de Zoete and W. Spies, *Dance and Drama in Bali*, p. 78.

7 Biren Bonnerjea, "Materials for the Study of Garo Ethnology"; Verrier Elwin: "The Hobby Horse and the Ecstatic Dance," p. 211; *The Muria and Their Ghotul*, pp. 205–09.

8 "The Hobby Horse," pp. 212–13; *The Muria*, p. 208.

9 Shamrao Hivale, "The Laru Kaj," cited by Elwin, *The Muria*, p. 209. Cf. also W. Archer, *The Vertical Man: a Study in Primitive Indian Sculpture*, pp. 41 ff., on the ecstatic dance with images of horses (in Bihar).

horsemen on wooden tablets which they place by graves.[10] Among the Muria a funeral is accompanied by ritual songs announcing the deceased's arrival in the other world on horseback. The description includes a palace in which are a golden swing and a diamond throne. The deceased is brought there by an eight-legged horse.[11] Now, we know that the octopod horse is typically shamanic. According to a Buryat legend, a young woman takes as her second husband the ancestral spirit of a shaman, and after this mystical marriage one of the mares in her stud gives birth to a foal with eight legs. The earthly husband cuts off four of them. The woman cries: "Alas! It was my little horse on which I used to ride like a shamaness!" and vanishes, flying through the air, to settle in another village. She later became a guardian spirit of the Buryat.[12]

Eight-legged or headless horses are documented in the rites and myths of both Germanic and Japanese "men's societies." [13] In all these cultural complexes many-legged horses or phantom horses have a function that is at once funerary and ecstatic. The Morris "hobby horse" is also connected with the ecstatic—though not necessarily shamanic—dance.[14]

But even when the "horse" is not formally documented in the shamanic séance, it is symbolically present through the white horsehairs that are burned or through a white mareskin on which the shaman sits. Burning horsehairs is equivalent to evoking the magical animal that will carry the shaman into the beyond. Buryat

10 Cf. W. Koppers, "Monuments to the Dead of the Bhils and Other Primitive Tribes in Central India"; Elwin, *The Muria*, pp. 210 ff., figs. 27, 29, 30.

11 Elwin, *The Muria*, p. 150. Concerning the horse in North Indian shamanism, see also R. Rahmann, "Shamanistic and Related Phenomena in Northern and Middle India," pp. 724–25.

12 G. Sandschejew, "Weltanschauung und Schamanismus der Alaren-Burjaten," p. 608. In Tungus belief, the shamans' Mother of the Beasts gives birth to an eight-legged kid; cf. G. V. Ksenofontov, *Legendy i rasskazy o shamanakh u yakutov, buryat i tungusov* (2nd edn.), pp. 64 f.

13 Höfler, pp. 51 ff.; Slawik, pp. 694 ff.

14 Cf. R. Wolfram, "Robin Hood und Hobby Horse"; A. van Gennep, *Le Cheval-jupon*.

legends tell of horses carrying dead shamans to their new home. In a Yakut myth the "devil" inverts his drum, sits down on it, pierces it three times with his stick, and the drum turns into a three-legged mare that carries him into the east.[15]

These few examples show in what way shamanism has made use of the mythology and rites of the horse. Psychopomp and funerary animal, the horse facilitated trance, the ecstatic flight of the soul to forbidden regions. The symbolic "ride" expressed leaving the body, the shaman's "mystical death."

Shamans and Smiths

The craft of the smith ranks immediately after the shaman's vocation in importance.[16] "Smiths and shamans are from the same nest," says a Yakut proverb. "A shaman's wife is respectable, a smith's wife is venerable," says another. Smiths have power to heal and even to foretell the future.[17] According to the Dolgan, shamans cannot "swallow" the souls of smiths because smiths keep their souls in the fire; on the other hand, a smith can catch a shaman's soul and burn it. In their turn, the smiths are constantly threatened by evil spirits. They are reduced to working unintermittingly, handling fire, keeping up a constant noise, to drive away the hostile spirits.[18]

According to Yakut myths, the smith received his craft from the "evil" divinity K'daai Maqsin, the chief smith of the underworld.

15 Propp, p. 286.

16 Cf. M. A. Czaplicka, *Aboriginal Siberia*, pp. 204 ff. On the past importance of the smith among the Yenisei peoples, cf. W. Radlov, *Aus Sibirien*, I, 186 ff. See also F. Altheim, *Geschichte der Hunnen*, I, 195 ff.; Dominik Schröder, "Zur Religion der Tujen des Sininggebietes (Kukunor)," art. 3, pp. 828, 830; H. Findeisen, *Schamanentum*, pp. 94 ff. For what follows, see Eliade, *The Forge and the Crucible*, especially pp. 53 ff. See also Hummel, "Der göttliche Schmied in Tibet."

17 W. Sieroszewski, "Du chamanisme d'après les croyances des Yakoutes," p. 319. Cf. also W. I. Jochelson, *The Yakut*, pp. 172 ff.

18 A. A. Popov, "Consecration Ritual for a Blacksmith Novice among the Yakuts," pp. 258–60.

He lives in an iron house, surrounded by fired slag iron. K'daai Maqsin is a famous master; it is he who repairs the broken or amputated limbs of heroes. He sometimes takes part in initiating the famous shamans of the other world, by tempering their souls as he tempers iron.[19]

According to Buryat beliefs, the nine sons of Boshintoi, the celestial smith, came down to earth to teach men metallurgy; their first pupils were the ancestors of the families of smiths.[20] According to another legend the "white" Tängri himself sent Boshintoi and his nine sons to earth to reveal the art of metalworking to mankind.[21] Boshintoi's sons married daughters of earth, and thus became the ancestors of the smiths; no one can become a smith unless he is descended from one of these families.[22] The Buryat also have "black smiths" who daub their faces with soot for certain ceremonies; the people are particularly afraid of them.[23] The smiths' tutelary gods and spirits do not merely help them in their work, they also defend them against evil spirits. The Buryat smiths have their special rites: a horse is sacrificed by opening its belly and tearing out its heart (this last rite is distinctly "shamanic"). The soul of the horse goes to the celestial smith, Boshintoi. Nine youths play the parts of Boshintoi's nine sons, and a man, who incarnates the celestial smith himself, falls into ecstasy and recites a long monologue in which he tells how, *in illo tempore*, he sent his nine sons to earth to help mankind, and so on. Then he touches the fire with his tongue. Sandschejew was told that in the

19 Ibid., pp. 260–61. The role of smiths-shamans ("devils") in the initiatory dreams of future shamans will be remembered. As for K'daai Maqsin's house, we know that in his ecstatic descent to the underworld of Erlik Khan, the Altaic shaman hears metallic noises. Erlik puts iron chains on the souls captured by the evil spirits (Sandschejew, p. 953). According to Tungus and Orochon traditions, the future shaman's head is forged with the ornaments of his costume, in the same furnace; cf. A. Friedrich and G. Buddruss, *Schamanengeschichten aus Sibirien*, p. 30.

20 Sandschejew, pp. 538–39.

21 The Tibetans likewise have a divine protector of the smith and his nine brothers. Cf. R. de Nebesky-Wojkowitz, *Oracles and Demons of Tibet*, p. 539.

22 Sandschejew, p. 539.   23 Ibid., p. 540.

old days the man representing Boshintoi took molten iron in his hand.[24] But Sandschejew only saw him touch red-hot iron with his foot.[25] Shamanic exhibitions are easy to recognize in such feats; like the smiths, the shamans are "masters over fire." But their magical powers are notably greater.

Popov has described the séance of a shaman curing a smith. The sickness was brought on by the smith's "spirits." After the sacrifice of a black bull to K'daai Maqsin, all the smith's implements were daubed with blood. Seven men lighted a great fire and threw the bull's head among the coals. Meanwhile the shaman began his incantation and prepared to go on his ecstatic journey to visit K'daai Maqsin. The seven men retrieved the bull's head, put it on the anvil, and fell to striking it with hammers. Is not this a symbolic forging of the shaman's "head," parallel to that performed by the "demons" in the future shaman's initiatory dreams? The shaman goes down to K'daai Maqsin's underworld, succeeds in embodying a spirit, and the latter, through the shaman's mouth, answers the questions asked it regarding the sickness and the treatment to be given.[26]

Their "power over fire," and especially the magic of metals, have everywhere given smiths the reputation of redoubtable sorcerers.[27] Hence the ambivalent attitude entertained toward them; they are at once despised and venerated. This antithetical behavior is found especially in Africa.[28] Among a number of tribes the smith is spurned, regarded as a pariah, and can safely be killed;[29] in

24 Dogon smiths pick up red-hot iron to re-enact the practice of the first smiths; cf. M. Griaule, *Dieu d'eau*, p. 102.

25 "Weltanschauung und Schamanismus," pp. 550 ff.

26 "Consecration Ritual," pp. 262 ff.

27 Cf. Eliade, *The Forge and the Crucible*, pp. 53 ff. and passim.

28 Cf. Walter Cline, *Mining and Metallurgy in Negro Africa*. Cf. also B. Gutmann, "Der Schmied und seine Kunst im animistischen Denken"; H. Webster, *Magic*, pp. 165–67.

29 For example, among the Bari of the White Nile (Richard Andree, *Die Metalle bei den Naturvölkern; mit Berücksichtigung prähistorischer Verhältnisse*, pp. 9, 42); among the Wolof, the Tibbu (ibid., pp. 41–43); among the Wanderobo, the Masai (Cline, p. 114); etc.

others, on the contrary, he is respected, assimilated to the medicine man, and even becomes the political chief.[30] This ambivalence is explained by the contradictory reactions aroused by metals and metallurgy, and by the differences in level between various African societies—some of which came to know metallurgy late and in complex historical contexts. What is of interest to us here is that in Africa, too, smiths sometimes form secret societies with their own initiation rituals.[31] In some cases we even find a symbiosis between smiths and shamans or medicine men.[32] The presence of smiths in the initiatory societies (*Männerbünde*) is documented among the ancient Germans [33] and the Japanese.[34] Similar relations between metallurgy, magic, and the founders of dynasties have been found in Chinese mythological tradition.[35] The same connections, though now infinitely more complex, are decipherable between the Cyclopes, the Dactyli, the Curetes, the Telchines, and metalworking.[36] The demonic, *āsuric* nature of metallurgy is well brought out in the myths of the aboriginal peoples of India (Birhor, Munda, Oraon), where emphasis is laid on the pride of the smith and his final defeat by the Supreme Being, who succeeds in burning him in his own forge.[37]

30 The Balolo of the Congo attribute royal origin to smiths (Cline, p. 22). The Bantu Wachaga at once honor and fear them (ibid., p. 115). The partial identification of smiths with chiefs is found in several Congo tribes—the Basongo, Baholoholo, etc. (ibid., p. 125).

31 Cf. ibid., p. 119; Eliade, *The Forge and the Crucible*, pp. 97 ff.

32 Cline, p. 120 (Bayeke, Ila, etc.).

33 Höfler, *Kultische Geheimbünde der Germanen*, pp. 54 ff. On the relations between metallurgy and magic in Finnish mythological traditions, cf. K. Meuli, "Scythica," p. 175.

34 Slawik, "Kultische Geheimbünde der Japaner und Germanen," pp. 597 ff.

35 M. Granet, *Danses et légendes de la Chine ancienne*, II, 609 ff. and passim.

36 Cf. L. Gernet and A. Boulanger, *Le Génie grec dans la religion*, p. 79; Bengt Hemberg, *Die Kabiren*, pp. 286 ff. and passim. On the relations among smith, dancer, and sorcerer, cf. Robert Eisler, "Das Qainszeichen und die Qeniter."

37 Cf. Sarat Chandra Roy, *The Birhors*, pp. 402 ff. (Birhor); E. T. Dalton, *Descriptive Ethnology of Bengal*, pp. 186 ff. (Munda); Rev. P. Dehon, *Religion and Customs of the Uraons*, pp. 128 ff. (Oraon). On this whole problem

The "secrets of metallurgy" are reminiscent of the professional secrets transmitted among the shamans by initiation; in both cases we have a magical technique that is esoteric. This is why the smith's profession is usually hereditary, like the shaman's. A more thorough analysis of the historical relations between shamanism and metalworking would carry us too far from our subject. Here it suffices—and it is important—to bring out the fact that metallurgical magic, by the "power over fire" that it involved, assimilated a number of shamanic exploits. In the mythology of smiths we find many themes and motifs borrowed from the mythologies of shamans and sorcerers in general. This state of things is also seen in the folklore traditions of Europe, whatever be the case as to their origins; the smith is often assimilated to a demonic being, and the devil is famed for shooting flame from his mouth. In this image we see a negative re-evaluation of the magical power over fire.

"Magical Heat"

Like the devil in the beliefs of the European peoples, shamans are not merely "masters over fire"; they can also incarnate the spirit of fire to the point where, during séances, they emit flames from their mouths, their noses, and their whole bodies.[38] This sort of feat must be put in the category of shamanic wonders connected with the "mastery over fire," of which we have given many examples. The magical power involved expresses the "spirit condition" obtained by shamans.

As we saw, however, the idea of "mystical heat" is not an exclusive possession of shamanism; it belongs to magic in general. Many "primitive" tribes conceive of magico-religious power as "burning" or express it in terms meaning "heat," "burn," "very hot," and the like. In Dobu the idea of "heat" always accompanies

see Walter Ruben, *Eisenschmiede und Dämonen in Indien*, pp. 11 ff., 130 ff., 149 ff., and passim.

38 Propp, *Le radici storiche dei racconti di fate*, pp. 284 ff., citing examples of Gilyak and Eskimo shamans.

that of sorcery.[39] The same is true of Rossel Island, where "heat" is the attribute of magicians.[40] In the Solomon Islands anyone possessing a large quantity of *mana* is regarded as *saka*, "burning." [41] Elsewhere—in Sumatra and the Malay Archipelago, for example—words designating "heat" also express the idea of evil, while the notions of bliss, peace, serenity are all rendered by words meaning coolness.[42] This is why many magicians and sorcerers drink salted or spiced water and eat highly aromatic plants; they hope thus to increase their inner "heat." [43] For a like reason certain Australian sorcerers and sorceresses are forbidden "burning" substances; they already have enough "inner fire." [44]

The same ideas have survived in more complex religions. The Hindus of today give an especially powerful divinity the epithets *prakhar*, "very hot," *jājval*, "burning," or *jvalit*, "possessing fire." [45] The Mohammedans of India believe that a man in communication with God becomes "burning." [46] A man who performs miracles is called *sahib-josh*, *josh* meaning "boiling." [47] By extension, all kinds of persons or actions involving one or another magico-religious "power" are regarded as "burning." [48]

Relevant here are the initiatory steam baths of the North American mystical brotherhoods and, in general, the magical role of the steam bath during the preparatory period of future shamans in a number of North American tribes. We have found the ecstatic function of the vapor bath, combined with intoxication from hemp smoke, among the Scythians. Still in the same context, we again refer to the *tapas* of the cosmogonic and mystical traditions of

39 R. F. Fortune, *Sorcerers of Dobu*, pp. 295 ff. Cf. also A. R. Brown, *The Andaman Islanders*, pp. 266 ff. Cf. above, pp. 363, 437–38.

40 Webster, *Magic*, p. 7, citing W. E. Armstrong, *Rossel Island*, pp. 172 ff.

41 Webster, p. 27; cf. R. H. Codrington, *The Melanesians*, pp. 191 ff.

42 Webster, p. 27.　　　　43 Ibid., p. 7.

44 Ibid., pp. 237–38. On "inner heat" and "mastery over fire," cf. Eliade, *The Forge and the Crucible*, pp. 79 ff.

45 J. Abbott, *The Keys of Power: a Study of Indian Ritual and Belief*, pp. 5 ff.

46 Ibid., p. 6.　　　　47 Ibid.

48 Ibid., pp. 7 ff., and Index, s.v. "heat."

ancient India; "inner heat" and "sweating" are "creative." Certain Indo-European heroic myths could also be cited, with their *furor*, their *wut*, their *ferg*. The Irish hero Cuchulain emerges so "heated" from his first exploit (which, as Dumézil has shown, is equivalent to an initiation of the martial type) that three vats of cold water are brought him. "He was put in the first vat, and he made the water so hot that it broke the staves and the copper hoops of the vat as one cracks a walnut. In the second vat the water made bubbles as big as a fist. In the third vat the heat was of the kind that some men can bear and some cannot. Then the little boy's wrath (*ferg*) lessened, and they gave him his clothes." [49] The same "mystical heat" (of the "martial" type) distinguishes the hero of the Nart, Batradz.[50]

All these myths and beliefs have their counterparts, we should note, in initiatory rituals that involve a real "mastery over fire." [51] The future Manchurian or Eskimo shaman, like the Himalayan or tantric yogin, must prove his magical power by resisting the most severe cold or drying wet sheets on his bare body. Then too, a whole series of ordeals imposed on future magicians complement this mastery over fire in the opposite direction. Resistance to cold through "mystical heat" denotes obtaining a superhuman state in the same measure as insensibility to fire.

Often the shamanic ecstasy is not attained until after the shaman is "heated." As we have had occasion to observe, the exhibition of fakiristic powers at certain moments during the séance springs from the shaman's need to authenticate the "second state" obtained through ecstasy. He gashes himself with knives, touches

49 *Tâin Bô Cuâlnge*, summarized and tr. by Georges Dumézil, *Horace et les Curiaces*, pp. 35 ff.

50 Cf. Dumézil: *Légendes sur les Nartes*, pp. 50 ff., 179 ff.; *Horace et les Curiaces*, pp. 55 ff.

51 The Australian medicine men are held to be "fire walkers"; cf. A. P. Elkin, *Aboriginal Men of High Degree*, pp. 62 ff. On fire walking, cf. the bibliography in R. Eisler, *Man into Wolf*, pp. 134–35. The Magyar name for shaman probably derives from an etymon meaning "heat, ardor," etc.; cf. János Balázs, "A magyar samán réülete" (Die Ekstase der ungarischen Schamanen), pp. 438 ff. (German summary).

white-hot iron, swallows burning coals, because he cannot do otherwise; he is obliged to test the new, superhuman condition to which he has now attained.

There is every reason to believe that the use of narcotics was encouraged by the quest for "magical heat." The smoke from certain herbs, the "combustion" of certain plants had the virtue of increasing "power." The narcotized person "grows hot"; narcotic intoxication is "burning." Mechanical means were sought for obtaining the "inner heat" that led to trance. We must also take into consideration the symbolic value of narcotic intoxication. It was equivalent to a "death"; the intoxicated person left his body, acquired the condition of ghosts and spirits. Mystical ecstasy being assimilated to a temporary "death" or to leaving the body, all intoxications that produced the same result were given a place among the techniques of ecstasy. But closer study of the problem gives the impression that the use of narcotics is, rather, indicative of the decadence of a technique of ecstasy or of its extension to "lower" peoples or social groups.[52] In any case, we have observed that the use of narcotics (tobacco, etc.) is relatively recent in the shamanism of the far Northeast.

"Magical Flight"

Siberian, Eskimo, and North American shamans fly.[53] All over the world the same magical power is credited to sorcerers and medicine men.[54] In Malekula the sorcerers (*bwili*) are able to change

52 We hope to return to this problem in the course of a fuller comparative study of the ideologies and techniques of "inner heat." On imaginary structures of fire, cf. G. Bachelard, *La Psychanalyse du feu.*

53 See, for example, Czaplicka, *Aboriginal Siberia*, pp. 175 ff., 238, etc.; A. L. Kroeber, "The Eskimo of Smith Sound," pp. 303 ff.; W. Thalbitzer, "Les Magiciens esquimaux," pp. 80–81; John W. Layard, "Shamanism: an Analysis Based on Comparison with the Flying Tricksters of Malekula," pp. 536 ff.; A. Métraux, "Le Shamanisme chez les Indiens de l' Amérique du Sud tropicale," p. 209; T. I. Itkonen, *Heidnische Religion und späterer Aberglaube bei den finnischen Lappen*, p. 116.

54 Australia: W. J. Perry, *The Children of the Sun* (2nd edn.), pp. 396,

into animals, but they usually choose to change into hens and falcons, for the faculty of flight makes them like spirits.[55] The Marind sorcerer "goes to a sort of lodge that he has built in the forest from palm leaves, and equips his upper arms and forearms with long plumes from a heron. Finally, he sets fire to his hut, without leaving it . . . the smoke and flames are to lift him into the air, and, like a bird, he flies where he will. . . ."[56]

All this makes us think of the ornithomorphic symbolism of the Siberian shamans' costumes. The Dyak shaman, who escorts the souls of the deceased to the other world, also takes the form of a bird.[57] We have seen that the Vedic sacrificer, when he reaches the top of the ladder, spreads his arms as a bird does its wings and cries: "We have come to the heaven," and so forth. The same rite is found in Malekula: at the culminating point of the sacrifice the sacrificer spreads his arms to imitate the falcon and sings a chant in honor of the stars.[58] According to many traditions, the power of flight extended to all men in the mythical age; all could reach heaven, whether on the wings of a fabulous bird or on the clouds.[59] There is no need to repeat all the details of flight symbolism recorded earlier in these pages (feathers, wings, etc.). We will add that a universal belief, amply documented in Europe, gives wizards and witches the ability to fly through the air.[60] We have seen that

403 ff.; Trobriand Islands: B. Malinowski, *The Argonauts of the Pacific*, pp. 239 ff. The *nijamas* of the Solomon Islands change into birds and fly (A. M. Hocart, "Medicine and Witchcraft in Eddystone of the Solomons," pp. 231–32). See also the documents already cited (cf. Index, s.v. "flying").

55 Layard, "Malekula: Flying Tricksters, Ghosts, Gods and Epileptics," pp. 504 ff.

56 P. Wirz, *Die Marind-anim von Holländisch-Süd-Neu-Guinea*, II, 74, cited in L. Lévy-Bruhl, *La Mythologie primitive. Le Monde mythique des Australiens et de Papous*, p. 232.

57 H. M. and N. K. Chadwick, *The Growth of Literature*, III, 495; N. K. Chadwick, *Poetry and Prophecy*, p. 27.

58 Layard, *Stone Men of Malekula*, pp. 733–34.

59 So, for example, in Yap: see Max Walleser, "Religiöse Anschauungen und Gebräuche der Bewohner von Jap, Deutsche Südsee," pp. 612 ff.

60 See G. L. Kittredge, *Witchcraft in Old and New England*, pp. 243 ff., 547–48 (bibliography); N. M. Penzer, ed., *Somadeva's Kathā-sarit-sāgara* (or

the same magical powers are credited to yogins, fakirs, and al-chemists.[61] We should make it clear, however, that here such powers often take on a purely spiritual character: "flight" ex-presses only intelligence, understanding of secret things or meta-physical truths. "Among all things that fly the mind [*manas*] is swiftest," says the *Ṛg-Veda*.[62] And the *Pañcaviṃśa Brāhmaṇa* adds: "Those who know have wings." [63]

An adequate analysis of the symbolism of magical flight would lead us too far. We will simply observe that two important mythi-cal motifs have contributed to give it its present structure: the mythical image of the soul in the form of a bird and the idea of birds as psychopomps. Negelein, Frazer, and Frobenius have assembled much material regarding these two myths of the soul.[64] What concerns us in this instance is the fact that sorcerers and shamans are able, *here on earth* and *as often as they wish*, to accom-plish "coming out of the body," that is, the death that alone has power to transform the rest of mankind into "birds"; shamans and sorcerers can enjoy the condition of "souls," of "disincarnate beings," which is accessible to the profane only when they die. Magical flight is the expression both of the soul's autonomy and of ecstasy. The fact explains how this myth could be incorporated into such different cultural complexes: sorcery, mythology of dream, solar cults and imperial apotheoses, techniques of ecstasy, funerary symbolisms, and many others. It is also related to the symbolism of ascension.[65] This myth of the soul contains in embryo

---

Oceans of Streams of Story), tr. C. H. Tawney, II, 104; Stith Thompson, *Motif-Index of Folk-Literature*, III, 217; Arne Runeberg, *Witches, Demons and Fertility Magic*, pp. 15 ff., 93 ff., 105 ff., 222 ff.

61 Above, pp. 407 ff.   62 VI, 9, 5 (tr. R. T. H. Griffith).

63 XIV, I, 13 (tr. W. Caland). On the symbolism of "flying through the air," see Ananda K. Coomaraswamy, *Figures of Speech or Figures of Thought*, pp. 183 ff.

64 Bird-soul: J. von Negelein, "Seele als Vogel"; J. G. Frazer, *Taboo and the Perils of the Soul*, pp. 33–36. Bird-psychopomp: L. Frobenius, *Die Welt-anschauung der Naturvölker*, pp. 11 ff.; Frazer, *The Fear of the Dead in Primi-tive, Religion*, I, 189 ff.

65 See below, pp. 490 ff.

a whole metaphysics of man's spiritual autonomy and freedom; it is here that we must seek the point of departure for the earliest speculations concerning voluntary abandonment of the body, the omnipotence of intelligence, the immortality of the human soul. An analysis of the "imagination of motion" will show how essential the nostalgia for flight is to the human psyche.[66] The point of primary importance here is that the mythology and the rites of magical flight peculiar to shamans and sorcerers confirm and proclaim their transcendence in respect to the human condition; by flying into the air, in bird form or in their normal human shape, shamans as it were proclaim the degeneration of humanity. For as we have seen, a number of myths refer to a primordial time when *all human beings* could ascend to heaven, by climbing a mountain, a tree, or a ladder, or flying by their own power, or being carried by birds. The degeneration of humanity henceforth forbids the mass of mankind to fly to heaven; only death restores men (and not all of them!) to their primordial condition; only then can they ascend to heaven, fly like birds, and so forth.

Once again, without undertaking a thorough analysis of this flight symbolism and the mythology of the bird-soul, we will remind the reader that the concept of the bird-soul and, hence, the identification of the deceased with a bird, are already documented in the religions of the archaic Near East. The Egyptian Book of the Dead describes the deceased as a falcon flying away,[67] and in Mesopotamia the dead were imagined as birds. The myth is probably even older. In the prehistoric monuments of Europe and Asia the Cosmic Tree is depicted with two birds in its branches; [68] in addition to their cosmogonic value, these birds seem to have symbolized the Ancestor-Soul. For, it will be remembered, in the mythologies of Central Asia, Siberia, and Indonesia the birds

66 See, for example, Bachelard, *L'Air et les songes. Essai sur l'imagination du mouvement*; Eliade, "Dūrohaṇa and the 'Waking Dream.'" Cf. also id., *Myths, Dreams and Symbols*, pp. 99 ff.

67 Ch. xxviii, etc.

68 Cf. G. Wilke, "Der Weltenbaum und die beiden kosmischen Vögel in der vorgeschichtlichen Kunst."

perched on the branches of the World Tree represent men's souls. Because shamans can change themselves into "birds," that is, because they enjoy the "spirit" condition, they are able to fly to the World Tree to bring back "soul-birds." The bird perched on a stick is a frequent symbol in shamanic circles. It is found, for example, on the tombs of Yakut shamans. A Hungarian *táltos* "had a stick or post before his hut and perched on the stick was a bird. He sent the bird wherever he would have to go." [69] The bird perched on a post is already found in the celebrated relief at Lascaux (bird-headed man) in which Horst Kirchner has seen a representation of a shamanic trance.[70] However this may be, it is certain that the motif "bird perched on a post" is extremely archaic.

From these few examples it is clear that the symbolism and mythologies of "magical flight" extend beyond the bounds of shamanism proper and also precede it; they belong to an ideology of universal magic and play an essential part in many magico-religious complexes. Yet we can understand the incorporation of this symbolism and of all these mythologies into shamanism; for did they not evince and emphasize the shaman's superhuman condition, his freedom, in the last analysis, to move safely among the three cosmic zones and to pass indefinitely from "life" to "death" and vice versa, exactly like the "spirits" whose abilities he had appropriated? The "magical flight" of sovereigns manifests the same autonomy and the same victory over death.

In this connection we may remember that the levitation of saints and magicians is also attested in both the Christian and Islamic traditions.[71] Roman Catholic hagiography has gone so far as to record a large number of "levitations" and even of "flights";

---

69 G. Róheim, "Hungarian Shamanism," p. 38; cf. id., *Hungarian and Vogul Mythology*, pp. 49 ff.

70 *Ein archäologischer Beitrag zur Urgeschichte des Schamanismus*, especially pp. 271 ff. J. Maringer (*Vorgeschichtliche Religion*, p. 128) considers that it is more probably a memorial image.

71 On levitation in primitive societies, cf. O. Leroy, *La Raison primitive*, pp. 174 ff.

Olivier Leroy's compilation of instances [72] is there to prove it. The outstanding example is that of St. Joseph of Cupertino (1603–1663). A witness describes his levitation as follows: ". . . he rose into space, and, from the middle of the church, flew like a bird onto the high altar, where he embraced the tabernacle. . . ." [73] "Sometimes, too, he was seen to fly to the altar of St. Francis and of the Virgin of the Grotello. . . ." [74] Another time he flew into an olive tree, "and he remained kneeling for half an hour on a branch, which was seen to sway as if a bird had perched on it." [75] In another ecstasy he flew, about seven feet above the ground, to an almond tree a hundred feet away.[76] Among the countless other examples of levitation or flight by saints or pious persons, we will also cite the experience of Sister Mary of Jesus Crucified, an Arabian Carmelite. She rose high into the air, to the tops of the trees, in the garden of the Carmelite nunnery in Bethlehem, "but she began by raising herself with the help of some branches and never floated free in space." [77]

The Bridge and the "Difficult Passage"

Shamans, like the dead, must cross a bridge in the course of their journey to the underworld. Like death, ecstasy implies a "mutation," to which myth gives plastic expression by a "perilous passage." We have seen a considerable number of examples. As we intend to return to this subject in a special work, we shall confine ourselves here to a few brief remarks. The symbolism of the funerary bridge is universally disseminated and extends far beyond the bounds of shamanic ideology and mythology.[78] This symbolism

72 *La Lévitation.*
73 Ibid., p. 125.
74 Ibid., p. 126.
75 Ibid., p. 127.
76 Ibid., p. 128.
77 Ibid., p. 178.

78 In addition to the examples given in this book, cf. Johannes Zemmrich, "Toteninseln und verwandte geographische Mythen," pp. 236 ff.; Rosalind Moss, *The Life after Death in Oceania and the Malay Archipelago,* s.v., "bridge"; Kira Weinberger-Goebel, "Melanesische Jenseitsgedanken," pp. 101 ff.; Martti Räsänen, *Regenbogen-Himmelsbrücke,* passim; Theodor Koch,

s linked, on the one hand, with the myth of a bridge (or tree, vine, etc.) that once connected earth and heaven and by means of which human beings effortlessly communicated with the gods; on the other hand, it is related to the initiatory symbolism of the "strait gate" or of a "paradoxical passage," which we shall illustrate by a few examples. We here have a mythological complex whose principal constituents would appear to be the following: (*a*) *in illo tempore*, in the paradisal time of humanity, a bridge connected earth with heaven [79] and people passed from one to the other without encountering any obstacles, because there was not yet *death*; (*b*) once the *easy* communications between earth and heaven were broken off, people could not cross the bridge except "in spirit," that is, either as dead or in ecstasy; (*c*) this crossing is difficult; in other words, it is sown with obstacles and not all souls succeed in traversing it; demons and monsters seeking to devour the soul must be faced, or the bridge becomes as narrow as a razoredge when the wicked try to cross it, and so on; only the "good," and especially the *initiates*, cross the bridge easily (these latter in some measure know the road, for they have undergone ritual death and resurrection); (*d*) certain privileged persons nevertheless succeed in passing over it during their lifetime, be it in ecstasy, like the shamans, or "by force," like certain heroes, or, finally, "paradoxically," through "wisdom" or initiation (we shall return to the "paradox" in a moment).

The important point here is that numerous rites are conceived of as symbolically "building" a "bridge" or a "ladder," and as accomplishing this by the sheer power of the rite itself. This idea is documented, for example, in the symbolism of the Brāhmanic sacrifice.[80] We saw that the cord connecting the ceremonial birches

---

Zum Animismus der südamerikanischen Indianer," pp. 129 ff.; F. K. umazawa, *Die Weltanfänge in der japanischen Mythologie*, pp. 151 ff., 313 ., 393; L. Vannicelli, *La religione dei Lolo*, pp. 179 ff.; S. Thompson, *Motif-index of Folk-Literature*, III, 22 (F 152).

79 Cf. Numazawa, pp. 155 ff.; H. T. Fischer, "Indonesische Paradies-mythen," pp. 207 ff.

80 Cf. *Taittirīya Saṃhitā*, VI, 5, 3, 3; VI, 5, 4, 2; VII, 5, 8, 5; etc.

set up for the shamanic séance is called the "bridge" and symbolizes the shaman's ascent to the heavens. In some Japanese initiations the candidates are made to construct a "bridge" upon seven
arrows and with seven boards.[81] This rite is comparable to the
ladders of knives climbed by candidates during their initiation as
shamans and, in general, to initiatory ascension rites. The meaning
of all these "dangerous passage" rites is this: communication between earth and heaven is established, in an effort to restore the
"communicability" that was the law *in illo tempore*. From one point
of view, all these initiation rites pursue the reconstruction of a
"passage" to the beyond and hence abolition of the break between
planes that is typical of the human condition after the "fall."

The vitality of this bridge symbolism is further demonstrated
by the part that it plays in Christian and Islamic apocalypses as well
as in the initiatory traditions of the western Middle Ages. The
Vision of St. Paul describes a bridge "narrow as a hair" connecting
our world with paradise.[82] The same image is found in the Arabic
writers and mystics: the bridge is "narrower than a hair," and
connects earth with the astral spheres and paradise; [83] just as in
Christian tradition, sinners cannot cross it and are cast into hell.
Arabic terminology clearly brings out the nature of the bridge or
the "path" as "difficult of access." [84] Medieval legends tell of a
"bridge under water" and of a "sword-bridge," which the hero
(Lancelot) must cross barefoot and bare-handed; it is "sharper
than a scythe" and it is crossed "with great pain and agony." The
initiatory character of crossing the sword-bridge is also confirmed
by another fact: before he starts over it, Lancelot sees two lions on
the further bank, but when he is there he sees only a lizard; successfully undergoing the initiatory ordeal in itself makes the "danger"

81 Among the shamanesses of Ryukyu; cf. A. Slawik, "Kultische Geheimbünde der Japaner und Germanen," p. 739.

82 Miguel Asín Palacios, *La escatología musulmana en la Divina Comedi*
(2nd edn.), p. 282.

83 Ibid., p. 182.

84 Ibid., pp. 181 f. The Islamic conception of the bridge (*ṣirāṭ*) is o
Persian origin (ibid., p. 180).

disappear.[85] In Finnish tradition, Väinämöinen and the shamans who journey to the other world (Tuonela) in trance must cross a bridge made of swords and knives.[86]

The "narrow passage" or "dangerous passage" is a common motif in both funerary and initiatory mythologies (we have seen how closely they may be connected, sometimes to the point of coalescence). In New Zealand the deceased must pass through a very narrow space between two demons that try to capture him; if he is "light" he gets through, but if he is "heavy" he falls and becomes the demons' prey.[87] "Lightness" or "swiftness"—as in the myths of passing very quickly through the jaws of a monster—is always a symbolic formula for "intelligence," "wisdom," "transcendence," and, in the last analysis, for initiation. "A sharpened edge of a razor, hard to traverse, / A difficult path is this—poets declare!" says the *Kaṭha Upaniṣad*.[88] This formula illuminates the initiatory nature of metaphysical knowledge. "Strait is the gate and narrow is the way which leadeth unto life, and few there be that find it." [89]

And indeed the symbolism of the "strait gate" and the "dangerous bridge" is bound up with the symbolism of what we have called the "paradoxical passage" because it sometimes proves to be an impossibility or a situation from which there is no escape. It will be remembered that candidate shamans or the heroes of certain myths sometimes find themselves in apparently desperate situations. They must go "where night and day meet," or find a gate in a wall, or go up to the sky through a passage that opens out for an instant, pass between two constantly moving millstones,

85 Cf. the texts quoted in H. Zimmer, *The King and the Corpse: Tales of the Soul's Conquest of Evil*, pp. 166 ff., 173 ff. Cf. ibid., p. 166, fig. 3, the fine representation of crossing the "sword-bridge," from a twelfth-century French manuscript.

86 M. Haavio, *Väinämöinen*, pp. 110 ff.

87 E. S. C. Handy, *Polynesian Religion*, pp. 73 ff.

88 III, 14 (tr. R. E. Hume, p. 353). On the Indian and Celtic symbolism of the bridge, see Luisa Coomaraswamy, "The Perilous Bridge of Welfare"; also Ananda K. Coomaraswamy, *Time and Eternity*, p. 28 and n. 36.

89 Matt. 7:14.

two rocks that clash together, through the jaws of a monster, and the like.[90] As Coomaraswamy rightly saw, all these mythical images express the need to transcend opposites, to abolish the polarity typical of the human condition, in order to attain to ultimate reality. "Whoever would transfer from this to the Otherworld, or return, must do so through the undimensioned and timeless 'interval' that divides related but contrary forces, between which, if one is to pass at all, it must be 'instantly.' "[91] In the myths the "paradoxical" passage emphatically testifies that he who succeeds in accomplishing it has transcended the human condition; he is shaman, a hero, or a "spirit," and indeed this "paradoxical" passage can be accomplished only by one who is "spirit."

These few examples throw light on the function of the myths, rites, and symbols of "passage" in shamanic techniques and ideologies. By crossing, in ecstasy, the "dangerous" bridge that connects the two worlds and that only the dead can attempt, the shaman proves that he is spirit, is no longer a human being, and at the same time attempts to restore the "communicability" that existed *in illo tempore* between this world and heaven. For what the shaman can do today *in ecstasy* could, at the dawn of time, be done by all human beings *in concreto*; they went up to heaven and came down again without recourse to trance. Temporarily and for a limited number of persons—the shamans—ecstasy re-establishes the primordial condition of all mankind. In this respect, the mystical experience of the "primitives" is a return to origins, a reversion to the mystical age of the lost paradise. For the shaman in ecstasy, the bridge or the tree, the vine, the cord, and so on—which, *in illo tempore*, connected earth with heaven—once again, for the space of an instant, becomes a present reality.

---

90 On these motifs, cf. A. B. Cook, *Zeus*, III, Pt. 2, Appendix P ("Floating Islands"), pp. 975–1016; A. K. Coomaraswamy, "Symplegades"; Eliade, *Birth and Rebirth*, pp. 64 ff., 130; G. Hatt, *Asiatic Influences in American Folklore*, pp. 78 f.

91 "Symplegades," p. 486.

The Ladder—The Road of the Dead—Ascension

We have seen countless examples of shamanic ascent to the sky by means of a ladder.[92] The same means is also employed to facilitate the gods' descent to earth or to ensure the ascent of the dead man's soul. Thus in the Indian Archipelago the Sun God is invited to come down to earth by a ladder with seven rungs. Among the Dusun the medicine man summoned to treat a patient sets up a ladder in the center of the room; it reaches the roof, and down it come the spirits that the sorcerer summons to possess him.[93] Some Malay tribes supply graves with upright sticks that they call "soul-ladders," no doubt to invite the deceased to leave his burial place and fly up to heaven.[94] The Mangar, a Nepalese tribe, use a symbolic stairway by making nine notches or steps in a stick, which they plant in the grave; by it the dead man's soul goes up to heaven.[95]

In their funerary texts the Egyptians preserved the expression *asken pet* (*asken* = step) to show that the ladder furnished them by Rā to mount into the sky is a real ladder.[96] "I set up a ladder to heaven among the gods," says the Book of the Dead.[97] The gods

92 See the photograph of such a ladder, used by a Gond sorcerer, in W. Koppers, *Die Bhil in Zentralindien*, Pl. XIII, fig. 1.

93 Frazer, *Folk-lore in the Old Testament*, II, 54–55.

94 W. W. Skeat and C. O. Blagden, *Pagan Races of the Malay Peninsula*, I, 108, 114.

95 H. H. Risley, *The Tribes and Castes of Bengal*, II, 75. The Russians of Voronezh bake little ladders of dough in honor of their dead, and sometimes represent seven heavens on them by seven bars. The custom has been borrowed by the Cheremis; cf. Frazer: *Folk-lore in the Old Testament*, II, 57; *The Fear of the Dead in Primitive Religion*, I, 188 ff. The same custom is found among the Siberian Russians; cf. G. Ränk, *Die heilige Hinterecke im Hauskult der Völker Nordosteuropas und Nordasiens*, p. 73. On the ladder in Russian funerary mythology, cf. Propp, *Le radici storiche dei racconti di fate*, pp. 338 ff.

96 Cf., for example, Wallis Budge, *From Fetish to God in Ancient Egypt*, p. 346; H. P. Blok, "Zur altägyptischen Vorstellung der Himmelsleiter."

97 Cited by R. Weil, *Le Champ des roseaux et le champ des offrandes dans la religion funéraire et la religion générale*, p. 52. (Tr. above is Budge's, p. 495).

"made a ladder for N., that he might ascend to heaven on it." [98] In a number of tombs from the archaic and medieval dynasties, amulets representing a ladder (*maqet*) or a stairway have been found.[99] Similar figurines were included in burials on the Rhine frontier.[100]

A ladder (*klimax*) with seven rungs is documented in the Mithraic mysteries, and we have seen [101] that the prophet-king Kosingas threatened his subjects that he would go up to the goddess Hera by a ladder. An ascent to heaven by ceremonially climbing a ladder probably formed part of the Orphic initiation.[102] In any case, the symbolism of ascension by means of stairs was known in Greece.[103]

W. Bousset long ago compared the Mithraic ladder with similar Oriental conceptions and demonstrated their common cosmological symbolism.[104] But it is no less important to show the symbolism of the "Center of the World" that is implicitly present in all ascents to heaven. Jacob dreams of a ladder whose top reaches heaven, "with the angels of God ascending and descending on it." [105] The stone on which Jacob goes to sleep is a *bethel* (that is, a sacred stone) and

Cf. also J. H. Breasted, *The Development of Religion and Thought in Ancient Egypt*, pp. 112 ff., 156 ff.; F. Max Müller, *Egyptian [Mythology]*, p. 176; W. J. Perry, *The Primordial Ocean*, pp. 263, 266; Jacques Vandier, *La Religion égyptienne*, pp. 71–72.

98 *The Pyramid Texts*, Utt. 572, §1474b (tr. A. S. B. Mercer, I, 234).

99 Cf., for example, Budge, *The Mummy* (2nd edn.), pp. 324, 327. A reproduction of funerary ladders to heaven is to be found in id., *The Egyptian Heaven and Hell*, II, 159 ff.

100 Cf. F. Cumont, *Lux perpetua*, p. 282.   101 Above, pp. 390.

102 At least this is the supposition of A. B. Cook (*Zeus*, II, Pt. 1, pp. 124 ff.), who, in his usual way, brings together a vast quantity of references to ritual ladders in other religions. But see also W. K. C. Guthrie, *Orpheus and Greek Religion*, p. 208.

103 Cf. Cook, II, Pt. 1, pp. 37, 127 f. Cf. also C. M. Edsman, *Le Baptême de feu*, p. 41.

104 "Die Himmelsreise der Seele," especially pp. 155–69; see also A. Jeremias, *Handbuch* (2nd edn.), pp. 180 ff. Vol. VIII of the *Vorträge* of the Bibliothek Warburg is devoted to the soul's celestial journeys in various traditions; cf. also F. Saxl, *Mithras*, pp. 97 f.; Benjamin Rowland, "Studies in the Buddhist Art of Bāmiyān," p. 48.

105 Gen. 28:12.

s situated "at the center of the world," for it is there that there was onnection among all the cosmic regions.[106] In Islamic tradition Mohammed sees a ladder rising from the temple in Jerusalem pre-eminently the "Center") to heaven, with angels to right and eft; on this ladder the souls of the righteous mounted to God.[107] The mystical ladder is abundantly documented in Christian tradion; the martyrdom of St. Perpetua and the legend of St. Olaf are ut two examples.[108] St. John Climacus uses the symbolism of the adder to express the various phases of spiritual ascent. A remarkbly similar symbolism is found in Islamic mysticism: to ascend to God, the soul must mount seven successive steps—repentance, bstinence, renunciation, poverty, patience, trust in God, satisction.[109] The symbolism of the "stair," of "ladders," and of asensions was constantly employed by Christian mysticism. In the eaven of Saturn Dante sees a golden ladder rising dizzyingly to he last celestial sphere and trodden by the souls of the blessed.[110]

106 Cf. Eliade, *Patterns in Comparative Religion*, pp. 229 ff., 380 ff. See lso above, ch. viii. Nor should we forget another type of ascension—that of ne sovereign or prophet to receive the "heavenly book" from the hands of ne Supreme God, an extremely important motif, studied by G. Widengren, *he Ascension of the Apostle of God and the Heavenly Book.*

107 Miguel Asín Palacios, *La escatología musulmana en la Divina Comedia*, . 70. In other traditions Mohammed reaches heaven on the back of a bird; us the *Book of the Ladder* says that he accomplished his journey astride "a rt of duck larger than a donkey and smaller than a mule," and guided by ne Archangel Gabriel; see Enrico Cerulli, *Il "libro della scala."* See above pp. 402 f.) similar tales of Moslem saints. "Magical flight," climbing, scension are, in any case, homologizable formulations of the same mystical xperience and the same symbolism.

108 Cf. C. M. Edsman, *Le Baptême de feu*, pp. 32 ff.

109 G. van der Leeuw, *La Religion dans son essence et ses manifestations*, . 484, with the references.

110 St. John of the Cross represents the stages of mystical perfection as a ifficult climb; his *Ascent of Mount Carmel* describes the necessary ascetic and piritual efforts in the form of a long, trying ascent of a mountain. In some astern European legends the Cross of Christ is regarded as a bridge or ladder by which the Lord descends to earth and souls mount to him U. Holmberg, *Der Baum des Lebens*, p. 133). On the Byzantine iconography f the heavenly ladder, cf. Coomaraswamy, "Svayamātṛṇṇā: Janua Coeli," 47.

The ladder with seven rungs was also preserved in alchemical tradition. A codex represents alchemical initiation by a seven-runged ladder up which climb blindfolded men; on the seventh rung stands a man with the blindfold removed from his eyes, facing a closed door.[111]

The myth of ascent to the sky by a ladder is also known in Africa,[112] Oceania,[113] and North America.[114] But stairs are only one of the numerous symbolic expressions for ascent; the sky can be reached by fire or smoke,[115] by climbing a tree [116] or a mountain,[117] or ascending by way of a rope [118] or vine,[119] the rainbow,[120] or even a sunbeam, for example. Finally, we must mention another group of myths and legends related to the theme of ascent—the "chain of

111 G. Carbonelli, *Sulle fonti storiche della chimica e dell'alchimia in Italia,* p. 39, fig. 47. The codex is in the Royal Library at Modena.

112 Cf. Alice Werner, *African [Mythology]*, p. 136.

113 Cf. A. E. Jensen and H. Niggemeyer, eds., *Hainuwele*, pp. 51 ff., 82, 84, etc.; Jensen, *Die drei Ströme*, p. 164; H. M. and N. K. Chadwick, *The Growth of Literature*, III, 481, etc.

114 S. Thompson, *Motif-Index*, III, 8.

115 Cf., for example, R. Pettazzoni, *Saggi di storia delle religioni e di mitologia*, p. 68, n. 1; A. Riesenfeld, *The Megalithic Culture of Melanesia*, pp 196 ff., etc.

116 Cf. A. van Gennep, *Mythes et légendes d'Australie*, nos. 17, 56; Pettazzoni, *Saggi*, p. 67, n. 1; H. M. and N. K. Chadwick, III, 486, etc.; Harry Tegnaeus, *Le Héros civilisateur*, p. 150, n. 1; etc.

117 The medicine man of the Wotjobaluk (Australia) tribe can mount as far as the "dark place," which resembles a mountain (A. W. Howitt, *The Native Tribes of South-East Australia*, p. 490). Cf. also W. Schmidt, *Der Ursprung der Gottesidee*, III, 845, 868, 871.

118 Cf. Pettazzoni, *Miti e leggende*, I, 63 (Thonga), etc.; H. M. and N. K. Chadwick, III, 481 (Sea Dyak); Frazer, *Folk-lore in the Old Testament*, II, 54 (Cheremis).

119 H. H. Juynboll, "Religionen der Naturvölker Indonesiens," p. 583 (Indonesia); Frazer, *Folklore*, II, 52–53 (Indonesia); Roland Dixon, *Oceanic [Mythology]*, p. 156; Alice Werner, *African [Mythology]*, p. 135; H. B Alexander, *Latin-American [Mythology]*, p. 271; S. Thompson, *Motif-Index* III, 7 (North America). Approximately the same regions present the myth of ascension by a spider web.

120 To the examples cited in the course of this study, add: Juynboll, p. 584 (Indonesia); Ivor H. N. Evans, *Studies in Religion, Folk-lore & Custom*, pp 51–52 (Dusun): H. M. and N. K. Chadwick, III, 272 ff., etc.

rrows." A hero goes up by fixing a first arrow in the celestial vault, a second in the first, and so on until he has made up a chain between heaven and earth. This motif is found in Melanesia, and North and South America; it does not occur in Africa and Asia.[121] The bow being unknown in Australia, its part in the myth is taken by a lance bearing a long strip of cloth; with the lance fixed in the celestial vault, the hero ascends by the trailing cloth.[122]

A volume would be required for an adequate exposition of these mythical motifs and their ritual implications. We will merely point out that the various roads are equally available to mythical heroes and to shamans (sorcerers, medicine men, etc.) and certain privileged persons among the dead. This is not the place to study the extremely complex problem of the variety of itineraries after death in the various religions.[123] We will only observe that for certain tribes, who are reckoned among the most archaic, the dead go to the sky, but that the majority of "primitive" peoples know at least two post-mortem routes—celestial for privileged beings (chiefs, shamans, "initiates") and horizontal or infernal for the rest of mankind. Thus, a certain number of Australian tribes—Narrinyeri, Dieri, Buandik, Kurnai, and Kulin—believe that the dead rise into the sky; [124] among the Kulin they go up by the rays of the setting sun.[125] But in Central Australia the dead haunt the familiar places where they had passed their lives; elsewhere, they go to certain regions in the west.[126]

121 Except among the Semang (cf. Pettazzoni, "La catena di frecce," p. 9) and the Koryak (cf. W. I. Jochelson, *The Koryak*, pp. 213, 304).

122 Pettazzoni, "The Chain of Arrows." See also Jochelson, *The Koryak*, p. 293, 304; ibid., supplementary references for the dissemination of the motif in North America. Cf. also G. Hatt, *Asiatic Influences in American Folk-re*, pp. 40 ff.

123 We shall study this problem in our book now in preparation, *Mythologies of Death*.

124 Cf. Frazer, *The Belief in Immortality and the Worship of the Dead*, I, 34, 138, etc.

125 Howitt, *The Native Tribes of South-East Australia*, p. 438.

126 According to F. Graebner (*Das Weltbild der Primitiven*, pp. 25 ff.) and W. Schmidt (*Der Ursprung*, I [2nd edn.], 334–476: III, 574–86, etc.), the most archaic Australian tribes are those of the southeast of the continent,

For the Maori of New Zealand the ascent of souls is long and difficult, for there are as many as ten heavens, and the gods dwell in the last. The priest employs several means to accomplish it: he sings, thus magically escorting the soul; at the same time, by a particular ritual, he tries to separate the soul from the body and send it upward. When the dead man is a chief, the priest and his assistants fasten feathers to the end of sticks and, as they chant gradually raise their sticks into the air.[127] We may note that, here again, only the privileged go up to the sky; the rest of mankind depart across the ocean or to a subterranean realm.

If we try to achieve a general view of all the myths and rites just briefly reviewed, we are struck by the fact that they have a dominant idea in common: communication between heaven and earth can be brought about—or could be *in illo tempore*—by some physical means (rainbow, bridge, stairs, ladder, vine, cord, "chain of arrows," mountain, etc., etc.). All these symbolic images of the connection between heaven and earth are merely variants of the World Tree or the *axis mundi*. In an earlier chapter we saw that the myth and symbolism of the Cosmic Tree imply the idea of a "Center of the World," of a point where earth, sky, and underworld meet. We also observed that the symbolism of the "Center," while playing a role of the first importance in shamanic ideology and techniques, is infinitely more widespread than shamanism itself and long preceded it. The symbolism of the "Center of the World" is also indissolubly connected with the myth of a primordial time when communications between heaven and earth, gods and mortals, were not merely possible but easy and within reach of all mankind. The myths we have just reviewed generally refer to this primordial *illud tempus*, but some of them tell of a celestial

that is, precisely those whose funerary conceptions are the most determinedly celestial (doubtless in connection with their beliefs in a Supreme Being of uranian structure); whereas the tribes of Central Australia—where the funerary conception is predominantly "horizontal," and related to the ancestor cult and totemism—are, from the ethnological point of view, the least "primitive."

127 Frazer, *The Belief in Immortality*, II, 24 ff.

scent performed by a hero or sovereign or sorcerer *after* communication was broken off; in other words, they imply the possibility, or certain privileged or elect persons, of returning to the origin of ime, of recovering the mythical and paradisal moment before the "fall," that is, before the break in communications between heaven nd earth.

It is in this category of the elect or the privileged that shamans belong. They are not alone in being able to fly up to heaven or to each it by means of a tree, a ladder, or the like; other privileged persons can match them here—sovereigns, heroes, initiates. The hamans differ from the other privileged categories by their particular technique, which is ecstasy. As we saw, shamanic ecstasy can be regarded as a recovery of the human condition before he "fall"; in other words, it reproduces a primordial "situation" ccessible to the rest of mankind only through death (since ascents o heaven by means of rites—compare the case of the Vedic Indian acrificer—are *symbolic*, not *concrete* like the shaman's). Although he ideology of shamanic ascent is perfectly consistent and forms n integral part of the mythical conception we have just reviewed "Center of the World," break in communications, degeneration of umanity, etc.), we have come upon numerous cases of aberrant hamanic practices; [128] we refer especially to rudimentary and mehanical means of obtaining trance (narcotics, dancing to the point f exhaustion, "possession," etc.). The question arises if, aside rom the "historical" explanations that could be offered for these berrant techniques (deterioration as the result of external cultural nfluences, hybridization, etc.), they cannot also be interpreted on

128 It is perhaps on account of the aberrant kinds of shamanic trance that Vilhelm Schmidt regarded ecstasy as an attribute of "black" shamans only cf. *Der Ursprung*, XII, 624). Since, according to his interpretation, the white" shaman did not enter into ecstasy, Schmidt did not consider him "a eal shaman" and proposed terming him a "Himmelsdiener" (ibid., pp. 365, 34 ff., 696 ff.). In all probability Schmidt denigrated ecstasy because, as a ood rationalist, he could not grant any validity to a religious experience hat involved "loss of consciousness." Cf. the discussion of his theses, as comared with those put forward in the French edition of the present work, in Dominik Schröder, "Zur Struktur des Schamanismus."

another plane. We may ask, for example, if the aberrant aspect of the shamanic trance is not due to the fact that the shaman seeks to experience *in concreto* a symbolism and mythology that, by their very nature, are not susceptible of being "realized" on the "concrete" plane; if, in short, the desire to obtain, at any cost and by any means, an ascent *in concreto*, a mystical and at the same time *real* journey to heaven, did not result in the aberrant trances that we have seen; if, finally, these types of behavior are not the inevitable consequence of an intense desire to "live," that is, to "experience" on the plane of the body, what in the present condition of humanity is no longer accessible except on the plane of "spirit." But we prefer to leave this problem open; in any case, it is one that reaches beyond the bounds of the history of religions and enters the domain of philosophy and theology.

CHAPTER FOURTEEN

Conclusions

The Formation of North Asian Shamanism

THE word "shaman," we saw, comes to us through Russian
from the Tungusic *šaman*. The derivation of this term from
the Pali *samaṇa* (Sanskrit *śramaṇa*) through the Chinese *sha-men*
(a mere transcription of the Pali word), which was accepted by the
majority of nineteenth-century Orientalists, was nevertheless questioned quite early (in 1842 by W. Schott, in 1846 by Dordji Banzarov) and rejected by J. Németh [1] in 1914 and by B. Laufer in
1917.[2] These scholars believed they had demonstrated that the
Tungusic word belonged to the group of Turko-Mongolian languages, by virtue of certain phonetic correspondences: the initial
s of archaic Turkic developing into Tatar *k*, Chuvash *j*, Yakut *x*
(a surd spirant, as in German *ach*), Mongolian *ts*, *č*, and Manchu-
Tungusic *s*, *ś*, or *š*, the Tungusic *šaman* would be the exact phonetic
equivalent of the Turko-Mongolian *kam* (*qam*), which is precisely
the term for "shaman" in the strict sense in most of the Turkic
languages.

But G. J. Ramstedt [3] has shown that Németh's phonetic law is

1 "Über den Ursprung des Wortes Šaman und einige Bemerkungen zur
türkisch-mongolischen Lautgeschichte." On the meaning of the term *šaman*
in the Islamic world, see V. F. Büchner, "Shaman."

2 "Origin of the Word Shaman." Laufer's article also contains a brief
history and bibliography of the problem. See also Jean-Paul Roux, "Le Nom
du chaman dans les textes turco-mongols." On the Turkic term *bögü*, cf.
Hans-Wilhelm Haussig, "Theophylakts Exkurs über die skythischen Völker," pp. 359 ff.

3 "Zur Frage nach der Stellung der tschuwassichen," pp. 20–21; cf. Kai

invalid. Then too, the discovery of similar words in Tokharian (*ṣamāne* "Buddhist monk") and in Sogdian (*šmn* = *šaman*) revived the theory of Indian origin.[4] Hesitating to pronounce upon the linguistic aspect of the question, and taking into account the difficulties in the way of explaining the migration of this Indian term from Central to Far Eastern Asia, we would add that the problem of Indian influences on the Siberian peoples should be posed as a whole and with use of the ethnographic as well as the historical data.

This has been done by Shirokogoroff for the Tungus, in a series of studies [5] of which we shall attempt to summarize the results and the general conclusions. The word *šaman*, Shirokogoroff argues, appears to be foreign to the Tungusic language. But, what is more important, the phenomenon of shamanism itself displays elements of southern origin, specifically Buddhist (Lamaist) elements. Now Buddhism had penetrated quite far into northeastern Asia—in the fourth century to Korea, in the second half of the first millennium to the Uigur, in the thirteenth century to the Mongols, in the fifteenth century into the Amur region (presence of a Buddhist temple at the mouth of the Amur River). The majority of the names of spirits among the Tungus are borrowed from the Mongols and the

---

Donner, "Über soghdisch *nōm* 'Gesetz' und samojedisch *nōm* 'Himmel Gott,' " p. 7. See also G. J. Ramstedt, "The Relation of the Altaic Languages to Other Language Groups."

4 Cf. Sylvain Lévi, "Étude des documents tokhariens de la Mission Pelliot," especially pp. 445–46; Paul Pelliot, "Sur quelques mots d'Asie Centrale attestés dans les textes chinois," especially pp. 466–69; A. Meillet ("Le Tokharien," p. 19) also points out the resemblance between the Tokharian *ṣamāne* and the Tungusic word. F. Rosenberg ("On Wine and Feasts in the Iranian National Epic," n., pp. 18–20) stresses the importance of the Sogdian term *šmn*.

5 N. D. Mironov and S. M. Shirokogoroff, "Śramaṇa-Shaman." Cf. also Shirokogoroff: "General Theory of Shamanism among the Tungus"; "Northern Tungus Migrations in the Far East"; "Versuch einer Erforschung der Grundlagen des Schamanentums bei den Tungusen"; *Psychomental Complex of the Tungus*, pp. 268 ff.

Manchu, who, in turn, had received them from the Lamaists.[6] In the costume, the drum, and the paintings of the Tungus shamans Shirokogoroff detects recent influences.[7] In addition, the Manchu state that shamanism appeared among them in the middle of the eleventh century but did not become widespread until the Ming Dynasty (14th-17th centuries). The southern Tungus, for their part, say that their shamanism is borrowed from the Manchu and the Dahor. Finally, the northern Tungus are influenced by their neighbors to the south, the Yakut. In support of his belief that the appearance of shamanism coincided with the dissemination of Buddhism in these countries of North Asia, Shirokogoroff cites the fact that shamanism flourished in Manchuria between the twelfth and seventeenth centuries, in Mongolia before the fourteenth century, among the Kirgiz and the Uigur probably between the seventh and eleventh centuries, that is, just before the official recognition of Buddhism (Lamaism) by these peoples.[8] The Russian ethnologist further cites several ethnographic elements of southern origin. The snake (in some cases, the boa constrictor), occurring in the shamanic ideology and the shaman's ritual costume, is not found in the religious beliefs of the Tungus, the Manchu, the Dahor, and others, and among some of these peoples the reptile itself is unknown.[9] The shamanic drum, whose center of dissemination the Russian scholar puts in the Lake Baikal region,

6 Mironov and Shirokogoroff, "Śramaṇa-Shaman," pp. 119 ff.; Shirokogoroff, *Psychomental Complex*, pp. 279 ff. Shirokogoroff's theory has been accepted by N. N. Poppe; cf. *Asia Major*, III (1926), 138. The southern (Sino-Buddhist) influence on the *burkhan* has also been brought out by J. Harva, *Die religiösen Vorstellungen der altaischen Völker*, p. 381. Cf. also W. Schmidt, *Der Ursprung der Gottesidee*, X, 573; Dominik Schröder, "Zur Religion der Tujen," last art., pp. 203 ff.

7 Mironov and Shirokogoroff, "Śramaṇa-Shaman," p. 122; Shirokogoroff, *Psychomental Complex*, p. 281.

8 "Śramaṇa-Shaman," p. 125.

9 Ibid., p. 126. A large number of the Tungus shamans' "spirits" are of Buddhist origin (*Psychomental Complex*, p. 278). Their iconographic representation on the shamanic costumes shows "a correct reproduction of the costumes of Buddhist priests" (ibid.).

plays a role of the first importance in Lamaist religious music; and the copper mirror,[10] itself of Lamaist origin, has become so important in shamanism that a shaman can perform without costume and drum so long as he has the mirror. Some of the shaman's head ornaments are also, Shirokogoroff finds, borrowed from Lamaism.

In conclusion Shirokogoroff considers Tungus shamanism "a relatively recent phenomenon which seems to have spread from the west to the east and from the south to the north. It includes many elements directly borrowed from Buddhism. . . ."[11] "Shamanism has its very profound roots in the social system and psychology of animistic philosophy characteristic of the Tungus and other shamanists. But it is also true that shamanism in its present form is one of the consequences of the intrusion of Buddhism among the North-Asiatic ethnical groups."[12] In his great synthesis, *Psychomental Complex of the Tungus*, Shirokogoroff arrives at the formula "shamanism stimulated by Buddhism."[13] This phenomenon of stimulation can still be observed today in Mongolia: the lamas advise the mentally unbalanced to become shamans, and a lama often becomes a shaman and uses the shamans' "spirits."[14] Hence we need not be surprised if the Tungus cultural complexes are saturated with elements borrowed from Buddhism and Lamaism. The coexistence of shamanism with Lamaism is also found among other Asian peoples. Among the Tuvas, for example, in many yurts, even those belonging to lamas, beside the images of the Buddha are others—those of the shamanic *éréni*, protectors against the evil spirit.[16]

We are in complete agreement with Shirokogoroff's formula "shamanism stimulated by Buddhism." Southern influences have, indeed, modified and enriched Tungus shamanism—but the latter *is not a creation of Buddhism*. As Shirokogoroff himself observes, before the intrusion of Buddhism the religion of the Tungus was

10 Cf. above, pp. 153 f.
11 "Śramaṇa-Shaman," p. 127.
12 Ibid., p. 130, n. 52.
13 P. 282.
14 Ibid.
15 Ibid.
16 V. Bounak, "Un Pays de l'Asie peu connu: le Tanna-Touva," p. 9. See also V. Diószegi, "Tuva Shamanism."

dominated by the cult of Buga, god of the sky; another element that played a certain part was the ritual of the dead. If there were no "shamans" in the present sense of the term, there were nevertheless priests who specialized in the sacrifices offered to Buga and in the cult of the dead. Today, Shirokogoroff observes, among all the Tungus tribes shamans do not take part in the sacrifices in honor of the celestial god; as for the cult of the dead, as we saw, shamans are invited only in exceptional cases, for example when a dead man refuses to leave the earth and must be summoned to the underworld by means of a shamanic séance.[17] If it is true that the Tungus shamans take no part in the sacrifices offered to Buga, it is none the less true that the shamanic séances still contain a number of elements that could be regarded as celestial; then too, the symbolism of ascent is amply documented among the Tungus. It is possible that this symbolism, *in its present form*, was borrowed from the Buryat and the Yakut, but this in no way proves that the Tungus did not possess it before they entered into contact with their neighbors to the south; the religious importance of the celestial god and the universality of myths and rites of ascent in the Far North of Siberia oblige us to assume precisely the contrary. The conclusion, then, that we are justified in drawing concerning the formation of Tungus shamanism would be as follows: Lamaist influences found expression chiefly in the importance that came to be ascribed to the "spirits" and in the technique employed to control and embody them. Hence we could regard Tungus shamanism, in its present form, as strongly influenced by Lamaism. But is it justifiable to hold that Asian and Siberian shamanism as a whole is the product of such Sino-Buddhist influences?

Before we answer this question, let us recall some results of the present study. We were able to find that the specific element of shamanism is not the embodiment of "spirits" by the shaman, but the ecstasy induced by his ascent to the sky or descent to the underworld; incarnating spirits and being "possessed" by spirits are universally disseminated phenomena, but they do not necessarily

17 *Psychomental Complex*, p. 282.

belong to shamanism in the strict sense. From this point of view, Tungus shamanism as it exists today cannot be considered a "classic" form of shamanism, precisely because of the predominant importance it accords to the incarnation of "spirits" and the small role played by the ascent to the sky. Now, we have seen that, according to Shirokogoroff, it is precisely the ideology and the technique employed to master and incarnate the "spirits"—that is, the southern (Lamaist) contribution—that have given Tungus shamanism its present aspect. Hence we are justified in regarding this modern form of Tungus shamanism as a hybridization of the ancient North Asian shamanism; besides, as we have seen, the myths are eloquent on the subject of the present decadence of shamanism, and such myths are found both among the Tatars of Central Asia and among the peoples of extreme northeastern Siberia.

As for influences from Buddhism (Lamaism), whose effect on Tungus shamanism has been decisive, they were also freely exercised on the Buryat and the Mongols. We have more than once pointed out evidence of such Indian influences on the mythology, cosmology, and religious ideology of the Buryat, the Mongols, and the Tatars. It was principally Buddhism that served as the vehicle for the religious contribution of India in Central Asia. But here an observation is necessary: Indian influences were neither the first nor the only southern influences to reach into Central and North Asia. From earliest prehistory, southern cultures and, later, the ancient Near East, influenced all the cultures of Central Asia and Siberia. The Stone Age in the circumpolar regions is dependent on the prehistory of Europe and the Near East.[18] The prehistoric and protohistoric civilizations of North Russia and North Asia are strongly influenced by the paleo-Oriental civilizations.[19] Ethnolog-

18 Cf. Gutorm Gjessing, *Circumpolar Stone Age*. See also A. P. Oklad-nikov, "Ancient Cultures and Cultural and Ethnic Relations on the Pacific Coast of North Asia," especially pp. 555 ff.; Karl Jettmar, "Urgeschichte Innerasiens," pp. 150–61; C. S. Chard, "An Outline of the Prehistory of Siberia," Pt. I.

19 Cf., for example, A. M. Tallgren, "The Copper Idols from Galich and

ically, all the cultures of the nomads are to be regarded as tribu-
taries of the discoveries made by the agricultural and urban civilizations; indirectly, the radiation of the latter extends very far into
the north and the northeast. And this radiation, begun in prehistory, continues down to our day. We have seen the importance
of Indo-Iranian and Mesopotamian influences on the formation of
the mythologies and cosmologies of Central Asia and Siberia.
Iranian terms have been documented among the Ugrians, the
Tatars, and even the Mongols.[20] Cultural contacts and reciprocal
influences between China and the Hellenistic East are, in any case,
well known. And Siberia profited in turn from this cultural exchange: the numerals used by the various Siberian peoples are
borrowed, indirectly, both from ancient Rome and China.[21] Influences from Chinese civilization penetrated as far as the Ob and
the Yenisei.[22]

It is in this historico-ethnological perspective that we must

---

Their Relatives." On the relations between the Proto-Turks and the peoples
of the Near East during the fourth millennium, see W. Koppers, "Urtürkentum und Urindogermanentum im Lichte der völkerkundlichen Universalgeschichte," pp. 488 ff. According to D. Sinor's linguistic studies, the primitive home of the Proto-Turks must be placed "much farther west than has
been done so far" ("Ouralo-altaïque-indo-européen," p. 244). Cf. also
Jettmar: "The Karasuk Culture and Its South-eastern Affinities"; "The
Altai before the Turks"; "Urgeschichte Innerasiens," pp. 154 ff. According
to L. Vajda, the North Asian shamanic complex is the result of exchanges between the agricultural cultures of the south and the traditions of the northern
hunters. But shamanism is not characteristic of either the former or the latter;
it is the result of a cultural integration, and it is more recent than its com-
ponents. North Asian shamanism is no earlier than the Bronze Age; cf. "Zur
phaseologischen Stellung des Schamanismus," p. 479. But as we shall soon
see (pp. 504, n. 31), the prehistorian Karl J. Narr believes he can prove that
North Asian shamanism originated at the moment of the transition from
Lower to Upper Paleolithic.

20 On the Iranian elements in the Mongolic vocabulary, see also B. Laufer,
Sino-Iranica, pp. 572–76. Cf. Otto Mänchen-Helfen, "Manichaeans in Siberia," on the rock monuments of the Sogdians in southern Siberia in the
ninth century. Cf. also P. Pelliot, "Influence iranienne en Asie Centrale et en
Extrême Orient."   21 Kai Donner, *La Sibérie*, pp. 215–16.

22 Cf., for example, F. B. Steiner, "Skinboats and the Yakut 'Xayik.'"

place the southern influences on the religions and mythologies of the peoples of Central and North Asia. As for shamanism proper, we have already seen the results of such influences, especially on magical techniques. The shamanic costume and drum [23] also underwent southern influences. But shamanism in its structure and as a whole cannot be considered a creation of these southern contributions. The documents that we have collected and interpreted in the present volume show that the ideology and the characteristic techniques of shamanism are attested in archaic cultures, where it would be difficult to admit the presence of paleo-Oriental influences. It is enough to remember, on the one hand, that Central Asian shamanism is part and parcel of the prehistoric culture of the Siberian hunters,[24] and, on the other, that shamanic ideologies and

23 In an unpublished study, summarized by W. Schmidt, *Der Ursprung*, III, 334–38, A. Gahs concludes that the shamanic drum of Central and North Asia has its prototype in the Tibetan double drum. Shirokogoroff (*Psychomental Complex*, p. 299) accepts Schmidt's theory (*Der Ursprung*, III, 338) that the round drum with wooden handle—of Tibetan origin—was the first to have reached Asia, including the Chukchee and the Eskimo. The Asian origin of the Eskimo drum was also proposed by W. Thalbitzer (*The Ammasalik Eskimo*, Pt. 2, 2nd half-vol., p. 580). W. Koppers ("Probleme der indischen Religionsgeschichte," pp. 805–07), though accepting Shirokogoroff's and Gahs's conclusions concerning the southern origin of the shamanic drum, does not believe that its prototype was Tibetan, but rather the drum in the shape of a winnowing basket that is also found among the magicians of the archaic peoples of India (Santal, Munda, Bhil, Baiga). See also R. Rahmann, "Shamanistic and Related Phenomena in Northern and Middle India," pp. 732–34. In regard to the shamanism of these aboriginal peoples (which, in any case, is strongly influenced by Indian magic), Koppers weighs the question ("Probleme," pp. 810–12) of a possible organic relation between the Turko-Tatar stem *kam* and a group of words designating magic, the magician, or the land of magic in the languages of the Bhil (*kāmru*, "the land of magic," etc.) and the Santal (*kamru*, the home of sorcery, Kamru, the First Magician, etc.), and also in Hindi (Kāmrūp, Sanskrit Kāmarūpa, etc.). He suggests (p. 783) a possible South Asian provenance for the word *kāmaru* (*kamru*) later explained, by a popular etymology, as *Kāmarūpa* (name of the district of Assam, famous for the importance of Shaktism there). See also A. Gahs, "Die kulturhistorischen Beziehungen der östlichen Paläosibirier zu den austrischen Völkern, insbesondere zu jenen Formosas."

24 Cf. H. Findeisen, *Schamanentum*, pp. 18 ff.; F. Hančar, "The Eurasian Animal Style and the Altai Complex"; K. J. Narr: "Nordasiatisch-euro-

techniques are documented among the primitive peoples of Australia, the Malay Archipelago, South America, North America, and other regions.

Recent researches have clearly brought out the "shamanic" elements in the religion of the paleolithic hunters. Horst Kirchner has interpreted the celebrated relief at Lascaux as a representation of a shamanic trance.[25] The same author considers that the "Kommandostäbe"—mysterious objects found in prehistoric sites—are drumsticks.[26] If this interpretation is accepted, the prehistoric sorcerers would already have used drums comparable to those of the Siberian shamans. In this connection we may mention that bone drumsticks have been found on Oleny Island, in Barents Sea, at a site dated ca. 500 B.C.[27] Finally, Karl J. Narr has reconsidered the problem of the "origin" and chronology of shamanism in his important study "Bärenzeremoniell und Schamanismus in der Älteren Steinzeit Europas."[28] He brings out the influence of notions of fertility ("Venus statuettes") on the religious beliefs of the prehistoric North Asian hunters; but this influence did not disrupt the paleolithic tradition.[29] His conclusions are as follows: Animal skulls and bones found in the sites of the European Paleolithic (before 50,000–ca. 30,000 B.C.) can be interpreted as ritual offerings. Probably about the same period and in connection with the same rites, the magico-religious concepts of the periodic return of animals to life from their bones crystallized, and it is in this "Vorstellungswelt" that the roots of the bear ceremonialism of Asia and North America lie. Soon afterward, probably about

---

päische Urzeit in archäologischer und völkerkundlicher Sicht," pp. 199 f.; "Interpretation altsteinzeitlicher Kunstwerke durch völkerkundliche Parallelen," pp. 544 ff. Cf. also A. M. Tallgren, *Zur westsibirischen Gruppe der "schamanistischen Figuren."*

25 "Ein archäologischer Beitrag zur Urgeschichte des Schamanismus," pp. 271 ff.

26 Ibid., pp. 279 ff. ("Kommandostäbe" = *bâtons de commandement.* Cf. S. Giedion, *The Eternal Present.* I: *The Beginnings of Art,* pp. 162 ff.)

27 See the reproduction in Findeisen, *Schamanentum,* fig. 14; cf. ibid. pp. 158 ff.

28 *Saeculum,* X (1959), 233–72.   29 P. 260.

25,000, Europe offers evidence for the earliest forms of shamanism (Lascaux) with the plastic representations of the bird, the
tutelary spirit, and ecstasy.[30]

It is for the specialists to judge the validity of this chronology
proposed by Narr.[31] What appears to be certain is the antiquity of
"shamanic" rituals and symbols. It remains to be determined
whether these documents brought to light by prehistoric discoveries represent the first expressions of a shamanism *in statu
nascendi* or are merely the earliest documents today available for
an earlier religious complex, which, however, did not find "plastic"
manifestations (drawings, ritual objects, etc.) before the period
of Lascaux.

In accounting for the formation of the shamanic complex in
Central and North Asia, we must keep in mind the two essential
elements of the problem: on the one hand, the ecstatic experience
as such, as a primary phenomenon; on the other, the historico-religious milieu into which this ecstatic experience was destined to be
incorporated and the ideology that, in the last analysis, was to
validate it. We have termed the ecstatic experience a "primary
phenomenon" because we see no reason whatever for regarding it
as the result of a particular historical moment, that is, as produced
by a certain form of civilization. Rather, we would consider it
fundamental in the human condition, and hence known to the whole
of archaic humanity; what changed and was modified with the different forms of culture and religion was the interpretation and
evaluation of the ecstatic experience. What, then, was the historico-religious situation in Central and North Asia, where, later on,
shamanism crystallized as an autonomous and specific complex?
Everywhere in those lands, and from the earliest times, we find
documents for the existence of a Supreme Being of celestial structure, who also corresponds morphologically to all the other Su-

30 "Bärenzeremoniell," p. 271.

31 Narr's chronology is accepted by Alois Closs, "Das Religiöse im Schamanismus." In this article the author discusses some recent interpretations of
shamanism: Findeisen, A. Friedrich, Eliade, D. Schröder, Stiglmayr.

preme Beings of the archaic religions.[32] The symbolism of ascent, with all the rites and myths dependent on it, must be connected with celestial Supreme Beings; we know that "height" was sacred as such, that many supreme gods of archaic peoples are called "He on High," "He of the Sky," or simply "Sky." This symbolism of ascent and "height" retains its value even after the "withdrawal" of the celestial Supreme Being—for, as is well known, Supreme Beings gradually lose their active place in the cult, giving way to religious forms that are more "dynamic" and "familiar" (the gods of storm and fertility, demiurges, the souls of the dead, the Great Goddesses, etc.). The magico-religious complex that has come to be called "matriarchy" accentuates the transformation of a celestial god into a *deus otiosus*. The reduction or even the total loss in religious currency of uranian Supreme Beings is sometimes indicated in myths concerning a primordial and paradisal time when communications between heaven and earth were easy and accessible to everyone; as the result of some happening (especially of a ritual fault), these communications were broken off and the Supreme Beings withdrew to the highest sky. Let us repeat: the disappearance of the cult of the celestial Supreme Being did not nullify the symbolism of ascent with all its implications. As we have seen, this symbolism is documented everywhere and in all historico-religious contexts. Now, the symbolism of ascent plays an essential part in the shamanic ideology and techniques.

We saw in the previous chapter in what sense the shamanic ecstasy could be considered a reactualization of the mythical *illud tempus* when men could communicate *in concreto* with the sky. It is indubitable that the celestial ascent of the shaman (or the medicine man, the magician, etc.) is a survival, profoundly modified and sometimes degenerated, of this archaic religious ideology centered on faith in a celestial Supreme Being and belief in concrete communications between heaven and earth. But, as we have seen, the shaman, because of his ecstatic experience—which enables him to relive a state inaccessible to the rest of mankind—is regarded, and

32 See Eliade, *Patterns in Comparative Religion*, ch. ii.

regards himself, as a privileged being. Furthermore, the myths refer to more intimate relations between the Supreme Beings and shamans; in particular, they tell of a First Shaman, sent to earth by the Supreme Being or his surrogate (the demiurge or the solarized god) to defend human beings against diseases and evil spirits.

The historical changes in the religions of Central and North Asia—that is, in general, the increasingly important role given to the ancestor cult and to the divine or semidivine figures that took the place of the Supreme Being—in their turn altered the meaning of the shaman's ecstatic experience. Descents to the underworld,[33] the struggle against evil spirits, but also the increasingly familiar relations with "spirits" that result in their "embodiment" or in the shaman's being "possessed" by "spirits," are innovations, most of them recent, to be ascribed to the general change in the religious complex. In addition, there are the influences from the south, which appeared quite early and which altered both cosmology and the mythology and techniques of ecstasy. Among these southern influences we must reckon, in later times, the contribution of Buddhism and Lamaism, added to the Iranian and, in the last analysis, Mesopotamian influences that preceded them.

In all probability the initiatory schema of the shaman's ritual death and resurrection is likewise an innovation, but one that goes back to much earlier times; in any case, it cannot be ascribed to influences from the ancient Near East, since the symbolism and ritual of initiatory death and resurrection are already documented in the religions of Australia and South America. But the innovations introduced by the ancestor cult particularly affected the structure of this initiatory schema. The very concept of mystical death was altered by the many and various religious changes effected by lunar mythologies, the cult of the dead, and the elaboration of magical ideologies.

33 The history of religions, of course, knows various types of *descensus ad inferos*. We need only compare the descent to hell undertaken by Ishtar or Herakles with the shaman's ecstatic descent to realize the difference. Cf Eliade, *Birth and Rebirth*, pp. 61 ff., 87 ff.

Hence we must conceive of Asiatic shamanism as an archaic technique of ecstasy whose original underlying ideology—belief in a celestial Supreme Being with whom it was possible to have direct relations by ascending into the sky—was constantly being transformed by a long series of exotic contributions culminating in the invasion of Buddhism. The concept of mystical death, furthermore, encouraged increasingly regular relations with the ancestral souls and the "spirits," relations that ended in "possession." [34] The phenomenology of the trance, as we have seen, underwent many changes and corruptions, due in large part to confusion as to the precise nature of ecstasy. Yet all these innovations and corruptions did not succeed in eliminating the possibility of the true shamanic ecstasy; and we have been able to find, here and there, examples of genuine mystical experiences of shamans, taking the form of "spiritual" ascents and prepared by methods of meditation comparable to those of the great mystics of East and West.

---

34 As Dominik Schröder has well shown, "possession" as a religious experience is not without a certain greatness; there is, in sum, an embodying of "spirits," that is, a making the "spiritual world" present, living, and "concrete"; cf. "Zur Struktur des Schamanismus," pp. 865 ff. It is possible that "possession" is an extremely archaic religious phenomenon. But its structure is different from the ecstatic experience characteristic of shamanism in the strict sense. And indeed, we can see how "possession" could develop from an ecstatic experience: while the shaman's soul (or "principal soul") was traveling in the upper or lower worlds, "spirits" could take possession of his body. But it is difficult to imagine the opposite process, for, once the spirits have taken "possession" of the shaman, his personal ecstasy—that is, his ascent to the sky or descent to the underworld—is halted. It is the "spirits" that, by their "possession," bring on and crystallize the religious experience. In addition, there is a certain "facility" about "possession" that contrasts with the dangerous and dramatic shamanic initiation and discipline.

Epilogue

THERE is no solution of continuity in the history of mysticism. More than once we have discerned in the shamanic experience a "nostalgia for paradise" that suggests one of the oldest types of Christian mystical experience.[1] As for the "inner light," which plays a part of the first importance in Indian mysticism and metaphysics as well as in Christian mystical theology, it is, as we have seen, already documented in Eskimo shamanism. We may add that the magical stones with which the Australian medicine man's body is stuffed are in some degree symbolic of "solidified light." [2]

But shamanism is important not only for the place that it holds in the history of mysticism. The shamans have played an essential role in the defense of the psychic integrity of the community. They are pre-eminently the antidemonic champions; they combat not only demons and disease, but also the black magicians. The exemplary figure of the shaman-champion is Dto-mba Shi-lo, the mythical founder of Na-khi shamanism, the tireless slayer of demons.[3] The military elements that are of great importance in certain types of Asian shamanism (lance, cuirass, bow, sword, etc.) are accounted for by the requirements of war against the demons, the true enemies of humanity. In a general way, it can be

---

This Epilogue has been added to the English translation.

[1] Cf. also Eliade, "Nostalgia for Paradise in the Primitive Traditions," pp. 59–72.

[2] Cf. id., "Significations de la 'lumière intérieure.' "

[3] See above, pp. 445 ff.

508

said that shamanism defends life, health, fertility, the world of "light," against death, diseases, sterility, disaster, and the world of "darkness."

The shaman's combativeness sometimes becomes an aggressive mania; in certain Siberian traditions shamans are believed to challenge one another constantly in animal form.[4] But such a degree of aggressiveness is rather exceptional; it is peculiar to some Siberian shamanisms and the Hungarian *táltos*. What is fundamental and universal is the shaman's struggle against what we could call "the powers of evil." It is hard for us to imagine what such a shamanism can represent for an archaic society. In the first place, it is the assurance that human beings are not alone in a foreign world, surrounded by demons and the "forces of evil." In addition to the gods and supernatural beings to whom prayers and sacrifices are addressed, there are "specialists in the sacred," men able to "see" the spirits, to go up into the sky and meet the gods, to descend to the underworld and fight the demons, sickness, and death. The shaman's essential role in the defense of the psychic integrity of the community depends above all on this: men are sure that *one of them* is able to help them in the critical circumstances produced by the inhabitants of the invisible world. It is consoling and comforting to know that a member of the community is able to *see* what is hidden and invisible to the rest and to bring back direct and reliable information from the supernatural worlds.

It is as a further result of his ability to travel in the supernatural worlds and to *see* the superhuman beings (gods, demons, spirits of the dead, etc.) that the shaman has been able to contribute decisively to the *knowledge of death*. In all probability many features of "funerary geography," as well as some themes of the mythology of death, are the result of the ecstatic experiences of shamans. The lands that the shaman sees and the personages that he meets during his ecstatic journeys in the beyond are minutely described by the shaman himself, during or after his trance. The unknown and terrifying world of death assumes form, is organized in accordance

4 See above, pp. 94 f.

with particular patterns; finally it displays a structure and, in course of time, becomes familiar and acceptable. In turn, the supernatural inhabitants of the world of death become *visible;* they show a form, display a personality, even a biography. Little by little the world of the dead becomes knowable, and death itself is evaluated primarily as a rite of passage to a spiritual mode of being. In the last analysis, the accounts of the shamans' ecstatic journeys contribute to "spiritualizing" the world of the dead, at the same time that they enrich it with wondrous forms and figures.

We have already referred to the likenesses between the accounts of shamanic ecstasies and certain epic themes in oral literature.[5] The shaman's adventures in the other world, the ordeals that he undergoes in his ecstatic descents below and ascents to the sky, suggest the adventures of the figures in popular tales and the heroes of epic literature. Probably a large number of epic "subjects" or motifs, as well as many characters, images, and clichés of epic literature, are, finally, of ecstatic origin, in the sense that they were borrowed from the narratives of shamans describing their journeys and adventures in the superhuman worlds.

It is likewise probable that the pre-ecstatic euphoria constituted one of the universal sources of lyric poetry. In preparing his trance, the shaman drums, summons his spirit helpers, speaks a "secret language" or the "animal language," imitating the cries of beasts and especially the songs of birds. He ends by obtaining a "second state" that provides the impetus for linguistic creation and the rhythms of lyric poetry. Poetic creation still remains an act of perfect spiritual freedom. Poetry remakes and prolongs language; every poetic language begins by being a secret language, that is, the creation of a personal universe, of a completely closed world. The purest poetic act seems to re-create language from an inner experience that, like the ecstasy or the religious inspiration of "primitives," reveals the essence of things. It is from such linguistic creations, made possible by pre-ecstatic "inspiration," that the

5 Cf. above, pp. 213 ff., 311 ff., 368 ff. See also R. A. Stein, *Recherches sur l'épopée et le barde au Tibet,* pp. 317 ff., 370 ff.

"secret languages" of the mystics and the traditional allegorical languages later crystallize.

Something must also be said concerning the dramatic structure of the shamanic séance. We refer not only to the sometimes highly elaborate "staging" that obviously exercises a beneficial influence on the patient.[6] But every genuinely shamanic séance ends as a *spectacle* unequaled in the world of daily experience. The fire tricks, the "miracles" of the rope-trick or mango-trick type, the exhibition of magical feats, reveal another world—the fabulous world of the gods and magicians, the world in which *everything seems possible*, where the dead return to life and the living die only to live again, where one can disappear and reappear instantaneously, where the "laws of nature" are abolished, and a certain superhuman "freedom" is exemplified and made dazzlingly *present*.

It is difficult for us, modern men as we are, to imagine the repercussions of such a *spectacle* in a "primitive" community. The shamanic "miracles" not only confirm and reinforce the patterns of the traditional religion, they also stimulate and feed the imagination, demolish the barriers between dream and present reality, open windows upon worlds inhabited by the gods, the dead, and the spirits.

These few remarks on the cultural creations made possible or stimulated by the experiences of shamans must suffice. A thorough study of them would exceed the limits of this work. What a magnificent book remains to be written on the ecstatic "sources" of epic and lyric poetry, on the prehistory of dramatic spectacles, and, in general, on the fabulous worlds discovered, explored, and described by the ancient shamans. . . .

6 Cf. also Lucile H. Charles, "Drama in Shaman Exorcism," especially pp. 101 ff., 121 ff.

LIST OF WORKS CITED

AA	*American Anthropologist* (Menasha)
AE	*Acta ethnographica* (Budapest)
AL	Acta lapponica (Stockholm)
ALat	*Annali lateranensi* (Vatican City)
AM	*Asia Major* (Leipzig)
AMNH	American Museum of Natural History (New York)
AN	Akademia Nauk Soyuza Sovetskikh Sotzialisticheskikh Respublik (Moscow, Leningrad, et al.)
L'Anthropologie	*L'Anthropologie* (Paris)
Anthropos	*Anthropos* (Salzburg; Mödling, Vienna; Fribourg)
AO	*Acta orientalia* (Leiden)
AOH	*Acta orientalia hungarica* (Budapest)
ArtA	*Artibus Asiae* (Leipzig)
ARW	*Archiv für Religionswissenschaft* (Leipzig)
AUFA	*Annales universitatis fennicae aboensis* (Turku)
AVK	*Archiv für Völkerkunde* (Vienna)
BBEW	*Bulletin of the Bureau of American Ethnology* (Washington)
BEFEO	*Bulletin de l'École française d'Extrême-Orient* (Hanoi)
BMB	Berenice P. Bishop Museum Bulletin (Honolulu)
BMFEA	*Bulletin of the Museum of Far Eastern Antiquities* (Stockholm)
BS	Bollingen Series (New York)
CPAAE	University of California Publications in American Archaeology and Ethnology
CPSP	University of California Publications in Semitic Philology

EJ	*Eranos-Jahrbuch* (Zurich)
Ethnographia	*Ethnographia* (Budapest)
Ethnos	*Ethnos* (Stockholm)
FFC	Folklore Fellows Communications (Hamina; later Helsinki)
FMNH	Field Museum of Natural History (Chicago)
FS	*Folklore Studies* (Peking; later Tokyo)
Globus	*Globus* (Brunswick)
GSA	General Series in Anthropology (Menasha)
HJAS	*Harvard Journal of Asiatic Studies* (Cambridge, Mass.)
HOS	Harvard Oriental Series (Cambridge, Mass., and London)
IA	*Indian Antiquary* (Bombay)
IAE	*Internationales Archiv für Ethnographie* (Leiden)
IPEK	*Jahrbuch für prähistorische ethnographische Kunst* (Berlin)
JA	*Journal asiatique* (Paris)
JAFL	*Journal of American Folklore* (Boston and New York; later Lancaster and New York)
JAOS	*Journal of the American Oriental Society* (New Haven)
JE	Jesup North Pacific Expedition
JMVK	*Jahrbuch des Museums für Völkerkunde* (Leipzig)
JPS	*Journal of the Polynesian Society* (Wellington)
JRAI	*Journal of the Royal Anthropological Institute* (London)
JRAS	*Journal of the Royal Asiatic Society* (London, et al.)
JSA	*Journal de la Société des Américanistes* (Paris)
JSFO	*Journal de la Société Finno-Ougrienne* (Helsinki)
KS	*Keletï szemle* (Budapest)
MAGW	*Mitteilungen der anthropologischen Gesellschaft in Wien*
MAR	Mythology of All Races (Boston and London)
MCB	*Mélanges chinois et bouddhiques* (Brussels)
MGVK	*Mitteilungen der Gesellschaft für Völkerkunde* (Leipzig)

MS	*Monumenta serica* (Peking; later Nagoya)
MSFO	Mémoires de la Société Finno-Ougrienne (Helsinki)
Numen	*Numen* (Leiden)
Paideuma	*Paideuma* (Bamberg)
PM	*Primitive Man* (Washington)
PTS	Pali Text Society Translation Series (London)
RBEW	*Reports of the Bureau of American Ethnology* (Washington)
RFTE	Report of the Fifth Thule Expedition
RHR	*Revue de l'histoire des religions* (Paris)
SBB	Sacred Books of the Buddhists (London)
SBE	Sacred Books of the East (Oxford)
Sinica	*Sinica* (Taipei)
SJA	*Southwestern Journal of Anthropology* (Albuquerque)
SMSR	*Studi e materiali di storia delle religioni* (Rome)
SO	Studia orientalia (Helsinki)
SS	*Studia septentrionalia* (Oslo)
TMIE	Travaux et mémoires de l'Institute d'ethnologie (Université de Paris)
TP	*T'oung Pao* (Leiden)
WBKL	Wiener Beiträge zur Kulturgeschichte und Linguistik
WPZ	*Wiener prähistorische Zeitschrift*
WVM	*Wiener Völkerkundliche Mitteilungen*
Zalmoxis	*Zalmoxis: revue des études religieuses* (Paris and Bucharest)
ZB	*Zeitschrift für Buddhismus* (Munich)
ZE	*Zeitschrift für Ethnologie* (Berlin)
ZMKRW	*Zeitschrift für Missionskunde und Religionswissenschaft* (Berlin)

AARNE, ANTTI. *Der tiersprachenkundige Mann und seine neugierige Frau: eine vergleichende Märchenstudie.* Hamina, 1914. (FFC II, 15.)

ABBOTT, J. *The Keys of Power: a Study of Indian Ritual and Belief.* London, 1932.

ABERLE, DAVID F. " 'Arctic Hysteria' and Latah in Mongolia," *Transactions of the New York Academy of Science,* ser. II, vol. XIV, 7 (May 1952), 291–97.

ACKERKNECHT, ERWIN H. "Medical Practices," in STEWARD, JULIAN H. ed., *Handbook of South American Indians* (q.v.), V, 621 ff.

ADRIANI, N., and KRUYT (KRUIJT, KRUJT), A. C. *De Bare'e-sprekende Toradja's van Midden-Celebes.* Batavia, 1912–14. 4 vols.

AGAPITOV, N. N., and KHANGALOV, M. N. "Materialy dlya izucheniia shamanstva v Sibiri. Shamanstvo u buryat Irkutskoi gubernii," *Izvestiia Vostochno-Sibirskovo Otdela Russkovo Geograficheskovo Obshchestva* (Irkutsk), XIV, 1–2 (1883), 1–61. Tr. and summarized in STIEDA, L. "Das Schamanentum unter den Burjaten" (q.v.).

ALEXANDER, HARTLEY BURR. *Latin-American* [*Mythology*]. 1920. (MAR XI.)

———. *North American* [*Mythology*]. 1916. (MAR X.)

ALFÖLDI, ANDRÁS. "The Bear Cult and Matriarchy in Eurasia," *Közlemények* (Budapest), L (1936), 5–17. (In Hungarian.)

ALMGREN, O. *Nordische Felszeichnungen als religiöse Urkunden.* Frankfur a. M., 1934.

ALTHEIM, FRANZ. *Geschichte der Hunnen.* Berlin, 1959–62. 4 vols. (2nd edn. of *Attila und die Hunnen,* Baden-Baden, 1951.)

———. *Römische Geschichte.* Baden-Baden, 1951–53. 2 vols.

——— and HAUSSIG, HANS-WILHELM. *Die Hunnen in Osteuropa.* Baden Baden, 1958.

AMANDRY, PIERRE. *La Mantique apollinienne à Delphes. Essai sur l fonctionnement de l'Oracle.* Paris, 1950.

AMSCHLER, WOLFGANG. "Über die Tieropfer (besonders Pferdeopfer der Telingiten im sibirischen Altai," *Anthropos,* XXVIII, 3–4 (1933) 305–13.

ANDREE, RICHARD. *Die Metalle bei den Naturvölkern; mit Berücksichtigung prähistorischer Verhältnisse.* Leipzig, 1884.

————. "Scapulimantia," in *Anthropological Papers Written in Honor of Franz Boas,* pp. 143–65. New York, 1906.

ANDRES, FRIEDRICH. "Die Himmelsreise der caräibischen Medizin-männer," *ZE,* LXX, 3–5 (1938; pub. 1939), 331–42.

ANISIMOV, A. F. "Predstavlenia evenkov o dushe i problema proiskho-zhdenia animisma," in *Rodovoye obshchestvo,* pp. 109–18. Moscow, 1951. (AN, Trudy Instituta Ethnografii, n.s. XIV.)

————. "Shamanskiye dukhi po vossreniam evenkov i totemichiskiye istoki ideologii shamanstva," in AN, *Sbornik Muzeya Antropologii i Etnografii,* XIII, 187–215. Moscow and Leningrad, 1951.

ANOKHIN, A. V. *Materialy po shamanstvu u altaitsev, sobranniye vo vremia puteshestvy po Altayu v 1910–1912 gg. po porucheniyu Russkogo Komiteta dlya Izuchenia Srednei i Vostochnoi Asii.* Leningrad, 1924.

ANUCHIN, V. I. *Ocherk shamanstva u yeniseiskikh ostyakov.* St. Petersburg, 1914.

ARBMAN, ERNST. *Rudra: Untersuchungen zum altindischen Glauben und Kultus.* Uppsala and Leipzig, 1922.

ARCHER, W. *The Vertical Man: a Study in Primitive Indian Sculpture.* London, 1947.

ARMSTRONG, W. E. *Rossel Island.* Cambridge, 1928.

ASÍN PALACIOS, MIGUEL. *La escatalogía musulmana en la Divina Comedia.* 2nd edn., Madrid and Granada, 1943.

BACHELARD, GASTON. *L'Air et les songes. Essai sur l'imagination du mouvement.* Paris, 1943.

————. *La Psychanalyse du feu.* Paris, 1935.

BACOT, JACQUES. *Les Mo-so.* Leiden, 1913.

BALÁZS, JÁNOS. "A magyar samán reülete" (German summary, "Die Ekstase des ungarischen Schamanen"), *Ethnographia,* LXV, 3–4 (1954), 416–40.

BARBEAU, MARIUS. "Bear Mother," *JAFL,* LIX, 231 (Jan.–Mar., 1946), 1–12.

BARTELS, MAX. *Die Medizin der Naturvölker.* Leipzig, 1893.

BARTHÉLEMY, M. A., tr. *Artâ Vîrâf-Nâmak ou livre d'Ardâ Vîrâf.* Paris, 1887. (Bibliothèque orientale elzévirienne LIV.)

BARTHOLD, W. *Histoire des Turcs d'Asie Centrale.* Paris, 1945.

BAUMANN, HERMANN. "Afrikanische Wild- und Buschgeister," *ZE,* LXX, 3–5 (1938; pub. 1939), 208–39.

BAUMANN, HERMANN. "Likundu, die Sektion der Zauberkraft," *ZE*, LX (1928), 73–85.

———. *Lunda. Bei Bauern und Jägern in Inner-Angola.* Berlin, 1935.

———. *Schöpfung und Urzeit des Menschen im Mythus der afrikanischen Völker.* Berlin, 1936.

BAWDEN, C. R. "On the Practice of Scapulimancy among the Mongols," *Central Asiatic Journal* (The Hague), IV (1958), 1–31.

BEAGLEHOLE, ERNEST and PEARL. *Ethnology of Pukapuka.* 1938. (BMB 150.)

BEAL, SAMUEL, tr. *Si-yu-ki: Buddhist Records of the Western World.* From the Chinese of Hiuen Tsiang (A.D. 629). London, 1884. (Trübner's Oriental Series.) 2 vols.

BENEDICT, RUTH. *The Concept of the Guardian Spirit in North America.* Menasha, 1923. (Memoirs of the American Anthropological Association 29.)

———. "The Vision in Plains Culture." *AA*, n.s. XXIV (1922), 1–23.

BERGEMA, HENDRIK. *De Boom des Levens in Schrift en Historie.* Hilversum, 1938.

BERNARDINO DE SAHAGÚN. *Historia general de las cosas de Nueva España.* Mexico, 1829–39. (*General History of the Things of New Spain*, tr Arthur J. O. Anderson and Charles E. Dibble. Santa Fe, 1950–59. [Monographs of the School of American Research 14.]) 13 parts in 9 vols.

BESTERMAN, E. See CRAWLEY, E.

BIALLAS, P. FRANZ. "K'üh Yüan's 'Fahrt in die Ferne' (Yüan-yu)," *AM*, VII (1932), 179–241.

BICKERMANN, E. "Die römische Kaiserapotheose," *ARW*, XXVII (1929), 1–24.

BIDEZ, JOSEPH. *Eos, ou Platon et l'Orient.* Brussels, 1945.

——— and CUMONT, FRANZ. *Les Mages hellénisés: Zoroastre, Ostanè et Hystaspe d'après la tradition grecque.* Paris, 1938. 2 vols.

BILBY, J. W. *Among Unknown Eskimos.* London, 1923.

BIOT, ÉDOUARD, tr. *Le Tcheou-li, ou Rites des Tcheou.* Paris, 1851. 2 vols.

BIRKET-SMITH, KAJ. "Über die Herkunft der Eskimos und ihre Stellung in der zirkumpolaren Kulturentwicklung," *Anthropos*, XXV (1930), 1–23.

BLAGDEN, C. O. See SKEAT, W. W.

BLEICHSTEINER, ROBERT. *L'Église jaune.* Paris, 1937. (Orig.: *Die gelbe Kirche.* Vienna, 1937.)

BLEICHSTEINER, ROBERT. "Rossweihe und Pferderennen im Totenkult der kaukasischen Völker," in *Die Indogermanen- und Germanenfrage: neue Wege zu ihrer Lösung*, pp. 413–95. 1936. (WBKL IV.)

BLOK, H. P. "Zur altägyptischen Vorstellung der Himmelsleiter," *AO*, VI (1928), 257–69.

BOAS, FRANZ. "The Central Eskimo," *6th RBEW* (1884–85; pub. 1888), pp. 399–675.

———. *The Eskimo of Baffin Land and Hudson Bay.* 1901. (AMNH Bulletin XV.)

———. *Indianische Sagen von der nord-pacifischen Küste Amerikas.* Berlin, 1895.

———. "The Salish Tribes of the Interior of British Columbia," in *Annual Archaeological Report, 1905, being part of Appendix to the Report of the Minister of Education, Ontario*, pp. 219–25. Toronto, 1906.

———. "The Shushwap," in his "The Indians of British Columbia: Lku'-ñgen, Nootka, Kwakiutl, Shushwap," in British Association for the Advancement of Science, *Sixth Report on the North-Western Tribes of Canada* (1890; pub. 1891), pp. 553–715. (Also printed in separate of *Sixth Report*, pp. 93 ff.)

BODE, FRAMROZE ARDESHIR, and NANAVUTTY, PILOO, trs. *Songs of Zarathushtra: the Gathas. Translated from the Avesta.* London, 1952. (Ethical and Religious Classics of East and West 6.)

BOEHM, FRITZ. "Spatulimantie," in *Handwörterbuch des deutschen Aberglaubens*, ed. Hanns Bächtold-Staubli, VII, 125 ff. Berlin, 1927–42. 10 vols.

BOGORAS, WALDEMAR G. (V. G. BOGORAZ). *The Chukchee.* 1904. (AMNH Memoirs XI; JE VII.)

———. *Chukchee Mythology.* 1910–12. (AMNH Memoirs XII; JE VIII.)

———. "The Folklore of Northeastern Asia, as compared with that of Northwestern America," *AA*, n.s. IV, 4 (Oct.–Dec., 1902), 577–683.

———. "K psikhologii shamanstva u narodov severo-vostochnoi Azii," *Etnograficheskoye obozreniye* (Moscow), LXXXIV–LXXXV, 1–2 (1910), 1–36.

———. "The Shamanistic Call and the Period of Initiation in Northern Asia and Northern America," in *Proceedings of the 23rd International Congress of Americanists* (1928), pp. 441–44. New York, 1930.

BOLTE, J., and POLÍVKA, G. *Anmerkungen zu den Kinder- und Hausmärchen der Brüder Grimm.* Leipzig, 1913–32. 5 vols.

BONNERJEA, BIREN. "Hunting Superstitions of the American Aborigines," *IAE*, XXXII, 3-6 (1934), 167-84.

———. "Materials for the Study of Garo Ethnology," *IA*, LVIII (1929), 121-27.

BOULANGER, A. See GERNET, L.

BOUNAK, V. "Un Pays de l'Asie peu connu: le Tanna-Touva," *IAE*, XXIX (1928), 1-16.

BOURKE, JOHN G. "The Medicine-Men of the Apache," *9th RBEW* (1887-88; pub. 1892), pp. 443-603.

BOUSSET, WILHELM. "Die Himmelsreise der Seele," *ARW*, IV (1901), 136-69, 229-73.

BOUTEILLER, MARCELLE. *Chamanisme et guérison magique.* Paris, 1950.

———. "Don chamanistique et adaptation à la vie chez les Indiens de l'Amérique du Nord," *JSA*, n.s. XXXIX (1950), 1-14.

———. "Du 'chaman' au 'panseur de secret,'" in *Actes du XXVIII Congrès International des Américanistes* (1947), pp. 237-45. Paris, 1948.

BOUVAT, L. "'Les Premiers Mystiques dans la littérature turque' de Kieuprilizâdé, analyse critique," *Revue du monde musulman* (Paris), XLIII (Feb., 1921), 236-66.

BRAND, J. *Introduction to the Literary Chinese.* 2nd edn., Peking, 1936.

BREASTED, JAMES H. *The Development of Religion and Thought in Ancient Egypt.* London, 1912.

BREUIL, H., and OBERMAIER, H. "Crânes paléolithiques façonnés e coupe," *L'Anthropologie*, XX (1909), 523-30.

BRIGGS, GEORGE W. *Gorakhnāth and the Kānphāṭa Yogis.* Calcutta and London, 1938.

BRODEUR, ARTHUR GILCHRIST. See SNORRI STURLUSON.

BROWN, A. R. *The Andaman Islanders.* Cambridge, 1922.

BÜCHNER, V. F. "Shaman," in *The Encyclopaedia of Islam*, IV, 302-3. 1st edn., Leiden and London, 1913-34. 4 vols.

BUCK, PETER H. See HIROA, TE RANGI.

BUDDHAGHOṢA. See TIN, PE MAUNG.

BUDDRUSS, GEORG. See FRIEDRICH, ADOLPH.

BUDGE, SIR E. A. WALLIS, ed. and tr. *The Book of the Dead; an English Translation of the Chapters, Hymns, etc. of the Theban Recension.* 2nd edn., rev. and enlarged, London, 1949. 3 vols in 1.

———. *The Book of Paradise.* London, 1904. 2 vols.

BUDGE, SIR E. A. WALLIS. *The Egyptian Heaven and Hell*. London, 1925. 3 vols.

------. *From Fetish to God in Ancient Egypt*. London, 1934.

------. *The Mummy: a Handbook of Egyptian Funerary Archaeology*. 2nd. edn., rev. and enlarged, Cambridge, 1925.

BURKERT, WALTER. "ΓΟΗΣ. Zum griechischen 'Schamanismus,'" *Rheinisches Museum für Philologie* (Frankfurt a. M.), n.s. CV (1962), 36–55.

BURROWS, EDWIN G. "Culture-Areas in Polynesia," *JPS*, XLIX (1940), 349–63.

BURROWS, FATHER ERIC. "Some Cosmological Patterns in Babylonian Religion," in *The Labyrinth: Further Studies in the Relation between Myth and Ritual in the Ancient World*, S. H. Hooke, ed., pp. 43–70. London and New York, 1935.

BUSCHAN, GEORG, ed. *Illustrierte Völkerkunde*. Stuttgart, 1922, 1926. 2 vols.

CALAND, WILLEM. *Altindischer Ahnenkult*. Leiden, 1893.

CALLAWAY, REV. CANON [HENRY]. *The Religious System of the Amazulu*. London and Springvale (Natal), 1870.

CARBONELLI, GIOVANNI. *Sulle fonti storiche della chimica e dell'alchimia in Italia*. Rome, 1925.

CARPENTER, RHYS. *Folk Tale, Fiction and Saga in the Homeric Epics*. Berkeley and Los Angeles, 1946.

CASTAGNÉ, J. "Magie et exorcisme chez les Kazak-Kirghizes et autres peuples turcs orientaux," *Revue des études islamiques* (Paris), (1930), 53–151.

CASTRÉN, ALEXANDER M. *Nordische Reisen und Forschungen*. II: *Reiseberichte und Briefe aus den Jahren 1845-49*; III: *Vorlesungen über die finnische Mythologie*; IV: *Ethnologische Vorlesungen über die altaischen Völker, nebst samojedischen Märchen und tatarischen Heldensagen*. St. Petersburg, 1852–62. 12 vols. (Vol. II, 1856; III, 1853; IV, 1857.)

CERULLI, ENRICO, ed. *Il "libro della scala" e la questione delle fonti arabospagnole della Divina Commedia*. Vatican City, 1949. (Studi e testi CL; Biblioteca Apostolica Vaticana.)

CHADWICK, H. MUNRO and NORA K. *The Growth of Literature*. Cambridge, 1932–40. 3 vols.

CHADWICK, NORA K. "The Kite: a Study in Polynesian Tradition," *JRAI*, LXI (1931), 455–91.

CHADWICK, NORA K. "Notes on Polynesian Mythology," *JRAI*, LX (1930), 425–46.

———. *Poetry and Prophecy*. Cambridge, 1942.

———. "Shamanism among the Tatars of Central Asia," *JRAI*, LXVI (1936), 75–112.

CHALMERS, ROBERT, tr. *Further Dialogues of the Buddha* [*Majjhima-nikāya*]. 1926, 1927. (SBB V, VI.) 2 vols.

CHARD, CHESTER S. "An Outline of the Prehistory of Siberia. Pt. I: The Pre-metal Periods," *SJA*, XIV (1958), 1–33.

CHARLES, LUCILE HOERR. "Drama in Shaman Exorcism," *JAFL*, LXVI, 260 (Apr.–June, 1953), 95–122.

CHAVANNES, ÉDOUARD, tr. *Les Mémoires historiques de Se-ma-Ts'ien* [*Ssu-ma Ch' ien*]. Paris, 1895–1905. 5 vols.

———. See also LÉVI, SYLVAIN.

CHRISTENSEN, ARTHUR. *Les Types du premier homme et du premier roi dans l'histoire légendaire des Iraniens*. Stockholm, 1917, 1934. (Archives d'études orientales XIV, 1; XIV, 2.) 2 vols.

CHRISTENSEN, H. H. See HASLUND-CHRISTENSEN, HENNING.

CHRISTIANSEN, REIDAR T. "Ecstasy and Arctic Religion," *SS*, IV (1953), 19–92.

———. "Myth, Metaphor and Simile," in *Myth: a Symposium*, ed. Thomas A. Sebeok, pp. 39–49. Philadelphia, 1955.

CLARK, WALTER EUGENE. "Śākadvīpa and Śvetadvīpa," *JAOS*, XXXIX (1919), 209–42.

CLEMEN, CARL. "Zalmoxis," *Zalmoxis*, II (1939), 53–62.

CLEMENTS, FORREST E. *Primitive Concepts of Disease*. Berkeley, 1932. (CPAAE XXXII, 2.)

CLINE, WALTER. *Mining and Metallurgy in Negro Africa*. 1937. (GSA 5.)

CLOSS, ALOIS. "Die Religion der Germanen in ethnologischer Sicht," in *Christus und die Religionen der Erde: Handbuch der Religionsgeschichte*, II, 267–366. Vienna, 1951. 3 vols.

———. "Die Religion des Semnonenstammes," in *Die Indogermanen- und Germanenfrage: neue Wege zu ihrer Lösung*, pp. 549–673. 1936. (WBKL IV.)

———. "Das Religiöse im Schamanismus," *Kairos* (Salzburg), II (1960), 29–38.

CODRINGTON, R. H. *The Melanesians: Studies in Their Anthropology and Folk-lore*. Oxford, 1891.

ᴏᴇ, Michael D. "Shamanism in the Bunun Tribe, Central Formosa," *Ethnos*, XX, 4 (1955), 181–98.

ᴏèᴅᴇs, G. *Les États hindouisés d'Indochine et d'Indonésie.* Paris, 1948.

ᴏʟᴇ, Fay-Cooper. *The Peoples of Malaysia.* New York, 1945.

ᴏʟᴇᴍᴀɴ, Sister Bernard. "The Religion of the Ojibwa of Northern Minnesota," *PM*, X (1937), 33–57.

ᴏʟʟɪɴs, Col. *English Colony of New South Wales.* London, 1804.

ᴏᴍᴀɴ, Jean. "Orphée, civilisateur de l'humanité," *Zalmoxis*, I (1938), 130–76.

——. "Zalmoxis," *Zalmoxis*, II (1939), 79–110.

ᴏɴᴢᴇ, Edward. *Buddhism, Its Essence and Development.* New York, 1951.

ᴏᴏᴋ, Arthur Bernard. *Zeus: a Study in Ancient Religion.* Cambridge, 1914–40. 3 vols.

ᴏᴏᴍᴀʀᴀsᴡᴀᴍʏ, Ananda K. *Elements of Buddhist Iconography.* Cambridge (Mass.), 1935.

——. *Figures of Speech or Figures of Thought.* London, 1946.

——. *Hinduism and Buddhism.* New York, 1943.

——. "The Inverted Tree," *Quarterly Journal of the Mythic Society* (Bangalore), XXIX, 2 (1938), 1–38.

——. "Svayamātṛṇṇā: Janua Coeli," *Zalmoxis*, II (1939), 1–51.

——. "Symplegades," in *Studies and Essays in the History of Science and Learning Offered in Homage to George Sarton on the Occasion of His Sixtieth Birthday, 31 August 1944*, ed. Ashley M. F. Montague, pp. 463–88. New York, 1946.

——. *Time and Eternity.* Ascona, 1947.

ᴏᴏᴍᴀʀᴀsᴡᴀᴍʏ, Luisa. "The Perilous Bridge of Welfare," *HJAS*, VIII (1944), 196–213.

ᴏᴏᴘᴇʀ, John M. "Areal and Temporal Aspects of Aboriginal South American Culture," *PM*, XV, 1–2 (Jan.–Apr., 1942), 1–38.

——. "Northern Algonkian Scrying and Scapulimancy," in *Festschrift: Publication d'hommage offerte au P [ère] W. Schmidt*, ed. W. Koppers, pp. 205–17. Vienna, 1928.

ᴏʀᴅɪᴇʀ, Henri. See Yule, Sir Henry.

ᴏʀɴғᴏʀᴅ, Francis Macdonald. *Principium Sapientiae: the Origins of Greek Philosophical Thought.* Cambridge, 1952.

ᴏᴜᴠʀᴇᴜʀ, S., tr. *Li ki; ou, mémoires sur les bienséances et les cérémonies.* 2nd edn., Ho-kien-fu, 1927. 2 vols.

COXWELL, C. FILLINGHAM, comp. and ed. *Siberian and Other Folk-Tale* London, 1925.

CRAWLEY, ERNEST. *Dress, Drinks and Drums: Further Studies of Savage and Sex*, ed. Theodore Besterman. London, 1931.

CREEL, HERRLEE GLESSNER. *The Birth of China: a Survey of the Formative Period of Chinese Civilization*. London, 1936.

CROOKE, WILLIAM. *Popular Religion and Folk-Lore of Northern India* Westminster, 1896. 2 vols. (Rev. edn., retitled *Religion & Folklore Northern India*. London, 1926. 2 vols. in 1.)

CUISINIER, JEANNE. *Danses magiques de Kelantan*. 1936. (TMIE XXII

CUMONT, FRANZ. *Lux perpetua*. Paris, 1949.

——. *Les Religions orientales dans le paganisme romain*. 3rd edn., Pari 1929.

——. See also BIDEZ, JOSEPH.

CURTIN, JEREMIAH. *A Journey in Southern Siberia*. London, 1909.

CZAPLICKA, M. A. *Aboriginal Siberia: a Study in Social Anthropolog* Oxford, 1914.

DÄHNHARDT, OSKAR. *Natursagen: eine Sammlung naturdeutender Sage Märchen, Fabeln, und Legenden*. Leipzig, 1907–12. 4 vols.

DALTON, E. T. *Descriptive Ethnology of Bengal*. Calcutta, 1872.

DAVID-NEEL, ALEXANDRA. *With Mystics and Magicians in Tibe* London, 1931. (Original: *Mystiques et Magiciens du Thibet*. Pari 1929.)

DAVIDSON, D. S. "The Question of Relationship between the Culture of Australia and Tierra del Fuego," *AA*, n.s. XXXIX, 2 (Apr.–Jun 1937), 229–43.

DAWA-SAMDUP, LAMA KAZI. See EVANS-WENTZ, W. Y.

DEACON, A. BERNARD. *Malekula: a Vanishing People in the New Hebride* London, 1934.

DE ANGULO, JAIME. "La Psychologie religieuse des Achumawi. IV: I Chamanisme," *Anthropos*, XXIII (1928), 561–82.

DEFRÉMERY, CHARLES FRANÇOIS, and SANGUINETTI, B. R., eds. and tr *Voyages d'ibn Batoutah*. Paris, 1853–79. 4 vols.

DEHON, REV. P. *Religion and Customs of the Uraons*. Calcutta, 190 (Memoirs of the Asiatic Society of Bengal I, 9.)

DIETERICH, ALBRECHT. *Eine Mithrasliturgie*. 2nd edn., Leipzig and Berli 1910.

DIETERLEN, GERMAINE. *Les Âmes de Dogon*. 1941. (TMIE XL.)

Diószegi, Vilmos. "Golovnoi ubor nanaiskikh (goldskikh) shamanov," *A néprajzi értesítö* (Budapest), XXXVII (1955), 81–108.

——. "K voprosu o borbe shamanov v obraze zhivotnykh," *AOH*, II (1952), 303–16.

——. "Problems of Mongolian Shamanism (Report of an Expedition Made in 1960 in Mongolia)," AE, X, fasc. 1–2 (1961), 195–206.

——. *A sámánhit emléki a magyar népi müveltségben.* Budapest, 1958.

——. "Tunguso-manchzhurskoye zerkalo shamana," *AOH*, I (1951), 359–83.

——. "Tuva Shamanism," *AE*, XI (1962), 143–90.

——. "Die Typen und interethnischen Beziehungen der Schamanentrommeln bei den Selkupen (Ostjak-Samojeden)," *AE*, IX (1960), 159–79.

——. "Die Überreste des Schamanismus in der ungarischen Volkskultur," *AE*, VII (1958), 97–135.

——. "A viaskodó táltosbika és a samán állatalakú életlelke (La Lutte du taureau miraculeux et l'âme vitale du chaman susceptible de revêtir la forme d'un animal)," *Ethnographia*, LXIII (1952), 308–57.

——. "Der Werdegang zum Schamanen bei den nordöstlichen Sojoten," *AE*, VIII (1959), 269–91.

Dirlmeier, Franz. "Apollon, Gott und Erzieher des hellenischen Adels," *ARW*, XXXVI, 2 (1940), 277–99.

Dirr, A. "Der kaukasiche Wild- und Jagdgott," *Anthropos*, XX (1925), 139–47.

Dixon, Roland B. *The Building of Cultures.* New York, 1928.

——. *The Northern Maidu.* New York, 1905.

——. *Oceanic [Mythology].* 1916. (MAR IX.)

——. *The Shasta.* 1907. (AMNH Bulletin XVII, Pt. V.)

——. "Some Aspects of the American Shaman," *JAFL*, XXI (Jan.–March, 1908), 1–12.

Dodds, E. R. *The Greeks and the Irrational.* Berkeley and Los Angeles, 1951. (Sather Classical Lectures XXV.)

Doerr, Erich. "Bestattungsformen in Ozeanien," *Anthropos*, XXX (1935), 369–420, 727–65.

Dombart, Theodor. *Der babylonische Turm.* Leipzig, 1930.

——. *Der Sakralturm.* I: *Ziqqurat.* Munich, 1920.

Donner, Kai. "Beiträge zur Frage nach dem Ursprung der Jenissei-Ostjaken," *JSFO*, XXXVIII, 1 (1928), 1–21.

DONNER, KAI. *Ethnological Notes about the Yenisey-Ostyak* (*in the Turu khansk Region*). 1933. (MSFO LXVI.)

―――. "Ornements de la tête et de la chevelure," *JSFO*, XXXVII, (1920), 1–23.

―――. *La Sibérie. La Vie en Sibérie, les temps anciens.* Paris, 1946

―――. "Über soghdisch *nōm* 'Gesetz' und samojedisch *nōm* 'Himmel' Gott,'" *SO*, I (1925), 1–8.

―――. "Zu der ältesten Berührung zwischen Samojeden und Türken," *JSFO*, LX, 1 (1924), 1–24.

DORÉ, P. H. *Manuel des superstitions chinoises.* Shanghai, 1936.

DOWNS, R. E. *The Religion of the Bare'e-speaking Toradja of Central Celebes.* Diss., Leiden, 1956.

DRUCKER, PHILIP. *The Northern and Central Nootkan Tribes.* 1951. (BBEW 144.)

DUBOIS, CONSTANCE GODDARD. *The Religion of the Luiseño Indians of Southern California.* Berkeley, 1908. (CPAAE VIII, 3.)

DU BOIS, CORA ALICE. *The 1870 Ghost Dance.* Berkeley, 1939. (University of California Anthropological Records III, 1.)

―――. *Wintu Ethnography.* Berkeley, 1935. (CPAAE XXXVI, 1.

DUCHESNE-GUILLEMIN, JACQUES. *Zoroastre. Étude critique, avec une traduction commentée des Gâthâ.* Paris, 1948.

DUMÉZIL, GEORGES. "Les 'Enarees' scythiques et la grossesse du Narte Hamyc," *Latomus* (Brussels), V (July–Dec., 1946), 249–55.

―――. *Horace et les Curiaces* (*les mythes romains*). Paris, 1942.

―――. *Jupiter, Mars, Quirinus.* Paris, 1940–48. 4 vols.

―――. *Légendes sur les Nartes. Suivies de cinq notes mythologiques.* Paris, 1930. (Bibliothèque de l'Institut français de Léningrad.)

―――. *Loki.* Paris, 1948.

―――. *Mythes et dieux des Germains. Essai d'interprétation comparative.* Paris, 1939. (Mythes et religions I.)

―――. *Le Problème des centaures. Étude de mythologie comparée indo-européenne.* Paris, 1929. (Annales du Musée Guimet. Bibliothèque d'études XLI.)

―――. *La Saga de Hadingus, Saxo Grammaticus I, v-viii, etc.* Paris 1953. (Bibliothèque de l'École des Hautes Études. Section des sciences religieuses LXVI.)

―――. *Tarpeia. Essai de philologie comparative indo-européenne.* Paris 1947.

ƆUMONT, LOUIS. *Une Sous-caste de l'Inde du Sud. Organisation sociale et religion des Pramalai Kallar.* Paris, 1957.

ƆUMONT, PAUL ÉMILE. *L'Aśvamedha.* Paris, 1927.

ƆURME, P. J. VAN. "Notes sur le Lamaïsme," *MCB,* I (1931–32), 263–319.

ƆYRENKOVA, N. P. "Bear Worship among Turkish Tribes of Siberia," in *Proceedings of the 23rd International Congress of Americanists* (1928), pp. 411–40. New York, 1930.

ᴇBERHARD, WOLFRAM. *Lokalkulturen im alten China.* Part I: *Die Lokalkulturen des Nordens und Westens.* Leiden, 1942. Part II: *Die Lokalkulturen des Südens und Ostens.* Peking, 1942. (MS III.) 2 vols.

——. *Typen chinesischer Volksmärchen.* 1937. (FFC L, 120.)

ᴅER, MATTHIAS. "Schamanismus in Japan," *Paideuma,* VI, 7 (May, 1958), 367–80.

ᴅSMAN, CARL MARTIN. "Arbor inversa," *Religion och Bibel* (Uppsala), III (1944), 5–33.

——. "Återspeglar Voluspá 2:5–8 ett schamanistikt ritual eller en keltisk åldersvers?" *Arkiv för Nordisk Filologi* (Lund), LXIII (1948), 1–54.

——. *Le Baptême de feu.* Uppsala and Leipzig, 1940.

——. *Ignis divinus: le Feu comme moyen de rajeunissement et d'immortalité: contes, légendes, mythes et rites.* Lund, 1949.

ᴇLLS, REV. MYRON. *A Few Facts in Regard to the Twana, Clallam and Chemakum Indians of Washington Territory.* Chicago, 1880.

ɢɢELING, JULIUS, tr. *The Satapatha Brâhmaṇa: According to the Text of the Mâdhyandina School.* Oxford, 1882–1900. (SBE XII, XXVI, XLI, LXIII, LXIV.) 5 vols.

ʜNMARK, ERLAND. *Anthropomorphism and Miracle.* Uppsala and Leipzig, 1939.

ʜRENREICH, PAUL. *Die allgemeine Mythologie und ihre ethnologischen Grundlagen.* Leipzig, 1910. (Mythologische Bibliothek IV, 1.)

ɪSENBERGER, ELMAR JAKOB, "Das Wahrsagen aus dem Schulterblatt," *IAE,* XXXV (1938), 49–116.

ɪSLER, ROBERT. *Man into Wolf.* London, 1951.

——. "Das Qainszeichen und die Qeniter," *Le Monde orientale* (Uppsala), XXIII, fasc. 1–3 (1929), 48–112.

——. *Weltenmantel und Himmelszelt.* Munich, 1910. 2 vols.

ELIADE, MIRCEA. *Birth and Rebirth: the Religious Meanings of Initiation in Human Culture*, tr. Willard R. Trask. New York, 1958.

―――. *Cosmologie şi alchimie babiloniană*. Bucharest, 1937.

―――. "Dūrohaṇa and the 'Waking Dream,' " in *Art and Thought: a Volume in Honour of the Late Dr. Ananda K. Coomaraswamy on the Occasion of His 70th Birthday*, ed. Iyer K. Bharatha, pp. 209–13. London, 1947.

―――. "Einführende Betrachtungen über den Schamanismus," *Paideuma*, V, 3 (July, 1951), 88–97.

―――. *The Forge and the Crucible*. London and New York, 1962.

―――. *Images and Symbols: Studies in Religious Symbolism*. London and New York, 1961.

―――. *The Myth of the Eternal Return*, tr. Willard R. Trask. 1954 (BS XLVI.) Also London, 1954. (Reprinted as *Cosmos and History: The Myth of the Eternal Return*, Torchbooks paperback, New York, 1960. With orig. title, Princeton/Bollingen paperback, 1972.)

―――. *Myths, Dreams and Mysteries: the Encounter between Contemporary Faiths and Archaic Realities*. London, 1960; New York, 1961.

―――. "Nostalgia for Paradise in the Primitive Traditions," in his *Myths, Dreams and Mysteries* (q.v.), pp. 59–72.

―――. *Patterns in Comparative Religion*, tr. Rosemary Sheed. London and New York, 1958.

―――. "Le Problème du chamanisme," *RHR*, CXXXI, 1, 2–3 (1946), 5–52.

―――. "Recent Works on Shamanism: a Review Article," *History of Religions* (Chicago), I (summer, 1961), 152–86.

―――. "Remarques sur le 'rope trick,' " in *Culture in History: Essays in Honor of Paul Radin*, ed. Stanley Diamond, pp. 541–51. New York, 1960.

―――. "Sapta padāni kramati . . . ," in *The Munshi Diamond Jubilee Commemoration Volume*, Pt. I, pp. 180–88. Bombay, 1948. (Bhāratīya Vidyā IX.)

―――. "The Seven Steps of the Buddha," in his *Myths, Dreams and Mysteries* (q.v.), pp. 110–15.

―――. "Shamanism," in *Forgotten Religions*, ed. Vergilius Ferm, pp. 299–308. New York, 1950.

―――. "Significations de la 'lumière intérieure,' " *EJ*, XXVI (1957), 189–242.

ELIADE, MIRCEA. *Techniques du Yoga*. Paris, 1948.

———. *Yoga: Immortality and Freedom*, tr. Willard R. Trask. 1958. (BS LVI.) Also London, 1958. (Princeton/Bollingen paperback, 1970.)

ELKIN, ADOLPHUS PETER. *Aboriginal Men of High Degree*. Sydney, n.d. (1946?).

———. *The Australian Aborigines: How to Understand Them*. Sydney and London, 1938.

———. "The Rainbow-Serpent Myth in North-West Australia," *Oceania* (Melbourne), I, 3 (1930), 349–52.

ELLIOTT, ALAN J. A. *Chinese Spirit-Medium Cults in Singapore*. London, 1955. (London School of Economics and Political Science, Department of Anthropology. Monographs on Social Anthropology, n.s. 14.)

ELLIS, HILDA RODERICK. *The Road to Hel: a Study of the Conception of the Dead in Old Norse Literature*. Cambridge, 1943.

ELLIS, WILLIAM. *Polynesian Researches during a Residence of Nearly Eight Years in the Society and Sandwich Islands*. 3rd edn., London, 1853. 4 vols.

ELMENDORF, WILLIAM W. "Soul Loss Illness in Western North America," in *Indian Tribes of Aboriginal America: Selected Papers of the 29th International Congress of Americanists*, ed. Sol Tax, III, 104–14. Chicago, 1952.

ELWIN, VERRIER. "The Hobby Horse and the Ecstatic Dance," *Folklore* (London), LIII (Dec., 1942), 209–13.

———. *The Muria and Their Ghotul*. Bombay, 1947.

———. *Myths of Middle India*. London, 1949.

———. *The Religion of an Indian Tribe*. London and New York, 1955.

EMSHEIMER, ERNST. "Schamanentrommel und Trommelbaum," *Ethnos*, IV (1946), 166–81.

———. "Eine sibirische Parallele zur lappischen Zaubertrommel?" *Ethnos*, XII, 1–2 (Jan.–June, 1948), 17–26. .

———. "Zur Ideologie der lappischen Zaubertrommel," *Ethnos*, IX, 3–4 (1944), 141–69.

———. See also HASLUND-CHRISTENSEN, HENNING.

ERKES, EDUARD. "Die alt-chinesischen Jenseitsvorstellungen," *MGVK*, I (1933), 1–5.

———. "The God of Death in Ancient China," *TP*, XXXV (1940), 185–210.

———. "Der Hund im alten China," *TP*, XXXVII (1944), 186–225.

ERKES, EDUARD. "Der Primat des Weibes im alten China," *Sinica*, IV (1935), 166–76.

———. "Der schamanistische Ursprung des chinesischen Ahnenkultus," *Sinologica* (Basel), II, 4 (1950), 253–62.

———. *Das "Zurückrufen der Seele" (Chao-Hun) des Sung Yüh*. Inaugural diss., Leipzig, 1914.

EVANS, IVOR H. N. *Papers on the Ethnology and Archaeology of the Malay Peninsula*. Cambridge, 1927.

———. "Schebesta on the Sacerdo-Therapy of the Semang," *JRAI*, LX (1930), 115–25.

———. *Studies in Religion, Folk-Lore, & Custom in British North Borneo and the Malay Peninsula*. Cambridge, 1923.

EVANS-PRITCHARD, E. E. *Witchcraft, Oracles and Magic among the Azande*. Oxford, 1937.

EVANS-WENTZ, W. Y., ed. *The Tibetan Book of the Dead (Bardo Thödol)* tr. Lama Kazi Dawa-Samdup. London, 1927; 2nd edn., 1949; 3rd edn. 1957.

———, ed. *Tibetan Yoga and Secret Doctrines; or, Seven Books of Wisdom of the Great Path*, tr. Lama Kazi Dawa-Samdup. London and New York, 1935; 2nd edn., London, 1958.

FAIRCHILD, WILLIAM P. "Shamanism in Japan," *FS*, XXI (1962), 1–122

FILLIOZAT, JEAN. *La Doctrine classique de la médecine indienne. Ses origines et ses parallèles grecs*. Paris, 1949.

———. "Les Origines d'une technique mystique indienne," *Revue philosophique de la France et de l'étranger* (Paris), CXXXVI (1946) 208–20.

FINDEISEN, HANS. "Der Adler als Kulturbringer im nordasiatischen Raum und in der amerikanischen Arktis," *ZE*, LXXXI (1956), 70–82

———. "Der Mensch und seine Teile in der Kunst der Jennisseje (Keto)," *ZE*, LXIII (1931), 296–315.

———. *Schamanentum, dargestellt am Beispiel der Besessentheitspriester nordeurasiatischer Völker*. Stuttgart, 1957.

———. "Zur Geschichte der Bärenzeremonie," *ARW*, XXXVII (1941) 196–200.

FISCHER, H. T. "Indonesische Paradiesmythen," *ZE*, LXIV, 1–3 (1932) 204–45.

FLANNERY, REGINA. "The Gros Ventre Shaking Tent," *PM*, XVI (1944), 54–84.

FORDE, C. DARYLL. *Ethnography of the Yuma Indians.* Berkeley, 1931. (CPAAE XXVII, 4.)

FORTUNE, R. F. *Sorcerers of Dobu.* London, 1932.

FOY, W. "Indische Kultbauten als Symbole des Götterbergs." In *Festschrift Ernst Windisch zum siebzigsten Geburtstag am 4. September 1914,* pp. 213–16. Leipzig, 1914.

FRAZER, SIR JAMES GEORGE. *Aftermath: a Supplement to The Golden Bough.* London, 1936.

——. *The Belief in Immortality and the Worship of the Dead.* London, 1913–24. 3 vols.

——. *The Fear of the Dead in Primitive Religion,* London, 1933–36. 3 vols.

——. *Folk-lore in the Old Testament: Studies in Comparative Religion, Legend and Law.* London, 1919. 3 vols.

——. *Spirits of the Corn and of the Wild.* 3rd edn. of *The Golden Bough: a Study in Magic and Religion,* Pt. V. New York and London, 1955. 2 vols.

——. *Taboo and the Perils of the Soul.* 3rd edn. of *The Golden Bough,* Pt. II. New York and London, 1951.

——. *Totemism and Exogamy: a Treatise on Certain Early Forms of Superstition and Society.* London, 1910. 4 vols.

FRIEDERICI, GEORG. "Zu den vorkolumbischen Verbindungen der Südsee-Völker mit Amerika," *Anthropos,* XXIV (1929), 441–87.

FRIEDRICH, ADOLF. *Afrikanische Priestertümer.* Stuttgart, 1939.

——. "Das Bewusstsein eines Naturvolkes von Haushalt und Ursprung des Lebens," *Paideuma,* VI, 2 (Aug., 1955), 47–54.

——. "Knochen und Skelett in der Vorstellungswelt Nordasiens," *WBKL,* V (1943), 189–247.

—— and BUDDRUSS, GEORG. *Schamanengeschichten aus Sibirien* (tr. of KSENOFONTOV, G. V., *Legendy i rasskazy o shamanakh u yakutov, buryat i tungusov* [q.v.].) Munich and Planegg, 1955.

FRITZNER, JOHAN. *Lappernes Hedenskab og Trolddomskunst sammenholdt med andre Folks, isaer Nordmaenes, Tro og Overtro.* Christiania, 1877. (Norsk Historisk Forening Tidsskrift IV.)

FROBENIUS, LEO. *Kulturgeschichte Afrikas. Prolegomena zu einer historischen Gestaltlehre.* Zurich, 1933.

——. *Die Weltanschauung der Naturvölker.* Weimar, 1898.

FÜHNER, H. "Solanazeen als Berauschungsmittel: eine historischethnologische Studie," *Archiv für experimentelle Pathologie und Pharmakologie* (Leipzig), III (1926), 281–94.

GAERTE, W. "Kosmische Vorstellungen im Bilde prähistorischer Zeit: Erdberg, Himmelsberg, Erdnabel und Weltströme," *Anthropos*, IX (1914), 956–79.

GAHS, ALEXANDER. "Blutige und unblutige Opfer bei den altaischen Hirtenvölkern," in *Semaine internationale d'ethnologie religieuse, IVe session (1925)*, pp. 217–32. Paris, 1926.

————. "Kopf-, Schädel- und Langknochenopfer bei Rentiervölkern," in *Festschrift. Publication d'hommage offerte au P[ère] W. Schmidt*, ed. W. Koppers, pp. 231–68. Vienna, 1928.

————. "Die kulturhistorischen Beziehungen der östlichen Paläosibirier zu den austrischen Völkern, insbesondere zu jenen Formosas," *MAGW*, LX (1930), pp. 3–6.

GANAY, SOLANGE DE. *Les Devises de Dogon*. Paris, 1941.

GAYTON, A. H. "The Orpheus Myth in North America," *JAFL*, XLVIII, 189 (July–Sept., 1935), 263–93.

GENNEP, ARNOLD VAN. *Le Cheval-jupon*. Paris, 1945. (Cahiers d'ethno-graphie folklorique I.)

————. *Mythes et légendes d'Australie*. Paris, 1906.

————. *The Rites of Passage*. Chicago and London, 1960. (Orig.: *Les Rites de passage*. Paris, 1909.)

GEORGI, J. G. *Bemerkungen einer Reise im russischen Reich im Jahre 1772*. St. Petersburg, 1775.

GERNET, L., and BOULANGER, A. *Le Génie grec dans la religion*. Paris, 1932.

GHEERBRANT, ALAIN. *Journey to the Far Amazon: an Expedition into Unknown Territory*. New York, 1954. (English edn., *The Impossible Adventure: Journey to the Far Amazon*. London, 1953.)

GIEDION, S. *The Eternal Present*. I: *The Beginnings of Art*. (A. W. Mellon Lectures in the Fine Arts, 1957.) 1962. (BS XXXV. 6.I.) Also London, 1962.

GIFFORD, E. W. "Southern Maidu Religious Ceremonies," *AA*, XXIX, 3 (1927), 214–57.

GJESSING, GUTORM. *Circumpolar Stone Age*. Copenhagen, 1944. (Acta arctica II, fasc. 2.)

GMELIN, JOHANN GEORG. *Reise durch Sibirien, von dem Jahr 1733 bis 1743*. Göttingen, 1751–52. 4 vols. in 3.

GODLEY, A. D., tr. *Herodotus*. London and New York, 1921–24. (Loeb Classical Library.) 4 vols.

GOEJE, C. H. DE. "Philosophy, Initiation and Myths of the Indians of Guiana and Adjacent Countries," *IAE*, XLIV (1943), 1–136.

GOLOUBEW (GOLUBEV), V. "Sur l'origine et la diffusion des tambours métalliques," *Praehistorica Asiae orientalia* (Hanoi), 1932, 137–50.

———. "Les Tambours magiques en Mongolie," *BEFEO*, XXIII (1923), 407–09.

GOLTHER, W. *Handbuch der germanischen Mythologie*. Leipzig, 1895.

GOMES, EDWIN H. *Seventeen Years among the Sea Dyaks of Borneo: a Record of Intimate Association with the Natives of the Bornean Jungles*. Philadelphia, 1911.

GORCE, M., MORTIER, R. (and others). *Histoire générale des religions*. Paris, 1944–51. 5 vols.

GRAEBNER, FRITZ. *Das Weltbild der Primitiven. Eine Untersuchung der Urformen weltanschaulichen Denkens bei Naturvölkern*. Munich, 1924.

GRANET, MARCEL. *Danses et légendes de la Chine ancienne*. Paris, 1926. 2 vols.

———. *La Pensée chinoise*. Paris, 1934.

———. "Remarques sur le taoïsme ancien," *AM*, II (1925), 145–51.

GREY, SIR GEORGE. *Polynesian Mythology and Ancient Traditional History of the New Zealanders as Furnished by Their Priests and Chiefs*. Reprint, Auckland, 1929.

GRIAULE, MARCEL. *Dieu d'eau. Entretiens avec Ogotommêli*. Paris, 1949.

GRIFFITH, RALPH T. H., tr. *The Hymns of the Rigveda*. Benares, 1889–92. 4 vols.

GRØNBECH, K. See HASLUND-CHRISTENSEN, HENNING.

GROOT, JAN J. M. DE. *The Religious System of China*. Leiden, 1892–1910. 6 vols.

GROUSSET, RENÉ. *L'Empire des steppes*. Paris, 1938.

GRUBE, W. "Das Schamanentum bei den Golden," *Globus*, LXXI (1897), 89–93.

GRÜNWEDEL, ALBERT. *Die Teufel des Avesta und ihre Beziehungen zur Ikonographie des Buddhismus Zentral-Asiens*. Berlin, 1924. 2 vols. (called parts).

GUDGEON, Col. W. E. "Te Umu-ti, or Fire-Walking Ceremony," *JPS*, VIII, 29 (Mar., 1899), 58–60.

GÜNTERT, HERMANN. *Der arische Weltkönig und Heiland*. Halle, 1923.

GÜNTERT, HERMANN. *Kalypso*. Halle, 1919.

GUNTHER, E. See HAEBERLIN, HERMAN.

GUSINDE, MARTIN. "Une École d'hommes-médecine chez les Yamanas de la Terre de Feu," *Revue Ciba* (Basel), No. 60 (Aug., 1947), pp. 2159–62.

———. *Die Feuerland Indianer*. I: *Die Selk'nam*, II: *Die Yamana*, Mödling (Vienna), 1931, 1937. 2 vols.

———. "Der Medizinmann bei den südamerikanischen Indianern," *MAGW*, LXII (1932), 286–94.

GUTHRIE, W. K. C. *The Greeks and Their Gods*. London, 1950. (Beacon paperback reprint, Boston, 1955.)

———. *Orpheus and Greek Religion: a Study of the Orphic Movement*. London, 1935.

GUTMANN, B. "Der Schmied und seine Kunst im animistischen Denken," *ZE*, XLIV (1912), 81–93.

HAAVIO, MARTTI. *Väinämöinen, Eternal Sage*. 1952. (FFC LXI, 144.)

HAEBERLIN, HERMAN. "Sbεtεtda'q, a Shamanistic Performance of the Coast Salish," *AA*, n.s. XX (1918), 249–57.

——— and GUNTHER, E. "Ethnographische Notizen über die Indianerstämme des Puget-Sundes," *ZE*, LVI (1924), 1–74.

HAEKEL, JOSEF. "Idolkult und Dualsystem bei den Ugriern (zum Problem des eurasiatischen Totemismus)," *AVK*, I (1946), 95–163.

———. "Initiationen und Geheimbünde an der Nordwestküste Nordamerikas," *MAGW*, LXXXIII (1954), 176–90.

———. "Kosmischer Baum und Pfahl im Mythus und Kult der Stämme Nordwestamerikas," WVM, VI, n.s. 1 (1958), 33–81.

———. "Schutzgeistsuche und Jugendweihe im westlichen Nordamerika," *Ethnos*, XII (1947), 106–22.

HAGUENAUER, M. C. *Origines de la civilisation japonaise. Introduction à l'étude de la préhistoire du Japon*, vol. I. Paris, 1956.

———. "Sorciers et sorcières de Corée," *Bulletin de la Maison Franco-Japonaise* (Tokyo), II, 1 (1929), 47–65.

HALLOWELL, A. IRVING. "Bear Ceremonialism in the Northern Hemisphere," *AA*, n.s. XXVIII (1926), 1–175.

HANČAR, FRANZ. "The Eurasian Animal Style and the Altai Complex," *ArtA*, XV (1952), 171–94.

HANDY, E. S. C. *The Native Culture in the Marquesas*. 1923. (BMB 9.)

HANDY, E. S. C. *Polynesian Religion.* 1927. (BMB 4.)

HARPER, EDWARD B. "Shamanism in South India," *SJA*, XIII (1957), 267–87.

HARVA (formerly HOLMBERG), UNO. *Der Baum des Lebens.* Helsinki, 1922–23. (Suomalaisen Tiedeakatemian Toimituksia. Annales Academiae Scientiarum Fennicae, ser. B, XVI.)

———. *Finno-Ugric [and] Siberian [Mythology].* 1927. (MAR IV.)

———. *Die religiösen Vorstellungen der altaischen Völker.* Helsinki, 1938. (FFC LII, 125.)

———. *The Shaman Costume and Its Significance.* 1922. (AUFA, ser. B, I, 2.)

———. "Über die Jagdriten der nordlichen Völker Asiens und Europas," *JSFO*, XLI, fasc. 1 (1925), 1–53.

HASLUND-CHRISTENSEN, HENNING; GRØNBECH, K.; and EMSHEIMER, ERNST. *The Music of the Mongols.* I: *Eastern Mongolia.* Stockholm, 1943.

HATT, GUDMUND. *Asiatic Influences in American Folklore.* Copenhagen, 1949. (Det Kongelige Danske Videnskabernes Selskab. Historisk-filologiske Meddelelser XXXI, 6.)

HAUER, J. W. *Die Anfänge der Yogapraxis.* Stuttgart, 1922.

———. *Der Vrātya. Untersuchungen über die nichtbramanische Religion Altindiens.* I: *Die Vrātya als nichtbramanische Kultgenossenschaften arischer Herkunft.* Stuttgart, 1927.

HAUG, MARTIN, ed. and tr. *The Aitareya Brahmanam of the Rigveda.* Bombay, 1863. 2 vols.

——— (with E. W. WEST), ed. and tr. *The Book of Ardâ-Vîrâf.* Bombay and London, 1872.

HAUSSIG, HANS-WILHELM. "Theophylakts Exkurs über die skythischen Völker," *Byzantion* (Brussels), XXIII (1953), 275–462.

———. See also ALTHEIM, FRANZ.

HAYANS, GUILLERMO. See HOLMER, NILS M., and WASSÉN, S. HENRY.

HEINE-GELDERN, ROBERT VON. "Bedeutung und Hernkunft der ältesten hinterindischen Mettalltrommeln (Kesselgongs)," *AM*, VIII (1933), 519–37.

———. "Cultural Connections between Asia and Pre-Columbian America," *Anthropos*, XLV (1950), 350–52.

———. "Das Problem vorkolumbischer Beziehungen zwischen Alter und Neuer Welt und seine Bedeutung für die allgemeine Kulturge-schichte," *Anzeiger der Osterreichischen Akademie der Wissenschaften* (Vienna), phil.-hist. Klasse, XCI, 24 (1955), 343–63.

———. Review of *Antler and Tongue: an Essay on Ancient Chinese Symbolism and Its Implications*, by A. Salmony, *ArtA*, XVIII (1955), 85–90.

———. "Uhrheimat und früheste Wanderungen der Austronesier," *Anthropos*, XXVII (1932), 543–619.

———. "Weltbild und Bauform in Südostasien," *Wiener Beiträge zur Kunst- und Kulturgeschichte Asiens*, IV (1930), 28–78.

———. See also LOEB, E. M.: *Sumatra . . .*

HEISSIG, WALTHER. "A Mongolian Source to the Lamaist Suppression of Shamanism in the 17th Century," *Anthropos*, XLVIII (1953), 1–29, 493–536.

———. "Schamanen und Geisterbeschwörer im Küriye–Banner," *FS*, III (1944), 39–72.

HEMBERG, BENGT. *Die Kabiren*. Uppsala, 1950.

HENNING, W. B. *Zoroaster; Politician or Witch-Doctor?* London, 1951.

HENRY, A. "The Lolos and Other Tribes of Western China," *JRAI*, XXXIII (1903), 96–107.

HENTZE, CARL. *Bronzegerät, Kultbauten, Religion im ältesten China der Shang-Zeit.* Antwerp, 1951.

———. "Le Culte de l'ours et du tigre et le t'ao-t'ié," *Zalmoxis*, I (1938), 50–68.

———. *Frühchinesische Bronzen und Kultdarstellungen.* Antwerp, 1937.

———. *Mythes et symboles lunaires.* Antwerp, 1932.

———. *Objets rituels, croyances et dieux de la Chine antique et de l'Amérique.* Antwerp, 1936.

———. *Die Sakralbronzen und ihre Bedeutung in den frühchinesischen Kulturen.* Antwerp, 1941.

———. "Eine Schamanendarstellung auf einem Han-Relief," *AM*, n.s. I (1944), 74–77.

———. "Schamanenkronen zur Han-Zeit in Korea," *Ostasiatische Zeitschrift* (Berlin), n.s. IX, 5 (1933), 156–63.

———. "Eine Schamanentracht in ihrer Bedeutung für die altchine-sische Kunst und Religion," *IPEK*, XX(1960–63), 55–61.

———. "Zur ursprünglichen Bedeutung des chinesischen Zeichens *t'oû* = Kopf," *Anthropos*, XLV (1950), 801–20.

HERMANNS, MATTHIAS. *The Indo-Tibetans*. Bombay, 1954.

———. *Mythen und Mysterien, Magie und Religion der Tibeter*. Cologne, 1956.

HERODOTUS. See GODLEY, A. D.

HILLEBRANDT, ALFRED. *Vedische Mythologie*. 2nd rev. edn., Breslau, 1927–29. 2 vols.

HIROA, TE RANGI (PETER H. BUCK). *Ethnology of Mangareva*. 1938. (BMB 157.)

HIVALE, SHAMRAO. "The Laru Kaj," *Man in India* (Ranchi), XXIV (1944), 122 ff.

HOCART, ARTHUR MAURICE. "Flying Through the Air," *IA*, LII (1923), 80–82.

———. "Medicine and Witchcraft in Eddystone of the Solomons," *JRAI*, LV (1925), 221–70.

HOFFMAN, W. J. "The Midē'wiwin or 'Grand Medicine Society' of the Ojibwa," *7th RBEW* (1885–86; pub. 1891), pp. 143–300.

———. "Pictography and Shamanistic Rites of the Ojibwa," *AA*, I (1888), 209–29.

HOFFMANN, HELMUT. "Gšen. Eine lexikographisch- religionswissenschaftliche Untersuchung," *Zeitschrift der deutschen morgenländischen Gesellschaft* (Leipzig), XCVIII (1944), 340–58.

———. *Quellen zur Geschichte der tibetischen Bon-Religion*. Wiesbaden, 1950. (Abhandlungen der Akademie der Wissenschaften und der Literatur in Mainz, geistes- und sozialwissenschaftlichen Klasse 4.)

———. *The Religions of Tibet*, tr. Edward Fitzgerald. New York, 1961. (Orig.: *Die Religionen Tibets; Bon und Lamaismus in ihrer geschichtlichen Entwicklung*. Freiburg and Munich, 1956.)

HOFFMANN, REV. JOHN (with REV. ARTHUR VAN EMELEN). *Encyclopaedia Mundarica*. Patna, 1930–38. 4 vols.

HÖFLER, OTTO. *Kultische Geheimbünde der Germanen*, vol. I. Frankfurt a. M., 1934.

HOLM, G. "Ethnological Sketch of the Angmagsalik Eskimo," in THALBITZER, WILLIAM, ed., *The Ammassalik Eskimo: Contributions to the Ethnology of the East Greenland Natives*, pt. I, pp. 1–147. Copenhagen, 1914.

HOLMER, NILS M., and WASSÉN, S. HENRY, eds. and trs. *Nia-Ikala: Canto mágico para curar la locura. Texto en lengua cuna, anotado por el indio Guillermo Hayans con traduccion española y commentarios por Nils*

M. Holmer y S. Henry Wassén. Göteborg, 1958. (Etnologiska Studier XXIII.)

HOLT, CATHARINE. See KROEBER, A. L.

HONKO, LAURI. *Krankheitsprojectile: Untersuchung über eine urtümliche Krankheitserklärung*. 1959. (FFC LXXII, 178.)

HOPKINS, EDWARD WASHBURN. "Yoga-Technique in the Great Epic," *JAOS*, XXII (1901), 333–79.

HOPKINS, L. C. "The Bearskin, Another Pictographic Reconnaisance from Primitive Prophylactic to Present-day Panache: a Chinese Epigraphic Puzzle," *JRAS*, Pts. I–II (1943), pp. 110–17.

———. "The Shaman or Chinese Wu: His Inspired Dancing and Versatile Character," *JRAS*, Pts. I–II (1945), 3–16.

HORNELL, JAMES. "Was There Pre-Columbian Contact between the Peoples of Oceania and South America?" *JPS*, LIV (1945), 167–91.

HORNER, I. B., tr. *Majjhimanikāya*. 1959. (PTS XXXI.)

HOUSSE, ÉMILE. *Une Épopée indienne. Les Araucans du Chili*. Paris, 1939.

HOWELL, REV. W. "A Sea-Dayak Dirge," *Sarawak Museum Journal*, I, 1 (Jan., 1911), 5–73. (Extracts in CHADWICK, H. M. and N. K., *The Growth of Literature* [q.v.], III.)

HOWITT, A. W. *The Native Tribes of South-East Australia*. London, 1904.

———. "On Australian Medicine Men," *JRAI*, XVI (1887), 23–58.

HUART, CLÉMENT. *Les Saints des derviches tourneurs. Récits traduits du persan*. Paris, 1918–22. 2 vols.

HULTKRANTZ, ÅKE. *Conceptions of the Soul among North American Indians: a Study in Religious Ethnology*. Stockholm, 1953.

———. *The North American Indian Orpheus Tradition: a Contribution to Comparative Religion*. Stockholm, 1957.

HUME, ROBERT ERNEST, tr. *The Thirteen Principal Upanishads*. London, 1921.

HUMMEL, SIEGBERT. "Die Bedeutung der Na-khi für die Erforschung der tibetischen Kultur," *MS*, XIX (1960), 307–34.

———. "Eurasiatische Traditionen in der tibetischen Bon-Religion," in *Opuscula ethnologica memoriae Ludovici Biro sacra*, pp. 165–212. Budapest, 1959.

———. *Geheimnisse tibetischer Malereien*. II: *Lamaistische Studien*. Leipzig, 1949–59. 2 vols.

———. "Der göttliche Schmied in Tibet," *FS*, XIX (1960), 251–72.

HUMMEL, SIEGBERT. "Grundzüge einer Urgeschichte der tibetischen Kultur," *JMVK*, XIII (1954: pub. 1955), 73–134.

———. "Der Hund in der religiösen Vorstellungswelt des Tibeters," *Paideuma*, VI, 8 (Nov., 1958), 500–09; VII, 7 (July, 1961), 352–61.

IBN BATŪTAH. See DEFRÉMERY, C. F., and SANGUINETTI, B. R.

IM THURN, EVERARD F. *Among the Indians of Guiana, Being Sketches, Chiefly Anthropological, from the Interior of British Guiana.* London, 1883.

ITKONEN, TOIVO IMMANUEL. *Heidnische Religion und späterer Aberglaube bei den finnischen Lappen.* 1946. (MSFO LXXXVII.)

IVANOV, S. V. *Materialy po isobrazietelnomu iskusstvu narodov Sibiri XIX-nachala XX v.* Moscow and Leningrad, 1954. (AN, Trudy Instituta Etnografii, n.s. XXII.)

JACOBY, ADOLF. "Der Baum mit den Wurzeln nach oben und den Zweigen nach unten," *ZMKRW*, XLIII (1928), 78–85.

———. "Zum Zerstückelungs- und Wiederbelebungswunder der indischen Fakire," *ARW*, XVII (1914), 455–75.

JENNESS, DIAMOND. "Prehistoric Culture Waves from Asia to America," in *Annual Report of the Smithsonian Institution, 1940,* pp. 383–96. Washington, 1941.

JENSEN, A. E. *Die drei Ströme.* Leipzig, 1948.

——— and NIGGEMEYER, H., eds. *Hainuwele: Volkserzählungen von der Molukken-Insel Ceram.* Frankfurt a. M., 1939.

JEREMIAS, ALFRED. *Handbuch der altorientalischen Geisteskultur.* 2nd edn., Berlin and Leipzig, 1929.

JETTMAR, KARL. "The Altai before the Turks," *BMFEA*, No. 23 (1951), pp. 135–223.

———. "The Karasuk Culture and Its South-eastern Affinities," *BMFEA*, No. 22 (1950), pp. 83–126.

———. "Urgeschichte Innerasiens," in NARR, KARL J., *Abriss der Vorgeschichte* (q.v.), pp. 150–61.

———. "Zur Herkunft der türkischen Völkerschaften," *AVK*, III (1948), 9–23.

JOCHELSON, WALDEMAR (VLADIMIR) I. *The Koryak.* Leiden and New York, 1905–8. (AMNH Memoirs X; JE VI.)

———. *The Yakut.* 1933. (AMNH Anthropological Papers XXXIII, Pt. II.)

Jochelson, Waldemar (Vladimir) I. *The Yukaghir and the Yukaghirized Tungus.* Leiden and New York, 1924–26. (AMNH Memoirs XIII, 2–3; JE IX.) 2 vols.

John of the Cross, St. "Ascent of Mount Carmel," in *The Complete Works of Saint John of the Cross,* I, ed. and tr. E. Allison Peers. London, 1934–35. 3 vols.

Johnson, Frederick. "Notes on Micmac Shamanism," *PM,* XVI (1943), 53–80.

Juynboll, H. H. "Religionen der Naturvölker Indonesiens," *ARW,* XVII (1914), 582–606.

Kagarow (Kagarov), E. "Der umgekehrte Schamanenbaum," *ARW,* XXVII (1929), 183–85.

Kahn, Charles H. "Religion and Natural Philosophy in Empedocles' Doctrine of the Soul," *Archiv für Geschichte der Philosophie* (Berlin), XLII (1960), 3–35.

Kaltenmark, Max, ed. and tr. *Le Lie-sien tchouan* (*Biographies légendaires des Immortels taoïstes de l'antiquité*). Peking, 1953.

Karjalainen, K. F. *Die Religion der Jugra-Völker.* 1921–27. (FFC VIII, 41; XI, 44; XX, 63.) 3 vols.

Karsten, Rafael. *The Civilization of the South American Indians.* London, 1926.

———. *The Religion of the Samek.* Leiden, 1955.

———. "Zur Psychologie des indianischen Medizinmannes," *ZE,* LXXX, 2 (1955), 170–77.

Keith, Arthur Berriedale. *The Religion and Philosophy of the Veda and Upanishads.* 1925. (HOS XXXI, XXXII.) 2 vols.

———, tr. *Rigveda Brāhmaṇas: the Aitareya and Kauṣītaki Brāhmaṇas of the Rigveda.* 1920. (HOS XXV.)

———, tr. *The Veda of the Black Yajus School Entitled Taittirīya Saṇhitā.* Pt. I: *Kandas I–III*; Pt. II: *Kandas IV–VII.* 1914. (HOS XVIII, XIX.) 2 vols.

Kerényi, Carl (Karl). *Pythagoras und Orpheus.* 3rd edn., Zurich, 1950. (Albae Vigilae, n.s. IX.)

Khangalov, M. N. See Agapitov, N. N.

Kirchner, Horst. "Ein archäologischer Beitrag zur Urgeschichte des Schamanismus," *Anthropos,* XLVII (1952), 244–86.

Kirfel, Willibald. *Die Kosmographie der Inder, nach den Quellen dargestellt.* Bonn and Leipzig, 1920.

KITTREDGE, GEORGE LYMAN. *Witchcraft in Old and New England.* Cambridge (Mass.), 1929.

KLAPROTH, J. H., ed. "Description du Tubet," *JA*, Ser. II, IV (Aug., 1829), 81–158, 241–324; VI (Sept., 1830), 161–246; (Nov., 1830), 321–50.

KNOLL-GREILING, URSULA. "Berufung und Berufungserlebnis bei den Schamanen," *Tribus* (Stuttgart), n.s. II–III (1952–53), 227–38.

KOCH, THEODOR. "Zum Animismus der südamerikanischen Indianer," *IAE*, Suppl. XIII (1900).

KOLLANTZ, ARNULF. "Der Schamanismus der Awaren," *Palaeologia* (Osaka), IV, 3–4 (1955), 63–73.

KOPPERS, WILHELM. *Die Bhil in Zentralindien.* Horn (Austria) and Vienna, 1948.

———. "Die Frage eventueller alter Kulturbeziehungen zwischen südlichen Südamerika und Südost-Australien," in *Proceedings of the 23rd International Congress of Americanists* (1928), pp. 678–86. New York, 1930.

———. "Der Hund in der Mythologie der zirkumpazifischen Völker," *WBKL*, I (1930), 359–99.

———. "Monuments to the Dead of the Bhils and Other Primitive Tribes in Central India: a Contribution to the Study of the Megalith Problem," *ALat*, VI (1942), 117–206.

———. "Pferdeopfer und Pferdekult der Indogermanen," in *Die Indogermanen- und Germanenfrage: neue Wege zu ihrer Lösung*, pp. 279–411. 1936. (WBKL IV.)

———. "Probleme der indischen Religionsgeschichte," *Anthropos*, XXXV–XXXVI (1940–41), 761–814.

———. Review of *The Building of Cultures*, by Roland B. Dixon, *Anthropos*, XXIV (1929), 695–99.

———. "Tungusen und Miao," *MAGW*, LX (1930), 306–19.

———. *Unter Feuerland-Indianern. Eine Forschungsreise zu den südlichsten Bewohnern der Erde mit M. Gusinde.* Stuttgart, 1924.

———. "Urtürkentum und Urindogermanentum im Lichte der völkerkundlichen Universalgeschichte," *Belleten* (Ankara), V, 20 (Oct., 1941), 481–525.

KÖPRÜLÜZADÉ, MEHMED FUAD. *Influence du chamanisme turco-mongol sur les ordres mystiques musulmans.* Istanbul, 1929. (Mémoires de l'Institut de Turcologie de l'Université de Stamboul, n.s. I.)

KÖPRÜLÜZADÉ, MEHMED FUAD. *Les Premiers Mystiques dans la littérature turque*. Constantinople, 1919. (In Turkish.)

KÖRNER, THEO. "Das Zurückrufen der Seele in Kuei-chou," *Ethnos*, III, 4–5 (July–Sept., 1938), 108–12.

KRADER, LAWRENCE. "Buryat Religion and Society," *SJA*, X, 3 (1954), 322–51.

KREMSMAYER, HEIMO. "Schamanismus und Seelenvorstellungen im alten China," *AVK*, IX (1954), 66–78.

KRETSCHMAR, FREDA. *Hundestammvater und Kerberos*. Stuttgart, 1938. 2 vols.

KROEBER, ALFRED LOUIS. "The Eskimo of Smith Sound," *AMNH Bulletin*, XII (1899), 265–327.

———. *Handbook of the Indians of California*. 1925. (BBEW 78.)

———. "A Karok Orpheus Myth," *JAFL*, LIX (1946), 13–19.

——— and HOLT, CATHARINE. "Masks and Moieties as a Culture Complex," *JRAI*, L (1920), 452–60.

KROEF, JUSTUS M. VAN DER, "Transvestitism and the Religious Hermaphrodite in Indonesia," *Journal of East Asiatic Studies* (Manila), III (1959), 257–65.

KROHN, KAARLE. *Kalevalastudien*. 1924–28. (FFC XVI, 53; XXI, 67; XXIII, 71–72; XXVI, 75–76.) 6 vols. (Vol. V: *Väinämöinen*.)

KROLL, JOSEF. *Gott und Hölle*. Leipzig, 1932.

———. *Die Himmelfahrt der Seele in der Antike*. Cologne, 1931.

KRUYT (KRUIJT, KRUJT), A. C. *Het Animisme in den Indischen Archipel*. The Hague, 1906.

———. "Indonesians," in *Encyclopaedia of Religion and Ethics*, ed. James Hastings, VII, 232–50. New York, 1951.

———. See also ADRIANI, N.

KSENOFONTOV, G. V. *Legendy i rasskazy o shamanakh u yakutov, buryat i tungusov*. 2nd edn., Moscow, 1930. (German tr., FRIEDRICH, A., and BUDDRUSS, GEORG, *Schamanengeschichten aus Sibirien* [q.v.].)

LAFONT, PIERRE-BERNARD. "Pratiques médicales des Thai noirs du Laos de l'ouest," *Anthropos*, LIV (1959), 819–40.

LAGERCRANTZ, ELIEL. "Die Geheimsprachen der Lappen," *JSFO*, XLII, 2 (1928), 1–13.

LALOU, MARCELLE. "Le Chemin des morts dans les croyances de Haute-Asie," *RHR*, CXXXV (1949), 42–48.

LAMOTTE, ÉTIENNE, tr. *Le Traité de la Grande Vertu de sagesse de Nāgārjuna* (*Mahāprajñāpāramitāśāstra*). Louvain, 1944, 1949. 2 vols.

LANDTMAN, G. *The Kiwai Papuans of British New Guinea*. London, 1927.

LANKENAU, H. VON. "Die Schamanen und das Schamanenwesen," *Globus*, XXII (1872), 278–83.

LANTERNARI, V. "Il Serpente Arcobaleno e il complesso religioso degli Esseri pluviali in Australia," *SMSR*, XXIII (1952), 117–28.

LARSEN, HELGE. "The Ipiutak Culture: Its Origin and Relationship," in *Indian Tribes of Aboriginal America: Selected Papers of the 29th International Congress of Americanists*, ed. Sol Tax, III, 22–34. Chicago, 1952.

LATTIMORE, OWEN. "Wulakai Tales from Manchuria," *JAFL*, XLVI (1933), 272–86.

LAUFER, BERTHOLD. "Burkhan," *JAOS*, XXXVI (1917), 390–95.

———. *Chinese Clay Figures*. 1914. (FMNH Anthropological Series XIII, 2.)

———. "Columbus and Cathay, and the Meaning of America to the Orientalist," *JAOS*, LI, 2 (June, 1931), 87–103.

———. "Origin of the Word Shaman," *AA*, XIX (1917), 361–71.

———. *The Prehistory of Aviation*. 1928. (FMNH Anthropological Series XVIII, 1.)

———. *Sino-Iranica: Chinese Contributions to the History of Civilization in Ancient Iran*. 1919. (FMNH Anthropological Series XV, 3.)

———. *Use of Human Skulls and Bones in Tibet*. 1923. (FMNH Department of Anthropology Publication X.)

LAVAL, HONORÉ. *Mangareva. L'Histoire ancienne d'un peuple polynésien*. Braine-le-Comte and Paris, 1938.

LAVIOSA-ZAMBOTTI, P. *Les Origines et la diffusion de la civilisation*. Paris, 1949. (Orig.: *Origini e diffusione della civiltà*. Milan, 1947.)

LAYARD, JOHN W. "Malekula: Flying Tricksters, Ghosts, Gods and Epileptics," *JRAI*, LX (July–Dec., 1930), 501–24.

———. "Shamanism: an Analysis Based on Comparison with the Flying Tricksters of Malekula," *JRAI*, LX (July–Dec., 1930), 525–50.

———. *Stone Men of Malekula*. London, 1942.

LEEUW, GERARDUS VAN DER. *La Religion dans son essence et ses manifestations*. Paris, 1948. (French tr. of German text, rev. by author. English tr.: *Religion in Essence and Manifestation*. London, 1938.)

LEHMANN, WALTER. "Die Frage völkerkundlicher Beziehungen zwischen der Südsee und Amerika," *Orientalische Literaturzeitung* (Berlin), XXXIII (1930), 322–39.

LEHTISALO, T. "Beobachtungen über die Jodler," *JSFO*, XLVIII, 2 (1936–37), 1–34.

———. *Entwurf einer Mythologie der Jurak-Samojeden.* 1924. (MSFO LIII.)

———. "Der Tod und die Wiedergeburt des künftigen Schamanen," *JSFO*, XLVIII, fasc. 3 (1937), 1–34.

LEROY, OLIVIER. *Les Hommes salamandres. Recherches et réflexions sur l'incombustibilité du corps humain.* Paris, 1931.

———. *La Lévitation.* Paris, 1928.

———. *La Raison primitive. Essai de réfutation de la théorie du prélogisme.* Paris, 1927.

LESSING, F. D. "Calling the Soul: a Lamaist Ritual," in *Semitic and Oriental Studies: a Volume Presented to William Popper on the Occasion of his Seventy-Fifth Birthday, October 29, 1949,* ed. Walter J. Fischel, pp. 263–84. Berkeley and Los Angeles, 1951. (CPSP XI.)

LÉVI, SYLVAIN. *La Doctrine du sacrifice dans les Brāhmaṇas.* Paris, 1898.

———. "Étude des documents tokhariens de la Mission Pelliot," *JA,* ser. X, vol. XVII (May–June, 1911), 431–64.

——— and CHAVANNES, ÉDOUARD. "Les Seize Arhats protecteurs de la loi," *JA,* ser. XI, vol. VIII (July–Aug., 1916), 5–50, 189–304.

LEVY, GERTRUDE R. *The Gate of Horn: a Study of the Religious Conceptions of the Stone Age, and Their Influence upon European Thought.* London and Chicago, 1948.

LÉVY, ISIDORE. *La Légende de Pythagore de Grèce en Palestine.* Paris, 1927.

LÉVY-BRUHL, LUCIEN. *La Mythologie primitive. Le Monde mythique des Australiens et des Papous.* Paris, 1935.

LI AN-CHE. "Bon: the Magico-Religious Belief of the Tibetan-Speaking Peoples," *SJA,* IV, 1 (1948), 31–41.

LINDGREN, E. J. "The Reindeer Tungus of Manchuria," *Journal of the Royal Central Asian Society* (London), XXII (April, 1935), 221–31.

———. "The Shaman Dress of the Dagurs, Solons and Numinchens in N. W. Manchuria," *Geografiska annaler* (Stockholm), I, 1935.

LINDQUIST, SIGURD. *Siddhi und Abhiññā: eine Studie über die klassischen Wunder des Yoga.* Uppsala, 1935.

LINTON, RALPH. "Marquesan Culture," in *The Individual and His*

Society: the Psychodynamics of Primitive Social Organization, ed. Abram Kardiner, pp. 137–96. New York, 1939.

Liungman, Waldemar. *Traditionswanderungen, Euphrat-Rhein: Studien zur Geschichte der Volksbräuche*. 1937–38. (FFC XLVIII, 118; XLIX, 119.) 2 vols.

Loeb, Edwin Meyer. *Pomo Folkways*. Berkeley, 1926. (CPAAE XIX, 2.)

————. "The Shaman of Niue," *AA*, n.s. XXVI, 3 (July–Sept., 1924), 393–402.

————. "Shaman and Seer," *AA*, n.s. XXXI, 1 (Jan.–Mar., 1929), 60–84.

————. *Sumatra: Its History and People* (with "The Archaeology and Art of Sumatra," by Robert Heine-Geldern). 1935. (WBKL III.)

————. *Tribal Initiations and Secret Societies*. Berkeley, 1929. (CPAAE XXV, 3.)

Lommel, Hermann. "Bhrigu im Jenseits," *Paideuma*, IV (1950), 93–109.

————. "Yasna 32," *Wörter und Sachen* (Heidelberg), XIX = n.s. I (1938), 237–65.

Lopatin, Ivan A. *Goldy amurskiye, ussuriskiye i sungariiskiye*. Vladivostok, 1922.

————. "A Shamanistic Performance to Regain the Favor of the Spirit," *Anthropos*, XXXV–XXXVI (1940–41), 352–55.

————. "A Shamanistic Performance for a Sick Boy," *Anthropos*, XLI–XLIV (1946–49), 365–68.

Lot-Falck, Eveline. "À propos d'Ätügän, déesse mongole de la terre," *RHR*, CXLIX, 2 (1956), 157–96.

————. "À propos d'un tambour de chaman tongouse," *L'Homme* (Paris), No. 2 (1961), pp. 23–50.

————. "L'Animation du tambour," *JA*, CCXLIX (1961), 213–39.

————. *Les Rites de chasse chez les peuples sibériens*. Paris, 1953.

Lowie, Robert H. *Notes on Shoshonean Ethnography*. 1924. (AMNH Anthropological Papers XX, Pt. III.)

————. "On the Historical Connection between Certain Old World and New World Beliefs," in Congrès International des Américanistes, *Compte-Rendu de la XXIe session, part 2* (1924), pp. 546–49. Göteborg, 1925.

————. *Primitive Religion*. New York, 1924.

LOWIE, ROBERT H. "Religious Ideas and Practices of the Eurasiatic and North American Areas," in *Essays Presented to C. G. Seligman*, ed. E. E. Evans-Pritchard, et al., pp. 183–88. London, 1934.

LUBLINSKI, IDA. "Der Medizinmann bei den Naturvölkern Südamerikas," *ZE*, LII–LIII (1920–21), 234–63.

LUOMALA, KATHARINE. *Maui-of-a-Thousand-Tricks: His Oceanic and European Biographers.* 1949. (BMB 198.)

MACCHIORO, VITTORIO. *Zagreus. Studi intorno all'orfismo.* Florence, 1930.

McMAHON, LIEUT.-COLONEL A. R. *The Karens of the Golden Chersonese.* London, 1876.

MADDOX, JOHN LEE. *The Medicine Man: a Sociological Study of the Character and Evolution of Shamanism.* New York, 1923.

MADSEN, W. "Shamanism in Mexico," *SJA*, XI (1955), 48–57.

MALINOWSKI, BRONISLAW. *The Argonauts of the Pacific.* London, 1932.
———. *Myth in Primitive Psychology.* London and New York, 1926. (Reprinted in his *Magic, Science and Religion, and Other Essays*, pp. 93–148. Anchor Books paperback, New York, 1954.)
———. *The Sexual Life of Savages in NW Melanesia.* New York, 1929.

MALTEN, LUDOLPH. "Das Pferd im Totenglauben," *Jahrbuch des kaiserlich deutschen archäologischen Instituts* (Berlin), XXIX (1914), 179–256.

MÄNCHEN-HELFEN, OTTO. "Manichaeans in Siberia," in *Semitic and Oriental Studies Presented to William Popper on the Occasion of His Seventy-Fifth Birthday, October 29, 1949*, ed. Walter J. Fischel, pp. 311–26. Berkeley and Los Angeles, 1951. (CPSP XI.)
———. *Reise ins asiatische Tuwa.* Berlin, 1931.

MANKER, ERNST. *Die lappische Zaubertrommel.* I: *Die Trommel als Denkmal materieller Kultur;* II: *Die Trommel als Urkunde geistigen Lebens.* 1938, 1950. (AL I, VI.) 2 vols.

MANNHARDT, JOHANN WILHELM EMANUEL. *Germanische Mythen.* Berlin, 1858.

MARCEL-DUBOIS, CLAUDIE. *Les Instruments de musique de l'Inde ancienne.* Paris, 1941.

MARINER, W. *An Account of the Natives of the Tonga Islands.* London, 1817; Boston, 1820. 2 vols.

MARINGER, JOHANNES. *Vorgeschichtliche Religion: Religionen im Steinzeitlichen Europa.* Zurich and Cologne, 1956.

MARSHALL, Rev. HARRY IGNATIUS. *The Karen People of Burma: a Study in Anthropology and Ethnology*. Columbus, 1922.

MARSTRANDER, CARL. "Deux Contes irlandais," in *Miscellany Presented to Kuno Meyer by Some of His Friends and Pupils on the Occasion of His Appointment to the Chair of Celtic Philology in the University of Berlin*, eds. Osborn Bergin and Carl Marstrander, pp. 371–486. Halle, 1912.

MARTINO, ERNESTO DE. *Il mondo magico. Prolegomena a una storia del magismo*. Turin, 1948.

MASPERO, HENRI. *La Chine antique*. Paris, 1927.

———. "Légendes mythologiques dans le *Chou king*," *JA*, CCIV (1924), 1–100.

———. *Les Religions chinoises*. Paris, 1950. (*Mélanges posthumes sur les religions et l'histoire de la Chine* I.)

MASSIGNON, LOUIS. *Essai sur les origines du lexique technique de la mystique musulmane*. Paris, 1922. (2nd edn., rev. and enlarged, Paris, 1954.)

———. *La Passion d'al-Hosayn-ibn-Mansour al-Hallaj, martyr mystique de l'Islam, exécuté à Bagdad le 26 mars 922: étude d'histoire religieuse*. Paris, 1922. 2 vols.

MAUSS, MARCEL. "L'Origine des pouvoirs magiques dans les sociétés australiennes," *Année sociologique* (Paris), VII (1902–03), 1–140. (Reprinted in HUBERT, HENRI, and MAUSS, MARCEL, *Mélanges d'histoire des religions*, pp. 131–87. 2nd edn., Paris, 1929.)

MAX MÜLLER, F. *Egyptian [Mythology]*. 1918. (MAR XII.)

MEILLET, A. "Le Tokharien," *Indogermanisches Jahrbuch* (Strassburg), I (1913), 1–19.

MEISEN, KARL. *Die Sagen vom Wütenden Heer und Wilden Jaeger*. Münster, 1935.

MELNIKOW (MELNIKOV), N. "Die ehemaligen Menschenopfer und der Schamanismus bei den Burjaten des irkutskischen Gouvernements," *Globus*, LXXV (1899), 132–34.

MENASCE, JEAN DE. "The Mysteries and the Religion of Iran," in *The Mysteries* (Papers from the Eranos Yearbooks, 2), pp. 135–48. 1955. (BS XXX.2.) Also London, 1955.

MENGES [KARL HEINRICH]. See POTAPOV, L. P.

MERCER, SAMUEL A. B., ed. and tr. *The Pyramid Texts, in Translation and Commentary*. New York, 1952. 4 vols.

MÉTRAUX, ALFRED, "Les Hommes-dieux chez les Chiriguano et dans l'Amérique du Sud," *Revista del Instituto de Etnología de la Univers* *dad nacional de Tucumán*, II (1931), 61–91.

———. "Religion and Shamanism," in *Handbook of South Americ* *Indians*. V: *The Comparative Ethnology of South American Indians*, p 559–99. Washington, 1949.

———. *La Religion des Tupinamba et ses rapports avec celle des autr* *tribus Tupi-Guarani*. Paris, 1928.

———. "Le Shamanisme araucan," *Revista del Instituto de Antropolog* *de la Universidad nacional de Tucumán*, II, 10 (1942), 309–62.

———. "Le Shamanisme chez les Indiens de l'Amérique du Sud trop cale," *Acta americana* (Mexico), II, 3–4 (1944), 197–219, 320–4

———. "The Social Organization of the Mojo and Manasi," *PM*, X\ (1943), 1–30.

MEULI, KARL. "Griechische Opferbräuche," in *Phyllobolia für Peter v* *der Mühll zum 60. Geburtstag am 1. August 1945*, pp. 185–288. Base 1946.

———. "Maske," in *Handwörterbuch des deutschen Aberglaubens*, e Hanns Bächtold-Stäubli, V. Berlin, 1927–42. 10 vols.

———. *Schweizer Masken*. Zurich, 1943.

———. "Scythica," *Hermes* (Berlin), LXX (1935), 121–76.

MIKHAILOWSKI, V. M. "Shamanism in Siberia and European Russi Being the Second Part of *Shamanstvo*," *JRAI*, XXIV (1894), 62–10 126–58. (Tr. from Russian by Oliver Wardrop.)

MIRONOV, N. D., and SHIROKOGOROFF (SHIROKOGOROV), S. M., "Šraman Shaman: Etymology of the Word 'Shaman,' " *JRAS, North-Chi* *Branch* (Shanghai), LV (1924), 105–30.

MODI, JIVANJI JAMSHEDJI. "The Tibetan Mode of the Disposal of th Dead," in his *Memorial Papers*, pp. 1 ff. Bombay, 1922.

MOERENHOUT, JACQUES A. *Voyages aux îles du Grand Océan*. Paris, 183 2 vols.

MOGK, E. *Germanische Mythologie*. Strassburg, 1898.

MONSEN, ERLING, and SMITH, A. H. See SNORRI STURLUSON.

MONTANDON, GEORGES. *Traité d'ethnologie culturelle*. Paris, 1934.

MOONEY, JAMES. "The Ghost-Dance Religion and the Sioux Outbrea of 1890," *14th RBEW*, Pt. II (1892–93; pub. 1896), pp. 641–113

MORÉCHAND, GUY. "Principaux Traits du chamanisme mèo blanc Indochine," *BEFEO*, XLVII, 2 (1955), 509–46.

Morris, J. *Living with the Lepchas*. London, 1938.

Moss, Rosalind. *The Life after Death in Oceania and the Malay Archipelago*. London, 1925.

Moulton, James Hope. *Early Zoroastrianism: Lectures Delivered at Oxford and in London February to May 1912*. London, 1913.

Mühlmann, Wilhelm Emil. *Arioi und Mamaia. Eine ethnologische, religionssoziologische und historische Studie über polynesische Kultbünde*. Wiesbaden, 1955.

Müller, F. Max. See Max Müller, F.

Müller, Werner. *Die blaue Hütte*. Wiesbaden, 1954.

——. *Weltbild und Kult der Kwakiutl-Indianer*. Wiesbaden, 1955.

Munkácsi, Bernhardt. " 'Pilz' und 'Rausch,' " *KS*, VIII (1907), 343–44.

Münsterberger, Werner. *Ethnologische Studien an indonesischen Schöpfungsmythen. Ein Beitrag zur Kulturanalyse Südostasiens*. The Hague, 1939.

Murray, Margaret Alice. *The God of the Witches*. London, 1934.

Mus, Paul. *Barabuḍur. Esquisse d'une histoire du Bouddhisme fondée sur la critique archéologique des textes*. Hanoi, 1935 ff. 2 vols.

Muster, Wilhelm. "Der Schamanismus bei den Etruskern," *Frühgeschichte und Sprachwissenschaft* (Vienna), I (1948), 60–77.

——. "Der Schamanismus und seine Spuren in der Saga, im deutschen Brauch, Märchen und Glauben." Diss., Graz.

Nachtigall, H. "Die erhöhte Bestattung in Nord- und Hochasien," *Anthropos*, XLVIII, 1–2 (1953), 44–70.

——. "Die kulturhistorische Wurzel der Schamanenskelettierung," *Zeitschrift für Ethnologie* (Berlin), LXXVII (1952), 188–97.

Nadel, S. F. "A Study of Shamanism in the Nuba Mountains," *JRAI*, LXXVI, Pt. I (1946), 25–37.

Nāgārjuna. See Lamotte, Etienne.

Nanavutty, P. See Bode, Dastur Framroze Ardeshir.

Narr, Karl J. "Bärenzeremoniell und Schamanismus in der Älteren Steinzeit Europas," *Saeculum* (Freiburg and Munich), X, 3 (1959), 233–72.

——. "Interpretation altsteinzeitlicher Kunstwerke durch völkerkundliche Parallelen," *Anthropos*, L (1955), 513–45.

——. "Nordasiatisch-europäische Urzeit in archäologischer und völkerkundlicher Sicht," *Studium generale* (Berlin), VII, 4 (Apr 1954), 193–201.

——— (and others), eds. *Abriss der Vorgeschichte*. Munich, 195

NEBESKY-WOJKOWITZ, RENÉ DE. "Ancient Funeral Ceremonies of th Lepchas," *Eastern Anthropologist* (Lucknow), V, 1 (Sept.–Nov 1951), 27–39.

———. *Oracles and Demons of Tibet: the Cult and Iconography of t Tibetan Protective Deities*. The Hague, 1956.

———. "Tibetan Drum Divination, 'Ngamo,'" *Ethnos*, XVII (1952 149–57.

———. "Die tibetische Bön-Religion," *AVK*, II (1947), 26–68.

———. "Das tibetische Staatsorakel," *AVK*, III (1948), 136–5

NEGELEIN, JULIUS VON. "Seele als Vogel," *Globus*, LXXIX, 23 (1901 357–61, 381–84.

NEHRING, ALFONS. "Studien zur indogermanischen Kultur und Urhe mat," in *Die Indogermanen- und Germanenfrage: neue Wege zu ihr Lösung*, pp. 7–229. 1936. (WBKL IV.)

NELSON, EDWARD WILLIAM. "The Eskimo about Bering Strait," *18 RBEW*, Pt. I (1896–97; pub. 1899), 19–518.

NÉMETH, JULIUS. "Über den Ursprung des Wortes Šaman und eini Bemerkungen zur türkisch-mongolischen Lautgeschichte," *KS*, XI (1913–14), 240–49.

NEWBOLD, T. J. *Political and Statistical Account of the British Settlemen in the Straits of Malacca, viz. Pinang, Malacca, Singapore, with History of the Malayan States on the Peninsula*. London, 1839. 2 vol

NGUYỄN-VĂN-KHOAN. "Le Repêchage de l'âme, avec une note sur l hôn et les phách d'après les croyances tonkinoises actuelles," *BEFE XXXIII* (1933), 11–34.

NIGGEMEYER, H. See JENSEN, A. E.

NILSSON, MARTIN P. *Geschichte der griechischen Religion*. Munich, 194 50. 2 vols.

NIORADZE, GEORG. *Der Schamanismus bei den sibirischen Völkern*. Stut gart, 1925.

NÖLLE, W. "Iranisch-nordasiatische Beziehungen im Schamanismus *JMVK*, XII (1953), 86–90.

———. "Schamanistische Vorstellungen im Shaktismus," *JMVK*, ? (1952), 41–47.

Nordenskiöld, Erland. *Origin of the Indian Civilization in South Amerika*. Göteborg, 1931. (Comparative Ethnographical Studies IX, 9.)

Nourry, Émile (pseud. P. Saintyves). *Les Contes de Perrault*. Paris, 1923.

Numazawa, Franz Kiichi. *Die Weltanfänge in der japanischen Mythologie*. Paris and Lucerne, 1946.

Nyberg, H. S. "Questions de cosmogonie et de cosmologie mazdéennes," *JA*, CCXIX (July–Sept., 1931), 1–134.

———. *Die Religionen des alten Iran*. Leipzig, 1938.

Nyuak, Leo. "Religious Rites and Customs of the Iban or Dyaks of Sarawak," *Anthropos*, I (1906), 11–23, 165–84, 403–25.

Obermaier, H. See Breuil, H.

Oesterreich, T. K. *Possession, Demoniacal and Other, among Primitive Races in Antiquity, the Middle Ages, and Modern Times*. London and New York, 1930.

Ohlmarks, Åke. "Arktischer Schamanismus und altnordischer Seidhr," *ARW*, XXXVI, 1 (1939), 171–80.

———. *Studien zum Problem des Schamanismus*. Lund, 1939.

Oka, Masao. "Kulturschichten in Altjapan." (German tr., unpublished, from Japanese MS.)

Okladnikov, A. P. "Ancient Cultures and Cultural and Ethnic Relations on the Pacific Coast of North Asia," in *Proceedings of the 32nd International Congress of Americanists (1956)*, pp. 545–56. Copenhagen, 1958.

Oldenberg, Hermann. *Die Religion des Veda*. 2nd edn., Berlin, 1917.

Olsen, Magnus. "Le Prêtre-magicien et le dieu-magicien dans la Norvège ancienne," *RHR*, CXI (1935), 177–221.

Opler, Morris Edward. "The Creative Role of Shamanism in Mescalero Apache Mythology," *JAFL*, LIX, 233 (July–Sept., 1946), 268–81.

———. "Notes on Chiricahua Apache Culture. I: Supernatural Power and the Shaman," *PM*, XX, 1–2 (Jan.–Apr., 1947), 1–14.

O'Rahilly, Thomas F. *Early Irish History and Mythology*. Dublin, 1946.

Pallas, P. S. *Reise durch verschiedene Provinzen des russischen Reiches*. St. Petersburg, 1771–76. 3 vols.

Pallisen, N. "Die alte Religion der Mongolen und der Kultus Tchingis-Chans," *Numen*, III (1956), 178–229.

PANDER, EUGEN. "Das lamaische Pantheon," *ZE*, XXI (1889), 44–78

PARK, WILLARD Z. "Paviotso Shamanism," *AA*, n.s. XXXVI, 1 (Jan.–Mar., 1934), 98–113.

———. *Shamanism in Western North America: a Study in Cultural Relationships*. Evanston and Chicago, 1938. (Northwestern University Studies in the Social Sciences 2.)

PARKER, K. LANGLOH. *The Euahlayi Tribe: a Study of Aboriginal Life in Australia*. London, 1905.

PARROT, A. *Ziggurats et Tour de Babel*. Paris, 1949.

PARSONS, ELSIE CLEWS. *Pueblo Indian Religion*. Chicago, 1939. 2 vols

PARTANEN, JORMA. *A Description of Buriat Shamanism*. Helsinki, 1941–42. (*JSFO* LI.)

PÂRVAN, VASILE. *Getica. O protoistorie a Daciei*. Bucharest, 1926.

PAUL, OTTO. "Zur Geschichte der iranischen Religionen," *ARW* XXXVI (1940), 215–34.

PAULSON, IVAR. *Die primitiven Seelenvorstellungen der nordeurasischen Völker*. Stockholm, 1958.

———. *Schutzgeister und Gottheiten des Wildes (der Jagdtiere und Fische) in Nordeurasien*. Uppsala, 1961.

PELLIOT, PAUL. "Influence iranienne en Asie Centrale et en Extrême-Orient," *Revue d'histoire et de littérature religieuses* (Paris), 1912.

———. Review of *Der Hund in der Mythologie der zirkumpazifischen Völker*, by W. Koppers, *TP*, XXVIII, 3–5 (1931), 463–70.

———. "Sur quelques mots d'Asie Centrale attestés dans les textes chinois," *JA*, ser. XI, vol. I (Mar.–Apr., 1913), 451–69.

———. "Tängrim>tärim," *TP*, XXXVII (1944), 165–85.

PENZER, NORMAN MOSLEY, ed. *The Ocean of Story, being C. H. Tawney's translation of Somadeva's Kathā Sarit Sāgara (or Oceans of Streams of Story)*. London, 1924–28. 10 vols.

PERHAM, ARCHDEACON J. "Manangism in Borneo," *JRAS, Straits Branch* (Singapore), No. 19 (1887), 87–103.

PERING, BIRGER. "Die geflügelte Scheibe," *Archiv für Orientforschung* (Graz), VIII (1935), 281–96.

PERRY, W. J. *The Children of the Sun: a Study of the Early History of Civilization*. 2nd edn., London, 1926.

———. *The Megalithic Culture of Indonesia*. Manchester, 1918.

———. *The Primordial Ocean*. London, 1935.

PESTALOZZA, UBERTO. "Il manicheismo presso i Turchi occidentali ed orientali," *Reale Instituto Lombardo di Scienze e Lettere, rendiconti* (Milan), ser. II, vol. LXVII, fasc. 1–5 (1934), 417–97.

ᴇᴛʀɪ, Hᴇʟᴍᴜᴛ. "Der australische Medizinmann," *ALat*, XVI (1952), 159–317; XVII (1953), 157–225.

ᴇᴛʀᴜʟʟᴏ, Vɪɴᴄᴇɴᴢᴏ. "The Yaruros of the Capanaparo River, Venezuela," *Smithsonian Institution, BBEW 123, Anthropological Papers*, No. 11 (1939), 161–290.

ᴇᴛᴛᴀᴢᴢᴏɴɪ, Rᴀꜰꜰᴀᴇʟᴇ. "The Chain of Arrows: the Diffusion of a Mythical Motive," *Folklore* (London), XXXV (1924), 151–65. (Reprinted, with additions, as "La catena di frecce: saggio sulla diffusione di un motivo mitico," in his *Saggi di storia delle religioni e di mitologia* [q.v.], pp. 63–79.)

————. *Dio. Formazione e sviluppo del monoteismo nella storia delle religioni.* Rome, 1922.

————. *Essays on the History of Religions.* Leiden, 1954.

————. "Io and Rangi." In *Pro regno pro sanctuario, hommage à Van der Leeuw*, pp. 359–64.

————. *I Misteri: saggio di una teoria storico-religiosa.* Bologna, 1924. (Storia delle religione VII.)

————. *Miti e leggende.* I: *Africa, Australia.* Turin, 1948.

————. *Mitologia giapponese.* Bologna, 1929.

————. *L'onniscienza di Dio.* Turin, 1955.

————. *Saggi di storia delle religioni e di mitologia.* Rome, 1946.

ᴇᴛᴛᴇʀssᴏɴ, Oʟᴏꜰ. *Jabmek and Jabmeaime: a Comparative Study of the Dead and the Realm of the Dead in Lappish Religion.* Lund, 1957.

ʜɪʟʟɪᴘs, E. D. "The Legend of Aristeas: Fact and Fancy in Early Greek Notions of East Russia, Siberia, and Inner Asia," *ArtA*, XVIII, 2 (1955), 161–77.

ɪᴅᴅɪɴɢᴛᴏɴ, Rᴀʟᴘʜ. See Wɪʟʟɪᴀᴍsᴏɴ, R. W.

ɪʟsᴜᴅsᴋɪ, Bʀᴏɴɪsʟᴀᴠ. "Der Schamanismus bei den Ainu-Stämmen von Sachalin," *Globus*, XCV, 1 (1909), 72–78.

ɪᴘᴘɪᴅɪ, D. M. "Apothéoses impériales et apothéose de Pérégrinos," *SMSR*, XX (1947–48), 77–103.

————. *Recherches sur le culte impérial.* Bucharest, 1939.

ᴏʟíᴠᴋᴀ, G. See Bᴏʟᴛᴇ, J.

ᴏᴘᴏᴠ, A. A. "Consecration Ritual for a Blacksmith Novice among the Yakuts," *JAFL*, XLVI, 181 (July–Sept., 1933), 257–71.

————. *Seremonia ozhivlenia bubna u ostyak-samoyedov.* Leningrad, 1934.

Popov, A. A. *Tavgytzy: Materialy po etnografii avamskikh i vedeyevskikh tavgytzev.* Moscow and Leningrad, 1936. (AN, Trudy Instituta Anthropologii i Etnografii I, 5.)

Poppe, Nicholas N. Review of *Der Schamanismus bei den sibirischen Völkern,* by Georg Nioradze, *AM,* III (1926), 137–40.

————. Review of *Der Ursprung der Gottesidee,* vol. X, by W. Schmidt. *Anthropos,* XLVIII (1953), 327–32.

————. "Zum khalkhamongolischen Heldenepos," *AM,* V, 2 (1928) 183–213.

Potanin, G. N., *Ocherki severo-zapadnoi Mongolii.* St. Petersburg, 1881-83. 4 vols.

Potapov, L. P. "Obryad ozhivlenia shamanskovo bubna u tyurkoyazych nykh plemen Altaya," in AN, *Trudy Instituta Etnografii,* n.s. I, 159-82. Moscow, 1947.

———— and Menges, [Karl Heinrich]. *Materialien zur Volkskunde der Türkvölker des Altaj.* Berlin, 1934. (Mitteilungen des Seminars für orientalische Sprachen zu Berlin XXXVII.)

Pozdneyev, A. M. *Dhyāna und Samādhi im mongolischen Lamaismus.* Hannover, 1927. (Untersuchungen zur Geschichte des Buddhismus und verwandter Gebiete XXII.)

————. *Mongolskaya khrestomatia dlya pervonachalnavo prepodavani* (Mongolian Chrestomathy). St. Petersburg, 1900.

Priklonsky, V. L. "O shamanstve u yakutov," *Izvestia Vostochno Sibirskovo Otdela Russkovo Geograficheskovo Obshchestva* (Irkutsk) XVII, 1–2 (1886), 84–119. (German tr., "Das Schamanenthum der Jakuten,"*MAGW,* XVIII [1888], 165–82.)

Pripuzov, N. V. *Svedenia dlya izuchenia shamanstva u yakutov.* Irkutsk 1885.

Propp, V. I. [Vladimir Yakovlevich]. *Le radici storiche dei racconti di fate.* Turin, 1949. (Russian edn., Leningrad, 1946.)

Przyluski, Jean. "Un Ancien Peuple du Penjab: les Udumbara," *JA* CCVIII (Jan.–Mar., 1926), 1–59.

————. "Les Sept Terrasses de Barabuḍur," *HJAS,* I, 2 (July, 1936) 251–56.

Pulver, Max. "The Experience of Light in the Gospel of St. John, in the 'Corpus hermeticum,' in Gnosticism, and in the Eastern Church," in *Spiritual Disciplines* (Papers from the Eranos Yearbooks, 4), pp 239–66. 1960. (BS XXX.4.) Also London, 1960.

QUIGSTAD, J. *Lappische Heilkunde*. Oslo, 1932.

RADCLIFFE-BROWN, A. R. *The Andaman Islanders: a Study in Social Anthropology*. Cambridge, 1922.

RADIN, PAUL. *Primitive Religion: Its Nature and Origin*. New York, 1937. 2nd edn. (new foreword), New York, 1957.

———. *The Road of Life and Death: a Ritual Drama of the American Indians*. 1945. (BS V.)

RADLOV (RADLOFF), WILHELM. *Aus Sibirien: lose Blätter aus dem Tagebuche eines reisenden Linguisten*. Leipzig, 1884. 2 vols. in 1.

———. *Proben der Volksliteratur der türkischen Stämme Süd-Sibiriens und der tsungarischen Steppe*. St. Petersburg, 1866–1907. 10 vols.

RAHMANN, RUDOLF. "Shamanistic and Related Phenomena in Northern and Middle India," *Anthropos*, LIV (1959), 681–760.

RAINGEARD, P. *Hermès psychagogue. Essai sur les origines du culte d'Hermès*. Paris, 1935.

RAMSTEDT, G. J. "The Relation of the Altaic Languages to Other Language Groups," *JSFO*, LIII, 1 (1946–47), 15–26.

———. "Zur Frage nach der Stellung der tschuwassichen," *JSFO*, XXXVIII (1922–23), 1–34.

RÄNK, GUSTAV. *Die heilige Hinterecke im Hauskult der Völker Nordosteuropas und Nordasiens*. 1949. (FFC LVII, 137.)

———. "Lapp Female Deities of the Madder-Akka Group," *SS*, VI (1955), 7–79.

RANKE, KURT. *Indogermanische Totenverehrung*. I: *Der dreissigste und vierzigste Tag im Totenkult der Indogermanen*. 1951. (FFC LIX, 140.)

RÄSÄNEN, MARTTI. *Regenbogen-Himmelsbrücke*. 1947. (SO XIV, 1.)

RASMUSSEN, KNUD. *Across Arctic America*. New York and London, 1927.

———. *Intellectual Culture of the Copper Eskimos*, tr. W. E. Calvert. Copenhagen, 1932. (RFTE IX.)

———. *Intellectual Culture of the Iglulik Eskimos*, tr. William Worster. Copenhagen, 1930. (RFTE VII, 1.)

———. *The Netsilik Eskimos: Social Life and Spiritual Culture*, tr. W. E. Calvert. Copenhagen, 1931. (RFTE VIII, 1–2.)

———. *Die Thulefahrt*. Frankfurt a. M., 1926.

REAGAN, ALBERT B. *Notes on the Indians of the Fort Apache Region*. 1930. (AMNH Anthropological Papers XXXI, Pt. V.)

REINHOLD-MÜLLER, F. G. "Die Krankheits- und Heilgottheiten des Lamaismus," *Anthropos*, XXII (1927), 956–91.

RENEL, C. "L'Arc-en-ciel dans la tradition religieuse de l'antiquité," *RHR*, XLVI (1902), 58–80.

RIBBACH, S. H. *Drogpa Namgyal. Ein Tibeterleben.* Munich and Planegg, 1940.

RICHTHOFEN, BOLKO, FREIHERR VON. "Zur Frage der archäologischen Beziehungen zwischen Nordamerika und Nordasiens," *Anthropos*, XXVII (1932), 123–51.

RIESENFELD, A. *The Megalithic Culture of Melanesia.* Leiden, 1950.

RISLEY, H. H. *The Tribes and Castes of Bengal.* Calcutta, 1891–92. 4 vols.

RIVET, PAUL. "Les Australiens en Amérique," *Bulletin de la Société de Linguistique de Paris*, XXVI (1925), 23–63.

———. "Les Malayo-Polynésiens en Amérique," *JSA*, n.s. XVII (1926), 141–278.

———. "Les Mélano-Polynésiens et les Australiens en Amérique," *Anthropos*, XX (1925), 51–54.

———. *Les Origines de l'homme américain.* Montreal, 1943; 2nd edn. Paris, 1957. (Also tr.: *Los origines del hombre americano.* Mexico, 1943.)

ROBLES RODRIGUEZ, EULOJIO. "Guillatunes, costumbres y creencias araucanas," *Anales de la Universidad de Chile* (Santiago), CXXVI (1910), 151–77.

RÖCK, FRITZ. "Neunmalneun und Siebenmalsieben," *MAGW*, LX (1930), 320–30.

ROCK, JOSEPH F. *The Ancient Na-khi Kingdom of Southwest China.* Cambridge (Mass.), 1947. (Harvard-Yenching Institute Monograph Series IX.) 2 vols.

———. "Contributions to the Shamanism of the Tibetan-Chinese Borderland," *Anthropos*, LIV (1959), 796–818.

———. "The Muan bpö Ceremony or the Sacrifice to Heaven as Practiced by the Na-khi," *MS*, XIII (1948), 1–160.

———. "Studies in Na-khi Literature: I. The Birth and Origin of Dto-mba Shi-lo, the Founder of the Mo-so Shamanism, According to Mo-so Manuscripts," *ArtA*, VII, fasc. 1–4 (1937), 5–85; *BEFEO*, XXXVII (1937), 1–39; ". . . II. The Na-khi ¹Hă ²zhi ¹p'i or the Road the Gods Decide," *BEFEO*, XXXVII (1937), 40–119.

———. *The Zhi Mä Funeral Ceremony of the Na-khi of Southwest China Described and Translated from Na-khi Manuscripts.* Vienna and Mödling, 1955.

ROCKHILL, WILLIAM WOODVILLE. *The Land of the Lamas: Notes of a Journey through China, Mongolia, and Tibet.* New York and London, 1891.

———. "On the Use of Skulls in Lamaist Ceremonies," *Proceedings of the American Oriental Society* (New Haven), XL (1888; pub. 1890), xxiv–xxxi.

RÖDER, JOSEPH G. *Alahatala. Die Religion der Inlandstämme Mittelcerams.* Bamberg, 1948.

RODRÍGUEZ, EULOJIO ROBLES. See ROBLES RODRÍGUEZ, EULOJIO.

ROHDE, ERWIN. *Psyche: the Cult of Souls and Belief in Immortality among the Greeks,* tr. from 8th German edn. by W. B. Hillis. New York and London, 1925.

RÓHEIM, GÉZA. *The Eternal Ones of the Dream: a Psychoanalytic Interpretation of Australian Myth and Ritual.* New York, 1945.

———. "Hungarian Shamanism," *Psychoanalysis and the Social Sciences* (New York), III, 4 (1951), 131–69.

———. *Hungarian and Vogul Mythology.* New York, 1954. (Monographs of the American Ethnological Society XXIII.)

ROSENBERG, F. "On Wine and Feasts in the Iranian National Epic," *Journal of the K. R. Cama Oriental Institute* (Bombay), No. 19 (1931), pp. 13–44. (Tr. from Russian by L. Bogdanov.)

ROSETTI, A. *Colindele Românilor.* Bucharest, 1920.

ROTH, H. LING. *The Natives of Sarawak and British North Borneo, Based Chiefly on the Mss. of the Late Hugh Brooke Low.* With a preface by Andrew Lang. London, 1896. 2 vols.

ROTH, WALTER E. "An Inquiry into the Animism and Folk-Lore of the Guiana Indians," *30th RBEW* (1908–9; pub. 1915), pp. 103–386.

ROUSSELLE, ERWIN. "Die Typen der Meditation in China," in *Chinesisch-deutscher Almanach für das Jahr 1932.* (China Institut, Frankfurt [a. M.] Universität.)

ROUX, JEAN-PAUL. "Eléments chamaniques dans les textes pré-mongols," *Anthropos,* LIII, 1–2 (1958), 440–56.

———. "Le Nom du chaman dans les textes turco-mongols," *Anthropos,* LIII, 1–2 (1958), 133–42.

———. "Tängri. Essai sur le ciel-dieu des peuples altaïques," *RHR,* CXLIX (1956), 49–82, 197–230; CL (1956), 27–54, 173–231.

ROWLAND, BENJAMIN, JR. "Studies in the Buddhist Art of Bāmiyān: the Bodhisattva of Group E," in *Art and Thought, Issued in Honour of Dr.*

Ananda K. Coomaraswamy on the Occasion of His 70th Birthday, pp. 46–54. London, 1947.

ROY, SARAT CHANDRA. *The Birhors: a Little-Known Jungle Tribe of Chota Nagpur*. Ranchi, 1925.

RUBEN, WALTER. "Eisenschmiede und Dämonen in Indien," *IAE*, Suppl. XXXVII (1939).

——. "Schamanismus im alten Indien," *AO*, XVII (1939), 164–205.

RUDOLF OF FULDA (with MEGINHART). *Translatio S. Alexandri*, in *Monumenta Germaniae historica* (ed. G. H. Pertz, 1826–   ), *Scriptorum Tomus* 2. Hannover. (For translation into German, see RICHTER, B. *Die Geschichtschreiber der deutschen Vorzeit*, VI. 2nd edn., Leipzig, 1889.)

RUNEBERG, ARNE. *Witches, Demons and Fertility Magic: Analysis of Their Significance and Mutual Relations in West-European Folk Religion.* Helsinki, 1947.

RUSSU, ION I. "Religia Geto-Dacilor," *Annuarul Institutului de Studii Clasice* (Cluj), V (1947), 61–137.

SAHAGÚN, BERNARDINO DE. See BERNARDINO DE SAHAGÚN.

SAINTYVES, P. (pseud.). See NOURRY, E.

SALMONY, ALFRED. *Antler and Tongue: an Essay on Ancient Chinese Symbolism and Its Implications.* Ascona, 1954.

SANDSCHEJEW, GARMA. "Weltanschauung und Schamanismus der Alaren-Burjaten," tr. from Russian by R. Augustin, *Anthropos*, XXVII (1927–28), 576, 613, 933–55; XXVIII (1928), 538–60, 967–86.

SANGUINETTI, B. R. See DEFRÉMERY, CHARLES FRANÇOIS.

SANJANA, DARAB DASTUR PESHOTAN, ed. and tr. "Dinkart IX," in his *The Dinkard, Bk. IX: Contents of the Gathic Nasks*, Pt. I. Bombay, 1922.

SAUVAGEOT, AURÉLIEN. "Eskimo et Ouralien," *JSA*, n.s. XVI (1924), 279–316.

SAXL, F. *Mithras*. Berlin, 1931.

SCHAEFNER, A. *Origine des instruments de musique*. Paris, 1936.

SCHÄRER, HANS. *Die Gottesidee der Ngadju Dajak in Süd-Borneo*. Leiden, 1946.

——. "Die Vorstellungen der Ober- und Unterwelt bei den Ngadju Dajak von Süd-Borneo," *Cultureel Indie* (Leiden), IV (1942), 73–81.

SCHEBESTA, PAUL. "Jenseitsglaube der Semang auf Malakka," in *Festschrift. Publication d'hommage offerte au P[ère]. W. Schmidt*, ed. W. Koppers. Vienna, 1928.

ЅCHEBESTA, PAUL. *Les Pygmées*. Paris, 1940. (Tr. from German by F. Berge.)

ЅCHLERATH, BERNFRIED. "Der Hund bei den Indogermanen," *Paideuma*, VI, 1 (Nov., 1954), 25–40.

ЅCHMIDT, J. "Das Etymon des persischen Schamane," *Nyelvtudományi közlemények* (Budapest), XLIV, 470–74.

ЅCHMIDT, LEOPOLD. "Der 'Herr der Tiere' in einigen Sagenlandschaften Europas und Eurasiens," *Anthropos*, XLVII (1952), 509–39.

———. "Pelops und die Haselhexe," *Laos* (Stockholm), I (1951), 67–78.

ЅCHMIDT, WILHELM. *Grundlinien einer Vergleichung der Religionen und Mythologien der austronesischen Völker*. Vienna, 1910. (Denkschriften der kaiserlichen Akademie der Wissenschaften in Wien, Phil.-hist. Klasse LIII.)

———. *Handbuch der Methode der kulturhistorische Ethnologie*. Münster, 1937.

———. "Der heilige Mittelpfahl des Hauses," *Anthropos*, XXXV–XXXVI (1939–41), 966–69.

———. "Das Himmelsopfer bei den innerasiatischen Pferdezüchtervölkern," *Ethnos*, VII (1942), 127–48.

———. "Die kulturhistorische Methode und die nordamerikanische Ethnologie," *Anthropos*, XIV–XV (1919–20), 546–63.

———. "Kulturkreise und Kulturschichten in Süd-Amerika," *ZE*, XLV (1913), 1014–1124.

———. *Der Ursprung der Gottesidee: eine historisch-kritische und positive Studie*. Münster, 1912–55. 12 vols.

ЅCHRAM, L. M. J. *The Monguors of the Kansu-Tibetan Border*. Pt. II: *Their Religious Life*. Philadelphia, 1957.

ЅCHRÖDER, DOMINIK. "Zur Religion der Tujen des Sininggebietes (Kukunor)," *Anthropos*, XLVII (1952), 1–79, 620–58, 822–70; XLVIII (1953), 202–59.

———. "Zur Struktur des Schamanismus," *Anthropos*, L (1955), 849–81.

ЅCHURTZ, HEINRICH. *Altersklassen und Männerbünde*. Berlin, 1902.

ЅCHUSTER, CARL. *Joint-Marks: a Possible Index of Cultural Contact between America, Oceania and the Far East*. Amsterdam, 1951. (Koninklijk Instituut voor de Tropen, Mededeling 94.)

———. "A Survival of the Eurasiatic Animal Style in Modern Alaskan

561

Eskimo," in *Indian Tribes of Aboriginal America: Selected Papers of the 29th International Congress of Americanists*, ed. Sol Tax, III, 34–45. Chicago, 1952.

SELER, EDWARD. *Gesammelte Abhandlungen zur amerikanischen Sprach- und Alterthumskunde*. Berlin, 1902–13. 5 vols.

———. "Zauberei im alten Mexiko," *Globus*, LXXVIII, 6 (Aug. 11, 1900), 89–91. (Reprinted in his *Gesammelte Abhandlungen* [q.v.], II, 78–86.)

SELIGMAN, C. G. *The Melanesians of British New Guinea* (with a chapter by F. R. Barton and an appendix by E. L. Giblin). Cambridge, 1910.

SHASHKOV, S. *Shamanstvo v Sibirii*. St. Petersburg, 1864.

SHIMKEVICH, P. P. *Materialy dlya izucheniya shamanstva u goldov*. Khabarovsk, 1896.

SHIMKIN, B. D. "A Sketch of the Ket, or Yenisei 'Ostyak,' " *Ethnos*, IV (1939), 147–76.

SHIROKOGOROFF (SHIROKOGOROV), SERGEI M. "General Theory of Shamanism among the Tungus," *JRAS, North-China Branch* (Shanghai), LIV (1923), 246–49.

———. "Northern Tungus Migrations in the Far East (Goldi and Their Ethnical Affinities)," *JRAS, North-China Branch* (Shanghai), LVI (1926), 123–83.

———. *Psychomental Complex of the Tungus*. London, 1935.

———. "Versuch einer Erforschung der Grundlagen des Schamanentums bei den Tungusen," *Baessler-Archiv* (Berlin), XVIII, Pt. II (1935), 41–96. (Tr. of article in Russian published at Vladivostok, 1919.)

———. See also MIRONOV, N. D.

SIEROSZEWSKI, WENCESLAS. "Du chamanisme d'après les croyances des Yakoutes," *RHR*, XLVI (1902), 204–33, 299–338.

———. *Yakuty*. St. Petersburg, 1896. (See abridged tr. by WILLIAM G. SUMNER [q.v.], "The Yakuts.")

SINOR, D. "Ouralo-altaïque-indo-européen," *TP*, XXXVII (1944), 226–44.

SKEAT, W. W. *Malay Magic*. London, 1900.

———. and BLAGDEN, C. O. *Pagan Races of the Malay Peninsula*. London, 1906. 2 vols.

SLAWIK, ALEXANDER. "Kultische Geheimbünde der Japaner und Germanen," in *Die Indogermanen- und Germanenfrage: neue Wege zu ihrer Lösung*, pp. 675–763. 1936. (WBKL IV.)

SMITH, A. H. See SNORRI STURLUSON.

SNELLGROVE, DAVID L. *Buddhist Himalaya*. New York, 1957.

SNORRI STURLUSON. *The Prose Edda*, tr. Arthur Gilchrist Brodeur. New York and London, 1916; 2nd printing, 1923. (Scandinavian Classics V.)

————. "Ynglinga Saga," in *Heimskringla, or the Lives of the Norse Kings*, ed. and tr. Erling Monsen (with the assistance of A. H. Smith). Cambridge, 1932.

SÖDERBLOM, N. *La Vie future d'après le mazdéisme*. Paris, 1901.

SOMADEVA. See PENZER, NORMAN MOSLEY.

SPEISER, FELIX. "Melanesien und Indonesien," *ZE*, LXX, 6 (1938), 463–81.

SPENCER, BALDWIN, and GILLEN, F. J. *The Arunta: a Study of a Stone Age People*. London, 1927. 2 vols.

————. *The Native Tribes of Central Australia*. London, 1899.

————. *The Northern Tribes of Central Australia*. London, 1904.

SPIER, LESLIE. *Klamath Ethnography*. Berkeley, 1930. (CPAAE XXX.)

————. *The Prophet Dance of the Northwest and Its Derivatives: the Source of the Ghost Dance*. 1935. (GSA 1.)

————. *Yuman Tribes of the Gila River*. Chicago, 1933.

SPIES, WALTER. See ZOETE, BERYL DE.

SSÛ-MA CH'IEN. See CHAVANNES, ÉDOUARD.

STEFÁNSSON, VILHJÁLMUR. "The MacKenzie Eskimo," in *The Stefánsson-Anderson Arctic Expedition of the American Museum. Preliminary Ethnological Report*, pp. 133–50. (AMNH Anthropological Papers XIV.)

STEIN, ROLF A. "Leao-Tche," *TP*, XXXV (1940), 1–154.

————. *Recherches sur l'épopée et le barde au Tibet*. Paris, 1959.

STEINEN, KARL VON DEN. *Unter den Naturvölkern Zentral-Brasiliens. Reiseschilderung und Ergebnisse der zweiten Schingu-Expedition, 1887–1888*. Berlin, 1894.

STEINER, F. B. "Skinboats and the Yakut 'Xayik,'" *Ethnos*, IV (1939), 177–83.

STEINMANN, ALFRED. "Eine Geisterschiffmalerei aus Südborneo," *Jahrbuch des Bernischen Historischen Museums in Bern*, XXII (1942), 107–12. (Also published separately.)

————. "Das kultische Schiff in Indonesien," *IPEK*, XIII–XIV (1939–40), 149–205.

STERNBERG, LEO. "Der Adlerkult bei den Völkern Sibiriens: Vergleich
ende Folklore-Studie," *ARW*, XXVIII (1930), 125–53.

———. "Die Auserwählung im sibirischen Schamanismus," *ZMKRW*
L (1935), 229–52.

———. "Divine Election in Primitive Religion," in Congrès Inter
national des Américanistes, *Compte-Rendu de la XXIᵉ session, Pt.*
(1924), pp. 472–512. Göteborg, 1925.

STEVENSON, MATILDA COXE. *The Zuñi Indians: Their Mythology, Esoter*
Fraternities, and Ceremonies. 1904. (23rd RBEW [1901–02].)

STEWARD, JULIAN H. "Shamanism among the Marginal Tribes," in hi
Handbook of South American Indians (q.v.), pp. 650 ff.

———, ed. *Handbook of American Indians North of Mexico.* 1907, 1910
(BBEW 30, Pts. I–II.) 2 vols.

———. *Handbook of South American Indians.* Washington, 1949.

STEWART, C. S. *A Visit to the South Seas, in the United States' Shi*
Vincennes, during the Years 1829 and 1830. New York, 1831; London
1832. 2 vols.

STIEDA, L. "Das Schamanenthum unter den Burjäten," *Globus*, LII, 1
(1887), 250–53.

STIGLMAYR, ENGELBERT. "Schamanismus bei den Negritos Südostasiens,"
WVM, II, 2 (1954), 156–64; III, 1 (1955), 14–21; IV, 1 (1956), 135
47. (With English summary.)

———. "Schamanismus in Australien," *WVM*, V, 2 (1957), 161–90

STIRLING, MATTHEW W. "Jivaro Shamanism," *Proceedings of the America*
Philosophical Society (Philadelphia), LXXII, 3 (1933), 137–45.

STÖHR, WALDEMAR. *Das Totenritual der Dajak.* Cologne, 1959. (Ethno
gica, n.s. I.)

STRÖMBÄCK, DAG. *Sejd. Textstudier i nordisk religionshistoria.* Stockholr
and Copenhagen, 1935.

SUMMERS, MONTAGUE. *The Werewolf.* London, 1933.

SUMNER, WILLIAM G., tr. "The Yakuts. Abridged from the Russian c
Sieroszewski," *JRAI*, XXXI (1901), 65–110.

SWANTON, JOHN R. "Shamans and Priests," in STEWARD, JULIAN H., ed
Handbook of American Indians North of Mexico (q.v.), II, 522–24.

———. "Social Conditions, Beliefs, and Linguistic Relationship of th
Tlingit Indians," *26th RBEW* (1904–5; pub. 1908), pp. 391–485

SYDOW, C. W. VON. "Tors färd till Utgard. I: Tors bockslaktning,"
Danske Studier (Copenhagen), 1910, pp. 65–105, 145–82.

ᴛALLGREN, Aarne Michael. "The Copper Idols from Galich and Their Relatives," *Studia orientalia* (Helsinki), I (1925), 312–41.

——. *Zur westsibirischen Gruppe der "schamanistischen Figuren."* Prague, 1931. (Seminarium Kondakovianum IV.)

ᴛAWNEY, Charles Henry. See Penzer, Norman Mosley.

ᴛCHENG-TSU Shang. "Der Schamanismus in China." Diss., Hamburg, 1934.

ᴛEGNAEUS, Harry. *Le Héros civilisateur. Contribution à l'étude ethnologique de la religion et de la sociologie africaines.* Uppsala, 1950.

ᴛEIT, James A. *The Lillooet Indians.* Leiden, 1906. (AMNH Memoirs IV; JE II, 5.)

——. "The Thompson Indians of British Columbia," *AMNH Memoirs*, II (1900), 163–392. (JE I.)

ᴛHALBITZER, William, "Cultic Games and Festivals in Greenland," in Congrès International des Américanistes, *Compte-Rendu de la XXIᵉ session, Pt. 2* (1924), pp. 236–55. Göteborg, 1925.

——. "The Heathen Priests of East Greenland (Angakut)," in *Verhandlungen des XVI Internationalen Amerikanisten-Kongresses, Pt. 2* (1908), pp. 447–64. Vienna and Leipzig, 1910.

——. "Le Magiciens esquimaux, leurs conception du monde, de l'âme et de la vie," *JSA*, n.s. XXII (1930), 73–106.

——. "Parallels within the Culture of the Arctic Peoples," in *Annaes do XX Congresso Internacional de Americanistas, Pt. 1* (1924), 283–87. Rio de Janeiro, 1925.

——, ed. *The Ammasalik Eskimo: Contributions to the Ethnology of the East Greenland Natives.* Copenhagen, 1914.

ᴛHOMPSON, B. *The Figians.* London, 1908.

ᴛHOMPSON, Stith. *Motif-Index of Folk-Literature.* Helsinki and Bloomington, 1932–36. (FFC 106–09, 116–17; Indiana University Studies 96, 97, 100, 101, 105, 106, 108, 110–12.) 6 vols. (2dn edn., rev. and enlarged, 1955–57. 6 vols. in 4.)

ᴛHORNDIKE, Lynn. *A History of Magic and Experimental Science.* New York, 1923–58. 8 vols.

ᴛHURN, Everard F. Im. See Im Thurn, Everard F.

ᴛIN, Pe Maung, tr. *The Path of Purity, Being a Translation of Buddhaghoṣa's Visuddhimagga.* London, 1923–31. (PTS XI, XVII, XXI.) 3 vols.

TOIVOINEN, Y. H. "Le Gros Chêne des chants populaires finnois," *JSFO* LIII (1946–47), 37–77.

TRETYAKOV, P. I. *Turukhansky krai, evo priroda i zhiteli.* St. Petersburg 1871.

TUCCI, GUISEPPE. *Tibetan Painted Scrolls.* Rome, 1949. 2 vols.

VAJDA, LÁSZLO. "Zur phaseologischen Stellung des Schamanismus," *Ural-altaische Jahrbücher* (Wiesbaden), XXXI (1959), 455–85.

VAN EMELEN, REV. ARTHUR. See HOFFMANN, REV. JOHN.

VAN DER KROEF, JUSTUS M. "Transvestitism and the Religious Hermaph rodite in Indonesia," *Journal of East Asiatic Studies* (Manila), III, (Apr., 1954), 257–65.

VANDIER, JACQUES. *La Religion égyptienne.* Paris, 1944.

VANNICELLI, LUIGI. *La religione dei Lolo.* Milan, 1944.

VASILYEV, V. N. *Shamansky kostyum i buben u yakutov.* St. Petersburg 1910. (Sbornik Muzeya po Antropologii i Etnografii pri Imperator skoi Akademii Nauk I, 8.)

VISSER, MARINUS WILLEM DE. *The Arhats in China and Japan.* Berlin 1923.

VRIES, JAN DE. *Altgermanische Religionsgeschichte.* Berlin and Leipzig 1935–37; 2nd edn., 1956–57. 2 vols.

WALES, H. G. QUARITCH. *The Mountain of God: a Study in Early Religio and Kingship.* London, 1953.

———. *Prehistory and Religion in South-East Asia.* London, 1957

WALEY, ARTHUR. *The Nine Songs: a Study of Shamanism in Ancient China* London, 1955.

WALLESER, MAX. "Religiöse Anschauungen und Gebräuche der Be wohner von Jap, Deutsche Südsee," *Anthropos*, VII (1913), 607–29

WARNECK, J. *Die Religion der Batak.* Leipzig, 1909.

WASSÉN, S. HENRY. See HOLMER, NILS M.

WATSON, WILLIAM. "A Grave Guardian from Ch'ang-sha," *Britis Museum Quarterly* (London), XVII, 3 (1952), 52–56.

WEBSTER, HUTTON. *Magic: a Sociological Study.* Stanford, 1948.

———. *Primitive Secret Societies: a Study in Early Politics and Religion* New York, 1908; 2nd, rev. edn., 1932.

———. *Taboo: a Sociological Study.* Stanford, 1942.

WEHRLI, HANS J. "Beitrag zur Ethnologie der Chingpaw (Kachin) vo Ober-Burma," *IAE*, Suppl. XVI (1904).

Weil, Raymond. *Le Champ des roseaux et le champ des offrandes dans la religion funéraire et la religion générale*. Paris, 1936.

Weinberger-Goebel, Kira. "Melanesische Jenseitsgedanken," *WBKL*, V (1943), 95–124.

Weisser-Aall, Lily. "Hexe," in *Handwörterbuch des deutschen Aberglaubens*, ed. Hanns Bächtold-Stäubli, III. Berlin, 1927–42. 10 vols.

Wensinck, A. J. *The Ideas of the Western Semites concerning the Navel of the Earth*. Amsterdam, 1917.

———. *Tree and Bird as Cosmological Symbols in Western Asia*. Amsterdam, 1921.

Werner, Alice. *African [Mythology]*. 1925. (MAR VII.)

Wernert, P. "L'Anthropophagie rituelle et la chasse aux têtes aux époques actuelle et paléolithique," *L'Anthropologie*, XLVI (1936), 33–43.

———. "Culte des crânes. Représentations des esprits des défunts et des ancêtres," in Gorce, M., and Mortier, R., *L'Histoire générale des religions* (q.v.), pp. 51–102.

West, E. W., tr. *Pahlavi Texts*. I: *The Bundahiš, Bahman Yašt, and Shâyast lâ-Shâyast*; II: *The Dâdistân-î Dînîk and The Epistles of Mânûškîhar*. 1880–97. (SBE, V, XVIII, XXIV, XXXVII, XLVII.) 5 vols. (Vol. I, 1880; Vol. II, 1882.)

———. See also Haug, Martin.

Weyer, Edward Moffatt, Jr. *The Eskimos: Their Environment and Folkways*. New Haven and London, 1932.

White, C. M. N. "Witchcraft, Divination and Magic among the Balovale Tribes," *Africa* (London), XVIII (1948), 81–104.

Whitehead, George. *In the Nicobar Islands*. London, 1924.

Widengren, George. *The Ascension of the Apostle of God and the Heavenly Book*. Uppsala and Leipzig, 1950.

———. *Hochgottglaube im alten Iran*. Uppsala and Leipzig, 1938.

———. *The King and the Tree of Life in Ancient Near Eastern Religion*. Uppsala, 1951.

———. "Stand und Aufgaben der iranischen Religionsgeschichte," *Numen*, I (1954), 26–83; II (1955), 47–134.

Wieschoff, Heinz. *Die afrikanischen Trommeln und ihre ausserafrikanischen Beziehungen*. Stuttgart, 1933.

Wikander, Stig. *Der arische Männerbund*. Lund, 1938.

WIKANDER, STIG. *Vayu; Texte und Untersuchungen zur indo-iranischen Religionsgeschichte.* Uppsala, 1941.

WILHELM, RICHARD, tr. *Chinesische Volksmärchen.* Jena, 1927 (Märchen der Weltliteratur, ser. II.)

WILKE, GEORG. "Der Weltenbaum und die beiden kosmischen Vögel in der vorgeschichtlichen Kunst," *Mannus-Bibliothek* (Leipzig), XIV (1922), 73–99.

WILKEN, G. A. *Het Shamanisme bij de Volken van den Indischen Archipel.* The Hague, 1887. (Reprint of article in *Bijdragen tot de Taal- Land- en Volkenkunde van Nederlandsch Indie* [The Hague], V, Pt. II [1887], 427–97.)

WILLIAMSON, ROBERT W. *Essays in Polynesian Ethnology,* ed. Ralph Piddington. Cambridge, 1939.

———. *Religion and Social Organization in Central Polynesia,* ed. Ralph Piddington. Cambridge, 1937.

WILSON, HORACE HAYMAN, tr. *Ṛig-Veda Sanhitá: a Collection of Ancient Hindu Hymns, Constituting the First Ashtake, or Book of the Ṛig-Veda.* London, 1854–88. 6 vols.

WINSTEDT, SIR RICHARD O. "Indian Influence in the Malay World," *JRAS,* Pts. III–IV (1944), pp. 186–96.

———. "Kingship and Enthronement in Malaya," *JRAS,* Pts. III–IV (1945), pp. 134–45.

———. *Shaman, Saiva and Sufi: a Study of the Evolution of Malay Magic.* London, 1925.

WIRZ, PAUL. *Exorzismus und Heilkunde auf Ceylon.* Bern, 1941.

———. *Die Marind-anim von Hollandisch-Süd-Neu-Guinea.* Hamburg, 1922–25. 2 vols.

WISSLER, CLARK. *The American Indian.* New York, 1917; 2nd edn., 1922; 3rd edn., 1938.

———. *General Discussion of Shamanistic and Dancing Societies.* 1916. (AMNH Anthropological Papers XI, Pt. XII.)

WOLFRAM, R. "Robin Hood und Hobby Horse," *WPZ,* XIX (1932).

WOLTERS, PAUL. *Der geflügelte Seher.* Munich, 1928. (Sitzungsberichte der Akademie der Wissenschaften, Phil.-hist. Klasse I.)

WOODWARD, FRANK LEE, tr. *The Book of the Gradual Sayings (Anguttara-Nikāya) or More Numbered Suttas.* 1932–36. (PTS 22, 24–27.) 5 vols.

WRIGHT, ARTHUR FREDERICK. "Fo-tʻu-têng: a Biography," *HJAS,* XI (1948), 321–71.

Wüst, Walther. "Bestand die zoroastrische Urgemeinde wirklich aus berufsmässigen Ekstatikern und schamanisierenden Rinderhirten der Steppe?" *ARW*, XXXVI, 2 (1940), 234–49.

———. "Yasna XLII 4, 2/3," *ARW*, XXXVI, 2 (1940), 250–56.

Wylick, Carla van. *Bestattungsbrauchs und Jenseitsglaube auf Celebes.* The Hague, 1941. (Diss., Basel, 1940.)

Yasser, J. "Musical Moments in the Shamanistic Rites of the Siberian Pagan Tribes," *Pro-Musica Quarterly* (New York), Mar.–June, 1926, 4–15.

Yule, Sir Henry, tr. *The Book of Ser Marco Polo*, ed. Henri Cordier. London, 1921. 2 vols.

Zelenin, D. "Ein erotischer Ritus in den Opferungen der altaischen Tuerken," *IAE*, XXIX, 4–6 (1928), 83–98.

———. *Kult ongonov v Sibiri. Perezhitki totemisma v ideologii sibirskikh narodov.* Moscow, 1936.

Zemmrich, Johannes. "Toteninseln und verwandte geographische Mythen," *IAE*, IV (1891), 217–44.

Zerries, Otto. "Krankheitsdämonen und Hilfsgeister des Medizinmannes in Südamerika," in *Proceedings of the 30th International Congress of Americanists*, pp. 162–78. London, 1955.

———. *Wild- und Buschgeister in Südamerika.* Wiesbaden, 1954.

Zimmer, Heinrich. *The King and the Corpse: Tales of the Soul's Conquest of Evil*, ed. Joseph Campbell. New York, 1948. (BS XI.) (Princeton/Bollingen paperback, 1971.)

Zoete, Beryl de, and Spies, Walter. *Dance and Drama in Bali.* London, 1938.

INDEX

INDEX

A

Aarne, Antti, 98n
abagaldei, 151
Abakan Tatars, 153n, 193, 208, 266, 270
Abaris, 388, 389n
abassy, 74f, 206; -oibono, 234; /ojuna
(oyuna), 184
Abbott, J., 475n
Aberle, David F., 24n
aberration, shamanic, 12, 493f
abhijñās, 409n
"above" and "below," 186 & n
Abyrga, 122n
accidents: and initiation/vocation, 45, 81;
medicine man and, 32
acham, 435
Achomawi, 105, 305ff
Ackerknecht, Erwin H., 323n
Adam, 161, 268
Adam of Bremen, 375
Adriani, N., and Kruyt, A. C., 354n, 358n
Aegean, 379, 388
aerobates, 390
Africa, 374n; children's souls, 273; lad-
der in, 490; mentality of shamans, 31;
origin of man from trees, 273n; shamanic
costume, 178; smiths in, 472f; South,
21; West, 92
Agapitov, N. N., and Khangalov, M. N.,
69n, 115n, 150, 152, 185n, 250n
Agaricus muscarius, 400
age, paradisal, see time
aggressiveness, 509
Aghorīs, 434n
ahistoricity, of religious life, xix
Ahlbrinck, W., 127n
Ahmed ibn Fadlan, 384
Ahriman, 122n, 271n
Ahura-Mazda, 399
Ai Oyuna, see Ajy Ojuna
Ai/Ajy, 70n
Aïjä/Aijo/Aije, 71n
Ainu, 262
Aisyt, 80n, 185n
Aitareya Brāhmaṇa, 403n, 412n
Ai Toyon, 69f, 275

Ajy Ojuna/Ai Oyuna/ajy oyuna, 71n, 184
akarata, 370n, 371
Ak Ayas, 9
ak kam, 189
Akwaala, 109
Alarsk Buryat, see Buryat
Alaska, 336; southern, 334n; see also Es-
kimo, Alaskan
Alcestis, 391
alchemy: and flight, 411, 479; Indian,
410; ladder in, 490
Alchera/Alcheringa, 46, 48
alcohol, 401
Alekseyev, Gavril, 36
Alexander, Hartley Burr, 163n, 262n,
490n
Alföldi, András, 459n
Algonkin, 262, 321, 334
Alibamu, 312f
allara kyrar, 234
alligator bench, 128
a'lma, 245
Almgren, O., 355n
Alpine countries, 161n
Altai/Altaians/Altaic shamans, 44, 84,
166, 181, 208, 263, 278; and
Araucanians, comparison, 326; ascent to
sky, xiv, 275; bow, 175; costume, 146,
152ff, 155, 156; and death, 206;
"flues," 262; gods, 10, 277; groups of,
189; and heavens, 406; recruiting, 20;
refrains of, 96; sacrifices, 182, 198f;
séances among, 190ff; and souls/spirits
of dead, 84, 88, 89, 169; and Supreme
Being, 198ff
Altai Kan, 193
Altai mountains, 201
Altai Tatars, 9, 120, 182f, 205, 261, 266
alter ego, 94, 170
Altheim, Franz, 165n, 396n, 460n, 470n;
and Haussig, Hans-Wilhelm, 70n
Ama, 226
āmägät, 16, 90, 149, 231, 233
Amahuaca, 83
Amana, 129
Amandry, Pierre, 387n

Amazonian: region, 327; shamans, 30; tribes, 21

Amazulu, 55

Ambat, 361

America, peopling of, 332*n*

America, Central, 92

America, North, 5, 21, 92, 97, 122*n*, 139, 182, 184, 297*ff*, 338*n*, 491, 503; caves, 52, 101; costume, shamanic, 178*f*; initiation rites, 65, 108, 125, 436; ladder in, 490; séance in, 300*ff*; shaman's quest in, 99*ff*, 108*f*; sources of shamanic power, 102, 104; transvestitism, 258

America, South, 161, 310, 323*ff*, 332*n*, 335, 491, 503, 506; costume, shamanic, 178; initiation, 82, 84, 97, 131, 141; initiatory illness, 53*ff*, 65; rock crystals, 52*f*, 91, 139; spirits, guardian, 91; transvestitism, 258

Amīn Ahmad Rāzi, *see* Rāzi

Ammasalik, *see* Eskimo

Amschler, Wolfgang, 197*n*

amulets, 488

Amur region, 496

Anakhai, 37*n*

An Alaï Chotoun, 187

Anavatapta, lake, 409

ancestors: choice of shamans by, 67, 71, 82; cult of, 12, 67, 506; and drum, 170*f*; lunar, 277; mythical, tiger as, 339, 344; of nations, 40*n*; reintegration into, 18*n*; theriomorphic, 171; *see also* dead

Anchimalen, 329

Andaman Islands, 25, 68*n*, 86, 342

Andean region, 327

Andree, Richard, 164*n*, 472*n*

Andres, Friedrich, 127*n*, 128*n*, 129*n*, 130*n*

androgynization, ritual, 153*n*; *see also* transvestitism

androgyny, 329, 352

angakok (*angakut*), 58, 90, 288*ff*, 435, 438

angakoq, 60*f*

angga, 354

Anguttara-nikāya, 408*n*

animal(s): behavior, and ecstasy, 385; bones, 161*n*; burial of, 159; and Chinese shamanism, 458*f*; cries, 440; dance and, 459, 461; in dreams, 104; and drum, 170; friendship with, 99; human solidarity with, 94; language of, *see* language; mythical, 460; shamanic, 254; shaman's relation with, 184, 459; and shaman's "death," 93*f*; as helping spirits, 89, 92*ff*, 104; torture by, 44;

transformation into 18*n*, 93, 94, 328*f*, 381, 385, 459*f*, 467, 477*f*; *see also* antelope; ants; bat; bear; bee; bird; boa constrictor; buffaloes; bull; cat; centaurs; chicken; cock; colt; coyote; crow; cuckoo; deer; dog; duck; eagle; elk; emu; ermine; falcon; fish; fly; fox; gander; goat; goose; grebe; gull; hare; hens; heron; horse; jaguars; kingfisher; lambs; leopard; lions; lizard; mouse; ostrich; otter; owl; panther; parrots; pig, pigeon; ram; reindeer; roebuck; sea serpents; serpents; shark; sheep; snake; sparrow; sparrow-hawk; spider; squirrel; stag; swan; tiger; toad; vulture; walrus; wildcat; wolf; worms

Animals, Goddess/Lady/Mother of the, 41*n*, 42, 81, 294, 459, 460

Anisimov, A. F., 94*n*

Anokhin, A. V., 20*n*, 44*n*, 76, 153*n*, 155*n*, 173*n*, 189, 197*n*, 200, 201, 208*n*, 263*n*, 275, 276

Antarctic, 332

antar jyotih, 61

antelope, 105; -charming, 184*n*

Anthony, St., 377

ants, poisonous, 129

Anuchin, V. I., 153*n*, 223*n*

anvils, 41

Apache, 178, 299

Apapocuva, 83

Apinaye, 83, 327 & *n*

apocalypses, 484

Apollo, 387*n*, 388

Apollodorus, 66*n*

apples, magical, 78

Apsarases, 408

Arabs, and "bridge," 484

Aranda, 46, 48, 161

Arapaho, 102*n*, 258

Araucanians, 233*n*, 467; initiation among, 25, 51, 53, 54, 122*ff*; initiatory journey, 141; *ngillatun* ceremony, 324*f*, 325*n*; transvestitism, 258

arba, 153

Arbman, Ernst, 407*n*, 418*n*, 466*n*

Archer, W., 468*n*

archetype(s), xvii; of gaining existential consciousness, 394; and hierophany, xvii; of magician, 412; of shaman, 160

Arctic peoples: nervous constitution, 24; religion, 7

arhats, 408, 410, 434

ariki, 366

Arimaspeia, 388*n*, 395

Aristât, 397
Aristeas of Proconnesus, 388*f*
Aristophanes, 390
Arjuna, 420
Arnobius, 392*n*
aroettawaraare, 82
arrow(s), 100, 152 & *n*, 175*n*, 217, 227, 388; chain of, 121, 362, 430, 490*f*; magical, and sickness, 364
Arsari, 37*n*
art: of N.W. America and Asia, 334*n*; Renaissance, 34
Artay Virâf (*Book of*), 142*n*, 393, 398, 399, 400, 419
Art Toyon Aga, 186*f*, 188
Arunta, *see* Aranda
ascension/ascent: celestial, xiv, 5, 24, 51, 58, 76*ff*, 85, 89, 112, 119*ff*, 132, 135*ff*, 139*ff*, 177, 194*ff*, 198*ff*, 242, 430, *et passim*; evaluations of, 377; and flying, 479, *see also* flying; in India, 403*ff*; and initiation, 34, 38, 43, 49*f*, 61, 121; and Sky God, 505; *see also* flying; journey; ladder; levitation; tree
Ascension of Isaiah, 142
ashes, daubing with, 64
Asia, *passim*: influence on Polynesia, 366; masks in, 166; shaman as healer in, 182
Asia, Central, 4, 6, 109, 120, 244, 276, *et passim*; divination, 257*n*; healing, 215; influences from South, 237, 266, 500; initiation in, 110; passage rites, 65; pillar in, 262; religions of, 7
Asia, North, 4, 6, 120, 184, 215, 244, 266, *et passim*; decadence of shamans in, 237; drum in, 176; eagle in, 245; formation of shamanism in, 495*ff*; instruction, shamanic, 110; and North America, 333; passage rites, 65; religions of, 7; sacrifices, 198; shaman as psychopomp in, 209; southern influences, 500
Asia, South, 179, 366; Southeast, 279
Asín Palacios, Miguel, 484*n*, 489*n*
Assam, 263, 442*n*
Assiniboin, 108*n*, 109
astodan, 163
Aštôvidatu, 163*n*
asuras, 271
Aśvaghoṣa, 428
aśvamedha, 80*n*, 199, 420*n*; *see also* horse sacrifice
Aśvins, 10
Atharva Veda, 261*n*, 408, 414*f*, 418*n*, 419*n*

ātman, 61
atmosphere, gods of, 199; *see also* Sky God; storms, god of
atnongara, 47 & *n*, 48
Atsugewi, 102
Aua/aua, 90*f*
Aukelenuiaiku, 133
auṣadhi, 416
Australia(ns), 31, 82, 84, 85, 92, 108, 134, 250, 503; Central, 491, 492*n*; fate of dead in, 491; initiation in, 45*ff*, 50*f*, 64, 65, 135*ff*; and South America, 332; *see also names of peoples*
Austria, 161*n*
Austroasiatic civilization, 287*n*
Austronesians, 361*n*
autoeroticism, 27
Avalokiteśvara, 440
Avam Samoyed, *see* Samoyed
Axis, Cosmic/*axis mundi*/Axis of World, 120, 169, 194*n*, 224, 239*n*, 259*f*, 261*ff*, 280, 404, 430, 439, 447, 492; *see also* Center of the World
ayami, 71*ff*, 80*f*
Aztecs, 163*n*

B

Baba, Barak, *see* Barak Baba
Babylonia: and cosmic pillar/mountain, 264, 267; cosmology, 406; hair of kings in, 152*n*; and number seven, 122*n*, 134
Bacchanalia, 387
bacchantes, 391
Bacham, 281
Bachelard, Gaston, 477*n*, 480*n*
backbone, 150
Bacot, Jacques, 444*n*
Baffinland, 161*n*, 292
Baholoholo, 473*n*
Baiame, 135, 137, 138
Bai Baianai, 187, 276*n*
Baiga, 421*n*, 425, 426, 502*n*
Baikal, Lake, 238, 497
Bai Ülgän, 76, 77, 88, 153, 182, 191, 192*f*, 196, 197, 198*ff*, 201, 266, 270, 275, 276, 278, 325, 403, 407
bajasa, 353*f*
Bakairi, 53, 326
Bakchai, 387
Balagansk, 117, 119
Balan Bacham, 281
Balázs, János, 225*n*, 476*n*
Balder, 383
Baldrs draumar, 382*n*

Bali, 468
balian, 340, 352*f*, 357
Balkans, 379
Balolo, 473*n*
Bamiyan frescoes, 134
Bandopal, 468
bangha, 399*ff*
Banks Islands, 364*f*
banquet: at Buryat initiation, 120; funerary, 208, 210
Banzarov, Dordji, 495
baqça, 20, 30, 44, 97, 155*n*, 157, 175
Barak Baba, 402*f*
Barama, 91
Barbeau, Marius, 459*n*
bardo/Bardo thödol, 435, 438, 442
Bare'e Toradja, 353
Barents Sea, 503
bari (Bororo shaman), 82
Bari (of White Nile), 472*n*
barich, 350
Bartels, Max, 21*n*
Barthélemy, M. A., 399*n*
Barthold, W., 11*n*
Bartle Bay, 365*n*
barua, 426
Bashkir, 261
basil shrub, 426
basir, 352*f*
Basongo, 473*n*
baš-tut-kan-kiši, 191, 195, 197
Basuto, 141
bat(s), 129
bata ilau, 350
Batak, 21, 25, 82*n*, 96, 273, 346–47*n*;
cosmology, 286; dancing, 340; funerary beliefs, 340*f*; and horse-stick, 467; position of shaman among, 346*ff*
Batarov, P. P., 218*n*
Batavia, 429
bath, steam/vapor, 322, 334*n*, 335, 394, 475*f*
bâtons de commandement, 503*n*
Batradz, 476
Batu Herem, 280
Batu Ribn, 280
Baudhāyana Dharma Sūtra, 412*n*
Baumann, Hermann, 81*n*, 273*n*, 374*n*
Bawden, C. R., 165*n*
Bayeke, 473*n*
Beaglehole, Ernest and Pearl, 371*n*, 372*n*
Beal, Samuel, 420*n*
bear(s), 44, 59, 62, 72, 93, 101, 105, 153;
ceremonialism, 458, 459, 461, 503;
•sacrifice, 166; and shamanic costume,

156; spirit as, 59, 89, 90, 103, 106, 221, 458
bearskin, 452*n*, 458
Bebrang, 282
Bechuana, 21
bee, 256*n*
beer, 170
beginning of world, 103, 406; *see also* creation of world
begu, 346*f*
behavior: change in, and initiation, 35;
study of, xviii
bekliti, 57, 58
Bektashi, 402
Belet, 281
Belgium, 161*n*
belian, 351; *see also* dances
bells, 177, 278, 453*n*
belt, 146
Beltir, 9, 183, 205, 208
Belyavsky, —, 16*n*, 29
Benedict, Ruth, 92*n*, 157
Benua, 344
Benua-Jakun, 342*n*
Bergema, Hendrik, 270*n*
Bernardino de Sahagún, 429
Berndt, R. M., 127
berserkir, 385, 399*n*
Besisi, 282, 346
Bessarabia, 161
besudi, 57
bethel, 488
Bethlehem, 482
"beyond": orientation of, 356; sea as, 235
Bhaiga, 44*n*
bhakti, 416*n*
Bharhut, 430
Bhil, 177*n*, 421*n*, 425, 468, 502*n*
Bhṛgu, 419
Bhuiya, 425
Bhutan, 432, 433*n*
Biallas, P. Franz, 451*n*
Bible, *see* Genesis; Job; Judges; Matthew; Revelation; *also* Ascension of Isaiah
Bickermann, E., 392*n*
Bidez, Joseph, 393*n*; and Cumont, Franz, 393*n*
Bilby, J. W., 59*n*
Binbinga, 48, 51
Biot, Édouard, 452*n*
Birartchen, 147, 149*n*, 153

birch tree, 39, 116*ff*, 191, 194, 232; and
first shaman, 70; and World Tree,
xiv, 169, 173, 270, 403
bird(s)/Bird, 39, 82, 89; aquatic, 234;
Black, 196; giant, 38; Lord of the, 70;
as psychopomp, 98, 479; and snake, 273,
285; on stick, 481; transformation into,
403; and Tree, 273, 480*f*; water, on
shaman's costume, 153; wooden, 357;
see also costume, ornithomorphic;
Märküt; Thunder Bird; *and list s.v.*
animals
bird-fairy, 158*n*
Bird-Mother, 36–38
bird song, 97*f*
bird-soul, *see* soul
bird-spirit, 204*n*
Birhor, 424*n*, 425, 473
Birket-Smith, Kaj, 288*n*
birth, of shamans, initiatory, 37*f*
bis, 186
bisexuality, 352
biunity, divine, 352
Blackfoot Indians, 262*n*
blacksmiths, *see* smiths
Blagden, C. O., *see* Skeat, W. W.
Bleichsteiner, Robert, 164*n*, 395*n*, 396*n*,
434*n*, 436
Blok, H. P., 487*n*
blood: goat's, 121; pig's, 73; purification
with, 117; sucking, 306*f*
boa constrictor, 149*n*, 497
Boas, Franz, 59*n*, 101*n*, 104*n*, 138,
257*n*, 309*n*
boat: bone, 164; of the dead, 355*ff*, 360,
417; drum as, 172; ritual, uses of,
356; "of the spirits," 356
bodhisattvas, 434
body: entering another's, 416; intrusion
of object into, 45, 47, 50, 52, 57, 132,
135, 215, 301, 316, 327, 330, 343,
373, *see also* rock crystals; naming parts
of, 62; voluntary abandonment of, 480
Boehm, Fritz, 165*n*
bögä, see *bügä*
Bogdan, 161*n*
Bogoras, Waldemar G. (V. G. Bogoraz),
24, 93*n*, 108 & *n*, 125*n*, 216*n*, 219*n*,
252, 253*ff*, 258*n*, 262*n*, 333*n*, 351*n*
bögü, 495*n*; see also *bügä*
boiling: of initiate, 41*ff*, 44*n*, 159; of
Pelops, 66
Bö-Khân, 77
Bö-Khâ-näkn, 77
Bolivia, 161*n*, 323

Bolot Khan, 214*n*
Bolte, J., and Polívka, G., 66*n*
bomor, 25, 93, 339; *bomor belian*, 339*n*,
345
Bondo, 425
Bon dtkar, 432
Bon-po/Bon religion, 410, 431*ff*, 440,
444, 453*n*; priests, 177; White, 432
bonds, magic of, 419
bones: animal, breaking, 161*n*; cult of
shaman's, 324; divination by, 164*f*,
246*n*, 249, 257*n*; in India, 163*f*; iron
symbolic, 36, 158*f*; naming, 62*f*; rebirth from, 160*ff*; replacement of, 57; as
source of life, 63, 159; soul and, 159;
see also skeleton
Bonnerjea, Biren, 81*n*, 468*n*
Bonsu, 339
"book, heavenly," 393, 489*n*
Book: *of Artay Virāf*, *see s.v.*; of Fate,
see s.v.; of the Ladder, 489*n*; of Life, 273
Book of the Dead, 392; Egyptian, 163*n*,
480, 487; Tibetan, *see* Tibetan Book of
the Dead
books, *datu*'s, 347
boot, shaman's, 156
Borneo, 334*n*, 349*ff*, 358*n*; *see also*
Dusun; Dyak; Sarawak
Borobodur, 267
Bororo, 92
Borsippa, 267
Boshintoi, 471*f*
Botiugne, 188
bottle, girl's soul in, 68
Boulanger, A., *see* Gernet, L.
Bounak, V., 498*n*
Bourke, John G., 179*n*
Bousset, Wilhelm, 488
Bouteiller, Marcelle, 22*n*, 101*n*, 178*n*,
299*n*, 301*n*, 302*n*, 313*n*
Bouvat, L., 402*n*
bow: drum as, 174; shaman's, 175
Boyerb, 137
Brahmalokas, 430
brahman, 183*n*
Brāhmaṇas, see *Aitareya*; *Jaiminīya*;
Pañcaviṃśa; *Śatapatha*; *Taittirīya*
Brāhmanism, 406; *see also* Hinduism
brāhmarandhra, 164
brain washing, 57
Brand, J., 451*n*
brandy, 210, 232
break-through in plane, 173, 251*n*, 259*f*,
265, 269, 296, 467, 484
Breasted, James H., 488*n*

breath, control of, 412*f*
Breuil, H., and Obermaier, H., 434*n*
B*r*hadāra*n*yaka Upani*s*ad, 406*n*, 408*n*
bridge, 121, 202, 282, 311, 417, 430, 431, 441, 447, 482*ff*; Činvat, 396*f*, 399; and drum, 135, 173; Gjallar, 383*n*; hair-breadth, 202, 203*f*, 287, 395, 396*n*, 397*f*, 483; Islamic conception, 484*n*; see also rainbow; swords
Briggs, George W., 163*n*
brimures, 132
British Columbia, 100, 104, 308, 309, 334*n*
Brodeur, Arthur Gilchrist, 162*n*
Brown, A. R., 86*n*, 475*n*
bü, see *bügä*
Buandik, 491
Buchacheyev, Bulagat, 44
Büchner, V. F., 495*n*
Buck, Peter H., see Hiroa, Te Rangi
Buddha, 119*n*, 407, 436; and magic flight, 409; miracles, 428, 430; Nativity of, 400, 405*f*; and rainbow, 134
Buddhaghoṣṣa, 409*n*
Buddhism, 440, 458; and Amur Tungus, 119*n*; in Central and North Asia, 496, 506, 507; and magical flight, 408*f*, 411; and miracles, 428*ff*; Mongolian, 435; Tibetan, see Lamaism; and Tungus shamanism, 498*f*; yoga of, 61, 164, 407
Buddruss, Georg, see Friedrich, Adolph
Budge, E. A. Wallis, 487*n*, 488*n*
buffaloes, black, 187
bügä/bögä/buge/bü, 4
Buga (Supreme Being), 9, 242, 499
bull, 90
Bundahišn, 397*n*
Bundjil, 134
burial, symbolic, 64, 343; see also death; initiation
Burkert, Walter, 387*n*
burkhan, 119 & *n*, 497*n*
Burma, 442, 443, 455
"burning," 475; sorcerer, 363
Burrows, Edwin G., 366*n*
Burrows, Eric, 268*n*, 269*n*
Buryat, 28, 30, 35*n*, 37*n*, 42*n*, 43*f*, 67, 68, 69, 94, 100*n*, 112, 115*ff*, 122 & *n*, 133*n*, 159, 165, 182*n*, 194*n*, 197*n*, 206, 213, 217, 242, 250*n*, 261, 263, 266, 271, 276, 277, 469, 500; Alarsk, 18; costume, 149*ff*; dualism among, 185, 186; election among, 75*f*; gods of, 10; initiation among, 43*ff*, 75, 110, 115*ff*; and origin of shamans, 69; religion, 9;

"shaman's horse," 173, see also horse; shamans and politics, 181*n*; shamanic recruiting, 18*ff*; and smiths, 471*f*; three souls, 216*n*; see also Olkhonsk
"bush soul," 92
Buschan, Georg, 357*n*
Bushmen, 161
butchu, 211
bwili, 25, 56, 477

C

caftan, 148, 149*n*, 152
Cahuilla, 103
Caingang, 327*n*
Caland, Willem, 415*n*
caldron, 41, 43, 44*n*, 50, 282, 446
California: Central, 262; Northern, 21, 31, 102, 105, 262; Southern, 103, 109
"call" to shamanic career, see vocation
Callaway, Henry, 56*n*
Calypso, 79
Campa, 83
candle flame, 345
cannibalism, 434*n*
canoes, 369*f*; for dead, 355*f*; drum as, 254
cap, shaman's, 146, 148, 150, 154*f*, 462; see also headdress; hat
Carbonelli, Giovanni, 490*n*
Carib, 91, 128*n*, 326; first shaman, 97; initiation among, 54, 127*ff*; séance, 329*n*
Caribou, Mother of the, 62
Car Nicobar, 343*f*
Carpenter, Rhys, 390*n*
carpets, 340
Cashinawa, 83
casque, 150
Castagné, J., 20*n*, 30*n*, 97, 155*n*, 158*n*, 175*n*, 219*n*
Castrén, Alexander M., 15*n*, 67*n*, 213*n*, 227
cat, 287
Caucasus/Caucasians, 161*n*, 395*f*
caul, birth with, 16
cave(s), 41; and initiation, 46*f*, 51*f*, 136*n*; painted, 51*n*; retirement to, 389; temples, 204
Celebes, 353
Celsus, 121
Celts, 82, 382
Cenoi/Chenoi/Chinoi/Cinoi/*cenoi*, 52*n*, 96, 125, 138, 280, 337*ff*
centaurs, 387

Center of World, 37n, 42, 71, 75, 120, 134, 168ff, 171, 194n, 224, 226, 259ff, 265, 266, 269, 274, 492, et passim; Buddha and, 406; inverted, 418; and North, 279; see also Axis; Tree, Cosmic
Ceram, 354n
Cerulli, Enrico, 489n
Ceylon, 179
Chadwick, H. Munro and Nora K., 30n, 31n, 78n, 133n, 204n, 214n, 287n, 360n, 478n, 490n
Chadwick, Nora K., 30n, 31n, 110n, 133n, 141n, 179n, 204n, 367n, 381n, 478n
chain, golden, 431n
Chakât-i-Dâitîk, see Kakâd-i-Dâitîk
Changsha, 460
Chao, King, 51
Chard, Chester S., 500n
chariots, flying, 449f
Charlemagne, 263
Charles, Lucile H., 511n
chastity, ordeal of, 311f
Chavannes, Édouard, 448n, 449n; and Lévi, Sylvain, 410n
hebuch, 339
Chenoi, see Cenoi
Cheremis, 276, 487n
chest, 151
Cheyenne Indians, 258, 335
hicken, sacrifice of, 351
'Chief of the Religion," 455
hild(ren): sacrifice of, 347; souls of, 272, 273n, 281f; torture of, by spirits, 18
childbirth: difficult, 181; divinities of, 10
Chile, 25, 51
Chimariko, 21
China/Chinese, 122, 164n, 179, 264, 270n, 386n, 410, 419, 452n, 453n, 457f, 461n, 501; ancient, and America, 334n; artistic influence, 334n; divination in ancient, 257n; influence of, on Manchu, 113; kite in, 133n; magic, 442f; matriarchy, 449; and Polynesian religion, 366n; rope trick in, 429; shamanism in, 448ff; —, modern, 456f; Tree of Life in, 271n; and Tungus shamanism, 237
Chingpaw, 443
Chinoi, see Cenoi
Chinoi-Sagar, 281
Chivalkov, —, 201
höd (gchod), 108n, 436f
Cholko, Ivan, 43

Chou li, 458
Christensen, Arthur, 267n
Christianity: ecstatic experience and, 8; and Ghost-Dance Religion, 320; influence, on Altaians, 208n; —, on Lapps, 224; inner light in, 61; ladder in, 489; levitation in, 481f; temptations of saints in, 377; see also saints
Christiansen, Reidar T., 24n, 133n
Chronicon Norvegiae, 383, 384
chronology, and history of religion, xviiff
Ch'uang, 455n
Chudyakov, I. A., 187n
Chukchee, xii, 35n, 93, 96, 97, 165, 176, 181n, 206, 235, 247, 260, 262, 288, 335; and after-death state, 216; religion, 9; séances among, 252ff; transvestitism, 125n, 351 & nn
Chung-li, 451
Chuvash, 37n, 276
Ch'ü Yüan, 451
Cinoi, see Cenoi
Činvat, see bridge
circle, magic, 345
clairvoyance, 184, 304
Clark, Walter Eugene, 409n
clay, lumps of, 426
Clemen, Carl, 390n
Clements, Forrest E., 215n, 300n, 310n, 327n, 415n
Cline, Walter, 472n, 473n
Closs, Alois, 381n, 382n, 390n, 504n
coals, walking on, see fire-walking
coat, shaman's, 226; see also costume
Cobeno, 21, 52, 327n
Cocama, 327n
cock, 384, 426
coconut, 58, 368; palm, 78n
Cocopa, 109
Codrington, R. H., 364n, 365n, 475n
Coe, Michael D., 456n
Coèdes, G., 280n
coincidentia oppositorum, 352
cold, resistance to, 113, 335; see also heat; sheets
Cole, Fay-Cooper, 337n, 341n
Collins, Col. —, 45
Coleman, Sister Bernard, 317n
colors: of Buryat costume, 185; of celestial regions, 261; seven, 134; sibaso and, 347
colt, 90
Coman, Jean, 390n, 391n
concentration, 29, 167, 175, 179, 420
confession, 60, 296; collective, 289

Confucianism, 454

Congo tribes, 473*n*

Conibo, 83

contraries, opposition of, 285

Conze, Edward, 429*n*

Cook, Arthur Bernard, 486*n*, 488*n*

cooking, *see* boiling

Coomaraswamy, Ananda K., 169*n*, 262*n*, 268*n*, 270*n*, 274*n*, 404*n*, 405*n*, 430*n*, 479*n*, 485*n*, 486, 489*n*

Coomaraswamy, Luisa, 485*n*

Cooper, John M., 164*n*, 323*n*

cord, *see* rope; threads

Cornford, Francis Macdonald, 387*n*

corpse(s): exposing, 163; sleeping near, 358

Cosmic: Axis, *see s.v.*; Mountain, *see s.v.*; Tree, *see s.v.*

cosmogony in reverse, 413

costume, shamanic, 29, 111, 145*ff*, 460*n*, 497; Altaic, 152*f*; in Africa, 178; of "black" and "white" shamans, 185; Buryat, 149*ff*; buying, 147; degeneration in making, 147*n*; disuse of special, 252; eagle and, 71, 156, 178; finding, 147; Goldi, 156, 157; Manchu, 157, 158; in North America, 178*f*; ornithomorphic elements in, 71, 131, 156*ff*, 404, 478; sacred, outside shamanism, 179; Siberian, 148*f*; Soyot, *see s.v.*; *spákona*, 386; and "spirits," 147; submarine motifs in, 294; Tungus, 146, 147*ff*, 154*f*, 156; of "white" shamans, 189; Yakut, *see s.v.*; Yukagir, *see s.v.*

Coto, 327*n*

Couvreur, S., 448*n*

Coxwell, C. Fillingham, 161*n*, 163*n*

coyote, 100, 103, 105; "language," 100

Crawley, Ernest, 177*n*, 420*n*

creation of world, 284, 412; *see also* beginning of world

Creator: of the Earth, 250; of Light, 248

Cree Indians, 335

Creel, Herrlee Glessner, 164*n*

cries: animal, 440; shamanic, 97*f*

crisis, and shamanic vocation, xii, 253

Croats, 225*n*

Crooke, William, 426

Cross, of Christ, 268, 489*n*

crow(s), 89, 106, 232, 389; Odin's, 381

Crow Indians, 102*n*, 335*n*

crystal gazing, 363

crystals: volcanic, 364; *see also* rock; quartz

Cuchulain, 476

cuckoo, 176, 196

Cuisinier, Jeanne, 25*n*, 27*n*, 93*n*, 286*n*, 339*n*, 345*n*, 346*n*, 356*n*

Cumont, Franz, 121*n*, 392*n*, 488*n*; *see also* Bidez, Joseph

Curetes, 473

Curtin, Jeremiah, 69*n*, 198*n*

"cutting," 55

cushion, see *fanya*

cycles, cultural, xiii

Cyclopes, 473

Czaplicka, M. A., 24, 25, 35*n*, 90*n*, 148*n*, 184, 470*n*, 477*n*

D

Dactyli, 473

Dähnhardt, Oskar, 66*n*

Dahor, 497

Dākinī/*dākinīs*, 410, 437, 440

Dakota (Indians) 161*n*

dalabči, 150

Dalton, E. T., 473*n*

damagomi, 105*f*, 305

damaru, 420*n*

dance: and animal, 459, 461; among Batak, 340; *belian*, 344; of dead, 312; ecstatic, in China, 449, 451; among Goldi, 73; on horse-stick, 467*f*; initiatory, 128*f*; among Kirgiz, 175; Paviotso, 304; skeleton, 164, 434*f*; among Tungus, 29, 247; *see also* Ghost-Dance Religion

dancer, woman, 303

Dante Alighieri, 399, 489

Daramulun, 137

Darkness, Spirit of, 114

Dasuni, 422

Dātastān i dēnīk, 397*n*

David-Neel, Alexandra, 436*n*, 438*n*

Davidson, D. S., 332*n*

Dawa-Samdup, Lama Kazi, 437*n*, 438*n*

daya beruri, 350

Dayachan, 242

Deacon, A. Bernard, 126*n*, 361*n*

dead: ambivalence toward, 207; canoes for, 355*f*; converse with, and initiation, 34; Eskimo beliefs, 291; fate of, in Australia, 491; Indian beliefs concerning, 417*f*; possession by, 365*f*; precautions against return of, 207; Pygmy beliefs concerning, 281; ships of the, 285; souls of, and recruiting of shamans, 81*ff*, 102; *see also* ancestors; souls; spirits

Dead: Boat of the, *see s.v.*; Book of the, *see s.v.*; King of the, 270, *see also* Erlik Khan; Land of the, 61, *see also* Shades; Lord of the, 173; Mountain of the, 457

De Angulo, Jaime, 105n, 106, 305ff

death: Central and North Asian conception of, 10; and initiation, 33ff, 64, 76, 206, 506; knowledge of, shaman and, 509f; ritual, repetition of, 95; simulated, and resurrection, 36, 45, 53ff, 59, 64, 76, 84; symbolic/ritual, 33, 34, 53, 80, 84; *see also* burial; initiation

death watch, 208n

Death, Waters of, 355

decadence, of shamans, 67, 68, 112, 130, 237, 249, 250, 252, 254, 256, 258, 290, 364, 376, 401, 500

deer, 101, 105; *see also* antelope; stag

degeneration, of humanity, 480

Dehon, P., 473n

deities, *see* gods; goddess(es)

Delphi, oracle of, 387n

Demeter, 66

demons: converse with, and initiation, 34; expulsion of, by boat, 356; Moso and, 445f; shamans as enemies of, 508; *see also* devil(s)

descent, *see* journey; underworld

deus otiosus, 9, 286, 505

Devas, 453n

Devata Sangiang, 285

devil(s): and first shaman, 68; and initiation, 37f, 113; shoots flame from mouth, 474

"devil's hand," 47

Dhurwa, 468

dialogue: between shaman and God, 199; in initiation, 34; with gods and spirits, 227

diamonds, 139

Diegueno, 109

Dieri, 491

Dieterich, Albrecht, 122n

dīkṣā, 413f

dinang tree, 354

Dinkart, 397n

Diomede Islands, 22n

Dionysus, 388

Dioscuri, 10

Diószegi, Vilmos, 94n, 154, 168n, 223n, 225n, 461n, 498n

Dirr, A., 81n

disease(s): children's, divinities of, 10; classification, 300, 305; soul and, 215;

spirits of dead and, 206; *see also* epilepsy; hysteria; hysteroid; illness; mental disease; psychopathy; sickness; "sickness-vocation"; syphilis

disks, iron, 148

dismemberment, 430n; and initiation, 34, 36ff, 53ff, 108, 130, 429, *et passim*; rejuvenation by, 66; *see also* initiation

displayed object, identity with, 179

divination, 184, 257n, 382; by bones, 164f, 246n, 249; in Dobu, 364; drums and, 176, 239; epileptics and, 25; Epimenides and, 389; among Eskimo, 257n, 297; among Koryak, 164; Lolo, 442; among Samoyed, 228; by skulls, *see s.v.*; among Yukagir, 249, 391, 435n

divinities, feminine, *see* goddesses

Dixon, Roland B., 104n, 105n, 302n, 323n, 490n

Djangar, 426

Djara, 108n

dMu, 431

dmu-t'ag, 431

Dobrudja, 161

Dobu, 363f, 474

Dodds, E. R., 387n, 389n, 391n

Doerr, Erich, 355n

dog(s), 153; as helping spirit, 90; sacrifice of, 188; underworld, 203, 248, 251, 295, 466ff; Yama's, 417

Dogon, 472n

Dolgan, 40, 41, 156, 191n, 272, 470; séance among, 233ff

dolls, on shaman's costume, 153

Dombart, Theodor, 267n

Dongson, 177

Donner, Kai, 30, 122n, 145n, 148n, 152n, 154n, 155n, 158, 171n, 172n, 181n, 223n, 228n, 232n, 277n, 278n, 496n, 501n

door(s), 52 & n, 340; *see also* gate; strait; passage, difficult

Doré, P. H., 456n

double, shaman's, 94

Downs, R. E., 354 & n

dragon, 122n; bearded, 449

dreams: flying, 225n; initiatory, 14, 33ff, 104, 168, 377, 429, 446; —, Buryat, 43f; —, Samoyed, 38ff; instruction and, 103f; premonitory, 109; sickness, 43; and vocation, 67, 101ff

drinks: to produce unconsciousness, 64; *see also* alcohol; beer; brandy; narcotics; *tarasun*

Drucker, Philip, 138n, 309n

drugs, *see* narcotics
drum(s), xiii, 121, 168*ff, et passim;*
animating, 170; Bon, 433; choice of
wood for, 169*f;* description of, 171*ff;*
and divination, 176, 239; double, Tibetan, 502*n;* family, 247, 252; and
feminine magic, 465; in India, 420, 426;
and initiation, 38, 40; lacking among
Eskimo, 289; Lamaist, 176, 497*f;* Lapp,
172, 175*ff,* 334; metal, 442*n;* and rainbow, 135; as shaman's horse, 173*f,* 233,
407; Soyot, 173, 174; and spirits,
174; symbols on, 172*ff,* 224; and World
Tree, 40*n,* 168*ff*
Drum, Masters of the, 192
drumsticks, 503
dto-mba, 446, 447
Dto-mba Shi-lo, 445*ff,* 508
dualism: Buryat, 185, 186; cosmological,
284; Iranian, 68, 163*n;* Yakut, 186*ff*
DuBois, Constance Goddard, 55*n*
Du Bois, Cora Alice, 31*n,* 320*n*
Duchesne-Guillemin, Jacques, 398*n*
duck(s), 39; costume, 149
duels, intershamanic, 290
dukun, 348
Dumézil, Georges, 378*f,* 380*n,* 383*n,*
384*n,* 385*n,* 386*n,* 387*n,* 395*n,* 396*n,*
397*n,* 476
Dumont, Louis, 424*n*
Dumont, Paul Émile, 80*n,* 420*n*
Dunin-Gorkavich, A. A., 15
Durme, P. J. van, 410*n*
dūrohaṇa, 403
Dusadh, 426
Dusun, 97, 178, 283, 287, 349, 357, 487
dwarf, 102
Dyak, 21, 31, 273*n,* 350*ff,* 358, 359*ff,*
478; initiation, 57; Ngadju, 284, 352*f;*
Sea, 138, 177, 258, 350; and World
Tree, 285
Dyaus, 199
Dyrenkova, N. P., 44*n,* 459*n*
Dzhe Manido, 316
Dzokuo, Mount, 37*n*

E

eagle, 140, 153, 204*n,* 218; feathers of,
101, 155, 179, 302, 321*f;* as helping
spirit, 89, 90, 105, 106; and origin of
shamans, 69*ff,* 160, 185*f;* and shaman's
costume, 71, 156, 178; and shaman,
mythical relations, 128*n,* 157*f;* Supreme

Being as, *see s.v.;* two-headed, 70
ears, piercing of, 42, 363
earth/Earth: Creator of the, 250; goddess, 10; Lord of the, 39; -Owner,
248; Spirit(s), 243, 277
Eberhard, Wolfram, 449*n,* 451*n,* 453*n,*
457 & *n,* 458*n,* 462*n*
ecstasy, 200, 221*ff,* 243, 493*f, et passim;*
and animal behavior, 385; and cosmic
opening, 265*f;* first, 18; foundation for,
190; as initiation, 33*f,* 35*ff;* Iranian,
400; martial, 385; nonshamanic, 5, 7*n,*
379; parashamanic, 253; and ritual
death, 95; séance and, 12; shaman as
master of, 4, 107; and shaman's prestige, 236; sovereign and, 449; symbols
of, 174; technique of, 4; *see also*
journey; trance
ecstatic: Chinese, 448; and shaman,
distinction, 5
Edda, Prose (Gylfaginning), 161, 162*n,*
383
Eder, Matthias, 462, 463*n,* 464 & *n*
Edsman, Carl Martin, 66*n,* 161*n,* 162*n,*
270*n,* 386*n,* 488*n,* 489*n -*
Eells, Myron, 309*n*
effigy, of deceased, 439
egg, birth of shaman from, 37
Egypt(ians), 163*n,* 264, 487*f*
Ehatisaht Nootka, 138
Ehnmark, Erland, 296*n*
Ehrenreich, Paul, 133*n,* 260*n*
Eiriks Saga Rautha, 386
Eisenberger, Elmar Jakob, 164*n*
Eisler, Robert, 260*n,* 473*n,* 476*n*
Elbruz, 267, 397
election: illness and, 28; resistance to, 23,
109; of shamans, 13*ff,* 67*ff;* signs of, in
medicine man, 32; supernatural, in
India, 425; *see also* initiation
Eliade, Mircea (other works): *Birth and
Rebirth,* 64*n,* 126*n,* 132*n,* 136*n,*
465*n,* 486*n,* 506*n; Cosmologie çi alchimie
babiloniană,* 262*n,* 267*n,* 268*n,* 269*n;
Death and Initiation,* xxi, 64*n;* "*Dūro-
haṇa* and the 'Waking Dream,' "
403*n,* 480*n;* "Einführende Betrachtungen über den Schamanismus," xxi;
The Forge and the Crucible, 139*n,* 461*n,*
470*n,* 472*n,* 473*n,* 475*n; Images and
Symbols,* 260*n,* 419*n; The Myth of the
Eternal Return,* 265*n,* 267*n,* 269*n,*
325*n,* 357*n,* 446*n; Mythology of Death,*
xxi, 205*n,* 491*n; Myths, Dreams and
Mysteries,* 33*n,* 99*n,* 134*n,* 319*n,* 377*n,*

410n, 480n; "Nostalgia for Paradise in the Primitive Traditions," 509n; *Patterns in Comparative Religion*, xiv, xvii, 9n, 10n, 19n, 23, 31n, 107n, 133n, 134n, 139n, 169n, 187n, 199n, 260n, 265n, 269n, 270n, 271n, 272n, 273n, 277n, 313n, 337n, 352n, 358n, 398n, 442n, 489n, 505n; "Le Problème du chamanisme," xxi, 24n; "Recent Works on Shamanism," xxii; "Remarques sur le 'rope trick,' " 428n, 430n; "Sapta padāni kramati . . . ," 406n; "The Seven Steps of Buddha," 406n; "Shamanism," xxi; "Significations de la 'lumière intérieure,' " 61n, 137n, 509n; *Techniques du Yoga*, 413n, 416n; *Yoga: Immortality and Freedom*, 61n, 164n, 287n, 407n, 409n, 410n, 413n, 416n, 428n, 430n, 434n, 436n, 453n

lk, 90

lkin, Adolphus Peter, 31n, 46n, 86n, 87n, 108n, 127 & n, 132n, 136n, 138n, 476n

lliott, Alan J. A., 456n

llis, Hilda R., 224n, 381n, 382n, 383n, 384n

llis, William, 371 & n

lmendorf, William W., 300n

lwin, Verrier, 58n, 421, 426, 468, 469n

mpyrean, 122

msheimer, Ernst, 39n, 70n, 168n, 169n, 170n, 243n

mu, 46

nareis, 395

ieñalan, 251

ngishiki, 463

ngland, 161n

nstasis, 417

nthusiasm/*enthousiasmos*, 387, 388

ntrance, difficult, 292; *see also* gate, strait; passage, difficult

pic: origins of, 214, 395; themes, and shamanism, 510f; *see also* literature; poetry

pidemics, 344, 356f, 442, 443

pilepsy/epileptics, xi, 15, 20, 24, 25, 27, 31; as diviners/magicians, 25; in Sudan, 27; *see also* psychopathy

pimenides, 389

r, 393f

rénī, 498

rkes, Eduard, 448n, 449n, 451n, 452n, 466n

rlik Khan, 10, 153, 173, 199, 200ff, 218, 471n; *see also* Irle Kan

ermine, 39, 41

eroticism, mystical, 416n

Eruncha, 46, 47

erunchilda, 47

eschatology, 322

Eskimo, 22, 82, 93, 161n, 184, 229n, 235, 261, 288ff; Alaskan, 90, 166; American, 257n; Ammasalik, 58; Asiatic, 258; Copper, 289n; drums, 176; Habakuk, 231n; and helping spirits, 90; Iglulik, 21, 60f; initiation among, 44f, 58ff, 288, 435; Labrador, 59, 438; and mask, 166; and resistance to cold, 113; and ritual nudity, 146; séance among, 290; and secret language, 96, 97; Smith Sound, 51; songs of shaman, *see* songs; and submarine journey, 254

Estonians, 261

ethnologist, approach to shamanism, xiif

Etruscans, 394n

Euahlayi, 45, 134, 137

Europe: incursion of shamanizing horsemen, 396n; rope trick in medieval, 429, 430n

Eurydice, 391

Evans, Ivor H. N., 21n, 52n, 91n, 93n, 96n, 97n, 177n, 178n, 231n, 280, 281, 282n, 283n, 337n, 338n, 339n, 340n, 341n, 342n, 349n

Evans-Pritchard, E. E., 374n, 490n

Evans-Wentz, W. Y., 61n, 437n, 438n

Evenki, 41, 94n

evil, powers of, struggle against, 508

experience, religious, variety of, xviii

"Exposition of the Road of Death," 438ff

eyes: change of, 42, 54; tearing out, 54

Ezekiel, 162f, 163n

F

face, anointing/daubing of, 64, 166

fainting spells, 53

Fairchild, William P., 463n

fairy wife, 77f, 361; *see also* wives, celestial

fakirism, 228, 254, 256, 428, 479

Falahi, 348

falcon(s), 478, 480

Fall, the, 99, 133, 484, 493

family head, and domestic cult, 4, 247

fan, winnowing, *see* winnow

fanya (cushion), 210ff

fasting, and initiation/vocation, 43, 84, 129

fat, daubing face with, 166

Fate, Book of, 272, 273
fatigue, 84
fault, ritual, 505
feathers, 492; and ascension, 177; chicken, 343; in China, 450; owl, 57; on shaman's cap, 155; and shamanic costume, 156; *see also* eagle
fee, shaman's, 302
female line, transmission in, 15
feminization, 395; *see also* transvestitism
ferg, 476
fertility: Bai Ülgän and, 198, 199; goddess, 80*n*; gods, 505; and prehistoric hunters, 503; rites, 79, 80*n*
Fiji, 365*n*, 372*f*, 456
fili, 382
Filliozat, Jean, 415*n*, 417*n*
Findeisen, Hans, 44*n*, 70*n*, 114*n*, 145*n*, 158*n*, 159, 168*n*, 459*n*, 470*n*, 502*n*, 503*n*, 504*n*
Finns, 71*n*, 261, 473*n*, 485
fir tree: giant, 37; ninefold, 270
fire: and celestial destiny, 206; cult of, 10; inner, 475; and magic, 363; mastery over, 5, 257, 316*n*, 335, 373, 412, 438, 472, 474*ff*; meditation by, 412; origin from vagina, 363*n*; "playing with," 232*n*, 335; smiths and, 472–73
Fire, Master of the, 193
fireball, 21
fire-handlers, 315
fire-walking, 54, 112, 206, 372, 442, 456
Fischer, H. T., 133*n*, 483*n*
fish, 93
flame, emission of, 474
Flannery, Regina, 335*n*
flight, *see* flying
Florida (Solomon Islands), 364
flues, 262
fly, 256*n*
flying: in alchemy, *see* alchemy; bird costume and, 157; in China, 448, 450*f*; Freudianism and, 225*n*; in India, 407*ff*; magical, 5, 121, 136, 138*f*, 140*f*, 154, 160, 239*n*, 245, 289, 400, 405, 408*f*, 477*ff*, *et passim*; power of, 56, 57, 126; spiritual, 479; *see also* ascension; levitation
folklore: European, smith in, 474; Indian, bones in, 163; shamanic adventures and, 180
footsteps, four, 400
Forde, C. Daryll, 103*n*, 310*n*
forgetfulness, 64*f*
Formosa, 456*n*

Fornander, A., 369
Forrest River, 131
Fortune, R. F., 363*n*, 364*n*, 475*n*
forty-nine (number), 208*n*
Fo-t'u-têng, 453*n*
fountain of youth, 78
four, footsteps, 400
fox, 90, 103
Fox Indians, 335
Foy, W., 268*n*
France, 161*n*, 244
Fravaši-yašt, 399
Frazer, James G., 92*n*, 102*n*, 160, 309*n*, 354*n*, 355*n*, 366*n*, 479, 487*n*, 490*n*, 491*n*, 492*n*
Freudianism, and shamanic flight, 22*t*
Freyja, 385, 386*n*
Friederici, Georg, 332*n*
Friedrich, Adolf, 94*n*, 159*n*, 161, 163 *n*, 164*n*, 171*n*, 177*n*, 209*n*, 374*n*, 504*n*; and Buddruss, Georg, 37*n*, 94*n*, 95*n*, 114*n*, 160 & *n*, 170, 176*n*, 275*n*, 471*n*
Fritzner, Johan, 224*n*
Frobenius, Leo, 133*n*, 160*f*, 479
Fruit Island, 281*n*, 282
Fuegians, 333; *see also* Tierra del Fuego
Fühner, H., 130*n*
function, alteration of, 174
funerary beliefs; Batak, 340*f*; Japanese, 355; Sea Dyak, 359*ff*
funerary ceremonies: Goldi, 207, 209, 210*ff*; Malayan/Indonesian, 355; shaman and, 181, 207*f*; Yurak, 212*f*
funerary geography, 509
fur(s), 150, 179
furor, 476

G

Gabriel, Archangel, 489*n*
Gabrielino, 109, 312
Gaerte, W., 280*n*
Gagauzi, 161
Gahs, Alexander, 81*n*, 167*n*, 187*n*, 192, 199*n*, 228*n*, 264*n*, 277, 502*n*
galdr, 98
Galla, 263
gam, see *kam*
gamana, 409
gander, 405
gandharvas, 408
Ganjkka (Ganykka), 38, 228
Gaokērēna, 122*n*, 271*n*
garabancias, 225*n*

Garide/Garuda, 267
garment, new, 447
Garo, 415n, 442n, 468
Garôdmân, 400
Garuda, see Garide
ashes, seven, 277
gate, strait, 260n, 293, 295, 483; see also
door; passage, difficult
gāthās, 397, 398n, 399
gawei antu, 360
Gayton, A. H., 311n, 312n
gaze, Platonic, 402n
gchod, see chöd
Genesis, Book of, 488n
Gennep, Arnold van, 64n, 137n, 469n,
490n
"Gentle Mother Creatress," 187
"Gentle Lady of Birth," 187
geography, funerary, 509
Georgi, J. G., 172
Gerizim, Mount, 268
Germans, ancient, 161n, 162, 224, 267,
273, 355, 380ff, 473
Gernet, L., and Boulanger, A., 473n
Gesser Khan, 161n
Getae, 389f
ghanṭa, 420
Gheerbrant, Alain, 129n
Gheranda Saṃhitā, 409n
ghosts, 229; incarnating, 454; possession
by, 462
"Ghost Ceremony" society, 54
Ghost Dance, 311
Ghost-Dance Religion, 142f, 299, 314,
320ff, 391n
giant, visit to underworld, 383
Gibbet, 380
Giedion, S., 503n
Gifford, E. W., 54n
Gilgamesh legend, 78, 313n
Gilgit, 431n
Gillen, F. J., see Spencer, Baldwin
gilyak, 474n
Gisla Saga, 382
gjallar, bridge, 383n
Gjessing, Gutorm, 500n
glove, 278
Gmelin, Johann Georg, 150n, 234n, 236n
gña-k'ri-bstan-po, 430
goat(s): black, 240; blood of, 121; hair
of, 16; sacrifice of, 119; Thor's, 161f
god(s)/God: of atmosphere, 199; "binding," 419; bipartition of, 186; Buryat,
10; celestial, 9, 12; —, replacement of,
199; the Father, 329; fertility, 505; and

first shaman, 68; Great/celestial, of
Asian nomads, 9; —, names of, 9;
groups of seven or nine, 275ff; Indian,
267; invocation of, 88; marriage with,
464; messengers of, 9, 10; multiplication of, 10; "nephews" of, 337; ninety-
nine, 277; renunciation of, 113;
"sons"/"daughters" of, 9, 10; of
storms, see storms; Sun, 487; thirty-
three, 276; uranian, 199; —, and telluric,
186ff; village of, 353; visits from, 324;
Yakut, 186ff, 276; see also Supreme
Being; names of specific gods
Goddess of the Animals, see Animals
goddess(es): earth, 10; fertility, 80n;
Great, 505; Turko-Tatar, 10
Goeje, C. H. de, 127n
gold dust, 57
Goldi, 28, 82n, 97, 166, 204n, 439n; and
Cosmic Tree, 270f, 272; election
among, 71ff; funerary ceremonies, 207,
209, 210ff; initiation among, 114, 120;
shaman's costume, 156, 167
Golgotha, 268
Goloubew, V., 177
Golther, W., 355n
Gomes, Edwin H., 57n, 126n
Gond, 44n, 58n, 425n, 426, 468; see also
Nodora
Gond-Pardhan, 468
Gondatti, N. L., 15
gong, 179
goose, 89, 191f, 195, 203, 204
Gorakhnāth, 163
gourd, 312
Graebner, Fritz, xiii, 262n, 491n
grana nour, 232
"Grandfather, Indian," 128
"Grandfather Vulture," 128f
Grand Medicine Society, 315ff; see also
Midē'wiwin
Granet, Marcel, 269n, 449, 458n, 461n,
473n
grave: lying by, 82; sleeping on, 45,
102n, 382
Great Basin, 102, 104
Great Crow, 250
Great Hell, 438f
Great Medicine Lodge, 317
grebe, 234
Greece, 264, 387ff, 488
Greeks, migrations of, 379
Greenland, 59, 90
"green man, little," 102
Grey, George, 78n

Griaule, Marcel, 472n
Grimnismál, 383
Grønbech, K., 243n
Groot, Jan J. M. de, 448n, 452n, 453, 454n, 455n, 456n
Gros Ventre Indians, 102n
Grousset, René, 11n
Grube, W., 212n
Grünwedel, Albert, 163 & n
gShen rab mi bo, 433
gtüm-mõ, 437n
Guarani, 83, 324
Guardians of the Sky, 276
Gudgeon, W. E., 372n
Guiana, 21, 97, 329n; Dutch, 127, 326
guitar, 220, 221f
gull, 153, 234
Güntert, Hermann, 405n, 466n
Gunther, E., see Haeberlin, Herman
guru, 347
Gusinde, Martin, 26n, 53n, 84n, 331n
Guthrie, W. K. C., 388n, 391n, 392n, 488n
Gutmann, B., 472n
gydhjur, 385
Gylfaginning, see Edda, Prose

H

Haavio, Martti, 485n
Hades, 387, 389, 391, 392, 399
Hadia, 263
Hadingus, 383f
Haeberlin, Herman, 310n; and Gunther, E., 107n
Haekel, Josef, 99n, 126n, 278n, 313n
Haguenauer, Charles, 462n, 464
Haida, 178
hair: horse, 469; long, 152n, 407; and shamanizing for reindeer, 41; Takánakapsâluk's, 295f
hala/halak, 52n, 93, 96, 125, 138, 337ff, 341
Halak Gihmal, 340
Halliday, W. R., 395n
Hallowell, A. Irving, 334, 458n
Hamites, 161
Han period, 461
Hančar, Franz, 502n
hand, father's, image of, 15
Handy, E. S. C., 287n, 366n, 367n, 368n, 369n, 370n, 371n, 372n, 485n
hanging, of initiation candidate, 380
Haraberezaiti (Elbruz), see Elbruz

hare(s): guardian spirit as, 89; hunt, 19 & n; among Winnebago, 319
Harper, Edward B., 424n
Harva (Holmberg), Uno, xi, 10n, 14n, 24n, 27n, 37n, 68n, 69n, 70n, 81n, 82n, 89n, 92n, 94n, 114n, 115n, 116n, 120n, 121 & n, 122n, 133n, 135n, 145n, 146n, 148n, 152n, 153n, 155n, 156n, 158 & n, 159n, 166n, 167, 169n, 171n, 172n, 173n, 174 & n, 175n, 176n, 184, 185n, 189n, 190n, 191n, 197n, 198n, 201n, 204n, 205n, 206n, 207n, 208n, 211n, 212n, 213n, 217n, 218n, 229n, 232n, 233n, 234n, 235n, 260n, 261n, 262n, 263n, 266n, 267n, 268n, 270n, 271n, 272, 273n, 274n, 275n, 276n, 277n, 279n, 489n, 497n
harvest ritual, 468
hashish, 402
hašira, 464
Haslund-Christensen, Henning, et al., 243n
hat, lambskin, 189
Hatibadi, 421
Hatt, Gudmund, 333n, 486n, 491n
Hauer, J. W., 407n, 413n, 420n
Haussig, Hans-Wilhelm, 396n, 495n; see also Altheim, Franz
Hávamál, 380n
Hawaii, 78n, 133, 369, 372 & n
"He Above," 249
head: forging of shaman's, 41, 471n; opening, 55; sacrifices of, 199; spirit o 89
headcloth, 146f
headdress: two-horned, 402; see also cap hat
head-holder, 191, 195
healing, magical/shamanic, 5, 182, 215ff, 283, 289, 300ff, 326ff, et passim
heat: and evil, 475; in France, 244; inner, 412; and magic, 363, 474ff; mystical, 437f; —, in South America, 335; physical, 113; see also tapas
heaven(s): ascent to/through, 197, se also ascent, journey; —, in China, 449 and earth, communication, 449n; nine 233, 274, 383, 406; number of, 275; planetary, 271, 274; sacrifice to, 444; seven, 122, 134, 274, 275, 383, 405; shaman's knowledge of, 278; ten, 492 thirty-three, 277; Trayastriṃśa, 430
"heavenly book," see "book, heavenly"
Hebrus, 391

Ieine-Geldern, Robert von, 268n, 333n, 334n, 361n, 442n, 460n

Ieissig, Walther, 154n, 174n, 461n

Iel, 382, 383

Iell, 397, 446f; and ancestor cult, 458; see also Hades; underworld

Iell, Great, 438f

Iellenistic East, 501

Iemberg, Bengt, 473n

Iemorrhage, hysterical, 308

Iemp, see smoke

Ienning, W. B., 398n

Ienry, A., 442n

Iens, transformation into, 56, 478

Ientze, Carl, 94n, 179n, 270n, 271n, 272n, 273n, 334n, 435n, 449n, 458n, 459n, 460n, 461n

Iera, 391, 488

Ierakles, xvi, 392, 506n

Ierb, miraculous, 78

Ieredity, transmission of power by, 13, 21, 372

Iermanns, Matthias, 431n, 432n

Iermaphrodites, 352

Iermes Psychopompos, 392

Iermódhr, 380, 383

Iermotimos of Clazomenae, 389

Iero(es): and animal, 94; ascent of, 491; civilizing, 361, 362; and crystal mountains, 139; culture, Orpheus as, 391; descent to underworld, 94, 367f; fairy women and, 78, 81; journey of, 94, 204n; long hair and, 152n

Ierodotus, 389n, 394, 395, 434n

Ieron, 478

Iierogamy, heaven/earth, 285

Iierophanies: dialectic of, xii, 32, 107; and history, xvi; repetition of, xviii; spontaneity of, xix

Iih, 452

Iiku, 368

Iilden, K., 197n

Iillebrandt, Alfred, 413n

Iimingbjörg, 267

Iimmelsdiener, 493n

Iinduism, 286, 408

Iiroa, Te Rangi (Peter H. Buck), 370n, 371n

Iistoriography, xvf

Iistory: and myth, 355, 362; polyvalence of term, xvi; of religions, see religions; and transformation of archaic religious schema, 376f

Iiung-Nu, 183

Iivale, Shamrao, 468n

hobby-horse, Morris, 469; see also horse

Hocart, Arthur Maurice, 410n, 478n

Hoffman, W. J., 313n, 315 & n, 316n, 317n, 318n

Hoffmann, Helmut, 165n, 177, 274n, 431n, 432n, 433n

Hoffmann, John, 425n

Höfler, Otto, 355n, 380, 384n, 467n, 469n, 473n

"Hole of the Spirits," 234

Holm, G., 289n

Holmberg, Uno, see Harva, Uno

Holmer, Nils M., and Wassén, S. Henry, 323n

Holt, Catharine, see Kroeber, Alfred Louis

homosexuality, see inverts; pederasty

Honko, Lauri, 215n

Hopkins, Edward Washburn, 409n

Hopkins, L. C., 452n

Hornell, James, 332n, 366n

horns; on shaman's cap, 155, 462; stag, 462

horse, 217, 407, 467ff; eight-hooved/-legged, 380, 469; gray, 89; hairs of, 469; mythology of, 467; Odin's, 380; religious importance, 11; sacrificial, 405, see also horse sacrifice; shaman's, 151, 173f, 175, 325, 408, 467; see also drum; skull of, 232; stars as, 261; and tree, 270n; white, 55, 154; wooden, 325, 408; see also drum; hobby-horse

horse sacrifice, 79f, 182, 183, 190ff, 198ff, 325, 471; agrarianization of, 197n; in India, 199; see also asvamedha

Horse-stick, Lord and Lady of the, 118

house: and Center of World, 265; purification after death in, 208

Housse, Émile, 25, 53, 123, 124n, 325n, 330

Howell, W., 360n

Howitt, A. W., 45 & n, 136, 137n, 138n, 490n, 491n

Huai-nan Tse, 451

Huart, Clément, 401 & n

Huang Ti, 449

Huchnom, 54

Hudson Bay, 161n

Huginn, 381

Hultkrantz, Åke, 241n, 300n, 310n, 311n, 313n, 391n

humanism, and spiritual tradition, xx

Hummel, Siegbert, 432n, 438n, 444n, 466n, 470n

Hungarian shamans, see táltos

hunters: and guardian spirits, 104; ideology of, 435; paleolithic, 503; Siberian, 502
hunting: rites, 10, 12, 184, 385; shaman and, 299, 459
Huottarie, 39
Hupa, 21, 105
hurricane, 359
hut: initiatory, 128, 131; leaf, 341; shaking of, 335, 338
Hu Ti, 457
Hutu, 367*f*
hymns, shamanic, 19; *see also* songs
Hyperboreans, 388
hysteria, 31; arctic, 24
hysteroid: crisis, and vocation, 17; disease, xi

I

Ibn Baṭūṭah, 429
ice, diving in, 113
Ichirō, Hori, 462
ichiya-tsuma, 463
Ida, Mount, 389
ideology: religious, 7; shamanic, 300, 310, 373, 378, 413, 504, 507
ié-kyla, 89*f*
Iglulik, *see* Eskimo
ikikuchi, 462
Ila, 473*n*
illness: and shamanic election, 28; shamans and, 31; and violation of taboos, 289; *see also* disease; epilepsy; hysteria; hysteroid; insanity; mental disease; psychopathy; sickness; "sickness-vocation"; syphilis
illud tempus, see time
illumination, shaman's, 90, 91, 420
Ilpailurkna, 47*f*
immersion, 235
Immortality: Medicine of, 446; Tree of, 271; *see also* soul
Im Thurn, Everard F., 97*n*
incisions, seven, 283
India: aboriginals, 287*n*; bones in, 163*f*; "burning" concept, 475*f*; drum in, 420, 426; fire-walking, 372; influence of, 4, 165, 279, 496, 500; —, on Batak, 286, 346, 348; —, on Buryat ritual, 122*n*; —, on China, 453*n*; journey to, 204; magical flight in, 407*ff*; possession in, 424; psychopomp in, 418; rope trick in, 127, 428*ff*; seven colors and, 134; Vedic, 328; —, sacrifice in, 199;

skulls in, 421, 434*n*; and World Pillar, Center, 264, 266, 268, 272
"Indian Grandfather," 128
Indians: North American, *see* America, North; South American, *see* America, South; *for both, names of specific tribes*
Indochina, 443
Indo-Europeans, 10*f*, 375*ff*; contact with urban culture, 379; and horse sacrifice 198; religion of, 10, 375*ff*; and Turko Tatars, resemblances, 10*f*, 378
Indonesia(ns), 5, 182, 273, 279, 355, 357, 455; Chinese art and, 334*n*; drumming, 177; eternal return, 246*n*; mourners, 396*n*; multiple souls, 215; rainbow in, 133; shamanism, and sickness, 25; transvestitism, 258
Indra, 199, 267, 439
Ingjugarjuk, 59–60*n*
inheritance, of shamanic profession, 13 15*ff*, 20*ff*; *see also* heredity; initiation
inhibition, neurotic, 402*n*
Ini, 352
initiation, 14, 110*ff*, 343, *et passim*; and accidents, 45, 81; celestial and infernal 34; dreams and, 33*ff*; ecstasies and, 33*ff*; fasting and, 43, 84, 129; martial, military, 385, 467; and medicine man 32; morphological similarities, 362*n*; and shaman's journey, 236; and shamanic powers, 109; sickness and, 33*ff* 38*ff*; tribal, and guardian spirits, 107 —, and shamanic, 64, 65; *see also* dismemberment
insanity, 365*n*; *see also* psychopathy; mental disease
insensibility, physical, 244
inspiration, 253
instruction, of shaman, 13*f*, 31, 33, 34, 110*ff*, 425; *see also* initiation
integrity, psychic, 508*f*
interpreter, shaman's, 302*f*, 306
Interpreters of the Sky, 276
intoxication, 223, 395, 399*ff*; *see also* alcohol; mushrooms; narcotics; smoke toxins
inverts, sexual, as shamans, 125*n*
invisibility, 86, 140
invulnerability, 100
Ipiutak culture, 334*n*
Iran(ians): and Cosmic Axis/Mountain 266, 267, 272; dualism, 68, 163*n*; and hemp, 395; influence of, 501; —, on Buddhist India, 163; —, on Buryat, 122 —, on shamanism, 68, 122, 400, 506

—*ₛ* on Yakut, 186; Islamized, 401; otherworld ideas, 396*ff*
Ireland, prophets, 179
i'rkeye, 245
Irkutsk, 28
Irle Kan, 213, 270; *see also* Erlik Khan
Irminsūl, 261*n*, 263
iron/Iron, 50, 231; bones fastened with, 36, 158*f*; Man-Pillar of, 263; Mountain of, *see s.v.*; on shamanic costumes, 29, 148, 150, 152, 158; snake, 426
Irtysh, 9, 15, 183, 220
Iruntarinia, 46*f*, 48
Ishtar, 506*n*
Islam: "bridge" in, 484; in Central Asia, 402; influence on Altaians, 208*n*; — on Menangkabau, 286; levitation in, 481; *see also* Mohammedanism
isolation: psychic, 33; of shamanic candidates, 128, 131
Israel, 393*n*; *see also* Jews; Judaism
Issedones, 434*n*
Itkonen, Toivo Immanuel, 15*n*, 30*n*, 90*n*, 93*n*, 175*n*, 176*n*, 224*n*, 278*n*, 477*n*
Itonama, 327*n*
Ivanov, Pyotr, 36
Ivanov, S. V., 146*n*

J

Jacob's Fountain, 268
Jacob's Ladder, 488
Jacoby, Adolf, 70*n*, 428*n*, 429*n*, 430*n*
jaguars, 129
Jaiminīya Brāhmaṇa, 415*n*, 419*n*
Jaiminīya Upaniṣad Brāhmaṇa, 405*n*
Jajyk (Yaik) Kan, 88
Jakun, 21, 91, 177*n*, 283, 341; *see also* Malay Peninsula; Negritos
Jambudvīpa, 439
Jangmai, 421*f*
Japan(ese), 285*n*, 380*n*; and bridge, 484; funerary beliefs, 355; and rainbow, 133, 134; shamanism in, 462*ff*; smiths, 473
Jäschke, H. A., 431*n*
Jātakas, 436
Java, 429, 467
Jenness, Diamond, 333*n*
Jensen, A. E., and Niggemeyer, H., 490*n*
Jeremias, Alfred, 134*n*, 267*n*, 269*n*, 488*n*
Jerusalem, 489
jĕs'sakkīd', 315*f*, 318
Jesus Christ, 66
Jettmar, Karl, 11*n*, 500*n*, 501*n*
Jews, 161*n*; *see also* Israel; Judaism

jhānas, 406
jimson weed, 109
jīvan-mukta, 413
Jivaro, 26, 84
Job, Book of, 261*n*
Jochelson, Waldemar I., 24*n*, 145*n*, 156*n*, 186*n*, 216*n*, 221*n*, 229*n*, 232*n*, 234*n*, 245*n*, 246*n*, 247, 248*n*, 249*n*, 250*n*, 251*n*, 252, 262*n*, 435*n*, 470*n*, 491*n*
John Climacus, St., 489
John of the Cross, St., 489*n*
Johnson, Frederick, 302*n*
Johore, 342*n*
Joseph of Cupertino, St., 126*f*, 482
journey, shamanic/ecstatic, 8, 72*n*, 114, 127*ff*, 182, 223, 236, 289, *et passim*; and birds, 98; to Center of World, 269; drum and, 173*ff*; "for joy alone," 291; and guardian spirits, 95, 103, 157; undersea/underwater, 289, 293; *see also* ascent; underworld; sky
Juaneno, 109
Juang, 425
Judaism, 134; *see also* Israel; Jews
Judges, Book of, 268*n*
jugglers, 315
jungle, 343
juniper, 116, 118*n*, 192, 445
Jupiter, pillars of, 261*n*
jutpa, 153
Juynboll, H. H., 354*n*, 490*n*

K

Kachin, 426*n*, 442*n*
Kadang baluk, 339*n*
Kagarow, E., 169*n*, 270*n*
Kahn, Charles H., 389*n*
Kahtyr-Kaghtan Bouraï-Toyon, 188
kahu, 371, 372
Kaira Kan, 88, 192, 193, 198*f*, 275, 276
Kakâd (Chakât)-i-Dâitîk, 397, 399
Kakhyen, 455*n*
Kalau, 249, 251
Kalmyk, 122*n*, 164, 261, 266, 267, 271
Kaltenmark, Max, 450*n*
kam/gam/kami/qam, 4, 20, 76, 190*ff*, 495, 502*n*
kāmaru, 502*n*
Kamchadal, 100*n*, 165, 257*n*, 258
kami, see *kam*
kamikuchi, 462
Kamilaroi, 134
kamlanie, 155*n*
Kaniṣka, 420

Kānphaṭā Yogis, 164
Kāpālikas, 434n
Kapilavastu, 428
kapnobatai, 390
Karagas, 155, 156, 174, 279
karain bö, 185
kara kam, 189
Karakuš, 196
Karei, 231n, 337, 338
Karen, 442, 455
Karginz, 208
Kari, 337
Karjalainen, K. F., 15, 29, 89 & n, 145n,
   154n, 164n, 182n, 183n, 220n, 221,
   222, 262n, 263n, 276n, 278n, 279n
Karsten, Rafael, 26n, 169n, 176n, 224n,
   323n, 329n
Karšüt, 197n
katā.na, 465
Katanov, N. V., 277
Kaṭha Upaniṣad, 405n, 485
Katshina, 183
kaula, 370n
Kawaiisu, 109
Kawelu, 368
Kazak Kirgiz, see Kirgiz
kazatauri, 210
K'daai Maqsin, 470ff
Kebrenoi, 390
Keith, Arthur Berriedale, 413n, 417n,
   418n
Kelantan, 25, 93, 231n, 338, 339, 344
ké'let, 255, 257
kemoit, 281
Kena, 368
kennikî oyuna, 185n
Kenta, 341
Kenya, 263
kerchief, 148, 167
kerei, 85
Kerényi, Carl, 392n
Keres, 316n
Ket, 70n, 216n, 223n
khamu-at, 174
Khangalov, M. N., 115, 120; see also
   Agapitov, N. N.
Khans: black and white, 185, 186; west-
   ern, 118, 119n
khärägä-khulkhä, 117
Khara-Gyrgän, 68
Khargi, 17
Khasi, 263
Khingan, 153
Khond, 425
Khosru, Emir, 410n

khubilgan/khubilkhu, 94
King: of the Dead, see s.v.; of the
   Underworld, see s.v.
kings: and ascent to heaven, 431; flying,
   408, 481
kingfisher, 232
Kintara, 421f
Kirchner, Horst, 156n, 382n, 396n, 481,
   503
Kirfel, Willibald, 267n, 406n
Kirgiz, 97, 164, 175, 261, 497; Kazak, 30,
   44, 155n, 157; —, recruitment
   among, 20
kite/kiteflying, 78n, 133, 367, 373
Kittredge, George Lyman, 92n, 93n,
   164n, 478n
Kiwai, 57
Klallam, 21
Klamath, 21
Klaproth, J. H., 431n
klimax, 488
knives, ladder of, 442, 443, 484
Knoll-Greiling, Ursula, 14n
knots, 419
kobuz, 175
Koch, Theodor, 326n, 482n
Koch-Grünberg, T., 30
Koita, 365n
Kojiki, 463
Kolarians, 424
Kommandostäbe, 503
Kollantz, Arnulf, 396n
koori, 204n, 211
Koppers, Wilhelm, xiii, 11n, 53n, 80n,
   177n, 198n, 243n, 323n, 327n, 332,
   421n, 425n, 426n, 466n, 469n, 487n,
   501n, 502n
Köprülüzadé, Mehmed Fuad, 67n, 402,
   403n
Koran, 163n
Korea, 461f, 496
Korku, 424n, 425, 468
Körmös, 197, 206
Körner, Theo, 449n
Korwa, 425
Koryak, 206, 261, 491n; divination
   among, 164; family shamanism, 247;
   and masks, 165; ritual transformation
   into woman, 258; séances among, 249ff;
   and sky god, 9
Kosingas, 390, 488
kotchaĭ, 233
kougos, 232
Krader, Lawrence, 186n, 218n
kratophanies, dialectic of, 32

Kremsmayer, Heimo, 452n
Kretschmar, Freda, 466
Krivoshapkin, —, 24
Kroeber, Alfred Louis, 52n, 103n, 105n, 109n, 311n, 477n; and Holt, Catharine, 167n
Kroef, Justus M. van der, 352n
Krohn, Kaarle, 71n
Kroll, Josef, 392n
Kruyt/Kruijt/Krujt, A. C., 347n, 358n; see also Adriani, N.
Ksenofontov, G. V., 37n, 38n, 43, 44n, 114, 469n
Kuala Langat, 282
Kubaiko, 213f
Kubu, 285, 349
kuei, 454
kuei-ju, 453
kujur, 55
Kuksu, 55
Kulin (Australian tribe), 134, 491
kulin ("snakes"), 149
Kumandin, 79, 176n, 197n
Kunlun, Mount, 457
Kuo yu, 451
kupitja, 48
Kurkutji, 49
Kurnai, 491
kut, 206
Kwakiutl, 138
Kwangsi, 455n
Kysugan Tengere, 275

L

Laborde, —, 131
Labrador, 164n
labyrinth, 51
laces, 419
Lä-ch'ou, 447
ladder, 58, 123, 126, 129, 326, 328, 391, 410, 430f, 487ff; in India, 407, 426; Mithraic, 121f; soul, 283, 285, 487; see also knives; sword-ladder
Ladder, Book of the, 489n
Lady: of the Animals, see s.v.; "of the Earth," 187; "Gentle, of Birth," 187; Great, of the Night, 367; of the Underworld, 368; of the Waters, 39, 42; "of the White Colt," 188; see also mother
Lafont, Pierre-Bernard, 443n
Lagercrantz, Eliel, 96n
laghiman, 409
Lakher, 442n
Lalou, Marcelle, 438

Lamaism, 208n, 266, 506; drum in, 176, 497f; Mongols and, 461, 500; skulls in, 421, 434f; and soul, 440f; sutura frontalis in, 164; and Tungus shamanism, 112, 237, 497; see also Tibet
lamas: and shamanism, 433ff, 498; and shamans, compared, 440
lambs, sacrifice of, 123
Lamotte, Étienne, 409n
lance, 47, 285, 343, 491
Lancelot, 484
Land: of the Dead, see s.v.; "pure," 409; of the Shamanesses, 39
Landtman, G., 57n
language: animal/secret/shaman's, 62, 93ff, 96ff, 290, 338n, 511; Eskimo, 288n; Lapp, 96; Sogdian, 496; of the spirits, 347, 440; Tibetan secret, 440; "twilight," 440
Lankenau, H. von, 20n, 173n, 219n
Lanternari, V., 132n
Laos, 443n
Lapp(s), 93, 161n, 224, 235, 261, 263, 278, 288, 335; and American tribes, 334; and drum, 172, 175ff, 334; helping spirits, 90n; recruiting of shamans, 15; séance among, 223; secret language, 96
Larsen, Helge, 334n
Laru Kaj, 468
Lascaux, 481, 503, 504
Lattimore, Owen, 241n
Laufer, Berthold, 119n, 133n, 164n, 333n, 430n, 434n, 448n, 449n, 451n, 460n, 495, 501n
laurel, 130n
Laval, Honoré, 370n
Laviosa-Zambotti, Pia, 279n, 280n
Law, Tables of the, 393n
Layard, John W., 25, 27n, 56n, 126n, 361n, 477n, 478n
laymen, imitation of shamanism by, 252f
leap(s), ceremonial, 338, 443
Lebed Tatars, see Tatars
Leeuw, Gerardus van der, 489n
Lehmann, Walter, 332n
Lehtisalo, T., 16n, 37n, 38 & n, 39n, 42n, 44n, 93n, 96n, 97n, 98, 145n, 161n, 174, 213n, 226n, 228, 264n, 277n, 278n
leopard, 55
Lepers Island, 365n
Lepcha, 432n, 433n
Leroy, Olivier, 373n, 481n, 482
Lesbos, 391
Lessing, F. D., 433n

Lévi, Sylvain, 403, 405n, 413n, 496n;
  and Chavannes, É., 410n
levitation, 61, 243, 481f; see also ascen-
  sion; flying
Levy, Gertrude R., 51n, 272n
Lévy, Isidore, 393n
Lévy-Bruhl, Lucien, 478n
liana, 328
Li An-che, 432n
Li byin ha ra, 37n
Lie, House of the, 398
Lietard, Fr., 443
Life: Book of, see s.v.; Master of, see s.v.;
  Tree of, 271 & n, 282
life-substance, 160
Light/light: Creator of, see s.v.; inner,
  61, 420, 508; mystical, 60f; solidified,
  137f, 508; white, 9
lightness, 485
lightning, 19, 55, 81, 100 & n, 170, 206
Ligoi, 280
Lillooet Indians, 102
Lindgren, E. J., 30, 110n, 145n
Lingo Pen, 468
Lindquist, Sigurd, 409n
Linton, Ralph, 371n, 372n
lions, mountain, 101
Li Shao-kun, 451
literature, traditional, 361; see also epic;
  poetry; Saga
Liu An, 451
Liungman, Waldemar, 161n
liver, eating, 250
lizard(s), 122n, 155n, 271n, 484
Llü-bu, 444n
Loeb, Edwin Mayer, 21n, 25n, 54n, 55n,
  64n, 65n, 82n, 86n, 87n, 96n, 97n,
  126n, 140n, 178n, 286n, 287n, 347n,
  348n, 349n, 369n
log, rotten, 311f
Loima-Yékamush, 54n
Lokasenna, 385
Loki, 386n
Lol-narong, 56
Lolo, 164n, 209, 426n, 441f
Lommel, Hermann, 417n
Lopatin, Ivan A., 115n, 210n, 212n, 244f
Lord(s): Universal, 42, 168; of the Birds,
  see s.v.; of the Dead, see s.v.; of the
  Earth, see s.v.; and Lady of the
  Horse-stick, see Horse-stick; of Mad-
  ness, see s.v.; of the Sea, see s.v.; of the
  Tree, see s.v.; of the Underworld, see
  s.v.; of the Water, see s.v.; of the World,
  see s.v.; see also "White Lord Creator"

Losun, 267
Lot-Falck, Eveline, 10n, 81n, 149n, 168n
Lotuko, 25
Lowie, Robert H., 310n, 334 & n, 335
Lublinski, Ida, 54n, 84n, 97n, 141n, 326n
Lucifer, 139
Luiseno, 55, 109
Lunga, 108n
Luomala, Katharine, 367n
lupa, 344, 345f
Lushai, 442n
lycanthropy, 467; see also werewolves
lyric poetry, 510

M

Maanyan, 357
Macchioro, Vittorio, 391n
machi, 53, 123ff, 141, 325, 327, 329f, 467
McMahon, A. R., 455n
Macusi, 21
Madagascar, 309n
Maddox, John Lee, 21n, 177n
Madness: Lord of, 39; Spirit of, 149
Madsen, W., 323n
maga, 398
magic: Chinese, 442f; fire and, 363; heat
  and, 363, 474ff; Indian, 348; powers,
  acquisition of, 21f; —, quest for, 107;
  primitive, 3; shamanic elements in, 6f,
  universality of, 5
magician(s): black, 297ff, 362, 508; and
  shaman, distinction, 5; use of term, 3;
  women as, 363
magico-religious powers, methods of
  acquiring, 22f
Magna Mater, 121
Magyars, see Hungarian shamans
Mahābhārata, 409, 410n, 420n
Mahīdhara, 405n
Maidu, 54, 102n, 104, 179, 262
maiqabči, 151
Majjhima-nikāya, 405, 406, 437n
Maki, 126
Malacca, 358n
malakhaī, 155n
Malakot, 468
Malay Peninsula/Archipelago/Malays/
  Malaysia, 177n, 281, 282, 344ff, 355ff,
  475, 487, 503; see also Jakun; Negritos
Malekula, 25, 51, 56, 126, 362n, 477, 478
Maler, 425
males, initiation of, 65
Malinowski, Bronislaw, 283n, 478n
Malten, Ludolph, 467n

malu, 165
Mampes, 281
Mampüi, 200
mana, 475
Manabozho, 321
Manacica, 326
manang, 57, 126, 350*ff*
manang bali, 258, 351
manas, 479
Manasi, 141, 323, 324
Mänchen-Helfen, Otto, 173, 501*n*
Manchu/Manchuria, 214*n*, 240, 497;
 initiation among, 110, 112*f*, 438;
 Northern, 154, 242; recruiting among,
 17*f*; shamanic costume, 157, 158; *see
 also* Tungus
mane kisu, 364*f*
Mangaian, 368
Mangar, 487
Mangareva, 369, 370*n*
Mani, 119*n*
Manidou, 317
Man in the Moon, *see* Moon
Manker, Ernst, 168*n*, 173*n*, 175, 176*n*
Mankova, 240
Männerbünde, 467, 473; *see also* men's
 societies
Mannhardt, Johann Wilhelm Emanuel,
 162*n*
Man-Pillar of Iron, *see* Iron
Manquilef, Manuel, 330*n*
"Manual," of Buryat shamans, 115 & *n*,
 150
Manyak, 189
m'ao, 241
Maori, 367, 369, 492; *see also* New
 Zealand
Mapic Tree, 281, 282
maqet, 488
Mara, 49*f*, 51, 137
maraca, 178
marae, 370*n*
marang deora, 426
maraque, 129
Marcel-Dubois, Claudie, 420*n*
marebito, 463
Maricopa, 103
Marind, 478
Mariner, W., 371 & *n*
Maringer, Johannes, 51*n*, 168*n*, 434*n*,
 481*n*
Marka Pandum, 468
Märküt, 193
Marquesas Islands/Marquesans, 368,
 371, 372

marriages: initiatory, 421; of shamaness
 to god, 463; spirit, 424; *see also* wives,
 celestial
Mars (planet), 83
Marshall, Harry Ignatius, 442*n*
Marstrander, Carl, 66*n*
Martino, Ernesto de, 255*n*, 290*n*, 372*n*
Mary of Jesus Crucified, Sister, 482
marya, 399*n*
Masai, 472*n*
masks, 93, 148, 149, 151, 165*ff*, 177, 179
Maspero, Henri, 441*n*, 448*n*, 449*n*, 453
massage, 123, 364
Massignon, Louis, 402*n*, 429*n*
Massim, 365*n*
Master(s): of the Fire, 193; of Life, 142,
 320, 321; of the Drum, 192
Mat Chinoi, 340
matriarchy: and celestial god, 505; "ce-
 lestial wife" and, 78, 81; Chinese, 449;
 Japanese elements, 464; and Sea
 Dyak, 352; and secret societies, 166*f*;
 and sex change, 258; and Tree of
 Life, 282
Matthew, Gospel of, 485*n*
Maui, 362, 367
Mauss, Marcel, 45*n*, 85, 136*n*
Max Müller, Frederick, 488*n*
māyayā, 410
May-junk-kān, 222
Mazdaism, 396*n*
Më, 444
meal, celestial wife and, 77, 80
meaning, transfer of, 152*n*
Medea, 66
Medicine of Immortality, 446
medicine man: Australian, consecration,
 50*ff*, 65; hereditary profession, 21*f*;
 Melanesian, 362; psychopathy of, 26;
 and shaman, distinction, 300; special
 character, 31*f*; use of term, 3
Medicine Rite, Winnebago, 319*f*
meditation: on bones, 62*f*; Buddhist, 407;
 by fire, 412; yogic, 406
Mediterranean civilizations, 379
mediumship, 370, 456; spontaneous, 347
Meier, Fritz, 402*n*
Meillet, A., 496*n*
Meisen, Karl, 384*n*
Melanesia(ns), 358; and ascent to sky,
 491; Asiatic art and, 334*n*; rainbow
 in, 133; and ritual boat, 356; shamanism
 in, 361*ff*; three cultural types, 361
Melnikow, N., 218*n*
Melton, E., 429

memory, loss of, 65
"men, wooden," 246
Menangkabau, 86, 286, 348
Menasce, Jean de, 398n
Mendes Correa, 332
menerik, 24, 29
Menghin, O., 280n
Menomini, 55, 97, 316, 335
Menri, 231n, 338
men's societies, 166f, 469; see also
  Männerbünde
mental capacity, of shamans, 29f
mental disease: shamanism and, xif;
  24f; see also insanity; psychopathy
Mentawei(ans), 25, 85, 87, 96, 140,
  178, 349
Menteg, 282
Meo, 443
"Merciful Emperor Heaven," 198, 275
Mergen Tengere, 276
Meru, Mount, 266, 409, 439
meryak, 24, 29
meshibitsu, 463
Mesopotamia, 393n, 480, 501, 506; and
  India, 268; and rainbow, 134; and
  world Center/Pillar, 264, 266, 274
messengers of god, see god
Messenger, Spirit, 137
metallurgy: and Africa, 473; Chinese,
  461n; secrets of, 474; and shamanism,
  42n; see also smith(s)
Metawand, 468
meteors/meteorites, 139, 260
Métraux, Alfred, 21n, 26n, 30, 51n, 52n,
  53 & n, 54n, 83n, 91n, 92n, 97n, 98n,
  123n, 125n, 129n, 130n, 131, 141n,
  178n, 323n, 324n, 325n, 327n, 328n,
  329n, 330, 331n, 351n, 477n
Meuli, Karl, 159n, 160, 166n, 180n,
  192n, 193n, 334n, 388n, 390n, 394, 395,
  413n, 460n, 473n
Mexico, 92, 319, 429, 430n
microcosm, 261, 265, 415; drum as, 172f
midē, 316ff
midēwigan, 317
Midē'wiwin, 103n, 143, 299, 313n, 314,
  315ff, 321
mīgis, 316ff
migrations, ancestral, and boat of the
  dead, 355
Mikhailof, A. N., 75
Mikhailowski, V. M., 13n, 15n, 16n,
  17n, 19n, 20n, 68n, 69n, 89n, 90n,
  100n, 114n, 115n, 145n, 148n, 150n,
  153n, 155n, 173n, 181n, 185n, 190n,

201n, 218n, 219n, 220n, 224n, 226n,
  227n, 228n, 236n, 243n, 255n, 278n
Mikkulai, 38
miko, 463, 464
mikogami, 463
Mi-la ras-pa, 433
military elements, 508
milk, oblations of, 263
Milk, Ocean of, 409
Milky Way, 260, 271n, 292
Mimir, head of, 382, 391
Mi'nabō'zho, 316f
Mindanao, 25
Ming dynasty, 241, 497
Minitari Indians, 159n
Minnungarra, 49
Minusinsk Tatars, 156
miracles, 4, 67, 228, 324, 412, 511
Mironov, N. D., and Shirokogoroff,
  S. M., 496n, 497n
mirror(s), 151, 153f, 498
Mithraic mysteries, 121, 488
miwi, 86
Miwok, 54
Mjöllnir, 162
Modi, Jivanji Jamshedji, 163
Moerenhout, Jacques A., 371n
Moesbach, —, 123, 124
Mogk, E., 71n
Mohaghir, 426
Mohammed, ascent to heaven, 377, 489
  & n
Mohammedans, Indian, 475
Mohave, 103
Mojo, 323
mompanrilangka, 353
mompemate, 354
Mongolia/Mongols, 10, 261, 267, 276,
  277, 497, 498; and Buddhism, 496;
  Cosmic Mountain, 266, 270, 271;
  divination, 164; Iranian influence, 501;
  and Lamaism, 461, 500
Monguor, 461
Mono, 21
monotheism, in religious history, xviii
monster, cannibal, 251–52n
Montandon, Georges, 167n
mood changes, 20
moon/Moon: 196, 327; Man in the, 292;
  Spirit of the, 62
Mooney, James, 142n, 320n, 321n, 322n
Mordo Kan, 193
Moréchand, Guy, 443n
Mori, 354
Morris, J., 432n

Morris horse, 469; *see also* horse
Moses, 393*n*
Moso, 392, 444*f*
Moss, Rosalind, 355*n*, 356*n*, 358*n*, 482*n*
Mota Lava, 365
mother(s)/Mother(s): animal, 89; of the Animals, *see s.v.*; Bird-, *see s.v.*; of the Caribou, 62; "Creatress, Gentle," 187; Divine/Holy, 463; and Father Tree, *see* Tree; Goddesses, 379; Queen, of the West, 457; of the Sea Beasts, *see s.v.*; Tasygan, 193; *see also* Lady
notion, imagination of, 480
Mount of the Lands, 267
mountain(s)/Mountain(s): artificial, 267; Cosmic, 41, 42, 266*ff*, *et passim*, *see also* Axis, Center of the World, Tree; crystal, 139; of the Dead, *see s.v.*; in funerary mythology, 283, 355; as guardian spirits, 90, 106; Iron, 201, 266, 270, 439*n*; of Siva, 420; Taliang, 441
mourners: Indonesian, 396*n*; women, 358, 359*f*
mouse, 39, 41
Mu, King of Chu, 457
muday, 464
Mühlmann, Wilhelm Emil, 286*n*
Mukat, 103
Mula djadi na bolon, 286
Mu-lian, 457, 458
Müller, F. Max, see Max Müller, Frederick
Müller, Werner, 138*n*, 313*n*, 317*n*, 318*n*, 319*n*
Mu-monto, 213
Munda, 424*n*, 425, 426*f*, 473, 502*n*
Mundadji, 49
muni, 152*n*, 407*f*, 411
Muninn, 381
Munkácsi, Bernhardt, 401*n*
Munkaninji, 49
Münsterberger, Werner, 284*n*, 286*n*
Muria, 325, 380, 425, 469
Murray, Margaret Alice, 92*n*
Mus, Paul, 267*n*, 268*n*, 269*n*, 405*n*, 406*n*
Musaeus, 388
mushrooms, 220*f*, 223, 228, 278, 400*f*
music: and ecstasy, 223; magic of, 175, 180
musical instruments, autonomy of, 180
Muster, Wilhelm, 386*n*, 397*n*
Mwod Mod, 443*n*
Mysore, 424*n*
mystic, unsuccessful, 27

mysticism, xviii, xix; agricultural, 379; Buddhist, 64; Christian, 63, 489, 508; and inner light, 61; Islamic, 402, 489; North American, 299*f*; primitive, 3; shamans and, 265; and shamanism, 8, 508
Mytchyll, 29
myth, *see* history
mythical personage, incarnation of, 167*f*
mythology: of horse, 467; lunar, 285, 358*n*, 506; matriarchal, 10, 78, 351; Scandinavian, 176, 224; and shamanism, 7; *see also* woman

N

Nachtigall, H., 159*n*
Naciketas, 418
Nadel, S. F., 21*n*, 26*n*, 27, 31, 55*n*, 141*n*, 373*n*
nāga (snake-spirit), 420
Nāgārjuna, 409*n*
Nagas (tribe), 287*n*
Nagatya, 45
nagual, 92
Nail Star, 261
Na-khi, 431, 444*ff*, 508
Nam, 188
name-card, 439
Nandi, 263
Nandimitra, 410*n*
Nārada, 409
narcotics, xiii, 24, 64, 84, 109, 130*n*, 220, 402*n*, 417, 477; in yoga, 416
Na-ro bon-č'un, 433
Narr, Karl J., 501*n*, 502–03*n*, 503, 504
Narrinyeri, 491
Nart, 476
Nda-pa, 444
Nebesky-Wojkowitz, René de, 37*n*, 175*n*, 177*n*, 432*n*, 433
necromancy: Greek, 387; Odin and, 382
Negelein, Julius von, 479
Negritos, 21, 138, 337, 340; *see also* Jakun; Malay Peninsula
Nehring, Alfons, 390*n*
Nelson, Edward William, 292*n*
Németh, Julius, 495
Nepal, 487
nervous disorders, *see* psychopathy
Nespelem, 179
net, 419
Newbold, T. J., 344*n*
New Guinea, 65, 334*n*, 363, 365; *see also* Papuans

New Hebrides, 21
New Ireland, 334n
New Year, 357
New Zealand, 133n, 368, 485, 492; see also Maori
Nez Perce, 21
Ngadju Dyak, see Dyak
Ngenechen, 53
ngillatun ceremony, 324f, 325n
Nguyẽn-văn-Khoan, 442n
Nias/Niassans, 140, 287, 348
Nicobar Islands, 342ff, 356n
Nicola Valley, 100
Niggemeyer, H., see Jensen, A. E.
Night, Great Lady of the, 367
"night, spirit of the," 104f
nigurasun, 150
Nihongi, 463
nijamas, 478n
Nil, Archbishop of Yaroslavl, 151, 165
Nilsson, Martin P., 387n, 388n
nimgan, 210
nine: gods, 275ff; heavens, see s.v.; levels of underworld, 383; the number, 274ff; Seas, 39; sons/brothers, 471; trees, 233
Nine Seas, 39
ninety-nine gods, 277
Ninwa, 348
Nioradze, Georg, 14n, 24n, 89n, 145n, 147n, 148n, 150n, 153n, 166n
Nirṛti, 415, 419
Nirvāṇa, 406, 407
Nišan, 241
Nišan šaman, 241
Niue, 25
Nodora Gond, 58n
noise, magic of, 174f
Nölle, W., 396n, 420n
nomads/nomadism, 9, 501
Nootka Indians, 138, 309
Nordenskiöld, Erland, 323n
north: birth of shamans in, 37; as "Center," 279
North America, see America, North
nose, piercing of, 48
Nourry, Émile, 161n
Nuba, 141; Mountains, 55
nudity, ritual, 146, 224
Num, 9, 199, 213n, 227, 264n
Numazawa, Franz Kiichi, 133n, 441n, 483n
numbers: mystical, 36; see also three; four; seven; nine; thirty-three; forty-nine; ninety-nine
numerals, 501

Num-tôrem, 276
Nü Ying, 448
Nyberg, H. S., 396n, 398, 399n
nyen-jomo, 432
Nyima, 21
Nyuak, Leo, 57n

O

Ob, 501
Obermaier, H., see Breuil, H.
óboro, 57
"obstacles," initiatory, 384; see also passage, difficult; pudak
ocean, cosmic, 456
Ocean of Milk, 409
Oceania, 5, 25, 257n, 279, 362, 419; initiation in, 65; ladder in, 490; rock crystals in, 139; and South America, 332n
Ochirvani, 267
Odin, 71n, 270n, 375, 380ff, 385; shamanic attributes, 381n
Oesterreich, T. K., 25n, 347n
offerings, ritual, paleolithic, 503
Ohlmarks, Åke, 14n, 24, 26, 89n, 145n, 157, 158n, 166n, 167n, 223n, 224n, 231n, 386n
O Huang, 448
oĭbonküngätä, 148
oigös timir, 149
ojha, 426
Ojibwa, 143, 315ff
ojuna (oyuna), 4
Oka, Masao, 462
Okanagon, 21, 104n
Okladnikov, A. P., 500n
oko-jumu, 342
öksökjou, 232
Oktu Kan, 193
Olaf, St., 489
Old Dixie, 105f, 109n
Oldenberg, Hermann, 413n
Oleny Island, 503
Olkhonsk Buryat, 151
oloh, 232
Olsen, Magnus, 386n
omnipotence, 299
ontological separation, 32
opening: cosmic/central, 259, 265; in earth and sky, 251
"Opening into the Earth," 234
opposites, transcending, 486
Opler, Morris Edward, 300n, 302n
O'Rahilly, Thomas F., 382n

Oraon, 415, 425, 426f, 473
orations, funeral, 358
ordeals: initiatory, 14, 17; see also tortures
organs, mystical, 328
orgiski, 238
orgoï, 150
Oriental civilizations, and Indo-Europeans, 379
Oriental religion, xiv
Origen, 121n
Orissa, 421
ornaments, metal, on shaman's costume, 149
Orochi, séances among, 244f
Orochon, 70, 471n
r.o-s.u, 464
Orpheus, 389n, 391f; "motif," 214n, 241; —, in China, 457f; myth, 383; —, North American, 311; —, Polynesian, 368
Orphic plates, see plates
Orphism, 391f; initiation, 488
orto oyuna, 185n
Osmanli Turks, see Turks
Osset, 395
ostrich, 402f
Ostyak, 30, 89, 96, 152n, 154n, 222, 262, 263, 264n, 273, 275, 278; drum among, 171; Eastern, 15; initiation among, 114; Irtysh, 9, 183, 220; and number seven, 278; recruiting of shamans, 15, 16; séance among, 220, 225ff; Yenisei, 70, 172, 223; see also Vasyugan
otherworld: Iranian ideas of, 396ff; as reverse of this world, 205
otter, 360; skin, 316f, 319
owl, 89, 90, 103, 105, 155, 156; feathers, 57
oyuna, see ojuna

P

Padmasaṃbhava, 434
Pahang, 338
pain, as symbolic death, 33
"pains," 105
Paisyn Kan, 193
palaces, crystal, 139
Palaung, 442n
Palawan, 340
Paleolithic: age, 11, 503; hunters, 503; man, 332n
Palestine, 268

Pallas, P. S., 149
Pallisen, N., 199n
pana, 360
panáptu, 154
Pañcaviṃśa Brāhmaṇa, 404, 415n, 479
Pander, Eugen, 432n
pânkh/panga/pango/pongo, 401
panther, 72
Papuans, 57, 361
paradise(s): Buddhist, 409; lost, 431; myth, 99, 133, 171, 282n, 486; nostalgia for, 508f; see also time
paradox, difficult passage and, 483, 485f
parapurakāyapraveśa, 416
Pare, 367f
Park, Willard Z., 21, 22n, 52n, 101 & n, 102n, 103n, 104n, 105n, 106n, 109 & n, 178n, 179n, 184n, 298, 301, 302n, 303n, 304n, 305n, 310n
Parker, K. Langloh, 46n, 137n
Parrot, A., 267n
parrots, 82
Parsons, Elsie Clews, 316n
Partanen, Jorma, 115 & n, 120n, 145n, 150, 152n, 168n
Pârvan, Vasile, 390n
passage: death as, 510; difficult/dangerous/narrow, 482ff; paradoxical, see paradox; rite(s) of, 64f, 486; see also bridge; gate
Pasuka, 84
Patagonians, 258
Patañjali, 409, 411, 416
patriarchal society, 10
Patwin, 262; River, 55
Paul, St., Vision of, 484
Paul, Otto, 398n
Paulson, Ivar, 81n, 159n, 209n, 210n, 215n, 216n, 243n
Paviotso, 101, 102, 104, 184n, 299, 301, 302ff
pawang, 341, 345f
Pawnee Indians, 313n, 319
pawo, 432
pebbles, see stones
pectoral, 148
pederasty, 258
Pekarsky, E. K., 148n, 158
Pelias, 66
Pelliot, Paul, 199n, 466n, 496n, 501n
Pelops, 66
Penard, F. P. and A. P., 127n
Penzer, Norman Mosley, 98n, 405n, 409n, 478n
Perham, J., 57n, 126, 351, 360n

Pering, Birger, 269n
Perpetua, St., 489
Perry, W. J., 69n, 356n, 477n, 488n
Pestalozza, Uberto, 70n, 119n
Petri, B. E., 120
Petri, Helmut, 136n
Petrullo, Vincenzo, 325n
Petrus Comestor, 268
Pettazzoni, Raffaele, 68n, 122n, 134n, 136n, 137n, 138n, 143n, 337n, 490n, 491n
Pettersson, Olof, 385n
phallus, 79
phenomenologist, attitude of, xv
Phillips, E. D., 389n
Philostratus, 98n
piai, 91, 97
Piddington, Ralph, 361n, 366n
pig, blood of, 73; sacrifice of, 114
pigeon, 267
pillar/Pillar(s): central, of dwelling, 262f; Golden/Iron/Solar, 261; World, 122n, 261ff, see also Axis; Center of World
Pilsudski, Bronislav, 244n
pimo, 441
Pindar, 66n
Piṇḍola, 410n
pine bark, 116
Pineday Bascuñan, Nuñes de, 330n
pipe-smoking, ritual, 303f
Pippidi, D. M., 392n
pitaras, 417
planetnik, 225n
planets, nine, 274n; see also Mars
planes: and man, solidarity, 282; seven, 40; use in yoga, 416
Plateau Indians, 21, 102
plates, Orphic, gold, 391f, 438
platform, 326, 362n; incantation, 381n
Plato, 393
Pliny, 389n
plowshares, hot, 442
poem, shamanist, 241
poetry: lyric, 510; see also epic
Poland, 225n
pole, tent, 261f
Pole Star, 254, 260ff, 266, 267
Polívka, G., see Bolte, J.
Polyaenus, 390
Polynesia(ns), 133, 214n, 312, 355, 358, 361; and America, 366n; Hindu influences, 286n; séance in, 371f; shamanism in, 366ff
Pomo, 54, 97, 125; Eastern, 262

Pomponius Mela, 390n
Pon, 246
Pondo, 69n
pongo, see pánkh
Popov, A. A., xx, 38, 168n, 169n, 470n, 471n, 472
Poppe, Nicholas N., 214n, 461n, 497n
Porphyry, 390n
porter, underworld, 202, 203
Porter Spirit, 194
Port Jackson, 45, 50
possession: 5f, 236, 346, 507; among Batak, 346–47n; in China, 450, 453; by dead person, 365f; and disease, 215; and helping spirits, 93, 328; in India, 424; in Polynesia, 368ff; spontaneous 371; and vocation, 82, 85
post: bird on, 481; sacrificial, see yūpa
Potanin, G. N., 13n, 19n, 20n, 120, 152 153n, 155n, 166n, 173n, 191n, 192n, 201, 203, 204, 218, 267n
Potapov, L. P., 170 & n, 189
pouch, otterskin, 316f, 319
Pouru-bangha, 399
power, shamanic: definition of, 101; sources of, 102, 106ff; see also spirits, guardian
poyang, 91, 341, 342, 344
Pozdneyev, A. M., 115 & n, 120, 164n
Prajāpati, 199, 412
prakṛti, 413
prāṇāyāma, 413, 437
prayer, 92, 183
prelithic period, 11
prestige, and shamanism, xii
pretaloka, 439
pride, smith's, 473
priest(s): colleges of, 369; in North America, 297ff; replaced by shaman, 183; sacrificing, 4
priestesses, Dusun, 349
Priklonsky, V. L., 114n, 234n, 276n
Pripuzov, N. V., 16, 68n, 113, 148n, 185 276n
Prose Edda, see Edda
prophet(s): Irish, 179; Polynesian, 370n, 371; see also taula
Propp, V. I., 44n, 467n, 470n, 474n, 487n
prostitution, 352
Proto-Turks, 11, 183, 501n
Prudentius, 121n
Przyluski, Jean, 268n, 420n
psychologist, approach of, to shamanism xi–xii

psychopathy/psychopathology, shamanic, 14, 23*ff*; *see also* epilepsy; insanity; mental disease
psychophoria, 199, 236
psychopomp, 354, 445; ancestral spirit as, 85; animals as, 93; birds as, 98, 479; horse as, 467, 470; in India, 418; mourner as, 359; shaman as, 4, 182, 205*ff*, 208*f*, 237, 283, 326, 354, 358, 392*f*, 442, 445, 447; Valkyries as, 381*n*; Vayu as, 397; Zarathustra as, 398
pudak, 201, 205, 275, 279
Puë di Songe, 353
pujai/püyéi, 127 & *n*, 130, 131, 133*n*
Pukapuka, 372
puntidir, 48
pûra, *see* horse sacrifice
purification, 116*f*; of deceased's house, 208
puteu, 337*n*, 341
Puyallup, 22
püyéi, see *pujai*
Pygmies, *see* Batak: Semang
Pyramid Texts, 488*n*
pyramids, 341
Pythagoras, 389*n*, 393

Q

qam, see *kam*
Qat, 361*f*
qaumaneq, 60, 62, 420
qilaneq, 296
qolbugas, 150, 151
quartz, 47, 50, 52*n*, 125, 339, 350; liquefied, 138; *see also* rock crystals
Quebec, 164*n*
Queen Mother of the West, 457
quest, voluntary, for shamanic power, 14, 101, 108*f*
Quigstad, J., 224*n*
Qutb ud-dīn Haydar, 126, 402*n*

R

Rā, 487
Radcliffe-Brown, A. R., 342
Radesco, General N., xxi
Radin, Paul, 26, 56*n*, 142*n*, 319
Radlov, Wilhelm, 20*n*, 44*n*, 88*n*, 146, 166*n*, 173*n*, 181, 189, 190 & *n*, 200, 205*n*, 208*n*, 209*f*, 266*n*, 270*n*, 275*n*, 276*n*, 395, 470*n*
Rahmann, Rudolf, 44*n*, 421*n*, 424*ff*, 455*n*, 469*n*, 502*n*

rainbow, 78*n*, 118, 132*ff*, 173, 490
Rainbow-Serpent, 132, 138
Raingeard, P., 392*n*
rain rites, 420
rākṣasa, 439
Ral gcing ma, 37*n*
ram, 213; divination by bone of, 164; rejuvenation of, 66
Rāmāyaṇa, 409*n*
Ramree Island, 351*n*
Ramstedt, G. J., 495, 496*n*
Ränk, Gustav, 10*n*, 80*n*, 210*n*, 487*n*
Ranke, Kurt, 166*n*
raqs, 402*n*
Räsänen, Martti, 135*n*, 173*n*, 482*n*
Rasmussen, Knud, 22*n*, 59*n*, 60*n*, 61*n*, 62 & *n*, 67*n*, 90–91 & *n*, 93*n*, 96*n*, 100*n*, 146*n*, 184*n*, 231*n*, 289*n*, 290, 291*n*, 293*n*, 296*n*, 297*n*
Rasuno, 424
rattle, 91, 178
Rāzi, Amīn Ahmad, 402*n*
Reagan, Albert B., 299*n*
rebirth, 246
recruitment, of shamans, 13*ff*; *see also* election; initiation
regeneration: perpetual, 319; universal, 321
regions, cosmic, *see* zones
reindeer, 41, 93, 147*n*, 248; costume, 149, 156; horns, 155; sacrifice of, 239; shaman's battle animal, 95*n*
Reindeer Tungus, *see* Tungus
Reinhold-Müller, F. G., 432*n*
rejuvenation, 66
religion: chronological perspective, xvii*ff*; of Indo-Europeans, 10, 375*ff*; Polynesian, sources, 366*n*; primitive, and shamanism, 3, 6, 7; Samoyed, 9, 199; Turco-Tatar, 7, 9, 10; *see also* "Chief of the Religion"
religions, history of, xiii*ff*, 11
Rémusat, Abel, 432*n*
Renaissance art, 34
Renel, C., 133*n*
renewal: nonshamanic, 66; physical, 34
resurrection, as initiation, 33, 38, 45, 55, 64, 76; *see also* death
return, eternal, xvi*f*, 246, 285
Revelation, Book of, 134*n*
reversibility, of religious positions, xviii*f*
rewe, 123*f*, 325
Ṛg-Veda, 152*n*, 264*n*, 272*n*, 404, 407*f*, 408*n*, 412, 414*f*, 417*n*, 418, 479
rgyal·rabs, 431*n*

Rhine frontier, 488
Ribbach, S. H., 433*n*
ribbons, 149, 150, 152*n*; colored, 117*f*, 121, 135
rice: sicknesses of, 442; soul of, 353
Richthofen, Bolko, Freiherr von, 333*n*
Riesenfeld, A., 126*n*, 356*n*, 361*n*, 362*n*, 490*n*
rishis, 409
Risley, H. H., 487*n*
rite(s)/ritual(s): fertility, 79, 80*n*; harvest, 468; hunting, *see s.v.*; initiatory, 64; Medicine, *see s.v.*; of passage, *see s.v.*; of "road," *see s.v.*
Rivers, W. H. R., 361*n*
Rivet, Paul, 53*n*, 288*n*, 323*n*, 332
"road": ritual of the, 441; for spirits, 111*f*, 369
"Road desire," 446
Robles Rodriguez, Eulojio, 123 & *n*, 124
Röck, Fritz, 274*n*
Rock, Joseph F., 431*n*, 444*n*, 445*n*, 446–47*n*
rock crystals, 47, 50*n*, 52, 91 & *n*, 132, 135, 136, 137, 138*f*; *see also* quartz
Rockhill, William Woodville, 432*n*, 434*n*
Rocky Mountain tribes, 21
Röder, Joseph G., 284*n*, 354*n*
Rodriguez, E. Robles, *see* Robles Rodriguez
roebuck, shaman's, 174
Rohde, Erwin, 387*n*, 388*n*, 389*n*, 390*n*, 394*n*
Róheim, Géza, 126*n*, 174*n*, 224–25*n*, 481*n*
Romania, 225*n*
Romanov, Timofei, 36
Rome, ancient, 501
rope, 117, 232; for celestial ascent, 50, 78*n*, 121, 136, 226, 484*f*, 490; as emblem of celestial marriage, 75; for tree climbing, 127; as "spirit road," 111*f*; in Tibet, 430*f*
rope trick: in Europe, 429, 430*n*; Indian, 127, 428*ff*; shamanic, 511
Roro, 365*n*
Rosales, Juan de Dios, 54
Rosenberg, F., 496*n*
Rosetti, A., 261*n*
Rossel Island, 475
Roth, H. Ling, 21*n*, 57*n*, 97*n*, 126*n*, 350*n*, 351*n*, 352*n*, 360*n*
Rousselle, Erwin, 164*n*, 452*n*
Roux, Jean-Paul, 9*n*, 199*n*, 461*n*, 495*n*
Rowland, Benjamin, Jr., 134*n*, 488*n*

Roy, Sarat Chandra, 473*n*
Ruben, Walter, 406*n*, 407*n*, 408*n*, 421*n*, 474*n*
Rudolf of Fulda, 261*n*
Rudra-Śiva, 418
Runeberg, Arne, 93*n*, 385*n*, 386*n*, 479*n*
runes, 380
Russia, North, 500
Russians, 40, 487*n*
Russu, Ion I., 390*n*
Ryukyu, 484*n*

S

saargi, 43
Saaytani, Assembly of the, 44
saber, 465
sacrifice(s), 198*ff*, 444; at Araucanian initiation, 123*f*; bear, 166; blood, 263, 275, 277; Brāhmanic, and bridge, 483; —, and ecstatic experience, 411; at Buryat initiation, 118, 119; Central and North Asian, 11; of chicken, 351; of child, 347; directions for, 249–50*n*; of dog, 188; of goat, 119; at Goldi initiation, 115; in India, 403*ff*, 411; not shaman's function, 181; Olympian, 11; among Semites, xvi; shamans and, 183; and shaman's journey, 235; of sheep, 118, 123, 331; *soma*, 413*f*; and soul recovery, 216; spirits and, 92; Tungusic, 238*ff*; Vedic, 126, 183*n*, 199, 478, 493; Vogul, 183; of white animals, 188; at Yakut initiation, 114, 275; Yurak-Samoyed, 264*n*; *see also* horse sacrifice
Saga Hjálmthérs ok Olvers, 381*n*; see also *Gisla; Sturlaugs; Ynglinga*
Sagai, 208
sagani bö, 185
Sahagún, *see* Bernardino de Sahagún
sahib-josh, 475
Sahor, 357
sai kung, 455, 456
saingy, 80*n*
saints, Christian, 377; *see also* Anthony; John; Joseph; Olaf; Paul; Perpetua
Saintyves, P., 161*n*
Śaivism, 434*n*; *see also* Śiva
saka, 475
Sakai, 93, 282, 285, 337, 341
Salish, 100, 104, 106
Salmony, Alfred, 460*n*
Salym, 264*n*
samādhi, 416, 417

šaman, 4, 237, 495, 496
samaṇa, 4, 495
ša-men, 495
Saṃhitās, see *Gheraṇḍa*; *Taittirīya*
Samoa, 25, 369
Samoyed, 30, 136*n*, 205, 232*n*, 260, 262, 288; Avam, 39; drum, 171; initiation among, 38*ff*, 114; recruiting among, 15; religion, 9, 199; séance among, 227*f*; shaman's cap and mask, 154*n*, 155, 167*n*; Tadibei, *see s.v.*; Tavgi, *see s.v.*; *see also* Yurak-Samoyed
Samson, 152*n*
Sanchi, 430
Sandschejew, Garma, 18, 19*n*, 28, 30*n*, 69*n*, 119*n*, 120, 145*n*, 181*n*, 182*n*, 185*n*, 216*n*, 218*n*, 277*n*, 469*n*, 471*f*
Sangiang, 352, 353
Sängimäghiz, 163
sänke/Sänke, 9, 15, 220*f*, 263*n*, 278*n*
Sanpoil, 179
Santa Cruz (Solomons), 364
Santal, 421*n*, 424*n*, 425, 426, 427, 502*n*
Saora, *see* Savara
Sarawak, 126, 138
särgä, 118
Śatapatha Brāhmaṇa, 403*n*, 404, 415, 419*n*
sattāvāsas, 406
Saturn, heaven of, 489
Saulteaux, 335
Sauvageot, Aurélien, 288*n*
Savara/Saora, 73*n*, 421*ff*, 424*n*, 426, 464; séance among, 424
Saxl, F., 488*n*
Saxo Grammaticus, 383*f*
sayan, 69
Sayan steppe, 213
Saymali Taš, 95
Scandinavia(n), 176, 224, 380*ff*; and America, 335
scapulimancy, 164 & *n*
scarf/scarves, 136, 444*n*
scepter, 343
Schaefner, A., 177*n*
Schärer, Hans, 21*n*, 273*n*, 284*n*, 285*n*, 352*n*, 360*n*
Schebesta, Paul, 52*n*, 96*n*, 280*n*, 281*n*, 337*n*, 338*n*, 339*n*
Schlerath, Bernfried, 466*n*
Schmidt, J., 398*n*
Schmidt, Leopold, 161*n*, 165*n*
Schmidt, Wilhelm, xiii, 20*n*, 89*n*, 95*n*, 110*n*, 114*n*, 115*n*, 118*n*, 119*n*, 145*n*, 148*n*, 150*n*, 153*n*, 156*n*, 167*n*, 168*n*,

172*n*, 173*n*, 183*n*, 184*n*, 185*n*, 189*n*, 190*n*, 192*n*, 197*n*, 198*n*, 199*n*, 200*n*, 201*n*, 218*n*, 227*n*, 228*n*, 234*n*, 237*n*, 262*n*, 263*n*, 274*n*, 275*n*, 276*n*, 280*n*, 323*n*, 332*n*, 337*n*, 358*n*, 461*n*, 490*n*, 491*n*, 493*n*, 497*n*, 502*n*
Schoolcraft, H. R., 143*n*
Schott, W., 495
Schram, L. M. J., 461*n*
Schröder, Dominik, 95*n*, 177*n*, 433*n*, 461*n*, 470*n*, 493*n*, 497*n*, 504*n*, 507*n*
Schurtz, Heinrich, 64*n*
Schuster, Carl, 332*n*, 334*n*
Scythia(ns), 388, 390, 394*ff*
sea: as "beyond," 235; endless, 40
Sea Beasts, Mother of the, 289, 294; *see also* Animals, Mother of the
Sea Dyak, *see* Dyak
Sea(s): Lord of the, 193; Nine, 39
seal, 164
Sea Serpents, 348
séance(s), 190*ff*, 209*f*, 249*ff*, *et passim*; animal spirits in, 92*f*; dramatic structure of, 511; and ecstasy, 12; "little," 237; role of drum in, 168, 171, 173; and sickness, 217*ff*
seclusion, 64, 128, 131
second sight, 124
second state, 476, 510
secret societies, 313*ff*; and dog, 467; and initiation, 65, 109; and masks, 166; Melanesian, 362; men's 166*f*, 398–99*n*; of smiths, 473; see also *Männerbünde*; Midē'wiwin
secrets, professional, 17, 34, 474
sects, mystical, and shamanism, 315
Seed Eaters, 102
Seerradeetta, Vyriirje, 213*n*
seidhmenn/*seidhkonur*, 385*f*
seidhr, 224, 385*f*
Selangan, 282
Seler, Edward, 429*n*
Seligman, C. G., 363*n*, 364*n*, 365*n*
Selk'nam, 26, 84, 131, 331*n*
Semang, 52, 68*n*, 93, 125, 337*ff*, 491*n*; cosmology of, 280; and secret language, 96
Semites, sacrifice among, xvi
Semurgaon, 468
Serbs, 225*n*
serpents: diamonds and, 139; *see also* snake
Servants, Spirit, 137
séven, 240; see also *syvén*

seven (number), 121, 122*n*, 134, 264*n*, 274*ff*, 279, 341; branches, 285; gashes, 277; gods, 275*ff*; heavens, *see s.v.*; incisions, 283; planes, 40; stairs, 275; stones, 40*f*; strides, 405*f*; virgins, 153

sex, change of, 257*f*

sexual energy, transmutation of, 437

sexuality, and shamanism, 71*ff*, 79*ff*

sexual organs, drawings on shaman's costume, 153

Shades/Shadows, Kingdom/Realm of, 8, 166, 246*ff*; *see also* Dead, Land of the

Shakers, 321

shaman(s): "black," 69, 114*n*, 493*n*; —, and descent to underworld, 200*ff*; —, and "white," 19, 184*ff*, 189; "common," "great," and "last," 185*n*; dancing, 452; decadence of, *see s.v.*; distinguishing features of, 107, 188*f*; etymology of word, 4, 495*f*; Father, 19, 115*ff*; first, xii, 18, 69, 70, 71, 77, 97, 160, 391, 445*ff*, 506; "great," 17; Greek, 389*n*; Hungarian, see *táltos*; instruction of, 13*f*; and laymen, difference, 315; North American, distinguishing features, 298*f*; "prince of," 188; recruitment, 13*ff*; "self-made," 13; "summer," 80*n*; treatment at death, 341; tying, 229; use of term, 3–4; "white," 493*n*, *see also* "black"

Shaman, Great, celestial, 125

shamaness(es), 221, 241, 256; Altaic, 189; Araucanian, 53, 123, 325, see also *machi*; Buryat, 69; in China, 452*n*; Japanese, functions, 462*f*; in Korea, 462; Land of the, 39; tutelaries and, 423*f*; Yukagir, 246

shamanism: aberrant, 12, 493*f*; Arctic and sub-Arctic, 24; family/domestic, 246, 252*f*; and guardian spirits, 106*f*; identification of, 5; imitation of, 456; Indo-Aryan, 162; "little," 237, 238, 240, 242; and mental disease, xi–xii; origin in America, 333*ff*; "primitive" elements in, 6; use of term, 4, 5

"shamanizing, great," 24

Shang period, 334*n*

shark, 90, 91

Shashkov, S., 68*n*, 148, 198*n*

Shasta, 21, 102

Shawano, 321

sheep: sacrifice of, 118, 123, 331; *see also* ram

sheets, drying on body, 113, 437–38*n*, 476

shell(s): shooting into body, 319; as substitute for drum, 179; see also *mīgis*

shen, 452, 453, 454

Shimkevich, P. P., 212*n*

Shimkin, B. D., 70*n*, 153*n*, 186*n*, 206*n*, 216*n*, 223*n*, 226*n*

shinikuchi, 462

Shipibo, 21

Shirokogoroff, Sergei M., 17, 18*n*, 70*n*, 73, 110, 111*ffnn*, 119*n*, 145*n*, 147*n*, 149, 154*n*, 156*f*, 157, 158*n*, 165, 172, 176*n*, 236*n*, 237, 238*n*, 239*n*, 240, 241, 242, 243*n*, 244*n*, 420*n*, 456*n*, 496*ff*, 502*n*; *see also* Mironov, N. D.

shirts, ghost, 322

Shor, 146

Shoshone, 102

Shun, Emperor, 448

Shuswap, 21, 100, 102, 308

sibaso, 346*f*

Siberia(ns), 4, 220, 501; drum in, 176; costume, 146; psychopomp in, 418; rites of passage, 65; shamans, 53, 84, 89, 108, 509; shamanic initiation, 34, 50*f*, 110; Southern influence, 237; Western, 15*f*, 155; *see also names of specific tribes*

Sibo, 120, 275

sickness(es): dreams, 43; "female," 395; pathological, as initiation, 33*ff*, 38*ff*; Polynesian conception, 373; of rice, 442; and shamanic vocation, 25*ff*, 67; *see also* disease; epilepsy; hysteria; hysteroid; illness; mental disease; psychopathy; syphilis

"sickness-vocation," 33*f*

siddhis, 409, 410*n*, 416

Siduri, 78

Sieroszewski, Wenceslas, 16, 28, 29, 70*n*, 80*n*, 82, 90, 148, 170*n*, 172*n*, 182*n*, 185*n*, 186*n*, 187*n*, 188*n*, 206*n*, 229, 232, 233, 260*n*, 276*n*, 470*n*

sikerei, 25

Sikkim, 432, 433*n*

Sila, 289*f*, 294

sin(s): expulsion of, 357; of first man, 441

Sinkyone, 102

Singapore, 456

Sining, 461

sinners: punishment of, 399; torture of, 202

Sinor, D., 501*n*

Sitakigagailau, 87

Śiva, 427; Mountain of, 420; *see also*
Rudra; Śaivism
sjaadai, 264*n*, 277
skambha, 261*n*
Skeat, W. W., 177*n*, 345 & *n*, 356*n*; and
Blagden, C. O., 281*n*, 337*n*, 341*n*, 342*n*,
346*n*, 487*n*
skeleton, 132; contemplating own, 45,
62*ff*; and Lamaism, 435; reduction to,
59, 63; and shaman's costume, 158*ff*;
see also bones; skulls
skies, superimposed, 133*n*
skin, rubbing, 53–54*n*
skulls: cult of, in India, 421, 434*n*; in
Lamaism, 421, 434*f*; shamans', divination by, 245, 383, 391
sky, 260*f*, 505; contemplation of, 321,
325; god of, 9, 10, 198; journey/ascent
to, *see* ascension; opening in, 251*n*, 260
Sky: Father, 325; God, 9, 226, 505, *see
also* sky, god of; House, 262; Nail, 260
slaughter, autumn, 252
Slawik, Alexander, 166*n*, 285*n*, 355*n*,
380*n*, 462*n*, 466*n*, 467*n*, 473*n*, 484*n*
sled, 211
sleep: candidate's, 53; hypnotic, 64;
"long," 225*n*
Sleipnir, 380, 382, 383, 386*n*
Sliepzova, N. M., 74
Slocum, John, 142, 321
smallpox, 39
"smell of the living," 368
Smith, Marian, 21
smith(s), 41*f*, 42*n*, 66, 470*ff*; ambivalence toward, 472; "black," 471; curing
of, 472; eagle and, 70; and fire, 472*f*;
mythology of, 474; and nine sons/
brothers, 471; *see also* metallurgy
smoke, 490; hemp, 390, 394, 395, 399*ff*,
475
snahud, 337*n*
snake(s), 55, 68, 98, 340; and bird, 273,
285; cosmic, 286; on shaman's costume,
152, 497; as helping spirit, 92; and
initiation, 48, 108*n*, 135; iron, 426;
and tree, 273
Snellgrove, David L., 439*n*, 440*n*
Snorri Sturluson, 380*f*, 383, 385
societies, secret, *see* secret societies
Society Islands, 372
sociologist, approach to shamanism, xii
Söderblom, Nathan, 396*n*, 397*n*
"soft men," 257
Sogdian(s), 122, 501*n*; language, 496
sokha, 427

Solboni, 75
solomonar, 225*n*
Solomon Islands, 364, 475, 478*n*
soma sacrifice, 413*f*
songs: and descent to underworld, 201*ff*,
358; of Eskimo shamans, 96, 303, 306*ff*;
magical, taught in dreams, 83; obscene, 91, 96*ff*, 180, 222,
225*ff*, 290; —, Lapp and North American, 335; —, Shuswap, 100; Zarathustra
and, 398; *see also* hymns
"sons, shaman's," 116*ff*
Sons of God, 276, 277
sorcerer(s), 301, 324; "burning," 363;
defense against, 299; Polynesian,
371*f*; use of term, 3
sorceresses, Chinese, 453*f*
soul(s), *passim*; as bird, 206, 392, 479,
480*f*; and bones, 159; bush, 92; calling
back, 217, 414, 442; capturing, 419*f*;
of children, 272, 273*n*, 281*f*; crushing,
372; of dead, 84, 88, 89, 169; destiny
of, 216; extraction of, 60; flight of, 350,
357, 448; immortality of, 480; instability of, 415; Lamaism and, 440*f*;
"life," 94; loss of, 8, 87, 300*f*, 307*f*, 310,
327, 335; multiple, 215*f*, 256*n*; plurality of, 417; projection into effigy,
212*n*; rape of, 215; restoring to body,
256*n*; of rice, 353; search for, 183, 208,
210, 217*ff*, 433; Semang beliefs, 281;
shaman and, 8; shaman as guardian of,
182; shaman's knowledge of, 216; theft
of, 289, 309, 348; three, 209, 246;
weighing of, 282
"soul ladder," *see* ladder
"soul-shade," 154
sounds, mystical, 453*n*
South America, *see* America, South
Sovereign, terrifying, 379
Soyot, 223*n*, 277, 279; drum, 173, 174;
and lightning, 19, 100*n*; and shaman's
costume, 155, 156, 157; tent pole, 261
spákona, 385*f*
sparrow, 245
sparrow-hawk, 39
specialization, infernal, 235
spectacle, séance as, 511
Speech, Tree of, 441
speed, miraculous, 174
Speiser, Felix, 358*n*, 361*n*
Spencer, Baldwin, and Gillen, F. J., 47 &
n, 48, 48–50*nn*, 136*n*
spider, 68; web, 78*n*, 490*n*
Spier, Leslie, 103*n*, 315*n*, 320*n*

"spindle of necessity," 393f
Spies, Walter, see Zoete, Beryl de
Spirit: of Madness, see s.v.; of the Moon, see s.v.; Messenger, see s.v.; "of the night," 104f; Porter, see s.v.; Servants, see s.v.; of Thunder, see s.v.; Wind, see s.v.
spirit(s), passim; abduction by, 87; acquiring, 21; "boat of," 356; consultation of, 296; of darkness, 226; descent of, 97; evil, drum and, 174; —, Eskimo and, 293; familiarity with, 81, 88; feminine, 73, 77, 79ff; guardian, 89, 91, 95, 100, 103, 106, 157, 197; helping/tutelary, 6, 28, 44, 52, 62, 63, 71, 72, 81, 88ff, 100n, 104, 157, 222, 226f, 249, 278, 297, 328, 341, 381, 425, 427; —, nonshamanic, 106f; "Hole of the," 234; language of, 347, 440; marine, 309; marriage with mortals, 73ff; mountain, 90; "road" for, 111f, 369; "seeing," 84, 85ff; sexual relations with, 74; shaman's relations with, 5f; torture of children by, 18; various kinds, 6; visions of, 85ff; of warriors, 104; world of, 179; see also damagomi; souls
spirituality, Chinese, 451
spirit-women, 133n, 344f; see also spirit(s), feminine
spittle, 114
spoon, 222
spouses, one-night, 463
squirrel, flying, 278
śramaṇa, 495
srung-ma, 444n
staff: guru's, 347; magical, 128
stag(s), 89, 156, 160 & n, 462; black, 164
stairs, 391, 400, 443; see also ladder; seven, 275
stairway, spiral, 136, 137
Star/stars, 260, 261; Pole, see s.v.
Stefánsson, Vilhjálmur, 59n
Stein, Rolf A., 155n, 208n, 431n, 466n, 510n
Steinen, Karl von den, 326n
Steiner, F. B., 501n
Steinmann, Alfred, 285n, 286n, 357n, 358n
Stepanov, Mikhail, 43
sterility, 181, 289
"Stern Woman with the Handled Stick," 222
Sternberg, Leo, 14n, 28, 67, 70n, 71 & n, 73ff, 74n, 76n, 156n
Stevenson, Matilda Coxe, 316n

Steward, Julian H., 323n
Stewart, C. S., 371n
stick(s): for divination, 228; eagle feather, 302f; horse-headed, see horse, magical, 177
"stick-horse," 150
Stieda, L., 115n, 145n, 218n
Stiglmayr, Engelbert, 136n, 337n, 342n, 504n
Stirling, Matthew W., 85n
Stöhr, Waldemar, 351n
stone(s), 135; cylindrical, 426; holding, 40; —, hot, 54; inserted in head/body, 46, 49; Jacob's, 488; "light," 138, 508; rubbing, 59; seven, 40f; striped, 124, 125; see also atnongara; quartz; rock crystals
Stone Age, 11, 500
ston-pa, 445
storms: controlling, 290; foreseeing, 342; god of, 10n, 198, 505; see also hurricane
Strabo, 390
strides, seven, 405f
Strömbäck, Dag, 224n, 385n, 386n
Sturlaugs Saga Starfsama, 381n
Subandhu, 415
Subanun, 25
suction, 243n, 256, 301, 304, 307, 329, 330, 331, 345, 348, 364
Sudan(ese), 21, 26n, 27, 31, 55
suet, 166
suffering, and initiation, 33
Sufism, 402n
sulde-tengri, 276
Sulta-Khan, 197n
Sumatra, 21, 25, 82n, 86, 96, 140, 178, 286f, 334n, 346ff, 358n, 475
Sumbur/Sumer/Sumur/Sumeru, 266, 267, 271, 277
Summers, Montague, 93n
Sumner, William G., 234n
Sumur, see Sumbur
Sun, 196, 276; as guardian spirit, 106; God, 487; orifice of, 148
sunbeam, ascent by, 490
Sungkai, 339n
Sung Yü, 448
Supreme Being, 81, 105n, 107, 128, 135f, 142, 220, 242, 249, 444, 504f; as eagle, 69, 70, 158; sacrifices to, 198; and trance, 34; see also Buga; god
Sūtras, see Bandhyāyana; Dharma; Patañjali
sutura frontalis, 164
Svadhilfari, 386n

Śvetadvīpa, 409
wan(s), 39, 68, 153, 155, 176
Swanton, John R., 55n, 82n, 178n, 298
weat-house, 100
weating, and creation, 334n, 412
Sweden, 161n
wiftness, 485
word-ladder, 455
words, bridge of, 456, 484
Sydow, C. W. von, 162n
Sykaiboai, 391
symbolism: degeneration of, 450; lunar, 272; uranian, 139
ymbols, on drum, 172ff, 224
yphilis, 39
yvén, 71, 92; see also séven

T

abjan (tabyan), 149n
aboos, 296; and initiation, 59n; violation of, and illness, 289
Tabor, Mount, 268
abyan, see tabjan
abytala, 149
Tadibei Samoyed, 148
adu, 353
Tagarao, 362
Tagaro, 365n
Tahiti, 78n, 369, 371n
ahu, 371
T'ai, Mount, 456
Taino, 323
Taittirīya Brāhmaṇa, 418n
Taittirīya Saṃhitā, 404n, 415n, 483n
Taittirīya Upaniṣad, 417n
Takánakapsâluk, 289, 294ff
akini, 130
Taliang mountains, 441
talker, shaman's, 302
Tallgren, Aarne Michael, 500n, 503n
áltos, 95n, 126, 174, 225n, 481, 509
amziq, 402n
angara, 186
Tangara, see Tengri
angata wotu, 372
Tängere, see Tengri
Tängri, 471
anjô, 463
Tantalus, 66
tantrism, 164, 373, 408, 420, 421, 434n, 436f; see also yoga
Tao, 449
Taoism/Taoists, 432n, 450f, 453ff; and animals, 460

tao shih, 455
tapas, 408, 412ff, 475
Ta Pedn/Tata Ta Pedn, 125, 280n, 282, 337f; see also Tapern
Tapern, 280, 340; see also Ta Pedn
Tapirape, 323n
tapti/tapty, 76, 191, 194f, 275
tapu, 371
tarasun, 19, 116
Tarō, Nakayama, 462
Tasygan, Mother, 193
Tata Ta Pedn, see Ta Pedn
Tatars: Abakan, see s.v.; Altai, see Altai/Altaians; Black, 146, 166; and descents to underworld, 213f; and drum, 172; Indian/Iranian influence, 500, 501; Lebed, 146, 175, 197n; Minusinsk, 156; Siberian, 205, 261, 266, 270, 273; Volga, see s.v.
taua, 370n
taula, 366, 369, 370n
taula atua, 369
Taulipang, 30, 327f
taura, 370n
taurobolion, 121
Tavgi Samoyed, 40, 41
Tawhaki, 78n, 133
Tawney, Charles Henry, 98n, 405n, 479n
Taz River, 226
Tchaky race, 188
Tcheng-tsu Shang, 456n
Tegnaeus, Harry, 490n
Teit, James A., 102n, 106n, 309n
Tekha Shara Matzkala, 75
Telchines, 473
Telenginsk, 150n
Telengit, 197n
Teleut, 44, 70, 79, 206, 207, 208, 217, 219n, 261; ascent to heaven among, 76f, 275; costume, 146, 155, 156; horse sacrifice, 192n, 197n
Telumni Yokuts, see Yokuts
Temir taixa, 201
ten heavens, 492
Teng, 339
Tengere Kaira Kan, see Kaira Kan
Tengri/Tengeri/Tängere/Tingir/Tangara (Great God), 9, 69, 199, 250n, 271, 276
Tenino, 22
terror: and helping spirits, 100n; and initiation, 91
Thai, Black, 443n

Thalbitzer, William, 58n, 59n, 90n, 96n, 261n, 288n, 289n, 290n, 293, 333, 477n, 502n
thief, discovery of, 365, 372
thirty-three (number), 276f
Thjālfi, 162
Thompson, B., 372n
Thompson, Stith, 64n, 78n, 92n, 93n, 98n, 134n, 158n, 479n, 483n, 490n
Thompson Indians, 21, 102, 106, 309
Thor, 161f
Thorndike, Lynn, 98n
Thought, Tree of, 441
Thracians, 389ff
thread(s), 217, 338f
three (number), 274; souls, 209, 246
throne, 343
thunder/Thunder: as guardian spirit, 106; Spirit of, 38
Thunder Bird, 106, 244, 245
thunderstones, 139
Thurn, Everard F. Im, see Im Thurn
thyme, wild, 116, 118n
t'iao-shen, 449
Tibbu, 472n
Tibet(an), 37n, 108f, 163, 164, 204, 212n, 392, 410, 430ff, 440, 502n; see also Bon
Tibetan Book of the Dead, 61, 208n, 418, 438, 444, 446
T'ien, 444
Tierra del Fuego, 26, 53, 131, 327, 336
Tiger/tiger(s): Ancestor, 339; evocation of, 345f; changing into, 93, 281, 339; as helping spirit, 72; spirit, 344
time(s), dream/mythical/paradisal/primordial, 94, 99, 103, 132, 144, 171, 265, 282, 287, 322, 354, 446n, 480, 483, 486, 492, 505
Tin, Pe Maung, 409n
tindalo, 365
Tingir, see Tengri
Tipiknits, 311f
Tlingit, 55, 82n, 178, 335n
toad, 68
Toba, 54
tobacco(juice), 54, 83, 84, 128, 129, 131, 220, 254, 330, 401
tobacco box, 340
tohunga, 366, 369, 370n
Toivoinen, Y. H., 271n
Tokharian, 496
toli, 151
Tomsk, 79, 166, 227
tondi, 346

Tongársoak, 59
tongue: perforation of, 46, 47; tearing out, 54
Tôrem-karevel, 276
Toradja, 286n, 358n; Bare'e, 353
tortures: infernal, 213; initiatory, 33ff, 64, 84, 109
totemism, 160; Chinese, 459
to t'ui, 455
toxins, and ecstasy, 221; see also mushrooms; narcotics; tobacco
Toyon Kötör, 70
trance, passim; Altaic shamans and, 200 cataleptic, 331, 393; deliberate, 24; epileptics and, 24; erotic, 73; among Eskimo, 291f; of Lapp shamans, 224; muni's, 411; as shamanic speciality, 8 Yurak-Samoyed, 227f; see also ecstasy lupa
Transbaikal, 16, 149, 242; Tungus, 10 110, 172
transformation, through display, 197f; into woman, 257f
transvestitism, 125n, 168, 258, 351 & nn 461; see also androgynization; feminiza tion
Transylvania, 161n
Trayastriṃśa Heaven, 430
tree(s): climbing, 123ff, 125ff, 137, 169 see also ascension, initiation; inverted, 169, 270n; nine, 233; relation to sha man, 70; snake and, 273; underworld, 270; see also birch; dinang; fir
Tree, Cosmic/Universal/World, xiv, 37n, 38, 42, 70, 71 & n, 120, 122n, 157 194n, 206, 211, 269ff, 282, 395, 492; and bird, 273; and boat, 357f; destruc tion of, 284; and drum, 40n, 168ff, 171 172f, 270; seven branches of, 285; an snake, 273; see also birch; drum
Tree: of Immortality, 271; of Life, 271 282; Lord of, 39f; —, Mapic, 281; — Mother and Father, 118n; of Speech, 441; of Thought, 441
Tree Yjyk-Mas, 37n
Tremyugan, 89, 183, 220
Tretyakov, P. I., 15n, 17n, 68n, 114, 225, 226n
tricks, shamanistic, 255n
trident, 426
tripartition, divine, 378
tripod, Delphic, 387n
Trobriands, 282n, 365n
Troshchansky, V. F., 73, 158, 234n
Tshe-spong-bza, Queen, 434

Tsingala, 221n, 263, 278n
Tubalares, 170
tube, bamboo, 96
Tucci, Giuseppe, 430n, 432n
Tucuna, 327n
T'u-jen, 461
Tukajana, 129, 130
tukang tawur, 353
Tukue, 183
Tuma, 282n
Tumnin river, 244
tumsa, 443n
Tungus, 40, 70–71n, 82n, 112, 149, 205,
    209, 212n, 235, 254, 272, 420, 471n,
    497, 498ff; drum, 172, 176; and helping
    spirits, 92, 249; and Indian influences,
    496; initiation among, 43ff, 110ff;
    masks, 165; recruiting among, 17ff;
    Reindeer, 29, 240, 242; religion, 9;
    séances among, 236ff; and secret lan-
    guage, 96; shamanic costume, 146,
    147ff, 154f, 156; shamanism, two strata,
    244; Transbaikal, 16, 110, 172;
    Turukhansk, 16, 68, 185, 208
Tun Huang, 438
Tuonela, 485
Tupi-Imba, 53f
Tupinamba, 178, 323n
Turkestan, 204
Turkic peoples, and sacrifice, 198
Turko-Mongol shamanism, and Oriental
    influences, 12
Turko-Tatar peoples, 198, 260, 274, 276,
    395; and Indo-Europeans, resem-
    blances, 10f, 378; religion of, 7, 9, 10
Turks, 135, 462; Osmanli, 273
turö, 111
Turukhansk, 16, 68, 185, 208
Tüspüt, 27, 82, 90, 229
Tuvas, 498
Twana Indians, 309
Tylor, Edward B., 333

U

Ubi-Ubi, 137
Ucayali, 83
udagan/udayan/udoyan, 4
Ude/Udekhe, 244
udeši-burkhan, 117, 194, 263
udoyan, see udagan
Uganda, 25
Ugrian peoples, 263, 276, 279n, 400,
    501; drums among, 175; ecstasy among,

222f; sacrifice among, 183; séance
    among, 220ff
Uigur, 135, 496, 497; Yellow, 207
Ukko, 71n
Ülgän, see Bai Ülgän
Ulka, 244
Ulū-Toyon, 185n, 187f
Ulū-tūyer Ulū-Toyon, 187
Ulysses, 79
unconsciousness, as symbolic death, 33
understaffing, effects of, 270f
underworld, passim; Altaic, 200ff; de-
    scent/journey to, 5, 24, 39, 50f, 211ff,
    234ff, 311ff, 418; —, in North America,
    308ff; —, hero's, 94, 367f; dogs, see
    s.v.; entrance to, 278; geography of,
    205f; initiation and, 34, 36f, 39, 43, 47,
    50, 51, 64; levels of, 279, 383; porter,
    202, 203; submarine, 153, 254; tree in,
    270; and Tungus, 238ff; see also
    Hades; hell
Underworld, King of the, 213; Lady of,
    see Lady; Lord of, 10, 39, 42, see also
    Erlik Khan; Tipiknits
unity of cosmos, 284
Unmatjera, 47
Universal Tree, see Tree
üör, 229
Upaniṣads, 61, 420; see also Bṛhadā-
    raṇyaka; Jaiminiya; Kaṭha; Taittirīya
Upi, 348
Ur, 267
uranian symbolism, 139
Uriankhai, 77
"Urkultur," 262n
Ürün/Ürüng, 187
üsa kyrar, 234
utcha, 18, 67
Ute, 258
Ut-Napishtim, 313n
üzüt pairamy, 208n

V

vada, 364n
Väinämöinen, 71n, 485
Vairocana, 434
Vajda, Lászlo, 145n, 168n, 501n
Valkyries, 381n
values, origin of, 263n
Vanaspati, 404
Vancouver Island, 138
Vandier, Jacques, 488n
Vannicelli, Luigi, 164n, 441n, 442n,
    443n, 451n, 483n

Varuṇa, 199, 375, 379, 419
Vasilyev, V. N., 145n, 148n, 234
Vasyugan, 15, 89, 164, 183, 221, 270, 276
vats, 476
Vayu, 397, 407
Vea Island, 309n
Vedas, see *Atharva Veda; Ṛg Veda*
Vedic: divinities, 88; sacrifices, 126,
    183n, 199, 478, 493
Venezuela, 30
ventriloquism, 255n, 335
Venus statuettes, 503
Verbitsky, V. L., 190 & n, 197n, 277
vertigo, 25
Vidēvdat, 397n, 398n, 399
vileo(s), 125
village: of the gods, 353; spirit, 348
vine: connecting earth and sky, 354, 362,
    430, 483, 490; connecting earth and
    underworld, 368
virgins, seven, 153
Viriga family, 369
Vishtâsp, narcotic of, 399
visions, 227f; of spirits, 85ff
Visser, Marinus Willem de, 409n, 410n
Vitashevsky, N. Y., 24, 229n, 234n
vocation: mystical, 35; and dreams, 67,
    101ff; necessity of, 65; and possession,
    82, 85; spontaneous, 13, 109; *see also*
    election
vodka, 170
Vogul, 29, 154n, 222, 264n, 275, 276;
    character of shamans, 29; mushrooms,
    401; number seven among, 278; re-
    cruiting of shamans, 15; sacrifice, 183
"voices, separate," 255n
Volga Tatars, 9
Völuspa, 382n
volva, 383, 386
Voronezh, 487n
Votyak, 15
Vourukasha, lake (sea), 122n, 271n
vrātya, 408n
Vries, Jan de, 98n, 380n, 385n
"Vulture, Grandfather," 128f

W

Wâbĕnō', 315f
Wachaga, 473n
waka, 370
Walapai, 103
Wales, H. G. Quaritch, 177, 268n, 280n,
    354n, 355n, 358n
Waley, Arthur, 452n
Walleser, Max, 478n
walrus, 21, 44, 381
Wanderobo, 472n
Wang Ch'ung, 454
Warburton Ranges, 46
Warneck, J., 273n, 347n, 467n
Warramunga, 48
Warrau, 54n
warriors, spirits of, 104
Washington (State), 309
Wassén, S. Henry, *see* Holmer, Nils M
water/Water: gazing into, 363; as
    guardian spirit, 106; Lords of the, 39
    purification by, 116; spiced, 475
Water-babies, 105
Waters: of Death, 355; Lady of the,
    see s.v.
Watson, William, 460n
weather control, 289f, 304
Webster, Hutton, 22n, 25n, 52n, 59n,
    64n, 82n, 85n, 90n, 92n, 177n, 178n,
    351n, 472n, 475n
weddings, shaman and, 181f
Wee, 455
Wehrli, Hans J., 443n
Weil, R., 487n
Weinberger-Goebel, Kira, 363n, 482n
Weisser-Aall, Lily, 93n
Wensinck, A. J., 268n, 269n, 273n
werewolves, 324, 381n; *see also*
    lycanthropy
Werner, Alice, 490n
Wernert, P., 434n
West, E. W., 397n
Weyer, Edward Moffatt, Jr., 22n, 58n
    59n, 90n, 96n, 184n, 289n, 290n
wheel, 433
whip, 151, 174
whirlwind, 92, 423f
White, C. M. N., 374n
Whitehead, George, 343n, 356n
"White Lord Creator," 187
Widengren, George, 273n, 385n, 393n
    397n, 398n, 399n, 407n, 489n
Wieschoff, Heinz, 177n
wife, fairy, 77f, 361; *see also* wives,
    celestial; spirit-women
wigiwam, 317
wigwan, 239
Wikander, Stig, 385n, 397n, 398n, 399n
    401n
wildcat, 46
Wilhelm, Richard, 457n
Wilke, Georg, 273n, 480n
Wilken, G. A., 25, 347n

Williamson, Robert W., 361n, 366n, 371n

wind, see hurricane

Wind Spirit, 359

wings, 392

Winnebago, 142, 319f

winnow, 425f

Winstedt, Richard O., 286n, 345n

Wintu, 21, 31, 102

Wiradjuri, 134, 135, 137

Wirz, Paul, 179n, 478n

Wissler, Clark, 298, 313n

witchcraft, 298

witches/wizards, 478

Witoto, 327n

wives, celestial, 76ff, 79ff, 133n, 168, 381n, 421; see also wife, fairy; spirit-women

wizards, see witches

wolf/wolves, 72, 89, 90, 93, 106, 241, 467

Wolfram, R., 469n

Wolof, 472n

Wolters, Paul, 388n

woman/women: dressing as, see transvestitism; as magicians, 363; as source of magic power, 449; mythological role/mythology of, 10, 78, 351; transformation into, 257f

Wombu, 136

Wongaibon, 127

wood, choice of, for drum, 169

world/World: beginning of, see beginning; Center of the, see s.v.; creation of, see s.v.; Lord of the, 70

worms, 89

Wotjobaluk, 45, 137, 490n

Wovoka, 142

Wright, Arthur Frederick, 453n

wu, 452, 454, 455

wu-ism, 454

wurake, 353

Wurundjeri, 137

wu-shih, 455

Wüst, Walther, 398n

wut, 476

Wütende Heer, 384n

Wylick, Carla van, 355n

Y

Yahgan, 327

Yahweh, 393n

Yaik Kan, see Jajyk Kan

yaika, 303

Yakṣas, 453n

Yakut, 40, 160n, 182n, 205, 249, 272, 288, 481, 497; bones, 158, 159; classes of gods, 186ff, 276; classes of shamans, 184f, 185n; drums, 172, 173, 174; eagle among, 70n; and earth divinity, 10; fertility goddess, 80n; gods, 9, 10; "first shaman," 68f; initiations, 35ff, 113f, 120; masks, 165; recruiting of shamans, 16; and sacrifices, 118, 275; séance among, 228ff; secret language, 96, 97; sex relations with spirits, 74; shaman, character of, 29; —, costume, 148f, 152n, 156; and smiths, 470f; and souls of dead, 206; and stars, 260; vocabulary, 30

yálgil, 247

Yama, 272, 417f, 419

Yamana, 26, 53, 131, 331

Yao, Emperor, 448

Yap, 478n

Yaralde, 86

Yaruro, 83, 178, 325n

Yasser, J., 243n

Yašt, 399

yawning, 415

Yayutši, 196

Yecuana, 328

yefatchel, 331

yékamush, 54n

yekush, 331

Yellow Emperor, 449

Yellow Uigur, see Uigur

Yenang, 282

Yenisei, 501; see also Ostyak

yer mesi/yer tunigi, 202

Yesevî, Ahmed, 402

Yggdrasil, 71n, 270n, 380, 383

Yima, 272

Yjyk-Mas, Tree, 37n

Ynglinga Saga, 381n, 382n

Yoga-sūtras, see Patañjali

yoga, 416f; baroque, 416; Buddhist, 61, 416; and flying, 409, 410, 411; and mastery over fire, 373; shamanic, 417; tantric, 413; and *tapas*, 413; see also tantrism

yogin(s), 113, 163f, 409, 436, 476, 479; Buddhist, 61, 164, 407

Yokuts, Telumni, 311

yorra, 212

Ysabel, 364

Yü the Great, 449, 458

Yuin, 137

Yukagir, 216; costume, 156; divination, 249, 391, 435n; masks, 165, 166; séances among, 97, 245ff
Yuki, 54
Yule, Henry, 429n, 432n, 443n
Yuma, 103, 309
Yunnan, 441, 444
yūpa, 403f
Yuracare, 161n
Yurak Samoyed, 89n, 209, 213n, 277, 278; cap, 154; drum, 135, 174; funerary ceremonies, 212f; initiation among, 38; recruiting among, 15; sacrifices, 264n; séance, 225ff
Yurok, 102

Z

Zalmoxis, 390
Zambu, 122n, 271

Zarathustra/Zoroaster, 119n, 393, 397f
Zateyev, Sofron, 36
Zelenin, D., 26, 70n, 79n, 166n, 197n
Zemmrich, Johannes, 482n
Zerries, Otto, 81n, 161n, 323n
Zhi-mä, 446
žiber, 151
ziggurat, 134, 264, 267
Zimmer, Heinrich, 485n
Zoete, Beryl de, and Spies, Walter, 468n
zones, cosmic: 37n, 259ff, 282, 284, 397; communication between, 265; and drum, 176
Zoroaster, see Zarathustra
Zulu, 21
Zuni, 316n

Index by A. S. B. Glover

MYTHOS: The Princeton/Bollingen Series in World Mythology

J. J. Bachofen / MYTH, RELIGION, AND MOTHER RIGHT

George Boas, trans. / THE HIEROGLYPHICS OF HORAPOLLO

Anthony Bonner, ed. / DOCTOR ILLUMINATUS: A RAMON LLULL
READER

Jan Bremmer / THE EARLY GREEK CONCEPT OF THE SOUL

Joseph Campbell / THE HERO WITH A THOUSAND FACES

Henry Corbin / AVICENNA AND THE VISIONARY RECITAL

F. M. Cornford / FROM RELIGION TO PHILOSOPHY

Mircea Eliade / IMAGES AND SYMBOLS

Mircea Eliade / THE MYTH OF THE ETERNAL RETURN

Mircea Eliade / SHAMANISM: ARCHAIC TECHNIQUES OF ECSTASY

Mircea Eliade / YOGA: IMMORTALITY AND FREEDOM

Garth Fowden / THE EGYPTIAN HERMES

Erwin R. Goodenough (Jacob Neusner, ed.) / JEWISH SYMBOLS IN THE
GRECO-ROMAN PERIOD

W.K.C. Guthrie / ORPHEUS AND GREEK RELIGION

Jane Ellen Harrison / PROLEGOMENA TO THE STUDY OF GREEK
RELIGION

Joseph Henderson & Maud Oakes / THE WISDOM OF THE SERPENT

Erik Iversen / THE MYTH OF EGYPT AND ITS HIEROGLYPHS IN
EUROPEAN TRADITION

C. G. Jung & Carl Kerényi / ESSAYS ON A SCIENCE OF MYTHOLOGY

Carl Kerényi / ELEUSIS: ARCHETYPAL IMAGE OF MOTHER AND
DAUGHTER

Stella Kramrisch / THE PRESENCE OF ŚIVA

Roger S. Loomis / THE GRAIL: FROM CELTIC MYTH TO CHRISTIAN
SYMBOL

Bronislaw Malinowski (Ivan Strenski, ed.) / MALINOWSKI AND THE
WORK OF MYTH

Erich Neumann / AMOR AND PSYCHE

Erich Neumann / THE GREAT MOTHER

Maud Oakes with Joseph Campbell / WHERE THE TWO CAME TO
THEIR FATHER

Dora & Erwin Panofsky / PANDORA'S BOX

Paul Radin / THE ROAD OF LIFE AND DEATH

Otto Rank, Lord Raglan, Alan Dundes / IN QUEST OF THE HERO

Gladys Reichard / NAVAHO RELIGION

Géza Róheim (Alan Dundes, ed.) / FIRE IN THE DRAGON

Robert A. Segal, ed. / THE GNOSTIC JUNG

Philip E. Slater / THE GLORY OF HERA

Daisetz T. Suzuki / ZEN AND JAPANESE CULTURE

Jean-Pierre Vernant (Froma I. Zeitlin, ed.) / MORTALS AND
IMMORTALS

Jessie L. Weston / FROM RITUAL TO ROMANCE

Heinrich Zimmer (Joseph Campbell, ed.) / THE KING AND THE
CORPSE: TALES OF THE SOUL'S CONQUEST OF EVIL

Heinrich Zimmer (Joseph Campbell, ed.) / MYTHS AND SYMBOLS IN
INDIAN ART AND CIVILIZATION